Writing First

PRACTICE IN CONTEXT

WITH READINGS

Third Edition

Laurie G. Kirszner

University of the Sciences in Philadelphia

Stephen R. Mandell

Drexel University

with additional teaching tips and ESL tips by

Linda Mason Austin

McLennan Community College

Bedford/St. Martin's

Boston ■ New York

For Bedford/St. Martin's

Developmental Editor: Joelle Hann
Senior Production Editor: Shuli Traub
Senior Production Supervisor: Dennis J. Conroy
Senior Marketing Manager: Rachel Falk
Art Direction: Lucy Krikorian
Text Design: Wanda Kossak and Wanda Lubelska
Cover Design: Donna L. Dennison
Copy Editor: Rosemary Winfield
Photo Research: S. Zuckerman/Photosearch, Inc.
Cover Art: Painting *Washington Square* © Richard H. Fox/Strata-art.com
Composition: Stratford Publishing Services, Inc.
Printing and Binding: R.R. Donnelley & Sons Company

President: Joan E. Feinberg
Editorial Director: Denise B. Wydra
Editor in Chief: Nancy Perry
Director of Marketing: Karen Melton Soeltz
Director of Editing, Design, and Production: Marcia Cohen
Managing Editor: Erica T. Appel

Library of Congress Control Number: 2005922478

Manufactured in the United States of America.

1 0 9 8 7 6
f e d c b a

For information, write: Bedford/St. Martin's, 75 Arlington Street, Boston, MA 02116 (617-399-4000)

ISBN: 0-312-44090-1 (Instructor's Annotated Edition)
      0-312-43655-6 (Student Edition with Readings)
      0-312-43412-X (Student Edition)

EAN: 978-0-312-44090-9 (Instructor's Annotated Edition)
      978-0-312-43655-1 (Student Edition with Readings)
      978-0-312-43412-0 (Student Edition)

Acknowledgments

Acknowledgments and copyrights are continued at the back of the book on pages 712–714, which constitute an extension of the copyright page.

Preface for Instructors

In college, writing comes first. In fact, as soon as students set foot in a classroom, they are asked to write—to take notes, to complete assignments, to write papers, to take exams. But writing is also crucial outside the classroom: in the community and in the workplace, writing empowers people, enabling them to participate more fully in every aspect of their lives. For these reasons, writing also comes first in *Writing First: Practice in Context,* where our organization and emphasis reflect our priorities as teachers as well as the importance of writing in college and in the wider world.

In *Writing First,* writing comes first chronologically: the book begins with thorough coverage of the writing process, and most chapters begin with writing prompts. Writing is also first in importance: extensive writing practice is central to the grammar chapters as well as to the writing process chapters. In addition to an abundance of practice exercises, each grammar chapter includes a unique three-step sequence of writing and editing prompts (Writing First/Flashback/Revising and Editing) that guides students in using the chapter's concepts in a piece of their own writing. One thing our years in the classroom have taught us is that students learn writing skills best in the context of their own written work. Here, by moving from their own writing to workbook-style mastery exercises and back to their own work, students learn more effectively and more purposefully.

Our goals in this edition of *Writing First* remain the same as they have been from the start: to motivate students to improve their writing for college and for everyday life, and to give them the tools they need to do so. It is our hope that by practicing these skills in the context of their own writing, students will come to see writing as something at which they can succeed. To achieve our goals, we worked hard in this revision to keep the text flexible enough to support a variety of teaching styles and to meet the needs of individual students. At the same time, we wanted to support students and instructors grappling with the realities of the developmental classroom, so we added more help with grammar, ESL, and assessment issues.

We wrote this book for adults—our own interested, concerned, hardworking students—and we tailored the book's approach and content to them. Consequently, we avoid exercises that present writing as a dull, pointless, and artificial activity, and we do our best to offer fresh, contemporary examples, writing assignments, and student models. In the book's style and tone, we try to show respect for our audience—to treat college students as adults who can take responsibility for their own learning and for their own development as writers.

Organization

Writing First: Practice in Context has a flexible organization that permits instructors to teach various topics in the order that works best for them and their students. The book is divided into three sections: "Writing Paragraphs and Essays," "Revising and Editing Your Writing," and "Becoming a Critical Reader." The first section is a comprehensive discussion of the writing process. The second section presents a thorough review of sentence skills, grammar, punctuation, mechanics, and spelling. The third section introduces students to critical reading skills and includes nineteen professional essays, each illustrating a particular pattern of development. Finally, three appendixes—Appendix A, "Strategies for College Success," Appendix B, "Writing a Research Paper," and Appendix C, "Taking Standardized Assessment Tests"—provide help with skills that students will need in other courses and on standardized tests.

Features

Central to *Writing First* is our "student writing first" philosophy, which is supported by innovative features designed to make students' writing practice meaningful, productive, and enjoyable.

The text's process approach guides students step by step through the writing process, providing comprehensive coverage in a flexible format. Eleven chapters on paragraph development (Units One and Two) feature many examples of student and professional writing, with separate chapters on each method of paragraph development. A comprehensive treatment of essay writing (Unit Three) starts with Chapter 12, "Writing an Essay." Chapter 13, "Introductions and Conclusions," offers guidance rarely found in developmental writing texts. In Chapter 14, "Patterns of Essay Development," each pattern is illustrated by a student essay.

Unique "practice in context" activities allow students to apply each new concept to their own writing. Most chapters begin with a *Writing First* activity, a writing prompt accompanied by a visual. Then, a series of *Flashback* exercises encourages students to practice skills introduced in the chapter by applying them to their own Writing First responses. At the end of the chapter, a *Revising and Editing* activity guides students through a final look at their Writing First responses.

***Writing First* makes information easy to find and use.** The engaging full-color design supports the text's pedagogy and helps students find information quickly. *Focus boxes* highlight key concepts and important information, *quick-reference corner tabs* make the book easy to navigate, and *marginal cross-references* to other parts of the text help students find and review key information. *Writing Tips* in the margins provide additional information, address common problem areas, and make connections between academic and everyday writing situations. For students who need additional practice with specific skills, *marginal cross-references to the* Exercise Central *online exercise collection* appear throughout the text.

Both native and nonnative writers get the grammar help they need. Thorough, accessible grammar explanations are complemented by clear, helpful examples. The book also offers stronger ESL coverage than any competing text: Chapter 30, "Grammar and Usage for ESL Writers," discusses concerns of special interest to nonnative writers, and *ESL Tips* in the *Instructor's Annotated Edition* guide instructors in helping ESL students get the most out of the text. The new ancillary *Bedford/St. Martin's ESL Workbook* provides even more ESL coverage for students who need it most.

Each chapter offers numerous opportunities for practice and review. Easy-to-grade *Practices* following each section of every chapter form a strand of workbook-style mastery exercises that let students hone specific skills. (These Practices can supplement or replace the Writing First strand, depending on an instructor's preference.) *Visual writing prompts* in Chapter 14's essay assignments serve as additional sources of inspiration for writing. *Self-Assessment Checklists* in the paragraph and essay chapters show students how to revise and edit their own writing. Three kinds of *Chapter Review* activities provide additional practice opportunities: an *Editing Practice* featuring a passage of student writing gives students an opportunity to edit to eliminate a specific writing problem; *Collaborative Activities* offer creative options for student-centered classroom learning; and a *Review Checklist* recaps the main points of each chapter for quick review. *Unit Reviews* at the end of units 4, 5, 6, and 7 allow students to edit and correct two-page essays that contain a variety of different kinds of errors. Finally, *Answers to Odd-Numbered Exercise Items* at the end of the book let students check their own work as they practice and review.

Writing First **helps students make the connection between reading and writing.** Chapter 35, "Reading for College," guides students step by step through the reading process and includes a sample annotated reading. Chapter 36, "Readings for Writers," contains nineteen professional readings that illustrate the patterns of development covered in the paragraph and essay chapters of the book. Questions following each reading test comprehension, help build vocabulary skills, and offer topics for student writing.

Writing First **respects students as serious writers.** This text has more student writing than any other developmental textbook: numerous paragraph-length examples as well as thirty-three complete essays provide realistic models. The tone and level of explanatory material, as well as the subject matter of examples and exercises, acknowledge the diverse interests, ages, and experiences of developmental writers.

Appendixes cover skills that students can also use in other courses. Appendix A, "Strategies for College Success" (unique in books of this type), introduces students to practical strategies they can use throughout their college careers. Appendix B, "Writing a Research Paper," teaches students the basics of researching and writing a paper and citing and documenting sources. The chapter includes an annotated sample student paper in MLA style. The new Appendix C, "Taking Standardized Assessment Tests," orients students to some of the major standardized tests and offers practical advice and strategies to help them prepare for—and take—these important exams.

New to This Edition

In revising *Writing First,* our goal was to expand and improve upon the features that students and instructors have found most helpful in previous editions, at the same time adding features to make the book address the realities of the developmental classroom more practically and more directly.

New Grammar in Context boxes in each paragraph and essay chapter. These boxes help students identify and correct common grammar problems related to the rhetorical pattern they are learning. The boxes are cross-referenced to *Writing First*'s grammar sections where students can get more help on the problems they find most challenging.

New Unit Reviews that test students in realistic situations. Two-page essays that contain multiple types of errors, the new Unit Reviews allow students to practice correcting and editing writing in realistic situations. More practice is available online in **extra Unit Reviews in the Exercise Central database.**

A unique appendix on high-stakes test taking. Appendix C, a new appendix that orients students to high-stakes tests—the Georgia Regents, the Florida CLAST, the Texas THEA, the CUNY/ACT, the Accuplacer, and the COMPASS/ASSET test—has been added to give students a spectrum of study skills, preparation, and test-taking strategies. A handy correlation guide shows students how to use *Writing First* to practice for taking any of these tests.

Visual glosses for every Editing Practice and Unit Review. Marginal photographs and illustrations provide cultural context for students who need additional background for their reading and more help with vocabulary.

Expanded ESL coverage and new ESL Workbook. The comprehensive ESL chapter, addressing concerns of special interest to nonnative writers, has been thoroughly revised and expanded and now includes new sections on gerunds and modal auxiliaries. The new ancillary *Bedford/St. Martin's ESL Workbook* provides even more ESL exercises and coverage for students who need it most.

New readings and student essays. Six professional essays in Chapter 36, chosen for their focus on timely topics likely to be of interest to students, are new to this edition. Also, many of the student essays featured in the twenty-two Chapter Reviews are new.

Thoroughly revised and updated exercise topics that engage students' interest. *Writing First*'s exercises have been refreshed to better cover the subjects of everyday life, the world of work, academics, and historical and cultural issues.

Ancillaries

Writing First is accompanied by a comprehensive teaching support package that includes the following items:

Print Resources

■ The *Instructor's Annotated Edition* includes answers to the Practice exercises as well as numerous teaching tips and ESL tips in the margins.

■ *Classroom Resources for Instructors Using WRITING FIRST* includes helpful teaching suggestions, sample syllabi, and additional teaching materials.

■ *Teaching Developmental Writing: Background Readings* offers more than two dozen professional articles on topics of interest to developmental writing instructors, accompanied by suggestions for practical applications to the classroom.

■ *Diagnostic and Mastery Tests to Accompany WRITING FIRST* offers diagnostic and mastery tests complementing the topic coverage in *Writing First*. This volume's perforated pages enable instructors to copy the material and distribute it to students.

■ *Supplemental Exercises to Accompany WRITING FIRST* offers additional grammar exercises (including material from the Exercise Central online exercise collection). Like *Diagnostic and Mastery Tests,* this book is offered as a workbook with perforated pages to make it easier for instructors to copy and distribute the exercises to students.

■ *The Bedford/St. Martin's ESL Workbook* provides ESL students with a broad range of exercises covering grammatical issues for multilingual students of varying language skills and backgrounds.

■ *Transparency Masters to Accompany WRITING FIRST,* including editable student writing samples from the text, are available as a printed package and as files downloadable from the Web site.

New Media Resources

■ **Exercise Central,** the largest collection of grammar exercises available with any writing text, includes multiple-exercise sets on every grammar topic to give students all the practice they need. This software can be accessed via the Internet at <bedfordstmartins.com/exercisecentral>.

■ *Exercise Central To Go: Writing and Grammar Practices for Basic Writers* is drawn from the popular Exercise Central resource. This CD-ROM includes hundreds of additional practice items to help students build their writing and editing skills. The practices have been extensively class-tested and no Internet access is necessary.

■ The *Writing First* companion Web site <bedfordstmartins.com/writingfirst> offers downloadable teaching aids and links to other useful materials.

■ *Testing Tool Kit: A Writing and Grammar Test Bank,* a comprehensive CD-ROM, allows instructors to create secure, customized tests and quizzes from a pool of nearly 2,000 questions. The ready-to-administer diagnostic tests and questions at two levels of difficulty make this a flexible resource.

Acknowledgments

In our work on *Writing First,* we have benefited from the help of a great many people.

Franklin E. Horowitz of Teachers College, Columbia University, drafted the earliest version of Chapter 30, "Grammar and Usage for ESL Writers," and his linguist's insight continues to inform that chapter. Linda Stine and Linda Stengle of Lincoln University devoted energy and vision to the preparation of *Classroom Resources for Instructors.* Linda Mason Austin of McLennan Community College drew on her extensive teaching experience to contribute teaching tips and ESL tips to the *Instructor's Annotated Edition.* Susan Bernstein's work on the compilation and annotation of *Teaching Developmental Writing* reflects her deep commitment to scholarship and teaching. Sapna Gandhi brought her enthusiasm and ESL expertise to developing the *ESL Workbook.* We are very grateful for their contributions.

We thank Judith Lechner for her work on Exercise Central and the accompanying exercise book. Carol Sullivan and Mark Gallaher, longtime friends and colleagues, made valuable contributions to the book's exercises, and we thank them as well.

Writing First could not exist without our students, whose words appear on almost every page of the book, whether in sample sentences, paragraphs, or essays. Our thanks go to Dan Brody, Joyce Chin, Daniel Corey, Andrea de Marco, Kim DiPialo, Jerry Doyle, Stella Drew, Ann Duong, Thaddeus Eddy, Margaret Farah, John Fleeger, Jorge Hernandez, Nisha Jani, Toni-Ann Marro, Ethan A. Nadelmann, Rob O'Neal, Sean Ragas, Scott Rathmill, Cheri Rodriguez, Jen Rossi, Neena Thomas, Kimberley Toomer, Mina Tran, Scott Wedkerly, Jared White, Kristin Whitehead, and Alisha Woolery.

Instructors throughout the country have contributed suggestions and encouragement at various stages of the book's development. For their collegial support, we thank Grisel Acosta, Hudson County Community College; Joy Bashore, Central Virginia Community College; Deborah Davis, Dallas County Community College; Denise Diamond, College of the Desert; Carmen Hall, St. Petersburg Junior College; Ken Halliday, Southern State Community College; Teresa Irvin, Columbus State University; Patricia Johnson, Broward Community College North; Frederick Jones, St. Augustine's College; Lisa Kekaha, Butte Community College; Brenda Kwon, Honolulu Community College; Ronald Leonardo, Modesto Junior College; Patricia A. Malinowski, Finger Lakes Community College; Patricia McDonald, Palm Beach Community College; David Merves, Miami-Dade College North; Julie Mix, Wayne State University; Jessica Nathanson, Kilian Community College; Barbara J. Nelson, Southeast Community College; Christine O'Hale, Chicago State University; Mike Periclakes, Heald College; Patti Plasket, Palm Beach Community College; Gail Watson, County College of Morris; and Justin Williamson, Pearl River Community College.

At Bedford/St. Martin's, we thank the editorial director, Denise Wydra, and president Joan Feinberg, who believed in this project and gave us support and encouragement from the outset. We thank Nancy Perry, editor in chief and our longtime friend, who continues to earn our respect as well as our affection. We also thank Paul Stenis, associate editor, for his diligent work in revising the book's ancillaries; Robin Butterhof, editorial assistant, for helping with numerous tasks, big and small; Erica Appel, managing editor, and Shuli Traub, senior project editor, for guiding the book ably through production; Lucy Krikorian, art director, for overseeing the beautiful and innovative design; Nick Carbone, director of New Media, for overseeing the production of the *Writing Guide Software;* and New Media editors Harriet Wald and Coleen O'Hanley for their work on the *Writing First* Web site. Thanks also go to Dennis Conroy, senior production supervisor; Karen Melton Soeltz, director of marketing; and Rachel Falk, senior marketing manager. Finally, we would like to thank our editor, Joelle Hann, who took over the project in this edition without missing a beat. Her insights, energy, and thoroughness have helped to make this book as good as it could possibly be.

We are grateful, too, for the continued support of our families — Mark, Adam, and Rebecca Kirszner and Demi, David, and Sarah Mandell. Finally, we are grateful for the survival and growth of the writing partnership we entered into in 1975, when we were graduate students. We had no idea then of the wonderful places our collaborative efforts would take us. Now, we know.

Laurie G. Kirszner
Stephen R. Mandell

Contents

REVISING AND EDITING YOUR WRITING   227

BECOMING A CRITICAL READER 579

UNIT EIGHT Reading Essays 579

A Student's Guide to Using Writing First

What *Writing First* Can Do for You

It is no secret that writing will be very important in most of the courses you take in college. Whether you write lab reports or English papers, midterms or final exams, your ability to organize your thoughts and express them in writing will help to determine how well you do. In other words, succeeding at writing is the first step toward succeeding in college. Perhaps even more important, writing is a key to success outside the classroom. On the job and in everyday life, if you can express yourself clearly and effectively, you will stand a better chance of achieving your goals and making a difference in the world around you.

Whether you write as a student, as an employee, as a parent, or as a concerned citizen, your writing almost always has a specific purpose. For example, when you write an essay, a memo, a letter, or a research paper, you are completing an exercise but you are also giving other people information or telling them your ideas or opinions. That is why, in this book, we do not ask you simply to do grammar exercises and fill in blanks. In each chapter, we also ask you to apply the skills you are learning to a piece of your own writing.

As teachers—and as former students—we know how demanding college can be and how hard it is to juggle assignments with work and family responsibilities. We also know that you do not want to waste your time or money. That is why in *Writing First* we make information easy to find and use and provide many different features to help you become a better writer.

The following sections describe the key features of *Writing First*. If you take the time now to familiarize yourself with these features, you will be able to use the book more effectively later on.

> **Teaching Tip**
> Go over this guide with students on the first day of class. Once they have looked through the book and located some of its helpful features, they are more likely to use the book as a resource during the semester.

How *Writing First* Makes Information Easy to Find and Use

Brief table of contents   Inside the front cover is a brief table of contents that summarizes the topics covered in this book. This feature can help you find a particular chapter quickly.

Detailed table of contents   The table of contents that starts on page xi provides a detailed breakdown of the book's topics. Use this table of contents to find a specific part of a particular chapter.

Index   The index, which appears at the back of the book starting on page 715, enables you to locate all the available information about a particular topic. The topics appear in alphabetical order; so, for example, if you wanted to find out how to use commas, you would find the *C* section and look up the word *comma*. (If the page number following a word is **boldfaced,** that tells you that on that page you can find a definition of the word.)

List of Self-Assessment Checklists   On page xxviii is a list of checklists designed to help you write, revise, and fine-tune the paragraphs and essays you compose. Use this list to help you find the checklist that is most useful for the particular writing assignment you are working on.

A handy cross-referencing system   Often, an *italicized marginal cross-reference* will point you to another section of the book (for example, "*See 26A and 26B*"). At the tops of most pages of *Writing First,* you will find *quick-reference corner tabs* consisting of green-and-blue boxes, each containing a number and a letter. This information tells you which chapter you have turned to and which section of that chapter you are looking at. Together, the cross-references and the tabs help you find information quickly. For example, if a cross-reference in the text suggests, "*See 10A for more on definition,*" you can use the tabs to help you locate section 10A.

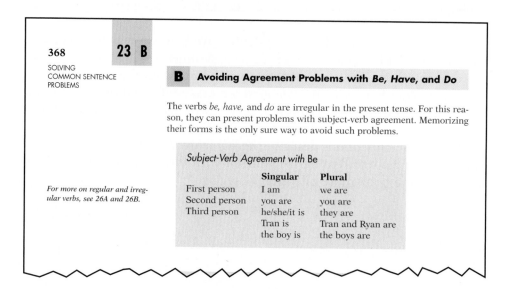

368

23 B

SOLVING
COMMON SENTENCE
PROBLEMS

B   Avoiding Agreement Problems with *Be, Have,* and *Do*

The verbs *be, have,* and *do* are irregular in the present tense. For this reason, they can present problems with subject-verb agreement. Memorizing their forms is the only sure way to avoid such problems.

For more on regular and irregular verbs, see 26A and 26B.

Subject-Verb Agreement with *Be*

	Singular	**Plural**
First person	I am	we are
Second person	you are	you are
Third person	he/she/it is	they are
	Tran is	Tran and Ryan are
	the boy is	the boys are

How *Writing First* Can Help You Become a Better Writer

Preview boxes   Each chapter starts with a list of key concepts that will be discussed in the chapter. Looking at these boxes before you skim the chapter will help you get an overview of the chapter.

PREVIEW

In this chapter, you will learn

■ to use apostrophes to form contractions (32A)

■ to use apostrophes to form possessives (32B)

■ to revise incorrect use of apostrophes (32C)

Writing First activities   Most chapters include a three-part writing activity that helps you apply specific skills to your own writing. Each chapter starts with a *Writing First* assignment that asks you to write about a particular topic. (An accompanying photograph or other visual is included to stimulate your writing.) Beside each assignment, a Word Power box lists two or three vocabulary words (and their definitions) that you might find useful as you write your response. Throughout the chapter, *Flashback* exercises help you analyze your Writing First response so you can identify and correct specific writing problems. Finally, a *Revising and Editing* exercise asks you to fine-tune your writing. (See, for example, pages 229, 232, and 238 in Chapter 15.)

Focus boxes   Throughout the book, boxes with the word *Focus* in a red banner highlight useful information, identify key points, and explain difficult concepts.

FOCUS   **Using Specific Words**

One way to strengthen your writing is to avoid **utility words**—general words like *good, nice,* or *great.* Instead, take the time to think of more specific words. For example, when you say the ocean looked *pretty,* do you really mean that it *sparkled, glistened, rippled, foamed, surged,* or *billowed?*

Grammar in Context   In Chapters 3 to 14 you will find boxes that identify key grammar problems that you will encounter as you practice writing each pattern of development. Use these boxes to increase your understanding of important mechanics issues in your writing.

GRAMMAR IN CONTEXT **Narration**

When you write a narrative paragraph, you tell a story. As you become involved in your story, you may find yourself stringing incidents together without proper punctuation. The result will be a **run-on** or **comma splice**.

INCORRECT (RUN-ON)   We soon ran out of food and supplies I thought we would never make it at last we reached Malaysia.

CORRECT   We soon ran out of food and supplies. I thought we would never make it, but at last we reached Malaysia.

For information on how to identify and correct run-ons and comma splices, see Chapter 21.

Self-Assessment Checklists Chapters 1, 3 to 12, and 14 include Self-Assessment Checklists that offer you a handy way to check your work and measure your progress. Use these checklists to help you revise your writing before you hand it in.

☑ **SELF-ASSESSMENT CHECKLIST:**
Writing a Narrative Paragraph

Unity

☐ Does your topic sentence tell readers what the point of the paragraph is?

☐ Is your topic sentence specific enough?

☐ Do all details and events support your topic sentence?

Development

☐ Should you add more events or details to make your narrative clearer or livelier?

Marginal notes In the margins of *Writing First,* you will find several kinds of notes that give you additional information in an easy-to-read format. *Writing Tips* offer practical information and helpful hints, including definitions and examples. *Word Power* boxes define words you might choose to include in your Writing First response. Finally, if you need additional practice with specific skills, *marginal cross-references to the* Exercise Central *online exercise collection* have been added to the text.

● **Writing Tip**

Because narrative paragraphs tell what happened, they often use transitional words and phrases that indicate time, such as *after, before, now,* and *then*. (See 2D.)

Word Power

adapt   to adjust to new surroundings

mentor   an experienced and trusted adviser

facilitate   to make easy

A STUDENT'S GUIDE TO
USING *WRITING FIRST*

Review Checklists   Each grammar chapter ends with a summary of the most important information in the chapter. Use these checklists to review material for quizzes or to remind yourself of the main points in the chapter you have been studying.

☑ **REVIEW CHECKLIST:**
Run-Ons and Comma Splices

☐ A run-on is an error that occurs when two sentences are joined without punctuation. (See 21A.)

☐ A comma splice is an error that occurs when two sentences are joined with just a comma. (See 21A.)

☐ Correct a run-on or comma splice by creating two separate sentences, by using a coordinating conjunction, by using a semicolon, by using a semicolon followed by a conjunctive adverb or transitional expression, or by connecting clauses with a subordinating conjunction or relative pronoun. (See 21B.)

Answers to Odd-Numbered Exercise Items   Starting on page 701, you will find answers for some of the Practice items in the book. When you need to study a topic independently or when your instructor has you complete a Practice but not hand it in, you can consult these answers to see if you are on the right track.

How *Writing First* Can Help You Succeed in Other Courses

In a sense, this whole book is all about succeeding in other courses. After all, writing is the key to success in college. But *Writing First* also includes specific sections at the end of the book that you may find especially useful in courses you take later on in college. We have designed these sections so you can use them on your own as well as with your instructor's help.

Appendix A, "Strategies for College Success"   This practical guide offers specific, useful information on a wide variety of important topics, such as note-taking, study skills, time management, and using the Internet.

Appendix B, "Writing a Research Paper"   This appendix gives a short overview of the research process and shows how to document sources and create a list of works cited. A student paper complete with helpful marginal notes is also included.

Appendix C, "Taking Standardized Assessment Tests"   This appendix gives an overview of important placement tests and exit exams along with tips on how to prepare for them.

List of correction symbols   The chart inside the back cover lists marks that many instructors use when evaluating and marking student papers. Become familiar with these symbols so that you get the most out of your instructor's comments on your work.

Self-Assessment Checklists for Writing Paragraphs and Essays

Units 1–3 of *Writing First* include a number of Self-Assessment Checklists designed to help you write, revise, and fine-tune your paragraphs and essays. You can use these checklists both in your writing course and in other courses that include written assignments. The following list shows the page number for each checklist.

UNIT ONE

Focus on Paragraphs

Writing a Paragraph

■ WRITING FIRST

As the pictures above show, students in college today may find themselves either in a traditional classroom or in a more career-oriented setting. What do you think is the primary purpose of college—to give students a general education or to prepare them for specific careers? Look at the pictures, and think about this question carefully as you read the pages that follow. This is the topic you will be writing about as you move through this chapter.

PREVIEW

In this chapter, you will learn

■ to understand paragraph structure (1A)

■ to focus on your assignment, purpose, and audience (1B)

■ to find ideas (1C)

■ to identify your main idea (1D)

■ to choose and arrange supporting points (1E)

■ to draft a paragraph (1F)

■ to revise a paragraph (1G)

Word Power
primary most important

aspiration a strong desire for high achievement; an ambitious goal

Writing is not just something you do to get a grade in school; writing is a life skill. If you can write clearly, you can express your ideas convincingly to others—in school, on the job, and in the community.

Writing takes many different forms. In college, you might write a single paragraph, an essay exam, a short paper, or a long research paper. At work, you might write a memo, a proposal, or a report. In your daily life as a citizen of your community, you might write a letter or an email asking for information or explaining a problem that needs to be solved.

Writing is important. If you can write, you can communicate; if you can communicate effectively, you can succeed in school and beyond.

*For information on how
paragraphs work in an essay,
see 12A.*

A Understanding Paragraph Structure

Because **paragraphs** are central to almost every writing task, learning to write one is an important step in becoming a competent writer. This chapter takes you through the process of writing a paragraph. Although a paragraph can be a complete piece of writing in itself—as it is in a short classroom exercise or an exam answer—most of the time a paragraph is part of a longer piece of writing.

A paragraph is a group of sentences that is unified by a single main idea. The **topic sentence** states the main idea, and the rest of the sentences in the paragraph **support** the main idea. Often a final **concluding statement** sums up the paragraph's main idea.

> ● **Writing Tip**
> Try to write at least five or six sentences to support your topic sentence.

Paragraph

Topic sentence	A paragraph consists of a **topic sentence** and **support**. The topic sentence states the main idea of the paragraph. This idea unifies the paragraph. The
Supporting sentences	other sentences in the paragraph provide support. These sentences present details, facts, and examples. At the end of the paragraph is a final **con-**
Concluding statement	**cluding statement**, a sentence that sums up the paragraph's main idea. Many paragraphs follow this general structure.

> ● **Writing Tip**
> Sometimes a sentence ends with a question mark (?) or an exclamation point (!).

Note that the first sentence of a paragraph is **indented**, starting about one-half inch (five spaces) from the left-hand margin. Every sentence begins with a capital letter and, in most cases, ends with a period.

> **Teaching Tip**
> Newspaper paragraphs usually have fewer sentences than other paragraphs. Explain to students that this length is necessitated by the width of the columns.

◆ PRACTICE 1-1

Bring two paragraphs to class—one from a newspaper or magazine article and one from a textbook. Compare your paragraphs with those brought in by other students. What features do all your paragraphs share? How do the paragraphs differ from one another?

B Focusing on Your Assignment, Purpose, and Audience

> **Teaching Tip**
> Ask students to share with the class the writing tasks they have had in the past month in school, at work, and in the community.

In college, a writing task—whether it is a paragraph, an essay, or a research paper—usually begins with an assignment that gives you a topic to write about. Instead of plunging in headfirst and starting to write, take time to consider some questions about your **assignment** (*what* you are expected to write about), your **purpose** (*why* you are writing), and your **audience** (*for whom* you are writing). Finding out the answers to these questions at this point will save you time in the long run.

Questions about Assignment, Purpose, and Audience

Assignment

- What is your assignment?
- Do you have a word or page limit?
- When is your assignment due?
- Will you be expected to complete your assignment at home or in class?
- Will you be expected to work on your own or with others?
- Will you be allowed to revise before you hand in your assignment?
- Will you be allowed to revise after you hand in your assignment?

Purpose

- Are you expected to express your personal reactions—for example, to tell how you feel about a piece of music or a news event?
- Are you expected to present information—for example, to answer an exam question, describe a process in a lab report, or summarize a story or essay you have read?
- Are you expected to argue for or against a position on a controversial issue?

Audience

- Who will read your paper—just your instructor or other students as well?
- Do you have an audience beyond the classroom—for example, your supervisor at work or your landlord?
- How much will your readers know about your topic?
- Will your readers expect you to use formal or informal language?

◆ PRACTICE 1-2

Each of the following writing tasks has a different audience and purpose. Think about how you would approach each task. (Use the Questions about Assignment, Purpose, and Audience listed above to help you decide on the best strategy.) On the lines following each task, make some notes about your approach. Discuss your responses with your class or in a small group.

1. For the other students in your writing class, describe your best or worst educational experience.

   Answers will vary. Students will include personal experiences and will

   probably use informal language.

   _____

   _____

2. For the instructor of an introductory psychology course, discuss how early educational experiences can affect a student's performance throughout his or her schooling.

   Answers will vary. Students will probably use fairly formal language and

   may include facts and findings from studies.

> **Teaching Tip**
> Some students may be reluctant to write in the book because they are afraid of making mistakes. (They will also have been told in high school never to write in a textbook.) Encourage them to write directly in the text where it is required.

> **ESL Tip**
> Make sure at least one student from another culture shares his or her experience or idea. Nonnative speakers often feel isolated because of the language barrier. You may have to draw them in each time you have a class discussion.

3. Write a short letter to your community's school board in which you try to convince members to make two or three specific changes that you believe would improve the schools you attended or those your children might attend.

   Answers will vary. Students will probably use formal language and include

   both personal experiences and objective information.

4. Write a letter to a work supervisor—either past or current—telling what you appreciate about his or her supervision and how it has helped you develop and grow as an employee.

   Answers will vary. Students may use either informal or formal language

   and will include personal experiences.

C Finding Ideas

Once you know what, why, and for whom you are writing, you can begin the process of finding material to write about. This process is different for every writer.

Stella Drew, a student in an introductory writing course, was given this assignment:

> Should community service—unpaid work in the community—be a required part of the college curriculum? Write a paragraph in which you answer this question.

Before she drafted her paragraph, Stella used a variety of strategies to help her find ideas to write about. The pages that follow illustrate the four strategies she used: *freewriting, brainstorming, clustering,* and *journal writing.*

Freewriting

When you **freewrite**, you write for a set period of time—perhaps five minutes—without stopping, even if what you are writing doesn't seem to have a point or a direction. Your goal is to relax and let ideas flow without worrying about whether or not they are related. Sometimes you can free-write without a topic in mind, but at other times you will focus your attention on a particular topic. This strategy is called **focused freewriting**.

When you finish freewriting, read what you have written, and underline any ideas you think you might be able to use. If you find an idea you want to explore further, freewrite again, using that idea as a starting point.

Here is Stella's focused freewriting on the topic of whether or not community service should be a required part of the college curriculum.

Community service. Community service. Sounds like what you do instead of going to jail. Service to the community—service in the community. Community center. College community—community college. Community service—I guess it's a good idea to do it—but when? In my spare time—spare time—that's pretty funny. So after school and work and all the reading and studying I also have to do service? Right. And what could I do anyway? Work with kids. Or homeless people. Old people? Sick people? Or not people—maybe animals. Or work for a political candidate. Does that count? But when would I do it? Maybe other people have time, but I don't. OK idea, could work— but not for me.

Freewriting

◆ PRACTICE 1-3

Reread Stella's freewriting on the topic of community service for college students. If you were advising her, which of her ideas would you suggest she explore further? Underline these ideas in her freewriting, and then recopy them on the lines below.

Answers will vary.

_____

_____

_____

_____

_____

_____

_____

_____

_____

1 C

Teaching Tip
You may prefer to give students an alternate assignment or a choice of topics to
write about.

◆ **PRACTICE 1-4**

Now it is time for you to begin the work that will result in a finished paragraph. (You already have your assignment from the Writing First box on
page 3: to write about whether the primary purpose of college is to give
students a general education or to prepare them for careers.) Your first
step is to freewrite about this assignment. On a blank sheet of lined paper
(or on your computer), write for at least five minutes without stopping. If
you have trouble thinking of something to write, keep recopying the last
word you have written until something else comes to mind.

◆ **PRACTICE 1-5**

Reread the freewriting you did for Practice 1-4. Underline any ideas you
think you might use in your paragraph. Then, choose one of these ideas,
and use it as a starting point for another focused freewriting exercise.

Brainstorming

When you **brainstorm**, you record all the ideas about your topic that you
can think of. Unlike freewriting, brainstorming is often scattered all over
the page. You don't have to use complete sentences; single words or
phrases are fine. You can underline, star, or box important points. You can
also ask questions, list points, draw arrows to connect ideas, and even
draw pictures or diagrams.

Stella's brainstorming on the topic of community service appears below.

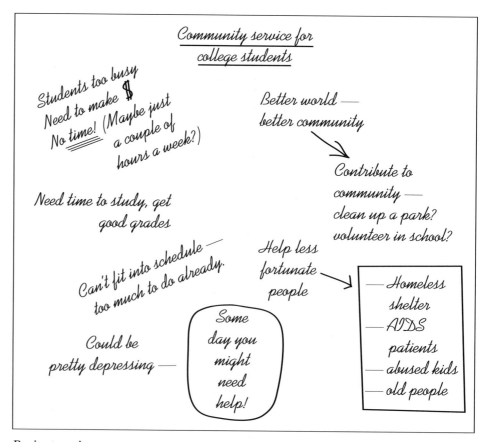

Brainstorming

ESL Tip
Suggest that students ask
a native-English-speaking
classmate to brainstorm into
a tape recorder. Have students try to write down exactly what was said and then
read the material aloud.
(This exercise develops
listening, speaking, and
writing skills.)

> **FOCUS Collaborative Brainstorming**
>
> You usually brainstorm on your own, but at times you may find it
> helpful to do **collaborative brainstorming**, working with other stu-
> dents to find ideas. Sometimes your instructor may ask you and an-
> other student to brainstorm together. At other times, the class might
> brainstorm as a group while your instructor writes ideas on the
> board. However you brainstorm, your goal is the same: to come up
> with as much material about your topic as you can.

◆ PRACTICE 1-6

Reread Stella's brainstorming notes on community service (page 8). How
is her brainstorming similar to her freewriting on the same subject
(page 7)? How is it different? If you were advising Stella, which ideas
would you suggest she write more about? Which ideas should she cross
out? Write your suggestions on the lines below.

Write more on these ideas: _____

Answers will vary.

_____

Cross out these ideas: _____

Answers will vary.

_____

◆ PRACTICE 1-7

On a sheet of *unlined* paper, brainstorm about your assignment: What do
you think is the primary purpose of college—to give students a general education or to prepare them for careers? (Begin by writing your topic, "The
purpose of college," at the top of the page.) Write quickly, without worrying about using complete sentences. Try writing on different parts of the
page, making lists, and drawing arrows to connect related ideas. When you
have finished, look over what you have written. Which ideas are the most
interesting? Did you come up with any new ideas as you brainstormed that
you did not discover while freewriting?

◆ PRACTICE 1-8

Working as a class or in a group of three or four students, practice collaborative brainstorming. First, decide as a group on a topic for brainstorming. (Your instructor may assign a topic.) Next, choose one person to write
down ideas on a blank sheet of paper or on the board. (If your group is
large enough, you might choose two people to write down ideas and have
them compare notes at the end of the brainstorming session.) Then, discuss the topic informally, with each person contributing at least one idea.

After fifteen minutes or so, review the ideas that have been written down. As a group, try to identify interesting connections among ideas and suggest ideas that might be explored further.

Clustering

Clustering, sometimes called *mapping*, is another strategy that can help you find ideas to write about. When you cluster, you begin by writing your topic in the center of a sheet of paper. Then, you branch out, writing related ideas on the page in groups, or clusters, around the topic. As you add new ideas, you circle them and draw lines to connect the ideas to one another and to the topic at the center. (These lines will look like spokes of a wheel or branches of a tree.) As you move from the center to the corners of the page, your ideas will get more and more specific.

Stella's clustering on the topic of community service for college students appears below.

Clustering

Note: Sometimes, one branch of your exercise will give you all the material you need. At other times, you may decide to write about the ideas from several branches—or to choose one or two from each branch. If you find you need additional material after you finish your first cluster exercise, you can cluster again on a new sheet of paper, this time beginning with a topic from one of the branches.

◆ PRACTICE 1-9

Reread Stella's clustering on community service (page 10). How is it similar to her brainstorming on the same subject (page 8)? How is it different? If you were advising Stella, which branches of the cluster diagram would you say seem most promising? Why? Can you add any branches? Can you extend any of her branches further? Write your suggestions on the following lines. Then, discuss them with your class or in a small group.

Answers will vary.

_____

_____

_____

_____

_____

◆ PRACTICE 1-10

Try clustering on your assignment: What do you think is the primary purpose of college—to give students a general education or to prepare them for careers? Begin by writing your topic in the center of a blank sheet of unlined paper. Circle the topic, and then branch out with specific ideas and examples, continuing to the edge of the page if you can. When you have finished, look over what you have written. What are the most interesting ideas in your cluster diagram? Which branches seem most promising as the basis for further writing? What new ideas have you come up with that you did not get from your freewriting or brainstorming?

Journal Writing

A **journal** is a notebook in which you keep an informal record of your thoughts and ideas. In a journal, you can reflect, question, summarize, or even complain. When you are involved in a writing project, your journal is a place where you jot down ideas to write about and think on paper about your assignment. Here you can try to resolve a problem, restart a stalled project, argue with yourself about your topic, or critique a draft. You can also try out different versions of sentences, keep track of details or examples, or keep a record of potentially useful things you read, see, or hear.

> ● **Writing Tip**
>
> If your instructor allows you to, you can keep your journal in a computer file.

Journal writing works best when you write regularly, preferably at the same time each day, so that it becomes a habit. Once you have started making regular entries in your journal, take the time every week or so to go back and reread what you have written. You may find material you want to explore in further journal entries—or even an idea for a paper.

FOCUS **Journals**

Here are some subjects you can write about in your journal:

- *Your school work*   You can use your journal to explore ideas for writing assignments. When you get a specific assignment, you can write a journal entry in which you record your thoughts about it and try to decide what you might write about. Your journal can also be a place where you think about what you have learned, ask questions about concepts you are having trouble understanding, and examine new ideas and new ways of seeing the world. Writing regularly in a journal about what you are studying in school can even help you become a better student.

- *Your job*   In your journal, you can record job-related successes and frustrations, examine conflicts with coworkers, or review how you handled problems on the job. Reading over these entries can help you understand your strengths and weaknesses and become a more effective employee. As an added bonus, you may discover work-related topics to write about in school.

- *Your ideas about current events*   Expressing your opinions in your journal can be a good way to explore complex ideas (or just to let off steam). Your entries may spur you to write letters to your local or school newspaper or to public officials—and even to become involved in community projects or political activities.

- *Your impressions of what you see around you*   Many professional and amateur writers carry their journals with them everywhere so they can record any interesting or unusual things they observe in the course of their daily lives. Rather than relying on memory, they jot down images of memorable people, places, or events as soon as possible after they observe them. If you get into the habit of recording such impressions, you can later incorporate them into essays or other pieces of writing.

- *Aspects of your personal life*   Although you may not want to record the intimate details of your life if your instructor plans to collect your journal, such entries are the most common of all in a private journal. Writing about relationships with family and friends, personal problems, hopes and dreams—all the details of your life—can help you develop a better understanding of yourself and others.

Teaching Tip
If students are reluctant to write about personal details in their journals, you might give them the option of labeling some pages "Do not read" or even taping them closed.

Here is Stella's journal entry on the topic of community service for college students.

> *I'm not really sure what I think about community service. I guess I think it sounds like a good idea, but I still don't see why we should have to do it. I can't fit anything else into my life. I guess it would be possible if it was just an hour or two a week. And maybe we could get credit and a grade for it, like a course. Or maybe it should just be for people who have the time and want to do it. But if it's not required, will anyone do it?*

Journal Entry

◆ PRACTICE 1-11

Buy a notebook to use as a journal. (Your instructor may require a specific size and format, particularly if journals are going to be collected at some point, or you may be permitted to keep your journal in a computer file.) Set a regular time to write for fifteen minutes or so in your journal—during your lunch break, for example, or before you go to bed. Make entries daily or several times a week, depending on your schedule and your instructor's suggestions. For your first journal entry, write down your thoughts about the topic you have been working on in this chapter: the primary purpose of college.

D   Identifying Your Main Idea

When you think you have enough material to write about, you can move on to the next stage of the writing process: finding a main idea to develop and selecting and organizing the points that will support that idea most effectively.

To find a main idea for your paragraph, begin by looking over what you have already written. As you read through your freewriting, brainstorming, clustering, and journal entries, look for the **main idea**—the central point that your material seems to support. If your assignment is to write a paragraph, the sentence that states your main idea and gives your writing its focus will be the paragraph's **topic sentence**.

When Stella Drew reviewed her notes, she saw that they included ideas about both the value of doing community service and the problems it presents. She thought her notes could support the idea that community service requires time and commitment but is basically worthwhile. She stated this idea in a sentence:

```
Community service takes time, but it is so important that
college students should be required to do it.
```

● **Writing Tip**

If at any stage of the writing process you run out of ideas, return to the strategies you found most helpful, and use them to help you find more material.

For more on topic sentences, see 2A.

◆ **PRACTICE 1-12**

In Practices 1-4, 1-7, and 1-10, you practiced freewriting, brainstorming, and clustering. Now, you are ready to write a paragraph in response to the following assignment:

> Do you think the primary purpose of college is to give students a general education or to prepare them for careers?

Your first step is to find a main idea for your paragraph. Look over the work you have done so far, and try to decide what main idea your material can best support. (This idea will be your paragraph's topic sentence.) Write the sentence that expresses this idea on the lines below.

Main idea: _Answers will vary._

● **Writing Tip**

Your paragraph's topic sentence should answer the question asked in the assignment.

E **Choosing and Arranging Supporting Points**

Choosing Supporting Points

After you identify your main idea, review your notes again. This time, look for specific facts, reasons, and examples to **support** your main idea. Write or type the topic sentence that states this main idea at the top of a blank page. As you review your notes, list all the supporting points you think you might be able to use.

Stella chose the following points from her notes to support her paragraph's main idea. After she read through her list of points, she crossed out three that she thought would not support her main idea.

```
Main idea: Community service takes time, but it is
so important that college students should be required
to do it.
```

- ~~Community service helps people~~.
- ~~Some community service activities could be boring~~.
- Community service can help the world.
- Community service helps the community.
- College students are busy.
- Community service takes a lot of time.
- ~~Community service might not relate to students' majors~~.
- Community service can be upsetting or depressing.
- Community service can be part of a student's education.

Arranging Supporting Points

After you have made a list of points you think you can use, your next step is to arrange them in the order in which you plan to discuss them in your paragraph.

When she read over her list of supporting points, Stella saw that she had two different kinds of points: some points identified the problems of doing community service, and other points identified the advantages of doing community service. When she arranged her points, she decided to group them in these two categories under the headings "problems" and "advantages."

Once you have made a list of points you can use, arrange your ideas in the order in which you plan to present them, as Stella did in the following list.

```
Main idea: Community service takes time, but it is
so important that college students should be required
to do it.
```

```
Problems
```
*   Community service takes a lot of time.
*   Students are busy (family and friends, studying, working).
*   Community service can be depressing and upsetting.

```
Advantages
```
*   Community service helps the community.
*   Community service can be part of a student's education.
*   Community service can make the world a better place.

● **Writing Tip**

You can arrange your points in time order, spatial order, or logical order. (See 2D.)

Teaching Tip
Remind students that they will need specific examples to support their main ideas. Have two or three students who have done community service talk about their experiences.

◆ PRACTICE 1-13

Now, continue your work on your own paragraph. Reread your freewriting, brainstorming, and clustering, and list the points you believe can best support your main idea.

Main idea: _Answers will vary._ _____

_____

_____

Supporting points:

*   _Answers will vary._ _____

*   _____

*   _____

*   _____

Can you think of any new points that could support your main idea? If so, list them below.

New points:

*   _Answers will vary._ _____

*   _____

● **Writing Tip**

Try to group related points together. For example, first list all your points about getting a general education, and then list all your points about preparing for a career.

Teaching Tip

Tell students that when they arrange their points, they may find themselves deleting or combining some—or even adding one or two new points.

Look over the material you listed above, and check to make sure each point supports your main idea. Cross out any ideas that do not support your main idea. Then, arrange your points below in the order in which you plan to write about them.

Getting a general education:

- *Answers will vary.*

- _____

- _____

- _____

Preparing for a career:

- *Answers will vary.*

- _____

- _____

- _____

F **Drafting Your Paragraph**

Once you have found a main idea for your paragraph, selected the points you will discuss, and arranged them in the order in which you plan to write about them, you are ready to write a first draft.

In a first draft, your goal is to get your ideas down on paper. Begin your paragraph with a topic sentence that states the paragraph's main idea. Then, keeping an eye on the list of points you plan to discuss, write or type without worrying about correct wording, spelling, or punctuation. If a new idea—one that is not on your list—occurs to you, write it down. Don't worry about where it goes or whether it fits with the other ideas. Your goal is not to produce a perfect piece of writing but simply to create a working draft. When you revise, you will have a chance to rethink ideas and rework sentences.

Because you will revise this first draft—adding or crossing out words and phrases, reordering ideas and details, clarifying connections between ideas—you should leave plenty of room for revision. Leave wide margins, skip lines, and leave extra blank lines in places where you might need to add material. Feel free to be messy and to cross out; remember, the only person who will see this draft is you. (If you are typing your draft, use large type and triple-space between lines to make the draft easier to edit.)

When you have finished your first draft, don't start revising right away. Take a break and think about something—anything—else. Then, return to your draft, and read it with a fresh eye.

Here is the first draft of Stella's paragraph on the topic of community service for college students.

> Why Community Service Should Be Required
>
> Community service takes time, but it is so important that college students should be required to do it. When college students do community service, they volunteer their time to do good for someone or for the community. Working in a soup kitchen, raking leaves for senior citizens, and reading to children are all examples of community service. Community service can require long hours and take time away from studying and jobs. It can also force students to deal with unpleasant situations, but overall it is rewarding and helpful to others. Community service is good for the community and can be more fulfilling than playing sports or participating in clubs. Community service can also be an important part of a college education. Students can even discover what they want to do with their lives. Community service can also make the world a better place.

First Draft

◆ PRACTICE 1-14

Reread Stella's draft paragraph. If you were advising her, what would you suggest that she change in the draft? What should she add? What should she cross out? Write your suggestions on the following lines. Then, discuss your ideas with your class or in a small group.

Answers will vary.

_____

_____

_____

_____

_____

◆ PRACTICE 1-15

Now, draft a paragraph about your own topic, using the material you came up with for Practice 1-12. Be sure your paragraph states your main idea and supports it with specific points. If you handwrite your draft, leave wide margins and skip lines; if you type your draft, triple-space. When you are finished, give your paragraph a title.

Revision is the process of reseeing, rethinking, reevaluating, and rewriting your work. Revision involves much more than substituting one word for another or correcting a comma here and there. Often, it means moving sentences, adding words and phrases, and even changing the direction or emphasis of your ideas. To get the most out of the revision process, begin by carefully rereading your draft, using the checklist below to guide your revision.

☑ SELF-ASSESSMENT CHECKLIST:
Revising Your Paragraph

- Have you stated your main idea clearly in your topic sentence?
- Do you have enough points to support your paragraph's main idea, or do you need to look back at your notes or try another strategy to find additional supporting material?
- Do you need to explain anything more fully or more clearly?
- Do you need to add more examples or details?
- Should you cross out any examples or details?
- Does every sentence say what you mean?
- Can you combine any sentences to make your writing smoother?
- Should you move any sentences?
- Are all your words necessary, or can you cut some?
- Should you change any words?
- Does your paragraph end with a sentence that sums up its main idea?

FOCUS   **Editing**

Don't confuse revision with editing. Revision often involves extensive rewriting and rearranging, and it can be hard work. Editing comes after revision.

When you **edit**, you concentrate on the surface features of your writing, checking for correct grammar, punctuation, mechanics, and spelling. You proofread carefully for typographical errors that a computer spell checker may not identify.

Remember, editing is a vital last step in the writing process. Many readers will not take your work seriously if it contains grammatical or mechanical errors.

⬤ **Writing Tip**

When you edit your paragraph, be sure you have indented the first sentence, and check to make sure every sentence begins with a capital letter and ends with a period.

Guided by the Self-Assessment Checklist on page 18, Stella revised her paragraph, writing her changes in by hand on her typewritten draft.

Why Community Service Should Be Required

Community service takes time, but it is so impor-

tant that college students should be required to do

it. When college students do community service, they

~~volunteer their time to~~ do good for someone or for

For example, they work ~~rake~~

the community. ~~Working~~ in a soup kitchen, ~~raking~~

                                or read

leaves for senior citizens, ~~and reading~~ to children.

                    These activities

~~are all examples of community~~ service. ~~Community~~

~~service~~ can require long hours and take time away

    important things like   *However, community service is worth*

from studying and jobs. ~~It can also force students to~~

the time it takes.

~~deal with unpleasant situations, but overall it is~~

~~rewarding and helpful to others.~~ Community service

                                        for students

~~is good for the community and~~ can be more fulfilling

    other college activities, such as

than playing sports or participating in clubs. Commu-

nity service can also be an important part of a col-

learn about themselves, about their communities, and about their world,

lege education. Students can even discover what they *and*

                                            they

want to do with their lives. ~~C~~ommunity service can *can*

~~also~~ make the world a better place. *For all these reasons,*

community service should be a required part of the college curriculum.

Revised Draft

When she revised, Stella did not worry about being neat. She crossed out words, added material, and made major changes in her words, sentences, and ideas. Then, she edited her paragraph, checking punctuation, mechanics, and spelling and looking for typos. The final typed version of Stella's paragraph appears below.

Why Community Service Should Be Required

Community service takes time, but it is so important **Topic sentence**

that college students should be required to do it. When

college students do community service, they do good for

someone or for the community. For example, they work in

a soup kitchen, rake leaves for senior citizens, or read

to children. These activities can require long hours and

Supporting sentences

take time away from important things, like studying
and jobs. However, community service is worth the time
it takes. Community service can be more fulfilling for
students than other college activities, such as playing
sports or participating in clubs. Community service
can also be an important part of a college education.
Students can learn about themselves, about their
communities, and about their world, and they can even
discover what they want to do with their lives. Finally,
community service can make the world a better place.

Concluding statement

For all these reasons, community service should be a
required part of the college curriculum.

◆ PRACTICE 1-16

Reread the final draft of Stella's paragraph about community service for
college students (above), and compare it with her first draft (page 17).
Then, answer the following questions about her revision.

1. Did Stella revise her paragraph's topic sentence? If so, why? If not, why
   not? Do you agree with her decision?

   Answers will vary. She did not revise her topic sentence.

   _____

2. Did Stella add any new material to her paragraph? List any new points
   or examples on the lines below.

   Answers will vary.

   _____

   Can you think of any new points she *should* have added? List them
   below.

   Answers will vary.

   _____

3. What did Stella cross out? Why do you think she deleted this material?
   Do you think she should cross out any additional material?

   Answers will vary.

   _____

4. Why do you think Stella added "For example" (line 4) and "However"
   (line 8)?

   These words are transitions. They tell readers that she is giving examples

   in line 4 and introducing her discussion of the advantages of community

   service in line 8.

5. Why do you think Stella added the word "Finally" in her next-to-last sentence?

She uses this word to introduce her last example in support of

community service for college students.

6. In her revision, Stella added a sentence at the end of the paragraph. Do you think this sentence is necessary?

Answers will vary. This sentence sums up the point she is making

in her paragraph.

◆ PRACTICE 1-17

Generally speaking, what kinds of changes did Stella make as she revised her paragraph? Which do you think are her most effective changes? Why? Do you think she needs to make any additional changes? Write your responses on the lines below. Then, with your class or in a small group, discuss your reactions to Stella's revised paragraph.

Answers will vary.

_____

_____

_____

_____

◆ PRACTICE 1-18

Use the Self-Assessment Checklist on page 18 to evaluate the paragraph you drafted for Practice 1-15. What additions can you make to support your main idea more fully? Should anything be crossed out because it does not support your main idea? Can anything be stated more clearly? On the following lines, list some of the changes you might make in your draft.

Answers will vary.

_____

_____

_____

_____

_____

_____

Now, revise your draft. Cross out unnecessary material and material you want to rewrite, and add new and rewritten material between the lines and in the margins. After you finish your revision, edit your paragraph, checking grammar, punctuation, mechanics, and spelling—and look carefully for typos. When you are satisfied with your paragraph, print out a clean copy to use in Chapter 2.

✔ **REVIEW CHECKLIST:**
Writing a Paragraph

- ☐ Learning to write a paragraph is an important step in becoming a competent writer. (See 1A.)

- ☐ Before you start to write, consider your assignment, purpose, and audience. (See 1B.)

- ☐ Use freewriting, brainstorming, clustering, and journal writing to help you find ideas. (See 1C.)

- ☐ Identify your main idea. (See 1D.)

- ☐ Choose points to support your main idea, and arrange them in a logical order. (See 1E.)

- ☐ Write a first draft. (See 1F.)

- ☐ Revise your draft. (See 1G.)

- ☐ Edit your draft. (See 1G.)

Fine-Tuning Your Paragraph

PREVIEW

In this chapter, you will learn

■ to write effective topic sentences (2A)

■ to write unified paragraphs (2B)

■ to write well-developed paragraphs (2C)

■ to write coherent paragraphs (2D)

■ WRITING FIRST

In Chapter 1, you wrote and revised a paragraph about the purpose of a college education. Keep a copy of the final draft of this paragraph handy so you can continue to work on it as you go through this chapter.

Word Power
pragmatic practical; active rather than passive

A Writing Effective Topic Sentences

As you learned in Chapter 1, a **paragraph** is a group of related sentences that develops one main idea. Every paragraph includes a **topic sentence** that states the paragraph's main idea. This topic sentence helps guide readers, and it also helps keep writers on track as they write.

The Topic Sentence in the Paragraph

The topic sentence is the most general sentence of your paragraph. The rest of the sentences in your paragraph support the topic sentence with details, facts, and examples. Many paragraphs also include a concluding statement that sums up the paragraph's main idea.

Topic sentence

<u>The modern roller coaster got its start in Coney Island in Brooklyn, New York.</u> The first economically successful roller coaster, the first high drop, and the first circuit coaster were all pioneered in Coney Island. In 1888, the Flip Flap Railway, which featured a circular loop, was built. This coaster was the first to go upside down, but it had a habit of injuring people's necks. In 1901, the Loop-the-Loop, which provided a safer ride than the Flip Flap Railway, was built. From 1884 through the 1930s, over thirty roller coasters were constructed in Coney Island. The most famous coaster in history, the Cyclone, was built at a cost of $100,000 in 1926. Although it opened in 1927, it is still the standard against which all other roller coasters are judged. It has steep drops, lots of angular momentum, and only a lap belt to hold riders in their seats. Still in operation, the Cyclone is the most successful ride in Coney Island history. It is also the last survivor of the classic wooden roller coasters that once drew crowds to Coney Island. Because of the advances that took place there, Coney Island made possible the many high-tech roller coasters in amusement parks today.

Support (details, facts, examples)

Concluding statement

Revising Topic Sentences

The first step in writing a good paragraph is learning to write an effective topic sentence. As you write and revise, keep in mind the following three characteristics of effective topic sentences:

1. ***A topic sentence should be a complete sentence.*** Like any sentence, a topic sentence must contain a subject and a verb and state a complete thought. Keep in mind that there is a difference between a *topic* and a *topic sentence.* The **topic** is what the paragraph is about; the **topic sentence** is the sentence that presents the paragraph's **main idea**—the idea the paragraph will develop.

Topic	Topic Sentence
Television violence	Violent television shows have a negative effect on my younger brother.
Animal testing	One reason not to buy products tested on animals is that most animal testing is not necessary.
Heroes	My heroes are people who take action instead of waiting for others to act.

2. ***A topic sentence should be more than just an announcement of what you plan to write about.*** It should make a point about the topic the paragraph discusses.

Announcement	Topic Sentence
In this paragraph, I will write about getting my first credit card.	When I got my first credit card, I had no idea of the problems it would cause.

3. *A topic sentence should present an idea that you can discuss in a single paragraph.* If your topic sentence is too broad, you will not be able to discuss it in just one paragraph. If your topic sentence is too narrow (for example, if it is a statement of fact), you will not be able to say much about it.

TOPIC SENTENCE TOO BROAD	Students with jobs have special needs.
TOPIC SENTENCE TOO NARROW	The tutoring center closes at 5 p.m.
EFFECTIVE TOPIC SENTENCE	Because many students have jobs, the tutoring center should remain open until 9 p.m.

FOCUS **Placing Topic Sentences**

A topic sentence can appear anywhere in a paragraph—at the beginning, in the middle, or at the end. As a beginning writer, however, you should place your topic sentences first in your paragraphs. This strategy will keep you on track as you write. In addition, by telling readers what your paragraph will be about, it will help readers follow your ideas.

◆ PRACTICE 2-1

Underline the topic sentence in each of the following paragraphs.

1.   Genetically modified crops, created by adding a desired trait from one plant to another, can be very beneficial. "Golden rice," for example, was created when scientists took genes from daffodils and other small plants and put them into a strain of rice. These genes gave the rice a golden color. More important, the new genes enabled the rice to produce beta-carotene, or vitamin A. The Swiss scientist who created golden rice wanted to produce a product containing this vitamin because he knew that about three hundred million people in China suffered from vitamin A deficiencies. The lack of vitamin A can cause a person to become sick easily or even to go blind, but in China vitamins were not easily available, and they were expensive. So, if the rice the Chinese people depended on already contained a vitamin that they needed, eating the rice would solve a number of medical problems.

2.   Perseverance is important if you want to publish a novel. J. K. Rowling, author of the Harry Potter books, first began writing the books in 1990. By 1993, she was the divorced mother of a young daughter. Rowling could not afford day care on the money she received in public assistance from the British government, and she could not get a job without paying someone to watch her child. As a result, she could write only when her daughter was asleep. When Rowling finished her first book five years later, she wanted to send a copy to publishers and keep a copy for herself, but

Word Power

perseverance   continued action over a long time, despite difficulties

she could not afford to make photocopies. She did not give up, though. Instead, she typed copies on her old typewriter. In 1997, *Harry Potter and the Philosopher's Stone* was bought by a publisher. Later, critics called Rowling an overnight sensation. They did not know how long that "night" had been.

3.   In the mid-nineteenth century, steamboats were an important means of transportation in America. These boats carried cargo and passengers between river towns. In some towns, passengers were met at the wharf by stage coaches that took them from place to place. In other towns, a railroad line came within walking distance of the wharf. Americans were pleased with this new type of transportation. Trips that had taken weeks by horse and carriage could now be completed in days.

4.   During the American Civil War, a camp was built at Andersonville, Georgia, to house prisoners of war. The Confederates selected the site because it was far from Richmond, Virginia, their capital, and near a railroad. Although the prison was built to house 10,000 prisoners, the number grew to over 32,000. There was no shelter from the weather, no source of fresh water (except for a small stream that ran through the camp and was also used as a sewer), no clothing other than what the prisoners arrived in, and no fruit or vegetables. Many prisoners dug holes in the ground to live in. Because of these conditions, nearly a third of the prisoners died of disease. Today, the Andersonville National Historic Site, built on the land occupied by the old prison, is a monument to all Americans who have been prisoners of war.

5.   Many experts believe that space travelers will not be able to fly to Mars until four problems have been overcome. First is the problem caused by a lack of gravity, which can lead to loss of bone strength, dizziness, and an inability to walk. Because we cannot create gravity on a spaceship, the astronauts who land on Mars might be unable to do their jobs once they arrive. Second, science cannot protect the astronauts from the cosmic rays they would be exposed to in deep space. Exposure to these rays would make the astronauts more likely to become ill or to develop serious diseases, such as cancer. Third, the astronauts would have very little help if they did become ill. They would not have access to the technology we use to treat such diseases here on earth. Finally, astronauts might develop psychological problems because of the length of time it would take to get to Mars. Until science can solve these problems, going to Mars will remain a dream.

◆ PRACTICE 2-2

Rearrange the following sentences into a logical paragraph by placing a *1* in front of the topic sentence, a *2* in front of the next sentence, and so on.

___6___ By the end of the war, the game had spread throughout the country, and standard rules had been established.

___1___ The first official baseball game was played in New York City in 1846.

___2___ In that game, the Knickerbocker Baseball Club played a team made up of its own members.

___5___ Soldiers even played baseball behind their own lines and in prisoner-of-war camps.

___3___ Between 1846 and the start of the Civil War, interest in the game grew slowly.

___7___ Several years after the war, in 1871, the first professional baseball league was formed.

___4___ During the war, however, the popularity of the game increased enormously.

◆ PRACTICE 2-3

Read the following items. Put a check mark next to each one that has all three characteristics of an effective topic sentence.

Examples:

The common cold. _____

Many people are convinced that large doses of vitamin C will prevent

the common cold. ___✔___

1. Global warming, a crisis for our cities. _____

2. If something is not done soon, the city of New Orleans could be under

water by the year 2010. ___✓___

3. In this paragraph, I will discuss global warming. _____

4. Buying books online. _____

5. College students can save money by buying their textbooks online. ___✓___

◆ PRACTICE 2-4

Decide whether each of the following statements could be an effective topic sentence for a paragraph. If a sentence is too broad, write "too broad" in the blank following the sentence. If the sentence is too narrow, write "too narrow" in the blank. If the sentence is an effective topic sentence, write "OK" in the blank.

Example: Thanksgiving always falls on the fourth Thursday in November. ___*too narrow*___

1. Wireless computer networks are changing the world. ___*too broad*___

2. There are five computer terminals in the campus library. ___*too narrow*___

3. Our school should set up a wireless network on campus. ___*OK*___

4. Soccer is not as popular in the United States as it is in Europe.

   too broad

5. Americans enjoy watching many types of sporting events on television.

   too broad

6. There is one quality that distinguishes a good coach from a bad one.

   _OK_

7. Vegetarianism is a healthy way of life. ____ _too broad_ ____

8. Uncooked spinach has fourteen times as much iron as steak does.

   too narrow

9. Fast-food restaurants are finally responding to the needs of customers

   who are vegetarians. ____ _OK_ ____

10. Medical schools in this country have high standards. ____ _too broad_ ____

◆ PRACTICE 2-5

The following paragraph has no topic sentence. Read it, and then choose the best topic sentence from the list below.

> Some people cannot bear to give away the books that they have read. They stack old paperbacks on tables, on the floor, and on their nightstands. Other people save magazines or newspapers. Who hasn't met someone who has a collection of old *National Geographic* magazines? Still others save movie-ticket stubs or postcards. Serious collectors hoard all sorts of things—including old toys, guns, knives, plates, figurines, Confederate currency, maps, stamps, commemorative medals, baseball cards, comic books, beer bottles, playbills, movie posters, dolls, clocks, old televisions, political campaign buttons, and even coffee mugs. Some things—such as matchbook covers or restaurant menus—may have value only to the people who collect them. Other items—such as stamps or coins—may be worth a lot of money. A very few collectors concentrate on items that are so large that housing a collection can present some real challenges. For example, people who collect automobiles or antique furniture may have to rent a garage or even a warehouse in which to store their possessions.

Put a check mark next to the topic sentence that best expresses the main idea of the paragraph above.

1. Everyone, regardless of age or occupation, seems to have the urge to

   collect. ____

2. Collecting things like matchbooks and restaurant menus can be fun,

   but collecting jewelry or coins can be very profitable. ____

3. The things people collect are as different as the people who collect them. ✓

4. In spite of the time and expense, collecting can be an interesting and fulfilling hobby. _____

5. Before you begin to collect things as a hobby, you should know what you are getting into. _____

◆ PRACTICE 2-6

The following paragraphs do not have topic sentences. Think of a topic sentence that expresses each paragraph's main idea, and write it on the lines above the paragraphs.

Example: Possible answer: Early rock and roll was a creation of both

black and white performers.

Early 1950s African-American musicians included performers such as Johnny Ace, Big Joe Turner, and Ruth Brown. Groups like the Drifters and the Clovers were also popular. By the mid-1950s, white performers such as Bill Haley and the Comets, Jerry Lee Lewis, and Elvis Presley imitated African-American music. Although their songs did not have the heavy back beat and explicit lyrics that most black music had, their music appealed to a white audience. Eventually, this combination of black and white musical styles became known as rock and roll.

1. Possible answer: For most Americans, television is the major source of

information, entertainment, and relaxation.

Most Americans own televisions. In fact, more people watch television than read magazines and newspapers. Television has even replaced the movies as the most popular form of entertainment. Not surprisingly, recent surveys have shown that most Americans get their news from television. Moreover, as anyone in the book industry knows, the best way for a book to become a best seller is for it to be promoted on a popular television show. For example, a book that is endorsed by Oprah Winfrey is almost sure to become an instant best-seller. Finally, Americans spend many hours a day staring at their televisions, just trying to unwind.

2. Possible answer: Applying for a job can be difficult, but the process can be

made easier and more rewarding if you follow a few simple steps.

First, you have to find a suitable job to apply for. Once you decide to apply, you have to type your résumé and send it to your potential employer. Then, when you are invited in for an interview, you need to decide what you are going to wear. At the interview, you need to speak slowly and clearly and answer all questions directly and honestly. After the interview, you need to send a note to the person who interviewed you, thanking him or her. Finally, if everything goes well, you will get a letter or a telephone call offering you the job.

3. *Possible answer: A lot of questions remain about Native Americans who were living in North America when the Europeans arrived.*

There are no written records left by the Native Americans themselves. Most of the early European settlers in North America were more interested in staying alive than in writing about the Native Americans. In addition, as the westward expansion took place, the Europeans met the Native Americans in stages, not all at once. Also, the Native Americans spoke at least fifty-eight different languages, which made it difficult for the Europeans to speak with them. Most important, by the time scholars decided to study Native American culture, many of the tribes no longer existed. Disease and war had wiped them out.

■ WRITING FIRST: Flashback

Look back at the paragraph you wrote for the Writing First exercise in Chapter 1. Does your paragraph have an effective topic sentence? Write that sentence on the lines below. If necessary, revise the topic sentence so that it states the main idea of your paragraph more clearly. (If your paragraph does not have a topic sentence, write one on the lines below.)

_____

_____

B Writing Unified Paragraphs

An effective paragraph focuses on a single main idea. A paragraph is **unified** when all its sentences support the main idea stated in the topic sentence.

Understanding Unity

To write a unified paragraph, state your main idea clearly in the topic sentence. Then, make sure the rest of the sentences in your paragraph relate directly to this idea.

Topic sentence

The population problem is one of the biggest causes for concern for scientists. In 1900, there were 1.6 billion people on earth, a quarter of today's population. In 1900, the average life expectancy was also much shorter than it is now. In some places, it was only twenty-three years. By the year 2000, the world's population had grown to over 6 billion. Today, average life expectancy worldwide is almost sixty-five years. This means that billions of people are living longer and using more of the earth's resources. The low death rate, combined with a high birth rate, is adding the equivalent of one new Germany to the world's population each year. According to a United Nations study, if present trends continue, by 2050 the world's population will be so large (between 7.3 and 10.5 billion) that most people in the world will be malnourished or starving.

The paragraph above is unified. The topic sentence states the paragraph's main idea, and the rest of the sentences present specific details to support the main idea.

Revising Paragraphs for Unity

A paragraph lacks unity when its sentences wander from the main idea. When you revise, you can make sure your paragraphs are unified by rewriting or deleting sentences that do not support the main idea that your topic sentence states.

Paragraph Not Unified

> The changing economic picture has caused many people to move away from the rural Pennsylvania community where I was raised. Over the years, farmland has become more and more expensive. Years ago, a family could buy each of its children twenty-five acres for a farm. Today, the price of land is so high that the average farmer cannot afford to buy this amount of land. I am tired of seeing my friends move away. After I graduate, I intend to return to my town and get a job there. Even though many factories have moved out of the area, I think I can get a job. My uncle owns a hardware store, and he told me that after I graduate, he will teach me the business. I think I can contribute something to the business and to the town.

Topic sentence

> ● **Writing Tip**
>
> Try boldfacing or underscoring the topic sentence of a paragraph before you start to revise. (See 2D.)

This paragraph is not unified. After presenting one reason why people are moving away, the writer strays from his paragraph's main idea, instead complaining about his friends and discussing his own future plans. These departures from the main idea do not support the topic sentence.

The following revised paragraph is unified. It discusses only what the topic sentence promises: the reasons why people have moved away from the writer's hometown.

Paragraph Unified

> The changing economic picture has caused many people to move away from the rural Pennsylvania community where I was raised. Over the years, farmland has become more and more expensive. Years ago, a family could buy each of its children twenty-five acres for a farm. Today, the price of land is so high that the average farmer cannot afford to buy this amount of land, and those who choose not to farm have few choices. They just cannot get good jobs anymore. Factories have moved out of the area and have taken with them the jobs that many young people used to get after high school. As a result, many eighteen-year-olds have no choice but to move to Pittsburgh to find employment.

Topic sentence

◆ PRACTICE 2-7

Read the following paragraphs, and then write an appropriate topic sentence for each.

Answers will vary.

1. *Possible answer: Good drivers have three ways to deal with road rage.* The first—and simplest way—is to move out of the way of the enraged driver. If the good driver does not do this, the angry driver may honk the horn, flash the lights, or tailgate the slower driver. Next, when the angry driver tries to get the good driver's attention, the defensive driver should avoid making eye contact. This lessens the chance that the furious driver will try to insult the good driver and make things worse. Finally, once the angry driver has passed, the good driver must consider whether or not to call the police.

2. *Possible answer: Some singers are more famous after death than in life.* For example, Jim Morrison, lead singer of the Doors, has been the subject of a big-budget movie and several books since his death in July 1971. His grave in France is visited around the clock by fans, including many who were not even born when he was alive. Kurt Cobain, who committed suicide in 1994, is now the subject of several books, and his group, Nirvana, has an album that continues to sell well. Another example is Tupac Shakur. He was killed in 1996, but his albums still sell well, and his poetry has been collected and published. Probably the biggest sign that all three singers are still remembered fondly is the number of Web sites that try to prove they are still alive.

3. *Possible answer: Patients are trying a variety of new methods to deal with their medical problems.* Some people who once turned to allergy shots now prefer to try vitamins and supplements. Some who suffer with back problems are trying to give up their pain relievers by visiting acupuncturists and chiropractors. Still other patients prefer to see if physical therapy can help them deal with a health problem instead of scheduling surgery. Some people also attend yoga classes to relieve stress instead of taking a prescription medication. Obviously, many patients are willing to try nontraditional methods to help them deal with their ailments.

◆ PRACTICE 2-8

The following paragraphs are not unified because some sentences do not support the topic sentence. Cross out any sentences in each paragraph that do not belong.

1. The one thing I could not live without is my car. In addition to attending school full time, I hold down two part-time jobs that are many miles from each other, from where I live, and from school. Even though my car is almost twelve years old and has close to 120,000 miles on it, I couldn't manage without it. ~~I'm thinking about buying a new car, and I always check the classified ads, but I haven't found anything I want that I can afford. If my old car breaks down, I guess I'll have to, though. I couldn't live without my portable tape recorder because I use it to record all the class lectures I attend. Then I can play them back while I'm driving or during my breaks at work.~~ Three nights a week and on weekends, I work as a counselor at a home for teenagers with problems, and my other job is in the tire department at Sears. Without my car, I'd be lost.

2. Studies conducted by Dr. Leonard Eron over the last thirty years suggest that the more television violence children are exposed to, the more aggressive they are as teenagers and adults. In 1960, Eron questioned parents about how they treated their children at home, including how much television their children watched. ~~There is more violence on television today than there was then.~~ Ten years later, he interviewed these families again and discovered that whether or not teenage sons were aggressive depended less on how they had been treated by their parents than on how much violent television programming they had watched as children. Returning in 1990, he found that these same young men, now in their thirties, were still more likely to be aggressive and to commit crimes. ~~Researchers estimate that a child today is likely to watch 100,000 violent acts on television before finishing elementary school.~~

3. Libraries today hold a lot more than just books. Of course, books still outnumber anything else on the shelves, but more and more libraries are expanding to include other specialized services. For example, many libraries now offer extensive collections of tapes and compact discs, ranging from classical music to jazz to country to rock. Many have also increased their holdings of videotapes, both instructional programs and popular recent and vintage movies. Some libraries also stock DVDs. ~~However, most people probably still get more movies from video stores than from libraries.~~ In addition, the children's section often has games and toys young patrons can play with in the library or even check out. Most important, libraries are offering more and more computerized data services, which can provide much more detailed and up-to-date information than printed sources. These expanding nonprint sources are the wave of the future for even the smallest libraries and will allow patrons access to much more information than books or magazines ever could. ~~People who don't know how to use a computer are going to be out of luck.~~

■ WRITING FIRST: Flashback

Look back at the paragraph you wrote for the Writing First exercise in Chapter 1. Review your paragraph for unity. Cross out any sentences that do not support the topic sentence. If necessary, rewrite sentences so they support your main point.

C Writing Well-Developed Paragraphs

A paragraph is **well developed** when it contains enough details, facts, and examples to support the topic sentence. A paragraph is not well developed when it lacks the support readers need to understand or accept its main idea.

Supporting the Topic Sentence

To decide on the amount and kind of support you need, ask yourself the following two questions:

1. *How complicated is your main idea?* A complicated main idea will need more support than a simple one. A relatively straightforward topic sentence—for example, "During the first week of school, registration is a nightmare"—would need only two or three well-chosen examples. A more far-reaching topic sentence—"Our community has to do much more to assist the physically challenged," for example—would call for a lot more support.

2. *How much do your readers know about your main idea?* If you know that your readers eat in your school's cafeteria, you do not need to give them many examples to convince them that the food needs to be improved. If you think that your readers are not familiar with the food at your school, however, you should supply more examples and possibly definitions (explaining what you mean by "mystery meat," for example) to support your point.

Revising Paragraphs for Development

A well-developed paragraph provides the support readers need to understand its points and to accept the statement the topic sentence makes. If your paragraph contains only general statements, it is not well developed. When you revise, be sure to support your general statements with details, facts, and examples.

The following paragraph is not well developed. It consists of a series of general statements that do not specifically explain or illustrate the main idea.

● **Writing Tip**

Hit the Enter or the Return key after your topic sentence and after each sentence that follows it. By highlighting each detail and example, you can evaluate the amount and kind of support you have used.

Undeveloped Paragraph

> Although pit bulls were originally bred to fight, they can make good pets. Today, many people are afraid of pit bulls. These dogs are sometimes mistreated. As a result, they become more aggressive. For this reason, they are misunderstood and persecuted. In fact, some cities have taken action against them. But pit bulls do not deserve their bad reputation. Contrary to popular opinion, they can make good pets.

Here is a revised version of this paragraph.

● **Writing Tip**

You can find the details, facts, and examples you need to support your topic sentence by reviewing the notes you took when you did freewriting, brainstorming, and clustering. (See 1C.)

Well-Developed Paragraph

> Although pit bulls were originally bred to fight, they can make good pets. It is true that their powerful jaws, short muscular legs, and large teeth are ideally suited to fighting, and they were used extensively for this purpose in the rural South and Southwest. It is also true that some pit bulls—especially males—can be aggressive toward other dogs. However, most pit bulls like human beings and are quite friendly. Owners report that pit bulls are affectionate, loyal, and good with children. When pit bulls behave viciously, it is usually because they have been mistreated. As a recent newspaper article pointed out, the number of reported bites by pit bulls is no greater than the number of bites by other breeds. In fact, some dogs, such as cocker spaniels, bite much more frequently. The problem is that whenever a pit bull attacks a person, the incident is reported. But pit bulls do not deserve their bad reputation. Contrary to popular opinion, they can make good pets.

The revised paragraph is now well developed. Because general statements are clarified by examples and details, readers are more likely to accept the idea that pit bulls can make good pets.

● **Writing Tip**
Length alone is no guarantee that a paragraph is well developed. A paragraph that contains one generalization after another can be long and yet still not well developed.

◆ PRACTICE 2-9

Underline the supporting details, facts, and examples in each of the following paragraphs.

1. Hearing people have some mistaken ideas about the deaf community. First, some hearing adults think that all deaf people consider themselves disabled and would trade anything not to be "handicapped." Hearing people do not realize that many deaf people do not consider themselves handicapped and are proud to be part of the deaf community. They have their own language, customs, and culture. Second, many hearing people think that all deaf people read lips, so there is no need to learn sign language to communicate with them. Lip reading—or speech reading, as deaf people call the practice—is difficult. Not all hearing people say the same words in the same way, and facial expressions can also change the meaning of the words. If hearing people make more of an attempt to understand the deaf culture, communication between them will improve.

2. In 1996, the National Basketball Association (NBA) approved a women's professional basketball league. Within fifteen months, eight teams had been formed, four in the Eastern Conference and four in the Western Conference. Next, the teams began to draft players for these teams and to select a logo and uniforms. The final logo selected, a red, white, and blue shield, showed the silhouette of a woman player dribbling the ball, with the letters "WNBA" above her. The uniforms consisted of shorts and jerseys in the colors of the different teams. That first season, games were played in the summer when the television sports schedule was lighter so they could be televised during prime time. At the end of that season, the Houston Comets became the first WNBA champions. Today, the WNBA consists of sixteen teams that play 256 regular season games televised to audiences worldwide.

3. A hurricane is a storm with winds of seventy-three miles per hour or greater that blow in a circle around the center, or eye, of the storm. These storms form near the equator and move along a curved path at anywhere from five to fifty miles per hour. To help weather forecasters talk about hurricanes to the general public, the storms are given names. Often, more than one storm will be active at a time, so the names help people understand which storm is being discussed. Since 1979, storms in the Atlantic have been given men's and women's names beginning with all the letters of the alphabet except q, x, y, and z. In the Pacific, the practice was the same until recently, when names common to the people in that area began to be used. So, while the second storm in the Atlantic in 2002 was named Bertha, the second in the Pacific Northwest was named Boris.

4. Turtles, among the oldest and most adaptable living reptiles, have been present on earth since even before the dinosaurs. They can live on land or in the water and are found everywhere in the world except Antarctica. In spring and summer, turtles search for food, including insects, fish, berries,

and water plants. In winter, they hibernate in the mud of lakes or creeks
or under piles of leaves and brush. Turtles range in size from several
inches to as large as eight feet, which is the average length of a sea turtle
called the leatherback. Unfortunately, pollution and population growth are
now threatening the existence of these fascinating and harmless creatures.

5.   One of the largest celebrations of the passage of young girls into womanhood occurs in Latin American and Hispanic cultures. This event is
called La Quinceañera, or the fifteenth year. It acknowledges that a young
woman is now of marriageable age. The day usually begins with a Mass of
Thanksgiving. The young woman wears a full-length white or pastel-
colored dress and is attended by fourteen friends and relatives who serve
as maids of honor and male escorts. Her parents and godparents surround
her at the foot of the altar. When the Mass ends, other young relatives give
small gifts to those who attended, while the Quinceañera places a bouquet
of flowers on the altar of the Virgin. Following the Mass is an elaborate
party, with dancing, cake, and toasts. Finally, to end the evening, the young
woman dances a waltz with her favorite escort.

◆ PRACTICE 2-10

Provide two or three supporting details for each of the following topic
sentences.

Answers will vary.

1. When it comes to feeding your family at the end of a hard day at work,
   there are several alternatives to fast food.

   _____

   _____

   _____

2. If you are involved in a romantic relationship at work, it is best not to
   let your coworkers know about it.

   _____

   _____

   _____

3. When scheduling classes, you need to keep several things in mind.

   _____

   _____

   _____

4. Although last year ten million people were victims of identity theft,
   there are steps you can take to protect yourself.

   _____

   _____

   _____

5. Choosing the right computer for my needs was harder than I thought it would be.

_____

_____

_____

◆ PRACTICE 2-11

The following two paragraphs are not well developed. On the lines that follow each paragraph, write three questions or suggestions that might help the writer develop his or her ideas more fully.

1. Computers can be a great help for students. Word processing can make writing assignments easier, and math drills can be fun when they are in the form of computer games. Also, when students have questions about almost anything, they can usually find the answer on the Internet. Even at a young age, children can do research by using computers. Computers are used so often by modern students that they cannot imagine what school was like before computers were invented.

Answers will vary. Students might suggest adding details about

the ways that word processing makes writing easier. For example, using

the cut-and-paste function helps them to move around parts of an

essay, and the spell checker helps them to catch spelling errors. Stu-

dents might include a specific question that could be answered on the

Internet, or note examples of computer research that could be done by

young children.

2. Sometimes it is impossible to tell much about people from the clothes they wear. For example, athletic clothing is popular today, but almost everyone wears these clothes, not just athletes. Also, worn-out clothes do not necessarily show that people do not have enough money to buy new clothes. Torn jeans are a popular style. In the past, black clothing was a symbol of mourning. Now, wearing black has nothing to do with being sad. Many times, clothing choices indicate that people want to be in style and not much else.

Answers will vary. Students might ask these questions: What are some

examples of athletic clothes often worn by nonathletes? What other

worn-out clothes do people wear besides torn jeans? Why do people wear

black clothing? What are some additional examples of clothing choices

that do not necessarily reveal much about a person?

■ WRITING FIRST: Flashback

Look back at the paragraph you wrote for the Writing First exercise in Chapter 1. Is your paragraph well developed? On the lines below, list the details, facts, and examples that you used to support your main idea. Then, list suggestions for revision, noting the kinds of facts, examples, and details you might add.

Details, Facts, and Examples in Your Paragraph:

Answers will vary.

_____

_____

_____

_____

_____

Suggestions for Revision:

Answers will vary.

_____

_____

_____

_____

_____

_____

D Writing Coherent Paragraphs

A paragraph is **coherent** if all its sentences are arranged in a clear, sensible order. You can make a paragraph coherent by arranging details in a definite order and by supplying transitional words and phrases that show the connections between sentences.

Arranging Details

You can help establish coherence by arranging the details in a paragraph according to *time order, spatial order,* or *logical order.*

Paragraphs that are arranged in **time order** present events in the order in which they occurred. Stories, historical accounts, and instructions are generally arranged in time order.

The following paragraph presents events in time order. Specific dates as well as the words *before, once, then, finally, later,* and *after* indicate the sequence of events in the paragraph.

In 1856, my great-great-great-grandparents, Anne and Charles McGinley, came to the United States to start a new life. Before they left Ireland, their English landlords had raised the taxes on their land so high that my ancestors could not afford to pay them. It took them three years to save the money for passage. Once they had saved the money, they had to look for a ship that was willing to take them. Then, my great-great-great-grandparents were on their way. They and their ten children spent four long months on a small ship. Storms, strong tides, and damaged sails made the trip longer than it should have been. Finally, in November of 1856, they saw land, and two days later they sailed into New York Harbor. After they were admitted to the United States, they took a train to Baltimore, Maryland, where some cousins lived.

See page 41 for a list of transitions that signal time order.

Paragraphs that are arranged in **spatial order** present details in the order in which a viewer sees them—from top to bottom, from near to far, from right to left, and so on. Spatial order is central to paragraphs that describe what an object, place, or person looks like.

The following paragraph presents events in spatial order. Notice how the phrases *directly in front of, next to, behind, in between, on top of, inside,* and *in the center of* establish the order—from far to near—in which the writer sees the details of the scene.

The day I visited the Amish school I knew it was unlike any other school I had seen before. A long, tree-lined dirt road led to the small one-room wooden schoolhouse. Directly in front of the school was a line of bicycles and metal scooters. A small baseball diamond had been carved into the dirt in the yard next to the schoolhouse. Behind the school, two little outhouses stood next to each other with a green water pump in between. The schoolhouse itself was a small one-story structure. White paint curled off its clapboard siding, and a short steeple, holding a brass bell, sat firmly on top of the roof. Inside the open door, a long line of black hats hung on pegs. In the center of the small schoolhouse was an iron potbellied stove surrounded by the children's desks.

See page 41 for a list of transitions that signal spatial order.

Paragraphs that are arranged in **logical order** present ideas in a sequence that indicates why one idea logically follows another. For example, a paragraph may move from least important to most important idea, from general to specific, or from most familiar to least familiar.

The following paragraph presents ideas in logical order. Here, the phrases *the first rule, an even sillier rule,* and *the most ridiculous rule* establish the order in which the rules are presented—from least silly to most silly—and thus help readers move from one point to another.

My high school had three rules that were silly at best and ridiculous at worst. The first rule was that only seniors could go outside the school building for lunch. In spite of this rule, many students went outside to eat because the cafeteria was not big enough to seat all the school's students at the same time. Understanding the problem, the teachers and the principal looked the other way as long as we returned to school before the lunch period was over. An even sillier rule was that we had to attend 95 percent of the classes for every course. This rule meant that a person could miss only about six days of class every semester. Naturally, this rule was never enforced because if it had been,

See page 41 for a list of transitions that signal logical order.

half the students would have failed. <u>The most ridiculous rule</u>, however, was that students could not throw their hats into the air during graduation. At some point in the past—no one seems to know when—a parent had complained that a falling hat could poke someone in the eye. As a result, graduating classes were told that under no circumstance could they throw their hats. Naturally, on graduation day we did what every previous graduating class had done—ignored the rule and threw our hats into the air.

◆ PRACTICE 2-12

Read each of the following sentences carefully. If you were writing a paragraph introduced by the sentence, how would you arrange the supporting details—in time order, spatial order, or logical order? Write your answer in the blank following the topic sentence.

Example: The work crews that built the Hoover Dam had to follow a definite procedure. _____time order_____

1. As a view from above shows, colonial Philadelphia was laid out as a series of squares. _____spatial order_____

2. The development of modern antibiotics took some interesting and unexpected turns. _____time order_____

3. There are three reasons why the king and queen of Spain gave Columbus the money for his voyage. _____logical order_____

4. By the time it was over, the 1918 flu epidemic was the deadliest in modern history. _____time order_____

5. Scientists are taking steps to stop Venice from sinking into the sea. _____logical order_____

6. The Guggenheim Museum in New York is an interesting and unusual building. _____spatial order_____

7. The life of Helen Keller is an inspiration to anyone who has a disability. _____time order_____

8. In order to build the first Ferris wheel at the 1893 Chicago World's Fair, George Ferris had to overcome several difficulties. _____logical order_____

9. Seeming to float above San Francisco Bay, the Golden Gate Bridge is an engineering marvel. _____spatial order_____

10. All young children go through the same stages as they develop language skills. _____time order_____

Using Transitional Words and Phrases

Within a paragraph, **transitional words and phrases** help to create coherence by indicating the relationships among sentences. By establishing the time order, spatial order, and logical order of the ideas in a paragraph, these words and phrases enable readers to see the connections among ideas.

Transitional Words and Phrases

Some Words and Phrases That Signal Time Order

after	finally	dates (for example, "In June")
afterward	later	
at first	next	
before	now	
during	soon	
earlier	then	
eventually	today	

Some Words and Phrases That Signal Spatial Order

above	in front	on the left
behind	in the center	on the right
below	inside	on top
beside	near	over
in back	next to	under
in between	on the bottom	

Some Words and Phrases That Signal Logical Order

also	last
although	moreover
consequently	next
first . . . second . . . third	not only . . . but also
for example	one . . . another
for instance	similarly
furthermore	the least important
in addition	the most important
in fact	therefore

Revising Paragraphs for Coherence

Because transitional words and phrases establish **coherence**, a paragraph without them is difficult to understand. You can correct this problem when you revise by including all the words and phrases that are needed to link the ideas in your paragraph.

Paragraph without Transitional Words and Phrases

During his lifetime, Jim Thorpe faced many obstacles. Thorpe was born in 1888, the son of an Irish father and a Native American mother. He was sent to the Carlisle Indian School in Pennsylvania. "Pop" Warner, the legendary coach at Carlisle, discovered Thorpe when he saw him jump more than six feet while he was wearing street clothes. Thorpe left Carlisle to play baseball for two seasons in the newly formed East Carolina minor league. Thorpe returned to Carlisle, played football, and was named to the All-American team. Thorpe went to the Olympic games in Stockholm, where he won two gold medals. Thorpe's career took a dramatic turn for the worse when a sportswriter who had seen him play baseball in North Carolina exposed him as a professional. The Amateur Athletic Union stripped him of his records and medals. The International Olympic Committee returned Thorpe's Olympic medals to his family.

The above paragraph is not as coherent as it should be because it does not include the transitional words and phrases needed to establish exactly how the events in Jim Thorpe's life relate to one another.

Paragraph with Transitional Words and Phrases

During his lifetime, Jim Thorpe faced many obstacles. Thorpe was born in 1888, the son of an Irish father and a Native American mother. In 1904, he was sent to the Carlisle Indian School in Pennsylvania. The next year, "Pop" Warner, the legendary coach at Carlisle, discovered Thorpe when he saw him jump more than six feet while he was wearing street clothes. Thorpe left Carlisle in 1909 to play baseball for two seasons in the newly formed East Carolina minor league. In 1911, Thorpe returned to Carlisle, played football, and was named to the All-American team. In 1912, Thorpe went to the Olympic games in Stockholm, where he won two gold medals. The next year, however, Thorpe's career took a dramatic turn for the worse when a sportswriter who had seen him play baseball in North Carolina exposed him as a professional. As a result, the Amateur Athletic Union stripped him of his records and medals. After years of appeals, the International Olympic Committee returned Thorpe's Olympic medals to his family in 1982.

The revised paragraph now contains transitional words and phrases— *in 1912, the next year,* and *after years of appeals,* for example—that establish the time order of the events in Thorpe's life.

◆ PRACTICE 2-13

Underline the transitional words and phrases in each of the following paragraphs. Then, decide what order—time order, spatial order, or logical order—the writer has chosen for arranging details in each paragraph. Write your answers in the blanks provided.

1. Alarmed that teenage girls today get only half as much exercise as boys, researchers are trying to find out why. One reason girls get little exercise, they say, is that they watch a lot of television. But this is not enough of an explanation because boys generally watch as much television as girls do. A more important reason is that many girls are not offered the sorts of organized athletic programs that are offered to boys. Furthermore, be-

cause both parents often work now, girls are more likely than boys to have responsibilities at home that leave them less free time to engage in physical activity. Most important, though, may be the attitude among girls that boys are not attracted to girls who are athletic. Being "feminine," for some girls, means avoiding anything that might mess up their hair or make them sweat. Unless these habits and attitudes change, the current generation of teenage girls may grow into a generation of women with serious health problems.

Order: _logical order_

2.   When I first came to New York, I looked for an apartment for three months. Just when I had nearly given up, I found one that I could afford. As you enter my apartment, the first thing you see on the left is a wooden loft that the former tenant painted red. It is attached to one of the apartment's cream-colored walls. On top of the loft is my mattress. Under my loft bed is storage space: on the left is my bicycle, and on the right are a small bookshelf and a tiny dresser. Across from the loft are five steps that lead down to the main level of the apartment. At the front of the apartment is my metal desk, which faces three large, curved windows. As I work at my desk, I look out at the people walking on West 100th Street. On the windowsill are two scraggly tomato plants and a miniature orange tree that I am trying to grow. In the middle of the apartment are two wooden chairs and a couch that I found in a used furniture store. At the back of the apartment is a small, open kitchen. A counter runs along the wall of the kitchen. Next to the counter are a refrigerator and a small closet. Above the counter are several cabinets that contain neatly stacked boxes and cans of food. I am very comfortable in this apartment, and I am lucky to have found it.

Order: _spatial order_

3.   The Caribbean island of Puerto Rico has a complex history. Before the 1400s, the island's inhabitants for centuries were the native Arawak Indians. In 1493, Christopher Columbus and his crew were the earliest Europeans to reach the island. Fifteen years later, Ponce de Leon conquered the island for Spain, and the Spanish subjected the Arawaks to virtual slavery to develop a sugar industry. Finally, these native people were completely wiped out, slaughtered by the sword and by European diseases to which they had no immunity. The Arawaks were soon replaced by African slaves as a European plantation culture flourished. In 1898, after the Spanish-American War, the island was given to the United States. The next year, the United States made Puerto Rico a colony under an American governor. Later, in 1917, Puerto Ricans were granted U.S. citizenship, and the country became a U.S. commonwealth in 1952. Since then, Puerto Ricans have debated this status, with some arguing for statehood and others for independence. For now, the island remains a commonwealth, and its citizens share most of the rights and obligations of U.S. citizenship.

Order: _time order_

■ WRITING FIRST: Flashback

Look back at the paragraph you wrote for the Writing First exercise in Chapter 1. Are all your sentences arranged in a clear, sensible order? Is this order time, spatial, or logical? List below the transitional words and phrases that signal this order to readers.

Answers will vary.

_____   _____

_____   _____

_____   _____

_____   _____

Now, add to your paragraph any transitions you think are needed, and rearrange your sentences if necessary.

■ WRITING FIRST: Revising and Editing

Review the work you did for the Flashback exercises on pages 30, 33, 38, and 44. Then, revise your paragraph for unity, development, and coherence, incorporating changes and corrections from your Flashback exercises.

CHAPTER REVIEW

◆ EDITING PRACTICE

Read the following paragraphs, and evaluate each in terms of its unity, development, and coherence. First, underline each topic sentence. Then, cross out any sentences that do not support the topic sentence. Add transitional words and phrases where needed. Finally, discuss in class whether additional details and examples could be added to each paragraph.

Teaching Tip
Assign groups of three or four students to rewrite the Editing Practice paragraphs, adding details and examples.

1. In 1979, a series of mechanical and human errors
    in Unit 2 of the nuclear generating plant at Three Mile
    Island, near Harrisburg, Pennsylvania, caused an
    accident that changed the nuclear power industry. A
    combination of stuck valves, human error, and poor

decisions caused a partial meltdown of the reactor core. *As a result, large* ~~Large~~ amounts of radioactive gases were released into the atmosphere. *Consequently, the* ~~The~~ governor of Pennsylvania evacuated pregnant women from the area. Other residents *then* panicked and left their homes. The nuclear regulatory agency claimed that the situation was not really dangerous and that the released gases were not a health threat. *However, activists* ~~Activists~~ and local residents disagreed with this. ~~The reactor itself remained unusable for more than ten years.~~ Large demonstrations followed the accident, including a rally of more than 200,000 people in New York City. ~~Some people came because the day was nice.~~ By the mid-1980s, new construction of nuclear power plants in the United States had stopped.

Nuclear reactor at Three Mile Island

2. A survey of cigarette advertisements shows how tobacco companies have consistently encouraged people to smoke. One of the earliest television ads showed two boxes of cigarettes dancing to an advertising jingle. The approach in this ad was simple: create an entertaining commercial, and people will buy the product. *However, other* ~~Many people liked these ads. Other~~ advertisements were more subtle. Some were aimed at specific audiences. *For example,* Marlboro commercials, with the rugged Marlboro man, targeted men. *In contrast,* Virginia Slims made an obvious pitch to women by saying, "You've come a long way, baby!" *Also,* Salem, a mentholated cigarette, showed rural scenes and targeted people who liked the freshness of the outdoors. *Similarly,* Kent, with its "micronite filter," appealed to those who were health conscious by claiming that Kent contained less tar and nicotine than any other brand. ~~This claim was not entirely true. Other brands had less tar and nicotine.~~ *Later,* Merit and other high-tar and high-nicotine cigarettes began to use advertisements

Ad featuring Joe Camel

that were aimed at minorities. ~~Cigarette~~ *Eventually, cigarette* companies responded to the national decline in smoking by directing advertising at young people. *For instance,* Camel introduced the cartoon character Joe Camel, which was aimed at teenagers and young adults.

3. <u>Cities created police forces for a number of reasons.</u> The first reason was status: after the Civil War, it became a status symbol for cities to have a uniformed police force. *Second, a* A police force provided a large number of political jobs. This meant that politicians were able to reward people who worked to support them. *Third, police* ~~Police~~ forces made people feel safe. *For example, police* ~~Police~~ officers helped visitors find their way. *In addition, they* ~~They~~ took in lost children and sometimes fed the homeless. They *also* directed traffic, enforced health regulations, and provided other services. *Finally, police* ~~Police~~ officers kept order. Without a visible, uniformed police force, criminals would have made life in nineteenth-century cities unbearable.

Nineteenth-century police officer in uniform

◆ COLLABORATIVE ACTIVITIES

1. Working in a group, list the reasons why you think students decide to attend your school. After working together to arrange these reasons from least to most important, write a topic sentence that states the main idea suggested by these reasons. Finally, on your own, draft a paragraph in which you discuss the factors that lead students to attend your school.

2. In a newspaper or magazine, find an illustration or photograph that includes a lot of details. Then, write a paragraph describing what you see in the photograph. (Include enough support—details, facts, and examples—so that readers will be able to "see" it almost as clearly as you can.) Decide on a specific spatial order—from top to bottom, from left to right, or another arrangement that makes sense to you. Use that spatial order to organize the details in your paragraph. Finally, trade paragraphs with another student, and offer suggestions that could improve his or her paragraph.

3. Bring to class a paragraph from a newspaper or a magazine. Working in a group, decide whether each of your paragraphs is unified, well developed, and coherent. If any paragraph does not conform to the guidelines outlined in this chapter, try as a group to revise it to make it more effective.

☑ REVIEW CHECKLIST:

Fine-Tuning Your Paragraph

- ☐ A topic sentence states the main idea of your paragraph. (See 2A.)

- ☐ A paragraph is unified when it focuses on a single main idea. (See 2B.)

- ☐ A paragraph is well developed when it contains enough details, facts, and examples to support the main idea. (See 2C.)

- ☐ A paragraph is coherent if its sentences are arranged in a clear, sensible order and it includes all necessary transitional words and phrases. (See 2D.)

Teaching Tip
Have students work in pairs to make up twenty test questions that Chapter 2 could answer. Discuss suggested questions (and how they might be answered).

Teaching Tip
Give an unannounced open-book test asking ten questions about the chapter's content. Allow the students to consult their notes as well as the text.

UNIT TWO

Patterns of Paragraph Development

Exemplification

PREVIEW

In this chapter, you
will learn to write
an exemplification
paragraph.

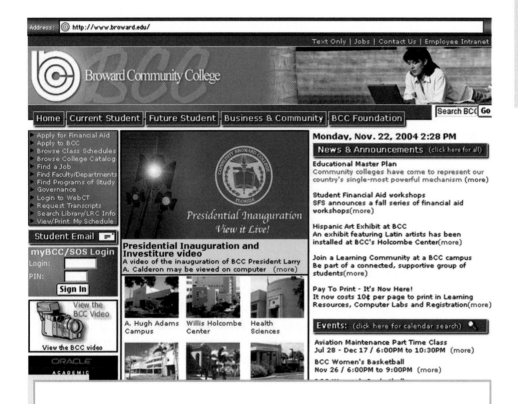

■ **WRITING FIRST**

The picture above shows the home page of Broward Community
College's Web site. Many students go to this site for information
about the school and the support services offered there. Look at the
image of the home page, and then write a paragraph about what
programs and services your school should offer to make it easier
for students to adjust to college. Make sure you review the writing
strategies discussed in Chapter 1 before you begin.

Word Power

adapt   to adjust to new surroundings

mentor   an experienced
and trusted adviser

facilitate   to make easy

In Chapters 1 and 2, you learned how to write paragraphs. In Chapters 3
through 11, you will learn different ways of organizing your ideas within
paragraphs.

As you write, your ideas tend to take shape in ways that reflect how your
mind works: you give examples, tell what happened, describe physical
characteristics, explain how something operates, identify causes or predict

51

effects, identify similarities and differences, classify information into categories, define, or persuade. Not surprisingly, these ways of presenting ideas match specific patterns of paragraph (and essay) development: *exemplification, narration, description, process, cause and effect, comparison and contrast, classification, definition,* and *argument.* Recognizing these patterns and understanding how they help you organize your ideas will help you become a more confident writer.

A Understanding Exemplification

● **Writing Tip**

Use a transitional phrase such as *for instance* or *for example* to let readers know you are going to use an example. (See 2D.)

An **example** is a specific illustration of a general idea. **Exemplification** is writing that explains a general statement by offering one or more specific examples. In an **exemplification paragraph**, you state a general idea in the topic sentence and then use examples to explain it. Thus, an example is always more specific than the idea expressed in the topic sentence. To be effective, examples must be *appropriate* (that is, they must support or explain your point), and they must be *specific* (that is, they must be precise).

You can use a number of short examples to support your topic sentence, or (if one example is particularly clear or forceful) you can use a single long example. The following paragraph about the 1969 Woodstock festival uses a series of short examples.

Topic sentence

Series of short examples

Teaching Tip

To help students understand the concept of exemplification, ask them to put brackets around all the specific examples in this paragraph. What is left? Discuss how specific examples enrich a paragraph.

> In most respects, after all, Woodstock was a disaster. To begin with, it rained and rained for weeks before the festival, and then, of course, it rained during the festival. The promoters lost weeks of preparation time when the site had to be switched twice. They rented Yasgur's field less than a month before the concert. The stage wasn't finished, and the sound system was stitched together perilously close to the start of the show. As soon as the festival opened, the water- and food-delivery arrangements broke down, the gates and fences disintegrated, and tens of thousands of new bodies kept pouring in. (One powerful lure was the rumor that the revered Bob Dylan was going to perform; he wasn't.) In response to an emergency appeal for volunteers, fifty doctors were flown in. The Air Force brought in food on Huey helicopters, and the Women's Community Center in Monticello sent thirty thousand sandwiches. One kid was killed as he was run over by a tractor, one died of appendicitis, and another died of a drug overdose.
>
> –HAL ESPEN, "The Woodstock Wars"

● **Writing Tip**

Many everyday tasks call for exemplification. In a letter to your local newspaper, you might give examples of quality-of-life improvements that need to be made in your neighborhood.

The writer of this paragraph presents a series of examples, one after the other, to support his paragraph's main idea. Each example gives a specific reason why Woodstock was a disaster: it rained, the promoters had to switch sites, water and food were not delivered as planned, and so on.

The next paragraph uses a single long example to support its main idea—that fear can move people to take action.

Topic sentence

Single extended example

> Sometimes, fear can be a great motivator. Once, when I was in high school, I tried out for a part in the school play. I was surprised and

thrilled when I was given one of the leads. Never for a moment, however, did I think about how long my part was or how hard I would have to work to learn it. All I could think of was how much attention I was getting from my friends. I even ignored the warnings of the play's director, who told me I would be in trouble if I did not begin to memorize my lines. The reality of my situation finally sank in during our first dress rehearsal when I stumbled all over my lines and the rest of the cast laughed at me. That night, and for the two weeks leading up to the play, I spent hours going over my lines. Miraculously, I got through the first night of the play without missing (at least obviously missing) many of my lines. As a result of that experience, I learned two things: first, that I could do almost anything if I was frightened enough, and second, that I would never try out for another play.

–JERRY DOYLE (student)

> **Writing Tip**
> Often a personal experience like this one can be an interesting and effective way to illustrate your ideas for your readers.

For information on how to write an exemplification essay as well as a list of transitions suitable for exemplification paragraphs and essays, see 14A.

FOCUS **Exemplification**

How many examples you need in a paragraph depends on your topic sentence. A complicated, far-reaching statement might require many supporting examples to support it. A simple, more direct statement might require fewer examples.

GRAMMAR IN CONTEXT **Exemplification**

When you write an exemplification paragraph, you may introduce your examples with transitional words and phrases like *for example* or *also*. If you do, be sure to use a comma after the introductory transitional word or phrase.

<u>For example</u>, the health-care field will have the greatest growth.

<u>Also</u>, many new employees will be needed in the retail and consumer service areas.

<u>In addition</u>, certain computer fields will need more workers.

For information on using commas with introductory transitional words and phrases, see 31B.

> **Teaching Tip**
> Before your students write exemplification paragraphs, you might want to explain the use of commas to set off introductory transitional elements (31B) and have them do Practice 31-2.

B   Writing an Exemplification Paragraph

◆ **PRACTICE 3-1**

Read this exemplification paragraph; then, follow the instructions below.

Jobs of the Future

   Working as a flight attendant on a spaceship to the moon
sounds exciting, but this job is not likely to be available
for many years. Most students are more concerned with jobs
that will actually be offered in the near future. <u>During
the next ten years, certain areas are expected to need
many more workers</u>. (For example,) the health-care field will
have the greatest growth. Hundreds of thousands of medical
workers—such as home-care aides, physician assistants, and
registered nurses—will be needed. (Also,) many new employees
will be needed in the retail and customer-service areas.
These are fields in which technology cannot completely
replace human beings. (In addition,) certain computer fields
will need many more workers. People who can work as
database administrators or information systems managers
will find many employment opportunities. (Furthermore,)
education will be an attractive area for new job seekers.
Many new teachers will be needed to replace the thousands
who are expected to retire during the next ten years.
Students who know what jobs will be available can prepare
themselves for the future.

1. Underline the topic sentence of the paragraph.

2. List the specific examples the writer uses to support her topic sentence. The first example has been listed for you.

   health-care jobs

   retail and customer-service jobs

   computer occupations

   jobs in education

3. Circle the transitions that the writer uses to connect ideas in the paragraph.

◆ **PRACTICE 3-2**

Teaching Tip
Give students a few minutes
to work on Practice 3-2.
Before they finish, ask some
of them to share what they
have written so far.

Following are four possible topic sentences for exemplification paragraphs. List three examples you could use to support each topic sentence. For example, if you were writing a paragraph about how difficult the first week of your new job was, you could mention waking up early, getting to know your coworkers, and learning new routines.

1. I really like my neighborhood.

   Answers will vary.

   _____

   _____

   _____

   _____

2. Internships give students valuable opportunities to develop job skills.

   Answers will vary.

   _____

   _____

   _____

   _____

3. Good health care is sometimes difficult to get.

   Answers will vary.

   _____

   _____

   _____

   _____

4. Some reality television shows insult the intelligence of their viewers.

   Answers will vary.

   _____

   _____

   _____

   _____

◆ PRACTICE 3-3

Choose one of the topics below (or one of your own choice) as the subject of an exemplification paragraph. Then, on a separate sheet of paper, use one or more of the strategies described in 1C to help you think of as many examples as you can for the topic you have chosen.

Effective (or ineffective) teaching	Things you can't do without
Qualities that make a great athlete	Terrible dates
Successful movies	The importance of recycling
Challenges that older students face	Role models
Traditions your family follows	Rude behavior
Unattractive clothing styles	Politicians
Peer pressure	Acts of bravery
The benefits of cell phones	Lying
	Credit-card debt

◆ PRACTICE 3-4

Review your notes from Practice 3-3, and list the examples that can best help you develop a paragraph on the topic you have chosen.

Answers will vary.

_____

_____

_____

◆ PRACTICE 3-5

Reread your list of examples from Practice 3-4. Now, draft a topic sentence that introduces your topic and communicates the main idea your paragraph will discuss.

Answers will vary.

_____

_____

◆ PRACTICE 3-6

Arrange the examples you listed in Practice 3-4 in a logical order—for example, from least important to most important.

1. *Answers will vary.* _____

2. _____

3. _____

4. _____

◆ PRACTICE 3-7

On a separate sheet of paper, draft your exemplification paragraph. Then, using the Self-Assessment Checklist on page 57, revise your paragraph for unity, development, and coherence.

◆ PRACTICE 3-8

On a separate sheet of paper, type a final, edited draft of your exemplification paragraph.

■ WRITING FIRST: Revising and Editing

Look back at your response to the Writing First exercise on page 51, and evaluate it for unity, development, and coherence. Then, prepare a final, edited draft of your paragraph.

☑ SELF-ASSESSMENT CHECKLIST:
Writing an Exemplification Paragraph

Unity

- [ ] Does your topic sentence state a general idea that can be supported with examples?

- [ ] Is your topic sentence specifically worded?

- [ ] Do all your examples support your topic sentence?

Development

- [ ] Do you need to find additional examples that more clearly support your topic sentence?

- [ ] Should you use one of the strategies discussed in 1C to help you come up with more ideas?

Coherence

- [ ] Are your examples arranged in an order that makes sense?

- [ ] Do you need to add transitional words or phrases?

Narration

PREVIEW

In this chapter, you will
learn to write a
narrative paragraph.

Teaching Tip
To help students understand
the concept of narration,
read aloud a tall tale or a
fairy tale—or a plot sum-
mary from *Soap Opera
Digest*.

Word Power

memorable worth remembering

moral a lesson of a fable
or story

■ WRITING FIRST

Look at the picture above, which illustrates a scene from *Goldilocks
and the Three Bears*. Then, write a paragraph in which you retell a
fairy tale or children's story, such as *Goldilocks and the Three Bears*,
that you know well. Make sure that your topic sentence states the
point of the story.

A Understanding Narration

Narration is writing that tells a story. In a **narrative paragraph**, you
relate a sequence of events. A narrative paragraph usually has a topic sentence that tells readers the point of the paragraph—that is, why you are
telling a particular story. The rest of the paragraph develops this point,
with ideas arranged in *time order*—that is, in the order in which they occurred.

58

In the following paragraph, writer Ron Kovic tells how he celebrated his birthday when he was a child.

> When the Fourth of July came, there were fireworks going off all over the neighborhood. It was the most exciting time of year for me next to Christmas. <u>Being born on the exact same day as my country I thought was really great.</u> I was so proud. And every Fourth of July, I had a birthday party and all my friends would come over with birthday presents and we'd put on silly hats and blow these horns my dad brought home from the A&P. We'd eat lots of ice cream and watermelon and I'd open up all the presents and blow out the candles on the big red, white, and blue birthday cake and then we'd all sing "Happy Birthday" and "I'm a Yankee Doodle Dandy." At night everyone would pile into Bobby's mother's old car and we'd go down to the drive-in, where we'd watch the fireworks display. Before the movie started, we'd all get out and sit up on the roof of the car with our blankets wrapped around us watching the rockets and Roman candles going up and exploding into fountains of rainbow colors, and later after Mrs. Zimmer dropped me off, I'd lie on my bed feeling a little sad that it all had to end so soon. As I closed my eyes I could still hear strings of firecrackers and cherry bombs going off all over the neighborhood.
>
> –RON KOVIC, *Born on the Fourth of July*

Topic sentence

Events presented in time order

● **Writing Tip**
Because narrative paragraphs tell what happened, they often use transitional words and phrases that indicate time, such as *after, before, now,* and *then.* (See 2D.)

In this paragraph, all the events and activities are related to the topic sentence, and transitional words and phrases—*at night, Before the movie started,* and *later*—clearly identify the order in which the events occurred.

In the next paragraph, the writer uses narration to question how prepared her state is to deal with the effects of hurricanes.

For information on how to write a narration essay as well as a list of transitions suitable for narration paragraphs and essays, see 14B.

> <u>The damage caused by hurricane Frances, a relatively small storm for a hurricane, raises concerns about how prepared we are for future storms.</u> The first that most people heard of hurricane Frances was when it was a tropical storm in the Caribbean. As the days passed and it moved closer to Florida, its strength increased. Twenty-four hours before the storm hit, the governor ordered everyone in Miami to evacuate the city. The massive traffic jams that occurred were made worse by cars that ran out of gas and blocked the roads. When hurricane Frances moved ashore, it was a category two storm with winds over one hundred miles an hour. During the first hours, the storm dropped over ten inches of rain. This rain, along with the high winds and the storm surge, caused a lot of damage. Houses that were not built to withstand hurricanes had their roofs torn off and, in some cases, were flattened. Mobile homes were blown over, and boats were crushed against the sides of piers. Many people who went to shelters to wait out the storm had to be evacuated when the shelters themselves began collapsing. When Frances finally passed, the damage was extensive, and fourteen people had died. Even now, questions remain. Why did the governor wait so long to evacuate Miami? Why has the state of Florida not made people upgrade their houses so they can withstand a category two hurricane? Finally, why were people moved into shelters that could not withstand the storm? These as well as other questions must be answered before another, even stronger, storm comes along.
>
> –MARGARET FARAH (student)

Topic sentence

Events presented in time order

In this paragraph, all the events are organized according to time order. By presenting events in the order in which they occurred and by using transitional words and phrases, the writer helps readers follow her discussion. The paragraph ends with a series of questions that reinforce the point made in the topic sentence—that the writer has concerns about how prepared Florida is for future storms.

GRAMMAR IN CONTEXT **Narration**

When you write a narrative paragraph, you tell a story. As you become involved in your story, you may find yourself stringing incidents together without proper punctuation. The result will be a **run-on** or **comma splice**.

INCORRECT (RUN-ON)	We soon ran out of food and supplies I thought we would never make it at last we reached Malaysia.
CORRECT	We soon ran out of food and supplies. I thought we would never make it, but at last we reached Malaysia.

For information on how to identify and correct run-ons and comma splices, see Chapter 21.

B **Writing a Narrative Paragraph**

◆ **PRACTICE 4-1**

Read this narrative paragraph; then, follow the instructions on page 61.

then, follow the instructions on page 61.

> The Trip to a Brand-New Life
>
> When I was seven, my family took a trip that changed our entire lives—the trip to America. Leaving our native Vietnam illegally, we (first) traveled three days in a small boat with about fifty other people. We (soon) ran out of food and supplies. I thought we would never make it, but (at last) we reached Malaysia. The people who met us on shore led us to a campsite where there were hundreds of other Vietnamese refugees. (For nine months,) my family stayed there, living in a shelter consisting of logs covered with thick plastic. (During this time,) we were called in to present our situation to representatives from a variety of countries so they could process our documents and decide whether to accept us as immigrants. We were among the fortunate ones accepted by the United States. (Next,) we were

---

Teaching Tip

Before your students write narrative paragraphs, you might want to explain how to identify and correct run-ons and comma splices (Chapter 21) and have them do Practices 21-1 and 21-4.

● **Writing Tip**

Many everyday writing tasks call for narration. In a complaint letter, you might summarize, in chronological order, the problems you had with a particular product.

Teaching Tip

Bring to class a magazine photograph that shows two people talking. Ask students to discuss what the people might be saying and to write out the conversation in dialogue format. Then, have students exchange papers and check each other's work. Explain how dialogue enriches narrative writing.

transferred to a camp in the Philippines, where the houses
were more stable and the floors were cement instead of
dirt. (For three months,) we continued to study English;
(then,) the happy moment came when we learned that we would
be leaving for America. (A few days later,) we were headed
for New York, changing planes in several countries before
reaching our destination. (As the last plane landed,) I was
overwhelmed by the realization that my family and I had
(finally) reached the land of our dreams. I knew that my
first step on the ground would lead me to a new future
and a completely new life. I was scared, but I did not
hesitate.

Ann Duong (student)

1. Underline the topic sentence of the paragraph.

2. List below the major events of the narrative. The first event has been
   listed for you.

   The family left Vietnam and spent three days on the water.

   When they reached Malaysia, they entered a refugee camp.

   For nine months, they waited to be accepted by another country.

   After being accepted by the United States, they moved to the Philippines
   for three months.

   Finally, they were flown to New York to begin their new life.

3. Reread the narrative, circling the transitional words and phrases the
   writer uses to link events in time.

◆ PRACTICE 4-2

Below are four possible topic sentences for narrative paragraphs. After
each topic sentence, list four events that could support the main idea. For
example, if you were recalling a barbecue that turned into a disaster, you
could tell about burning the hamburgers, spilling the soda, and forgetting
to buy paper plates.

> **Teaching Tip**
> Discuss how to format and
> punctuate dialogue. Show
> students how to indent each
> time the speaker changes.

1. One experience made me realize that I was no longer as young as I
   thought.

   Answers will vary.

2. The first time I _____, I got more than I bargained for.

   Answers will vary.

   _____

   _____

   _____

3. I did not think I had the courage to _____, but when I did, I felt proud of myself.

   Answers will vary.

   _____

   _____

   _____

4. I remember my reaction to one particular news story very clearly.

   Answers will vary.

   _____

   _____

   _____

◆ PRACTICE 4-3

Choose one of the topics below (or one of your own choice) as the subject of a narrative paragraph. On a separate sheet of paper, use one or more of the strategies described in 1C to help you recall events and details about the topic you have chosen.

A difficult choice	An embarrassing situation
A frightening situation	A surprise
A time of self-doubt	A sudden understanding or insight
A success	Something funny a friend did
An act of violence	Unexpected good luck
A lesson you learned	A conflict with authority
A happy moment	An event that changed your life
An instance of injustice	An important decision

◆ PRACTICE 4-4

List the events you recalled in Practice 4-3 that can best help you develop a narrative paragraph on the topic you have chosen.

Answers will vary.

_____

_____

_____

_____

_____

_____

◆ PRACTICE 4-5

Reread your list of events from Practice 4-4. Then, draft a topic sentence that introduces your topic and communicates the main idea your paragraph will discuss.

Answers will vary.
_____

_____

_____

◆ PRACTICE 4-6

Write down the events you listed in Practice 4-4 in the order in which they occurred.

1. *Answers will vary.*_____

2. _____

3. _____

4. _____

5. _____

Teaching Tip
Stop here, and have students share their ideas with the class.

◆ PRACTICE 4-7

On a separate sheet of paper, draft your narrative paragraph. Then, consulting the Self-Assessment Checklist on page 64, revise your paragraph for unity, development, and coherence.

Teaching Tip
For a quiz on dialogue, photocopy a comic strip, and have students rewrite the conversation in dialogue format.

◆ PRACTICE 4-8

On a separate sheet of paper, write a final, edited draft of your narrative paragraph.

ESL Tip
Remind students to copy the conversation exactly as it appears in the comic. Check to make sure they do not include double subjects or extra connecting words. (Incorrect: *Since it was late, so he didn't take the test.*)

■ WRITING FIRST: Revising and Editing

Look back at your response to the Writing First exercise on page 58, and evaluate your paragraph for unity, development, and coherence. Then, prepare a final, edited draft of your paragraph.

☑ SELF-ASSESSMENT CHECKLIST:
Writing a Narrative Paragraph

Unity

☐ Does your topic sentence tell readers what the point of the paragraph is?

☐ Is your topic sentence specific enough?

☐ Do all details and events support your topic sentence?

Development

☐ Should you add more events or details to make your narrative clearer or livelier?

Coherence

☐ Does your narrative proceed clearly in time order?

☐ Do you need to add transitional words or phrases?

Description

■ WRITING FIRST

Look at the picture above, which shows a street vendor selling food. Then, write a paragraph in which you describe a person you encounter every day—for example, a street vendor, a bus driver, or a worker in your school cafeteria. Before you begin writing, decide what general impression you want to convey about the person you are describing.

A   Understanding Description

Description is writing that paints a word picture of a person, place, or thing. In a **descriptive paragraph**, you use description to enable readers to see what you see, hear what you hear, smell what you smell, taste what you taste, and feel what you feel. Details in a descriptive paragraph are usually arranged in *spatial order*—that is, from top to bottom, near to far, front to back, and so on.

ESL Tip
Explain the correct placement of adverbs with verbs
and their objects. (Incorrect:
*The man moved quickly the
books.*)

When you write a descriptive paragraph, you try to create a single
dominant impression—a mood or feeling you want to communicate to
readers. For example, if you were describing an old house in your neighborhood and wanted to leave readers with the impression that it was
mysterious, your topic sentence would convey this idea: *The old house
stands dark and alone, with just one window lit.* The rest of the sentences
in the paragraph would reinforce this dominant impression.

In general, there are two kinds of descriptive paragraphs: *objective* and
subjective. Writers use **objective description** to describe something without conveying their own emotions or opinions. This kind of description is
used in technical or scientific writing but can also be used in other kinds
of writing. In the following paragraph, the writer uses precise language
and specific details to describe a scene to readers, but her writing does not
indicate any special meaning the scene may have for her.

Topic sentence

Events presented in spatial order

<u>One look at Bethany Beach, Delaware, shows the effect of con-
struction on the shoreline.</u> The small town is located just south of
Delaware Bay, where the land juts out and curves down the east coast.
On the Atlantic side of Bethany, the white beach slopes gradually up
from the ocean. In back of the beach are low rippling dunes that gradually blend into higher mounds of sand that have been planted with
several types of beach grass and stubby green shrubs. The town council hoped that these plants would stabilize the dune structure and stop
the erosion that threatens the beach every time there is a storm. Arching over the dunes are narrow gray boardwalks that protect the fragile
dunes from the human traffic that eventually would destroy them. Behind the dunes, however, nature seems to stop. Along the Atlantic
coast, as far south as Virginia Beach, the land has been divided into
sandy plots, each with its own beach house or apartment development.
The natural flow of the beach has been interrupted by geometrical
structures of shining glass and weathered gray wood.

–KIM DIPIALO (student)

● **Writing Tip**
Descriptive paragraphs often
use transitional words and
phrases that signal spatial
order, such as *in front of, in
back of, near,* and *next to.*
(See 2D.)

● **Writing Tip**
Descriptions often use language that conveys sensory
details—that tell what
something looks, smells,
sounds, tastes, or feels like
(*a <u>blue</u> sky, a <u>musty</u> smell*).

Because the writer's purpose is to help readers picture the scene she describes, her description is primarily objective. The topic sentence presents
the main idea of the paragraph. Then, the writer describes the beach, the
dunes, and finally the area behind the dunes. Transitional words and
phrases emphasize the spatial arrangement of details—*in back of the
beach, arching over the dunes,* and *behind the dunes*—and connect various
parts of the description. Specific visual details such as *stubby green shrubs,
narrow gray boardwalks,* and *weathered gray wood* give readers a clear picture of the scene.

Writers use **subjective description** to convey their feelings and opinions about a person, place, or thing, but subjective descriptions also contain precise language and specific details, just as objective descriptions do.
In the following paragraph, the writer describes her impression of a building that has strong emotional associations for her.

Topic sentence

<u>The school building was not a welcoming sight for someone used
to the bright colors and airiness of tropical architecture.</u> The building
looked functional. It could have been a prison, an asylum, or just what
it was: an urban school for the children of immigrants, built to with-

stand waves of change, generation by generation. Its red brick sides rose to four solid stories. The black steel fire escapes snaked up its back like exposed vertebrae. A chain link fence surrounded its concrete playground. Members of the elite safety patrol, older kids, sixth graders mainly, stood at each of its entrances, wearing their fluorescent white belts that criss-crossed their chests and their metal badges. No one was allowed in the building until the bell rang, not even on rainy or bitter-cold days. Only the safety patrol stayed warm.

–JUDITH ORTIZ COFER, *Silent Dancing: A Partial Remembrance of a Puerto Rican Childhood*

Events presented in spatial order

> **Teaching Tip**
> This descriptive paragraph works well with a minimum of transitional words and phrases. As an exercise, ask students to add some transitions to this paragraph.

In this paragraph, the topic sentence conveys the paragraph's dominant impression. The details of the paragraph are arranged in spatial order, starting with the school itself, moving to the chain link fence around it, and ending with the children standing outside. The paragraph includes enough specific details to give readers a clear picture of the school. At the same time, it also communicates the writer's strong negative response to the building she is describing.

For information on how to write a description essay as well as a list of transitions suitable for descriptive paragraphs and essays, see 14C.

GRAMMAR IN CONTEXT · Description

When you write a descriptive paragraph, you frequently use modifiers to help you describe your subject. If you place modifying words or phrases incorrectly, you may create a misplaced modifier that will confuse readers.

CONFUSING   Black with mildew, the hot sun curls the tan roof shingles. (Is the sun black with mildew?)

CLEAR   Black with mildew, the tan roof shingles curl in the hot sun.

For information on how to identify and correct misplaced modifiers, see 25D.

> **Teaching Tip**
> Before your students write descriptive paragraphs, you might want to explain how to identify modification errors (Chapter 25) and have them do Practice 25-5.

B   Writing a Descriptive Paragraph

◆ PRACTICE 5-1

Read this descriptive paragraph; then, follow the instructions on the next page.

> ● **Writing Tip**
> Most descriptive paragraphs mix objective description and subjective description. Although one kind of description may dominate, the other will probably be present as well.

```
              A House Left Behind

    I live in a neighborhood of well-maintained old houses.
They are carefully painted every few years and surrounded
by patches of thick, well-mown grass. The bushes are neatly
```

clipped, bright flowers line the front walks, and, in the back yards, vegetable gardens produce juicy red tomatoes and mountains of yellow squash every summer. <u>But right in the middle of one block is a house that looks sad and deserted.</u> Black with mildew, the tan roof shingles curl in the hot sun. Two broken windows on the second floor have been patched with pieces of wood, and the other windows are grey with dirt. On the side of the house dangles a battered basketball hoop. Once, the original white wood siding on the house must have been replaced by bright yellow aluminum, but now the color is faded, and the aluminum is scratched and dented. The front door was once bright yellow, too; now, the paint is cracked and peeling, and underneath, bare wood is visible. In the past, evergreen shrubs were planted around the house, but no one has trimmed them for a long time. They are straggly, with long, thin branches blocking some of the first-floor windows. The front yard shows what happens when no one fertilizes the grass: it keeps growing but gets thinner and more yellow. When it rains, patches of mud form on the grass. In the back yard, tomato plants from an old garden have reseeded themselves. They grow tall and narrow but do not produce any tomatoes. No one seems to care about this house anymore.

1. Underline the topic sentence of the paragraph.

2. In a few words, summarize the dominant impression the writer wants to give of the subject.

   Answers may vary.

3. What are some of the details the writer uses to create this dominant impression? The first detail has been listed for you.

   roof black with mildew

   broken windows

   windows grey with dirt

   battered basketball hoop

   faded aluminum siding

   straggly shrubs

◆ PRACTICE 5-2

Each of the five topic sentences below states a possible dominant impression for a paragraph. After each topic sentence, list three details that could help convey this dominant impression. For example, to support the idea that sitting in front of a fireplace is relaxing, you could describe the crackling of the fire, the pine scent of the smoke, and the changing colors of the flames.

1. One look at the stern face of the traffic-court judge convinced me that my appeal would be denied.

   Answers will vary.

   _____

   _____

   _____

2. The dog was at least ten years old and obviously had been living on the streets for a long time.

   Answers will vary.

   _____

   _____

   _____

3. The woman behind the department store makeup counter was a walking advertisement for almost every product she sold.

   Answers will vary.

   _____

   _____

   _____

4. One of the most interesting stores I know sells vintage clothing.

   Answers will vary.

   _____

   _____

   _____

5. Riding the roller coaster was so exciting that I immediately got back in line for another ride.

   Answers will vary.

   _____

   _____

   _____

◆ PRACTICE 5-3

Choose one of the topics below (or one of your own choice) as the subject of a descriptive paragraph. On a separate sheet of paper, use one or more of the strategies described in 1C to help you come up with specific details about the topic you have chosen. If you can, observe your subject directly and write down your observations.

A favorite place	A favorite article of clothing
A place you felt trapped in	An interesting object
An interesting spot on campus	A pet
An unusual person	A building you find interesting
Your dream house	Your car or truck
A family member or friend	The car you would like to have

A work of art   A statue or monument
A valued possession Someone you admire
Your workplace   A fashion disaster

◆ PRACTICE 5-4

List the details you came up with in Practice 5-3 that can best help you develop a descriptive paragraph on the topic you have chosen.

Answers will vary.

_____

_____

_____

_____

◆ PRACTICE 5-5

Reread your list of details from Practice 5-4. Then, draft a topic sentence that summarizes the dominant impression you want to convey in your paragraph.

Answers will vary.

_____

_____

◆ PRACTICE 5-6

Arrange the details you listed in Practice 5-4 in spatial order. You might arrange them in the order in which you are looking at them—for example, from left to right, near to far, or top to bottom.

1. *Answers will vary.* _____

2. _____

3. _____

4. _____

5. _____

6. _____

7. _____

Teaching Tip
Put a section of a descriptive piece of writing on an overhead transparency. Have students model their descriptions and sentence patterns on the sample.

◆ PRACTICE 5-7

On a separate sheet of paper, draft your descriptive paragraph. Then, consulting the Self-Assessment Checklist on page 71, revise your paragraph for unity, development, and coherence.

◆ PRACTICE 5-8

On a separate sheet of paper, write a final, edited draft of your descriptive paragraph.

■ WRITING FIRST: Revising and Editing

Look back at your response to the Writing First exercise on page 65, and evaluate your paragraph for unity, development, and coherence. Then, prepare a final, edited draft of your paragraph.

☑ SELF-ASSESSMENT CHECKLIST:
Writing a Descriptive Paragraph

Unity

☐ Does your topic sentence express the dominant impression you want to communicate?

☐ Do all the details in your paragraph support your topic sentence?

☐ Do all the details help to convey the dominant impression stated in your topic sentence?

Development

☐ Do you need to include more objective description to help readers see your subject?

☐ Do you need to add more subjective description to help readers understand your feelings and opinions about your subject?

Coherence

☐ Are your details arranged in a spatial order that makes sense?

☐ Do you need to add transitional words or phrases?

6

Process

PREVIEW

In this chapter, you will learn to write a process paragraph.

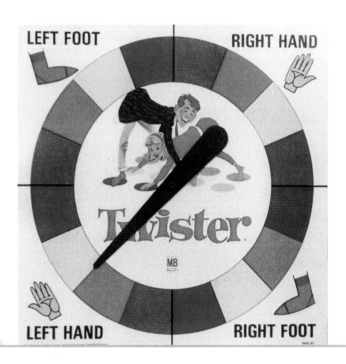

LEFT FOOT   RIGHT HAND

LEFT HAND   RIGHT FOOT

Word Power

compete to work against another person in pursuit of a goal

objective a purpose or goal

penalty a punishment or loss of advantage

■ WRITING FIRST

Look at the picture above, which shows a spinner from the game Twister. Then, write a paragraph in which you explain how to play your favorite board (or other indoor) game. Assume that your readers know nothing about the game.

Teaching Tip
To help students understand the concept of process, photocopy the operating instructions for an appliance or electronic device. (Students could also be asked to bring instruction booklets or operating manuals to class.) Have students take turns reading steps aloud, and ask the class to supply any missing transitions.

A   Understanding Process

A **process** is a series of steps that are presented in chronological order and that lead to a particular result. In a **process paragraph**, you explain how something works or tell how to do something. The topic sentence of your paragraph should identify the process (for example, "Frying chicken is easy" or "The typical job interview has three stages") and possibly communicate the point you want to make about it. The rest of the paragraph should discuss the steps in the process, one at a time, in the order in which they occur or the order in which they are to be performed.

In general, there are two kinds of process paragraphs: *process explanations* and *instructions*. In a **process explanation**, the writer's purpose is to help readers understand a process—for example, how something works or how something happens—not perform it. The following paragraph is a process explanation.

> <u>Once asleep, we go through four distinct stages.</u> The first stage of sleep is marked by an easing of muscle tension and a change in brain-wave activity. This transitional stage is especially light and typically lasts about twenty minutes, during which time you may be easily awakened. In stage two, brain waves slow and slumber grows deeper. Even with the eyes taped open, we are quite literally blind during this phase and would be incapable of seeing anything—even a hand passing over the face—since the eye-brain connection has been shut off. More than half of the time devoted solely to sleep is spent in stage two, and no dreaming occurs. Stages three and four are marked by even slower brain waves, but the deepest sleep occurs in stage four. Mysteriously, the highest levels of the body's growth hormone are released during this sleep stage. After cycling back for a few minutes of stage-two sleep, dreaming begins. The first dream phase, lasting only a few minutes, is the shortest of the night. When dreaming is over, the sleeper retraces all the stages back to lighter sleep and then repeats the deep-sleep stages back to dreaming.
>
> –MARK MCCUCHEN, *The Compass in Your Nose and Other Astonishing Facts about Humans*

Topic sentence
Stage 1

Stage 2

Stages 3 and 4

The topic sentence identifies the process, and the rest of the paragraph presents the steps in strict chronological order. Throughout the paragraph, transitional words and phrases—*the first stage*, *in stage two*, and *stages three and four*—clearly identify individual steps in the process.

Other process paragraphs present **instructions**. Here, the writer's purpose is to give readers the information they need to perform a task or activity. The following paragraph gives instructions for using a pair of chopsticks.

Teaching Tip
Mention the importance of using correct pronouns and avoiding shifts, especially from third person to second. Review when to use (and when not to use) *you* in process paragraphs.

> <u>With a little bit of patience, most people can learn how to use chopsticks in a short time.</u> Chopsticks are pointed pieces of wood that the Chinese use to eat their food. They are usually made of bamboo but can also be made of other materials. First used about five thousand years ago in China, chopsticks probably developed from sticks people used to retrieve hot food from cooking pots. Some people think that chopsticks reflect the influence of Confucianism, which sees knives and forks as resembling weapons and chopsticks as reflecting gentleness and kindness. Whatever their origin, chopsticks are easy to use:
>   1. First, place the lower chopstick in the V between the thumb and index finger, and rest its lower end below the first joint of the third finger. Support the chopstick with the little finger and the ring finger.
>   2. Next, hold the upper chopstick as if it were a pencil between your middle and index fingers. (Before you try using them, make sure

Topic sentence
Background

Teaching Tip
Ask the class to draw two or three diagrams to illustrate the process of using chopsticks. Then, discuss how diagrams can help readers understand certain processes.

Steps in process

that the tips of the two chopsticks are even. It will be difficult to hold food if the tip of one end extends farther than the other.)

3. To pick up food, move the upper chopstick with the middle and index fingers. The bottom chopstick should remain still.

When you begin, expect to drop food all over the table and yourself. Don't give up, though. After some practice, most people use chopsticks as easily as they do a fork. —JOYCE CHIN (student)

Concluding statement

Because the writer assumes that readers do not know much about her subject, she begins her paragraph by presenting a brief history of chopsticks. When she presents her instructions, she addresses readers directly, using commands to tell them what to do (for instance, "place the lower chopstick in the V between the thumb and index finger"). She also uses a numbered list as well as clear transitional words and expressions—*first, next, before*—to help readers see the exact sequence in which steps are to be performed. She includes a caution ("Before you try using them, make sure that the tips of the two chopsticks are even") and ends with some reassuring advice.

For information on how to write a process essay, as well as a list of transitions suitable for process paragraphs, see 14D.

● **Writing Tip**

Many everyday writing tasks call for outlining a process. For example, you might write a set of instructions telling your family members what to do in case of a fire.

FOCUS **Process**

Like narrative paragraphs, process paragraphs present a sequence of events. Unlike narrative paragraphs, however, process paragraphs describe a sequence that occurs—or should occur—in exactly the same way every time.

Teaching Tip

Before your students write process paragraphs, you might want to explain how to identify and avoid illogical shifts (Chapter 24) and have them do Practices 24-1 and 24-4.

GRAMMAR IN CONTEXT **Process**

When you write a process paragraph, you may have problems with illogical shifts in tense, person, number, and voice. If you shift from one tense, person, number, or voice to another without good reason, you will confuse readers.

CONFUSING Here, <u>workers</u> again <u>look</u> for bad spots, and any rotten pieces <u>are thrown away</u>. (illogical shift from active to passive voice)

CLEAR Here, <u>workers</u> again <u>look</u> for bad spots, and <u>they throw away</u> any rotten pieces. (consistent use of active voice)

For information on how to avoid illogical shifts in tense, person, number, and voice, see Chapter 24.

B Writing a Process Paragraph

◆ **PRACTICE 6-1**

Read this process paragraph; then, follow the instructions below.

```
                  An Order of Fries

    I never realized how much work goes into making French
fries until I worked at a potato processing plant in
Hermiston, Oregon. The process begins with freshly dug
potatoes being shoveled from trucks onto conveyor belts
leading into the plant. During this stage, workers must
pick out any rocks that may have been dug up with the
potatoes because these could damage the automated peelers.
After the potatoes have gone through the peelers, they
travel on a conveyor belt through the "trim line." Here,
workers cut out any bad spots, being careful not to waste
potatoes by trimming too much. Next, the potatoes are
sliced in automated cutters and then fried for about a
minute. After this, they continue along a conveyor belt
to the "wet line." Here, workers again look for bad spots,
and they throw away any rotten pieces. At this point, the
potatoes go to a second set of fryers for three minutes
before being moved to subzero freezers for ten minutes.
Then, it's on to the "frozen line" for a final inspection.
The inspected fries are weighed by machines and then sealed
into five-pound plastic packages, which are weighed again
by workers who also check that the packages are properly
sealed. The bags are then packed into boxes and made ready
for shipment to various restaurants across the western
United States. This process goes on twenty-four hours a
day to bring us consumers the tasty French fries we all
enjoy so much.

                          Cheri Rodriguez (student)
```

1. Underline the topic sentence of the paragraph.

2. Is this a process explanation or instructions? _process explanation_

   How do you know? _Verbs are not commands._

3. List the steps in the process. The first step has been listed for you.

   The potatoes are unloaded, and the rocks are sorted out.

   They are peeled and carried to the "trim line."

   They are sliced and fried for a minute.

   They are carried to the "wet line."

They are fried again and then frozen.

They get a final inspection on the "frozen line."

They are weighed, packaged, and boxed for shipment.

◆ PRACTICE 6-2

Following are four possible topic sentences for process paragraphs. After each topic sentence, list three or four steps that explain the process the sentence identifies. For example, if you were explaining the process of getting a job, you could list preparing a résumé, looking at ads in newspapers or online, writing a job application letter, and going on an interview. Make sure each step follows logically from the one that precedes it.

1. Downloading music from the Internet is a simple process.

   a. *Answers will vary.*

   b. _____

   c. _____

   d. _____

2. Getting the most out of a student-teacher conference can take some preparation.

   a. *Answers will vary.*

   b. _____

   c. _____

   d. _____

3. Breaking up with someone you are dating can be a tricky process.

   a. *Answers will vary.*

   b. _____

   c. _____

   d. _____

4. Choosing the perfect outfit for a job interview can be a time-consuming task.

   a. *Answers will vary.*

   b. _____

   c. _____

   d. _____

◆ PRACTICE 6-3

Choose one of the topics below (or one of your own choice) as the subject of a process paragraph. Use one or more of the strategies described in 1C to help you come up with as many steps as you can for the topic you have chosen, and list these steps on a separate sheet of paper.

Making a major purchase	How to use a digital camera
Strategies for winning an argument	How to perform a particular household repair
How to save money	How to apply for financial aid
Buying a book or CD online	A process involved in a hobby of yours
Your typical work or school day	
How to discourage telemarketers	Painting a room
Your morning routine	How to make your favorite dish
How to send a text message on a cell phone	How to drop (or add) a course
	How to prepare for a storm

◆ PRACTICE 6-4

Review your notes on the topic you chose in Practice 6-3, and decide whether to write a process explanation or a set of instructions. Then, on the lines below, choose the steps from the list you wrote in Practice 6-3 that can best help you develop a process paragraph on your topic.

Answers will vary.

_____   _____

_____   _____

_____   _____

_____   _____

◆ PRACTICE 6-5

Reread your list of steps from Practice 6-4. Then, draft a topic sentence that identifies the process you will discuss and communicates the point you will make about it.

Answers will vary.

_____

_____

_____

◆ PRACTICE 6-6

Review the steps you listed in Practice 6-4. Then, write them down in chronological order, moving from the first step to the last.

1. *Answers will vary.*   4. _____

2. _____   5. _____

3. _____   6. _____

6 B

Teaching Tip
Students have a tendency
to use short sentences in
process paragraphs. Take
this opportunity to do
a sentence-combining
exercise.

ESL Tip
Check drafts for correct article and preposition use.
(Nonnative speakers tend to
omit these parts of speech
or use them incorrectly.)
Have students circle articles
and prepositions so you can
check them quickly.

◆ **PRACTICE 6-7**

On a separate sheet of paper, draft your process paragraph. Then, consulting the Self-Assessment Checklist below, revise your paragraph for
unity, development, and coherence.

◆ **PRACTICE 6-8**

On a separate sheet of paper, write a final, edited draft of your process
paragraph.

■ WRITING FIRST: Revising and Editing

Look back at your response to the Writing First exercise on
page 72, and evaluate your paragraph for unity, development, and
coherence. Then, prepare a final, edited draft of your paragraph.

☑ SELF-ASSESSMENT CHECKLIST:
Writing a Process Paragraph

Unity

☐ Does your topic sentence identify the process you will discuss?
Does it state your main idea—the point you will make about
the process?

☐ Have you eliminated information that does not relate directly
to the process?

Development

☐ Have you included all the steps that readers need to know in
order to understand the process?

☐ Do you need to explain any steps in greater detail?

☐ If your paragraph is a set of instructions, do you need to include any cautions or reminders?

Coherence

☐ Is your process explained in exact chronological order, or do
you need to rearrange the steps?

☐ Do you need to add transitional words or phrases?

Cause and Effect

PREVIEW

In this chapter, you will learn to write a cause-and-effect paragraph.

Teaching Tip
To help students understand the concept of cause and effect, have them write a one-paragraph summary of a newspaper column or an editorial that deals with the causes or effects of a particular action or event.

■ WRITING FIRST

Look at the picture above, which shows a young woman talking on a cell phone. Then, write a paragraph in which you describe the impact of a particular electronic appliance or gadget on your life or the life of your family—for example, the ATM machine, the cell phone, or the television remote control. Be sure that your topic sentence identifies the item and that the rest of the paragraph discusses how it affects you or your family.

Word Power

gadget   a small specialized mechanical or electronic device

impact   the effect of one thing on another

simplify   to make easier

A | Understanding Cause and Effect

A **cause** is what makes a particular thing happen. An **effect** is what results from a particular cause: a situation, activity, or behavior. You write **cause-and-effect paragraphs** to help readers understand why something happened or is happening or to show readers how one thing affects something

79

else. You can also use cause-and-effect writing to speculate about future events.

The main difficulty you may have when planning a cause-and-effect paragraph is making sure that a **causal relationship** exists—that one event actually *caused* another event and did not just come before it in time. Another problem is making sure you consider all possible causes and effects, not just the most obvious ones. As you write, consider the importance of the causes or effects you discuss. Don't make a particular cause or effect seem more important than it actually is, just to strengthen your case. Finally, make sure you arrange causes (or effects) in a logical order—for example, from least important to most important.

A cause-and-effect paragraph can focus on causes or on effects. The following paragraph examines causes.

Topic sentence: effect

First (minor) cause: paper costs

Second (major) cause: illiteracy

Newspapers are folding. Paper costs are high, but loss of literate readers is much higher. Forty-five percent of adult citizens do not read newspapers. Only 10 percent abstain by choice. The rest have been excluded by their inability to read. Even the most distinguished daily papers are now written at an estimated tenth-grade level. Magazines such as the *Nation, New Republic, Time, Newsweek,* and the *National Review* are written at a minimum of twelfth-grade level. Circulation battles represent a competition for the largest piece of a diminished pie. Enlargement of that pie does not yet seem to have occurred to those who enter these increasingly unhappy competitions. The only successful major paper to be launched in the last decade, *USA Today,* relies on a simplistic lexicon, large headlines, color photographs, and fanciful weather maps that seek to duplicate the instant entertainment on TV.

–JONATHAN KOZOL, *Illiterate America*

Writing Tip

Many everyday writing tasks call for discussing causes and effects. For example, at work, you might write a memo describing how a new procedure might affect your job performance.

The topic sentence identifies the problem the paragraph will discuss. After mentioning one relatively minor cause of the problem (the cost of paper), the paragraph goes on to analyze the primary cause of the problem—illiteracy.

The paragraph below discusses effects.

Topic sentence: cause

First effect: pain disappears

Second effect: muscle damaged further

Professional athletes are sometimes severely disadvantaged by trainers whose job it is to keep them in action. The more famous the athlete, the greater the risk that he or she may be subjected to extreme medical measures when injury strikes. The star baseball player whose arm is sore because of a torn muscle or tissue damage may need sustained rest more than anything else. But his team is battling for a place in the World Series; so the trainer or team doctor, called upon to work his magic, reaches for a strong dose of butazolidine or other powerful pain suppressants. Presto, the pain disappears! The pitcher takes his place on the mound and does superbly. That could be the last game, however, in which he is able to throw a ball with full strength. The drugs didn't repair torn muscle or cause the damaged tissue to heal. What they did was to mask the pain, enabling the pitcher to throw hard, further damaging the torn muscle. Little wonder that so many star athletes are cut down in their prime, more the victims of overzealous treatment of their injuries than of the injuries themselves.

–NORMAN COUSINS,
"Pain Is Not the Ultimate Enemy"

The topic sentence identifies the cause of the problem the paragraph will consider. The paragraph then goes on to discuss two effects—the second more important than the first—of the trainer's actions.

For information on how to write a cause-and-effect essay, as well as a list of transitions suitable for cause-and-effect paragraphs and essays, see 14E.

GRAMMAR IN CONTEXT **Cause and Effect**

When you write a cause-and-effect paragraph, you may confuse the words *affect* and *effect*. *Affect* is a verb meaning "to influence"; *effect* is a noun meaning "result."

>   *effect*
> For me and for other experienced runners, the ~~affect~~ of running is pure pleasure. (*effect* is a noun)

>   *affected*
> As I begin, I am deeply ~~effected~~ by the clean, open air, and my lungs are immediately refreshed. (*affect* is a verb)

For more information on *affect* and *effect*, see 34E.

Teaching Tip
Before your students write cause-and-effect paragraphs, you might want to review the use of *affect* and *effect*, pointing them to the examples in 34E and to the relevant items in Practice 34-6.

B   **Writing a Cause-and-Effect Paragraph**

◆ **PRACTICE 7-1**

Read this cause-and-effect paragraph; then, follow the instructions on page 82.

The Ultimate High

    <u>For me and for other experienced runners, the effect of running is pure pleasure</u>. When I run, it may look as though I'm in agony, with my gaping mouth, soaked brow, and constantly contracting leg muscles. In fact, my daily half-hour run represents a time of complete physical and mental relaxation. As I begin my run, I am deeply affected by the clean, open air, and my lungs are immediately refreshed. The daily tensions built up in my body ease as my muscles stretch and pump, releasing all feelings of anger or frustration. I mentally dive into my run and feel as though I am lifting my feet from the pavement and ascending into the air. My mind wanders, and I seem to float, daydreaming about wherever my thoughts take me. I take pride in my effort, signified by the perspiration that trickles down my face and body. After I complete my run and cool down with long, deep breaths, my body tingles and feels energized, as if I had just come off a roller coaster. I am more alert, my concentration is sharper, and

I am relaxed and peaceful. I feel alive. Beginning runners initially experience soreness and fatigue rather than this kind of "high." They should be patient, however. As their bodies build up strength and tolerance, they will no longer equate running with pain but rather with relief from tension and with greater emotional well-being.

Scott Weckerly (student)

1. Underline the topic sentence of the paragraph.

2. Does this paragraph deal mainly with the causes or the effects of running? _____*effects*_____ How do you know? *The topic sentence says the*
   paragraph will focus on the "effect of running."

3. List some of the effects the writer describes. The first effect has been listed for you.

   His lungs are refreshed with clean air.

   Tension and frustrations are released.

   He escapes into another world.

   He feels proud of his effort.

   He feels energized afterward, alert and relaxed at the same time.

◆ PRACTICE 7-2

Following are four possible topic sentences for cause-and-effect paragraphs. After each topic sentence, list the effects that could result from the cause identified in the topic sentence. For example, if you were writing a paragraph about the effects of excessive drinking on campus, you could list low grades, health problems, and vandalism.

1. Having a baby can change your life.

   Answers will vary.

2. Learning a second language has many advantages.

   Answers will vary.

3. MP3 players have been a huge success for a number of reasons.

Answers will vary.

_____

_____

4. Impulse buying can have negative effects on a person's finances.

Answers will vary.

_____

_____

◆ PRACTICE 7-3

List three causes that could support each of the following topic sentences.

1. The causes of teenage obesity are easy to identify.

Answers will vary.

_____

_____

2. Chronic unemployment can have many causes.

Answers will vary.

_____

_____

3. The high cost of college tuition is not easy to explain.

Answers will vary.

_____

_____

4. There are several reasons why professional athletes' salaries are high.

Answers will vary.

_____

_____

5. Eighteen- to twenty-nine-year-olds tend not to vote in national elections for a number of reasons.

Answers will vary.

_____

_____

◆ **PRACTICE 7-4**

Choose one of the following topics (or one of your own choice) as the subject of a paragraph that examines causes or effects. Then, on a separate sheet of paper, use one or more of the strategies described in 1C to help you think of as many causes or effects as you can for the topic you have chosen.

> Why a current television show or movie is popular
> Some causes (or effects) of stress
> The negative effects of credit cards
> Why teenagers (or adults) drink
> The reasons you decided to attend college
> The effects of a particular government policy
> How becoming a vegetarian might change (or has changed) your life
> The benefits of home cooking
> Why a particular sport is popular
> How an important person in your life influenced you
> The effects of violent song lyrics on teenagers
> The benefits of email
> Why some people find writing difficult
> The major reasons that high school or college students drop out of school
> How managers can get the best (or the worst) from their employees

◆ **PRACTICE 7-5**

Review your notes on the topic you chose in Practice 7-4, and create a cluster diagram. Write the topic you have chosen in the center of the page, and draw arrows branching out to specific causes or effects.

◆ **PRACTICE 7-6**

For more on creating a cluster diagram, see 1C.

Choose a few of the most important causes or effects from the cluster diagram you made in Practice 7-5, and list them here.

Answers will vary.

_____

_____

_____

_____

_____

_____

◆ PRACTICE 7-7

Reread your list of causes or effects from Practice 7-6. Then, draft a topic sentence that introduces your topic and communicates the point you will make about it.

Answers will vary.

_____

_____

◆ PRACTICE 7-8

List the causes or effects you will discuss in your paragraph, arranging them in an effective order—for example, from least to most important.

1. *Answers will vary.* _____

2. _____

3. _____

4. _____

◆ PRACTICE 7-9

On a separate sheet of paper, draft your cause-and-effect paragraph. Then, consulting the Self-Assessment Checklist on page 86, revise your paragraph for unity, development, and coherence.

◆ PRACTICE 7-10

On a separate sheet of paper, write a final, edited draft of your cause-and-effect paragraph.

■ WRITING FIRST: Revising and Editing

Look back at your response to the Writing First exercise on page 79, and evaluate your paragraph for unity, development, and coherence. Then, prepare a final, edited draft of your paragraph.

ESL Tip
Do not just mark students' errors. Write in corrections, and have students rewrite the material. Toward the end of the semester, depending on how often students receive graded assignments, you can start asking them to make corrections on their own.

PATTERNS OF
PARAGRAPH
DEVELOPMENT

Teaching Tip
Ask students to exchange
drafts. Then, have them read
each others' paragraphs and
list the causes and effects
they find. Walk around the
room, checking as many lists
as you can.

☑ SELF-ASSESSMENT CHECKLIST:
Writing a Cause-and-Effect Paragraph

Unity

☐ Does your topic sentence clearly identify the cause or effect on which your paragraph will focus? Does it state your paragraph's main idea?

☐ Does all your information relate directly to the causes or effects you are discussing?

Development

☐ Do you need to add other important causes or effects?

☐ Does your audience need more information about any causes or effects you have included?

Coherence

☐ Are your causes and effects arranged in a logical order—for example, from least to most important?

☐ Do you need to add transitional words or phrases?

Comparison and Contrast

PREVIEW

In this chapter, you will learn to write a comparison-and-contrast paragraph.

■ WRITING FIRST

Look at the picture above, which depicts a scene from the classic 1950s television sitcom *Father Knows Best*. Then, write a comparison-and-contrast paragraph in which you explain how family life today is different from (or similar to) the life of the family pictured here.

Word Power

diverge to go in different directions; to differ

generation a group of individuals born and living about the same time

tradition a practice passed down from one generation to another

Writing Tip

Sometimes your purpose in a comparison-and-contrast paragraph is to analyze two subjects in order to clarify what makes each unique. At other times, your purpose may be to evaluate two subjects in order to determine which has greater merit or worth.

A Understanding Comparison and Contrast

A **comparison** tells how two things are similar. A **contrast** tells how they are different. A **comparison-and-contrast paragraph** can examine just similarities or differences, or it can examine both.

Before two things can be compared and contrasted, they need to have a **basis for comparison**—that is, they have to have enough in common so

87

Teaching Tip
To help students understand
the concept of comparison
and contrast, have them go
to the library and make
copies of the classified pages
of a newspaper printed on
the day they were born. In
class, discuss the differences
and similarities between
products and prices then
and now.

● **Writing Tip**

Make sure that with a
subject-by-subject comparison, you treat the points for
each subject in the same
order.

the comparison makes sense. Without at least one meaningful element in common, there can be no basis of comparison. For example, you would have a difficult time comparing people and bananas. (They do not share any meaningful characteristics.) You could, however, compare people and chimpanzees: both are mammals, both live in complex social groups, and both are capable of communication.

In general, there are two kinds of comparison-and-contrast paragraphs: *subject-by-subject comparisons* and *point-by-point comparisons*. In a **subject-by-subject comparison**, you discuss first all your points about one subject and then all your points about the other subject. When your points about both subjects correspond closely—and they often will—they should be presented in the same order. A subject-by-subject comparison has the following structure.

Subject-by-Subject Comparison

Subject A _____
   Point 1 _____
   Point 2 _____
   Point 3 _____
   Point 4 _____
Subject B _____
   Point 1 _____
   Point 2 _____
   Point 3 _____
   Point 4 _____

The following paragraph is an example of a subject-by-subject comparison.

Topic sentence
Subject 1 (women's conversations)

Subject 2 (men's conversations)

    First, it is important to note that men and women regard conver- sation quite differently. For women it is a passion, a sport, an activity even more important to life than eating because it doesn't involve weight gain. The first sign of closeness among women is when they find themselves engaging in endless, secretless rounds of conversation with one another. And as soon as a woman begins to relax and feel comfortable in a relationship with a man, she tries to have that type of conversation with him as well. However, the first sign that a man is feeling close to a woman is when he admits that he'd rather she please quiet down so he can hear the TV. A man who feels truly intimate with a woman often reserves for her and her alone the precious gift of one-word answers. Everyone knows that the surest way to spot a success- ful long-term relationship is to look around a restaurant for the table where no one is talking. Ah . . . now *that's* real love.

–Merrill Markoe, *Men, Women, and Conversation*

Teaching Tip
If you want students to
explore this topic further,
consider assigning "Men Are
from Mars, Women Are from
Venus" in 36F.

This paragraph begins with a topic sentence that states its main idea and indicates that the paragraph will focus on differences between men and women. The writer then discusses women's ideas about conversation and men's ideas about conversation separately. The transition *however* sig- nals the writer's shift from one subject to the other.

In a **point-by-point comparison**, you discuss each point for *both* subjects before going on to the next point. A point-by-point comparison has the following structure.

Point-by-Point Comparison

Point 1 _____

    Subject A _____

    Subject B _____

Point 2 _____

    Subject A _____

    Subject B _____

Point 3 _____

    Subject A _____

    Subject B _____

Point 4 _____

    Subject A _____

    Subject B _____

● **Writing Tip**

Many everyday writing tasks call for comparison and contrast. For example, you might write a paragraph comparing the qualifications of two people who are applying for the same job at your workplace.

The following paragraph is an example of a point-by-point comparison.

> After being a fan of both football and baseball for years, I have begun to understand how different these games really are. First, football is violent, and baseball is not. In football, the object is to tackle the opponent. The harder the hit, the better the tackle. As a result, many football players are injured each year. In baseball, however, violence is not the object of the game. If a player gets hurt, it is usually because of an accident, such as two players running into each other or a batter being hit by a pitch. The language used to describe each game is also different. The language of football is like the language of war: linemen "blitz," quarterbacks "throw bombs," tacklers "crush" receivers, and games end in "sudden-death" overtime. The language of baseball, however, is peaceful: hitters "bunt" or "sacrifice," runners "slide," and pitchers throw curves or sliders. Finally, the pace of each game is different. Football is played against the clock. When the clock runs down, the game ends, and the side with the most points wins. In baseball, however, the game does not end until nine innings have been completed or a tie has been broken. Theoretically, a game could go on for days—or even forever. Even though football and baseball are so different, I like them both. When I want to let off steam, I prefer football, and when I want to relax and sit in the sun, I prefer baseball.
>
>   —TRENT PATTERSON (student)

Topic sentence

Point 1 (level of violence is different)

Point 2 (language is different)

Point 3 (pace is different)

Concluding statement

Like a subject-by-subject comparison, this point-by-point comparison begins with a topic sentence that states the main idea of the paragraph and indicates whether the paragraph will focus on similarities or on differences. The rest of the paragraph discusses three points of contrast, with each point made about both subjects—first for football and then for baseball—before the writer moves on to the next point. Shifts from one

For information on how to write a comparison-and-contrast essay as well as a list of transitions suitable for comparison-and-contrast paragraphs and essays, see 14F.

subject to another are signaled by the transition *however* and the repetition of the words *football* and *baseball*.

FOCUS **Comparison**

A subject-by-subject comparison works well if you are discussing just a few points for each subject and if you can be sure that readers can keep these points in mind as they read. A point-by-point comparison is best for a paragraph in which you discuss many points because it enables readers to identify the individual points of the comparison as they are introduced.

GRAMMAR IN CONTEXT **Comparison and Contrast**

When you write a comparison-and-contrast paragraph, you should present the points you are comparing in **parallel** terms to highlight their similarities or differences.

CONFUSING A hundred years ago, most of the immigrants were <u>uneducated</u>, and also <u>many were unskilled and poverty was a problem</u>.

PARALLEL A hundred years ago, most of the immigrants were <u>uneducated</u>, <u>unskilled</u>, and <u>poor</u>.

For more information on revising to make ideas parallel, see Chapter 19.

Teaching Tip
Before your students write comparison-and-contrast paragraphs, you might want to explain the concept of parallelism (Chapter 19) and have them do Practices 19-1 and 19-2.

B   **Writing a Comparison-and-Contrast Paragraph**

◆ **PRACTICE 8-1**

Read this comparison-and-contrast paragraph; then, follow the instructions on the next page.

Comparing Past and Present
United States Immigration

<u>Immigration to the United States is quite different
today from what it was a century ago</u>. In the late
nineteenth and early twentieth centuries, immigrants to
the United States arrived mostly from southern and eastern

Europe. In the last fifty years, however, about 80 percent of the immigrants have come from Latin America, the Caribbean, and Asia. Although most immigrants a century ago came from Italy, Poland, Russia, and the Balkans, most recent immigrants come from Mexico, the Philippines, China, India, South Korea, Vietnam, and the Dominican Republic. In the early twentieth century, the majority of immigrants settled in the northeastern and midwestern regions of the United States. In recent years, however, most immigrants have settled in California, New York, Florida, Texas, New Jersey, or Illinois. A hundred years ago, most of the immigrants were uneducated, unskilled, and poor. Although some recent immigrants are in similar circumstances, many of the more recent arrivals are well-educated professionals who are not poor. Most immigrants a hundred years ago made a conscious effort to blend in. They saw the United States as a melting pot in which they would "melt down," lose their immigrant identities, and become like others in American society. More recent immigrants prefer the image of the United States as a mosaic of immigrant groups that maintain their distinctive identities while still taking part in the overall society. One thing has not changed. Most immigrants still come to the United States for the same reasons—to improve themselves economically and to find freedom.

Jorge Hernandez (student)

1. Underline the topic sentence of the paragraph.

2. Does this paragraph deal mainly with similarities or differences?

   _____*differences*_____ How do you know? *The topic sentence points*

   to differences.

3. Is this paragraph a subject-by-subject or point-by-point comparison?

   _____*point-by-point*_____ How do you know? *Discussion of points*

   alternates between immigrants of a century ago and those of recent

   years.

4. List some of the contrasts the writer describes. The first contrast has been listed for you.

   A century ago, most immigrants came from southern and eastern

   Europe; more recently, most have come from Latin America, the

   Caribbean, and Asia.

   A hundred years ago, most immigrants came from Italy, Poland,

   Russia, and the Balkans, and recent immigrants have come from Mexico,

8 B

the Philippines, China, India, South Korea, Vietnam, and the Dominican

Republic.

Earlier immigrants settled in the northeastern and midwestern regions,

but more recent arrivals have settled in California, New York, Florida,

Texas, New Jersey, and Illinois.

A century ago, most immigrants were uneducated, unskilled, and had

little money, while more recently many new arrivals are well-educated

professionals who are not poor.

◆ PRACTICE 8-2

Following are four possible topic sentences. List three similarities or differences for the two subjects being considered in the topic sentence. For example, if you were writing a paragraph comparing health care provided by a local clinic with health care provided by a private physician, you could discuss the cost, the length of waiting time, the quality of care, and the frequency of follow-up visits.

1. My mother (or father) and I are very much alike (or different).

   Answers will vary.

2. My friends and I have similar views on _____.

   Answers will vary.

3. Democrats and Republicans have two very different ways of trying to solve the country's problems.

   Answers will vary.

4. Two of my college instructors have very different teaching styles.

Answers will vary.

_____

_____

◆ **PRACTICE 8-3**

Choose one of the topics below (or one of your own choice) as the subject of a paragraph exploring similarities or differences. On a separate sheet of paper, use one or more of the strategies described in 1C to help you think of as many similarities and differences as you can for the topic you have chosen. (If you use clustering, create a separate cluster diagram for each of the two subjects you are comparing.)

Two popular television personalities or radio talk-show hosts
Dog owners versus cat owners
A common perception of something versus its reality
How you act in two different situations (home and work, for ex-
    ample) or with two different sets of people (such as your family
    and your friends)
Two ads for similar products directed at different audiences
Two different bosses
Men's and women's attitudes toward dating, shopping, or conversation
Your goals when you were in high school versus your goals today
Public school education versus home schooling
Two competing consumer items, such as two car models, two com-
    puter systems, or two types of cell phones
Two relatives who have very different personalities
Two different kinds of vacations
Two generations' attitudes toward a particular issue or subject (for
    example, how people in their forties and people in their teens view
    religion or politics)

◆ **PRACTICE 8-4**

Review your notes on the topic you chose in Practice 8-3, and decide whether to focus on similarities or differences. On the following lines, list the similarities or differences that can best help you develop a comparison-and-contrast paragraph on the topic you have selected.

Answers will vary.

_____

_____

_____

_____

8 B

◆ PRACTICE 8-5

Reread your list of similarities or differences from Practice 8-4. Then, draft a topic sentence that introduces your two subjects and suggests your purpose for comparing or contrasting them.

Answers will vary.

_____

_____

◆ PRACTICE 8-6

In the space below, outline a plan for your paragraph. Begin by deciding which subject you will discuss first. Then, decide on the order in which you will present your points—for example, from least important to most important.

Subject-by-Subject Comparison

    Subject A _____ _Answers will vary._ _____

        Point 1   _____

        Point 2   _____

        Point 3   _____

        Point 4   _____

    Subject B _____ _Answers will vary._ _____

        Point 1   _____

        Point 2   _____

        Point 3   _____

        Point 4   _____

Point-by-Point Comparison

    Point 1 _____ _Answers will vary._ _____

        Subject A   _____

        Subject B   _____

    Point 2 _____ _Answers will vary._ _____

        Subject A   _____

        Subject B   _____

    Point 3 _____ _Answers will vary._ _____

        Subject A   _____

        Subject B   _____

    Point 4 _____ _Answers will vary._ _____

        Subject A   _____

        Subject B   _____

◆ **PRACTICE 8-7**

On a separate sheet of paper, draft your comparison-and-contrast paragraph. Then, consulting the Self-Assessment Checklist below, revise your paragraph for unity, development, and coherence.

◆ **PRACTICE 8-8**

On a separate sheet of paper, write a final, edited draft of your comparison-and-contrast paragraph.

ESL Tip
Pay special attention to students' sentence structure and to their use of articles and prepositions. You might also spot-check verb forms. These areas often cause difficulties for nonnative speakers.

■ WRITING FIRST: Revising and Editing

Look back at your response to the Writing First exercise on page 87, and evaluate your paragraph for unity, development, and coherence. Then, prepare a final, edited draft of your paragraph.

☑ SELF-ASSESSMENT CHECKLIST:
Writing a Comparison-and-Contrast Paragraph

Unity

  ☐ Does your topic sentence indicate whether you are stressing similarities or differences? Does it state your paragraph's main idea?

  ☐ Does all your information relate directly to the similarities or differences between your two subjects?

Development

  ☐ Is there a basis for comparison between your two subjects?

  ☐ Do you need to include more similarities? More differences?

Coherence

  ☐ Have you used a subject-by-subject or a point-by-point comparison? Is this type of comparison appropriate for your subject?

  ☐ If your paragraph is a subject-by-subject comparison, have you treated the points for the second subject in the same order as the points for the first subject?

  ☐ Do you need to add any transitional words or phrases?

Classification

PREVIEW

In this chapter, you
will learn to write
a classification
paragraph.

Word Power

enthusiastic having great
excitement or interest in a
subject or cause

fanatic someone having
extreme enthusiasm for a
cause

■ WRITING FIRST

Look at the picture above, which shows fans at a baseball game.
Then, discuss the various types of fans that you see at a particular
sporting event—for example, those who concentrate on the game,
those who wave signs and banners, and those who wear costumes or
team gear.

Teaching Tip
To help students understand
the concept of classification,
give them lists of different
musical groups, foods,
sports figures, and so on,
and ask them to classify the
items on each list. (Each list
should include at least
twenty items.)

A   Understanding Classification

Classification is the activity of sorting items (people, things, ideas) into
categories. In a **classification paragraph**, you tell readers how a collection of items can be sorted into categories. Each of the categories into
which you classify information must be *distinct:* an item cannot fit into more
than one category. For example, you would not classify novels into mys-

teries, romance novels, and paperbacks because a mystery or romance novel could also be a paperback.

The topic sentence of a classification paragraph identifies the subject (the group of items being discussed) and the categories into which items will be sorted. The rest of the paragraph considers the categories in the order in which they are mentioned in the topic sentence. The following is an example of a classification paragraph.

My friends can be classified according to their attitudes toward life: those who know what they want out of life, those who don't have a clue, and those who are searching for goals. In the first category are those who know what they want; they are the most mature. They know exactly what they want to do for the rest of their lives. Although these friends will most likely be successful, they are the most predictable and therefore the most boring. In the second category are those who don't have a clue; they are the most immature. They seem to live for the minute and do not think much about the future. If there is a party the night before a big test, they will go to the party and then try to study when they get back. Although these friends can be a bad influence, they are the most fun. In the third category are those who are searching for goals; they are somewhere between the other two types when it comes to maturity. They do not know exactly what they want to do with their lives, but they realize that they should be trying to find a goal. Although these friends can sometimes be unpredictable, their willingness to try new things makes them by far the most interesting.

–DANIEL COREY (student)

Topic sentence

Category 1

Category 2

Category 3

The topic sentence clearly identifies the paragraph's subject—friends— and the three categories into which individual friends will be sorted. The rest of the paragraph discusses these three categories, one at a time. The shift from one category to another is signaled by the transitional phrases *the first category*, *the second category*, and *the third category*.

For information on how to write a classification essay, as well as a list of transitions suitable for classification paragraphs and essays, see 14G.

FOCUS Classification

Before you can classify information, you must decide what your focus will be. In other words, you must decide on a **principle of classification**. In the paragraph above, for example, friends are classified according to their attitudes toward life. Because the same information can be classified in more than one way, you must decide on a single principle of classification before you choose your categories. For instance, you could classify teachers according to the subjects they teach or their teaching ability, and you could classify computers according to how much memory they have or how much they cost.

GRAMMAR IN CONTEXT **Classification**

When you write a classification paragraph, you may want to list the categories you are going to discuss. If you use a colon to introduce your list, make sure that a complete sentence comes before the colon.

INCORRECT Shoppers can be broken into: pragmatic, recreational, and professional.

CORRECT Shoppers can be broken into three categories: pragmatic, recreational, and professional.

For more information on how to use a colon to introduce a list, see 33D.

B Writing a Classification Paragraph

◆ PRACTICE 9-1

Read this classification paragraph; then, follow the instructions on the next page.

Three Kinds of Shoppers

Shoppers can be broken into three categories: pragmatic, recreational, and professional. The first category is made up of pragmatic shoppers; they shop because they need something. Pragmatic shoppers are purposeful. You can recognize them because they go right to the item they are looking for in the store and then leave. They do not waste time browsing or walking aimlessly from store to store. For them, shopping is definitely a means to an end. The next category is made up of recreational shoppers; they shop for entertainment. Recreational shoppers usually have too much time on their hands. For them, shopping is like going to the movies or out to dinner. They do it because it is fun. They will spend hours walking through stores looking at merchandise. More often than not, they will not buy anything. For recreational shoppers, it is the activity of shopping that counts, not the purchase itself. The third category is made up of professional shoppers; they shop because they have to. Professional shoppers are on a mission For them, shopping is a serious business. You can see them in any mall, carrying four, five, or even six shopping bags. Frequently, an exhausted spouse who carries even more merchandise follows them. For merchants and for credit card companies, professional shoppers are a dream come true.

Kimberly Toomer (student)

1. Underline the topic sentence of the paragraph.

2. What is the subject of the paragraph? *shoppers*

3. What is the principle of classification? *attitudes toward shopping*

4. What three categories does the writer describe?

   pragmatic shoppers

   recreational shoppers

   professional shoppers

5. Circle the phrases the writer uses to introduce the three categories.

◆ PRACTICE 9-2

Classify the following groups of items into categories.

1. All the items on your desk

   Answers will vary.

2. Buildings on your college campus

   Answers will vary.

3. Magazines or newspapers you read

   Answers will vary.

4. The various parts of a piece of equipment you use for a course or on the job

   Answers will vary.

◆ PRACTICE 9-3

Choose one of the topics below (or one of your own choice) as the subject of a classification paragraph. Then, decide on a principle of classification. On a separate sheet of paper, use one or more of the strategies described in 1C to help you classify the members of the group you have chosen into as many categories as necessary.

Your friends	Popular music
Drivers	Fitness routines
Commuters on public transportation	Popular Web sites
Television shows	Part-time jobs
Employees or bosses	Teachers
Parents or children	Popular movies
Types of success	T-shirt slogans
Radio stations	

◆ PRACTICE 9-4

Review the information you came up with for the topic you chose in Practice 9-3. On the following lines, list three or four categories you can develop in your paragraph.

Category 1: *Answers will vary.* _____

Category 2: _____

Category 3: _____

Category 4: _____

◆ PRACTICE 9-5

Reread the list you made in Practice 9-4. Then, draft a topic sentence that introduces your subject and the categories you will discuss.

Answers will vary. _____

_____

_____

◆ PRACTICE 9-6

List below the categories you will discuss in your classification paragraph in the order in which you will discuss them.

1. *Answers will vary.* _____

2. _____

3. _____

4. _____

◆ PRACTICE 9-7

On a separate sheet of paper, write your classification paragraph. Then, consult the Self-Assessment Checklist below, and revise your paragraph for unity, development, and coherence.

Teaching Tip
If students are having trouble organizing their classification paragraphs, you might assign an essay from 36G and review it in class.

◆ PRACTICE 9-8

On a separate sheet of paper, write a final, edited draft of your classification paragraph.

■ WRITING FIRST: Revising and Editing

Look back at your response to the Writing First exercise on page 96, and evaluate your paragraph for unity, development, and coherence. Then, prepare a final, edited draft of your paragraph.

☑ SELF-ASSESSMENT CHECKLIST:
Writing a Classification Paragraph

Unity

☐ Have you decided on a principle of classification?

☐ Does your topic sentence identify the categories you will discuss? Does it state your paragraph's main idea—the point your classification paragraph makes?

☐ Does all your information support your topic sentence or relate to your subject and its categories?

Development

☐ Do you need to include additional categories?

☐ Do you need to include more examples or more specific information for any category?

Coherence

☐ Do you need to rearrange categories (or details within categories)?

☐ Do you need to add transitional words or phrases?

Teaching Tip
Divide the class into pairs, and have students use the checklist to critique each other's paragraphs.

10

Definition

PREVIEW

In this chapter, you
will learn to write a
definition paragraph.

Teaching Tip
To help students understand
the concept of definition,
photocopy a few pages from
a college dictionary. Ask
each student to choose
one noun from those pages
and to explain to the class
how the word's definition
might be expanded into a
paragraph.

Word Power

denote to indicate; to refer
to specifically

signify to have meaning or
importance

■ WRITING FIRST

Look at the picture above, which shows the pages of a dictionary.
Then, write a one-paragraph definition of a word you learned in
one of your college courses. Assume that your readers are not familiar with the term you are defining.

ESL Tip
This might be a good time to
review singular and plural
nouns and count and non-
count nouns. Refer students
to 30C and 30D.

A **Understanding Definition**

A **definition** explains what a term means. When you want readers to know
the exact meaning of a word or concept, you use definition.

When most people think of definitions, they think of the one- or two-
sentence **formal definitions** they see in a dictionary. These definitions
have a three-part structure that includes the term to be defined, the

general class to which the term belongs, and the characteristics that make the term different from all other terms in that class.

Term	Class	Differentiation
A pineapple	is a tropical fruit	that has large swordlike leaves and yellow edible fruit.
Basketball	is a game	played between two teams in which the object is to put a ball through an elevated basket on the opponent's side of a rectangular court.

● **Writing Tip**
Many everyday writing tasks call for definition. For a study group at your place of worship, for example, you might write short definitions of terms such as *morality, goodness,* and *repentance.*

A single-sentence formal definition may not be enough to define an abstract concept (*envy* or *democracy*, for example), a technical term, or a complex subject. In such cases, you may need to expand this definition by writing a definition paragraph. A **definition paragraph** usually includes the three components of a formal definition, but it does not follow a particular pattern of development. It may define a term or concept by using examples, by outlining a process, or by using any of the other patterns discussed in this text. A definition paragraph may even define a term by using **negation**, telling what the term is not before or after saying what it is. For example, good citizenship is not just obeying laws; it is also looking out for the welfare of others.

In a definition paragraph, the topic sentence identifies the term to be defined (and may briefly define it as well). The rest of the paragraph develops the definition by means of one or more of the patterns of development discussed in Chapters 3 through 11. The following paragraph defines the term *business casual.*

Teaching Tip
Remind students that the topic sentence does not always have to be the first sentence in a paragraph. Ask students what advantage the writer gains by postponing the topic sentence in the student paragraph below.

Many businesses allow business casual dress on Fridays; others permit it all the time. As a result, more and more people are finding themselves asking, "What is business casual?" Broadly speaking, business casual means dressing professionally but also looking relaxed. For women, this usually means wearing a skirt or pants with a blouse or sweater. For men, it means no tie—and certainly no suit. Khakis and a short-sleeved knit shirt are popular in the summer; in other seasons, men wear a jacket over a shirt left open at the collar. Business casual, however, is not an excuse for being sloppy or dressing inappropriately. In other words, it does not mean wearing shorts, low-cut shirts, tank or halter tops, sandals, flip-flops, jeans, or T-shirts.

             – MELISSA MORRIS (student)

Topic sentence

Series of examples

Negation

The topic sentence introduces the term the paragraph will define. The paragraph goes on to define the term, using several short examples to illustrate the definition. The paragraph ends with negation—telling what the term *business casual* does not mean.

For more information on how to write a definition essay, as well as a list of transitions suitable for definition paragraphs and essays, see 14H.

The following paragraph defines a piece of gymnastics equipment—the pommel horse.

<u>The pommel horse is of ancient origin.</u> The Romans used it for the very practical purpose of training soldiers to mount horses. Some suggest it was used even earlier, by the bull dancers of Minoan Crete. Jumping over the bulls by doing springs off the animals' horns, these dancers surely must have practiced on something a little tamer than a live bull. Today, the pommel horse events are less exciting. The gymnast performs intricate leg-swinging movements while supporting his weight on his hands, which are either grasping the pommels or lying flat on the leather of the horse. As he swings his legs so that one follows, or "shadows," the other, the gymnast demonstrates strength, balance, and timing. Exercises such as single or double leg circles and scissors must be done continuously and in both directions. The pommel horse is difficult to master and not a favorite among gymnasts; they call it "the beast."

—FORD HOVIS, *The Sports Encyclopedia*

Topic sentence

History and background: comparison and contrast

Explanation of current function: process

Here, the writer defines an object in terms of its history and its current function, using comparison and contrast and process to develop his definition.

FOCUS **Definition**

In general, avoid including a dictionary definition in your definition paragraph. After all, readers can look up a term themselves. Your definition paragraph should show how *you* define a term—not how a dictionary does.

GRAMMAR IN CONTEXT **Definition**

When you write a definition paragraph, you often begin with a one-sentence definition of the term or idea you are going to discuss in the rest of your paragraph. When you write your one-sentence definition, do not use the phrases *is where* or *is when*.

              the inability
Writer's block is ~~when you are unable~~ to start a piece of writing.

For more information on how to structure a definition sentence, see the box on page 103.

Teaching Tip
Before your students write definition paragraphs, you might want to review the correct structure for a one-sentence definition, pointing them to the box on page 103. Depending on the particular pattern students use to develop their definitions, you can also refer them to the specific exercises noted in the teaching tips beside the Grammar in Context boxes in Chapters 3 through 11.

B   Writing a Definition Paragraph

◆ PRACTICE 10-1

Read this definition paragraph; then, follow the instructions below.

                        Writer's Block

    Have you ever sat staring at a blank notebook page
or computer screen, searching your brain for words and
ideas, fidgeting with frustration, and longing to be
anywhere else? If so, you probably want to know more about
writer's block, a condition that afflicts ten out of ten
writers at some point during their lives. <u>Simply stated,
writer's block is the inability to start a piece of
writing</u>. For nonprofessionals, writer's block almost always
involves assigned writing, such as a paper for school or a
report for work. (People rarely feel blocked when they are
writing for pleasure.) Sometimes writer's block is caused
by poor preparation: the writer has not allowed enough time
to think and make notes that will pave the way for the
actual writing of a draft. However, even prepared writers
with many ideas already on paper can experience writer's
block. It is like being tongue-tied, only writer's block is
more like being brain-tied. All the ideas keep bouncing
around but will not settle into any order, and the writer
cannot decide what to say first. When writer's block
strikes, often the only cure is to give up for a while,
find something else to do, and try again later.

                              Thaddeus Eddy (student)

1. Underline the topic sentence of the paragraph.

2. What is the subject of this definition? _writer's block_____

3. What is the writer's one-sentence definition of the subject?

   Simply stated, writer's block is the inability to start a piece of writing.

   _____

4. List some of the specific information the writer uses to define his subject. The first piece of information has been listed for you.

   _It causes fidgeting and a desire to escape._____

   _It usually involves assigned writing._____

   _It can be caused by poor preparation._____

   _It's like being "brain-tied."_____

5. What patterns of development does the writer use in his definition? List them here.

uses description of writer's block

uses examples of writer's block

uses cause and effect to explain cause of writer's block

◆ PRACTICE 10-2

Following are four possible topic sentences for definition paragraphs. Each topic sentence includes an underlined word. In the space provided, list two possible patterns of development that you could use to expand a definition of the underlined word. For example, you could define the word *feminist* by giving examples (exemplification) and by telling a story (narration).

1. During the interview, the job candidate made a sexist comment.

   Possible strategy: *Answers will vary.*

   Possible strategy: *Answers will vary.*

2. Loyalty is one of the chief characteristics of golden retrievers.

   Possible strategy: *Answers will vary.*

   Possible strategy: *Answers will vary.*

3. More than forty years after President Johnson's Great Society initiative, we have yet to eliminate poverty in the United States.

   Possible strategy: *Answers will vary.*

   Possible strategy: *Answers will vary.*

4. The problem with movies today is that they are just too violent.

   Possible strategy: *Answers will vary.*

   Possible strategy: *Answers will vary.*

◆ PRACTICE 10-3

Teaching Tip
Encourage students to
choose a topic from one of
their other courses. By doing
so, students can see how
strategies they learn in this
course can be helpful in
other disciplines.

Choose one of the topics below (or one of your own choice) as the subject of a definition paragraph. On a separate sheet of paper, use one or more of the strategies described in 1C to help you define the term you have chosen to discuss. Name the term, and then describe it, give examples of it, tell how it works, explain its purpose, consider its history or future, or compare it to other similar things. In short, do whatever works best for defining your specific subject.

A negative quality, such as envy, dishonesty, or jealousy
An ideal, such as the ideal friend or neighborhood
A type of person, such as a worrier or a show-off
A social concept, such as equality, opportunity, or discrimination

An important play in a particular sport or game

A hobby you pursue or an activity associated with that hobby

A technical term or specific piece of equipment that you use in your job

An object (such as an article of clothing) that is important to your culture or religion

A basic concept in a course you are taking

A particular style of music or dancing

A controversial subject whose definition not all people agree on, such as affirmative action or date rape

A goal in life, such as success or happiness

◆ PRACTICE 10-4

Review your notes for the topic you chose in Practice 10-3. On the following lines, list the details that can best help you to develop a definition paragraph.

Answers will vary.

_____

_____

_____

_____

_____

_____

◆ PRACTICE 10-5

Reread your notes from Practice 10-4. Then, draft a topic sentence that summarizes the main point you want to make about the term you are going to define.

Answers will vary.

_____

_____

_____

◆ PRACTICE 10-6

List the ideas you will discuss in your paragraph, arranging them in an effective order.

1. *Answers will vary.* _____

2. _____

3. _____

4. _____

5. _____

ESL Tip
Remind students who critique nonnative writers' papers to write in their corrections. (You can refer them to the chart of correction symbols inside the back cover.) Then, check the students' revised papers for accuracy.

10 B

◆ **PRACTICE 10-7**

On a separate sheet of paper, write your definition paragraph. Then, using the Self-Assessment Checklist below, revise your paragraph for unity, development, and coherence.

◆ **PRACTICE 10-8**

On a separate sheet of paper, write a final, edited draft of your definition paragraph.

■ WRITING FIRST: Revising and Editing

Look back at your response to the Writing First exercise on page 102, and evaluate your paragraph for unity, development, and coherence. Then, prepare a final, edited draft of your paragraph.

☑ SELF-ASSESSMENT CHECKLIST:
Writing a Definition Paragraph

Unity

- Do you define your term clearly in your topic sentence?

- Does your topic sentence state your paragraph's main idea—the point you want to make about the term you are defining?

- Does all your information support your topic sentence?

Development

- Do you use an appropriate pattern (or patterns) of development in your paragraph?

- Would a different pattern of development be more effective?

- Should you use negation to help you define your term?

- Do you need to include more information about your term?

Coherence

- Would arranging the information in a different order make it clearer or more interesting to readers?

- Do you need to add transitional words or phrases?

Argument

PREVIEW

In this chapter, you will learn to write an argument paragraph.

■ WRITING FIRST

Look at the picture above, which shows a woman carrying a sign opposing a proposed change to California's election laws. Write a paragraph in which you argue for or against one of the following policies:

- Outlawing smoking in all public places
- Taxing all purchases made on the Internet
- Requiring everyone to carry a national identification card
- Reinstituting the military draft in the United States
- Enabling people to vote in federal elections on their home computers

Include examples from your experience or from your reading to support your position.

Word Power
controversy a dispute

debate to discuss or argue about

refute to prove false; argue against

Teaching Tip
To help students understand the concept of argument, photocopy a newspaper editorial or letter to the editor, and review it in class.

A   Understanding Argument

An **argument** takes a position on a debatable subject. When you write an **argument paragraph**, your purpose is to persuade readers that your particular position on an issue has merit. The topic sentence states your position. In the rest of the paragraph, you support the points you make with **evidence**—*facts, examples,* and *expert opinion*. The paragraph ends with a conclusion that sums up your position.

A **fact** is information that can be verified. For example, it is a fact that A comes before G in the alphabet and that the Canadian ice hockey team won a gold medal in the 2002 Olympics. If you make the point that students are less prepared for college today than they were twenty years ago, you should support it with facts—for example, SAT scores and college dropout rates. Avoid broad generalizations that are not supported by facts from encyclopedias, newspapers, or other reliable sources.

An **example** is a specific illustration of a general statement. To be convincing, an example should relate clearly to the point you are making. For example, to support a point that the quality of life in your neighborhood has improved recently, you could discuss a number of new businesses that have opened and several neighbors who have spent time and money improving their properties. Make sure, however, that your examples are typical, not exceptional. For instance, the fact that one new business has opened during the past two years is not enough to establish that your neighborhood is improving.

An **expert** is someone who is recognized as knowledgeable about a particular subject. The opinion of an expert who supports your view on a subject can be very persuasive. For example, if you wanted to argue that censoring the Internet would undercut people's freedom of speech, you could quote an expert on constitutional law such as Ruth Bader Ginsburg, a justice of the United States Supreme Court. Because Ginsburg is a recognized authority on constitutional issues, her opinion carries a great deal of weight. Remember, though, that an expert in one field is not necessarily an expert in another field. For instance, Ginsburg's personal opinion about the value of stem-cell research would have less value than the opinion of someone who has spent many years studying this subject.

The following paragraph argues against the use of Astroturf surfaces in sports stadiums.

> During the past twenty-five years, Astroturf or a similar synthetic surface has been installed in hundreds of indoor and outdoor fields throughout the country. The major reason for the popularity of Astroturf is that it requires little maintenance and creates a uniform playing surface. <u>But recently it has become clear that Astroturf has caused so many injuries that it should be eliminated from all sports stadiums.</u> Anyone who follows baseball or football knows that Astroturf causes many knee and ankle injuries. The main reason for this problem is that it does not absorb impact the way a natural grass surface does. Astroturf consists of a layer of rough artificial grass on top of a layer of padding. Beneath these layers is a cement pad. Players who fall on Astroturf—or, in the case of football, are thrown down onto it—risk se-

Writing Tip

At this point, your evidence will consist mainly of information from your own life. Later, when you become a more experienced writer, you will support your points with information you get from research. See Appendix B, section 4.

Teaching Tip

Remind students that many of the self-professed experts who post their ideas on the Internet are *not* authorities.

Writing Tip

Using *should* or *should not* in the topic sentence of your argument makes your position clear.

Topic sentence

Facts and examples

rious injury. The New York Giants, for example, lost tight end Mark Bavaro to knee injuries caused by his falling on the artificial surface of the Meadowlands Stadium. And the Astroturf surface in Philadelphia's old Veterans Stadium, which players felt was the worst in the country, caused the Eagles to lose a number of key players. As sports columnist Bill Lyon points out, when a player catches a foot on Astroturf, the result can be a painful sprain or worse. You can see this problem in every professional and amateur stadium that has an Astroturf playing surface. For this reason, both fans and players should insist that stadiums remove Astroturf and install natural grass surfaces.

Authority

Conclusion

–Toni-Ann Marro (student)

The paragraph begins with a sentence that gives some background. The topic sentence then states the writer's position. After stating that Astroturf causes injuries, the paragraph presents facts, examples, and comments by experts that support the writer's position. The paragraph ends with a conclusion based on the evidence presented. Throughout the paragraph, transitional words and phrases—*the main reason*, *for example*, and *for this reason*—lead readers through the argument.

For information on how to write an argument essay, as well as a list of transitions suitable for argument paragraphs and essays, see 14I.

FOCUS Audience

In addition to presenting evidence to support your argument, you need to consider the effect of your argument on your audience. Before you write, try to determine whether your readers are likely to be hostile, friendly, or neutral to your position. Let your analysis of your audience determine the approach you use.

For example, if you suspect your audience may not be receptive to your position, you might mention a possible objection in your topic sentence even before stating your position:

Although some people may argue that students will be shortchanged [*possible objection*], a core curriculum will actually benefit most students at Baker County Community College [*position*].

In your paragraph, you can go on to **refute** (argue against) this objection.

You can also address possible audience objections in the paragraph itself, stating the major argument against your position and then refuting it by showing that it is incorrect, shortsighted, or illogical. For example, you could say that people who object to a core curriculum fail to understand that students should receive a well-rounded education, not just training for a particular job.

● **Writing Tip**

Many everyday writing tasks call for argumentation. For example, in a letter to your local school board, you might argue against raising class size in the elementary school.

Teaching Tip

Point out the importance of being open-minded enough to include opposing arguments.

11 B

Teaching Tip
Before your students write
argument paragraphs, you
might want to explain how
to use subordinating con-
junctions and relative pronouns to form complex
sentences (Chapter 17) and
have students do Practices
17-3 through 17-6.

> **GRAMMAR IN CONTEXT** **Argument**
>
> When you write an argument paragraph, you need to show the re-
> lationships between your ideas by combining simple sentences to
> create both compound sentences and complex sentences.
>
> Every day, employees use their computers for work-related tasks/
> *, and every*
> ~~Every~~ keystroke they make is recorded.
>
> This monitoring creates an unpleasant work environment/ ~~Em-~~
> *because employees*
> ~~ployees~~ feel that someone is always watching them.
>
> For more information on how to create compound sentences, see
> Chapter 16. For information on how to create complex sentences,
> see Chapter 17.

B Writing an Argument Paragraph

◆ PRACTICE 11-1

Read this argument paragraph; then, follow the instructions on page 113.

```
            Big Brother in the Workplace

    Employers should not routinely monitor the computer use
of their employees. First of all, monitoring computer use
violates an employee's privacy. Every day, employees use
their computers for work-related tasks, and every keystroke
they make is recorded. In addition, companies routinely
read employees' private email files as well as monitor the
sites they visit on the Internet. This monitoring creates
an unpleasant work environment because employees feel
that someone is always watching them. At some companies,
employees have even been fired for sending personal emails
or for sending humorous pictures to one another. Of course,
companies that believe computers should be used only for
work-related tasks have a point. After all, the company
pays for both the computers and the employees' time. The
problem with this line of thinking, however, is that it
ignores the fact that workers need some downtime in order
to work effectively. It therefore makes sense that a
limited use of computers for personal reasons (to send
emails to friends, for example) should be allowed—just as
coffee breaks are. Unless the company has reason to suspect
```

misuse of company computers, it should not routinely
monitor all employees' computers. Putting an end to this
type of surveillance would not only create a more relaxed
workplace, but it would also make it possible for employees
to work more efficiently.

                    Scott Rathmill (student)

1. Underline the topic sentence of the paragraph.

2. What issue is the subject of the paragraph?

   personal privacy for computer use at work

   What is the writer's position?

   Employers should not routinely monitor the computer use of their

   employees.

3. What points does the writer use to support his topic sentence?

   Monitoring computer use violates an employee's privacy.

   Monitoring computer use creates an unpleasant work environment.

4. List some of the evidence that the writer uses to support his points.
   The first piece of evidence has been listed for you.

   Every keystroke an employee makes is recorded.

   Companies routinely monitor personal emails as well as other uses.

   Some companies have fired employees for sending personal emails or

   humorous pictures to one another.

5. What evidence (facts, examples, expert opinion) does the writer use to
   support his points?

   He uses facts and examples.

6. What other evidence could the writer have used?

   He could have presented statements by experts about the effects of

   monitoring employees' personal use of computers. He also could have

   presented additional factual information in the form of statistics. Finally,

   he could have given specific examples of workers who were fired.

7. What opposing argument does the writer address?

   Computers should be used only for work-related tasks.

8. How does the writer refute this argument?

   He shows how it is shortsighted because it ignores the fact that workers

   need downtime.

◆ **PRACTICE 11-2**

Following are four topic sentences for argument paragraphs. For each topic sentence, list two or three points that could support the topic sentence. For example, if you were arguing in support of laws requiring motorcycle riders to wear safety helmets, you could say they cut down on medical costs and save lives.

1. Marijuana use for certain medical conditions should be legalized.

   Answers will vary.

   _____

   _____

   _____

2. All student athletes should be paid a salary by their college or university.

   Answers will vary.

   _____

   _____

   _____

   _____

3. College students caught cheating should be expelled.

   Answers will vary.

   _____

   _____

   _____

   _____

4. The U.S. government should provide free health care for all citizens.

   Answers will vary.

   _____

   _____

   _____

   _____

◆ **PRACTICE 11-3**

Choose one of the topic sentences from Practice 11-2. Then, list two pieces of evidence that could support each point you listed. For example, if you said that wearing safety helmets saves lives, you could list accident statistics and statements by emergency room physicians.

Answers will vary.

   _____

   _____

   _____

◆ PRACTICE 11-4

Choose one of the topics below (or one of your own choice) as the subject of an argument paragraph. Then, on a separate sheet of paper, use one or more of the strategies described in 1C to help you focus on a specific issue to discuss in an argument paragraph.

An Issue Related to Your School

Grading policies   Financial aid
Required courses   Student activity fees
Entrance requirements   Childcare facilities
Attendance policies   Sexual harassment policies
Course offerings   The physical condition of classrooms

An Issue Related to Your Community

The need for a traffic signal, a youth center, or something else you think would benefit your community

An action you think local officials should take, such as changing school hours, cleaning up a public eyesore, or improving a specific service

A new law you would like to see enacted

A current law you would like to see repealed

A controversy you have been following in the news

◆ PRACTICE 11-5

Once you have chosen an issue in Practice 11-4, write a journal entry about your position on the issue. Consider the following questions: Why do you feel the way you do? Do you think many people share your views, or do you think you are in the minority? What specific actions do you think should be taken? What objections are likely to be raised against your position? How might you respond to these objections?

◆ PRACTICE 11-6

Review your notes for the topic you chose in Practice 11-4, and select the points that best support your position. List these points below. (You may also want to list the strongest objections to your position.)

Answers will vary.
_____

Supporting points: _____

_____

Objections: _____

_____

> **Teaching Tip**
> Divide students into pairs, and let each student take a turn arguing against the other's position on a particular topic (preferably the one the other student is writing about). Have students jot down their opponent's objections and later refute them in their own paragraphs.

◆ PRACTICE 11-7

Draft a topic sentence that clearly expresses the position you will take in your paragraph.

Answers will vary.

_____

_____

◆ PRACTICE 11-8

In the space provided, arrange the points that support your position in an order that you think will be convincing to your audience.

1. *Answers will vary.* _____

2. _____

3. _____

4. _____

5. _____

◆ PRACTICE 11-9

In the space provided, list the evidence (facts, examples, expert opinion) that you could use to support each of your points.

Answers will vary. _____

Evidence for point 1: _____

_____

Evidence for point 2: _____

_____

Evidence for point 3: _____

_____

◆ PRACTICE 11-10

On a separate sheet of paper, draft your argument paragraph. Then, consulting the Self-Assessment Checklist on page 117, revise your paragraph for unity, development, and coherence.

Teaching Tip
Because argument paragraphs can be hard to organize, you might require students to write outlines before they begin.

◆ PRACTICE 11-11

On a separate sheet of paper, write a final, edited draft of your argument paragraph.

■ WRITING FIRST: Revising and Editing

Look back at your response to the Writing First exercise on page 109, and evaluate your paragraph for unity, development, and coherence. Then, prepare a final, edited draft of your paragraph.

☑ SELF-ASSESSMENT CHECKLIST:
Writing an Argument Paragraph

Unity

- Does your topic sentence clearly state your position?
- Is all your information directly related to your topic sentence?
- Do you need to revise your topic sentence to include new ideas?

Development

- Have you made enough points to support your topic sentence?
- Do you need more facts or other evidence to convince your audience to accept any of your points?
- Have you mentioned the major arguments against your position?
- Have you refuted these arguments?
- Do you need to use one or more of the strategies discussed in 1C to help you come up with more ideas?

Coherence

- Would arranging ideas in a different order make your argument more convincing to readers?
- Do you need to add transitional words or phrases?

Teaching Tip
Hold a class debate. Divide the class into two groups, and have the groups take opposing positions on a controversial topic. Record each group's responses on the board under Arguments, Possible Objections, and Refutations.

UNIT THREE

Focus on Essays

Writing an Essay

PREVIEW

In this chapter, you will learn

- to think about paragraphs and essays (12A)

- to decide on a topic (12B)

- to find ideas to write about (12C)

- to state a thesis (12D)

- to arrange supporting points (12E)

- to draft an essay (12F)

- to revise and edit your essay (12G)

■ WRITING FIRST

The picture above shows a famous scene from an episode of *I Love Lucy* in which Lucy and Ethel go to work at a candy factory. Look at the picture, and think about the worst job you ever had. This is the topic you will be writing about as you move through this chapter. (If you have never had a job, you may write about a specific task that you disliked or a bad job that a friend or a relative has had.)

Word Power

dehumanize to deprive of human qualities; to render mechanical

exploit to make use of selfishly

Much of the writing you do in school will be longer than a single paragraph. Often, you will be asked to write an **essay**—a group of paragraphs on a single subject. When you write an essay, you follow the same process you do when you write a paragraph: you begin with finding something to say and then move to selecting and arranging ideas, drafting, revising, and editing. Chapters 12 through 14 will show you how to apply the paragraph skills you learned in Chapters 1 through 11 to writing essays.

For a discussion of writing a paragraph, see Chapter 1.

A Thinking about Paragraphs and Essays

● **Writing Tip**

Most writing situations outside of school require more than a paragraph. The skills you learn in this chapter can also be applied to these writing tasks.

In a sense, an essay is a paragraph that has been expanded. In fact, a paragraph is in many ways a miniature essay. Both paragraphs and essays have a single **main idea**. In a paragraph, the **topic sentence** presents the main idea, and the rest of the paragraph develops the main idea with details, facts, and examples. The paragraph often ends with a concluding statement.

Paragraph

A **topic sentence** states the main idea of the paragraph.

Supporting sentences develop the main idea with details, facts, and examples.

A **concluding statement** ends the paragraph.

An essay contains a number of paragraphs, each one carrying out a particular function. Even so, essay structure is similar to paragraph structure.

■ The first paragraph—the **introduction**—begins with **opening remarks** and closes with a **thesis statement**. This thesis statement, like a paragraph's topic sentence, presents the main idea.
■ The **body** of the essay contains several paragraphs that **support** the thesis statement. Each body paragraph begins with a **topic sentence** that states the main idea of the paragraph. The other sentences in the paragraph support the topic sentence with details, facts, and examples.
■ The last paragraph—the **conclusion**—ends the essay. The conclusion, which may restate the essay's thesis, offers the writer's final thoughts on the subject.

This **thesis-and-support** structure is central to nearly every essay you will write in college.

FOCUS Paragraphs and Essays

Keep in mind that an essay includes more ideas, more discussion, and more support than a paragraph does. Even so, because of their similarities, the skills you developed for writing paragraphs will also help you when you write essays.

Essay

Opening remarks introduce the subject being discussed.

Introduction

A **thesis statement** presents the main idea
of the essay.

A **topic sentence** states the essay's
first main point.

Supporting sentences present details,
facts, and examples.

A **topic sentence** states the essay's
second main point.

Body paragraphs

Supporting sentences present details,
facts, and examples.

A **topic sentence** states the essay's
third main point.

Supporting sentences present details,
facts, and examples.

The **restatement of the thesis** summarizes the essay's main point.

Conclusion

Closing remarks present the writer's final
thoughts on the subject.

Teaching Tip
Explain that conclusions do
not always restate the thesis
or summarize major points.
Refer students to 13B.

The following student essay by Mina Tran illustrates the thesis-and-
support structure diagrammed above.

Becoming Chinese American

Although I was born in Hong Kong, I never got to
know it because my parents came to America when I was
an infant. My parents and relatives always made sure

Introduction

that I did not forget where I came from, though. They told me stories of what it was like to live in Hong Kong, where they were surrounded by Chinese culture. To make sure that my brothers and sisters and I were aware of what was happening in our homeland, my parents even subscribed to Chinese cable TV. My siblings and I would watch the celebration of Chinese New Year, the news from Asia, and Chinese movies and music videos. As a result, I know how important it is to hold on to my Chinese cultural heritage even though I am living in America.

The Chinese language is one important part of my life as a Chinese American. Without the Chinese language, I would not be who I am. As a Chinese American, I feel it is my duty to learn Chinese and to pass it on to the next generation. Unlike some of my Chinese friends, I do not view the Chinese language as unimportant or embarrassing. It helps me to identify with my culture and also enables me to communicate with my relatives. Although I speak English most of the time, I speak Chinese at home. Because my parents and grandparents do not speak English well, Chinese is our only form of communication. If I abandoned this part of my culture, I would not be able to communicate with my family.

Food is another important part of my life as a Chinese American. Everyone knows that nothing brings a family together better than a traditional home-cooked meal. The ways we Chinese prepare and serve our food make my family different from many others. Everything we eat has a history and a meaning. For example, during a birthday meal for an elderly person, we end the meal by serving long noodles and buns in the shape of peaches. This is because we Chinese believe that long noodles represent long life and that peaches are served in heaven. As we Chinese know, in our culture food is not just food; it is a way of reinforcing the ties between families and friends. For example, during a wedding celebration, the bride and groom have to eat nine of everything. In our culture, the number nine represents "together forever." By taking part in this ritual, the bride and the groom accept the fact that Chinese customs will be a part of their life together.

Religion is probably the most important part of my life as a Chinese American because it brings together the people I care about the most. Every year during Chinese New Year, my whole family goes to temple. Along with hundreds of other families, we recite prayers and welcome one another with traditional New Year's greetings. After going to temple, we all go to Chinatown

and eat dim sum until the Lion Dance starts. People come
from everywhere to watch the colorful lion dance its way
up and down the many streets. As the lion dances, people
beat drums and throw firecrackers around it to drive off
any evil spirits that may be around. Afterward, we go
home and eat some more and talk. After the evening meal,
parents give children money in red envelopes that
symbolize joy and happiness for the coming year.

<u>My family and I know how important it is to hold
on to our culture.</u> When I was six, I was put into a
Chinese-American grade school because my parents wanted
me to learn my culture and my language. Every time I
went to class, my teacher thrilled me with stories of
Fa Mulan, the Shang Dynasty, and the Mood God. I will
never forget how happy I was when I thought how special
it was to be Chinese. This is how I want my own
children to feel. I want them to be proud of who they
are and to pass their language, history, and culture
on to the next generation.

This essay follows the pattern discussed above. The introduction includes
the essay's thesis statement. It presents the main idea of the essay—that
the writer, Mina Tran, will never give up her Chinese cultural heritage.
Each body paragraph supports this idea by discussing in detail one example of the things in Chinese culture that are important to Mina. The essay
ends by echoing the thesis statement in paragraph 1.

FOCUS   Writing Essays

Like a paragraph, an essay must be *unified, well developed,* and *coherent.*

- An essay is **unified** if all its body paragraphs discuss the main
  idea that is expressed in the thesis statement. Notice that the
  essay above is unified because each of its body paragraphs supports the thesis. In addition, the writer has not included material that is irrelevant to the essay's main idea.
- An essay is **well developed** if it contains enough support so
  readers will accept its thesis. The writer of the essay above
  knows that most readers will not be familiar with Chinese culture. For this reason, she provides imformation about the important part that Chinese language, food, and religion play in
  her life. The details, facts, and examples she presents help her
  readers accept her thesis.

(continued on the following page)

(continued from the previous page)

■ An essay is **coherent** if all its points are presented clearly and effectively. As in a paragraph, the points in an essay may be arranged according to *time order, spatial order,* or *logical order.* The points discussed in the essay above, for example, are organized in **logical order**—in the order of their importance to the writer. Transitional words and phrases signal this organization by indicating the relationships among the sentences. For instance, in the topic sentences, the phrases "one important part . . ."; "another important part . . ."; and "the most important part . . ." reinforce the logical organization of ideas.

◆ **PRACTICE 12-1**

Following is an essay organized according to the diagram on page 123. Read the essay, and then answer the questions that follow it.

Introduction

Maybe you have moved to a new city, so you need to find a new doctor for yourself and your family. Maybe your doctor has retired. Or maybe you need a specialist to deal with a difficult medical problem. In any case, your goal is clear—to find a doctor. Several strategies can help you in your search for a good doctor.

First, you need to find a well-qualified doctor. One way to begin is to identify the best hospital in the area and find a doctor on the staff there. Good doctors are attracted to good hospitals, so this is a good place to start your search. Recommendations from friends and neighbors can also be useful. Once you have some names, find out whether the doctors are board certified in their specific fields. Board certification means that doctors have had extensive training in their specialties. In addition, to maintain their certifications, doctors have to take part in continuing education programs each year. You can easily find out whether a doctor is board certified by going to the American Board of Medical Specialties Web site at http://www.ABMS.org.

Body paragraphs

Next, you need to decide what things are important to you. For example, think about how far you are willing to travel to see the doctor. Do you need a doctor with a convenient location? This might be important if you expect to see the doctor frequently or if you have a physical disability. Also consider when the doctor is available. Many doctors have office hours only on weekdays. Is this acceptable, or will you need evening or Saturday appointments? You should also find out the office policy concerning emergencies. Will you be able to see the doctor immediately, or will you have to go to a hospital emergency room? Finally, find out how you will pay for the medical care you receive. If you have medical insurance, find out if the doctor accepts your plan. Next, determine if someone at the doctor's office fills out insurance forms or if you have to do it yourself. If you do not have medical insurance, find out what payment options the doctor offers. Will you have to pay everything at once, or will you be able to stretch out payments?

If you are satisfied with the answers to all these questions, you should make an appointment to visit the office and meet the doctor. If the office seems crowded and disorganized, you should be on your guard. The doctor may be overscheduled, overworked, understaffed, or simply disorganized. Whatever the case, this situation does not make for good medical care. You should also see how long it takes for you to see the doctor. Unless the doctor is called away to an emergency, you should not have to sit in the waiting room for one or two hours before being called in. Finally, see if you feel comfortable talking to the doctor. If the doctor seems rushed or uninterested, you should take this as an indication of the type of medical care you will get. Good care takes time and patience, and quality doctors know this. Finally, see if you are treated with respect. Both the doctor and the office staff should treat you as an individual. They should take the time to ask about your general health and to update your medical records.

— Body paragraphs

Finding a good doctor requires careful planning and a lot of work. You may even have to take the time to see several doctors and assess each one. Remember, though, there are no short cuts. If the result of all your hard work is a qualified doctor who really cares about your well-being, then your time will have been well spent.

Conclusion

1. Underline the essay's thesis. Write it below in your own words.

Several strategies can help you find a good doctor.

2. Underline the topic sentence in each body paragraph.

3. What point does the first body paragraph make?

You should find out whether the doctor is well qualified.

4. What point does the second paragraph make?

You need to decide what things are most important to you—location,

office hours, cost, and so on.

5. What point does the third body paragraph make?

You should make an appointment to visit the office and meet the doctor.

6. At what point in the conclusion does the writer restate the essay's thesis?

The first sentence of the conclusion restates the essay's thesis.

7. How does the writer develop the points made in the body paragraphs?

Body paragraph 1: Examples of how to find a well-qualified doctor

Body paragraph 2: Examples of things that are important

Teaching Tip

Have students form groups of three. Ask each student in each group to make up an additional example for each body paragraph. Each group should then evaluate all the new examples and agree on the best addition to each paragraph. If time permits, students can share their examples with the class.

Body paragraph 3: Examples of things to look for when visiting the

doctor's office

_____

_____

_____

_____

B Deciding on a Topic

Most of the essays you will write in college begin as an **assignment** given to you by your instructor. The following assignments are typical of those you might be given in your composition class.

- Decide some things you would like to change about your school.
- What can college students do to improve the environment?
- Discuss an important decision you made during the past three years.

Because these assignments are so general, they would be difficult—if not impossible—to write about. What specific things would you change? Exactly what could you do to improve the environment? Which decision should you write about? Answering these questions will help you narrow these assignments into **topics** that you can write about.

Assignment	Topic
Discuss some things you would change about your school.	Three things I would change to improve the quality of life at Jackson County Community College
What can college students do to improve the environment?	The campus recycling project
Discuss an important decision you made during the past three years.	Deciding to go back to school

For each assignment you are given, try to list several possible topics so that you have choices. For example, if you were assigned to write a short essay about an important decision you made during the past three years, you could list the following topics.

- Deciding to go back to school
- Volunteering at a homeless center in my neighborhood
- Moving into my own apartment
- Deciding to quit smoking

For more on freewriting and brainstorming, see 1C and 12C.

After you make your list, review each topic and choose the one that you can write the best essay about. (The more you know about a topic, the more you will have to write about.) If you have difficulty coming up with a list of possible topics, try freewriting or brainstorming for a short period of time. If you still have difficulty, brainstorm with some of your classmates or make an appointment with your instructor.

◆ PRACTICE 12-2

Decide whether the following topics are suitable for an essay of four or five paragraphs. If a topic is suitable, write *OK* in the blank. If it is not, write in the blank a revised version of the same topic that is narrow enough for a brief essay.

Examples: Successful strategies for quitting smoking _____*OK*_____

Horror movies _____*1950s Japanese monster movies*_____

1. Violence in American public schools ___*Answers will vary.*___

   Example: the need for metal detectors in a local high school

2. Ways to improve your study skills ___*OK*___

3. Using pets as therapy for nursing-home patients ___*OK*___

4. Teachers ___*Answers will vary.*___

   Example: qualities of an effective teacher

5. Safe ways to lose weight ___*OK*___

6. Clothing styles ___*Answers will vary.*___

   Example: the influence of hip-hop on teenagers' clothing styles

7. Parent-child relationships ___*Answers will vary.*___

   Example: strategies for communicating with your child

8. Reasons children lie to their parents ___*OK*___

9. College education ___*Answers will vary.*___

   Example: the benefits of going to college

10. Television's impact on children ___*Answers will vary.*___

    Example: the influence of violent cartoons on children's behavior

---

■ **WRITING FIRST: Flashback**

Look back at the Writing First assignment on page 121. To narrow the topic to one you can write about, you need to decide which job to focus on. On the lines below, list all the possible jobs you could discuss.

_____

_____

_____

_____

C **Finding Ideas**

For a full discussion of ways of finding material to write about, see 1C.

Before you start writing about a topic, you need to find out what you have to say about it. Once you have done this, you will be ready to decide on a thesis for your essay. Sometimes, ideas may come to you easily. More often, you will have to use one or more strategies, such as *freewriting* or *brainstorming,* to help you come up with ideas about your topic.

Freewriting

When you **freewrite,** you write for a fixed period of time without stopping. When you engage in **focused freewriting,** you write with a specific topic in mind. Then, you read what you have written and choose the ideas you think you can use. Following is an example of focused freewriting by a student, Jared White, on the topic "Deciding to go back to school."

> Deciding to go back to school. When I graduated high school, I swore I'd never go back to school. Hated it. Pretty stupid—or maybe just immature. What did I know? Couldn't wait to get out. I wonder what I was thinking. How was I supposed to support myself? Lucky my dad's friend needed help. He taught me how to paint houses. I make good money, but it's boring. I can't picture myself doing it forever. My friends aren't much different from me, though. Kelly sells shoes at the mall, and Ahmed is thinking about becoming an electrician. I didn't have to be a genius to see that I needed to do something soon. Even though I knew I was going to have to go back to school, I kept putting off the decision. Maybe I was lazy. Maybe I was scared—probably both. I had this fear of being turned down. How could someone who had bad grades all through high school go to college? Also, I'd

been out of school for six years. And even if I did get
in (a miracle!), how would I pay for it? How would I
live? I met a guy while I was painting, who told me
that I could get into community college. I never really
considered community college. But it sounded like
something I should look at. Tuition was a lot lower
than I thought. Then, I just had to push myself to
go. Well, here I am—the first one in my family to go
to college.

◆ PRACTICE 12-3

Reread Jared White's freewriting. If you were advising Jared, which ideas
would you suggest that he explore further? Why? Write your answers below.

Answers will vary.

_____

_____

_____

_____

■ WRITING FIRST: Flashback

Choose two of the jobs you listed for the Flashback exercise on
page 130. Freewrite about each of them on separate sheets of paper.
Which job gave you the most interesting material? On the lines
below, write the name of the job, followed by the ideas that you
would like to develop further.

Job: _____

_____

Ideas: _____

_____

_____

_____

Brainstorming

When you **brainstorm** (either individually or in collaboration with others), you write down (or type) all the ideas you can think of about a particular topic. After you have recorded as much material as you can, you
look over your notes to figure out which ideas are useful and which ones
are not. Here is Jared White's brainstorming about his decision to go back
to school.

Deciding to Go Back to School

Money a problem
No confidence
Other students a lot younger
Paying tuition—how?
No one in family went to college
Friends not in college
Couldn't see myself in college
Have a serious relationship—Beth
Considered going to trade school
Computer programmer?
Grades bad in high school
Time for me to grow up
Wondered if I would get in
Found out about community college
Went to Web site
Web site answered questions
Admission requirements not bad
Afraid—too old, failing out, looking silly
Took time to get used to routine
Found other students like me
Liked studying

◆ PRACTICE 12-4

Reread Jared White's brainstorming. Which ideas would you advise him to explore further? Write them on the lines below.

Answers will vary.

_____

_____

_____

_____

■ WRITING FIRST: Flashback

Review the freewriting you did in the Flashback exercise on page 131. On a separate sheet of paper, brainstorm about the job for which you have found the most interesting ideas. What ideas about the job did you get from brainstorming that you did not get from freewriting? Write your response on the following lines.

_____

_____

_____

_____

D Stating Your Thesis

After you have gathered information about your topic, you have to decide exactly what you want to say about it. By choosing and rejecting ideas and by identifying connections among the ideas you keep, you can decide on the point you want to make. You can then express this point in a **thesis statement**: a single sentence that clearly expresses the main idea that you will discuss in the rest of your essay.

Topic	Thesis Statement
Three things I would change about Jackson County Community College	If I could change three things to improve Jackson County Community College, I would expand the food choices, decrease class size in first-year courses, and ship some of my classmates to the North Pole.
The campus recycling project	The recycling project recently begun on our campus should be promoted more actively.
The difficulty of going back to school	I decided that if I really wanted to attend college full-time, I could.

Like a topic sentence, a thesis statement tells readers what to expect. An effective thesis statement has two important characteristics.

For more on topic sentences, see 2A.

1. *An effective thesis statement makes a point about a topic or takes a stand on an issue. For this reason, it must do more than state a fact or announce what you plan to write about.*

STATEMENT OF FACT   Many older students are returning to school.

ANNOUNCEMENT   In this essay, I would like to discuss the difficulties many older students have going back to school.

EFFECTIVE THESIS STATEMENT   I decided that if I really wanted to attend college full-time, I could.

A statement of fact is not an effective thesis statement because it takes no position and gives you nothing to develop in your essay. After all, how much can you say about the *fact* that many older students are returning to school? Likewise, an announcement of what you plan to discuss gives readers no indication of the position you will take on your topic. An effective thesis statement makes a point.

2. *An effective thesis statement is clearly worded and specific.*

VAGUE THESIS STATEMENT   Television commercials are not like real life.

EFFECTIVE THESIS STATEMENT   Television commercials do not accurately portray women or minorities.

> **Teaching Tip**
> Spend extra time on writing effective thesis statements and on their placement. Remind students not to make an announcement and not to state the thesis in their essay's first sentence.

The vague thesis statement on the previous page says little about the ideas that the essay will discuss or how it will present those ideas. It does not say, for example, *why* television commercials are not realistic. The effective thesis statement is more focused. It signals that the essay will give examples of television commercials that present unrealistic portrayals of women and minorities.

● **Writing Tip**
Keep in mind that at this stage of the process, your thesis statement is not definite but tentative. You will probably change this tentative thesis statement as you write and revise your essay.

FOCUS **Stating Your Thesis**

You can sometimes revise a vague thesis statement by including in it a list of the specific points that you will discuss. Revised in this way, the thesis acts as a road map, telling readers what to expect as they read.

> VAGUE THESIS STATEMENT   Raising tropical fish is a good hobby.
>
> EFFECTIVE THESIS STATEMENT   Raising tropical fish is a good hobby because it is inexpensive, interesting, and educational.

The vague thesis statement above gives readers little information about the essay to follow. The effective thesis statement, however, lays out the plan of the essay and gives readers a clear idea of what the rest of the essay will discuss.

◆ **PRACTICE 12-5**

In the space provided, indicate whether each of the following items is a statement of fact (**F**), an announcement (**A**), a vague statement (**VS**), or an effective thesis (**ET**).

Examples:

My commute between home and school takes more than an hour each way. __F__

I hate my commute between home and school. __VS__

1. Students who must commute a long distance to school are at a disadvantage compared to students who live close by. __ET__

2. In this paper, I will discuss cheating and why students shouldn't cheat. __A__

3. Schools should establish specific policies that will discourage students from cheating. __ET__

4. Cheating is a problem. __VS__

5. Television commercials are designed to sell products. __F__

6. I would like to explain why some television commercials are funny. __A__

7. Single parents have a rough time. __VS__

8. An article in the newspaper says that young people are starting to abuse alcohol and drugs at earlier ages than in the past. __F__

9. Alcohol and drug abuse are major problems in our society. __VS__

10. Families can use several strategies to help children avoid alcohol and drugs. __ET__

◆ PRACTICE 12-6

Label each of the following thesis statements **VS** if it is too vague, **F** if it is factual, **A** if it is an announcement, or **ET** if it is an effective thesis. On a separate sheet of paper, rewrite those that are not effective thesis statements.

Answers to rewrites will vary.

1. Different types of amusement parks appeal to different types of people. __VS__

2. There are three reasons why Election Day should be a national holiday. __ET__

3. Every fourth year, the United States elects a new president. __F__

4. My paper will prove that DVDs are better than videotapes. __A__

5. The largest fish in the sea is the whale shark. __F__

6. Scientists once believed that the dinosaurs were killed off by the arrival of a new Ice Age. __F__

7. NASCAR drivers should take steps to make their sport safer than it is. __ET__

8. This paper will discuss the increase in the number of women in the military since the 1970s. __A__

9. Movies provide great entertainment. __VS__

10. Computers have made it easier for teachers and their students to communicate. __ET__

◆ **PRACTICE 12-7**

Rewrite the following vague thesis statements.

> **Example:**   My relatives are funny.
>
>   Rewrite: _My relatives think they are funny, but sometimes_
>   _their humor can be offensive._

Answers will vary.

1. Email can save time.

2. Airport security could be better.

3. Athletes are paid too much.

4. Many people get their identities from their cars.

5. Being single has advantages.

◆ **PRACTICE 12-8**

A list of broad topics for essays follows. Select five of these topics, narrow them, and generate a thesis statement for each.

Answers will vary.

1. Terrorism

2. Reality Television

3. U.S. Immigration Policies

4. Music

5. Dieting

6. Required Courses

7. Computer Games

8. Disciplining Children

9. Street Sense

10. Footwear

Teaching Tip
Have students read their thesis statements aloud, and let the class determine whether they are effective or not. Ask students to explain their decisions.

ESL Tip
Nonnative speakers may be reluctant to read their work aloud in front of the class. Having students exchange papers and read other students' thesis statements aloud may help them feel more comfortable.

■ WRITING FIRST: Flashback

Review your freewriting and brainstorming from the Flashback exercises on page 131 and page 132. Then, draft a thesis statement for your essay on the lines below.

Answers will vary.

E   Arranging Supporting Points

Once you have decided on a thesis statement, look over your freewriting and brainstorming again. Find the points that best support your thesis, and cross out those that do not. Here is Jared White's list of supporting points about his decision to go back to school.

```
              Deciding to Go Back to School
   Money a problem
   No confidence
   Other students a lot younger
   Paying tuition—how?
   No one in family went to college
   Friends not in college
   Couldn't see myself in college
   Have a serious relationship—Beth
   Considered going to trade school
   Computer programmer?
   Grades bad in high school
   Time for me to grow up
   Wondered if I would get in
   Found out about community college
   Went to Web site
   Web site answered questions
   Admission requirements not bad
   Afraid—too old, failing out, looking silly
   Took time to get used to routine
   Found other students like me
   Liked studying
```

After you have selected the points you think will best support your thesis, arrange them into groups. For example, after looking at the list of points above, Jared White saw that his points fell into three groups of excuses for not going back to school: excuse 1 was not being able to pay tuition, excuse 2 was not being a good student in high school, and excuse 3 was not being able to picture himself in college. After you have come up with your groups, arrange them in the order in which you will discuss them (for example, from general to specific, or from least important to most important). Then, arrange the supporting points for each group in the same way. This orderly list can serve as a rough outline to guide you as you write.

Jared grouped and listed his points in the following order.

```
   Excuse 1: Not being able to pay tuition
     Money a problem
     Found out about community college
     Went to Web site
   Excuse 2: Not being a good student in high school
     Grades bad in high school
     Wondered if I would get in
     Admission requirements not bad
```

> ● **Writing Tip**
> Indent items in your list of points to show how they are related. Use the Tab key on your computer keyboard.

```
Excuse 3: Not being able to picture myself in college
  No one in family went to college
  Friends not in college
  Afraid—too old
  Found other students in class like me
  Liked studying
```

◆ PRACTICE 12-9

Look over Jared's list of points above. Do you think his arrangement is effective? Can you suggest any other ways he might have arranged his points? Write your response on the lines below.

Answers will vary.

FOCUS **Preparing a Formal Outline**

The rough outline discussed and illustrated above is usually all you need to plan a short essay. However, some writers—especially when they are planning longer, more detailed essays—like to use a more formal outline. **Formal outlines** contain a combination of numbered and lettered headings and use roman numerals, capital letters, and Arabic numerals (and sometimes lower-case letters) to show the relationships among ideas. For example, the most important (and most general) ideas are assigned a roman numeral; the next most important ideas are assigned capital letters. Each level develops the idea above it, and each new level is indented. Here is a formal outline of the points that Jared planned to discuss in his essay.

Thesis statement: I decided that if I really wanted to attend college full-time, I could.
  I. Not being able to pay tuition
    A. Money a problem
    B. Community college
      1. Tuition low
      2. Expenses reasonable
  II. Not being a good student in high school
    A. Grades bad
      1. Didn't care about high school
      2. Didn't do homework
    B. Anxiety about getting in
    C. Admissions requirements
      1. High school diploma
      2. County residence
      3. Placement tests
  III. Not being able to picture myself in college
    A. Family no help
    B. Friends not in college

(continued on the following page)

(continued from the previous page)
    C. Fear of going
       1. Too old
       2. Couldn't keep up
       3. Never studied in high school
    D. Fears disappeared
       1. Found other students like me
       2. Liked studying

■ WRITING FIRST: Flashback

On the lines below, write the thesis statement you drafted in the
Flashback exercise on page 136.

Answers will vary.

Now, review your freewriting and brainstorming again, and list
below the points you plan to use to support your thesis statement.
Cross out any points that do not support your thesis statement.

Answers will vary.

Finally, group these points, and arrange them in an order in which
you could write about them.

Answers will vary.

F   Drafting Your Essay

After you have decided on a thesis for your essay and have arranged your
points in the order in which you will discuss them, you are ready to draft
your essay. At this stage of the writing process, you should not worry about

*For a discussion of introductions and conclusions, see
Chapter 13.*

spelling or grammar or about composing a perfect introduction or conclusion. Your main goal is to get your ideas down so you can react to them. Remember that the draft you are writing will be revised, so leave room for your changes: write on every other line, and triple-space if you are typing. Follow your rough outline, but don't hesitate to depart from it if you think of new points or if your ideas take an interesting or unexpected turn as you write.

For a discussion of thesis and support, see 12A.

As you draft your essay, be sure that it has a **thesis-and-support** structure—that is, it should state a thesis and support it with details, facts, and examples. (Because this structure enables you to present your ideas clearly and persuasively, it is central to much of the writing you do in college.) Regardless of the specific pattern of development you use to shape a particular essay, each of your essays should follow this basic structure.

For a discussion of patterns of essay development, see Chapter 14.

Notice that Jared White uses a thesis-and-support structure in the first draft of his essay.

Going Back to School

I have been out of school since I graduated from high school six years ago. The decision to return to school was one I had a lot of difficulty making. I had been around enough to know that without more education, I'd never get anywhere in life, but I always found reasons for not taking the plunge. However, after a lot of thinking, I realized that my reasons for not going to college were just excuses. I decided that if I really wanted to attend college full-time, I could.

My first excuse for not going to college was that I couldn't afford to go to school full-time. I had worked since I finished high school, but I hadn't put much money away. I kept wondering how I would pay for books and tuition. I also needed to support myself and pay for rent, food, and car expenses. I work as a house painter, and a house I was painting belonged to a college instructor. Painting wasn't hard work, but it was boring. I'd start in the morning and work without a break until lunch. During lunch break, we began talking. When I told him about my situation, he told me I should look at our local community college. I went online and looked at the college's Web site. I found out that tuition was forty dollars a credit, much less than I thought it would be.

Now that I had taken care of my first excuse, I had to deal with my second—that I hadn't been a good student in high school. When I was a teenager, I didn't care much about school. In fact, school bored me to death. Now that I was considering going back to school, though, I wondered what price I would have to pay for my laziness and immaturity. The answer to this question was not as bad as I thought it would be. According to the community college's Web site, all I needed to be

admitted was a high school diploma and county residence.
I would have to take some placement tests, but I would
be judged on my ability, not my high school grades. The
Web site was easy to navigate, and I had no problem
finding information.

I had a hard time picturing myself in college. No one
in my family had ever gone to college. My friends were
just like me; they all went to work right after high
school. I had no role model or mentor who could give
me advice. Besides, I thought I was just too old for
college. After all, I was probably at least six years
older than most of the students. How would I be able
to keep up with the younger students in the class?
I hadn't opened a textbook for years, and I'd never
really learned how to study. However, most of my fears
disappeared during my first few weeks of classes. I saw
a lot of students who were as old as I was, and some
were even older. Studying didn't seem to be a problem
either. I actually enjoyed learning. History, which
had put me to sleep in high school, suddenly became
interesting. So did math and English. It soon became
clear to me that I was going to like being in college.

Going to college as a full-time student has changed
my life, both personally and financially. I am no longer
the same person I was in high school. In the past, I
allowed laziness and insecurity to hold me back. Now,
I have options that I didn't have before. When I
graduate from community college, I plan to transfer
to the state university and get a four-year degree.

◆ PRACTICE 12-10

Reread Jared White's first draft. What changes would you suggest he
make? What might he add? What might he delete? Write your suggestions
on the lines below.

Answers will vary.

_____

_____

_____

_____

_____

_____

_____

■ **WRITING FIRST: Flashback**

On a separate sheet of paper, write a draft of an essay about the job you chose in the Flashback exercise on page 131. Be sure to include the thesis statement you developed in the Flashback exercise on page 136 as well as the points you listed in the Flashback exercise on page 139.

G **Revising and Editing Your Essay**

Writing Tip

Revise and edit on a hard copy of your essay before you type the changes into your document.

When you **revise** your essay, you resee, rethink, reevaluate, and rewrite your work. Some of the changes you make—such as adding, deleting, or rearranging several sentences or even whole paragraphs—will be major. Others will be small—for example, adding or deleting words or phrases.

Before you begin revising, put your paper aside for a time. This "cooling-off" period allows you to put some distance between yourself and what you have written so you can view your draft more objectively. (Keep in mind that revision is usually not a neat process. When you revise, feel free to write directly on your draft: draw arrows, underline, cross out, and write above lines and in the margins.)

When you **edit** your essay, you check grammar and sentence structure. Then, you look at punctuation, mechanics, and spelling.

As you revise and edit, think carefully about the questions in the two Self-Assessment Checklists that follow.

Writing Tip

When you edit your draft in a word-processing program, move unwanted material to the end of the draft or to a separate file. Do not delete it until you are sure you do not need it.

For a discussion of how to write paragraphs that are unified, well developed, and coherent, see Chapter 2.

☑ SELF-ASSESSMENT CHECKLIST:
Revising Your Essay

- ☐ Does your essay have an introduction, a body, and a conclusion?
- ☐ Does your essay have a clearly worded thesis statement?
- ☐ Does your thesis statement make a point about your topic?
- ☐ Does each body paragraph have a topic sentence?
- ☐ Does each topic sentence introduce a point that supports the thesis?
- ☐ Does each body paragraph contain enough details, facts, or examples to support the topic sentence?
- ☐ Are the body paragraphs unified, well developed, and coherent?
- ☐ Do you restate your thesis or summarize your main points in your conclusion?

(continued on the following page)

(continued from the previous page)

☐ Have you varied sentence type, structure, and length? (See Chapter 18.)

☐ Have you used effective parallel structure in your sentences? (See Chapter 19.)

☑ SELF-ASSESSMENT CHECKLIST:
Editing Your Essay

Editing for Common Sentence Problems

☐ Have you avoided run-ons and comma splices? (See Chapter 21.)

☐ Have you avoided sentence fragments? (See Chapter 22.)

☐ Do your subjects and verbs agree? (See Chapter 23.)
Have you avoided illogical shifts? (See Chapter 24.)

☐ Have you avoided dangling and misplaced modifers? (See Chapter 25.)

Editing for Grammar

☐ Are your verb forms and verb tenses correct? (See Chapters 26 and 27.)

☐ Have you used nouns and pronouns correctly? (See Chapter 28.)

☐ Have you used adjectives and adverbs correctly? (See Chapter 29.)

Editing for Punctuation, Mechanics, and Spelling

☐ Have you used commas correctly? (See Chapter 31.)

☐ Have you used apostrophes correctly? (See Chapter 32.)

☐ Have you used capital letters where they are required? (See Chapter 33.)

☐ Have you used quotation marks correctly where they are needed? (See Chapter 33.)

☐ Have you spelled every word correctly? (See Chapter 34.)

● **Writing Tip**

Use the Search function in your word-processing program to find spelling errors that you commonly make but that the spell checker will not catch—using *there* instead of *their*, for example.

When he typed the first draft of his essay about the difficulty he had deciding to return to college, Jared triple-spaced so he could write more easily in the space between the lines. Here is his draft, with his handwritten revision and editing changes.

~~Going Back to School~~ ∧*Starting Over*

The other day, my sociology instructor mentioned that half the students enrolled in college programs across the country were twenty-five or older. His remarks caught my attention because I am one of those students.

I have been out of school since I graduated from high school six years ago. The decision to return to school was one I had a lot of difficulty making. I had been around enough to know that without more education, I'd never get anywhere in life, but I always found reasons for not taking the plunge. However, after a lot of thinking, I realized that my reasons for not going to college were just excuses. *As I examined my excuses one by one,* ∧ I decided that if I really wanted to attend college full-time, I could.

My first excuse for not going to college was that I couldn't afford to go to school full-time. I had worked since I finished high school, but I hadn't put much money away. I kept wondering how I would pay for books and tuition. I also needed to support myself and pay for rent, food, and car expenses. *The solution to my problem came unexpectedly.* ∧ I work as a house painter, and a house I was painting belonged to a college instructor. ~~Painting wasn't hard work, but it was boring. I'd start in the morning and work without a break until lunch.~~ During my lunch break, we began talking. When I told him about my situation, he told me I should

In class, I would stare out the window or watch the second hand of the clock move slowly around the dial. I never bothered with homework. School just didn't interest me.

look at our local community college. I went online and looked at the college's Web site. I found out that tuition was forty dollars a credit, much less than I thought it would be. *The money I'd saved, along with what I could make painting houses on the weekends, could get me through.* ∧

Now that I had taken care of my first excuse, I had to deal with my second—that I hadn't been a good student in high school. When I was a teenager, I didn't care much about school. In fact, school bored me ~~to~~ ∧ ~~death.~~ Now that I was considering going back to school,

though, I wondered what price I would have to pay for
my laziness and immaturity. The answer to this question
was not as bad as I thought it would be. According to
the community college's Web site, all I needed to be
admitted was a high school diploma and county residence.
I would have to take some placement tests, but I would
be judged on my ability, not my high school grades. ~~The
Web site was easy to navigate, and I had no problem
finding information~~.
My biggest problem still bothered me;
            ∧
I had a hard time picturing myself in college. No one
in my family had ever gone to college. My friends were
just like me; they all went to work right after high
school. I had no role model or mentor who could give
me advice. Besides, I thought I was just too old for
college. After all, I was probably at least six years
older than most of the students. How would I be able
to keep up with the younger students in the class? I
hadn't opened a textbook for years, and I'd never
really learned how to study. However, most of my fears
disappeared during my first few weeks of classes. I saw
a lot of students who were as old as I was, and some
were even older. Studying didn't seem to be a problem
either. I actually enjoyed learning. History, which
had put me to sleep in high school, suddenly became
interesting. So did math and English. It soon became
clear to me that I was going to like being in college.

Going to college as a full-time student has changed
my life, both personally and financially. I am no longer
the same person I was in high school. In the past, I
allowed laziness and insecurity to hold me back. Now, I

have options that I didn't have before. When I graduate

from community college, I plan to transfer to the state

university and get a four-year degree. *The other day, one of my instructors asked me if I had ever considered becoming a teacher. The truth is, I never had, but now I might. I'd like to be able to give kids like me the tough, realistic advice that I wish someone had given me.* ∧

◆ PRACTICE 12-11

What kind of material did Jared White add to his draft? What did he delete? Why did he make these changes? Write your answers on the following lines.

Answers will vary.

_____

_____

_____

_____

When his revisions and edits were complete, Jared proofread his essay to be sure he had not missed any errors. The final revised and edited version of his essay appears below. (Marginal annotations have been added to highlight key structural features of his paper.)

Starting Over

Introduction —

Opening remarks

     The other day, my sociology instructor mentioned that half the students enrolled in college programs across the country are twenty-five or older. His remarks caught my attention because I am one of those students. I have been out of school since I graduated from high school six years ago. The decision to return to school was one I had a lot of difficulty making. I had been around enough to know that without more education, I would never get anywhere in life, but I always found reasons for not taking the plunge. However, after a lot of thinking, I realized that my reasons for not going to college were just excuses. As I examined my excuses one by one, I decided that if I really wanted to attend college full-time, I could.

Thesis statement

Body paragraph

Topic sentence

Supporting sentences (details, facts, examples)

     My first excuse for not going to college was that I couldn't afford to go to school full-time. I had worked since I finished high school, but I hadn't put much money away. I kept wondering how I would pay for books and tuition. I also needed to support myself and pay for rent, food, and car expenses. The solution to my problem came unexpectedly. I work as a house painter, and a house I was painting belonged to a college instructor. During my lunch break, we began talking. When I told him about my situation, he told me I should look at our local community college. I went online and looked at the college's Web site. I found out that tuition was forty dollars a credit, much less than I thought it would be. The money I'd saved, along with what I could make painting houses on the weekends, could get me through.

<u>Now that I had taken care of my first excuse, I had to deal with my second—that I hadn't been a good student in high school.</u> When I was a teenager, I didn't care much about school. In fact, school bored me. In class, I would stare out the window or watch the second hand on the clock move slowly around the dial. I never bothered with homework. School just didn't interest me. Now that I was considering going back to school, though, I wondered what price I would have to pay for my laziness and immaturity. The answer to this question was not as bad as I thought it would be. According to the community college's Web site, all I needed to be admitted was a high school diploma and county residence. I would have to take some placement tests, but I would be judged on my ability, not my high school grades.

<u>My biggest problem still bothered me; I had a hard time picturing myself in college.</u> No one in my family had ever gone to college. My friends were just like me; they all went to work right after high school. I had no role model or mentor who could give me advice. Besides, I thought I was just too old for college. After all, I was probably at least six years older than most of the students. How would I be able to keep up with the younger students in the class? I hadn't opened a textbook for years, and I'd never really learned how to study. However, most of my fears disappeared during my first few weeks of classes. I saw a lot of students who were as old as I was, and some were even older. Studying didn't seem to be a problem either. I actually enjoyed learning. History, which had put me to sleep in high school, suddenly became interesting. So did math and English. It soon became clear to me that I was going to like being in college.

<u>Going to college as a full-time student has changed my life, both personally and financially.</u> I am no longer the same person I was in high school. In the past, I allowed laziness and insecurity to hold me back. Now, I have options that I didn't have before. When I graduate from community college, I plan to transfer to the state university and get a four-year degree. The other day,

---

Margin annotations:

Topic sentence

Supporting sentences (details, facts, examples)

Body paragraph

Topic sentence

Supporting sentences (details, facts, examples)

Body paragraph

Restatement of thesis

Closing remarks

Conclusion

one of my instructors asked me if I had ever considered becoming a teacher. The truth is, I never had, but now I might. I'd like to be able to give kids like me the tough, realistic advice that I wish someone had given me.

◆ PRACTICE 12-12

Reread the final draft of Jared White's essay. Do you think this draft is an improvement over his first draft? What other changes could Jared have made? Write your ideas here.

Answers will vary.

_____

_____

_____

_____

_____

■ WRITING FIRST: Flashback

Using the Self-Assessment Checklist for revising your essay on pages 142–143 as a guide, evaluate the essay you wrote for the Flashback exercise on the same page. What points can you add to support your thesis more fully? What points can you delete? Can any ideas be stated more clearly? (You may want to get feedback by exchanging essays with another student.) On the following lines, list the changes you think you should make to your draft.

Answers will vary.

_____

_____

_____

_____

■ WRITING FIRST: Revising and Editing

Now, revise the draft of your essay, writing in new material between the lines or in the margins. Then, edit this revised draft, using the Self-Assessment Checklist for editing your essay on page 143 to help you find errors in grammar, sentence structure, punctuation, mechanics, and spelling. When you have finished, prepare a final draft of your essay.

CHAPTER REVIEW

◆ **EDITING PRACTICE**

1. After reading the following student essay, write an appropriate thesis statement on the lines provided. (Make sure your thesis statement clearly communicates the essay's main idea.) Then, fill in the topic sentences for the second, third, and fourth paragraphs. Finally, restate the thesis in different words in the conclusion.

Preparing for a Job Interview

I have looked at a lot of books and many Web sites that give advice on how to do well on a job interview. Some recommend practicing your handshake, and others suggest making eye contact. This advice is useful, but not many books tell how to get mentally prepared for an interview. [Thesis statement:] _Answers will vary._ _____

_____

_____

Woman at job interview

[Topic sentence for the second paragraph:] _____

Answers will vary. _____

_____

Feeling good about how I look is important, so I usually wear a jacket and tie to an interview. Even if you will not be dressing this formally on the job, try to make a good first impression. For this reason, you should never come to an interview dressed in jeans or shorts. Still, you should be careful not to overdress. For example, wearing a suit or a dressy dress to an interview at a fast-food restaurant might make you feel good, but it could also make you look as if you do not really want to work there.

[Topic sentence for the third paragraph:] _____

Answers will vary. _____

_____

Going on an interview is a little like getting ready to take part in a sporting event. You have to go in with the

*Man coming into a job
interview*

right attitude. If you think you are not going to be
successful, chances are that you will not be. So before
I go on any interview, I spend some time building my
confidence. I tell myself that I can do the job and that
I will do well in the interview. By the time I get to
the interview, I am sure I am the right person for
the job.

[Topic sentence for the fourth paragraph:] _____

Answers will vary.

_____

_____

Most people go to an interview knowing little or nothing
about the job. They expect the interviewer to tell them
what they will have to do. Once, an interviewer told me
that he likes a person who has taken the time to do his
or her homework. Since that time, I have always done some
research before I go on an interview—even for a part-time
job. (Most of the time, my research is nothing more than
a quick look at the company Web site.) This kind of
research really pays off. At my last interview, for
example, I was able to talk in detail about the job
I would do. The interviewer must have been impressed
because she offered me the job on the spot.

[Restatement of thesis:] _____

Answers will vary.

_____

_____

Of course, following my suggestions will not guarantee that
you get a job. You still have to do well at the interview
itself. Even so, getting mentally prepared for the
interview will give you an advantage over people who do
almost nothing before they walk in the door.

2. Write another body paragraph that you could add to the essay above.
   (This new paragraph will go right before the essay's conclusion.) The
   topic sentence has been written for you.

[Topic sentence for the fifth paragraph:]　*Another way to prepare*

yourself mentally is to anticipate and answer some typical questions

interviewers ask.

[Body paragraph for the fifth paragraph:]　_____

Answers will vary.

_____

_____

_____

_____

_____

_____

◆ COLLABORATIVE ACTIVITIES

1. On your own, find a paragraph in a magazine or a newspaper about an issue that interests you. Working in a group, select one of the paragraphs. Choose three points about the issue discussed that you could develop in a short essay, and then brainstorm about these points. Finally, write a sentence that could serve as the thesis statement for an essay.

2. Working in a group, come up with thesis statements suitable for essays on three of the following topics.

Living on a budget	Gun safety
The Internet	Dressing well
Safe driving	Patriotism
Parenthood	Bad habits
Honesty	How to prepare for a test

3. Exchange your group's three thesis statements with those of another group. Choose the best one of the other group's thesis statements. A member of each group can then read the thesis statement to the class and explain why the group chose the thesis statement it did.

For information on stating a thesis, see 12D.

☑ REVIEW CHECKLIST:
Writing an Essay

- Most essays have a thesis statement that presents the main idea, and the body paragraphs support the thesis. (See 12A.)

- Begin by deciding on a topic. (See 12B.)

(continued on the following page)

12 G

(continued from the previous page)

☐ Narrow your focus and find ideas to write about. (See 12C.)

☐ Develop an effective thesis statement. (See 12D.)

☐ List the points that best support your thesis, and arrange them in the order in which you plan to discuss them. (See 12E.)

☐ As you write your first draft, make sure your essay has a thesis-and-support structure. (See 12F.)

☐ Revise your essay. (See 12G.)

☐ Edit the final draft of your essay. (See 12G.)

Introductions and Conclusions

■ WRITING FIRST

Look at the picture above, in which Charlie Chaplin, in the film *Modern Times* (1936), is sucked into a factory machine. Then, print out a copy of the essay about your worst job that you wrote for Chapter 12. As you go through this chapter, you will be working on the introduction and conclusion of this essay.

Word Power

monotonous repetitious; lacking in variety

robotic mechanical; without original thought

routine a standard procedure; without any special quality

When you draft an essay, you usually focus on the **body** because it is the largest single section and because it is the section in which you develop your ideas. A well-constructed essay, however, is more than a series of body paragraphs. It also includes an **introduction** and a **conclusion**, both of which contribute to the overall effectiveness of your writing.

A Introductions

An **introduction** is the first thing people see when they read your essay. If your introduction is interesting and effective, it will make readers want to read further. If it is not, readers may get bored and stop reading.

Your introduction should prepare readers for your essay by giving them the information they need to follow your discussion. For this reason, the introduction should include a **thesis statement** that presents the main idea of your essay. This statement usually appears at the end of the introductory paragraph. (In each of the sample introductory paragraphs on pages 154–157, the thesis statement is underlined and labeled.)

Here are some options you can experiment with when you write your introductions.

● **Writing Tip**

Remind students that the introduction should be a full paragraph.

Teaching Tip

Find two introductory paragraphs (one that is catchy and one that is dull), and read each one to the class. After you read each introduction, ask students whether they would like to hear the rest of the essay—and why or why not.

FOCUS What to Avoid in Introductions

■ Do not begin your essay by announcing what you plan to write about.

Phrases to Avoid

This essay is about . . .

Today I will talk about . . .

In my essay I will discuss . . .

■ Do not apologize for your ideas.

Phrases to Avoid

Although I don't know much about this subject . . .

I might not be an expert but . . .

Beginning with a Direct Approach

The simplest way to start an essay is to present a few opening remarks and then list the points you will discuss. This straightforward approach moves readers directly to the main idea of your essay. (Once you feel comfortable with this strategy, you can experiment with other approaches.)

Television sitcoms are a part of most people's lives. Almost everyone watches these shows at one time or another. In addition to providing entertainment, sitcoms often show characters struggling with real-life situations. That is why it is disturbing to see how many sitcoms convey unrealistic images of men and women. These stereo-

Thesis statement

types not only misrepresent reality, but they also teach distorted values
that make it almost impossible for real men and women to relate to
one another.

–AMY DONOHUE (student)

Beginning with a Narrative

You can begin an essay with a narrative drawn from your own experience
or from a current news event. If your story is interesting, it will involve
readers almost immediately. Notice how the narrative in the following introduction sets the stage for an essay in which the writer discusses his experiences as a volunteer firefighter.

> On September 11, 2001, the unthinkable happened: terrorists
> crashed two commercial airplanes into the twin towers at the World
> Trade Center. Ignoring the danger to themselves, hundreds of fire-
> fighters rushed inside the buildings to try to save as many lives as pos-
> sible. Their actions enabled thousands of people to get out, but half the
> firefighters—over three hundred—died when the twin towers col-
> lapsed. Although I have never faced a catastrophe like the one in New   Thesis statement
> York, as a volunteer firefighter I am ready—day or night, whenever an
> alarm sounds—to deal with a dangerous situation.
>
> –RICHARD POGUE (student)

Beginning with a Question (or a Series of Questions)

Asking one or more questions at the beginning of your essay is an effective
strategy. Because readers expect you to answer the questions, they will
want to read further. Notice how two questions in the following introduction attract attention and draw readers into the essay.

> Imagine this scene: A child is sitting under a Christmas tree open-
> ing her presents. She laughs and claps her hands as she gets a doll, a
> pair of shoes, and a sweater. What could spoil this picture? What in-
> formation could cause the child's parents to feel guilt? The answer is   Thesis statement
> that children from developing countries probably worked long hours
> in substandard conditions so this child could receive her gifts.
>
> –MEGAN DAVIA (student)

Beginning with a Definition

A definition at the beginning of your essay can give valuable information
to readers. As the following paragraph shows, such information can explain a confusing concept or clarify a complicated idea.

> The term *good parent* is not easy to define. Some things about being
> a good parent are obvious—keeping your children safe, taking them to
> the doctor for regular checkups, helping them with their homework,
> being there for them when they want to talk, and staying up at night
> with them when they are sick, for example. Other things are not so

obvious, however. I found this out last year when I became a volunteer at my daughter's middle school. <u>Up until that time, I never would have dreamed that one morning a week could do so much to improve my daughter's attitude toward school.</u>   —RUSS HIGHTOWER (student)

FOCUS Beginning with a Definition

Avoid introducing a definition with a tired opening phrase such as "According to *Webster's* . . ." or "*The American Heritage Dictionary* defines. . . ."

Beginning with a Background Statement

A background statement can provide an overview of a subject and set the stage for the discussion to follow. As the following introduction illustrates, a background statement can also help prepare readers for a surprising or controversial thesis statement.

ESL Tip
Ask students why someone might think English is "crazy."

Thesis statement

English is the most widely spoken language in the history of our planet, used in some way by at least one out of every seven human beings around the globe. Half of the world's books are written in English, and the majority of international telephone calls are made in English. English is the language of over sixty percent of the world's radio programs, many of them beamed, ironically, by the Russians, who know that to win friends and influence nations, they're best off using English. More than seventy percent of international mail is written and addressed in English, and eighty percent of all computer text is stored in English. English has acquired the largest vocabulary of all the world's languages, perhaps as many as two million words, and has generated one of the noblest bodies of literature in the annals of the human race. <u>Nonetheless, it is now time to face the fact that English is a crazy language.</u>   —RICHARD LEDERER, "English Is a Crazy Language"

Beginning with a Quotation

An appropriate saying or an interesting piece of dialogue can draw readers into your essay. Notice how the quotation below creates interest and leads smoothly into the thesis statement at the end of the introduction.

Thesis statement

According to the comedian Jerry Seinfeld, "When you're single, you are the dictator of your own life. . . . When you're married, you are part of a vast decision-making body." In other words, before you can do anything, you have to discuss it with someone else. These words kept going through my mind as I thought about asking my girlfriend to marry me. The more I thought about Seinfeld's words, the more I hesitated. <u>I never suspected that I would pay a price for my indecision.</u>

—DAN BRODY (student)

Beginning with a Surprising Statement

You can begin your essay with a surprising or unexpected statement. Because your statement takes readers by surprise, it catches their attention. Notice in the following paragraph how a rather startling opening statement leads readers to the essay's thesis.

> Some of the smartest people I know never went to college. In fact, some of them never finished high school. Even so, they know how to save twenty percent on the price of a dinner, fix their own faucets when they leak, get discounted prescriptions, get free rides on a bus to Atlantic City, use public transportation to get anywhere in the city, and live on about twenty-two dollars a day. These are my grandparents' friends. Some people would call them old and poor. <u>I would call them survivors who have learned to make it through life on nothing but a Social Security check.</u>
>   —SEAN RAGAS (student)

Thesis statement

Beginning with a Contradiction

You can begin your introduction with an idea that many people believe to be true. Then, as the following paragraph does, you can capture readers' attention by demonstrating why this idea is untrue or questionable.

> Drugs and crime are so thoroughly intertwined in the public mind that to most people a large crime problem seems an inevitable consequence of drug use. But the historical link between the two is more a product of drug laws than of drugs. There are four clear connections between drugs and crime, and three of them would be much diminished if drugs were legalized. <u>This fact does not in itself make the case for legalization persuasive, of course, but it deserves careful attention in the emerging debate of whether prohibition of drugs is worth the trouble.</u>
>   —ETHAN A. NADELMANN, "Legalize Drugs"

Thesis statement

FOCUS   **Titles**

Every essay should have a **title** that suggests the subject of the essay and makes people want to read it.

Before you choose a title, reread your essay (especially your thesis statement) carefully. Then, jot down several possible titles and select the one you like the best. When you write your title, be sure to follow these guidelines.

- Capitalize all words except for articles (*a, an, the*), prepositions (*at, to, of, around,* and so on), and coordinating conjunctions (*and, but,* and so on), unless they are the first or last word of the title.
- Do not underline your title or enclose it within quotation marks.

(continued on the following page)

● **Writing Tip**

Do not underline or italicize the title of your own paper, and do not put quotation marks around it unless you are directly quoting a source. For more on punctuating titles, see 33C.

(continued from the previous page)

■ Center the title at the top of the first page. Double-space between the title and the first line of your essay.

As you consider a title for your paper, think about the following options.

■ A title can highlight a key word or term.

Guavas

Liars

■ A title can be a straightforward announcement.

Thirty-Eight Who Saw Murder Didn't Call the Police

The "Black Table" Is Still There

■ A title can set a scene.

Summer Picnic Fish Fry

■ A title can establish a personal connection with readers.

The Men We Carry in Our Minds

I Have a Dream

■ A title can offer an unusual perspective.

The New Prohibitionism

■ A title can be a familiar saying or a quotation from your essay itself.

Men Are from Mars, Women Are from Venus

Slice of Life

For more information on patterns of essay development, see Chapter 14.

■ A title can suggest the pattern of development used in the essay.

Three Ways to Make Your Neighborhood Better (exemplification)

The Rise and Fall of Doo-Wop (narrative)

My Grandfather (description)

How to Write an Effective Résumé (process)

Why the *Titanic* Sank (cause and effect)

Four-Year vs. Two-Year Colleges (comparison and contrast)

Types of Sports Fans (classification)

What It Means to Be Happy (definition)

Let's Stop Persecuting Smokers (argument)

◆ **PRACTICE 13-1**

Look at the student essays in Chapter 14, locating one introduction you think is particularly effective. On the lines below, explain the strengths of the introduction you chose.

Answers will vary.

_____

_____

_____

_____

◆ **PRACTICE 13-2**

Using the different options for creating titles discussed above, write two titles for each of the essays described below.

Answers will vary.

1. A student writes an essay about three people who disappeared mysteriously: Amelia Earhart, aviator; Ambrose Bierce, writer; and Jimmy Hoffa, union leader. In the body paragraphs, the student describes the circumstances surrounding their disappearances.

   _____

   _____

2. A student writes an essay arguing against doctors' letting people select the sex of their babies. In the body paragraphs, she presents reasons why she thinks it is unethical.

   _____

   _____

3. A student writes an essay to explain why America is ready to elect a woman president. In the body paragraphs, the writer gives reasons for his beliefs.

   _____

   _____

4. A student writes an essay describing the harmful effects of steroids on student athletes. In the body paragraphs, he shows the effects on the heart, brain, and other organs.

   _____

   _____

5. A student writes an essay explaining why she joined the Navy. In the body paragraphs, she discusses her need to earn money for college tuition, her wish to learn a trade, and her desire to see the world.

   _____

   _____

Teaching Tip
Read aloud several different
types of introductions, and
have the class categorize
them.

■ **WRITING FIRST: Flashback**

Look back at the essay you reprinted for the Writing First exercise on page 153. Evaluate your introduction. Does it prepare readers for the essay to follow? Does it include a thesis statement? Is it likely to interest readers? On a separate sheet of paper, draft a different opening paragraph using one of the options presented in 13A. Be sure to include a clear thesis statement. In the space provided below, indicate the kind of introduction you have drafted.

After you have finished drafting a new introduction, think of a new title that will attract your readers' attention. (Use one of the options listed in the Focus box on pages 157–158.) In the space provided below, write your new title, and then indicate the option you used.

Option used for new introduction: _____ *Answers will vary.* _____

New title: _____ *Answers will vary.* _____

Option used for new title: _____ *Answers will vary.* _____

B **Conclusions**

Because your **conclusion** is the last thing readers see, they often judge your entire essay by its effectiveness. For this reason, conclusions should be planned, drafted, and revised with care.

Your conclusion should give readers a sense of completion. One way you can accomplish this is by restating the essay's thesis. Keep in mind, however, that a conclusion is more than a word-for-word restatement of the thesis. If you return to your thesis here, you should summarize it, expand on it, and make some general concluding remarks; then, try to end with a final thought or observation that readers will remember.

Teaching Tip
Remind students that the
conclusion should be a full
paragraph.

● **Writing Tip**
In essay exams, when time
is limited, a one-sentence
restatement of your thesis
is often enough for a conclusion. Likewise, an essay
exam may require just a
one- or two-sentence introduction.

FOCUS **What to Avoid in Conclusions**

■ Do not introduce any new ideas. Your conclusion should sum up the ideas you discuss in your essay, not open up new lines of thought.
■ Do not apologize for your opinions, ideas, or conclusions. Apologies will undercut your reader's confidence in you.

(continued on the following page)

(continued from the previous page)

> *Phrases to Avoid*
>
> I may not be an expert . . .
>
> At least that's my opinion . . .
>
> I could be wrong, but . . .
>
> ■ Do not use overused phrases to announce your essay is coming to a close.
>
> *Phrases to Avoid*
>
> In summary, . . .
>
> In conclusion, . . .

Here are some options you can use when you write your conclusions.

Concluding with a Restatement of Your Thesis

This no-nonsense conclusion reinforces your essay's most important ideas by restating your thesis in different words and reviewing the main points of the discussion.

> It is unfortunate that television sitcoms do not show men and women relating to each other in a meaningful way. The use of male and female stereotypes does little to educate viewers. At best, television sitcoms teach viewers that sex can make any problem disappear. At worst, they reinforce behavior that makes it almost impossible for men and women to relate to each other. A more realistic response from characters would show viewers that honest communication can do more to resolve conflicts between men and women than stereotypical behavior can.
>
> —Neena Thomas (student)

Concluding with a Narrative

A narrative conclusion can bring an event discussed in the essay to a logical, satisfying close. The following conclusion uses a narrative to tie up the essay's loose ends.

> After twenty years, the tree began to bear. Although Grandfather complained about how much he lost because pollen never reached the poor part of town, because at the market he had to haggle over the price of avocados, he loved that tree. It grew, as did his family, and when he died, all his sons standing on each other's shoulders, oldest

to youngest, could not reach the highest branches. The wind could move the branches, but the trunk, thicker than any waist, hugged the ground.

—GARY SOTO, "The Grandfather"

Concluding with a Question (or a Series of Questions)

By ending with a question, you leave readers with something to think about. However, the question should build on the thesis statement and not introduce any new issues. Notice how the conclusion below asks a series of questions before restating the essay's thesis.

> Why is it that when the sun or the moon or the stars are out, they are visible, but when the lights are out, they are invisible, and that when I wind up my watch, I start it, but when I wind up this essay, I shall end it? English is a crazy language.
>
> —RICHARD LEDERER, "English Is a Crazy Language"

Concluding with a Prediction

This type of conclusion not only sums up the thesis but also looks to the future. The following conclusion uses this technique to paint a troubling picture of the future of American cities.

> On that little street were the ghosts of the people who brought me into being and the flesh-and-blood kids who will be my children's companions in the twenty-first century. You could tell by their eyes that they couldn't figure out why I was there. They were accustomed to being ignored, even by the people who had once populated their rooms. And as long as that continues, our cities will burst and burn, burst and burn, over and over again.   —ANNA QUINDLEN, "The Old Block"

Concluding with a Recommendation

Once you think you have convinced readers that a problem exists, you can make recommendations in your conclusion about how the problem should be solved. Notice how the following paragraph makes a series of recommendations about a cancer drug made from the Pacific yew tree.

> Every effort should be made to ensure that the yew tree is made available for the continued research and development of taxol. Environmental groups, the timber industry, and the Forest Service must recognize that the most important value of the Pacific yew is as a treatment for cancer. At the same time, its harvest can be managed in a way that allows for the production of taxol without endangering the continual survival of the yew tree.
>
> —SALLY THANE CHRISTENSEN, "Is a Tree Worth a Life?"

Concluding with a Quotation

Frequently, a well-chosen quotation—even a brief one—can add a lot to your essay. In some cases, quoted speech or writing can add authority to your ideas. In others, as in the following paragraph, it can reinforce the main point of the essay.

> It was 4:25 a.m. when the ambulance arrived to take the body of Miss Genovese. It drove off. "Then," a solemn police detective said, "the people came out."
>
> –MARTIN GANSBERG, "Thirty-Eight Who Saw Murder Didn't Call the Police"

◆ PRACTICE 13-3

Look at the student essays in Chapter 14, locating one conclusion you think is particularly effective. On the lines below, explain the strengths of the conclusion you chose.

Answers will vary.

_____

_____

_____

_____

■ WRITING FIRST: Flashback

Look again at the essay you reprinted for the Writing First exercise on page 153. Evaluate your conclusion. Is it suitable for your topic and thesis? Does it bring your essay to a clear and satisfying close that will leave a strong impression on readers? On a separate sheet of paper, try drafting a different concluding paragraph using one of the options presented in 13B. In the space provided, indicate what kind of conclusion you have drafted.

Option used for new conclusion: ___*Answers will vary.*___

● **Writing Tip**

Draft the body paragraphs before you spend much time writing the introduction or conclusion. After you have developed the body of your essay, you can revise your introduction and conclusion so they fit in with the direction that your essay has taken.

■ WRITING FIRST: Revising and Editing

Reread your responses to the Flashback exercise above and the one on page 160. Are the new paragraphs you wrote more effective than the introduction and conclusion of the essay you wrote in Chapter 12? If so, substitute them for the opening and closing paragraphs of that essay.

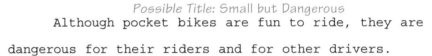

CHAPTER REVIEW

◆ **EDITING PRACTICE**

The following student essay has an undeveloped introduction and conclusion. Decide what introductory and concluding strategies would be most appropriate for the essay. Then, on a separate sheet of paper, rewrite both the introduction and the conclusion to make them more effective. Finally, add an interesting title for the essay.
Answers will vary.

Pocket bike

Possible Title: Small but Dangerous

Although pocket bikes are fun to ride, they are dangerous for their riders and for other drivers.

Like many other American fads, the pocket-bike craze started in California and has spread eastward across the United States. Pocket bikes weigh about fifty pounds and are about eighteen inches high. Even riders in their early teens have to hunch over them. Their tiny engines are similar to those used in leaf blowers. They buzz like chain saws as they speed down the street. Usually, pocket bikes can travel up to thirty-five miles per hour, but their engines can be modified to allow them to go faster. Owners of pocket bikes say that they are exciting to ride, burn very little gas, and cost a lot less than full-size motorcycles. They are so popular that dealers cannot keep them in stock.

However, police say that pocket bikes can be a hazard. They were originally developed to train professional motorcycle racers. Manufacturers say that they should be used only on closed tracks or in areas where there is no traffic. They are not meant to be driven on the street, and they do not meet federal safety standards. Many pocket bikers, though, ignore these restrictions and ride on residential streets.

Unfortunately, pocket bikes are so low that other drivers cannot see them. If a car or truck hits a pocket bike, the bike's rider is likely to be severely injured or even killed. Another danger is that pocket bikes look like toys. Unsuspecting parents buy them for their children, who are not ready to drive a vehicle of any type. Recently, a number of fatalities have occurred when young children lost control of their pocket bikes. Because of these dangers, several cities have banned pocket bikes. Other cities are starting to crack down on their use.

Although these bikes can be fun to ride, they present an unacceptable hazard.

Pocket bike with rider

◆ COLLABORATIVE ACTIVITIES

1. Bring to class several copies of an essay you wrote for another class. Have each person in your group comment on your essay's introduction and conclusion. Revise the introduction and conclusion in response to your classmates' suggestions.

2. Find a magazine or newspaper article that interests you. Cut off the introduction and conclusion, and bring the body of the article to class. Ask your group to decide on the best strategy for introducing and concluding the article. Then, collaborate on writing new opening and closing paragraphs and an interesting title.

3. Working in a group, think of interesting and appropriate titles for essays on each of the topics listed below. Try to use as many of the different options outlined in the Focus box on pages 157–158 as you can.

   The difficulty of living with a roommate
   The dangers of gambling
   The need for regular exercise
   The joys of living in the city (or in the country)
   The responsibilities of having a pet
   Things that make life easier
   The stress of job interviews
   The obligation to vote
   The advantages of wireless Internet
   The problems of being a parent
   The need for better public transportation

☑ REVIEW CHECKLIST:
Introduction and Conclusions

☐ The introduction of your essay should prepare readers for the ideas to follow and should include a thesis statement. It should also create interest. (See 13A.) You can begin an essay with any of the following options.

A direct approach	A definition
A narrative	A background statement
A question	A quotation
A surprising statement	A contradiction

☐ Your title should suggest the subject of your essay and make people want to read further. (See 13A.)

☐ The conclusion of your essay should restate the thesis and make some general concluding remarks. (See 13B.) You can conclude an essay with any of the following options.

A restatement of the thesis	A prediction
A narrative	A recommendation
A question	A quotation

Patterns of Essay Development

PREVIEW

In this chapter, you will learn to organize your essays according to different patterns of development:

- exemplification (14A)

- narration (14B)

- description (14C)

- process (14D)

- cause and effect (14E)

- comparison and contrast (14F)

- classification (14G)

- definition (14H)

- argument (14I)

As you learned in Chapters 3 through 11, writers have a variety of options for developing ideas within a paragraph. These options include *exemplification, narration, description, process, cause and effect, comparison and contrast, classification, definition,* and *argument.* When you write an essay, you can use these same patterns of development to help you organize your material.

In your college courses, different assignments and writing situations call for different patterns of essay development. For instance, if an essay exam question asked you to compare two systems of government, you would use *comparison and contrast.* If an English composition assignment asked you to tell about a childhood experience, you would use *narration.* If a section of a research paper on environmental pollution called for examples of dangerous waste disposal practices, you would use *exemplification.*

Each section in this chapter defines and explains one pattern of essay development, gives examples of how it is used in typical college writing assignments, provides several options for organizing an essay, lists some transitional words and phrases you can use to connect ideas, and offers "Grammar in Context" tips that apply to the particular pattern being discussed. A student essay illustrates each pattern, and a list of writing topics and a Self-Assessment Checklist give you opportunities for practice and review.

167

For information on writing an exemplification paragraph, see Chapter 3.

A　Exemplification

Exemplification illustrates a general statement with one or more specific examples. An **exemplification essay** uses specific examples to support a thesis.

FOCUS　**Topics for Exemplification**

The wording of your assignment may suggest exemplification. For example, you may be asked to *illustrate* or to *give examples*.

Assignment	Thesis Statement
Education　Should children be taught only in their native languages or in English as well? Support your answer with examples of specific students' experiences.	The success of students in a bilingual third-grade class suggests the value of teaching elementary-school students in English as well as in their native languages.
Literature　Does William Shakespeare's *Othello* have to end tragically? Illustrate your position with references to specific characters.	Each of the three major characters in *Othello* contributes to the play's tragic ending.
Composition　Discuss the worst job you ever had, including plenty of specific examples to support your thesis.	My summer job at a fast-food restaurant was my all-time worst job because of the endless stream of rude customers, the many boring and repetitive tasks I had to perform, and my manager's insensitive treatment of employees.

Teaching Tip
For each pattern of development, you can assign an appropriate reading from Chapter 36 and have students answer some of the questions that follow it.

Teaching Tip
For examples of exemplification essays by professional writers, see 36A.

● **Writing Tip**
Many everyday writing tasks call for exemplification. For example, in a parent committee report for your child's day-care center, you might present examples of possible environmental hazards in the school building.

In an exemplification essay, each body paragraph can develop a single example or discuss several related examples.

FOCUS　**Options for Organizing Exemplification Essays**

One Example per Paragraph	*Several Related Examples per Paragraph*
¶1 Introduction	¶1 Introduction
¶2 First example	¶2 First group of examples
¶3 Second example	¶3 Second group of examples
¶4 Third example	¶4 Third group of examples
¶5 Conclusion	¶5 Conclusion

Teaching Tip
Make sure students know that ¶ is the symbol for a paragraph.

In each body paragraph of your essay, a topic sentence should introduce the example (or group of related examples) that the paragraph will discuss. Each example you select should clearly support your thesis, and your topic sentence should help make this thesis-and-support connection clear. Transitional words and phrases should introduce your examples and indicate how one example is related to another.

FOCUS **Transitions for Exemplification**

Also	Furthermore	The most impor-
Besides	In addition	tant example
Finally	Moreover	The next example
First	One example . . .	
For example	Another example	
For instance	Specifically	

The following student essay, "Fighting Fire with Fire Safety Education" by Timothy E. Miles, uses a series of examples to illustrate the need to educate children about fire safety. Some paragraphs group several brief examples together; others develop a single example. Notice how Timothy uses clear topic sentences and helpful transitions to introduce his examples and link them to one another.

Fighting Fire with Fire Safety Education

Since young children suffer more fire-related   1
injuries and deaths than most others do, fire safety
education must be introduced at an early age. This can
be done both by parents and by local fire departments.
Fire safety for young children is very important, and
adults must take the responsibility for educating and
protecting them.

What should small children be taught? First, they   2
should understand what matches are and what the
consequences of playing with them can be. In addition,
they should be taught that matches are not toys and that
they can cause great damage. Children should also be
taught how to avoid contact burns from stove burners,
hot liquids, and electrical appliances.

Another essential part of fire safety education for 3
children is learning how to extinguish fires when their
clothing ignites. The chance of serious injury can be
prevented if they are taught to "Stop, drop, and roll."
One way of teaching this is for the adult to cut out
a "flame" from paper and tape it lightly to the child.
When the child actually stops, drops, and rolls on
the ground, the "flame" will fall off, thereby
"extinguishing" the "fire."

Exit drills in the home can <u>also</u> save lives. These   4
drills need to teach children how to crawl low to escape
smoke, how to feel for hot doors, and how to place
towels or clothing under doors to stop smoke from coming
into a room. (Children should also understand that smoke
and fumes, not the fire itself, cause most deaths.)
Deciding on a meeting place where all family members
can be accounted for is perhaps the most important.

Making sure children know the fire department phone   5
number is <u>another</u> way to reduce fire-related injuries
and deaths. It is important that children know the
correct number because not all areas have a 911 system.
The numbers of all emergency services should be posted
near each phone. Children should know how to dial these
numbers and should know the address from which they are
calling. To practice reporting a fire, a child can use
a toy phone, with an adult playing the role of the
operator.

<u>Finally</u>, children should be aware of what   6
firefighters look like in their equipment. Some
children, particularly very young ones, are afraid of
firefighters because of their unfamiliar appearance.
During a visit to any local firehouse, children can meet
firefighters who can answer questions and demonstrate
and explain their equipment and gear. If children are
familiar with firefighters and their equipment, they
will not run away from them or hide.

Of course, educating children is not enough in itself   7
to ensure fire safety; parents and other adults must
<u>also</u> educate themselves about what to do (and what not
to do) if a fire actually occurs. For example, do not
go back into a fire for any reason. Have a meeting place
where family members can be accounted for. Do not try to
put out a fire; instead, have someone notify the fire
department immediately. <u>In addition</u>, adults should take
the responsibility for getting children involved in
fire prevention. Many children learn best by example.
Handouts, displays, and videotapes are especially
helpful. Demonstration and practice of exit drills in
the home and of "Stop, drop, and roll" are <u>also</u> useful,
particularly during special fire hazard periods such
as Halloween and Christmas. Participating in designing
escape plans and inspecting their homes for potential
problems <u>also</u> make children feel they are helping. In
fact, children can sometimes see things that adults
overlook.

By keeping these points in mind, children and their   8
parents can join together to avoid potential disaster.
If family members learn about fire safety, and if they

practice and review what they have learned on a regular
basis, lives will be saved.

◆ PRACTICE 14-1

1. Underline the thesis statement of "Fighting Fire with Fire Safety Education." Restate it below in your own words.

   Adults should teach young children about fire safety.

2. (a) List the examples Tim uses to support his thesis. (b) Which examples does he group together? Why? (c) Which examples does he develop in paragraphs of their own? Why?

   (a) Young children should be taught the consequences of playing with

   matches, stove burners, hot liquids, and electrical appliances; how to

   extinguish fires; how to conduct exit drills in the home; the fire depart-

   ment phone number; and how firefighters look in their equipment.

   (b) Tim groups matches together with other burn-producing

   household items because they are all commonly found around the house

   and because teaching children not to use them as toys is the first step

   in fire prevention. (c) Tim develops full paragraphs on how to extinguish

   clothing fires, how to conduct exit drills, knowing the fire department

   phone number, and being aware of what firefighters look like in their

   equipment. He also includes a full paragraph on adults' responsibilities.

   Each of these examples requires some explanation because they deal

   with what to do if a fire occurs.

3. How does Tim link his examples to one another? Underline some of the transitional words that serve this purpose.

   Tim uses transitional words such as first, another, also, and finally to link

   examples and connect all his ideas to his thesis.

4. Is the straightforward introduction effective? How else might Tim have opened his essay?

   Answers will vary.

5. Is the conclusion effective? How else could Tim have ended his essay?

Answers will vary.

_____

_____

6. What is this essay's greatest strength? What is its greatest weakness?

Strength: ___*Answers will vary.*_____

Weakness: ___*Answers will vary.*_____

GRAMMAR IN CONTEXT **Exemplification**

When you write an exemplification essay, you may introduce your examples with transitional words and phrases like *First* or *In addition*. If you do, be sure to use a comma after the introductory word or phrase.

<u>First</u>, they should understand what matches are and what the consequences of playing with them can be.

<u>In addition</u>, adults should take the responsibility for getting children involved in fire prevention.

<u>Finally</u>, children should be aware of what firefighters look like in their equipment.

For information on using commas with introductory transitional words and phrases, see 31B.

Teaching Tip
Before your students write exemplification essays, you might want to explain the use of commas to set off introductory elements (31B) and have them do Practice 31-2 before they write their essays.

◆ **PRACTICE 14-2**

Following the writing process outlined in Chapter 12, write an exemplification essay on one of the following topics.

Reasons to start (or not to start) college right after high school
The three best products ever invented
What kinds of people or images should appear on U.S. postage stamps? Why?
Advantages (or disadvantages) of being a young parent
Athletes who really are role models
Four items students need to survive in college
What messages do various hip-hop artists send to listeners?
Study strategies that work
Traits of a good employee
Three or four recent national or world news events that upset or shocked you

◆ PRACTICE 14-3

The billboard pictured above shows a public service advertisement promoting HIV/AIDS awareness. Study the picture carefully, and then write an exemplification essay explaining how this advertisement appeals to its target audience. Is it effective? Why or why not? Begin by identifying the ad, the idea it promotes, and the audience you think it hopes to reach. Then, state your thesis. After briefly describing the ad, give specific examples to support your thesis.

☑ SELF-ASSESSMENT CHECKLIST:
Writing an Exemplification Essay

- Does your introduction give readers a clear idea of what to expect? If not, revise your introduction to clarify your essay's goals.

- Does your essay include a clearly stated thesis? If not, revise your thesis statement to clarify your essay's main idea.

- Do all your examples support your thesis? Eliminate any irrelevant examples.

- Do you have enough examples to support your thesis? Add examples where necessary.

- Does each example clearly support your essay's thesis? If not, reword your topic sentences to clarify the connection between thesis and support.

- Do transitional words and phrases clearly link your examples to one another? Add transitions where necessary.

- Does your conclusion sum up the main idea of your essay? If not, revise the conclusion to make this idea clear to your readers.

- What problems did you experience in writing your essay? What would you do differently next time?

*For information on writing
a narrative paragraph, see
Chapter 4.*

B   Narration

Narration tells a story, usually presenting a series of events in chronological (time) order, moving from beginning to end. A **narrative essay** can tell a personal story, or it can recount a recent or historical event or a fictional story.

FOCUS   Topics for Narration

The wording of your assignment may suggest narration. For example, you may be asked to *tell, trace, summarize,* or *recount.*

Assignment	Thesis Statement
Composition Tell about a time when you had to show courage even though you were afraid.	In extraordinary circumstances, a person can exhibit great courage and overcome fear.
American history Summarize the events that occurred during President Franklin Delano Roosevelt's first one hundred days in office.	Although many thought they were extreme, the measures enacted by Roosevelt during his first one hundred days in office were necessary to fight the effects of the economic depression.
Political science Trace the development of the Mississippi Freedom Democratic Party.	As the Mississippi Freedom Democratic Party developed, it found a voice that spoke for equality and justice.

Teaching Tip
For examples of narrative
essays by professional
writers, see 36B.

Writing Tip
Many everyday writing tasks
call for narration. For example, in a job-application
letter, you might summarize
your previous work experience.

When you write a narrative essay, you can discuss one event or several in each paragraph of your essay.

FOCUS   Options for Organizing Narrative Essays

One Event per Paragraph	*Several Events per Paragraph*
¶1 Introduction	¶1 Introduction
¶2 First event	¶2 First group of events
¶3 Second event	¶3 Second group of events
¶4 Third event	¶4 Third group of events
¶5 Conclusion	¶5 Conclusion

Sometimes, to add interest to your narrative, you may decide not to use exact chronological order. For example, you might begin with the end of your story and then move back to the beginning to trace the events that led to this outcome. However you arrange the events, carefully worded topic sentences and clear transitional words and phrases will help readers follow your narrative.

FOCUS **Transitions for Narration**

After	Finally	Now
As	First . . . Second . . .	Soon
As soon as	Third	Then
At the same time	Immediately	Two hours (days,
Before	Later	months, years)
By this time	Later on	later
Earlier	Meanwhile	When
Eventually	Next	

The following student essay, "Reflections" by Elaina Corrato, is a narrative that relates the events of the day of her thirtieth birthday. Transitional words and phrases link events in chronological order and help keep readers on track.

Reflections

Turning thirty did not bother me at all. My list of "Things to Do before I Die" was far from complete, but I knew I had plenty of time to do them. In fact, turning thirty seemed like no big deal to me. If anything, it was a milestone I was happy to be approaching. However, other people had different ideas about this milestone, and eventually their ideas made me rethink my own.

As the big day approached, my family kept teasing me about it. My sister kept asking me if I felt any different. She couldn't believe I wasn't upset. At first, I didn't pay any attention to her. After all, aging is a natural part of life, and if we're lucky, we age gracefully. (My mother always told me a few wrinkles would give me character.) I was looking forward to a new chapter in my life. I liked my job, I was making good progress toward my college degree, and I was healthy and happy. Why should turning thirty be a problem?

I had made no special plans for my birthday, and I decided to treat it as just another day. I was sure my husband would get me a cake and a few presents, and that was fine with me. I have never been one for a lot of fuss. I was sure I wouldn't react the way my husband did when he turned thirty. I invited a few of his friends to help him celebrate, but he was miserable. He sulked most of the evening and didn't even want to cut his cake.

My birthday fell on a Saturday that year, and I enjoyed the chance to sleep in. After I got up and had

1

Word Power
milestone an important event; a turning point

2

3

4

breakfast, I did my laundry and then set out to the
supermarket. I rarely put on makeup or fixed my hair on
Saturdays. I never saw the need. After all, I didn't
have to go to work or to school. I was only running
errands in the neighborhood. That day was no different.

<u>Later on</u>, though, as I waited in line at the deli   5
counter, I caught sight of my reflection in the mirrored
meat case. <u>At first</u>, I thought it wasn't really me. The
woman staring back at me looked so old! She had bags
under her eyes, and she even had a few gray hairs. I
was so upset by my reflection that I stopped and bought
a mud mask—guaranteed to make me look younger—on my way
home.

<u>As</u> I walked up the street toward my house, I saw   6
something attached to the front railing. <u>When</u> I got
closer, I realized that it was a bunch of balloons, and
they were black balloons. There was also a big sign that
said "Over the Hill" in big black letters. I'd been
trying to think about my birthday in positive terms, but
my family seemed to have other ideas. Obviously, it was
time for the mud mask.

<u>After</u> quickly unloading my groceries, I ran upstairs   7
to apply the mask. The box promised a "rejuvenating
look," and that was exactly what I wanted. I spread
the sticky brown mixture on my face, and it hardened
instantly. <u>As</u> I sat on my bed, waiting for the mask to
work its magic, I heard the doorbell ring. <u>Then</u>, I heard
familiar voices and my husband calling me to come down,
saying that I had company. I couldn't answer him. I
couldn't talk (or even smile) without cracking the mask.
I was hoping he would think I was taking a nap and tell
whoever was at the door to leave, but instead he ran
upstairs to get me. And right behind him came my
visitors: my neighbor Lucy, her husband, my parents,
and my sister.

<u>By this time</u>, the mask had turned a sickly green   8
color, and I'd started to resemble some kind of monster.
To make matters worse, Lucy had brought me a birthday
present tied in black ribbon with an "Over the Hill"
banner on top. She had seen the birthday decorations
outside and thought a milestone birthday should get
proper recognition.

<u>When</u> I washed the mask off, my face was covered with   9
little red pimples. Apparently, my sensitive skin
couldn't take the harsh chemicals. <u>At first</u>, I didn't
think the promise of "rejuvenated" skin was what I got.
I had to admit, though, that my skin did look a lot
younger. In fact, <u>when</u> I <u>finally</u> went downstairs to
celebrate my birthday, I looked as young as a teenager—
a teenager with acne.

◆ PRACTICE 14-4

1. Underline the thesis statement of "Reflections." Restate it below in your own words.

   Although Elaina was happy to be turning thirty, the reactions of her

   friends and family made her change her mind about her birthday.

2. Underline the specific transitional words and phrases Elaina uses to link events in chronological order.

3. What specific events and situations support Elaina's thesis? List as many as you can.

   Answers will vary. Family members teased her about her approaching

   birthday. Her sister kept asking her if she felt different. Her family tied

   black balloons and an "Over the Hill" banner on her front railing. Her

   friend Lucy tied black ribbon on her birthday present.

4. Do you think paragraph 2 is necessary? How would Elaina's essay be different without it?

   Paragraph 2 is necessary because it shows readers Elaina's positive

   outlook on turning thirty, which is contrasted in her essay with the

   negative reactions of her friends and family members.

5. Do you think Elaina's conclusion should restate her thesis and summarize all the events her essay discusses, or is her conclusion effective? Explain your answer.

   Answers will vary.

GRAMMAR IN CONTEXT **Narration**

When you write a narrative essay, you tell a story. When you get caught up in your story, you might sometimes find yourself stringing a list of incidents together without proper punctuation, creating a **run-on** or a **comma splice**.

(continued on the following page)

Teaching Tip
Before your students write narrative essays, you might want to explain how to identify and correct run-ons and comma splices (Chapter 21) and have them do Practices 21-1 and 21-4.

> *(continued from the previous page)*
>
> INCORRECT (COMMA SPLICES) As the big day approached, my family kept teasing me about it, my sister kept asking me if I felt any different, she couldn't believe I wasn't upset.
>
> CORRECT As the big day approached, my family kept teasing me about it. My sister kept asking me if I felt any different. She couldn't believe I wasn't upset.
>
> For information on how to identify and correct run-ons and comma splices, see Chapter 21.

◆ PRACTICE 14-5

Following the writing process outlined in Chapter 12, write a narrative essay on one of the following topics.

The story of your education
Your idea of a perfect day
The plot summary of a terrible book or movie
A time when you had to make a split-second decision
Your first confrontation with authority
An important historical event
A day everything went wrong
A story from your family's history
Your employment history, from first to most recent job
A biography of your pet

◆ PRACTICE 14-6

The picture on the following page shows a bride and groom at a Las Vegas wedding chapel. Study the picture carefully, and then write a narrative essay that tells the story behind it.

Word Power

impulsive acting without thought or without considering the consequences of one's actions

unique one of a kind

✓ SELF-ASSESSMENT CHECKLIST:
Writing a Narrative Essay

☐ Does your introduction make the purpose of your narrative clear to readers? Does it set the scene and introduce important people and places? Develop your opening paragraph further if you need to.

☐ What is your essay's thesis? If necessary, revise your thesis statement to make your main idea clear.

(continued on the following page)

(continued from the previous page)

- Have you included all the specific events you need? Discuss additional incidents, if necessary.

- Are all the events you discuss clearly related to your thesis statement? Delete any irrelevant events.

- Are the events you discuss arranged in clear chronological order? Rearrange events if necessary to reflect the order in which they occurred.

- Do topic sentences and transitional words and phrases make the sequence of events clear? Revise if necessary to clarify this sequence.

- Does your conclusion remind readers why you have told them your story? If necessary, revise your conclusion to make your purpose clear.

- What problems did you experience in writing your essay? What would you do differently next time?

C   Description

For information on writing a descriptive paragraph, see Chapter 5.

Description tells what something looks, sounds, smells, tastes, or feels like. A **descriptive essay** uses details to give readers a clear, vivid picture of a person, place, object, or scene.

Teaching Tip
For examples of descriptive essays by professional writers, see 36C.

● **Writing Tip**
Many everyday writing tasks call for description. For example, in a statement to your insurance company after an automobile accident, you might describe the damage to your car.

FOCUS   Topics for Description

The wording of your assignment may suggest description. For example, it may ask you to *describe* or to *tell what an object looks like.*

Assignment	Thesis Statement
Composition Describe a room that was important to you when you were a child.	Pink-and-white striped wallpaper, tall shelves of cuddly stuffed animals, and the smell of Oreos dominated the bedroom I shared with my sister.
Scientific writing Describe a piece of scientific equipment.	The mass spectrometer is a complex instrument, but every part is ideally suited to its function.
Art history Choose one modern painting, and describe its visual elements.	The disturbing images crowded together in Pablo Picasso's *Guernica* suggest the brutality of war.

When you plan a descriptive essay, you focus on selecting details that help your readers see what you see, feel what you feel, and experience what you experience. Your goal is to create a single **dominant impression**, a central theme or idea to which all the details relate. This dominant impression unifies the description and gives readers an overall sense of what the person, place, object, or scene looks like (and perhaps what it sounds, smells, tastes, or feels like). Sometimes—but not always—your details will support a thesis, making a point about the subject you are describing.

You can arrange details in a descriptive essay in many different ways. For example, you can move from least to most important details, from top to bottom (or from bottom to top or side to side), or from far to near (or near to far). Each of your essay's body paragraphs may focus on one key characteristic of the subject you are describing or on several related descriptive details.

FOCUS Options for Organizing Descriptive Essays

Least to Most Important	Top to Bottom	Far to Near
¶1 Introduction	¶1 Introduction	¶1 Introduction
¶2 Least important details	¶2 Details at top	¶2 Distant details
¶3 More important details	¶3 Details in middle	¶3 Closer details
¶4 Most important details	¶4 Details on bottom	¶4 Closest details
¶5 Conclusion	¶5 Conclusion	¶5 Conclusion

When you describe a person, place, object, or scene, you can use **objective description**, reporting only what your senses of sight, sound, smell, taste, and touch tell you ("The columns were two feet tall and made of white marble"). You can also use **subjective description**, conveying your attitude or your feelings about what you observe ("The columns were tall and powerful looking, and their marble surface seemed as smooth as ice"). Many essays combine these two kinds of description.

FOCUS Figures of Speech

Descriptive writing, particularly subjective description, is frequently enriched by **figures of speech**—language that creates special or unusual effects.

■ A **simile** uses *like* or *as* to compare two unlike things.

Her smile was like sunshine.

■ A **metaphor** compares two unlike things without using *like* or *as*.

Her smile was a light that lit up the room.

■ **Personification** suggests a comparison between a nonliving thing and a person by giving the nonliving thing human traits.

The sun smiled down on the crowd.

As you write, use transitional words and expressions to guide readers through your description. (Many of these useful transitions are prepositions or other words and phrases that indicate location or distance.)

FOCUS Transitions for Description

Above	In front of	Outside
Behind	Inside	Over
Below	Nearby	The least
Between	Next to	important
Beyond	On	The most
In	On one side . . . On	important
In back of	the other side	Under

The following student essay, "African Violet" by Alisha Woolery, uses description to create a portrait of a family member. By combining subjective and objective description and using specific visual details, Alisha conveys a vivid impression of her great-grandmother as physically frail yet emotionally spirited.

African Violet

The black-and-white picture of my great-grandparents is a picture I often bring into my mind when I have decided to look at the "big picture" of life and think all the "deep thoughts." I see their faces etched into the contrasting grays, so young, so hopeful for their new lives together. My mind then shifts to a more recent picture of my great-grandma's small, frail body, which in the end gave her more pain than she could handle. At this point, I realize how much she taught me about life and death—and about everything in between.

My great-grandfather died when I was quite young, and I have only a faint memory of riding his foot like a horse while he recited "Banbury Cross." I have to create an image of him from my relatives' memories. Fortunately, however, I knew my great-grandma well, and the conversations we had are among my favorite memories of her. Often, I picture her sitting with me in her parlor, telling me one of the numerous stories of her youth.

"One time I was getting to be about sixteen years old, and there was this boy who asked me on a picnic." Her eyes brightened as she told her story. "He was older than me, and he had a horse and buggy! And whoowee! That was really something."

The look of astonishment on my face must have

1

2

3

4

been apparent because we laughed until I thought we would keel over. There she was, ninety years old, with absolutely no teeth, telling me how hot this boy who had asked her out was. It was then I realized that the eyes looking out from her aging face were the same brown eyes that had flirted with boys, had fallen in love, and had seen her children and her children's children's children. She had years of experience, and I had very little, but on that warm summer evening, as we sat in her living room, her story bridged the gap between generations.

When I don't picture my great-grandma telling stories, I see her on her sunporch, engaged in her one true passion: caring for her plants. She loved them all, but her favorites were small plants with dark green leaves and purple blossoms, African violets. I didn't inherit her green thumb, so the miracles she worked with plants were a constant wonder to me. Stems and leaves seemed to thrive under her gentle touch. Her plants were her pride and joy, and until she was in her mid-eighties I often saw her, on hands and knees, digging around in the dirt in her front yard.

No, my great-grandma didn't resign herself to age and let life pass her by; she rode it for all it was worth. In fact, when I picture her, I often see her outside, behind the wheel of her car. The woman was a traffic hazard, not because she poked along as so many older folks do but because she was a speed demon! Poised for action, my great-grandma strapped herself into her brown 1972 Nova and sped out toward destinations unknown, with one foot on the gas and the other on the brake. I suppose, by all laws of nature, her driving escapades should have done her in, but my great-grandma died a peaceful death with quiet resolution and acceptance. In fact, she probably had a better outlook on the whole thing than anyone else in the family. I was only fifteen, and she was the closest person to me to die, so it was especially difficult for me to accept that our talks were over.

It wasn't until recently that I realized that even by her dying, my great-grandma was continuing to teach me about life. Now, when I picture her, I see not just her lively stories, caring hands, and daredevil spirit, but also her courage: I see how bravely she dealt with increasing pain as her body deteriorated.

The memories of my great-grandma are very important to me, and sometimes it scares me when a detail escapes my mind because remembering our time together and what I have learned from her is all I have left of her. It is virtually impossible to communicate the impact she has

had on me. The only way I feel I can repay her is by
someday telling her stories to my own grandchildren and
great-grandchildren, keeping her memory alive.

◆ PRACTICE 14-7

1. What dominant impression of her great-grandmother does Alisha convey to readers?

   Wise, high-spirited, strong, funny, and brave

   _____

2. List the specific visual details Alisha uses to convey her essay's dominant impression. What other details could she have included?

   Answers will vary. They might include her great-grandmother talking about

   a boy who asked her to go on a picnic, digging in the dirt in her front yard,

   and speeding in her brown 1972 Nova.

3. What determines the order in which details are presented in this essay? How else might Alisha have arranged details?

   The settings for Alisha's memories of her great-grandmother determine

   the order. She moves from indoors (the parlor) to the sunporch to the

   open road.

4. Is this essay primarily a subjective or an objective description?

   subjective

5. What is this essay's greatest strength? What is its greatest weakness?

   Strength: _____*Answers will vary.*_____

   Weakness: _____*Answers will vary.*_____

Teaching Tip
Before your students write
descriptive essays, you might
want to explain how to identify modifiers (25A–B) and
have them do Practices 25-1
and 25-2.

> **GRAMMAR IN CONTEXT** **Description**
>
> When you write a descriptive essay, you may use **modifiers** to describe your subject. If you place modifying words or phrases incorrectly, you create a misplaced modifier that may confuse your readers.
>
> ┌──────── MODIFIER ────────→
> CONFUSING   Often, <u>sitting with me in her parlor,</u> I picture her telling me one of the numerous stories of her youth. (Is the writer sitting with herself?)
>
> *(continued on the following page)*

(continued from the previous page)

CLEAR   Often, I picture her <u>sitting with me in her parlor</u> telling me one of the numerous stories of her youth.

————— MODIFIER —————

For information on how to identify and correct misplaced modifiers, see 25D.

◆ **PRACTICE 14-8**

Following the writing process outlined in Chapter 12, write a descriptive essay on one of the following topics.

An abandoned building

A person or character who makes you laugh (or frightens you)

Your room (or your closet or desk)

A family photograph

A historical site or monument

An advertisement

An object you cherish

Someone whom everyone notices

Someone whom no one notices

The home page of a Web site you visit often

◆ **PRACTICE 14-9**

The picture below shows a house surrounded by lush landscaping. Write a real-estate brochure for the house, using your imagination to invent details that describe its setting, exterior, and interior. Your goal in this descriptive essay is to enumerate the kind of positive details that might persuade a prospective buyer to purchase the house.

> **Word Power**
>
> **mansion**   a large, stately house
>
> **lush**   characterized by luxuriant growth

✔ SELF-ASSESSMENT CHECKLIST:
Writing a Descriptive Essay

☐ Does your introduction identify the subject of your description and convey your essay's dominant impression? Revise your introduction if necessary to clarify your essay's focus.

☐ Do you describe every significant aspect of your subject in detail? If necessary, add specific visual details to create a more complete, more vivid picture.

☐ Do all the details in your essay support your dominant impression? Eliminate any irrelevant details.

☐ Are your details arranged in a definite order within your essay and within paragraphs? Would another order be more effective? Rearrange the details if necessary.

☐ Do topic sentences and transitional words and phrases move readers smoothly from one part of your subject to another? Reword topic sentences, and add transitions where necessary.

☐ Does your conclusion leave readers with a clear sense of your essay's purpose? Revise if necessary to reinforce the dominant impression you want your description to convey.

☐ What problems did you experience in writing your essay? What would you do differently next time?

D Process

For information on writing a process paragraph, see Chapter 6.

A **process** is a series of chronological steps that produces a particular result. **Process essays** explain the steps in a procedure, telling how something is (or was) done. A process essay can be organized as either a *process explanation* or a set of *instructions*.

Teaching Tip
For examples of process essays by professional writers, see 36D.

● Writing Tip
Many everyday writing tasks describe a process. For example, in a training manual for new employees at your place of work, you might explain how to operate a piece of equipment or what to do in an emergency.

FOCUS Topics for Process

The wording of your assignment may suggest process. For example, you may be asked to *explain a process, give instructions, give directions,* or *give a step-by-step account.*

Assignment	Thesis Statement
American government Explain the process by which a bill becomes a law.	The process by which a bill becomes a law is long and complex, involving numerous revisions and a great deal of compromise.

(continued on the following page)

(continued from the previous page)

Assignment	Thesis Statement
Pharmacy practice Summarize the procedure for conducting a clinical trial of a new drug.	To ensure that drugs are safe and effective, scientists follow strict procedural guidelines for testing and evaluating them.
Technical writing Write a set of instructions for applying for a student internship in a state agency.	If you want to apply for a government internship, you need to follow several important steps.

If your purpose is simply to help readers understand a process, not actually perform it, you will write a process explanation. **Process explanations**, like the first two examples in the Focus box above, often use present tense verbs ("Once a bill *is* introduced in Congress" or "A scientist first *submits* a funding application") to explain how a procedure is generally carried out. However, when a process explanation describes a specific procedure that was completed in the past, it uses past tense verbs ("The next thing I *did*").

If your purpose is to enable readers to actually perform the steps in a process, you will write instructions. **Instructions**, like the last example in the Focus box above, always use present tense verbs in the form of commands to tell readers what to do ("First, *meet* with your adviser").

Whether your essay is a process explanation or a set of instructions, you can either devote a full paragraph to each step of the process or group a series of minor steps together in a single paragraph.

FOCUS **Options for Organizing Process Essays**

One Step per Paragraph	*Several Steps per Paragraph*
¶1 Introduction	¶1 Introduction
¶2 First step in process	¶2 First group of steps
¶3 Second step in process	¶3 Second group of steps
¶4 Third step in process	¶4 Third group of steps
¶5 Conclusion	¶5 Conclusion

● **Writing Tip**

Instructions also usually include a list of necessary materials or equipment as well as cautions and reminders that readers might need to know when performing the process.

As you write your process essay, discuss each step in the order in which it is performed, making sure your topic sentences clearly identify the function of each step or group of steps.

Transitions are extremely important in process essays because they enable readers to follow the sequence of steps in the process and, in the case of instructions, to perform the process themselves.

FOCUS **Transitions for Process**

After that	Later	The first (second,
As	Meanwhile	third) step
As soon as	Next	The last step
At the same time	Now	Then
Finally	Once	The next step
First	Soon	When
Immediately	Subsequently	While

The following student essay, Jen Rossi's "For Fun and Profit," explains the process of selling at a flea market. Because Jen thought most readers would be unlikely to share her interest in her hobby, she did not write her essay in the form of instructions. Instead, she wrote a process explanation, using past tense verbs. Notice how clear transitions move readers smoothly through the steps of the process.

For Fun and Profit

My first experience as a seller at a flea market was   1
both fun and profitable. In fact, it led to a hobby
that is also a continuing source of extra money. That
first time took a lot of work, but the routine I
established has made each flea market easier.

When my church advertised the event in its bulletin,   2
I thought immediately of all the junk cluttering up my
basement. At that time, my brother and I were living
in what had been our parents' house, and the basement
was full of things we had no use for—old toys and
games, sports equipment for sports no one in my family
had played in years, cassette tapes (and even record
albums), and boxes and boxes of old maps and magazines.
We didn't want these things, but it was just possible
that someone else might. Selling them at a flea market
seemed like a great idea.

The first thing I did, after getting my brother to   3
promise to help, was to call the church and reserve a
spot at the flea market. Then, we got to work.

The first and hardest job was sorting through all   4
the items. In addition to the things we expected to
find, we found everything from old Halloween costumes
to our grade school report cards to letters my parents
had written to each other when my father was in Vietnam.
We made three piles—keep, sell, and trash—and one by
one, we placed every item in a pile. (Before we decided
to sell or throw out an item, we checked with our

parents, just to make sure we weren't accidentally getting rid of one of their prized possessions.)

Next came pricing the items for sale. It was hard to accept the fact that we might need to set a low price on something that had sentimental value for us (my brother's first bike, for example). It was just as hard to set a high price on the hideous lamp or old record album that might turn out to be someone's treasure. That first time, we returned with a lot of unsold items, and we later realized we had sold others too cheaply.

The next step was (and still is) my least favorite: packing up items to be sold. As we packed, we tried to figure out how we would transport each item to the flea market. The old record albums were the worst. They were heavy and, it turned out, hard to sell (even at only a dollar each). We arranged to borrow a van for the bulky items (baby equipment, boxes of dishes, and so on) from one of my brother's friends. The small items (knickknacks, silk flower arrangements, a bag of mismatched teaspoons) could be transported in my brother's car.

The day before the event, we borrowed three card tables from friends of our parents. We also went to the bank and got lots of dollar bills and quarters, and we collected piles of newspaper and plastic supermarket bags. Now, our planning was complete.

On the day of the flea market, we got up early and loaded our two vehicles. When we arrived at the church parking lot where the event was to be held, we were surprised to find teenagers waiting to help us unload— for a price. Since we didn't need their help, we went directly to our reserved spot. As my brother unloaded the cars, I set things up, placing small items (like dishes and videotapes) on the card tables and large items (such as a high chair and a lawn mower) around and below the tables.

Then, the actual selling began. Even before I could set up our tables, people started picking through our things, offering us cash for picture frames, pots and pans, and toys. As the day went on, we developed a kind of system: I persuaded buyers that that old meat grinder or china figurine was just what they'd been looking for, and my brother negotiated with prospective buyers— haggling with some and holding firm to our set price with others. Then, while he wrapped small items in the newspapers or bags we had brought (and carried large items to people's cars), I took the money and made change.

At the end of the day, we had made over two hundred

dollars, and I was hooked on flea markets. We loaded all
the unsold items into the car and van and brought them
home. We were too tired to carry everything back down
into the basement, so we left it all in the garage,
where it would be easy to load up again for our next
flea market.

◆ PRACTICE 14-10

1. List the major steps in the process of selling at a flea market. Does Jen present them in strict chronological order?

Before the flea market: reserving a spot, sorting through items, pricing

items, packing items

At the flea market: unloading, setting up, selling, wrapping items

Yes, the steps are presented in strict chronological order.

2. What identifies Jen's essay as a process explanation rather than a set of instructions?

Verbs are not commands.

3. Underline some of the transitional words and phrases that link the steps in the process. Are any other transitions needed?

Answers will vary.

4. Underline Jen's thesis statement. Restate it below in your own words.

Having a routine makes the process of selling at a flea market easier.

5. Why does Jen devote the second paragraph of her essay to describing the contents of her basement? What purpose does this paragraph serve in her essay?

Answers will vary. The paragraph shows why Jen decides to try selling

at a flea market.

6. What is the essay's greatest strength? What is its greatest weakness?

Strength: _____*Answers will vary.*_____

Weakness: _____*Answers will vary.*_____

GRAMMAR IN CONTEXT   **Process**

When you write a process essay, you may have problems keeping tense, person, number, and voice consistent throughout. If you shift from one tense, person, number, or voice to another without good reason, you will confuse your readers.

CONFUSING   We made three piles—keep, sell, and trash—and one by one, every item is placed in a pile. (shift from active to passive voice and past to present tense)

CLEAR   We made three piles—keep, sell, and trash—and one by one, we placed every item in a pile. (consistent voice and tense)

For information on how to avoid illogical shifts in tense, person, number, and voice, see Chapter 24.

Teaching Tip
Before your students write process essays, you might want to explain how to avoid illogical shifts (Chapter 24) and have them do Practices 24-1 through 24-4.

◆ PRACTICE 14-11

Following the writing process outlined in Chapter 12, write a process essay on one of the following topics. (Note: Before you begin, decide whether a process explanation or a set of instructions will be more appropriate for your purpose.)

An unusual recipe
College registration
Finding an apartment
Applying for a job
Getting dressed for a typical Saturday night
A religious ritual or cultural ceremony
A task you often do at work
A do-it-yourself project that didn't get done
Your own writing process
A self-improvement program (past, present, or future)
How to find something on the Internet

◆ PRACTICE 14-12

The picture on the following page shows John Belushi as John "Bluto" Blutarsky in the infamous toga party scene from the 1978 film *Animal House.* Study the picture carefully, and then list the steps involved in planning the

Word Power

priorities   most important tasks

optimum   the most favorable condition for a particular situation

perfect party. Use this list to help you write a process essay that gives step-by-step instructions in the order in which they need to be done. (Hint: You can devote separate paragraphs to tasks to be done the week before, the day before, the morning of the party, and so on.) Be sure to include cautions and reminders to help your readers avoid potential problems.

☑ SELF-ASSESSMENT CHECKLIST:
Writing a Process Essay

- Does your introduction identify the process you will discuss and indicate its purpose? Revise your introduction if necessary to clarify your purpose.

- Is your essay a process explanation or a set of instructions? If your strategy is not appropriate for your essay's purpose, rewrite the essay using a different strategy.

- Does your thesis statement present an overview of the process? If not, revise the statement to make it as clear and specific as you can.

- Do you include every important step in the process? If not, add any steps readers may need to understand (or perform) the process.

- Are all the steps you present necessary? Delete any irrelevant or unimportant ones.

- Are the steps in the process presented in strict chronological order? Rearrange any that are out of order.

(continued on the following page)

(continued from the previous page)

- Are related steps grouped in individual paragraphs? If not, revise to make each paragraph unified.

- Do topic sentences clearly identify major stages in the process? Do they clarify the function of each step or group of steps? Revise topic sentences as necessary.

- Do transitional words and phrases clarify the relationship between steps? If necessary, add transitions to make connections clear.

- Have you included all necessary warnings or reminders? Add cautions or clarifications as needed.

- Does your conclusion effectively sum up your process? Revise as necessary to clarify your purpose.

- What problems did you experience in writing your essay? What would you do differently next time?

E Cause and Effect

A **cause** makes something happen; an **effect** is a result of a particular cause or event. **Cause-and-effect essays** identify causes or predict effects; sometimes they do both.

For information on writing a cause-and-effect paragraph, see Chapter 7.

FOCUS Topics for Cause and Effect

The wording of your assignment may suggest cause and effect. For example, the assignment may ask you to *explain why, predict the outcome, list contributing factors, discuss the consequences,* or tell what *caused* something else or how something is *affected* by something else.

Assignment	Thesis Statement
Women's studies What factors contributed to the rise of the women's movement in the 1970s?	The women's movement of the 1970s had its origins in the peace and civil rights movements of the 1960s.
Public health Discuss the possible long-term effects of smoking.	In addition to its well-known negative effects on smokers themselves, smoking also causes significant problems for those exposed to secondhand smoke.

(continued on the following page)

● **Writing Tip**

Many everyday writing tasks involve discussing causes and effects. For example, in a letter to your community's zoning board, you might discuss possible consequences of building a road, mall, or multiplex theater.

Teaching Tip

For examples of cause-and-effect essays by professional writers, see 36E.

(continued from the previous page)

Assignment	Thesis Statement
Media and society How has the Internet affected the lives of those who have grown up with it?	The Internet has created a generation of people who learn differently from those in previous generations.

A cause-and-effect essay can focus on causes or on effects. When you write about causes, be sure to examine *all* relevant causes. You should emphasize the cause you consider the most important, but do not forget to consider other causes that may be relevant to your topic. Similarly, when you write about effects, consider *all* significant effects of a particular cause, not just the first few that you think of.

If your focus is on finding causes, as it is in the first assignment in the Focus box on the previous page, your introductory paragraph should identify the effect (the women's movement). If your focus is on predicting effects, as it is in the second and third assignments listed there, you should begin by identifying the cause (smoking, the Internet). In the body of your essay, you can devote a full paragraph to each cause (or effect), or you can group several related causes (or effects) together in each paragraph.

FOCUS **Options for Organizing Cause-and-Effect Essays**

Identifying Causes
¶1 Introduction (identifies effect)
¶2 First cause
¶3 Second cause
¶4 Third (and most important) cause
¶5 Conclusion

Predicting Effects
¶1 Introduction (identifies cause)
¶2 First effect
¶3 Second effect
¶4 Third (and most important) effect
¶5 Conclusion

● **Writing Tip**

Be careful not to confuse *affect* (usually a verb) and *effect* (usually a noun) in your cause-and-effect essays. (See 34E.)

Transitions are important in cause-and-effect essays because they establish causal connections, telling readers that A caused B and not the other way around. They also make it clear that events have a *causal* relationship (A *caused* B) and not just a *sequential* one (A *preceded* B). Remember, when one event follows another, the second is not necessarily the result of the first.

FOCUS Transitions for Cause and Effect

Accordingly	For this reason	The most impor-
Another cause	Since	tant cause
Another effect	So	The most impor-
As a result	The first (second,	tant effect
Because	third) cause	Therefore
Consequently	The first (second,	
For	third) effect	

The following student essay, "How My Parents' Separation Changed My Life" by Andrea DeMarco, examines the effects of a significant event on the writer and her family. Andrea begins by identifying the cause—the separation—and then goes on to explain its specific effects on her family and on herself. Notice how transitional words and phrases make Andrea's causal connections clear to her readers.

How My Parents' Separation Changed My Life

Until I was eight, I lived the perfect all-American life with my perfect all-American family. I lived in a suburb of Albany, New York, with my parents, my sister and brother, and our dog, Daisy. We had a ping-pong table in the basement, a barbecue in the backyard, and two cars in the garage. My dad and mom were high school teachers, and every summer we took a family vacation. Then, it all changed. My parents' separation made everything different.

One day, just before Halloween, when my sister was twelve and my brother was fourteen (Daisy was seven), our parents called us into the kitchen for a family conference. We didn't think anything was wrong at first; they were always calling these annoying meetings. We figured it was time for us to plan a vacation, talk about household chores, or be nagged to clean our rooms. As soon as we sat down, though, we knew this was different. We could tell Mom had been crying, and Dad's voice cracked when he told us the news. They were separating—they called it a "trial separation"—and Dad was moving out of our house.

I hardly remember what else we talked about that day. But I do remember how things changed right after that. Every Halloween we always had a big jack-o'-lantern on our front porch. Dad used to spend hours at the kitchen table cutting out the eyes, nose, and mouth

1

2

3

and hollowing out the insides. That Halloween, <u>because</u> he didn't live with us, things were different. Mom bought a pumpkin, and I guess she was planning to carve it up. But she never did, and we never mentioned it. It sat on the kitchen counter for a couple of weeks, getting soft and wrinkled, and then it just disappeared. I suppose Mom threw it out.

Other holidays were also different <u>because</u> Mom and   4
Dad were not living together. Our first Thanksgiving without Dad was pathetic. I don't even want to talk about it. Christmas was different, too. We spent Christmas Eve with Dad and our relatives on his side, and Christmas Day with Mom and her family. Of course, we got twice as many presents as usual. I realize now that both our parents were trying to make up for the pain of the separation. The worst part came when I opened my big present from Mom: Barbie's Dream House. This was something I had always wanted. Even at eight, I knew how hard it must have been for Mom to afford it. The trouble was, I had gotten the same thing from Dad the night before.

The separation affected each of us in different ways.   5
The worst <u>effect</u> of my parents' separation on all three of us was not the big events but the disruption in our everyday lives. Dinner used to be a family time, a chance to talk about our day and make plans. But after Dad left, Mom seemed to stop eating. Sometimes she would just have coffee while we ate, and sometimes she would not eat at all. She would microwave some frozen thing for us or heat up soup or cook some hot dogs. We didn't care—after all, now she let us watch TV while we ate— but we did notice.

Other parts of our routine changed, too. <u>Because</u>   6
Dad didn't live with us anymore, we had to spend every Saturday and every Wednesday night at his apartment, no matter what else we had planned. Usually, he would take us to dinner at McDonald's on Wednesdays, and then we would go back to his place and do our homework or watch TV. That wasn't too bad. Saturdays were a lot worse. We really wanted to be home, hanging out with our friends in our own rooms in our own house. Instead, we had to do some planned activity with Dad, like go to a movie or a hockey game.

My parents were separated for only eight months, but   7
it seemed like forever. By the end of the school year, they had somehow worked things out, and Dad was back home again. That June, at a family conference around the kitchen table, we made our summer vacation plans. We decided on Williamsburg, Virginia, the all-American

vacation destination. So things were back to normal, but
I wasn't, and I'm still not. Now, ten years later, my
mother and father are all right, but I still worry
they'll split up again. And I worry about my own future
husband and how I will ever be sure he's the one I'll
stay married to. <u>As a result</u> of what happened in my own
family, it is hard for me to believe any relationship is
forever.

◆ PRACTICE 14-13

1. Underline Andrea's thesis statement. Restate it below in your own
   words.

   Everything changed for Andrea after her parents separated.

   _____

   _____

   _____

2. What specific effects of her parents' separation does Andrea identify?

   changes in holiday celebrations

   changes in dinner routine

   visits to father

   _____

3. Underline the transitional words and phrases that make the causal
   connections in Andrea's essay clear to her readers.

4. Is Andrea's relatively long concluding paragraph effective? Why or
   why not? Do you think it should be shortened or divided into two
   paragraphs?

   Answers will vary.

   _____

   _____

   _____

   _____

5. Is Andrea's straightforward title effective, or should she have used a
   more creative or eye-catching title? Can you suggest an alternative?

   Answers will vary.

   _____

   _____

   _____

6. What is this essay's greatest strength? What is its greatest weakness?

Strength: _____*Answers will vary.*_____

Weakness: _____*Answers will vary.*_____

Teaching Tip
Before your students write
cause-and-effect essays, you
might want to review the use
of *affect* and *effect*, pointing
them to the examples in 34E
and the relevant items in
Practice 34-6.

GRAMMAR IN CONTEXT   **Cause and Effect**

When you write a cause-and-effect essay, you may have trouble remembering the difference between *affect* and *effect*.

> The worst ~~affect~~ *effect* of my parents' separation on all three of us was not the big events but the disruption in our everyday lives. (*effect* is a noun)

> The separation ~~effected~~ *affected* each of us in different ways. (*affect* is a verb)

For information on *affect* and *effect*, see the Grammar in Context box in 7A.

◆ PRACTICE 14-14

Following the writing process outlined in Chapter 12, write a cause-and-effect essay on one of the following topics.

A teacher's positive (or negative) effect on you
Why you voted a certain way in a recent election (or why you did not vote)
Why the popularity of soap operas has been steadily declining
How your life would be different if you dropped out of school (or quit your job)
How a particular invention (for example, the cell phone) has changed your life
Why text messaging is so popular
A movie or book that changed the way you look at life
How a particular season (or day of the week) affects your mood
How having a child would change (or has changed) your life
How a particular event made you grow up

Word Power

annuity   the annual payment of an allowance or income

windfall   a sudden, unexpected piece of good luck

◆ PRACTICE 14-15

The picture on the following page shows a happy couple, recent lottery winners, with a sign announcing their prize. Imagine you have won a multi-million-dollar lottery. How would your life change? Write a cause-and-effect essay that discusses specific ways in which your life would be different.

☑ SELF-ASSESSMENT CHECKLIST:
Writing a Cause-and-Effect Essay

- Does your introduction identify the particular cause or effect on which your essay will focus? Revise your introduction if necessary to zero in on your topic.

- Does your essay focus on causes or effects? Does your thesis statement accurately convey this emphasis to readers? If not, revise your thesis statement to identify the key causes or effects that you will emphasize.

- Do you identify all causes or effects relevant to your topic? If not, revise to include all significant causes or effects.

- Do you discuss any irrelevant causes or effects? If necessary, revise to eliminate them.

- Which cause or effect is most important? Arrange causes or effects to indicate their relative importance.

- Does each body paragraph identify and explain one particular cause or effect (or several closely related causes or effects)? Revise where necessary to unify each body paragraph.

- Do your transitional words and phrases make causal connections clear? If not, revise to clarify the relationships between causes and effects.

- Does your conclusion reinforce the causal relationships you discuss? Revise to make your emphasis clearer.

(continued on the following page)

(continued from the previous page)

☐ What problems did you experience in writing your essay? What would you do differently next time?

F   Comparison and Contrast

For information on writing a comparison-and-contrast paragraph, see Chapter 8.

Comparison identifies similarities; **contrast** identifies differences. **Comparison-and-contrast essays** explain how two things are alike or how they are different; sometimes, they discuss both similarities and differences.

FOCUS   Topics for Comparison and Contrast

The wording of your assignment may suggest comparison and contrast—for example, by asking you to *compare, contrast, discuss similarities,* or *identify differences.*

Assignment	Thesis Statement
Philosophy What basic similarities do you find in the beliefs of Henry David Thoreau and Martin Luther King Jr.?	Although King was more politically active, both he and Thoreau strongly supported the idea of civil disobedience.
Nutrition How do the diets of native Japanese and Japanese Americans differ?	As they become more and more assimilated, Japanese Americans consume more fats than their native Japanese counterparts do.
Literature Contrast the two sisters in Alice Walker's short story "Everyday Use."	Unlike Maggie, Dee—her more successful, better-educated sister—has rejected her family's heritage.

> **● Writing Tip**
> Many everyday writing tasks call for comparison and contrast. For example, in a report to your supervisor at work, you might compare the merits of two procedures or two suppliers.

> **Teaching Tip**
> For examples of comparison-and-contrast essays by professional writers, see 36F.

> **● Writing Tip**
> In a comparison, your points must match up. If you discuss the appearance and behavior of one breed of dog, you also need to discuss the same two points for the other breed you are writing about.

When you organize a comparison-and-contrast essay, you can choose either a *point-by-point* or a *subject-by-subject* arrangement. A **point-by-point** comparison alternates between the two subjects you are comparing or contrasting, moving back and forth from one subject to the other. A **subject-by-subject** comparison treats its two subjects separately, first fully discussing one subject and then moving on to consider the other subject. In both kinds of comparison-and-contrast essays, the same points are discussed in the same order for both subjects.

FOCUS **Options for Organizing
Comparison-and-Contrast Essays**

*Point-by-Point
Comparison*

¶1 Introduction (identifies
subjects to be compared
or contrasted)

¶2 First point discussed for
both subjects

¶3 Second point discussed
for both subjects

¶4 Third point discussed
for both subjects

¶5 Conclusion

*Subject-by-Subject
Comparison*

¶1 Introduction (identifies
subjects to be compared
or contrasted)

¶¶2–3 First subject discussed

¶¶4–5 Second subject dis-
cussed

¶6 Conclusion

The transitional words and phrases you use in a comparison-and-
contrast essay tell readers whether you are focusing on similarities or on
differences. Transitions also help move readers through your essay from
one subject to the other and from one point of similarity or difference to the
next.

FOCUS **Transitions for Comparison and Contrast**

Although	Likewise
But	Nevertheless
Even though	On the contrary
However	On the one hand . . . On the other hand
In comparison	Similarly
In contrast	Unlike
Like	Whereas

The following student essay, "Another Ordinary Day" by Nisha Jani,
contrasts teenage boys and girls by going through a typical day in the
lives of "Johnny" and "Jane." A point-by-point comparison, Nisha's essay
alternates between her two subjects, treating the same points in the same
order for each. Notice that topic sentences identify the part of the day
under discussion in each paragraph and clearly signal shifts from one subject to the next.

Another Ordinary Day

"Boys are from Jupiter and get stupider/Girls are   1
from Mars and become movie stars/Boys take a bath and
smell like trash/Girls take a shower and smell like
a flower." As simple playground songs like this one

suggest, the two sexes see themselves very differently. As adults, men and women have similar goals, values, and occupations, but as children and teenagers, boys and girls often seem to belong to two different species. In fact, from the first moment of the day to the last, the typical boy and girl live very different lives.

The sun rises, and the alarm clock signals the beginning of another day for Johnny and Jane, two seventh-grade classmates. Johnny, an average thirteen-year-old boy, wakes up late and has to hurry. He throws on his favorite jeans, a baggy T-shirt, and a baseball cap. Then, he goes into the kitchen, has a hearty high-cholesterol breakfast, and runs out of the house to school, usually forgetting some vital book or homework assignment. Jane, unlike Johnny, wakes up early and takes her time. She takes a long shower and then blow-dries her hair. Then, there is the moment of truth: What should she wear today? Getting dressed can be a very difficult process, one that often includes taking everything out of her closet and calling friends for advice. After she makes her decision, she helps herself to some food (probably low- or no-fat) and goes off to school, making sure she has with her everything she needs.

School is a totally different experience for Johnny and Jane. Johnny will probably sit in the back of the classroom with a couple of guys, throwing paper airplanes and spitballs. These will be directed at the males they do not like and the females they think are kind of cute. (However, if their male friends ever ask the boys about these girls, they will say girls are just losers and deny that they like any of them.) On the opposite side of the classroom, however, Jane is focused on a very different kind of activity. At first it looks as if she is carefully copying the algebra notes that the teacher is putting on the board, but her notes have absolutely nothing to do with algebra. In actuality, she is writing about boys, clothes, and other topics that are much more important to her than the square root of one hundred twenty-one. She proceeds to fold the note into a box or other creative form, which can often put origami to shame. As soon as the teacher turns her back, the note is passed and the process begins all over again.

Lunch, a vital part of the school day, is also very different for Johnny and Jane. On the one hand, for Johnny and his friends, it is a time to compare baseball cards, exchange sports facts, and of course tell jokes about every bodily function imaginable. In front of them

2

3

4

Word Power

origami the Japanese art of folding paper into shapes representing birds or animals

on the table, their trays are filled with pizza, soda, fries, and chips, and this food is their main focus. For Jane, on the other hand, lunch is not about eating; it is a chance to exchange the latest gossip about who is going out with whom. The girls look around to see what people are wearing, what they should do with their hair, and so on. Jane's meal is quite a bit smaller than Johnny's: it consists of a small low-fat yogurt and half a bagel (if she feels like splurging, she will spread some cream cheese on the bagel).

After school, Johnny and Jane head in different   5
directions. Johnny rushes home to get his bike and meets up with his friends to run around and play typical "guy games," like pick-up basketball or touch football. Johnny and his friends play with every boy who shows up, whether they know them or not. They may get into physical fights and arguments; however, in the end it is all a game, and they plan to meet up again the next day. In contrast to the boys, Jane and her friends are very selective. Their circle is a small one, and they do everything together. Some days, they go to the mall (they will not necessarily buy anything there, but they will consider the outing productive anyway because they will have spent time together). Most days, though, they just talk, with the discussion ranging from school to guys to lipstick colors. When Jane gets home, she will most likely run to the phone and talk for hours to the same three or four girls.

At the age of twelve or thirteen, boys and girls   6
do not seem to have very much in common. Given this situation, it is amazing that boys and girls grow up to become men and women who coexist and interact as neighbors, friends, and coworkers. What is even more amazing is that so many grow up to share lives and raise families together, treating each other with love and respect.

◆ PRACTICE 14-16

1. Underline Nisha's thesis statement. Restate it below in your own words.

   Boys and girls are very different in their daily routines.

   _____

2. Does Nisha's opening paragraph identify the subjects she will discuss? Will she focus on similarities or on differences?

   Yes. She indicates that she will focus on differences.

   _____

3. Nisha's essay is a point-by-point comparison. What four points does she discuss for each of her two subjects?

difference in morning routine, school behavior, lunch routine, and after-

school activities

4. Underline some transitional words and phrases Nisha uses to move readers from one subject (Johnny) to the other (Jane).

5. Reread Nisha's topic sentences. What do they contribute to the essay?

The topic sentences remind readers that the essay's focus is on con-

trasting Johnny and Jane. They also tell readers which part of the day

will be discussed.

6. What is this essay's greatest strength? What is its greatest weakness?

Strength: _____*Answers will vary.*_____

Weakness: _____*Answers will vary.*_____

Teaching Tip
Before your students write comparison-and-contrast essays, you might want to explain the concept of parallelism (Chapter 19) and have them do Practices 19-1 and 19-2.

GRAMMAR IN CONTEXT **Comparison and Contrast**

When you write a comparison-and-contrast essay, you need to present the points you are comparing or contrasting in **parallel** terms to highlight their similarities or differences.

┌── PARALLEL ──┐
Johnny, an average thirteen-year-old boy, <u>wakes up late</u> and <u>has to hurry</u>.

┌── PARALLEL ──┐
Jane, unlike Johnny, <u>wakes up early</u> and <u>takes her time</u>.

For information on revising to make ideas parallel, see Chapter 19.

◆ **PRACTICE 14-17**

Following the writing process outlined in Chapter 12, write a comparison-and-contrast essay on one of the following topics.

Two coworkers
Two movie heroes
How you expect your life to be different from the lives of your parents
Men's and women's ideas about their body images
Two ways of studying for an exam
Risk-takers and people who play it safe

Library research and Internet research
Country and city living (or you can compare suburban living with either)
Two popular magazines (features, ads, target audiences, pictures)
Two professional athletes

◆ PRACTICE 14-18

The pictures below show two famous war memorials. Study the two photographs carefully, and then write an essay in which you compare them, considering both what the monuments look like and their emotional impact on you.

Iwo Jima memorial statue at Arlington National Cemetery

Vietnam Veterans Memorial in Washington, D.C.

☑ SELF-ASSESSMENT CHECKLIST:
Writing a Comparison-and-Contrast Essay

- Does your introduction identify the two subjects you will compare and contrast? If not, revise to make the focus of your essay clear.

- Does your essay examine similarities or differences? If necessary, revise your thesis statement to make your emphasis clear.

- Have you discussed all significant points of comparison or contrast that apply to your two subjects? Develop your discussion further if necessary.

- Are any points insignificant or irrelevant? If necessary, revise to eliminate any similarities or differences that do not support your thesis.

- Have you treated the same points for both of your two subjects? Revise if necessary to make your discussion balanced.

- Is your essay a point-by-point comparison or a subject-by-subject comparison? If necessary, revise to make your organization consistent with one of these two ways of organizing material.

- Does each topic sentence clearly identify the subject and the point of comparison or contrast being discussed? If necessary, revise topic sentences to clarify each paragraph's focus.

- Do transitional words and phrases move readers from one subject or point to another? Add transitions where necessary.

- Does your conclusion remind readers what your two subjects are and whether you have focused on similarities or differences? If not, revise to reinforce your essay's focus.

- What problems did you experience during the process of writing your essay? What would you do differently next time?

G Classification

For information on writing a classification paragraph, see Chapter 9.

Classification is the act of sorting items into appropriate categories. **Classification essays** divide a whole (your subject) into parts and sort various items into categories.

● **Writing Tip**

Many everyday writing tasks call for classification. For example, if you coach a youth sports team, you might write a recruitment flyer classifying player requirements by age, grade, and level of experience.

FOCUS Topics for Classification

The wording of your assignment may suggest classification. For example, you may be asked to consider *kinds, types, categories, components, segments,* or *parts of a whole.*

(continued on the following page)

(continued from the previous page)	
Assignment	**Thesis Statement**
Business What kinds of courses are most useful for students planning to run their own businesses?	Courses dealing with accounting, management, interpersonal communication, and computer science offer the most useful skills for future business owners.
Biology List the components of the blood, and explain the function of each.	Red blood cells, white blood cells, platelets, and plasma have distinct functions.
Education Classify elementary school children according to their academic needs.	The elementary school population includes special-needs students, students with reading and math skills at or near grade level, and academically gifted students.

Teaching Tip
For examples of classification essays by professional writers, see 36G.

As a rule, each paragraph of a classification essay examines a separate category—a different part of the whole. For example, a paragraph could focus on one kind of course in the college curriculum, one component of the blood, or one type of child. Within each paragraph, you discuss the individual items that you have assigned to a particular category—for example, accounting courses, red blood cells, or gifted students. If you consider some categories less important than others, you may decide to discuss those minor categories together in a single paragraph, devoting full paragraphs only to the most significant categories.

FOCUS   **Options for Organizing Classification Essays**

One Category in Each Paragraph	*Major Categories in Separate Paragraphs; Minor Categories Grouped Together*
¶1 Introduction (identifies whole and its major categories)	¶1 Introduction (identifies whole and its major categories)
¶2 First category	¶2 Minor categories
¶3 Second category	¶3 First major category
¶4 Third category	¶4 Second (and more important) major category
¶5 Conclusion	¶5 Conclusion

In a classification essay, topic sentences identify the category or categories discussed in each paragraph. Transitional words and phrases signal movement from one category to the next and may also tell readers which categories you consider most and least important.

FOCUS Transitions for Classification

One kind . . .	The first (second,	The most impor-
Another kind	third) category	tant component
The final type	The last group	The next part

The following student essay, "Selling a Dream" by Rob O'Neal, classifies American car names into categories on the basis of the kind of message they communicate to consumers. Notice that Rob discusses one category in each of his body paragraphs, using clear topic sentences to identify and define each kind of car name and relate each category to the group as a whole.

Selling a Dream

The earliest automobiles were often named after the men who manufactured them—Ford, Studebaker, Nash, Olds, Chrysler, Dodge, Chevrolet, and so on. More recently, however, American car makers have been competing to see what kinds of names will sell the most cars. Many car names seem to be chosen simply for how they sound: Alero, Corvette, Neon, Probe, Caprice. Many others, however, are designed to sell specific dreams to consumers. Americans always seem to want to be, do, and become something different. They want to be tough and brave, to explore new places, to take risks. With the names that auto manufacturers choose for their cars, they appeal to Americans' deepest desires.

1

Some American cars are named for places people dream of traveling to. Park Avenue, Malibu, Riviera, Seville, Tahoe, Yukon, Aspen, and Durango are some names that suggest escape—to New York City, California, Europe, the West. Other place names—Sebring, Daytona, and Bonneville, for example—are associated with the danger and excitement of car racing. And then there is the El Dorado, a car named for a fictional paradise: a city of gold.

2

Other car names convey rough and tough, even dangerous, images. Animal names fall into this category, with models like Ram, Bronco, and Mustang suggesting powerful, untamed beasts. (Car names associated with animals, such as Mercury's Cougar, Lynx, and Bobcat and Pontiac's Impala, tend to convey speed as well as

3

power.) Other cars in the "rough and tough" category include those that suggest the wildness of the Old West: Wrangler and Rodeo, for example. Because the American auto industry is centered near Detroit, Michigan, where many cities have Indian names, cars named for the cities where they are manufactured have inherited these names. Thus, cars called Cadillac, Pontiac, and Cherokee recall the history of Indian nations, and these too might suggest the excitement of the untamed West.

The most interesting car names in terms of the dream they sell, however, are those that suggest exploration and discovery. Years ago, some car names honored real explorers, like DeSoto and LaSalle. Now, model names only sell an abstract idea. Still, American car names like Blazer, Explorer, Navigator, Mountaineer, Expedition, Caravan, and Voyager (as well as the names of foreign cars driven by many Americans, such as Nissan's Pathfinder and Quest and Honda's Passport, Pilot, and Odyssey) have the power to make drivers feel they are blazing new trails and discovering new worlds—when in fact they may simply be carpooling their children to a soccer game or commuting to work.   4

Today, the car is an ordinary piece of machinery, a necessity for many people. Clearly, the car is no longer seen as the amazing invention it once was. Despite the fact that most people take the existence of cars for granted, however, manufacturers still try to make consumers believe they are buying more than just transportation. But whether we drive a Malibu, Mustang, Cherokee, or Expedition—or even a "royal" LeBaron or Marquis—we eventually realize that we are driving cars, not magic carpets.   5

◆ PRACTICE 14-19

1. What three categories of car names does Rob discuss in his essay?

Rob discusses names that suggest exciting destinations, names that

suggest danger, and names that suggest exploration.

2. Is Rob's treatment of the three categories similar? Does he give the same kind of information for each kind of car name?

Yes. In each of his three body paragraphs, Rob identifies a category of

car name, explains the dream with which it is associated, and gives a

series of examples.

3. How do Rob's topic sentences move readers from one category to the next? How do they link the three categories?

The topic sentence of each body paragraph includes the words car names

("Some American cars are named . . ."; "Other car names . . ."; "The most

interesting car names . . .") to link the three categories and move readers

from one category to the next.

4. Underline Rob's thesis statement. Restate it below in your own words.

Car manufacturers select model names to appeal to Americans' dreams

and desires.

5. Should Rob have included additional examples in each category? Should he have included any additional categories?

Answers will vary. Students will probably be able to suggest additional

examples for each category, and they may suggest additional categories

as well.

6. What is this essay's greatest strength? What is its greatest weakness?

Strength: _*Answers will vary.*_

Weakness: _*Answers will vary.*_

GRAMMAR IN CONTEXT **Classification**

When you write a classification essay, you may want to list the categories you are going to discuss or the examples in each category. If you do, use a **colon** to introduce your list, and make sure that a complete sentence comes before the colon.

> Many car names seem to be chosen simply for how they sound: Alero, Corvette, Neon, Probe, Caprice.

For information on how to use a colon to introduce a list, see 33D.

◆ **PRACTICE 14-20**

Following the writing process outlined in Chapter 12, write a classification essay on one of the following topics.

Types of teachers (or bosses)
Ways to lose (or gain) weight
Things hanging on your walls
Kinds of moods
Kinds of stores in your community shopping district or mall

Traits of oldest children, middle children, and youngest children
Kinds of desserts
Workers you encounter in a typical day
Popular music
How college students dress

◆ PRACTICE 14-21

The picture below shows a young man eating a taco. Look at the photo, and think about all the kinds of food you eat in a typical week. Then, write an essay in which you classify the food you eat. The categories you create can classify the food according to convenience, country of origin, ease of preparation, healthfulness, or where it is consumed.

> **Word Power**
> **finicky** hard to please
>
> **glutton** a person who eats without moderation

✔ SELF-ASSESSMENT CHECKLIST:
Writing a Classification Essay

☐ Does your introduction give readers an overview of the subject whose categories you will discuss? If necessary, revise to clarify the subject of your classification.

☐ Does your thesis statement identify the categories you will discuss? If not, revise your thesis statement to clarify your essay's focus.

(continued on the following page)

(continued from the previous page)

☐ Does each body paragraph discuss a single category (or a re-lated group of minor categories)? If not, revise to create unified paragraphs.

☐ Are any categories insignificant or irrelevant? Revise to eliminate any categories that are not central to your essay's purpose.

☐ Does each topic sentence identify and define the category or categories the paragraph discusses? If necessary, revise your topic sentences to clarify the focus of each paragraph.

☐ Have you treated each major category similarly and with equal thoroughness? If not, revise to make your discussion balanced.

☐ Do transitional words and phrases clearly lead readers from one category to the next? If not, revise to make your essay flow more smoothly.

☐ Does your conclusion review the major categories your essay discusses? If necessary, revise to sum up the categories and their relationships to your subject.

☐ What problems did you experience in writing your essay? What would you do differently next time?

H Definition

For information on writing a definition paragraph, see Chapter 10.

Definition explains the meaning of a term or concept. A **definition essay** presents an *extended definition*, using other patterns of development to move beyond a simple dictionary definition.

Teaching Tip
For examples of definition essays by professional writers, see 36H.

● **Writing Tip**
Many everyday writing tasks call for definition. For example, in a letter of complaint to a neighborhood business, you might define what you mean by terms like *excessive noise* and *rude behavior*.

FOCUS Topics for Definition

The wording of your assignment may suggest definition. For example, you may be asked to *define* or *explain* or to answer the question *What is x?* or *What does x mean?*

Assignment	Thesis Statement
Art Explain the meaning of the term *performance art*.	Unlike more conventional forms of art, *performance art* extends beyond the canvas.
Biology What did Darwin mean by the term *natural selection?*	*Natural selection*, popularly known as "survival of the fittest," is a good deal more complicated than most people think.

(continued on the following page)

(continued from the previous page)

Assignment	Thesis Statement
Psychology What is *attention deficit disorder?*	*Attention deficit disorder (ADD), once narrowly defined as a childhood problem, is now known to affect adults as well as children.*

Teaching Tip
Tell students that when they write a definition, the term being defined should be underlined to indicate italics.

As the thesis statements above suggest, definition essays can be developed in various ways. For example, you can define something by telling how it occurred (narration), by describing its appearance (description), by giving a series of examples (exemplification), by telling how it operates (process), by telling how it is similar to or different from something else (comparison and contrast), or by discussing its parts (classification). Some definition essays use a single pattern of development; others combine several patterns of development, perhaps using a different one in each paragraph.

FOCUS Options for Organizing Definition Essays

Single Pattern of Development

¶1 Introduction (identifies term to be defined)
¶2 Definition by example
¶3 Additional examples
¶4 Additional examples

¶5 Conclusion

Combination of Several Different Patterns of Development

¶1 Introduction (identifies term to be defined)
¶2 Definition by description
¶3 Definition by example
¶4 Definition by comparison and contrast
¶5 Conclusion

The kinds of transitions used in a definition essay depend on the specific pattern or patterns of development in the essay. (In addition to the transitional words and expressions listed in the following Focus box, you may also use those appropriate for the particular patterns you use to develop your definition essay. These transitions are listed in Focus boxes throughout this chapter.)

FOCUS Transitions for Definition

Also	Like
For example	One characteristic . . . Another characteristic
In addition	One way . . . Another way
In particular	Specifically

The following student essay, "Street Smart" by Kristin Whitehead, defines the term *street smart*. In the essay's introduction, Kristin defines her term briefly; in the essay's body paragraphs, she develops her definition further. Notice that the topic sentences of Kristin's three body paragraphs repeat a key phrase to remind readers of her essay's subject.

Street Smart

I grew up in a big city, so I was practically born street smart. I learned the hard way how to act and what to do, and so did my friends. To us, street smart meant having common sense. We wanted to be cool, but we needed to be safe, too. Now I go to college in a big city, and I realize that not everyone here grew up the way I did. Lots of students are from suburbs or rural areas, and they are either terrified of the city or totally ignorant of city life. The few suburban or rural kids who are willing to venture downtown are not street smart—but they should be. Being street smart is a vital survival skill, one that everyone should learn. 1

For me, being street smart means knowing how to protect my possessions. Friends of mine who are not used to city life insist on wearing all their jewelry when they go downtown. I think this is asking for trouble, and I know better. I always tuck my chain under my shirt and leave my gold earrings home. Another thing that surprises me is how some of my friends wave their money around. They always seem to be standing on the street, trying to count their change or stuff dollars into their wallets. Street-smart people make sure to put their money safely away in their pockets or purses before they leave a store. A street-smart person will also carry a backpack, a purse strapped across the chest, or no purse at all. A person who is not street smart carries a purse loosely over one shoulder or dangles it by its handle. Again, these people are asking for trouble. 2

Being street smart also means protecting myself. It means being aware of my surroundings at all times and looking alert. A lot of times I have been downtown with people who kept stopping on the street to talk about where they should go next or walking up and down the same street over and over again. A street-smart person would never do this. It's important that I look as if I know where I am going at all times, even if I don't. Whenever possible, I decide on a destination in advance, and I make sure I know how to get there. Even if I am not completely sure where I am headed, I make sure my body language conveys my confidence in my ability to reach my destination. 3

Finally, being street smart means protecting my 4

life. A street-smart person does not walk alone,
especially after dark, in an unfamiliar neighborhood.
A street-smart person does not ask strangers for
directions; when lost, he or she asks a shopkeeper for
help. A street-smart person takes main streets instead
of side streets. When faced with danger or the threat of
danger, a street-smart person knows when to run, when
to scream, and when to give up money or possessions to
avoid violence.

     So how does someone get to be street smart? Some   5
people think it is a gift, but I think it is something
almost anyone can learn. Probably the best way to learn
how to be street smart is to hang out with people who
know where they are going.

◆ PRACTICE 14-22

1. Underline Kristin's thesis statement. Restate it below in your own words.

   Everyone should learn how to be street smart.

2. In your own words, define the term *street smart*. Why does this term require more than a one-sentence definition?

   Answers will vary.

3. Where does Kristin use examples to develop her definition? Where does she use comparison and contrast?

   Answers will vary. Students may suggest that Kristin contrasts herself

   with people who are not street smart, giving examples of her behavior and

   theirs.

4. What phrase does Kristin repeat in the topic sentences to tie her three body paragraphs together?

   Being street smart means . . .

5. Kristin's conclusion is quite a bit shorter than her other paragraphs. What, if anything, do you think she should add to this paragraph?

   Answers will vary.

6. What is this essay's greatest strength? What is its greatest weakness?

   Strength: *Answers will vary.*

   Weakness: *Answers will vary.*

GRAMMAR IN CONTEXT   **Definition**

When you write a definition essay, you may begin with a one-
sentence definition that you expand in the rest of your essay. When
you write your definition sentence, do not use the phrases *is when*
or *is where.*

means knowing
For me, being street smart ~~is when I know~~ how to protect my
possessions.

means protecting
Being street smart ~~is~~ also ~~where I protect~~ myself.

For information on how to structure a definition sentence, see the
Grammar in Context box in 10A.

◆ **PRACTICE 14-23**

Following the writing process outlined in Chapter 12, write a definition
essay on one of the following topics.

Upward mobility	Responsibility	Courage
Peer pressure	Procrastination	Happiness
Competition	Security	Home
Success		

◆ **PRACTICE 14-24**

The pictures on the following page show various kinds of families. Look at
the pictures, and then write an essay in which you define *family.* In what
ways do the family groups shown on the following page fit or not fit into
your definition?

*For more on the patterns of
paragraph development, see
Chapters 3 through 11.*

☑ SELF-ASSESSMENT CHECKLIST:
Writing a Definition Essay

   ☐ Does your introduction identify the term your essay will define
   and provide a brief definition? If not, revise to make the scope
   of your essay clear.

   ☐ Does your thesis statement indicate why you are defining the
   term? If not, revise to clarify your purpose.

   ☐ What pattern or patterns of development do you use to develop
   your definition? Try exploring other options.

(continued on page 218)

(continued from page 216)

☐ Do topic sentences clearly introduce the different aspects of your definition? If necessary, revise to clarify the relationships between paragraphs.

☐ Are all your ideas clearly related to the term you are defining? If not, revise to eliminate any irrelevant ideas.

☐ Do transitional words and phrases clearly link your ideas? If necessary, add transitions to help guide readers through your essay.

☐ Does your conclusion sum up your essay's main points? Does it remind readers why you are defining the term? If necessary, revise to make your conclusion consistent with the rest of your essay.

☐ What problems did you experience in writing your essay? What would you do differently next time?

I   Argument

For information on writing an argument paragraph, see Chapter 11.

Argument takes a stand on a debatable issue. An **argument essay** uses different kinds of *evidence*—facts, examples, and expert opinion—to persuade readers to accept a position.

FOCUS   Topics for Argument

● **Writing Tip**

Many everyday writing tasks call for argument. For example, in a letter to the editor of a newspaper, you might take a stand on an issue—political, social, economic, religious, or environmental—that affects your family or community.

Teaching Tip

For examples of argument essays by professional writers, see 36I.

The wording of your assignment may suggest argument. For example, you may be asked to *debate, argue, consider, give your opinion, take a position,* or *take a stand.*

Assignment	Thesis Statement
Composition Explain your position on a current social issue.	People who contribute to Social Security should be able to invest some of their money in the stock market.
American history Do you believe that General Lee was responsible for the South's defeat at the Battle of Gettysburg? Why or why not?	Because Lee refused to listen to the advice given to him by General Longstreet, he is largely responsible for the South's defeat at the Battle of Gettysburg.

(continued on the following page)

> *(continued from the previous page)*
>
> | Assignment | Thesis Statement |
> |---|---|
> | *Ethics* Should physician-assisted suicide be legalized? | Although many people think physician-assisted suicide should remain illegal, it should be legal in certain situations. |

An argument essay can be organized *inductively* or *deductively*. An **inductive argument** moves from the specific to the general—that is, from a group of specific observations to a general conclusion based on these observations. An inductive argument responding to the first topic in the Focus box above, for example, could begin with a series of facts, examples, and opinions about the benefits of investing in the stock market and end with the conclusion that people should be able to invest part of their Social Security money in the stock market.

A **deductive argument** moves from the general to the specific. A deductive argument begins with a **major premise** (a general statement that the writer believes his or her audience will accept) and then moves to a **minor premise** (a specific instance of the belief stated in the major premise). It ends with a **conclusion** that follows from the two premises. For example, an essay that responds to the last topic in the Focus box above could begin with the major premise that all terminally ill patients who are in great pain should be given access to physician-assisted suicide. It could then go on to state and explain the minor premise that a particular patient is both terminally ill and in great pain, offering facts, examples, and the opinions of authorities to support this premise. The essay could conclude that this patient should, therefore, be allowed the option of physician-assisted suicide. In this way, the deductive argument presented in the essay goes through three steps.

MAJOR PREMISE   All terminally ill patients who are in great pain should be allowed to choose physician-assisted suicide.

MINOR PREMISE   John Lacca is a terminally ill patient who is in great pain.

CONCLUSION   Therefore, John Lacca should be allowed to choose physician-assisted suicide.

Before you present your argument, think about whether your readers are likely to be hostile to, neutral toward, or in agreement with your thesis. Once you understand your audience, you can decide which points to make in support of your argument.

Begin each paragraph of your argument essay with a topic sentence that clearly relates the discussion to the previous paragraph or to your thesis statement. Throughout your essay, try to include specific examples that will make your arguments persuasive. Keep in mind that arguments that rely just on generalizations are not as convincing as those that include vivid details and specific examples. Finally, strive for a balanced, moderate tone, and avoid name-calling or personal attacks.

In addition to presenting your case, your essay should also briefly identify arguments *against* your position and **refute** them (that is, argue against them or prove them false) by identifying factual errors or errors in logic. If an opposing argument is particularly strong, concede its strength—but try to point out some weaknesses as well. Dealing with the opposing point of view in this manner will help you overcome any objections your audience might have and also establish you as a fair and reasonable person.

FOCUS Options for Organizing Argument Essays

Inductive Argument	*Deductive Argument*
¶1 Introduction	¶1 Introduction
¶2 First point (supported by facts, examples, and expert opinions)	¶2 Major premise stated and explained
¶3 Second point	¶3 Minor premise stated and explained
¶4 Third point	¶4 Evidence supporting minor premise presented
¶5 Identification and refutation of opposing arguments	¶5 Opposing arguments identified and refuted
¶6 Conclusion	¶6 Conclusion

Transitions are extremely important in argument essays because they not only signal the movement from one part of the argument to another but also relate specific points to one another and to the thesis statement.

FOCUS Transitions for Argument

Accordingly	Granted	Of course
Admittedly	However	On the one hand
Although	In conclusion	. . . On the other
Because	Indeed	hand
But	In fact	Since
Certainly	In summary	Therefore
Consequently	Meanwhile	Thus
Despite	Moreover	To be sure
Even so	Nevertheless	Truly
Even though	Nonetheless	

The following student paper, "Why Isn't Pete Rose in the Hall of Fame?" by John Fleeger, is an argument essay. John takes a strong stand, and he supports his thesis with specific facts and examples. The deductive argument that underlies John's essay moves from the major premise (eligibility for the Hall of Fame should be based solely on a player's accomplishments as an athlete) to the minor premise (Pete Rose's accomplishments as an athlete are outstanding) to the conclusion (therefore, Pete Rose should be inducted into the Hall of Fame).

Why Isn't Pete Rose in the Hall of Fame?

The year 1992 was the first year Pete Rose would have been eligible for the National Baseball Hall of Fame. Not only was he not elected, but his name did not even appear on the ballot. Why? Had he not established himself as the all-time best hitter in baseball? Was he not a member of two championship teams with the Cincinnati Reds and one with the Philadelphia Phillies? Had he not helped build the foundation for the 1990 championship Reds team? Had he not set or tied several major-league and team records during his career? The answer to all of these questions is yes. His dedication to and enthusiasm for the game of baseball earned him the nickname "Charlie Hustle," but they did not earn him his rightful place in the Hall of Fame. Although Rose has made serious mistakes, he is still one of baseball's greats and therefore belongs in the Baseball Hall of Fame. 1

In the late summer of 1989, Pete Rose was banned from professional baseball. The legal agreement reached between major-league officials and Pete Rose did not offer any evidence that Rose bet on any baseball games, and Rose himself did not admit that he did. Even though it was not confirmed, A. Bartlett Giamatti, commissioner of baseball at that time, publicly stated that Rose bet not only on baseball but also on his own team. Betting on baseball is a violation of major-league rules that is punishable by lifetime banishment from baseball. This was the sentence Pete Rose received. 2

In 1991, the Hall of Fame Committee, along with Fay Vincent, who was then commissioner of baseball, decided that a player who has been banned from baseball is ineligible for Hall of Fame selection. This action was taken just a few weeks before Rose's name could have been placed on the ballot, and many believe that Vincent supported it specifically to make sure Rose could not be considered for selection. Several of the baseball writers who voted for the Hall of Fame candidates voiced their disapproval of this policy by writing in Rose's name on the ballot. Unfortunately, write-in votes are not counted. 3

Now, Rose's only hope of making the Hall of Fame seems to depend on his being readmitted to baseball. The current commissioner, Bud Selig, would have to review Rose's application and approve his reinstatement. 4

Chances that this will happen, however, have grown increasingly remote. <u>In fact</u>, new charges have surfaced. An acquaintance of Rose's has now accused him not only of having bet on baseball but also of having people forge his signature on baseball memorabilia.

<u>However</u>, although Rose has always admitted to betting on basketball and football games, he continues to deny that he ever placed a bet on baseball. <u>Moreover</u>, he has made it clear that he recognizes that his gambling is a serious psychological problem (a problem for which he has received counseling). Why is a player who has a gambling problem any worse than the many players who have tested positive for drugs? Those players are suspended from the game for a period of time and given a chance to recover and return to baseball. Pete Rose should have been treated the same way.

<u>Granted</u>, Pete Rose is no angel. <u>In fact</u>, he served a term in federal prison for tax-law violations after he failed to pay income tax on his gambling winnings and on the money he made at baseball-card shows. <u>Even so</u>, the Hall of Fame is not reserved for perfect people. Babe Ruth was an adulterer and a serious drinker, but he still holds a place in the Hall. Mickey Mantle and Willie Mays were barred from baseball for being employees of an Atlantic City casino (an obvious gambling connection), but this ruling was eventually overturned, and both men have been admitted to the Hall of Fame.

The truth is, the question of Rose's guilt or innocence is, and always has been, irrelevant. What matters is not whether he broke the rules (which it appears he did) but whether he is the kind of baseball player whose accomplishments on the field qualify him for Hall of Fame membership. And, <u>despite</u> his transgressions, he is still recognized, even by his critics, as a great baseball player.

<u>Certainly</u> Pete Rose has made some serious mistakes in his life, <u>but</u> this is no reason to keep him out of the Hall of Fame. His contributions to the game and his accomplishments as a player are all that should be considered, and these more than qualify him to occupy a place beside the greats of the game. Baseball should, in all fairness, let Pete Rose take his rightful place in the Hall of Fame.

5

6

7

8

Word Power

transgression a violation of law or duty

◆ **PRACTICE 14-25**

1. What position does John take in his essay?

He argues that Pete Rose should be in the Hall of Fame.

2. List the facts and examples John uses to support his thesis.

The Hall of Fame Committee may have intentionally discouraged Rose's

selection. Drug-addicted players are allowed to return to the game.

Other Hall of Famers had problems but were still allowed to play baseball.

Can you think of any that he doesn't mention?

Answers will vary.

3. Underline the transitional words and phrases John uses to move his argument along.

4. John's opening paragraph includes a series of questions he does not expect his readers to answer. Is this an effective opening strategy? Why or why not?

Answers will vary. Some students may argue that it is effective because

John proceeds to list facts that answer the questions for us.

5. Throughout his essay, John acknowledges Pete Rose's problems and shortcomings. Do you think this is a good idea? Why or why not?

Answers will vary.

6. Where does John address opposing arguments? What other arguments should he have addressed?

John addresses opposing arguments when he talks about Rose's

gambling problems and his prison term for tax evasion. He could have

gone into more detail about Rose's gambling and tax problems, but that

might have lessened the strength of his own argument.

7. What is this essay's greatest strength? What is its greatest weakness?

Strength: *Answers will vary.*

Weakness: *Answers will vary.*

GRAMMAR IN CONTEXT **Argument**

When you write an argument essay, you need to show the relationships between your ideas by combining simple sentences to create
both **compound sentences** and **complex sentences**.

His dedication to and enthusiasm for the game of baseball

earned him the nickname "Charlie Hustle." ~~They~~ did not earn
," but they

him his rightful place in the Hall of Fame.

(Two simple sentences are combined to create one compound
sentence.)

Although *, he*
Rose has made serious mistakes. ~~He~~ is still one of baseball's

greats and therefore belongs in the Baseball Hall of Fame.

(Two simple sentences are combined to create one complex
sentence.)

For information on how to create compound sentences, see Chapter 16. For information on how to create complex sentences, see
Chapter 17.

◆ PRACTICE 14-26

Following the writing process outlined in Chapter 12, write an argument
essay on one of the following topics.

The United States should (or should not) have an "open door" immigration policy, with no restrictions.

Teenagers who commit serious crimes should (or should not) be tried
as adults.

All citizens without criminal records should (or should not) be permitted to carry concealed weapons.

Welfare recipients with preschool children should (or should not) be
required to work.

Human beings should (or should not) be used in medical research
experiments.

Parents should (or should not) be permitted to use government vouch-
ers to pay private school tuition.

College financial aid should (or should not) be based solely on merit.

Government funds should (or should not) be used to support the arts.

Public high schools should (or should not) be permitted to distribute
condoms to students.

The minimim wage should (or should not) be raised to ten dollars an
hour.

◆ PRACTICE 14-27

The picture below shows a driver talking on a cell phone. Many states are considering (or have already adopted) a ban on cell phone use by drivers in moving vehicles. Look at the picture, and then write an argument essay in which you argue either that this ban is a good idea or that the convenience of cell phones outweighs the possible risk (which some consider remote) of accidents.

Word Power
multitasking doing several tasks at the same time

hazardous dangerous

☑ SELF-ASSESSMENT CHECKLIST:
Writing an Argument Essay

- Does your introduction present the issue you will discuss and clearly state your position? If necessary, revise to clarify your purpose.

- Is your topic debatable? Make sure you take a position on an issue that really has two sides.

- Does your thesis statement clearly express the stand you take on the issue? If necessary, revise to clarify your position.

- Are your readers likely to be hostile to, neutral toward, or in agreement with your position? Be sure you consider your audience's expectations when choosing the points you will make and deciding how you will present them.

(continued on the following page)

(continued from the previous page)

- [ ] Is your essay an inductive argument or a deductive argument? If necessary, revise the structure of your argument so it conforms to the requirements of the option you have chosen.

- [ ] Have you addressed the major arguments against your position? Identify any additional opposing arguments, and refute them if you can.

- [ ] Do you have enough evidence to support your points? If not, add facts, examples, and the opinions of experts if necessary.

- [ ] Do all your points clearly support your position? If not, revise to eliminate any points that are not directly related to your argument.

- [ ] Do transitional words and phrases help readers follow the logic of your argument? Add transitions if necessary.

- [ ] Does your conclusion follow logically from the points you have made in your essay? If necessary, revise so your concluding paragraph summarizes and reinforces your main points.

- [ ] What problems did you experience in writing your essay? What would you do differently next time?

☑ REVIEW CHECKLIST:
Patterns of Essay Development

- [ ] Exemplification essays use specific examples to support a thesis. (See 14A.)

- [ ] Narrative essays tell a story by presenting a series of events in chronological order. (See 14B.)

- [ ] Descriptive essays use details to give readers a clear, vivid picture of a person, place, or object. (See 14C.)

- [ ] Process essays explain the steps in a procedure, telling how something is (or was) done. (See 14D.)

- [ ] Cause-and-effect essays identify causes or predict effects. (See 14E.)

- [ ] Comparison-and-contrast essays explain how two things are alike or how they are different. (See 14F.)

- [ ] Classification essays divide a whole into parts and sort various items into categories. (See 14G.)

- [ ] Definition essays use various patterns of development to develop an extended definition. (See 14H.)

- [ ] Argument essays take a stand on a debatable issue, using evidence to persuade readers to accept a position. (See 14I.)

Teaching Tip
Give students an example of an essay that uses a combination of patterns. Have them work in groups to identify and label the patterns. In class discussion, compare the groups' responses.

UNIT FOUR

Writing Effective Sentences

Writing Simple Sentences

PREVIEW

In this chapter, you will learn

- to identify a sentence's subject (15A)

- to identify prepositions and prepositional phrases (15B)

- to distinguish a prepositional phrase from a subject (15B)

- to identify a sentence's verb (15C)

■ WRITING FIRST

The picture above shows ace pitcher Pedro Martinez, who helped lead the Boston Red Sox to World Series victory in 2004. Look at the picture, and then write about a person with whom you would like to trade places. What appeals to you about this person's life?

Word Power

idol someone who is admired or adored

role model a person who serves as a model for other people to imitate

emulate to strive to equal or excel

A **sentence** is a group of words that expresses a complete thought. Every sentence includes both a <u>subject</u> and a <u>verb</u>.

● **Writing Tip**

If a group of words does not include both a subject and a verb, it is a sentence fragment. See Chapter 22 for information on how to recognize and correct sentence fragments in your writing.

A Identifying Subjects

Every sentence includes a subject. The **subject** of a sentence tells who or what is being talked about in the sentence. Without a subject, a sentence is not complete.

<u>Derek Walcott</u> won the 1992 Nobel Prize in literature.

229

He was born in the Caribbean.

St. Lucia is an island in the Caribbean.

The subject of a sentence can be a noun or a pronoun. A **noun** names a person, place, or thing—*Derek Walcott, St. Lucia*. A **pronoun** takes the place of a noun—*I, you, he, she, it, we, they,* and so on.

The subject of a sentence can be *singular* or *plural*. A **singular subject** is one person, place, or thing (*Derek Walcott, St. Lucia, he*).

A **plural subject** is more than one person, place, or thing (*poems, people, they*).

Walcott's poems have been collected in books.

A plural subject that joins two subjects with *and* is called a **compound subject**.

St. Lucia and Trinidad are Caribbean islands.

*For information on subject-
verb agreement with com-
pound subjects, see 23A.*

FOCUS **Simple and Complete Subjects**

A sentence's **simple subject** is just a noun or a pronoun.

    poems   he

A sentence's **complete subject** is the simple subject along with all the words that describe it.

    Walcott's poems

A two-word name, such as *Derek Walcott*, is a simple subject.

◆ **PRACTICE 15-1**

In the paragraph below, underline the complete subject of each sentence once. Then, place a check mark above the simple subject.

Example: The poet's parents were both teachers.

(1) Derek Walcott was born in 1930. (2) His ancestors came from Africa, the Netherlands, and England. (3) Walcott's early years were spent on the Caribbean island of St. Lucia. (4) Writing poetry occupied much of his time. (5) His early poems were published in Trinidad. (6) He later studied in Jamaica and in New York. (7) Walcott eventually gained wide recognition as a poet. (8) He was a visiting lecturer at Harvard in 1981. (9) In 1990, the renowned poet published *Omeros*. (10) This long

poem about classical Greek heroes is set in the West Indies. (11) In 1992, the sixty-two-year-old Caribbean poet was honored with a Nobel Prize. (12) Walcott later collaborated with songwriter Paul Simon on *The Cape-man*, a Broadway musical.

Teaching Tip
Point out to students that in some cases a simple subject is also the sentence's complete subject.

◆ PRACTICE 15-2

Add a simple subject to each of the following sentences.

> **Example:** *Pets* can reduce stress, high blood pressure, and depression.
> *Answers may vary.*

1. For one thing, _____*animals*_____ allow us to express affection openly.

2. _____*We*_____ can stroke, cuddle, and talk baby talk to a kitten or puppy.

3. _____*Pets*_____ also love us unconditionally, no matter what our faults.

4. Our _____*animals*_____ do not care about our faults.

5. _____*Social workers*_____ sometimes bring animals into nursing homes and hospitals to visit patients.

6. For some patients, their only _____*visitors*_____ are these animals.

7. These _____*patients*_____ have better survival rates than those without animal visitors.

8. In prisons, _____*inmates*_____ sometimes train service dogs.

9. These _____*dogs*_____ help disabled people.

10. Their _____*trainers*_____ are making a positive contribution to society.

◆ PRACTICE 15-3

Underline the complete subject in each sentence. Then, write **S** above singular subjects and **P** above plural subjects. Remember, compound subjects are plural.

> **Example:** <u>Engineers</u> sometimes call the Channel Tunnel one of the seven wonders of the modern morld.

1. During the Ice Age, <u>a land bridge</u> connected the island of Great Britain to the continent of Europe.

2. Now, <u>Great Britain and the rest of Europe</u> are joined by the Channel Tunnel.

3. The Channel Tunnel consists of three concrete tubes that run under the
   English Channel.

4. Each tube is five feet thick.

5. The tubes extend from Coquelles, France, to Folkestone, England.

6. Double-decker trains travel through two of the tubes at one hundred
   miles per hour.

7. The third tube is used only by maintenance and emergency vehicles.

8. Passengers board the trains in their cars.

9. Next to the tracks, cold-water pipes drain off the heat caused by the
   trains' friction.

10. On the Channel Tunnel train, passengers can now travel from London
    to Paris in about two and a half hours.

■ WRITING FIRST: Flashback

Look back at your response to the Writing First exercise on page
229. Underline the complete subject of each of your sentences
once. Then, place a check mark above the simple subject. Finally,
list all the complete subjects on the lines below.

Answers will vary.

_____   _____

_____   _____

_____   _____

_____   _____

Now, write *S* beside each singular subject and *P* beside each plural
subject. (Remember that a compound subject is plural.)

---

*For more on prepositions, see
30M, 30N, and 30O.*

B   Identifying Prepositional Phrases

A **prepositional phrase** consists of a **preposition** (a word such as *on, to,
in,* or *with*) and its **object** (a noun or pronoun).

Preposition	+	Object	=	Prepositional Phrase
on		the stage		on the stage
to		Nia's house		to Nia's house
in		my new car		in my new car
with		them		with them

● **Writing Tip**

A phrase is a group of words
that is missing a subject
or a verb or both. For this
reason, a phrase cannot
stand alone as a sentence.
(See 22B.)

A prepositional phrase **modifies** (identifies, describes, or limits) another word or word group in the sentence.

> The girl <u>with long red hair</u> was first in line. (The prepositional phrase *with long red hair* modifies the noun *girl.*)

> Ken met his future wife <u>at Ted's house</u>. (The prepositional phrase *at Ted's house* modifies the verb *met.*)

Because the object of a preposition is a noun or a pronoun, it may appear to be the subject of a sentence. However, the object of a preposition can never be the subject of a sentence. To identify a sentence's true subject, cross out each prepositional phrase. (Remember, every prepositional phrase is introduced by a preposition.)

> *subject prep phrase*
> The <u>cost</u> ~~of the repairs~~ was astronomical.

> *prep phrase*   *prep phrase*   *subject*
> ~~At the end of the novel~~, ~~after an exciting chase~~, the <u>lovers</u> flee
> *prep phr*
> ~~to Mexico~~.

Frequently Used Prepositions

about	behind	except	off	toward
above	below	for	on	under
across	beneath	from	onto	underneath
after	beside	in	out	until
against	between	inside	outside	up
along	beyond	into	over	upon
among	by	like	through	with
around	despite	near	throughout	within
at	during	of	to	without
before				

◆ **PRACTICE 15-4**

Each of the following sentences includes at least one prepositional phrase. To identify each sentence's subject, begin by crossing out each prepositional phrase. Then, underline the simple subject of the sentence.

Example: ~~In presidential elections~~, third-party <u>candidates</u> have attracted many voters.

(1) ~~With more than 27 percent of the vote~~, <u>Theodore Roosevelt</u> was the strongest third-party presidential candidate ~~in history~~. (2) ~~In the 1912 race with Democrat Woodrow Wilson and Republican William H. Taft~~, <u>Roosevelt</u> ran second ~~to Wilson~~. (3) ~~Until Roosevelt~~, no third-party <u>candidate</u> had won a significant number ~~of votes~~. (4) ~~After 1912~~, however, some <u>candidates</u> ~~of other parties~~ made strong showings. (5) ~~For example~~, <u>Robert M. LaFollette</u> ~~of the Progressive Party~~ won ~~about 16~~

percent of the vote ~~in the 1924 race~~. (6) ~~In 1968,~~ ~~with more than 13 per-~~ ~~cent of the popular vote,~~ American Independent Party candidate George C. Wallace placed third ~~behind Republican Richard M. Nixon and Demo-~~ ~~crat Hubert H. Humphrey.~~ (7) ~~In 1980,~~ John B. Anderson, an Indepen- dent, challenged Republican Ronald Reagan and Democrat Jimmy Carter and got 6.6 percent ~~of the vote~~. (8) ~~With nearly 19 percent of the popular~~ ~~vote~~, Independent Ross Perot ran a strong race ~~against Democrat Bill~~ ~~Clinton and Republican George Bush~~ ~~in 1992~~. (9) ~~In 2000,~~ ~~with the sup-~~ ~~port of many environmentalists,~~ Ralph Nader challenged Al Gore and George W. Bush ~~for the presidency~~. (10) ~~In 2004,~~ Nader was also ~~on~~ ~~the ballot~~ ~~in many states~~. (11) ~~To this day,~~ the two-party system ~~of the~~ ~~United States~~ has remained intact ~~despite many challenges~~ ~~by third-~~ ~~party candidates~~.

■ WRITING FIRST: Flashback

Look back at your response to the Writing First exercise on page 229. Have you used any prepositional phrases? List them on the lines below.

Answers will vary.

_____

_____

_____

_____

C Identifying Verbs

For information on how to rec- ognize and correct incomplete sentences (sentence fragments), see Chapter 22.

In addition to its subject, every sentence also includes a verb. This **verb** (also called a **predicate**) tells what the subject does or connects the sub- ject to words that describe or rename it. Without a verb, a sentence is not complete.

Action Verbs

An **action verb** tells what the subject does, did, or will do.

Nomar Garciaparra <u>plays</u> baseball.

Renee <u>will drive</u> to Tampa on Friday.

Amelia Earhart <u>flew</u> across the Atlantic.

Action verbs can also show mental and emotional actions.

Travis always <u>worries</u> about his job.

Sometimes, the subject of a sentence performs more than one action. In this case, the sentence includes two or more action verbs joined to form a **compound predicate.**

He <u>hit</u> the ball, <u>threw</u> down his bat, and <u>ran</u> toward first base.

Linking Verbs

A **linking verb** does not show action. Instead, it connects the subject to a word or words that describe or rename it. The linking verb tells what the subject is (or what it was, will be, or seems to be).

A googolplex <u>is</u> an extremely large number.

Many linking verbs, like *is*, are forms of the verb *be*. Other linking verbs refer to the senses (*look, feel*, and so on).

The photocopy <u>looks</u> blurry.
Some students <u>feel</u> anxious about the future.

Frequently Used Linking Verbs		
act	feel	seem
appear	get	smell
be (am, is, are,	grow	sound
was, were)	look	taste
become	remain	turn

● **Writing Tip**
Some linking verbs, such as *look, smell, turn*, and *taste*, can also function as action verbs: *I will <u>look</u> for a clearer photocopy*.

Teaching Tip
Have students memorize these linking verbs.

◆ PRACTICE 15-5

In the following sentences, underline each action verb twice. Some sentences contain more than one action verb.

ON THE WEB
For more practice, visit Exercise Central *at* <*bedfordstmartins.com/ writingfirst*>.

1. Many critics <u>see</u> one romance novel as just like another.

2. The plot usually <u>involves</u> a beautiful young woman, or heroine, in some kind of danger.

3. A handsome stranger <u>offers</u> his help.

4. At first, she <u>distrusts</u> him.

5. Then, another man <u>enters</u> the story and <u>wins</u> the heroine's trust.

6. Readers, however, <u>see</u> this man as an evil villain.

7. Almost too late, the heroine too <u>realizes</u> the truth.

8. Luckily, the handsome hero <u>returns</u> and <u>saves</u> her from a nasty fate.

9. Many readers enjoy the predictable plots of romance novels.

10. However, most critics dislike these books.

◆ PRACTICE 15-6

In the following sentences, underline each linking verb twice.

1. Urban legends are folk tales created in our own time to teach a lesson.

2. One familiar urban legend is the story of Hookman.

3. According to this story, a young couple is alone in Lovers' Lane.

4. They are in a car, listening to a radio announcement.

5. An escaped murderer is nearby.

6. The murderer's left hand is a hook.

7. The young woman becomes hysterical.

8. Suddenly, Lovers' Lane seems very dangerous.

9. Later, they are stunned to see a hook hanging from the passenger door handle.

10. The purpose of this legend is to frighten young people into avoiding dangerous places.

◆ PRACTICE 15-7

Underline every verb in each of the following sentences twice. Remember that a verb can be an action verb or a linking verb.

Example: Some books have a great impact on their readers.

(1) In 1948, Betty Smith wrote *A Tree Grows in Brooklyn*. (2) The novel tells the story of Francie Nolan. (3) Francie is very poor but seems determined to succeed. (4) She loves books and is an excellent student. (5) Francie lives with her parents and her younger brother, Neely. (6) She dreams of a better life for herself and her family. (7) Tragically, Francie's father dies. (8) Her mother supports her family and does her best for her children. (9) She works as a janitor in their apartment building. (10) Eventually, Francie graduates from high school, with a bright future ahead of her.

Helping Verbs

Many verbs consist of more than one word. The verb in the following sentence consists of two words.

Minh <u>must make</u> a decision about his future.

In this sentence, *make* is the **main verb**, and *must* is a **helping verb**.

FOCUS Helping Verbs

Helping verbs (also called **auxiliary verbs**) include forms of *be*, *have*, and *do* as well as the words *must, will, can, could, may, might, should*, and *would*. Some helping verbs, like forms of *be* and *have*, combine with main verbs to give information about when the action occurs. Forms of *do* combine with main verbs to form questions and negative statements. Still other helping verbs indicate willingness (*can*), possibility (*may*), necessity (*should*), obligation (*must*), and so on.

A sentence's **complete verb** is made up of a main verb plus any helping verbs that accompany it. In the following sentences, the complete verb is underlined twice, and the helping verbs are checkmarked.

> ✔ ✔
> Minh <u>should have gone</u> earlier.

> ✔
> <u>Did</u> Minh <u>ask</u> the right questions?

> ✔
> Minh <u>will work</u> hard.

> ✔
> Minh <u>can</u> really <u>succeed</u>.

● **Writing Tip**

Every sentence must include a complete verb. For information on how to identify sentence fragments created by incomplete verbs, see 22C.

● **Writing Tip**

Sometimes, other words can come between the parts of a complete verb.

FOCUS Helping Verbs with Participles

Present participles, such as *thinking*, and many irregular **past participles**, such as *gone*, cannot stand alone as main verbs in a sentence. They need a helping verb to make them complete.

INCORRECT   Minh going to the library.

CORRECT   Minh <u>is going</u> to the library.

INCORRECT   Minh gone to the library.

CORRECT   Minh <u>has gone</u> to the library.

For information on past participles, see Chapter 27.

◆ **PRACTICE 15-8**

The verbs in the sentences that follow consist of a main verb and one or more helping verbs. In each sentence, underline the complete verb twice, and put a check mark above the helping verb(s).

Example: The Salk polio vaccine <u>was given</u> to more than a million schoolchildren in 1954.

(1) By the 1950s, parents <u>had become</u> terrified of polio. (2) For years, it <u>had puzzled</u> doctors and researchers. (3) Thousands <u>had become ill</u> each year in the United States alone. (4) Children <u>should have been playing</u> happily. (5) Instead, they <u>would get</u> very sick. (6) Polio <u>was</u> sometimes <u>called</u> infantile paralysis. (7) In fact, it <u>did cause</u> paralysis in children and in adults as well. (8) Some patients <u>could breathe</u> only with the help of machines called iron lungs. (9) Others <u>would remain</u> in wheelchairs for life. (10) By 1960, Jonas Salk's vaccine <u>had reduced</u> the incidence of polio in the United States by more than 90 percent.

■ **WRITING FIRST: Flashback**

Look back at your response to the Writing First exercise on page 229. In each sentence, underline the complete verb twice, and put a check mark above each helping verb. Then, copy the helping verbs on the lines below.

Answers will vary. _____ _____ _____

_____ _____ _____ _____

■ **WRITING FIRST: Revising and Editing**

Look back at your response to the Writing First exercise on page 229. Circle every action verb. Then, try to replace some of them with different action verbs that express more precisely what the subject of each sentence is, was, or will be doing. For example, you might replace *makes* with *builds* or *creates*.

CHAPTER REVIEW

◆ EDITING PRACTICE

Read the following student passage. Underline the complete subject of each sentence once, and underline the complete verb of each sentence twice. If you have trouble locating the subject, try crossing out the prepositional phrases. The first sentence has been done for you.

The Origin of Baseball

Baseball is an American sport. In many people's minds, Abner Doubleday started baseball in 1839. He decided on the rules of the game. However, baseball games were played before then. In fact, baseball was played in Pittsfield, Pennsylvania, in the late 1700s. According to historical records, Pittsfield had a new meeting house at that time. The building was damaged by baseballs. A new law banned baseballs within eighty yards of the meeting house.

Thousands of years earlier, baseball was played in ancient Egypt. Pharaohs played "batting the ball" with their priests in about 2400 B.C. Pictures of this game have been seen on the walls of Egyptian temples. The pictures resemble our game of stickball.

Today's game of baseball was actually derived from stickball. Stickball was usually played on city streets. Stickball players originally used broom handles for their bats. At the Museum of the City of New York, the Stickball Hall of Fame honors great stickball players. Abner Doubleday may have been a member of a stickball team. He did not really invent baseball. However, he changed stickball into our modern game of baseball.

Boy playing stickball

◆ COLLABORATIVE ACTIVITIES

1. Fold a sheet of paper in half vertically. Working in a group of three or four students, spend two minutes listing as many nouns as you can in the column to the left of the fold. When your time is up, exchange

papers with another group of students. Limiting yourselves to five minutes, write an appropriate action verb beside each noun. Each noun will now be the subject of a short sentence.

2. Choose five short sentences from those you wrote for Collaborative Activity 1. Working in the same group, collaborate to create more fully developed sentences. First, expand each subject by adding words or prepositional phrases that give more information about the subject. (For example, you could expand *boat* to *the small, leaky boat with the red sail*.) Then, expand each sentence further, adding ideas after the verb. (For example, the sentence *The boat bounced* could become *The small, leaky boat with the red sail bounced helplessly on the water.*)

3. Collaborate in a group of three or four students to write one original sentence for each of the linking verbs listed on page 235. When you have finished, exchange papers with another group. Now, try to add words and phrases to the other group's sentences to make them more interesting.

☑ REVIEW CHECKLIST:
Writing Simple Sentences

☐ A sentence expresses a complete thought. The subject tells who or what is being talked about in the sentence. (See 15A.)

☐ Prepositions connect words and groups of words in a sentence. A prepositional phrase consists of a preposition and its object (a noun or pronoun). (See 15B.)

☐ The object of a preposition cannot be the subject of a sentence. (See 15B.)

☐ An action verb tells what the subject does, did, or will do. (See 15C.)

☐ A linking verb connects the subject to a word or words that describe or rename it. (See 15C.)

☐ Many verbs are made up of more than one word. The complete verb in a sentence includes the main verb plus any helping verbs. (See 15C.)

Writing Compound Sentences

■ WRITING FIRST

In the picture above, which shows a high school graduation, some of the graduating students are also mothers. Look at the picture, and then write a letter to the president of your college explaining why your campus needs a day-care center. (If your school already has a day-care center, explain why it deserves continued—or increased—funding.)

A	**Forming Compound Sentences with Coordinating Conjunctions**

The most basic kind of sentence, a **simple sentence**, consists of a single **independent clause**: one <u>subject</u> and one <u>verb</u>.

European <u>immigrants</u> <u>arrived</u> at Ellis Island.

A **compound sentence** is made up of two or more simple sentences (independent clauses). One way to form a compound sentence is by joining two independent clauses with a **coordinating conjunction** preceded by a comma.

European immigrants arrived at Ellis Island, <u>but</u> Asian immigrants arrived at Angel Island.

Teaching Tip
Remind students that a comma alone cannot connect two independent clauses. Refer them to Chapter 21.

Coordinating Conjunctions

and	for	or	yet
but	nor	so	

Coordinating conjunctions join ideas of equal importance. They describe the relationship between two ideas, showing how and why the ideas are connected. Different coordinating conjunctions have different meanings:

■ If you want to indicate addition, use *and*.

He acts like a child, <u>and</u> people think he is cute.

■ If you want to indicate contrast or contradiction, use *but* or *yet*.

He acts like a child, <u>but</u> he is an adult.
He acts like a child, <u>yet</u> he longs to be taken seriously.

■ If you want to indicate a cause-and-effect relationship, use *so* or *for*.

He acts like a child, <u>so</u> we treat him like one.
He acts like a child, <u>for</u> he craves attention.

■ If you want to present alternatives, use *or*.

He acts like a child, <u>or</u> he is ignored.

■ If you want to eliminate alternatives, use *nor*.

He does not act like a child, <u>nor</u> does he look like one.

Teaching Tip
Remind students that when a compound sentence is formed with *nor*, the verb comes before the subject in the second clause.

Teaching Tip
Remind students that in a compound sentence, there is a complete sentence on each side of the coordinating conjunction.

FOCUS **Using Commas with Coordinating Conjunctions**

When you use a coordinating conjunction to link two independent clauses into a single compound sentence, always put a comma before the coordinating conjunction.

We can stand in line all night, or we can go home now.

(continued on the following page)

(continued from the previous page)

Remember, though, not to use a comma before a coordinating conjunction unless it links two *complete independent clauses.*

INCORRECT   We can stand in line all night, or go home now.

CORRECT   We can stand in line all night or go home now.

◆ PRACTICE 16-1

Fill in the coordinating conjunction—*and, but, for, nor, or, so,* or *yet*—that most logically links the two parts of each compound sentence. Remember to insert a comma before each coordinating conjunction.

ON THE WEB
*For more practice, visit
Exercise Central at
<bedfordstmartins.com/
writingfirst>.*

Example: Fairy tales have been told by many people around the

world, <u>*but*</u> the stories by two German brothers may be the most
     ^

famous.

Answers will vary.

(1) Jakob and Wilhelm Grimm lived in the nineteenth century, <u>*and*</u>
                                                         ^

they wrote many well-known fairy tales. (2) Most people think fondly of

fairy tales, <u>*but/yet*</u> the Brothers Grimm wrote many unpleasant and vio-
        ^

lent stories. (3) In their best-known works, children are abused, <u>*and*</u>
                                                            ^

endings are not always happy. (4) Either innocent children are brutally

punished for no reason, <u>*or*</u> they are neglected. (5) For example, in
                   ^

"Hansel and Gretel," the stepmother mistreats the children, <u>*and*</u> their
                                                      ^

father abandons them in the woods. (6) In this story, the events are

horrifying, <u>*but/yet*</u> the ending is still happy. (7) The children outwit the
       ^

evil adults, <u>*so/and*</u> they escape unharmed. (8) Apparently, they are not
        ^

injured physically, <u>*nor*</u> are they harmed emotionally. (9) Nevertheless,
               ^

their story can hardly be called pleasant, <u>*for*</u> it remains a story of child
                                      ^

abuse and neglect.

◆ PRACTICE 16-2

Join each of the following pairs of independent clauses with a coordinating conjunction. Be sure to place a comma before the coordinating conjunction.

                                                           , and it
Example: A computer can make drafting essays easier, ~~It~~ also lets
                                                      ^

you revise as often as possible.

1. Training a dog to heel is difficult, *, for dogs* ~~Dogs~~ naturally resist strict control.

2. A bodhran is an Irish drum, *, and it* ~~It~~ is played with a wooden stick.

3. Students should spend two hours of study time for each hour of class time, *, or they* ~~They~~ may not do well in the course.

4. Years ago, students wrote their lessons on slates, *, so the* ~~The~~ teacher could correct each student's work.

5. Each state in the United States has two senators, *, but the* ~~The~~ number of representatives depends on a state's population.

6. In 1973, only 2.5 percent of those in the U.S. military were women, *,* *but by* ~~By~~ 1999, that percentage had increased to 14.1 percent.

7. A "small craft advisory" warns boaters of bad weather conditions, *,* *for these* ~~These~~ conditions can be dangerous to small boats.

8. A digital video disc (DVD) looks like a compact disk, *, but it* ~~It~~ can hold fifteen times as much information.

9. Hip-hop fashions include sneakers and baggy pants, *, but these* ~~These~~ styles are very popular among today's young men.

10. Multiple births have become more and more common, *, and even* ~~Even~~ septuplets have a reasonable chance of survival today.

◆ PRACTICE 16-3

Add coordinating conjunctions to combine independent clauses where necessary to relate one idea to another. Remember to put a comma before each coordinating conjunction you add.

Example: Years ago, few Americans lived to be one hundred, *, but today,* ~~Today,~~ there are over 32,000 centenarians.

Answers will vary.

(1) Diet, exercise, and family history may account for centenarians' long lives, *, but this* (2) ~~This~~ is not the whole story. (3) Recently, a study conducted in Georgia showed surprising common traits among centenarians. (4) They did not necessarily avoid tobacco and alcohol, *, nor* (5) ~~They~~ did *they* ~~not~~ have low-fat diets. (6) In fact, they ate relatively large amounts of fat, cholesterol, and sugar, *, so diet* (7) ~~Diet~~ could not explain their long lives. (8) They did, however, share four key survival characteristics. (9) First, all of the centenarians were optimistic about life, *, and all* (10) ~~All~~ of them were positive thinkers.

(11) They were also involved in religious life and had deep religious faith. (12) In addition, all the centenarians had continued to lead physically active lives/ *, and they* (13) They remained mobile even as elderly people. (14) Finally, all were able to adapt to loss. (15) They had all experienced the deaths of friends, spouses, or children/ *, but they* (16) They were able to get on with their lives.

◆ PRACTICE 16-4

Write another simple sentence to follow each of the sentences below. Then, connect the sentences with a coordinating conjunction and the correct punctuation.

> **Example:** Many patients need organ transplants/ *, but there is a* ___ serious shortage of organ donors. ___
> *Answers will vary.*

1. Smoking in bed is dangerous. ___

2. Many cars are equipped with navigation systems. ___

3. Diamonds are very expensive. ___

4. Kangaroos carry their young in pouches. ___

5. Dancing is good exercise. ___

6. Motorcycle helmet laws have been dropped in some states. ___

7. Some businesses sponsor bowling leagues for their employees. ___

8. Pretzels are a healthier snack than potato chips. ___

9. Many so-called juices actually contain very little real fruit juice. ___

10. Human beings tend to resist change. ___

■ WRITING FIRST: Flashback

Look back at your response to the Writing First exercise on page 241. If you see any compound sentences, bracket them. If you see any pairs of simple sentences that could be combined into one compound sentence, rewrite them below, joining them with appropriate coordinating conjunctions.

Answers will vary.

1. _____

   _____

2. _____

   _____

3. _____

   _____

Be sure each of your new compound sentences includes a comma before the coordinating conjunction.

B Forming Compound Sentences with Semicolons

Another way to create a **compound sentence** is by joining two independent clauses with a *semicolon*.

> The AIDS quilt contains thousands of panels; each panel is rectangular.

A semicolon generally connects clauses whose ideas are closely linked.

For information on avoiding sentence fragments, see Chapter 22.

FOCUS Avoiding Sentence Fragments

Remember that a semicolon can join only two complete sentences (independent clauses). A semicolon cannot join a sentence and a fragment.

	FRAGMENT
INCORRECT	Because thousands are dying of AIDS; more research is clearly needed.
CORRECT	Thousands are dying of AIDS; more research is clearly needed.

◆ PRACTICE 16-5

Combine each pair of independent clauses below into one compound sentence by adding a semicolon in the appropriate place.

Example: People become famous for complicated reasons; just being the first to accomplish something is no guarantee of fame.

1. Sometimes runners-up are better remembered than winners; the triumphant are forgotten.

2. The race to reach the South Pole is a perfect example; it illustrates this well.

3. Roald Amundsen was a Norwegian explorer; Robert Falcon Scott was a British naval officer.

4. Amundsen's men used dogs to drag equipment to the Pole; Scott's men used Siberian ponies.

5. Amundsen's men buried food all along the trail; Scott's men left food in only a few locations.

6. The Norwegian team skied to the Pole; the British team tried to walk.

7. Amundsen's men made it to the Pole in December 1911; Scott's party arrived in January 1912.

8. The Norwegians found their supplies on the way back; the men arrived back at their ship in good condition.

9. Scott's exhausted party could not get to their provisions; none of the men survived the trek.

10. Nevertheless, Scott and his men are remembered for trying to get to the Pole; the Norwegians—the "winners"—have been almost forgotten.

◆ PRACTICE 16-6

Each of the following independent clauses can be joined with a semicolon to another independent clause to form a compound sentence. In each case, add a semicolon; then, complete the compound sentence with another independent clause.

Example: My brother is addicted to fast food; he eats it every day.

1. Fast-food restaurants are an American institution _____

Answers will vary.

Teaching Tip
Students may enjoy this exercise more if they work in pairs—and if they are encouraged to generate sentences that are humorous (and not necessarily factually accurate).

2. Families eat at these restaurants _____

_____

3. Many teenagers work there _____

_____

4. McDonald's is known for its hamburgers _____

_____

5. KFC is famous for its fried chicken _____

_____

6. Taco Bell serves Mexican-style food _____

_____

7. Pizza Hut specializes in pizza _____

_____

8. Many fast-food restaurants offer some low-fat menu items _____

_____

9. Some offer recyclable packaging _____

_____

10. Some even have playgrounds _____

_____

■ WRITING FIRST: Flashback

Look back at your response to the Writing First exercise on page 241. Do you see any pairs of simple sentences that you could connect with semicolons? If so, rewrite them on the lines below, linking each pair with a semicolon.

Answers will vary.

_____

_____

_____

_____

_____

C   Forming Compound Sentences with Conjunctive Adverbs and Transitional Expressions

Another way to combine two independent clauses into one **compound sentence** is with a **conjunctive adverb** or **transitional expression**. When you use a conjunctive adverb to join two independent clauses, a semicolon always comes *before* the conjunctive adverb, and a comma always comes *after* it.

> Some college students receive grants; <u>however</u>, others must take out loans.

Frequently Used Conjunctive Adverbs

also	instead	still
besides	later	subsequently
consequently	meanwhile	then
eventually	moreover	therefore
finally	nevertheless	thus
furthermore	now	
however	otherwise	

Adding a conjunctive adverb makes the connection between ideas in a sentence clearer and more precise than it would be if the ideas were linked with just a semicolon. Different conjunctive adverbs convey different meanings:

- Some conjunctive adverbs signal addition (*also, besides, furthermore, moreover*).

  > I have a lot on my mind; <u>also</u>, I have a lot of things to do.

- Some conjunctive adverbs make causal connections (*therefore, consequently, thus*).

  > I have a lot on my mind; <u>therefore</u>, it is hard to concentrate.

- Some conjunctive adverbs indicate contradiction or contrast (*nevertheless, however, still*).

  > I have a lot on my mind; <u>still</u>, I must try to relax.

- Some conjunctive adverbs present alternatives (*instead, otherwise*).

  > I have a lot on my mind; <u>otherwise</u>, I could relax.

  > I will try not to think; <u>instead</u>, I will relax.

- Some conjunctive adverbs indicate time sequence (*eventually, finally, later, meanwhile, now, subsequently, then*).

  > I have a lot on my mind; <u>meanwhile</u>, I still have work to do.

● **Writing Tip**

Do not forget to place a
semicolon before every conjunctive adverb or transitional expression that joins
two independent clauses. If
you leave out the semicolon,
you create a run-on sen-
tence. (See 21B.)

ON THE WEB

For more practice, visit
Exercise Central *at*
<bedfordstmartins.com/
writingfirst>.

Like conjunctive adverbs, **transitional expressions** can also link two
independent clauses into one compound sentence.

He had a miserable time at the party; in addition, he drank too much.

The transitional expression is preceded by a semicolon and followed by a
comma.

Frequently Used Transitional Expressions

after all	in comparison
as a result	in contrast
at the same time	in fact
for example	in other words
for instance	of course
in addition	on the contrary

◆ **PRACTICE 16-7**

Add semicolons and commas where required to set off conjunctive adverbs
or transitional expressions that join two independent clauses.

Example: Ketchup is a popular condiment; therefore, it is available in

almost every restaurant.

(1) Andrew F. Smith, a food historian, wrote a book about the

tomato; subsequently, he wrote a book about ketchup. (2) This book, *Pure

Ketchup,* was a big project; in fact, Smith worked on it for five years.

(3) The word *ketchup* may have come from a Chinese word; however,

Smith is not certain of the word's origins. (4) Ketchup has existed since

ancient times; in other words, it is a very old product. (5) Ketchup has

changed a lot over the years; for example, special dyes were developed in

the nineteenth century to make it red. (6) Smith discusses many other

changes; for instance, preservative-free ketchup was invented in 1907.

(7) Ketchup is now used by people in many cultures; still, salsa is more

popular than ketchup in the United States. (8) Today, designer ketchups

are being developed; meanwhile, Heinz has introduced green and purple

ketchup in squeeze bottles. (9) Some of today's ketchups are chunky; in

addition, some ketchups are spicy. (10) Ketchup continues to evolve;

however, Smith is now working on a book about the history of popcorn.

◆ PRACTICE 16-8

Consulting the list of conjunctive adverbs on page 249 and the list of transitional expressions on page 250, choose a word or expression that logically connects each pair of independent clauses below into one compound sentence. Be sure to punctuate appropriately.

Example: Every year since 1927, *Time* has designated a Man of the

       ; however, the
Year, ~~The~~ Man of the Year has not always been a man.

Answers may vary.
(1) The Man of the Year has had great influence over the previous

       ; consequently, the
year's events, ~~The~~ choice is often a prominent politician. (2) In the 1920s

         ; for example,
and 1930s, world leaders were often chosen, Franklin Delano Roosevelt

was chosen twice, and Ethiopia's Haile Selassie once. (3) During the war

         ; in fact,
years, Hitler, Stalin, Churchill, and Roosevelt were all chosen, Stalin was

featured twice. (4) Occasionally, the Man of the Year was not an individ-

      ; for instance, in
ual, ~~In~~ 1950, it was The American Fighting Man. (5) In 1956, The Hun-

         ; then, in
garian Freedom Fighter was Man of the Year, ~~In~~ 1966, *Time* editors chose

The Young Generation. (6) Only a few individual women have been

      ; for example,
selected, Queen Elizabeth II of England was featured in 1952, and

Corazon Aquino, president of the Philippines, in 1986. (7) In 1975, Amer-

         ; nevertheless, the
ican Women were honored as a group, ~~The~~ Man of the Year has nearly

always been male. (8) Very few people of color have been designated

      ; still,
Man of the Year, Martin Luther King Jr. was honored in 1963. (9) The

         ;
Man of the Year has almost always been one or more human beings,
however, the
~~The~~ Computer was selected in 1982 and Endangered Earth in 1988.

         ;
(10) More recently, prominent politicians have once again been chosen,
for example, in
~~In~~ 2001, New York City mayor Rudy Giuliani was *Time*'s Man of the Year

(now called Person of the Year). (11) In 2003, *Time* did not choose a

      ; instead, it
politician, ~~It~~ honored The American Soldier.

◆ PRACTICE 16-9

Add the suggested conjunctive adverb or transitional expression to each of the simple sentences below. Then, add a new independent clause to follow it. Be sure to punctuate correctly.

Example: (however) Commuting students do not really experience campus life.

Commuting students do not really experience campus life; however, there are some benefits to being a commuter.

Answers will vary.

1. (still) Campus residents may have a better college experience.

   Campus residents may have a better college experience; still, being a commuter has its advantages.

2. (in contrast) Living at home gives students access to home-cooked meals.

   Living at home gives students access to home-cooked meals; in contrast, dorm residents eat dining hall food or takeout.

3. (on the other hand) Commuters have a wide choice of jobs in the community.

   Commuters have a wide choice of jobs in the community; on the other hand, students living on campus may have to take on-campus jobs.

4. (however) Commuters get to live with their families.

   Commuters get to live with their families; however, dorm students may live far from home.

5. (for example) There are also some disadvantages to being a commuter.

   There are also some disadvantages to being a commuter; for example, commuters may have trouble joining study groups.

6. (in fact) Unlike dorm students, most commuters have family responsibilities.

   Unlike dorm students, most commuters have family responsibilities; in fact, they may have children of their own.

7. (in addition) Commuters might have to help take care of their parents or grandparents.

   Commuters might have to help take care of their parents or grandparents; in addition, they might have to babysit for younger siblings.

8. (consequently) Commuters might need a car to get to school.

   Commuters might need a car to get to school; consequently, they might have higher expenses than dorm students.

9. (of course) Younger commuters may be under the watchful eyes of their parents.

Younger commuters may be under the watchful eyes of their parents; of course, parents are likely to be stricter than dorm counselors.

10. (therefore) Commuting to college has pros and cons.

Commuting to college has pros and cons; therefore, commuters are not necessarily at a disadvantage.

◆ PRACTICE 16-10

Using the specified topics and conjunctive adverbs or transitional expressions, create five compound sentences. Be sure to punctuate appropriately.

Example:
Topic: fad diets
Transitional expression: for example

People are always falling for fad diets; for example, some people eat only pineapple to lose weight.

1. *Topic:* laws to protect people with disabilities
   Transitional expression: in addition

   Answers will vary.

Teaching Tip
Have students write these sentences on the board. Get at least two versions of each sentence.

2. *Topic:* single men and women as adoptive parents
   Conjunctive adverb: however

3. *Topic:* prayer in public schools
   Conjunctive adverb: therefore

4. *Topic:* high school proms
   Conjunctive adverb: also

5. *Topic:* course requirements at your school
   Conjunctive adverb: instead

■ WRITING FIRST: Flashback

Look back at your response to the Writing First exercise on page 241. Have you used any conjunctive adverbs or transitional expressions to link independent clauses? If so, check to make sure that you have punctuated them correctly. Then, check to see that you have used the word or expression that best shows the relationship between the ideas in the two independent clauses. Revise your work if necessary.

■ WRITING FIRST: Revising and Editing

Look back at your response to the Writing First exercise on page 241. Now, try to add one of the new compound sentences you created in the Flashback exercises on pages 246 and 248. Then, check each compound sentence to make sure you have used the coordinating conjunction, conjunctive adverb, or transitional expression that best conveys your meaning and that you have punctuated these sentences correctly. When you have finished, look over a piece of writing you have done in response to another assignment, and try combining some pairs of simple sentences into compound sentences.

CHAPTER REVIEW

◆ EDITING PRACTICE

Read the following student essay. Then, create compound sentences by linking pairs of simple sentences where appropriate, joining them with a coordinating conjunction, a semicolon, or a semicolon followed by either a conjunctive adverb or a transitional expression. Remember to put commas before coordinating conjunctions and to use semicolons and commas correctly with conjunctive adverbs and transitional expressions. The first two sentences have been combined for you.
Answers may vary.

My Father's Life

My grandparents were born in Ukraine, *but they* ~~They~~ raised my father in western Pennsylvania. The ninth of their ten children, he had a life I cannot begin to imagine. To me,

Teaching Tip
For a short writing assignment, ask students to write a similar passage about the life of one of their parents.

he is my big, strong, powerful father/ ~~In reality, he is a~~
                  ; however, he is also a
child of poverty.

    My grandfather worked for the American Car Foundry.
The family lived in a company house/ ~~They~~ shopped at the
            , and they
company store. In 1934, my grandfather was laid off/ ~~He~~
               , so he
went to work digging sewer lines for the government. At
that time, the family was on welfare. Every week, they were
entitled to get food rations/ ~~My~~ father would go to pick
         , and my
up the food. They desperately needed the prunes, beans,
flour, margarine, and other things.

    For years, my father wore his brothers' hand-me-down
clothes/ ~~He~~ wore thrift-shop shoes with cardboard over the
    ; in addition, he
holes in the soles. He was often hungry/ ~~He~~ would sometimes
                , so he
sit by the side of the railroad tracks, waiting for the
engineer to throw him an orange. My father would do any
job to earn a quarter/ ~~Once, for example,~~ he weeded a
           ; for example, once
mile-long row of tomato plants. For this work, he was paid
twenty-five cents and a pack of Necco wafers.

    My father saved his pennies/ ~~Eventually,~~ he was able
              ; eventually,
to buy a used bicycle for two dollars. He dropped out of
school at fourteen and got a job/ ~~The~~ family badly needed
           , for the
his income. He woke up every day at 4 a.m. ~~He~~ rode his
                 , and he
bike to his job at a meatpacking plant. He worked for
fifty cents a day.

    In 1943, at the age of seventeen, my father joined the
U.S. Navy/ ~~He~~ discovered a new world. For the first time
    ; thus, he
in his life, he had enough to eat. He was always first in
line at the mess hall/ ~~He~~ went back for seconds and thirds
        ; in fact, he
before anyone else. After the war ended in 1945, he was
discharged from the Navy. He went to work in a meat market
in New York City/ ~~The~~ only trade he knew was the meat
    ; the
business. Three years later, he had saved enough to open
his own store, Pete's Quality Meats.

Map of Ukraine

World War II sailor

◆ COLLABORATIVE ACTIVITIES

1. Working in a small group, pair each of the simple sentences in the left-hand column below with a sentence in the right-hand column to create ten compound sentences. Use as many different coordinating conjunctions as you can to connect the independent clauses. Be sure each coordinating conjunction you choose conveys a logical relationship between ideas, and remember to put a comma before each one. You may use some of the listed sentences more than once. *Note:* Many different combinations—some serious and factually accurate, some humorous—are possible.

Some dogs wear little sweaters.	Many are named Hamlet.
Pit bulls are raised to fight.	They live in groups.
Bonobos are pygmy chimpanzees.	One even sings Christmas carols.
	They can wear bandanas.
Many people fear Dobermans.	They can play Frisbee.
Leopards have spots.	Many live in equatorial Zaire.
Dalmations can live in firehouses.	Some people think they are gentle.
Horses can wear blankets.	They don't get cold in winter.
All mules are sterile.	They are half horse and half donkey.
Great Danes are huge dogs.	
Parrots can often speak.	They can be unpredictable.

2. Work in a group of three or four students to create a cast of five characters for a movie, a television pilot, or a music video. Working individually, write five descriptive short sentences—one about each character. Then, exchange papers with another student. Add a coordinating conjunction to each sentence on the list to create five new compound sentences.

Example:

ORIGINAL SENTENCE Mark is a handsome heartthrob.

NEW SENTENCE Mark is a handsome heartthrob, but he has green dreadlocks.

Next, select the three characters who sound most interesting. Write a few additional descriptive sentences about those characters, using compound sentences whenever possible. Your new sentences can provide information about the characters' relationships with one another as well as about their personalities and physical traits.

☑ REVIEW CHECKLIST:
Writing Compound Sentences

☐ A compound sentence is made up of two simple sentences (independent clauses). (See 16A.)

☐ A coordinating conjunction—*and, but, for, nor, or, so,* or *yet*—can join two independent clauses into one compound sentence. A comma always comes before the coordinating conjunction. (See 16A.)

☐ A semicolon can join two independent clauses into one compound sentence. (See 16B.)

☐ A conjunctive adverb or transitional expression can also join two independent clauses into one compound sentence. When it joins two independent clauses, a conjunctive adverb or transitional expression is always preceded by a semicolon and followed by a comma. (See 16C.)

Writing Complex Sentences

Word Power

courtesy polite behavior

infringe to go beyond the limits of

offend to cause anger or resentment

■ WRITING FIRST

In March 2003, the state of New York passed a law that banned smoking in bars and restaurants. The picture above shows a person lighting a candle in 2004 to celebrate the one-year anniversary of this tough antismoking law. Look at the picture, and then describe something that you believe needs to be changed—for example, a rule, a law, a policy, a situation, or a custom. First, identify what you think needs to be changed; then, explain why you think a change is necessary.

A   Identifying Complex Sentences

As you learned in Chapter 16, an **independent clause** can stand alone as a **simple sentence**.

INDEPENDENT   The exhibit <u>was</u> controversial.
CLAUSE

However, a **dependent clause** cannot stand alone as a sentence. It needs an independent clause to complete its meaning.

DEPENDENT   Because the exhibit was controversial
CLAUSE

What happened because the exhibit was controversial? To answer this question, you need to add an independent clause that completes the idea begun in the dependent clause. The result is a **complex sentence**—a sentence that consists of one independent clause and one or more dependent clauses.

┌─────────── DEPENDENT CLAUSE ───────────┐ ┌─ INDEPENDENT CLAUSE ─┐
COMPLEX   Because the exhibit was controversial, many people came
SENTENCE   └─────────────────────┘
            to see the paintings.

◆ PRACTICE 17-1

In the blank following each of the items below, indicate whether the group of words is an independent clause (***IC***) or a dependent clause (***DC***).

Example: Gymnastics became popular in the United States in the twentieth century. _*IC*_

1. Gymnastics exercises help develop all parts of the body. _*IC*_

2. The practice of gymnastics dates back to the athletes of ancient Greece. _*IC*_

3. Because a German named Frederick Jahn popularized gymnastics in the nineteenth century. _*DC*_

4. Although German immigrants to the United States participated in gymnastics. _*DC*_

5. Gymnastics later became an event in the Olympic games. _*IC*_

6. Even though women's gymnastics once stressed physical grace rather than strength. _*DC*_

7. In the 1970s, women Olympic gymnasts began to dominate the games. _*IC*_

8. When Mary Lou Retton became the first American woman to win a gold medal for gymnastics in 1984. _*DC*_

9. Who was only sixteen years old at the time of her gold-medal win. _*DC*_

ESL Tip
Review the concept of subordination. Discuss how adding a subordinating conjunction can make one idea depend on another for completion.

10. The first U.S. women's gymnastics team to win a gold medal competed in the 1996 games. _IC_

◆ PRACTICE 17-2

In the blank following each of the items below, indicate whether the group of words is an independent clause (**IC**) or a dependent clause (**DC**).

> **Example:** When novelist Toni Morrison was born in Ohio in 1931. _DC_

1. As a young reader, Toni Morrison liked the classic Russian novelists. _IC_

2. After she graduated from Howard University with a bachelor's degree in English. _DC_

3. Morrison based her novel *The Bluest Eye* on a childhood friend's prayers to God for blue eyes. _IC_

4. While she raised two sons as a single mother and worked as an editor at Random House. _DC_

5. As her reputation as a novelist grew with the publication of *Song of Solomon* and *Tar Baby*. _DC_

6. Her picture appeared on the cover of *Newsweek* in 1981. _IC_

7. Before her novel *Beloved* won the 1988 Pulitzer Prize for fiction. _DC_

8. *Beloved* was later made into a film starring Oprah Winfrey. _IC_

9. In 1993, Morrison became the first black woman to win the Nobel Prize in Literature. _IC_

10. Who published the novel *Paradise* in 1998 to mixed reviews. _DC_

B	**Forming Complex Sentences with Subordinating Conjunctions**

One way to form a complex sentence is to use a **subordinating conjunction**—a word like *although* or *because*—to join two simple sentences (independent clauses). When you add a subordinating conjunction to an independent clause, it can no longer stand alone. It becomes a dependent clause, which needs an independent clause to complete its meaning. A dependent clause joined with an independent clause creates a **complex sentence**.

TWO SIMPLE SENTENCES   Muhammad Ali was stripped of his title for refusing to go into the army. Many people admired his antiwar position.

DEPENDENT CLAUSE

COMPLEX SENTENCE   <u>Although Muhammad Ali was stripped of his title for refusing to go into the army,</u> many people admired his antiwar position.

● **Writing Tip**

A clause introduced by a subordinating conjunction does not express a complete thought. Used by itself, it is a sentence fragment. (See 22D.)

Frequently Used Subordinating Conjunctions

after	even though	since	whenever
although	if	so that	where
as	if only	than	whereas
as if	in order that	that	wherever
as though	now that	though	whether
because	once	unless	while
before	provided that	until	
even if	rather than	when	

Teaching Tip
Have students create sentences that start with the subordinating conjunctions listed here.

Different subordinating conjunctions express different relationships between dependent and independent clauses.

Teaching Tip
Have students memorize the subordinating conjunctions and the relationships they express.

ESL Tip
Make sure students understand the subtle differences in meaning between different subordinating conjunctions.

Relationship between Clauses	Subordinating Conjunction	Example
Time	after, before, since, until, when, whenever, while	When the whale surfaced, Ahab threw his harpoon.
Reason or cause	as, because	Scientists scaled back the project <u>because the government cut funds.</u>
Result or effect	in order that, so that	<u>So that students' math scores will improve,</u> many schools have begun special programs.
Condition	even if, if, unless	The rain forest may disappear <u>unless steps are taken immediately.</u>

Relationship between Clauses	Subordinating Conjunction	Example
Contrast	although, even though, though	<u>Although Thomas Edison had almost no formal education</u>, he was a successful inventor.
Location	where, wherever	Pittsburgh was built <u>where the Allegheny and Monongahela Rivers meet</u>.

FOCUS **Punctuating with Subordinating Conjunctions**

Use a comma after the dependent clause when it comes *before* the independent clause in the sentence. Do not use a comma when the dependent clause comes *after* the independent clause in the sentence.

┌──────── DEPENDENT CLAUSE ────────┐ ┌──── INDEPENDENT CLAUSE ────┐
Although she wore the scarlet letter, Hester carried herself proudly.

┌──── INDEPENDENT CLAUSE ────┐ ┌──── DEPENDENT CLAUSE ────┐
Hester carried herself proudly although she wore the scarlet letter.

◆ **PRACTICE 17-3**

ON THE WEB
For more practice, visit
Exercise Central *at*
*<bedfordstmartins.com/
writingfirst>.*

In the blank in each of the sentences below, write an appropriate subordinating conjunction. Look at the list of subordinating conjunctions on page 261 to help you choose a conjunction that establishes a logical relationship between the two clauses it links. (The required punctuation has been provided.)

Example: _____*When*_____ he was only six years old, Freddy Adu was playing informal soccer games with grown men.

Answers may vary.

(1) His family moved from Ghana to the United States _____*when*_____ he was still a young boy. (2) Freddy did not play organized soccer _____*until*_____ he was in the fourth grade. (3) _____*Although*_____ he is still a teenager, Freddy is already one of America's most famous soccer players.

(4) His remarkable talent excites even professional players and coaches
_____whenever_____ they see him play. (5) _____Since_____ he was thirteen, he has been recruited by some of the greatest teams in the world. (6) One team offered his mother $750,000 _____if_____ Freddy would play for them. (7) _____Although_____ she needed the money, his mother turned down every offer. (8) The offers kept coming in _____as_____ Freddy continued to excel in major competitions for young players. (9) He and his mother finally agreed to a professional contract _____that_____ runs for six years. (10) _____Now that_____ Freddy has joined DC United, he is the highest-paid player in American soccer.

◆ PRACTICE 17-4

Form one complex sentence by combining each of the following pairs of sentences. Use a subordinating conjunction from the list on page 261 to clarify the relationship between the dependent and independent clauses in each sentence. Make sure you include a comma where one is required.

Example: Orville and Wilbur Wright built the first powered plane,
although they
~~They~~ had no formal training as engineers.

Although professional   *, in*
1. ~~Professional~~ midwives are used widely in Europe, ~~In~~ the United States,

   they usually practice only in areas with few doctors.
   When   *, a*
2. John Deere constructed his first steel plow in 1837, ~~A~~ new era began in

   farming.
                                                       even though he
3. Stephen Crane describes battles in *The Red Badge of Courage,* ~~He~~ never

   experienced a war.
   When   *, thousands*
4. Elvis Presley died suddenly in 1977, ~~Thousands~~ of his fans gathered in

   front of his mansion.
   After   *, the*
5. Jonas Salk developed the first polio vaccine in the 1950s, ~~The~~ number of polio cases declined in the United States.
   As the   *, some*
6. ~~The~~ salaries of baseball players rose in the 1980s, ~~Some~~ sportswriters

   predicted a drop in attendance.
   Before the
7. ~~The~~ Du Ponts arrived from France in 1800, American gunpowder was

   inferior to the kind manufactured by the French.

8. Margaret Sanger opened her first birth-control clinic in America in *After*
1916, ~~She~~ , she was arrested and put in jail.

9. Thaddeus Stevens thought plantation land should be given to freed *Because*
slaves, ~~He~~ , he disagreed with Lincoln's peace terms for the South.

10. Steven Spielberg directed some very popular movies, ~~He~~ , he did not win *Even though*
an Academy Award until *Schindler's List*.

■ WRITING FIRST: Flashback

Look back at your response to the Writing First exercise on page 258. Identify two pairs of simple sentences that could be combined with subordinating conjunctions. On the lines below, combine each pair into a complex sentence by making one sentence a dependent clause. Check to make sure you have punctuated your new sentences correctly.

Answers will vary.

_____

_____

_____

_____

C | **Forming Complex Sentences with Relative Pronouns**

Another way to form a complex sentence is to use **relative pronouns** (*who, that, which,* and so on) to join two simple sentences (independent clauses). The relative pronoun introduces a dependent clause that describes a noun or pronoun in the independent clause.

TWO SIMPLE SENTENCES | Pit bulls were originally bred in England. They can be very aggressive.

————————— DEPENDENT CLAUSE ———————————

COMPLEX SENTENCE | Pit bulls, <u>which were originally bred in England</u>, can be very aggressive.

Note: The relative pronoun always refers to a word in the independent clause.

Relative Pronouns			
that	which	whoever	whomever
what	who	whom	whose

Different relative pronouns show different relationships between the ideas in the independent and dependent clauses that they link.

TWO SIMPLE SENTENCES	Nadine Gordimer comes from South Africa. She won the Nobel Prize in Literature in 1991.
COMPLEX SENTENCE	Nadine Gordimer, who won the Nobel Prize in Literature in 1991, comes from South Africa.
TWO SIMPLE SENTENCES	Last week I had a job interview. It went very well.
COMPLEX SENTENCE	Last week I had a job interview that went very well.
TWO SIMPLE SENTENCES	Transistors have replaced vacuum tubes in radios and televisions. They were invented in 1948.
COMPLEX SENTENCE	Transistors, which were invented in 1948, have replaced vacuum tubes in radios and televisions.

● **Writing Tip**
Remember, *who* refers to people, and *that* and *which* refer to things.

Teaching Tip
Tell students that when they create a complex sentence, the relative pronoun substitutes for a noun or another pronoun in one of the original simple sentences.

◆ **PRACTICE 17-5**

In each of the following complex sentences, underline the dependent clause once, and underline the relative pronoun twice. Then, draw an arrow from the relative pronoun to the noun or pronoun to which it refers.

ON THE WEB
For more practice, visit Exercise Central *at* <bedfordstmartins.com/ writingfirst>.

Example: MTV, which was the first TV show devoted to popular music videos, began in 1981.
Answers will vary.

1. MTV's very first music video, which was performed by a group called the Buggles, contained the lyric "Video killed the radio star."

2. MTV's early videos were simple productions that recorded the singers in live studio performances.

3. Recording executives, who had been suspicious of MTV at first, soon realized the power of music videos.

4. Music videos became elaborate productions that featured multiple settings, special effects, and large casts of dancers.

5. The Cars' song "You Might Think" won the award for best video at the first MTV music awards, which aired in September 1984.

6. The game show *Remote Control*, which made fun of *Jeopardy*, began on MTV in 1987.

7. The fashion program *House of Style* became popular in 1989 because of supermodel Cindy Crawford, who was its first host.

8. *The Real World*, a reality series that featured a group of young people living together in New York City, also became popular then.

9. This same year, governor Bill Clinton, who would soon be elected president, met with young voters on MTV.

10. Today, MTV, which devotes less and less time to music videos, produces many hours of original programming.

◆ **PRACTICE 17-6**

Combine each of the following pairs of simple sentences into one complex sentence, using the relative pronoun that follows each pair.

Example: Many young Americans perform community service as part of their education. They are learning valuable skills. (who)

Many young Americans who perform community service as part of their education are learning valuable skills.

Answers will vary.

1. Their work is called service-learning. It benefits both the participants and the communities. (which)

Their work, which benefits both the participants and the communities, is called service-learning.

2. A service-learning project meets a community need. It is sponsored either by a school or by the community. (which)

A service-learning project, which is sponsored either by a school or by the community, meets a community need.

3. The young people work at projects such as designing neighborhood playgrounds. They are not paid. (who)

The young people, who are not paid, work at projects such as designing neighborhood playgrounds.

4. It is challenging work. It gives young people satisfaction. (that)

It is challenging work that gives young people satisfaction.

5. Designing a playground teaches them to communicate. It requires teamwork. (which)

Designing a playground, which requires teamwork, teaches them to communicate.

6. Communicating with the public is an important skill. It is a skill they can use throughout their lives. (that)

   Communicating with the public is an important skill that they can use

   throughout their lives.

7. They also learn to solve problems. These are problems the community cannot solve by itself. (that)

   They also learn to solve problems that the community cannot solve by

   itself.

8. Being in charge of a project gives participants a sense of responsibility. It is a hard job. (which)

   Being in charge of a project, which is a hard job, gives participants a

   sense of responsibility.

9. The young participants gain satisfaction from performing a valuable service. They often lack self-confidence. (who)

   The young participants, who often lack self-confidence, gain satisfaction

   from performing a valuable service.

10. The community gets help solving its problems. It appreciates the young person's work. (which)

    The community, which gets help solving its problems, appreciates the

    young person's work.

D Punctuating with Relative Pronouns

Sometimes you place a comma before and after a clause introduced by a relative pronoun, and sometimes you do not. If the clause is **restrictive**—that is, it contains information that is essential to the meaning of the sentence—do **not** set it off with commas.

RESTRICTIVE CLAUSE The class <u>that I signed up for</u> is supposed to be interesting. (no commas)

In the sentence above, the writer is not talking about just any class. He is talking about the specific class that he signed up for. Without the clause *that I signed up for,* the sentence's meaning would be different. Because the dependent clause is necessary to convey the sentence's meaning, it is restrictive and not set off by commas.

If, however, the clause is **nonrestrictive**—that is, if it contains information that is *not* essential to the meaning of the sentence—you **must** set it off with commas.

NONRESTRICTIVE CLAUSE   *On the Waterfront,* which was released in 1954, is one of Marlon Brando's best films. (commas needed)

In this sentence, the dependent clause *which was released in 1954* gives extra information. Even without it, the sentence communicates the same idea: *On the Waterfront* is one of Marlon Brando's best films. Because the dependent clause is not necessary to convey the sentence's meaning, it is nonrestrictive and must be set off with commas.

FOCUS   **Punctuating with *Which, That,* and *Who***

In general, *which* introduces a nonrestrictive clause, which is set off with commas. *That* introduces a restrictive clause, which is not set off with commas. Because *who* can introduce either a restrictive or a nonrestrictive clause, a dependent clause introduced by *who* may or may not be set off with commas.

> My laptop, <u>which weighs only five pounds</u>, fits into my backpack. (*Which* introduces a nonrestrictive clause.)
>
> The laptop <u>that I bought yesterday</u> weighs only five pounds. (*That* introduces a restrictive clause.)
>
> My grandfather, <u>who worked two jobs most of his life</u>, came to this country in 1955. (*Who* introduces a nonrestrictive clause.)
>
> The comedian <u>who opened the show</u> wasn't very funny. (*Who* introduces a restrictive clause.)

◆ PRACTICE 17-7

Read the following sentences. If the dependent clause in the sentence is restrictive, write **R** in the blank. If the clause is nonrestrictive, write **N**.

Example: The United States, which is seen as a country of gun owners, is frightening to many Japanese. __N__

1. This image of the United States is reinforced by a Japanese television show that started several years ago. __R__

2. Every Sunday night, viewers watch Hoyota, who is a Japanese tourist trying to survive in America, overcome his latest disaster. __N__

3. One Sunday, Hoyota was walking the streets of New York, which were full of people, looking for someone to help him. __N__

Teaching Tip
Remind students that the clause introduced by a relative pronoun does not always interrupt the independent clause; often, as in item 1 in Practice 17-7, it comes *after* the independent clause.

4. His questions, which were in broken English, were not easily under-

   stood. _N_

5. This television program, which teaches American English to viewers,

   is very popular. _N_

6. Most Japanese learn English in high school by reading textbooks that

   are designed to help them get into universities. _R_

7. The English they learn, which is very formal, is not very useful in the

   real world. _N_

8. Many Japanese who come to the United States find that they cannot

   understand spoken English. _R_

9. For example, police once shot a Japanese exchange student who did

   not understand the command "freeze." _R_

10. For this reason, many Japanese want to learn "usable English" that

    will help them survive in the United States. _R_

◆ PRACTICE 17-8

Combine each of the following pairs of simple sentences into one complex
sentence, using a relative pronoun (*who, which,* or *that*). Be sure to add
proper punctuation.

> **Example:**   Emiliano Zapata was a leader of the 1911 Mexican Revo-
> lution. He is a hero to many Mexicans.
>
> _Emiliano Zapata, who was a leader of the 1911 Mexican Revolution, is a_
>
> _hero to many Mexicans._

Answers will vary.

1. Zapata was a sharecropper. He could not read or write.

   Zapata was a sharecropper who could not read or write.

2. He built an army. The army fought for the idea of "Tierra y Libertad"

   ("Land and Liberty").

   He built an army that fought for the idea of "Tierra y Libertad"

   ("Land and Liberty").

3. Mexican peasants wanted to regain their land. They felt foreigners had

   taken it from them.

   Mexican peasants wanted to regain their land, which they felt foreigners

   had taken from them.

4. Zapata helped the revolution succeed. He did not think the new government would return the land to the peasants.

Zapata, who helped the revolution succeed, did not think the new

government would return the land to the peasants.

5. He created his own program for returning the land. It was known as the "Plan of Ayala."

He created his own program, which was known as the "Plan of Ayala,"

for returning the land.

6. He continued to resist the government. The government did not agree with his plan.

He continued to resist the government, which did not agree with

his plan.

7. Zapata entered Mexico City in 1914. He had already gained control of almost all of southern Mexico.

Zapata, who had already gained control of almost all of southern Mexico,

entered Mexico City in 1914.

8. A year later, the government began a major campaign. It drove Zapata's army out of Mexico City.

A year later, the government began a major campaign that drove

Zapata's army out of Mexico City.

9. The government wanted to get rid of Zapata. It tricked him into meeting with one of its generals.

The government, which wanted to get rid of Zapata, tricked him into

meeting with one of its generals.

10. Zapata was murdered at that meeting. He is now the subject of many stories and songs.

Zapata, who was murdered at that meeting, is now the subject of many

stories and songs.

◆ PRACTICE 17-9

Fill in the blanks in the sentences that follow with a dependent clause that begins with a relative pronoun (*who, which,* or *that*). The new dependent clause should help complete the meaning of the original sentence. Be sure to add the proper punctuation.

Example: People *who are talking on cell phones* may not be paying close attention to their driving.
Answers will vary.

1. People _____

should have their driver's licenses revoked.

2. A speeding car is like a weapon _____

_____.

3. Teenagers _____

could be required to take driver's education first.

4. New drivers should be taught safety tips _____

_____.

5. One activity _____

is eating while one is driving.

6. A driver _____

cannot possibly keep both hands on the steering wheel.

7. Putting on makeup while driving is another activity _____

_____.

8. To encourage safe driving, the police should be allowed to pull over

any driver _____.

9. For a first offense, a driver _____

could be given only a warning.

10. A second offense, however, would result in a fine _____

_____.

■ WRITING FIRST: Flashback

Look back at your response to the Writing First exercise on page 258. Identify two simple sentences that could be combined with a relative pronoun. (If you cannot find two appropriate sentences, write two new ones.) On the lines below, write the new complex sentence.

Answers will vary.

_____

_____

_____

■ WRITING FIRST: Revising and Editing

Look back at your response to the Writing First exercise on page
258. Incorporating one of the new complex sentences you created
in the Flashback exercises on pages 264 and 271, revise your work.
Then, check to make sure there are no errors in your use of subordinating conjunctions and relative pronouns. When you have finished, look over a piece of writing you have done in response to
another assignment, and try combining some simple sentences into
complex sentences. Make sure that you have added the correct
punctuation.

CHAPTER REVIEW

◆ EDITING PRACTICE

Read the following student essay. Then, revise it by combining pairs of
simple sentences with subordinating conjunctions or relative pronouns
that indicate the relationship between them. Be sure to punctuate correctly. The first sentence has been revised for you.

Answers may vary.

Community Artist

When
I was in tenth grade at West Philadelphia High School

in Philadelphia, I took an art class. One day, my teacher

started to talk about the free Philadelphia Mural Arts
that we
Program, We could sign up for it. I needed something to
Although
do after school and during the summer. I didn't know much

about the program, I signed up and was accepted. It turned

out to be a rewarding experience.

My teacher told us about the beginning of the program,
which
It started in 1984. Philadelphia had a serious problem,
which
The problem was graffiti. Graffiti artists had painted

their designs on buildings all over the city. A solution

to the problem was the Philadelphia Anti-Graffiti Network,
which   *If they*
This program offered graffiti artists an alternative. They
they
could give up graffiti, They would not be prosecuted. *Since they* They
they
clearly enjoyed painting, They could use their skills to

serve the community by painting murals on public buildings.

Graffiti on wall

They could create scenic landscapes, portraits of local
heroes, and abstract designs. ~~The~~ *Although the* former graffiti artists
had once been lawbreakers~~.~~ *, they* ~~They~~ could now take a
constructive role in building community spirit.

By 1996, the Philadelphia Anti-Graffiti Network was
concentrating on eliminating graffiti, and the Mural Arts
Program continued to improve the community. *While it* ~~It~~ no longer
worked with graffiti offenders~~.~~ *, it* ~~It~~ started after-school and
summer programs for students. The Mural Arts Program
achieved national recognition in 1997~~.~~ *, when* President Clinton
visited the program and took part in painting murals. The
Mural Arts Program has so far completed more than 2,300
indoor and outdoor murals~~.~~ *, which* ~~This~~ is more than any other
public art program in the country.

I joined the Mural Arts program in 2001. My fellow
students *, who came from all parts of the city,* and I visited some of the murals. ~~We came from~~
~~all over the city.~~ The best part of the program was in
the summer~~.~~ *, when we* ~~We~~ learned to use computer-generated design
programs to turn artistic concepts into works of art. *When we* ~~We~~
worked with an artist~~.~~ *, we* ~~We~~ actually got to paint parts of
her mural on the walls of a building. *When people* ~~People~~ walk or drive
by the building~~.~~ *, they* ~~They~~ can see our work.

I learned a lot in this program. *Although all* ~~All~~ the students had
to work together~~.~~ *, we* ~~We~~ also worked with artists and community
residents. We helped the community come together to create
a mural. *Although at* ~~At~~ first~~.~~ I didn't care about art~~.~~ *, now* ~~Now~~ I really
appreciate it. I am grateful to my tenth-grade art
teacher~~.~~ *, who* ~~He~~ got me interested in the mural program.

*Mural created by Philadelphia
Mural Arts Program*

◆ COLLABORATIVE ACTIVITIES

1. Working in a group of four students, make a list of three or four of
   your favorite television shows. Divide into pairs, and with your partner, write two simple sentences describing each show. Next, use subordinating conjunctions or relative pronouns to combine each pair of
   sentences into one complex sentence. With your group, discuss how
   the ideas in each complex sentence are related, and make sure you
   have used the subordinating conjunction or relative pronoun that best
   conveys this relationship.

EXAMPLE: *The Brady Bunch* portrays a 1970s family. It still appeals to many viewers.

Although *The Brady Bunch* portrays a 1970s family, it still appeals to many viewers.

2. Imagine that you and the members of your group live in a neighborhood where workers are repairing underground power lines. As they work, the workers talk loudly and use foul language. Write a letter of complaint to the power company in which you explain that the workers' behavior is offensive to you and to your children. Tell the company that you want the offensive behavior to end. Write the first draft of your letter in simple sentences. After you have written this draft, work as a group to combine as many sentences as you can with subordinating conjunctions and relative pronouns.

3. Assume you are in a competition to determine which collaborative group in your class is best at writing complex sentences. Working in a group, prepare a letter to your instructor in which you present the strengths of your group. Be sure to use a subordinating conjunction or relative pronoun in each of the sentences in your letter. Finally, as a class, evaluate the letters from the groups, and choose the letter that most successfully convinces you that its group is best.

☑ REVIEW CHECKLIST:
Writing Complex Sentences

- A clause is a group of words that contains a subject and a verb. An independent clause can stand alone as a sentence. A dependent clause cannot stand alone as a sentence because it needs other words to complete its meaning. (See 17A.)

- A complex sentence consists of one independent clause (simple sentence) combined with one or more dependent clauses. (See 17A.)

- Subordinating conjunctions—such as *although, after, when, while,* and *because*—can join two independent clauses into one complex sentence. (See 17B.)

- Always use a comma after a dependent clause when it comes *before* the independent clause in the sentence. Do not use a comma when the dependent clause comes *after* the independent clause. (See 17B.)

- Relative pronouns—such as *who, which,* and *that*—can also join two independent clauses into one complex sentence. The relative pronoun shows the relationship between the ideas in the two independent clauses that it links. (See 17C.)

- When you link two independent clauses with a relative pronoun, use commas with nonrestrictive clauses; do not use commas with restrictive clauses. (See 17D.)

Achieving Sentence Variety

PREVIEW

In this chapter, you will learn

■ to vary sentence types (18A)

■ to vary sentence openings (18B)

■ to combine sentences (18C)

■ to vary sentence lengths (18D)

■ WRITING FIRST

The picture above shows items recovered from a 1950s time capsule. Plan a time capsule that your children will open when they are adults. What items would you include? How would you expect each item to communicate to your children what you and your world were like? Look at the picture, and then explain your decisions.

In Chapters 15 through 17, you learned to write simple, compound, and complex sentences. Now, you are ready to work on **sentence variety** by using sentences of different types and lengths in your writing. A passage of varied sentences flows more smoothly, is easier to read and understand, and is more interesting than one in which all the sentences are the same length and begin with the subject.

275

A Varying Sentence Types

Most English sentences are **statements**. Others are **questions** or **exclamations**. One way to vary your sentences is to use an occasional question or exclamation where it is appropriate.

In the following paragraph, a question and an exclamation add variety.

Question

Over a period of less than twenty years, the image of African Americans in television sitcoms seemed to change dramatically, reflecting the changing status of black men and women in American society. But had anything really changed? In *Beulah*, the 1950 sitcom that was the first to star an African-American woman, the title character was a maid. Her friends were portrayed as irresponsible and not very smart. *Amos 'n' Andy*, which also appeared in the 1950s, continued these negative stereotypes of black characters. In 1968, with the civil rights movement at its height, the NBC comedy hit *Julia* portrayed a black woman in a much more favorable light. A widowed nurse, raising a small boy on her own, Julia was a dedicated professional and a patient and devoted mother. The image of the African American was certainly more positive, but the character was no more balanced or three-dimensional than earlier black characters had been. Julia was not an object of ridicule; instead, she was a saint!

Exclamation

◆ **PRACTICE 18-1**

Revise the following passage by changing one of the statements into a question and one of the statements into an exclamation.

Example: Some people pursue two different careers at the same time. (statement)

Why do some people pursue two different careers at the same time?

(question)

Answers will vary.

(1) Many working people have more than one job. (2) For example, a police officer might moonlight as a security guard, an actor might also work as a waiter, and an artist or a writer might also teach. (3) These workers need their second jobs for survival. (4) In recent years, however, more and more successful professionals have decided to begin a second career without abandoning the first one. (5) Often, the second career seems to be very different from the first one. (6) For example, a teacher might also work as a professional model. (7) Sometimes, however, the two careers really do have something in common. (8) After all, both

teaching and modeling involve performing for an audience. (9) Similarly, a lawyer may be drawn to the ministry, another career that is dedicated to justice. (10) ~~Many things motivate~~ *What motivates* people to combine two seemingly different professions^ (11) Those who do so say they do it not for the money but for professional satisfaction. (12) Obviously, these workers are very lucky people^

■ WRITING FIRST: Flashback

Look back at your response to the Writing First exercise on page 275. What questions does your writing answer? Write one or two questions on the lines below.

Question 1: *Answers will vary.* _____

_____

Question 2: _____

_____

If you can, add one of these questions to your discussion. (You may need to substitute it for a sentence that is already there.)

If you think an exclamation would be an appropriate addition to your writing, suggest one below.

Exclamation: _____

_____

Where could you add this exclamation?

B   Varying Sentence Openings

Varying the way you begin your sentences is another way to add life to your writing. When all the sentences in a paragraph begin in the same way, your writing is likely to seem dull and repetitive. In the following paragraph, for example, every sentence begins with the subject.

> Scientists have been observing a disturbing phenomenon. The population of frogs, toads, and salamanders has been declining. This decline was first noticed in the mid-1980s. Some reports blamed chemical pollution. Some biologists began to suspect that a fungal disease was killing these amphibians. The most reasonable explanation seems to be that the amphibians' eggs are threatened by solar radiation. This radiation penetrates the thinned ozone layer, which used to shield them from the sun's rays.

Teaching Tip
Caution students against using too many of any kind of sentence opening. Starting every sentence with an adverb can be just as dull as always starting with the subject.

● **Writing Tip**
Circle every *The, This, He, She,* and *It* that begins a sentence. Then, revise as necessary to vary sentence openings.

*For more on adverbs, see
Chapter 29.*

Teaching Tip
Remind students that they
can use conjunctive adverbs,
such as *however* and *thus*, to
open sentences. Refer students to the list of conjunctive adverbs in 16C.

*For more on prepositions, see
15B.*

● Writing Tip
An adverb or a prepositional
phrase that opens a sentence
is followed by a comma.
However, if an introductory
prepositional phrase has
only one or two words, the
comma is not required.
(See 31B.)

ON THE WEB
For more practice, visit
Exercise Central *at
<bedfordstmartins.com/
writingfirst>.*

Beginning with Adverbs

Instead of opening every sentence with the subject, try beginning with one
or more **adverbs**, as the following paragraph illustrates.

> Scientists have been observing a disturbing phenomenon. Gradu-
> ally but steadily, the population of frogs, toads, and salamanders has
> been declining. This decline was first noticed in the mid-1980s. Some
> reports blamed chemical pollution. Some biologists began to suspect
> that a fungal disease was killing these amphibians. However, the most
> reasonable explanation seems to be that the amphibians' eggs are
> threatened by solar radiation. This radiation penetrates the thinned
> ozone layer, which used to shield them from the sun's rays.

Beginning with Prepositional Phrases

You can also begin some sentences with prepositional phrases. A **prepositional phrase** (such as *along the river* or *near the diner*) is made up of a
preposition and its object.

> In recent years, scientists have been observing a disturbing phe-
> nomenon. Gradually but steadily, the population of frogs, toads, and
> salamanders has been declining. This decline was first noticed in the
> mid-1980s. At first, some reports blamed chemical pollution. After a
> while, some biologists began to suspect that a fungal disease was
> killing these amphibians. However, the most reasonable explanation
> seems to be that the amphibians' eggs are threatened by solar radia-
> tion. This radiation penetrates the thinned ozone layer, which used to
> shield them from the sun's rays.

FOCUS   Sentence Openings

Note that in addition to adding variety, adverbs and prepositional
phrases at the beginnings of sentences can also function as transitions, joining the sentences smoothly into a paragraph. (See 2D.)

◆ PRACTICE 18-2

Underline the adverb in each of the following sentences, and then rewrite
the sentence so that the adverb appears at the beginning. Be sure to punctuate correctly.

Example: It is sometimes difficult to buy a gift for someone in a distant city.

Sometimes, it is difficult to buy a gift for someone in a distant city.

1. One way to deal with this problem, <u>however</u>, is to shop online.

   However, one way to deal with this problem is to shop online.

2. It may be intimidating, <u>initially</u>, to realize that almost anything can be purchased online.

   Initially, it may be intimidating to realize that almost anything can be

   purchased online.

3. Access to a wide variety of products can <u>nevertheless</u> be exhilarating.

   Nevertheless, access to a wide variety of products can be exhilarating.

4. Online shoppers must <u>first</u> use a search engine to find the category of product they want to purchase.

   First, online shoppers must use a search engine to find the category

   of product they want to purchase.

5. The search can <u>then</u> be narrowed.

   Then, the search can be narrowed.

6. Items with a wide variety of prices appear on the screen <u>next</u>.

   Next, items with a wide variety of prices appear on the screen.

7. Customer reviews are <u>often</u> available to help shoppers make a choice.

   Often, customer reviews are available to help shoppers make a choice.

8. A variety of shipping choices is <u>usually</u> possible, and the buyer can even have the item gift-wrapped.

   Usually, a variety of shipping choices is possible, and the buyer can even

   have the item gift-wrapped.

9. Payment is <u>generally</u> by credit card.

   Generally, payment is by credit card.

10. Online shopping <u>now</u> brings the world to everyone with access to a computer.

   Now, online shopping brings the world to everyone with access to a

   computer.

◆ **PRACTICE 18-3**

In each of the following sentences, fill in the blank with an appropriate adverb. Be sure to punctuate correctly.

Example: _____Slowly,_____ the sun crept over the horizon.
Answers will vary.

1. _____ the speeding car appeared from out of nowhere.

2. _____ it crashed into the guard rail.

3. _____ the car jackknifed across the highway.

4. _____ drivers behind the crashed car slammed on their brakes.

5. _____ someone used a cell phone to call 911.

6. _____ a wailing siren could be heard.

7. _____ the ambulance arrived.

8. _____ emergency medical technicians went to work.

9. _____ a police officer was on hand to direct traffic.

10. _____ no one was badly hurt in the accident.

◆ **PRACTICE 18-4**

Underline the prepositional phrase in each of the following sentences, and then rewrite the sentence so that the prepositional phrase appears at the beginning. Be sure to punctuate correctly.

Example: Very few American women worked in factories <u>before the 1940s.</u>

Before the 1940s, very few American women worked in factories.

1. Many male factory workers became soldiers <u>during World War II.</u>

During World War II, many male factory workers became soldiers.

2. War-related industries faced a labor shortage <u>as a result.</u>

As a result, war-related industries faced a labor shortage.

3. The U.S. government encouraged women to take factory jobs <u>in the war's early years.</u>

In the war's early years, the U.S. government encouraged women to take factory jobs.

4. Women met this challenge <u>with great eagerness and patriotic pride.</u>

With great eagerness and patriotic pride, women met this challenge.

5. They entered the industrial workplace <u>in unprecedented numbers</u>.

In unprecedented numbers, they entered the industrial workplace.

6. Over six million women took factory jobs <u>between 1942 and 1945</u>.

Between 1942 and 1945, over six million women took factory jobs.

7. Productivity rose and quality improved <u>with their efforts</u>.

With their efforts, productivity rose and quality improved.

8. A new female image emerged <u>alongside this greater responsibility and</u>

<u>independence</u>.

Alongside this greater responsibility and independence, a new female

image emerged.

9. Many women felt comfortable wearing pants <u>for the first time</u>.

For the first time, many women felt comfortable wearing pants.

10. Most lost their factory jobs <u>after the war</u> and had to return to "women's

work."

After the war, most lost their factory jobs and had to return to

"women's work."

◆ PRACTICE 18-5

In each of the following sentences, fill in the blank with an appropriate prepositional phrase. Be sure to punctuate correctly.

Example: *At the start of the New York marathon,* I felt as if I could run forever.
Answers will vary.

1. _____ the morning was bright, cool, and clear.

2. _____ I warmed up by stretching and bending.

3. _____ it was hard to run because all the runners were crowded together.

4. _____ the route went through the city.

5. _____ we crossed a bridge over the Hudson River.

6. _____ I noticed that we were running uphill.

7. _____ the route became more and more steep.

8. _____ my leg muscles started to ache, and I worried that I might get a bad cramp.

9. _____ I grabbed some water from a helpful onlooker.

10. _____ I staggered across the finish line, happy and

relieved that my first marathon was over.

◆ PRACTICE 18-6

Several sentences in the following passage contain prepositional phrases and adverbs that could be moved to the beginnings of sentences. As you revise the passage to vary the sentence openings, move prepositional phrases to the beginnings of three sentences. Move adverbs to the beginnings of two other sentences. Be sure to place a comma after these prepositional phrases and adverbs.

Example: *In the Cuban-American community, people*
~~People in the Cuban-American community~~ often mention

José Julian Martí as one of their heroes.

Answers will vary.

(1) Martí was born in Havana in 1853, at a time when Cuba was a
By the time he was sixteen years old, he
colony of Spain. (2) He had started a newspaper demanding Cuban
In 1870, the
freedom ~~by the time he was sixteen years old.~~ (3) ~~The~~ Spanish authori-
Openly continuing his fight, he
ties forced him to leave Cuba and go to Spain ~~in 1870.~~ (4) He published

his first pamphlet calling for Cuban independence while in Spain, ~~openly~~

~~continuing his fight.~~ (5) Working as a journalist and professor, he re-

turned to Cuba but was sent away again. (6) He then lived for fourteen
During his time in New York, he
years in New York City. (7) He started the journal of the Cuban Revolu-

tionary Party ~~during his time in New York.~~ (8) Martí's essays and poems

argued for Cuba's freedom and for the individual freedom of Cubans.
Passionately following up his words with actions, he
(9) He died in battle against Spanish soldiers in Cuba, ~~passionately fol-~~

~~lowing up his words with actions.~~ (10) Today, his ideas are still very

much alive in the dreams of many Cubans.

◆ PRACTICE 18-7

Listed below are two adverbs and four prepositional phrases. In the passage that follows, add each of these words or phrases to the beginning of a sentence in order to vary the sentence openings. Be sure your additions connect ideas clearly and logically. Remember to add commas where they are needed.

Occasionally	Sadly
For example	In fact
With their screams and chants	Of course

Example: ~~Pro~~ football players face great danger.
Sadly, pro
Answers may vary.

(1) Professional football is one of the most popular sports in the country; it is also one of the most dangerous. (2) *Sadly,* Bob Utley and Darryl Stingley are now paraplegics because of injuries they suffered on the field, and the disabled list increases each season.

(3) The league has established new rules to make the game safer, and some of these have cut down on serious injuries. (4) *For example, a* A player cannot tackle a kicker after he has kicked the ball, and a player cannot tackle a quarterback after he has thrown the ball or a runner after he has gone out of bounds. (5) These precautions, however, do not always protect players. (6) *Occasionally, players* ~~Players~~ still tackle other players in violation of the rules. (7) Sometimes they do this because they are angry and frustrated, but sometimes it is a calculated strategy. (8) *In fact, one* ~~One~~ coach was rumored to have paid team members to put opposing players out of commission for the entire game.

(9) *Of course, the* ~~The~~ fans also share the blame for the violence of football. (10) *With their screams and chants, they* ~~They~~ encourage players to hit harder and play with more intensity. (11) They believe their team should do anything to win. (12) The unfortunate fact is that as football becomes more dangerous to players, it becomes more popular with fans.

■ WRITING FIRST: Flashback

Look back at your response to the Writing First exercise on page 275. Identify one sentence that you could begin with an adverb and one that could open with a prepositional phrase. (Note that the adverb or prepositional phrase may already be somewhere in the sentence.) Write the revised sentences on the lines below.

1. *Answers will vary.* _____, _____
   (Adverb)

   _____

2. _____, _____
   (Prepositional phrase)

   _____

C Combining Sentences

You can also create sentence variety by experimenting with different ways of combining sentences. You have already learned to combine simple sentences to create compound sentences (Chapter 16) and complex sentences (Chapter 17). Now, you will learn to use *present participles, past participles, compounds,* or *appositives* to combine sentences. These different techniques will help you create varied, interesting sentences.

Using Present Participles

The **present participle** is the *-ing* form of a verb: *carrying, using.* You can use a present participle to combine two sentences.

TWO SENTENCES Duke Ellington composed more than a thousand songs. He worked hard to establish his reputation as a musician.

COMBINED <u>Composing</u> more than a thousand songs, Duke Ellington worked hard to establish his reputation as a musician. (present participle)

When the sentences are combined, the present participle *(composing)* introduces a phrase that describes the sentence's subject *(Duke Ellington).*

Using Past Participles

Past participles of verbs are usually formed with *-ed (carried)* or *-d (used),* but there are also many irregular past participle forms *(known, written).* Two sentences can often be combined when one of them contains a past participle.

TWO SENTENCES Nogales is located on the border between Arizona and Mexico. It is a bilingual city.

COMBINED <u>Located</u> on the border between Arizona and Mexico, Nogales is a bilingual city. (past participle)

When the sentences are combined, the past participle *(located)* introduces a phrase that describes the sentence's subject *(Nogales).*

◆ PRACTICE 18-8

Use a present participle to combine each of the following pairs of sentences into a single sentence. Eliminate any unnecessary words, and use a comma to set off each phrase that is introduced by a present participle. When you are finished, underline the present participle in each new sentence.

Example: The cost of operating America's prisons is rising steadily. It is getting higher as more people go to prison.

<u>Rising</u> steadily, the cost of operating America's prisons is getting higher

as more people go to prison.

For more on present participles, see 25A.

Teaching Tip
Once they are introduced to present and past participles, students tend to overuse them. Caution students against starting too many sentences with participles.

● Writing Tip
Place a comma after a phrase that is introduced by a present or past participle.

For more on past participles, see 25B. For a list of irregular past participles, see 27B.

● Writing Tip
Make sure that modifiers that are introduced by present or past participles refer clearly to the words they describe. (See 25C and 25D.)

ON THE WEB
For more practice, visit Exercise Central *at <bedfordstmartins.com/ writingfirst>.*

Answers will vary.

1. Most prisoners do little while in prison. They feel useless to themselves and to everyone else.

   Feeling useless to themselves and everyone else, most prisoners do little while in prison.

2. Some private businesses are taking advantage of this situation. They hire prisoners to work for them.

   Taking advantage of this situation, some private businesses hire prisoners to work for them.

3. About two thousand U.S. prisoners are working for private businesses. They are performing a variety of other jobs.

   Performing a variety of other jobs, about two thousand U.S. prisoners are working for private businesses.

4. Prisoners are working for airlines. They are handling travel reservations over the phone.

   Working for airlines, prisoners are handling travel reservations over the phone.

5. These prisoners are able to repay part of their cost to the public. This continues a practice that once was common.

   Continuing a practice that once was common, these prisoners are able to repay part of their cost to the public.

6. The prisoners learn new skills as they work. They are better prepared to find jobs after prison.

   Learning new skills as they work, the prisoners are better prepared to find jobs after prison.

7. This arrangement improves prisoners' chances of staying out of prison. It works well for everyone.

   Improving prisoners' chances of staying out of prison, this arrangement works well for everyone.

8. Prisons with working inmates benefit taxpayers. They cost less to run.

   Costing less to run, prisons with working inmates benefit taxpayers.

9. Many businesses fear competition from low-cost prison labor. They are opposed to prison work programs.

   Fearing competition from low-cost prison labor, many businesses are opposed to prison work programs.

Teaching Tip
In Practice 18-8, students may need to change a noun to a pronoun or vice versa when they combine sentences. Review the example sentences carefully.

10. Others see such programs as a smart way to turn a problem into a solution. They want more prisoners to work for private businesses.

Seeing such programs as a smart way to turn a problem into a

solution, others want more prisoners to work for private

businesses.

◆ **PRACTICE 18-9**

In sentences 1 through 5, fill in the blank with a phrase that is introduced by an appropriate present participle. Be sure to punctuate correctly.

Example: *Selling candy door to door,* the team raised money for new uniforms.
Answers will vary.

1. _____ the judge called for order in the courtroom.

2. _____ the miners found silver instead.

3. _____ migrating birds often travel long distances in the early fall.

4. _____ fans waited patiently to buy tickets for the concert.

5. _____ the child seemed frightened.

In sentences 6 through 10, fill in the blank with an appropriate independent clause. Be sure to punctuate correctly.

Example: Blasting its siren, *the fire truck raced through the busy streets.*
Answers will vary.

6. Stepping up to home plate _____

_____

7. Traveling at high speeds _____

_____

8. Broiling in the ninety-degree weather _____

_____

9. Looking both ways _____

_____

10. Talking to a group of news reporters _____

_____

◆ **PRACTICE 18-10**

Use a past participle to combine each of the following pairs of sentences into a single sentence. Eliminate any unnecessary words, and use a comma to set off each phrase that is introduced by a past participle. When you are finished, underline the past participle in each new sentence.

Example: Sacajawea was born in about 1787. She lived among her Shoshone tribespeople until the age of eleven.

<u>Born</u> in about 1787, Sacajawea lived among her Shoshone tribespeople until

the age of eleven.
Answers will vary.

1. She was captured as a young girl by a rival tribe. Sacajawea was later sold into slavery.

<u>Captured</u> as a young girl by a rival tribe, Sacajawea was later sold into

slavery.

2. She was saved by a French Canadian fur trader named Charbonneau. Sacajawea became his wife.

<u>Saved</u> by a French Canadian fur trader named Charbonneau, Sacajawea

became his wife.

3. The explorers Lewis and Clark hired Charbonneau in 1806. He brought his pregnant wife along on their westward expedition.

<u>Hired</u> by the explorers Lewis and Clark in 1806, Charbonneau brought his

pregnant wife along on their westward expedition.

4. Sacajawea was skilled in several native languages. She helped Lewis and Clark trade for horses and other goods.

<u>Skilled</u> in several native languages, Sacajawea helped Lewis and Clark

trade for horses and other goods.

5. The expedition was guided by Sacajawea's knowledge of the rugged terrain. It also benefited from her familiarity with native food plants.

<u>Guided</u> by Sacajawea's knowledge of the rugged terrain, the expedition

also benefited from her familiarity with native food plants.

6. Clark's journals were rescued by Sacajawea when the party's boat overturned in whitewater. They would have been lost otherwise.

<u>Rescued</u> by Sacajawea when the party's boat overturned in whitewater,

Clark's journals would have been lost otherwise.

7. Lewis and Clark were protected by the presence of the Shoshone woman and her infant. They encountered little hostility from the tribes they met.

<u>Protected</u> by the presence of the Shoshone woman and her infant, Lewis

and Clark encountered little hostility from the tribes they met.

8. Clark was indebted to Sacajawea for the success of the journey. He wrote afterward that she deserved much credit.

Indebted to Sacajawea for the success of the journey, Clark wrote afterward that she deserved much credit.

9. Sacajawea has been celebrated for many years as an American hero. She recently received an additional honor.

Celebrated for many years as an American hero, Sacajawea recently received an additional honor.

10. The U.S. dollar coin now bears her likeness. It was minted in 2000.

Minted in 2000, the U.S. dollar coin now bears her likeness.

◆ **PRACTICE 18-11**

In sentences 1 through 5, fill in the blank with a phrase that is introduced by an appropriate past participle. Be sure to punctuate correctly.

Example: *Buried away for many years,* the treasure was discovered by accident.
Answers will vary.

1. _____ the child started crying when the storm began.

2. _____ the hikers rested wearily on the rocks at the top of the mountain.

3. _____ the small boat almost capsized.

4. _____ the balloons in Macy's Thanksgiving Day parade soared above the crowds.

5. _____ family stories help families keep their traditions alive.

In sentences 6 through 10, fill in the blank with an appropriate independent clause. Be sure to punctuate correctly.

Example: Promoted as children's books, *the Harry Potter stories also appeal to adults* .
Answers will vary.

6. Annoyed by her parents _____

_____ .

7. Lost in the woods for three days _____

_____.

8. Bored by the same old routine _____

_____.

9. Confronted with the evidence _____

_____.

10. Asked whether they supported the president _____

_____.

Using Compound Subjects or Compound Predicates

A **compound subject** consists of two nouns or pronouns, usually joined by *and*. A **compound predicate** consists of two verbs, usually joined by *and*. You can use a compound subject or a compound predicate to combine two sentences.

TWO SENTENCES   Elijah McCoy was an African-American inventor. Garrett Morgan was also an African-American inventor.

COMBINED   <u>Elijah McCoy and Garrett Morgan</u> were African-American inventors. (compound subject)

TWO SENTENCES   Arundhati Roy's first novel, *The God of Small Things*, appeared in 1997. It won the Pulitzer Prize.

COMBINED   Arundhati Roy's first novel, *The God of Small Things*, <u>appeared</u> in 1997 <u>and won</u> the Pulitzer Prize. (compound predicate)

> ● **Writing Tip**
> Remember that a compound subject takes a plural verb. (See 23A.)

◆ PRACTICE 18-12

Create a compound subject by combining each of the following pairs of sentences into one sentence.

ON THE WEB
For more practice, visit Exercise Central *at* <bedfordstmartins.com/ writingfirst>.

Example: In prehistoric times, Pacific Islanders from Samoa came to Hawaii, crossing thousands of miles in their canoes. Pacific Islanders from Fiji also came to Hawaii, crossing thousands of miles in their canoes.

In prehistoric times, Pacific Islanders from Samoa and Fiji came to

Hawaii, crossing thousands of miles in their canoes.

1. About 1200, a new language came to the Hawaiian Islands, brought by travelers from the island of Tahiti. At the same time, new customs came to the Hawaiian Islands, brought by travelers from the island of Tahiti.

About 1200, a new language and new customs came to the Hawaiian

Islands, brought by travelers from the island of Tahiti.

2. After the British explorer Captain Cook arrived in 1778, other explorers followed. European traders also followed.

After the British explorer Captain Cook arrived in 1778, other explorers

and European traders followed.

3. At this time, the Hawaiians' culture supported common land ownership for the benefit of all the people. The Hawaiians' religion also supported common land ownership for the benefit of all the people.

At this time, the Hawaiians' culture and religion supported common land

ownership for the benefit of all the people.

4. A trading system was introduced by Captain Cook and the other Europeans. The concept of private ownership was also introduced by Cook and his fellow traders and explorers.

A trading system and the concept of private ownership were introduced

by Cook and his fellow traders and explorers.

5. A Hawaiian alphabet was created by Christian missionaries. A Hawaiian-language Bible was also created by Christian missionaries.

A Hawaiian alphabet and a Hawaiian-language Bible were created by

Christian missionaries.

6. By the mid-nineteenth century, pineapple plantations were established in Hawaii. By the same time, sugar plantations were established in Hawaii.

By the mid-nineteenth century, pineapple and sugar plantations were

established in Hawaii.

7. By 1900, many Japanese people had immigrated to Hawaii to find work on the plantations. Many Chinese people had also immigrated to Hawaii to find work.

By 1900, many Japanese and Chinese people had immigrated to Hawaii

to find work on the plantations.

8. Today, people of many different races live in Hawaii. Followers of many different religions live in Hawaii as well.

Today, people of many different races and followers of many different

religions live in Hawaii.

9. Tolerance for others is a result of the diversity of the Hawaiian population. Ethnic harmony is also a result of the diversity of the Hawaiian population.

Tolerance for others and ethnic harmony are results of the diversity of

the Hawaiian population.

10. Genuine warmth remains central to the Hawaiian concept of *aloha*. Kindness in everyday relationships also remains central to the Hawaiian concept of *aloha*.

Genuine warmth and kindness in everyday relationships are parts of the

Hawaiian concept of aloha.

◆ PRACTICE 18-13

Create a compound predicate by combining each of the following pairs of sentences into a single sentence.

Example: The inventor Thomas Edison left school at an early age. He first made his living selling newspapers.

The inventor Thomas Edison left school at an early age and first made his

living selling newspapers.

1. Despite his lack of formal education, Edison had a quick mind. He also showed a talent for problem solving.

Despite his lack of formal education, Edison had a quick mind and showed

a talent for problem solving.

2. His early work as a telegraph operator stimulated his interest in electricity. It also led him to experiment with inventions.

His early work as a telegraph operator stimulated his interest in electricity

and led him to experiment with inventions.

3. Edison patented the earliest phonograph in 1878. He created the first practical light bulb the following year.

Edison patented the earliest phonograph in 1878 and created the first

practical light bulb the following year.

4. His invention of a power distribution network brought electricity into people's homes. This invention led to many conveniences.

His invention of a power distribution network brought electricity into

people's homes and led to many conveniences.

5. Edison later developed an electric railroad. He also produced one of the first batteries to store long-term power.

Edison later developed an electric railroad and produced one of the first

batteries to store long-term power.

6. His early moving picture machine fascinated audiences. It became quite popular.

His early moving picture machine fascinated audiences and became quite popular.

7. His early experiments with sound pictures were surprisingly successful. They eventually led to "talking pictures" (movies).

His early experiments with sound pictures were surprisingly successful and eventually led to "talking pictures" (movies).

8. Edison held many patents. He made a fortune from his inventions.

Edison held many patents and made a fortune from his inventions.

9. Edison did much of his work in New Jersey. He had laboratories there in West Orange and Menlo Park.

Edison did much of his work in New Jersey and had laboratories there in West Orange and Menlo Park.

10. A number of his enterprises were combined after his death. They were renamed the General Electric Company.

A number of his enterprises were combined after his death and were renamed the General Electric Company.

◆ PRACTICE 18-14

Combine each of the following pairs of sentences into one sentence by creating a compound subject or a compound predicate. Remember that a compound subject takes a plural verb.

● **Writing Tip**

Do not put a comma between the two parts of a compound subject or between the two parts of a compound predicate. (See 31F.)

Teaching Tip

Show students that using a compound subject to combine two sentences often results in a more concise sentence. Refer them to 20B.

Example: Several years ago, the NCAA Presidents Commission wanted to reform college athletic programs, ~~It~~ *and* recommended a number of measures for doing so. (compound predicate)

(1) These college presidents *and their supporters* wanted to improve the academic performance of college athletes. ~~Their supporters also wanted to improve the academic performance of college athletes.~~ (2) Their first proposal raised the number of required core courses for entering freshmen, ~~It~~ *and* increased the SAT scores necessary for admittance. (3) A second proposal required athletes to earn a certain number of credits every year, ~~It~~ *and* mandated a minimum grade point average for them. (4) At first, many athletic

directors saw the changes as unfair. *and* ~~They~~ resisted them. (5) Many Big East coaches believe standardized test scores are biased. *and* ~~They~~ want their use in screening student athletes banned. (6) Some coaches also feared that *and other opponents of these requirements* the new rules would force many athletes to choose easy majors. ~~Other opponents of these requirements feared the same thing.~~ (7) According to supporters, however, many athletes under the old system have failed to advance academically. *and* ~~They~~ often finish their eligibility fifty or more hours short of graduation. (8) The new rules, they say, would give student athletes a fair chance. *and* ~~They~~ also keep them on the graduation track. *and lack of support for academic excellence were* (9) In the supporters' view, poor supervision by athletic directors ~~was~~ to blame for the poor performance of student athletes. ~~Lack of support for academic excellence was also to blame.~~

Using Appositives

An **appositive** is a word or word group that identifies, renames, or describes a noun or pronoun. Using an appositive is often a good way to combine two sentences about the same subject.

● **Writing Tip**

When you combine sentences with an appositive, set off the appositive with commas. (See 31C.)

TWO SENTENCES   C. J. Walker was the first American woman to become a self-made millionaire. She marketed a line of hair-care products for black women.

COMBINED   C. J. Walker, <u>the first American woman to become a self-made millionaire</u>, marketed a line of hair-care products for black women. (appositive)

Notice that in addition to appearing in the middle of a sentence, an appositive can also come at the beginning or at the end of a sentence.

<u>The first American woman to become a self-made millionaire</u>, C. J. Walker marketed a line of hair-care products for black women.

Several books have been written about C. J. Walker, <u>the first American woman to become a self-made millionaire</u>.

◆ PRACTICE 18-15

Use appositives to combine each of the following pairs of sentences into one sentence. Note that the appositive may appear at the beginning, in the middle, or at the end of the sentence. Be sure to use commas appropriately.

ON THE WEB
For more practice, visit **Exercise Central** *at* <*bedfordstmartins.com/writingfirst*>.

Example: Lorraine Hansberry's *A Raisin in the Sun,* ~~was~~ one of the first American plays to focus on the experiences of African Americans. ~~It~~ was produced on Broadway in 1959.

Answers will vary.

A playwright who wrote the prize-winning A Raisin in the Sun,

(1) Lorraine Hansberry was born in Chicago in 1930. ~~She was a playwright who wrote the prize-winning *A Raisin in the Sun.*~~ (2) Hansberry's father was a successful businessman, He moved the family from the south side of Chicago to a predominately white neighborhood when Hansberry was eight. (3) Hostile neighbors there were responsible for throwing a brick through a window of their house, ~~This was~~ an act Hansberry never forgot. (4) Such experiences inspired *A Raisin in the Sun,* ~~It is~~ the story of a family's struggle to escape a cramped apartment in a poor Chicago neighborhood. (5) Lena Younger is the mother of the family, ~~She~~ is about to receive a ten-thousand-dollar insurance payment following her husband's death. (6) Her son wants to use the money to invest in a liquor store, ~~This is~~ a business Lena finds unacceptable. (7) Her dream is a house with a yard her grandson can play in, ~~This dream~~ leads her to purchase a home in a white neighborhood. (8) Her plans are almost shattered when Walter invests the rest of the insurance money in a scheme to obtain a liquor license illegally, ~~This is~~ a deal that quickly goes bad. (9) One of their new white neighbors has offered the Younger family a bribe not to move into the neighborhood, ~~It is~~ a deal Walter now decides to accept. (10) Lena is a woman who knows her son's heart, ~~She~~ makes Walter realize that to accept this money and give up their dream would be a betrayal of his father's memory.

■ WRITING FIRST: Flashback

Look back at your response to the Writing First exercise on page 275. Underline two or three pairs of sentences that you think could be combined. On the lines below, combine each pair of sentences into a single sentence, using one of the methods discussed in 18C. Use a different method for each pair of sentences.

1. _*Answers will vary.*_____

_____

2. _____

_____

(continued on the following page)

(continued from the previous page)

3. _____

_____

D Varying Sentence Length

A paragraph of short, choppy sentences—or a paragraph of long, rambling sentences—can be monotonous. By mixing long and short sentences, perhaps combining some simple sentences to create compound and complex sentences, you can create a more interesting paragraph.

In the following paragraph, the sentences are all short, and the result is a dull passage.

> The world's first drive-in movie theater opened on June 6, 1933, in Camden, New Jersey. Automobiles became more popular. Drive-ins did too. By the 1950s, there were more than four thousand drive-ins in the United States. Over the years, the high cost of land led to the decline of drive-ins. So did the rising popularity of television. Now, the drive-in movie theater has been replaced by the multiplex. There are no drive-ins at all in Alaska. There are none in Rhode Island or Delaware, either. New Jersey's last drive-in closed in 1991.

The revised paragraph that appears below is more interesting because it mixes long and short sentences.

> The world's first drive-in movie theater opened on June 6, 1933, in Camden, New Jersey. As automobiles became more popular, drive-ins did too, and by the 1950s, there were more than four thousand drive-ins in the United States. Today, there are very few left. Over the years, the high cost of land, along with the rising popularity of television, led to a decline in the number of drive-ins. Now, the drive-in movie theater has been replaced by the multiplex and the VCR. There are no drive-ins at all in Alaska, Rhode Island, or Delaware, and New Jersey's last drive-in closed in 1991.

To increase sentence variety, the writer combined some of the original paragraph's short sentences, creating longer simple, compound, and complex sentences. He also added a new short sentence ("Today, there are very few left") for emphasis after a long one.

◆ PRACTICE 18-16

The following passage contains a series of short, choppy sentences that can be combined. Revise it so that it mixes long and short sentences. Be sure to use commas and other punctuation appropriately.

● **Writing Tip**

For information on creating compound and complex sentences, see Chapters 16 and 17.

ON THE WEB
For more practice, visit
Exercise Central *at*
<bedfordstmartins.com/
writingfirst>.

Example: Kente cloth has special significance for many African Americans/ *, but many* Many other people do not understand this significance.

Answers will vary.
(1) Kente cloth is made in western Africa/ *and* (2) It is produced primarily by the Ashanti people. (3) It has been worn for hundreds of years by African royalty/ *, who* (4) They consider it a sign of power and status. (5) Many African Americans wear kente cloth/ *because they* (6) They see it as a link to their heritage. (7) Each pattern on the cloth has a name/ *, and each* (8) Each color has a special significance. (9) For example, red and yellow suggest a long and healthy life/ *while green* (10) Green and white suggest a good harvest. (11) *Although* African women may wear kente cloth as a dress or head wrap/ (12) African-American women, like men, usually wear strips of cloth around their shoulders. (13) Men and women of African descent wear kente cloth as a sign of racial pride/ *; in fact, it* (14) It often decorates college students' gowns at graduation.

■ WRITING FIRST: Flashback

Look back at your response to the Writing First exercise on page 275. Count the number of words in each sentence, and write the results on the following lines.

Answers will vary.

Sentence 1 _____	Sentence 6 _____
Sentence 2 _____	Sentence 7 _____
Sentence 3 _____	Sentence 8 _____
Sentence 4 _____	Sentence 9 _____
Sentence 5 _____	Sentence 10 _____

Now, write a new short sentence to follow your longest sentence.

New sentence: _____

_____

_____

_____

■ WRITING FIRST: Revising and Editing

Look back at your response to the Writing First exercise on page
275. Using any strategies from this chapter that seem appropriate,
revise your writing so that your sentences are varied, interesting,
and smoothly connected. (You may want to incorporate sentences
you wrote for the Flashback exercises on pages 277, 283, 294, and
296.) When you are finished, revise the sentences in an assignment
you have completed for another course.

CHAPTER REVIEW

◆ EDITING PRACTICE

The following student essay lacks sentence variety. All of its sentences are
statements beginning with the subject, and it contains a number of short,
choppy sentences. Using the strategies discussed in this chapter, revise the
essay to achieve greater sentence variety. The first sentence has been edited for you.

Answers will vary.

Toys by Accident

    Many popular toys and games are the result of accidents/
when people
~~People~~ try to invent one thing, but they discover something

else instead. Sometimes they are not trying to invent
        and
anything at all/ ~~They~~ are completely surprised to find a

new product.
        , a popular preschool toy,
    Play-Doh is one example of an accidental discovery.

~~Play-Doh is a popular preschool toy.~~ Play-Doh first
       , where a
appeared in Cincinnati/ ~~A~~ company made a compound to clean
  and
wallpaper/ ~~They~~ sold it as a cleaning product. The company
                     Molding
then realized that this compound could be a toy. ~~Children~~
        , children
~~could mold~~ it like clay/ ~~They~~ could use it again and
               Since
again. The new toy was an immediate hit. Play-Doh was first

sold in 1956/ ~~Since then,~~ more than two billion cans ~~of~~

~~Play-Doh~~ have been sold.

    The Slinky was discovered by Richard James/ ~~He was~~ an

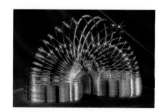
Slinky

engineer, *who* He was trying to invent a spring to keep ships'
instruments steady at sea. *Although he* He tested hundreds of springs of
varying sizes, metals, and tensions, *, none* None of them worked.
One spring fell off the desk *and* "walked" down a pile of
books, *, and* It went end over end onto the floor. *Thinking* He thought his
children might enjoy playing with it, James took the spring
home. They loved it. Every child in the neighborhood wanted
one. *When the* The first Slinky was demonstrated at Gimbel's Department
Store in Philadelphia in 1945, *, all* All four hundred Slinkys on
hand were sold within ninety minutes. *Simple* The Slinky is simple
and inexpensive, *, the* The Slinky is still popular with children.

Have you ever thrown a Frisbee? Almost everyone has. It
was discovered by accident, too. According to one story, a
group of Yale University students were eating pies from a
local bakery, The bakery was called Frisbies. *After they* They finished
eating the pies, *, they* They started throwing around the empty pie
tins. A carpenter in California made a plastic version,
which he He called it the Pluto Platter. The Wham-O company bought
the patent on the product, *and* Wham-o renamed it the Frisbee
after the bakery that made the pies eaten by the Yale
students. This was how the Frisbee came to be.

Some new toys are not developed by toy companies.
Play-Doh, the Frisbee, and the Slinky are examples of very
popular toys that resulted from accidental discoveries.
Play-Doh started as a cleaning product, *, the* The Slinky was
discovered by an engineer who was trying to invent
something else, *, and the* The Frisbee was invented by students just
having fun. *Discovered* The toys were discovered unexpectedly, *, all* All
three toys have become classics.

Frisbee

◆ **COLLABORATIVE ACTIVITIES**

1. Read the following list of sentences. Working in a small group, add to
   the list one related sentence that is a question or an exclamation. Then,
   add an appropriate adverb or prepositional phrase to one or more of
   the sentences on the list.

Many well-known African-American writers left the United States in the years following World War II.

Many went to Paris.

Richard Wright was a novelist.

He wrote *Native Son* and *Black Boy.*

He wrote *Uncle Tom's Children.*

He left the United States for Paris in 1947.

James Baldwin wrote *Another Country, The Fire Next Time,* and *Giovanni's Room.*

He also wrote essays.

He came to Paris in 1948.

Chester Himes was a detective story writer.

He arrived in Paris in 1953.

William Gardner Smith was a novelist and journalist.

He also left the United States for Paris.

These expatriates found Paris more hospitable than America.

They also found it less racist.

2. Continuing to work in your group, combine all the sentences on the list to create a varied and interesting paragraph. Use the strategies illustrated in 18C as a guide.

3. When your group's revisions are complete, trade paragraphs with another group and further edit the other group's paragraph to improve sentence variety.

☑ REVIEW CHECKLIST:
Achieving Sentence Variety

- Vary sentence types, using an occasional question or exclamation. (See 18A.)

- Vary sentence openings. (See 18B.)

- Combine sentences. (See 18C.)

- Vary sentence length. (See 18D.)

Using Parallelism

■ WRITING FIRST

Look at the picture above, which shows a street scene in the Old Town neighborhood of Chicago. Then, discuss three positive things about your own neighborhood, school, or workplace. Support your statements with specific examples.

A Recognizing Parallel Structure

Parallelism is the use of matching grammatical constructions to present comparable or equivalent ideas. For example, nouns are used with nouns, verbs with verbs, adjectives with adjectives, phrases with phrases, and clauses with clauses. By using similar grammatical structures, you identify how two or more ideas are alike and show what relationships exist among them.

Parallel

Casey is a <u>snowboarder</u>, not a <u>skier</u>. (two nouns)

We saw the ducks <u>fly</u>, <u>swim</u>, and <u>fish</u>. (three verbs)

The road of life is <u>long</u>, <u>bumpy</u>, and <u>steep</u>. (three adjectives)

<u>Making the team</u> was one thing; <u>staying on it</u> was another. (two phrases)

My, what big eyes you have, grandma! My, what big ears you have! My, what big teeth you have! (three independent clauses)

Faulty parallelism occurs when different grammatical constructions are used to present comparable or equivalent ideas.

Not Parallel

Casey is a snowboarder, but skiing is not something that interests him.

We saw the ducks fly, and some swam, and we saw others fishing.

The road of life is long, and a lot of bumps are found on it, and it climbs steeply.

Making the team was one thing, but she was worried about staying on the team.

My, what big eyes you have, Grandma! And you do have big ears. Your teeth are also quite large.

To correct faulty parallelism, reword the comparable ideas in your sentences so that they are expressed in matching grammatical constructions.

We saw the ducks fly, ~~and some swam, and we saw others~~ *swim, and* fish~~ing~~.

ESL Tip
Have students write five sentences illustrating each method of creating parallel structure—by using nouns with nouns, verbs with verbs, and so on. Students should identify the kinds of parallel constructions they are using in each sentence.

◆ **PRACTICE 19-1**

In the following sentences, decide whether the underlined words and phrases are parallel. If so, write *P* in the blank. If not, rewrite the sentences so that the ideas they express are presented in parallel terms.

ON THE WEB
For more practice, visit Exercise Central *at* <bedfordstmartins.com/ writingfirst>.

Examples: Our mailman is <u>sloppy</u>, <u>unfriendly</u>, and <u>undependable</u>.

_P_

When choosing a candidate, voters may think about whether the candidates are likable, ~~their trustworthiness~~ *trustworthy,*, and ~~if they are~~ honest. ____

1. I just bought <u>some lettuce</u> *a head of* ~~and~~ *, a pint of* <u>mushrooms</u>, and <u>three pounds of to-matoes</u>. ____

2. Do you want it done <u>quickly</u>, or do you want it done <u>well</u>? _P_

3. The plumber needs to <u>fix a leaky pipe</u>, <u>replace a missing faucet</u>, and *fix a running toilet.* ~~a toilet that is running should be fixed.~~ ____

4. When John was a college student, he ~~was on the football team and~~ *played*
~~played baseball, and~~ ~~was on the basketball team.~~ _____

5. Our vacation turned out to be relaxing but expensive. *P*

6. On my refrigerator are magnets from my accountant, *my new* ~~the doctor I went~~
~~to see for the first time last week~~, and my dentist. _____

7. Show me a neat desk, and I will show you an empty mind. *P*

8. At my tenth class reunion, I was surprised to find that I enjoyed meeting my old classmates, walking around the school, and ~~I even~~ ~~had a good time~~ talking with the principal. _____

9. I just washed the floor. Can you vacuum the rug? *P*

10. Our old car has poor gas mileage, *a leaky* ~~its windshield~~ leaks when it rains, *bad*
and ~~its brakes~~ ~~don't work very well.~~ _____

■ **WRITING FIRST: Flashback**

Look back at your response to the Writing First exercise on page 300, and underline the parallel words, phrases, and clauses. Revise, if necessary, to make sure that comparable ideas are presented in parallel terms.

B | **Using Parallel Structure**

● **Writing Tip**

Many everyday writing tasks require parallelism. For example, items listed on a résumé should be in parallel form.

Parallel structure is especially important for emphasizing the relationships in *paired items, comparisons,* and *items in a series.*

Paired Items

Use parallel structure when you connect ideas with a coordinating conjunction—*and, but, for, nor, or, so,* and *yet.*

> George believes in doing a good job *and* minding his own business.
> You can pay me now *or* pay me later.

Also use parallel structure for paired items joined by correlative conjunctions, such as *both . . . and, not only . . . but also, either . . . or, neither . . . nor,* and *rather . . . than.*

> Jan is *both* artistically talented *and* mechanically inclined.

The group's new recording *not only* has a dance beat *but also* has thought-provoking lyrics.

I'd *rather* eat one worm by itself *than* eat twenty with ice cream.

Comparisons Formed with *Than* or *As*

Use parallel structure for comparisons formed with *than* or *as*.

Working hard is more important *than* being lucky.

She cares about her patients as much *as* she cares about her family.

For information on punctuating items in a series, see 31A.

Items in a Series

Use parallel structure for items in a series—words, phrases, or clauses.

Every Wednesday I have English, math, and psychology.

Increased demand, high factory output, and a strong dollar help the economy.

She is a champion because she stays in excellent physical condition, puts in long hours of practice, and has an intense desire to win.

Items in a List or in an Outline

Use parallel structure for items in a numbered or bulleted list.

There are three reasons to open an IRA:
1. To save money
2. To pay fewer taxes
3. To be able to retire

Use parallel structure for the elements in an outline.

A. Basic types of rocks
   1. Igneous
   2. Sedimentary
   3. Metamorphic

◆ PRACTICE 19-2

Fill in the blanks in the following sentences with parallel words, phrases, or clauses of your own that make sense in context.

Example: At the lake, we can _____*go for a swim*_____, _____*paddle a canoe*_____, and _____*play volleyball*_____.
Answers will vary.

1. When I get too little sleep, I am _____, _____, and _____.

2. I am good at _____ but not at _____.

Teaching Tip
Practice 19-2 works well as a test and is quick and easy to grade. You may want to save this exercise for the end of the chapter.

ON THE WEB
For more practice, visit Exercise Central at <bedfordstmartins.com/ writingfirst>.

3. My ideal mate is _____ and _____.

4. I define success not only as _____ but also as

_____.

5. I use my computer for both _____ and _____.

6. I like _____ as much as _____.

7. You need three qualities to succeed at college: _____,

_____, and _____.

8. I enjoy_____ as much as _____.

9. _____ is more important to me than _____.

10. Football _____, but baseball _____.

◆ **PRACTICE 19-3**

Rewrite the following sentences so that the ideas are presented in parallel
terms. Add punctuation as needed.

> **Example:** California's San Gabriel Valley is close to mountains, and
> beaches and deserts are nearby.
>
> *California's San Gabriel Valley is close to mountains, beaches, and*
>
> *deserts.*

1. Pasadena and Claremont are major cities in the valley. So is Pomona.

   Pasadena, Claremont, and Pomona are major cities in the valley.

2. Pasadena offers the famous Rose Bowl stadium, and the Norton
   Simon Museum and the historic Wrigley house are also there.

   Pasadena offers the famous Rose Bowl stadium, the Norton Simon

   Museum, and the historic Wrigley house.

3. Watching the big Tournament of Roses Parade is more exciting than it
   is to watch the Macy's Thanksgiving parade.

   Watching the big Tournament of Roses Parade is more exciting than

   watching the Macy's Thanksgiving parade.

4. You can watch from the crowded parade route. The comfort of your
   living room is also a possibility.

   You can watch from the crowded parade route or from the comfort of your

   living room.

5. Judges rate the rose-covered floats on their originality, what artistic merit they have, and the overall impact they make.

   Judges rate the rose-covered floats on their originality, artistic merit, and

   overall impact.

6. Some people enjoy going to the parade more than when they go to the Rose Bowl game.

   Some people enjoy going to the parade more than they enjoy going to the

   Rose Bowl game.

7. The Rose Bowl game is not only America's oldest collegiate championship but also the bowl game that is the country's most popular.

   The Rose Bowl game is not only America's oldest collegiate championship

   but also the country's most popular bowl game.

8. Held every fall in Pomona, the Los Angeles County Fair offers carnival rides, popular performers, and there are agricultural shows included.

   Held every fall in Pomona, the Los Angeles County Fair offers carnival rides,

   popular performers, and agricultural shows.

9. Visitors come to play challenging skill games, and they also can enjoy various ethnic foods.

   Visitors come to play challenging skill games and enjoy various ethnic foods.

10. The starting gate was introduced at the San Gabriel Valley's Santa Anita Race Track, and so was electrical timing, as well as the photo finish.

    The starting gate, electrical timing, and the photo finish were introduced at

    the San Gabriel Valley's Santa Anita Race Track.

■ **WRITING FIRST: Flashback**

Look back at your response to the Writing First exercise on page 300. On the lines on the next page, write three new sentences that you could add to your response, and then revise them as follows: (1) In one sentence, use a coordinating conjunction, such as *and* or *but;* (2) in another sentence, create a comparison using *than* or *as;* (3) in a third sentence, present items in a series. When you have finished, check to make sure that you have used parallel structure in each sentence and that you have punctuated correctly.

(continued on the following page)

(continued from the previous page)

1. _Answers will vary._ _____

   _____

   _____

   _____

2. _____

   _____

   _____

   _____

3. _____

   _____

   _____

   _____

■ WRITING FIRST: Revising and Editing

Look back at your response to the Writing First exercise on page 300, and try to add one or more of the sentences you wrote for the Flashback exercise above. Then, revise your work, correcting faulty parallelism and adding parallel constructions where necessary to emphasize a relationship or increase clarity. When you are finished, do the same for another assignment you are currently working on.

CHAPTER REVIEW

◆ **EDITING PRACTICE**

Read the following student essay, which contains examples of faulty parallelism. Identify the sentences you think need to be corrected, and make the changes required to achieve parallelism. Be sure to supply all words necessary for clarity, grammar, and sense. Add punctuation as needed. The first error has been edited for you.
Answers will vary.

Questionable Heroes

The heroes we learn about in school are usually

historical figures. We look up to them for their

for
outstanding achievements, and their personal qualities ~~are~~
~~also admired.~~ When we were young children, we admired
people who helped start the country, and we also admired
brave leaders. Our heroes included American colonists and
brave
soldiers ~~who were thought of as brave.~~ After the terrorist
attacks on September 11, 2001, we realized that anyone who
helps in a disaster can be a hero. However, some people
often confuse heroes with ~~people who are~~ celebrities. It is
to be
much harder to be a hero than ~~becoming~~ famous. Heroes often
become famous, of course, but many people who are famous do
heroically.
not act ~~the way that heroes should act.~~ Unfortunately, many
figures
entertainers and ~~people who play~~ professional sports are
are
famous, but they ~~should~~ not ~~be thought of as~~ heroes.

To be a real hero, a person should be a model for

Martin Luther King Jr.

others. A genuine hero like George Washington was brave and
determined
~~showed determination~~ throughout his life. Martin Luther
King Jr. lost his life while fighting for equal rights.
or even die
Soldiers often risk their lives to save other people, ~~and~~
~~sometimes death even results.~~ During the terrorist attacks
of September 11, 2001, heroic firefighters climbed up the
stairs of the burning World Trade Center buildings, and
saved
many lives ~~were able to be saved.~~ Even the thousands of
Americans who pitched in to help during the clean-up can be
and food
thought of as heroes. They brought supplies to the rescue
workers, ~~and in addition, food was brought.~~
people are
On the other hand, ~~to be~~ famous ~~does~~ not always ~~mean~~
~~that people are~~ heroes. Nowadays, when people are in the
news, it does not mean that they have done something
heroic. In fact, it can mean the opposite. Some athletes,
for example, get a lot of attention for their misbehavior.
curse at
Sometimes, they fight with their coaches, the media ~~may be~~
fail
~~cursed at,~~ drug tests ~~may be failed,~~ and ~~they may even~~ get

Firefighters in ruins of World Trade Center

arrested for serious crimes. Similarly, some entertainers get news coverage for their worst behavior. Sometimes, they get married many times, or ~wear~ very provocative clothes ~are worn by them~. Fame may also be achieved from notorious court cases. However, this kind of fame is not heroic. Although sports ~and entertainment~ superstars can earn millions of dollars, ~and so can entertainers,~ many parents would not want them to be role models for their children. Nevertheless, to some people, the lure of fame can be strong. Sometimes it seems as if ~when people get a lot of~ publicity, ~it~ is more important than integrity.

Clearly, the image of the hero has changed over time. The heroes of the past were dedicated ~and courageous~ leaders ~and acted with courage~. Now, they have often been replaced by superstars who are famous for all the wrong reasons—for example, selfishness and ~they cannot control their own~ ~lack of self-control.~ ~actions~. These people may be fascinating, but they should not be thought of as heroes.

◆ COLLABORATIVE ACTIVITIES

1. Working in a group, list three or four qualities that you associate with each word in the following pairs.

   Brothers/sisters
   Teachers/students
   Parents/children
   City/country
   Baseball/football
   The Internet/television
   Work/play

2. Write a compound sentence comparing each of the above pairs of words. Use a coordinating conjunction to join the clauses, and make sure each sentence uses clear parallel structure, mentions both words, and includes the qualities you listed for the words in Collaborative Activity 1.

3. Choose the three best sentences your group has written for Collaborative Activity 2. Assign one student from each group to write these sentences on the board so the entire class can read them. The class can then decide which sentences use parallelism most effectively.

✔ REVIEW CHECKLIST:
Using Parallelism

- Use matching grammatical constructions to present comparable or equivalent ideas. (See 19A.)

- Use parallel structure with paired items. (See 19B.)

- Use parallel structure in comparisons formed with *than* or *as*. (See 19B.)

- Use parallel structure for items in a series. (See 19B.)

- Use parallel structure for items in a list and for the elements in an outline. (See 19B.)

20

Using Words Effectively

PREVIEW

In this chapter, you will learn

- to use specific words (20A)

- to use concise language (20B)

- to avoid clichés (20C)

- to use similes and metaphors (20D)

- to avoid sexist language (20E)

Word Power

appealing   attractive or interesting

ideal   a model of perfection; the best of its kind

practical   useful

■ WRITING FIRST

Look at the picture above, and then describe your dream house. Would it resemble the house in the picture, or would it be different? How? What would be inside the house? Be as specific as possible.

A   Using Specific Words

To write well, you need to use specific words that convey your ideas (and sometimes your feelings) with precision and clarity.

Specific words refer to particular people, places, things, ideas, or qualities; **general** words refer to entire classes or groups. Sentences that contain specific words are more vivid and more memorable than those that contain only generalities. The following sentences use general words.

Sentences with General Words

While walking in the woods, I saw an <u>animal</u>.

<u>Someone</u> decided to run for Congress.

<u>Weapons</u> are responsible for many murders.

Denise bought new <u>clothes</u>.

I really enjoyed my <u>meal</u>.

Darrell had always wanted a <u>classic car</u>.

Specific words make the following revised sentences clearer and more precise.

Sentences with Specific Words

While walking in the woods, I saw a <u>baby skunk</u>.

<u>Rebecca</u> decided to run for Congress.

<u>Saturday night specials</u> are responsible for many murders.

Denise bought a new <u>blue vest</u>.

I really enjoyed my <u>pepperoni pizza</u>.

Darrell had always wanted a <u>black 1957 Chevy convertible</u>.

Teaching Tip
Put a sentence on the board (for example, *The man was injured in an accident involving a shark*), and have students work as a team to make the sentence more specific and concrete. Asking students to write a news story about the sentence usually results in excellent paragraphs.

FOCUS   Using Specific Words

One way to strengthen your writing is to avoid **utility words**—general words like *good, nice,* or *great.* Instead, take the time to think of more specific words. For example, when you say the ocean looked *pretty,* do you really mean that it *sparkled, glistened, rippled, foamed, surged,* or *billowed?*

Teaching Tip
Warn students that the synonyms they see listed in a thesaurus almost never have the same meanings. For example, ask students to discuss the differences in meaning of the words in this Focus box.

◆ PRACTICE 20-1

In the following passage, the writer describes an old store in the town of Nameless, Tennessee. Underline the specific words in the passage that help you imagine the scene the writer describes. The first sentence has been done for you.

ON THE WEB
For more practice, visit **Exercise Central** *at <bedfordstmartins.com/ writingfirst>.*

(1) The old store, lighted only by <u>three fifty-watt bulbs</u>, smelled of <u>coal oil</u> and <u>baking bread</u>. (2) In the middle of the <u>rectangular room</u>, where the <u>oak floor</u> sagged a little, stood an <u>iron stove</u>. (3) To the right was a <u>wooden table</u> with an <u>unfinished game of checkers</u> and a stool made from an <u>apple-tree stump</u>. (4) On shelves around the walls sat <u>earthen jugs</u> with <u>corncob stoppers</u>, a few <u>canned goods</u>, and some of the <u>two thousand old clocks and clockworks</u> Thurmond Watts owned. (5) Only one was ticking; the others he just looked at.

–WILLIAM LEAST HEAT-MOON, *Blue Highways*

ESL Tip
Nonnative speakers often have trouble with adjective order. Explain why they should write *The tall, slender man drove away in a shiny new car.* Refer them to 30L.

◆ **PRACTICE 20-2**

In the blank beside each of the five general words below, write a more specific word. Then, use the more specific word in a sentence of your own.

Example: child _____six-year-old_____

All through dinner, my six-year-old chattered excitedly about his first day

of school.

Answers will vary.

1. emotion _____

_____

_____

2. building _____

_____

_____

3. said _____

_____

_____

4. animal _____

_____

_____

5. went _____

_____

_____

◆ **PRACTICE 20-3**

The following letter of application for a job uses general words. Choose a job that you might want to apply for. As you rewrite the paragraph on a separate page, substitute specific language for the general language of the original, and add details where necessary. Start by making the first sentence, which identifies the job, more specific: for example, "I would like to apply for the dental technician position you advertised on March 15 in the *Post*." Go on to include specific information about your background and qualifications, expanding the original paragraph into a three-paragraph letter.

   I would like to apply for the position you advertised in today's paper. I graduated from high school and am currently attending college. I have taken several courses that have prepared me for the duties the position requires. I also have several personal qualities that I think you would find useful in a person holding this position. In addition, I have had certain experiences that qualify me for such a job. I would appreciate the opportunity to meet with you to discuss your needs as an employer. Thank you.

■ **WRITING FIRST: Flashback**

Look back at your response to the Writing First exercise on page 310. Find several general words, and write those words on the lines below. For each word, substitute another word that is more specific.

General Words

Answers will vary.

_____

_____

_____

Specific Alternatives

_____

_____

_____

B   Using Concise Language

Concise writing says what it has to say in as few words as possible. Too often, writers use empty phrases that add nothing to a sentence's meaning. A good way to test a sentence for these nonessential words is to see if crossing out the words changes the sentence's meaning.

> ~~It is a fact that~~ the United States was not prepared to fight World War II.

If the sentence's meaning does not change, you can assume that the words are nonessential and that the sentence is better off without them.

WORDY   Due to the fact that I was tired, I missed my first class.

CONCISE   Because I was tired, I missed my first class.

WORDY   In order to follow the plot, you must make an outline.

CONCISE   To follow the plot, you must make an outline.

● **Writing Tip**

A short sentence is not necessarily a concise sentence. A sentence is concise when it contains only the words it needs to convey its ideas.

● **Writing Tip**

Avoid flowery language and complicated sentences. Good writing is clear and concise.

FOCUS   Using Concise Language

The following phrases add nothing to a sentence. You can usually delete or condense them with no loss of meaning.

(continued on the following page)

(continued from the previous page)	
Wordy	*Concise*
It is clear that	(delete)
It is a fact that	(delete)
The reason is because	Because
The reason is that	Because
It is my opinion that	I think/I believe
Due to the fact that	Because
Despite the fact that	Although
At the present time	Today/Currently
At that time	Then
In most cases	Usually
In order to	To
In the final analysis	Finally
Subsequent to	After

Nonessential words are sometimes the result of unnecessary repetition. Although repetition can be used effectively—for example, to emphasize important ideas—unnecessary repetition should be eliminated. Notice how easily these sentences can be edited to eliminate unnecessary repetition.

WORDY   My instructor told me the book was <u>old-fashioned and outdated</u>. (An old-fashioned book *is* outdated.)

CONCISE   My instructor told me the book was outdated.

WORDY   The <u>terrible tragedy</u> of the fire could have been avoided. (A tragedy is *always* terrible.)

CONCISE   The tragedy of the fire could have been avoided.

◆ PRACTICE 20-4

To make the following sentences more concise, eliminate any unnecessary repetition, and delete or condense wordy expressions.

Example: ~~Despite the fact that~~ ^{Even though} people buy used cars whenever they

need ~~or have a requirement for~~ them, many do not know how to choose

a good car.
Answers will vary.

(1) ~~In order to~~ ^{To} become an informed, ~~knowledgeable~~ used-car buyer,

the first thing a person should do is to look on the Internet and in the

local newspapers ~~in the area~~ to get an idea of the prices. (2) ~~As a matter

of fact, another~~ ^{Another} good source of information is a consumer magazine that

may have a ~~consumer's~~ buyer's guide for used cars. (3) When first seeing and inspecting the car, search ~~and inspect carefully and thoroughly~~ for new paint that looks different from the paint in the surrounding area. (4) ~~The reason is that this~~ ^This^ sign could mean ~~or suggest~~ that the car has ~~experienced or~~ been in an accident. (5) ~~Look at and check~~ ^Check^ the engine for problems like broken wires, cracked hoses, and leaks. (6) If, when you start the car ~~up and running~~, gray smoke keeps coming ~~and does not stop coming~~ from the exhaust pipe, do not buy the car. (7) Push down suddenly~~, all at once,~~ on the accelerator while the car is running, and see ~~and observe~~ if the car hesitates. (8) While on a straight and level road, check the steering by letting go ~~and taking your hands off~~ of the steering wheel and seeing if the car keeps going straight ahead ~~without going from side to side~~. (9) ~~Despite the fact that~~ ^Even if^ there does not seem to be anything wrong with the car, take ~~and drive~~ it to a ~~car~~ mechanic you trust to inspect it ~~and give it a close look~~. (10) If the owner refuses to allow you to ~~take it to a mechanic,~~ ^do this^ ~~the very best thing to do at that time is to~~ leave and start looking for another car.

■ WRITING FIRST: Flashback

Look back at your response to the Writing First exercise on page 310. Identify a sentence that contains unnecessary repetition. Rewrite the sentence on the lines below, editing it so it is more concise.

Answers will vary.

_____

_____

C   Avoiding Clichés

One way of making your writing more effective is to avoid **clichés**, expressions that have been used so often they have lost their ability to affect readers. Writers tend to plug in such ready-made phrases—for example, "easier said than done," "last but not least," and "work like a dog"—without giving them much thought, but these worn-out expressions deaden writing and do little to create interest.

● **Writing Tip**
Your computer's grammar
checker might be able to
flag clichés and wordy constructions. Remember, however, that you—not the
computer—must decide
whether (and how) to revise.

When you identify a cliché in your writing, replace it with a direct statement—or, if possible, substitute a fresher expression.

CLICHÉ   When school was over, she felt <u>free as a bird</u>.

REVISED   When school was over, she felt free.

CLICHÉ   These days, you have to be <u>sick as a dog</u> before you are admitted to a hospital.

REVISED   These days, you have to be seriously ill before you are admitted to a hospital.

FOCUS **Avoiding Clichés**

Here are examples of some clichés you should avoid in your writing.

better late than never	hit the nail on the head
beyond a shadow of a doubt	last but not least
break the ice	pass the buck
busy as a bee	sadder but wiser
cold, hard facts	sink or swim
easier said than done	the bottom line
face the music	tried and true
give 110 percent	wake up and smell the coffee
happy as a clam	water under the bridge
hard as a rock	what goes around comes around

ON THE WEB
For more practice, visit
Exercise Central *at*
<bedfordstmartins.com/
writingfirst>.

Teaching Tip
Have students keep a list of
overused expressions that
they encounter in their reading (or in their own writing).
They can refer to this list as
they revise their own work.

◆ **PRACTICE 20-5**

Cross out any clichés in the following sentences, and either substitute a fresher expression or restate the idea in more direct language.

Example: Lottery winners often think they will be ~~on easy street~~ for
                                                              free of financial worries
the rest of their lives.

Answers will vary.

(1) Many people think that a million-dollar lottery jackpot allows the
                                          long hours   *a comfortable life.*
winner to stop working ~~like a dog~~ and start living ~~high on the hog.~~ (2) ~~All~~
                                      In fact,
~~things considered, however,~~ the reality for lottery winners is quite different.
                                        win big prizes
(3) For one thing, lottery winners who ~~hit the jackpot~~ do not receive their

winnings all at once; instead, payments—for example, $50,000—are usually

spread out over twenty years. (4) Of that $50,000 a year, close to $20,000
                                            winner
goes to taxes and anything else the ~~lucky stiff~~ owes the government, such

as student loans. (5) Next come relatives and friends ~~with their hands~~ *who ask for money,*
~~out,~~ leaving winners ~~between a rock and a hard place.~~ *with difficult choices to make.* (6) They can either
give
~~cough up~~ gifts and loans or ~~wave bye-bye to~~ *lose the friendship of* many of their loved ones.
Even worse,
(7) ~~Adding insult to injury,~~ many lottery winners have lost their jobs

because employers thought that once they were "millionaires," they no

longer needed to draw a salary. (8) Many lottery winners wind up ~~way~~
serious   *Faced with financial difficulties,*
~~over their heads~~ in debt within a few years. (9) ~~In their hour of need,~~ many

would like to sell their future payments to companies that offer lump-sum

usually impossible,
payments of forty to forty-five cents on the dollar. (10) This is ~~easier said~~

~~than done,~~ however, because most state lotteries do not allow winners to

sell their winnings.

■ WRITING FIRST: Flashback

Look back at your response to the Writing First exercise on page
310. If you have used any clichés, list them below. Then, either replace each cliché with a more direct statement, or think of a more
original way of expressing the idea.

Cliché	*Revised*
Answers will vary.	

D   Using Similes and Metaphors

A **simile** is a comparison of two unlike things that uses *like* or *as*.

> His arm hung at his side <u>like</u> a broken branch.

> He was <u>as</u> content <u>as</u> a cat napping on a windowsill.

A **metaphor** is a comparison of two unlike things that does *not* use *like*
or *as*.

> Invaders from another world, the dandelions conquered my garden.

> He was a beast of burden, hauling cement from the mixer to the
> building site.

● **Writing Tip**

Both similes and metaphors
compare two *dissimilar*
things. If the items being
compared are *alike*, the result is a statement of fact
(*Your boat is like my boat*)
and is not a simile or a
metaphor.

The force of similes and metaphors comes from the surprise of seeing two seemingly unlike things being compared and, as a result, seeing
a hidden or unnoticed similarity between them. Used in moderation,
similes and metaphors can make your writing more lively and more
interesting.

◆ PRACTICE 20-6

Use your imagination to complete each of the following by creating three
appropriate similes.

Example: A boring class is like *toast without jam.* _____

a straitjacket. _____

a bedtime story. _____

Answers will vary.
1. A good friend is like _____

_____

_____

2. A thunderstorm is like _____

_____

_____

3. Falling in love is like _____

_____

_____

◆ PRACTICE 20-7

Think of a person you know well. Using that person as your subject, fill in
each of the following blanks to create metaphors. Try to complete each
metaphor with more than a single word, as in the example.

Example: If ___*my baby sister*___ were an animal, ___*she*___ would be

a curious little kitten.
_____
Answers will vary.
1. If _____ were an animal, _____ would be _____

_____.

2. If _____ were a food, _____ would be _____

_____.

3. If _____ were a means of transportation, _____ would be

_____.

4. If _____ were a natural phenomenon, _____ would be _____

_____.

5. If _____ were a toy, _____ would be _____

_____.

■ WRITING FIRST: Flashback

Look back at your response to the Writing First exercise on page 310. Find two sentences that could be enriched with a simile or a metaphor. On the lines below, rewrite these two sentences, adding a simile to one sentence and a metaphor to the other.

1. *Answers will vary.* _____

_____

2. _____

_____

E   Avoiding Sexist Language

Sexist language refers to men and women in insulting terms. Sexist language is not just words like *stud* or *babe*, which many people find objectionable. It can also be words or phrases that unnecessarily call attention to gender or that suggest a job or profession is exclusively male or female when it actually is not.

You can avoid sexist usage by being sensitive and using a little common sense. There is always an acceptable nonsexist alternative for a sexist term.

Sexist	*Nonsexist*
man, mankind	humanity, humankind, human race
businessman	executive, business person
fireman, policeman, mailman	firefighter, police officer, letter carrier
male nurse, woman engineer	nurse, engineer
congressman	member of Congress, representative
stewardess, steward	flight attendant
man and wife	man and woman, husband and wife
manmade	synthetic
chairman	chair, chairperson
anchorwoman, anchorman	anchor
actor, actress	actor

● **Writing Tip**

It is also sexist to give information about a woman—for example, her marital status or how she dresses—that you would not give about a man.

● **Writing Tip**

In addition to avoiding sexist language, avoid potentially offensive references to a person's age, physical condition, or sexual orientation.

For a discussion of subjects like everyone *(indefinite pronoun antecedents), see 28E.*

FOCUS Avoiding Sexist Language

Do not use *he* when your subject could be either male or female.

Everyone should complete <u>his</u> assignment by next week.

You can correct this problem in three ways:

■ Use *he or she* or *his or her*.

Everyone should complete <u>his or her</u> assignment by next week.

■ Use plural forms.

Students should complete <u>their</u> assignment by next week.

■ Eliminate the pronoun.

Everyone should complete <u>the</u> assignment by next week.

◆ PRACTICE 20-8

ON THE WEB
For more practice, visit
Exercise Central *at*
<bedfordstmartins.com/
writingfirst>.

Edit the following sentences to eliminate sexist language.

Answers will vary.

1. Many people today would like to see more ~~policemen~~ *police officers* patrolling the streets.

2. A doctor should be honest with his *or her (or omit "his")* patients.

3. The attorneys representing the plaintiff are Geraldo Diaz and ~~Mrs.~~ Barbara Wilkerson.

4. Chris Fox is the ~~female~~ mayor of Port London, Maine.

5. Travel to other planets will be a significant step for ~~man.~~ *humanity.*

■ WRITING FIRST: Flashback

Look back at your response to the Writing First exercise on page 310. Have you used any words or phrases that unnecessarily call attention to gender? Have you used *he* when your subject could be either male or female? Rewrite on the following lines any sentences in which these problems occur. Then, cross out the sexist language, and substitute acceptable nonsexist alternatives.

(continued on the following page)

(continued from the previous page)

_____

_____

_____

_____

■ WRITING FIRST: Revising and Editing

Look back at your response to the Writing First exercise on page 310. Revise the paragraph, making sure your language is as specific as possible, and avoid using clichés or sexist expressions. Be sure to incorporate the revisions you made in this chapter's Flashback exercises. When you have finished, revise another writing assignment you are currently working on.

CHAPTER REVIEW

◆ EDITING PRACTICE

Read the following student essay carefully, and then revise it. Make sure that your revision is concise, uses specific words, and includes no sexist language or clichés. Add an occasional simile or metaphor to increase interest. The first sentence has been edited for you.

Answers will vary.

Unexpected Discoveries

When we hear the word "accident," we think of bad
like dented fenders and broken glass.   *lucky,*
things. But accidents can be ~~good,~~ too. Modern science has

made important advances as a result of lucky accidents. ~~It~~
                                    A   *hard*
~~is a fact that a~~ scientist sometimes works ~~like a dog~~ for
        the   *an accidental*   *.*
years in ~~his~~ laboratory, only to make ~~a weird~~ discovery

~~because of a mistake.~~

The most famous example of a ~~good,~~ beneficial accident

is the discovery of penicillin. A scientist, Alexander

Fleming, had seen many soldiers die of infections after

Alexander Fleming

they were wounded in World War I. ~~All things considered,~~ *In fact,*
many more soldiers died ~~due to the fact that~~ *from* infections
~~occurred~~ than from their wounds. Fleming wanted to find a
drug that could ~~put an end to~~ *cure* these ~~terrible,~~ fatal
infections. One day in 1928, Fleming went on vacation,
leaving a pile of dishes in the lab sink. ~~As luck would~~
~~have it,~~ *Luckily,* he had been growing bacteria in those dishes. When
he came back, he noticed that one of the dishes looked
moldy. ~~What was strange was that~~ *Strangely,* near the mold, the
bacteria were dead ~~as a doornail.~~ ~~It was crystal clear to~~
Fleming *realized* that the mold had killed the bacteria. He had
discovered penicillin, the first antibiotic.

Charles Goodyear

Everyone has heard the name "Goodyear." ~~It was~~ Charles
Goodyear ~~who~~ made a discovery that ~~changed and~~
revolutionized the rubber industry and made our modern
tires last ~~so long.~~ *for years.* In the early nineteenth century, rubber
products ~~became thin and runny~~ *melted* in hot weather and cracked
in cold weather. One day in 1839, Goodyear accidentally
dropped some rubber mixed with sulfur on a hot stove. It
~~changd color and~~ turned black, but after being cooled, it
could be stretched, *, like a rubber band,* and ~~it~~ would return to its original
size and shape. This kind of rubber is now used in tires
and in many other products.

Another ~~thing~~ *product* was discovered because of a *messy* lab accident
involving rubber. In 1953, Patsy Sherman, a ~~female~~ chemist
for the 3M company, was trying to find a new type of
rubber. She created a batch of ~~man-made,~~ synthetic liquid
rubber. Some of the liquid accidentally spilled onto a lab
assistant's new white canvas sneaker. According to one
story, her assistant tried everything ~~but the kitchen sink~~
to clean the shoe, but nothing worked. ~~Over time,~~ *After a few weeks,* the rest
of the shoe became dirty, but the part where the spill had

Patsy Sherman

hit was still clean as a whistle. Sherman realized that she
a chemical
had found something that could actually keep fabrics clean

by keeping off and repelling dirt. The 3M Corporation named

this new product Scotchguard.
Scientists   *their*
A scientist can be clumsy and sloppy, but sometimes his

mistakes lead to great and significant discoveries.

Penicillin, long-lasting tires, and Scotchguard are

examples of successful products that were the result of

scientific accidents.

◆ COLLABORATIVE ACTIVITIES

1. Photocopy two or three paragraphs of description from a romance novel, a western novel, or a mystery novel, and bring your paragraphs to class. Working in a group, choose one paragraph that seems to need clearer, more specific language.

2. As a group, revise the paragraph you chose for Collaborative Activity 1, making it as clear and specific as possible and eliminating any clichés or sexist language.

3. Exchange your revised paragraph from Collaborative Activity 2 with the paragraph revised by another group, and check the other group's work. Make any additional changes you think your paragraph needs.

☑ REVIEW CHECKLIST:
Using Words Effectively

- Use specific words that convey your ideas clearly and precisely. (See 20A.)

- Use concise language that says what it has to say in the fewest possible words. (See 20B.)

- Avoid clichés. (See 20C.)

- Whenever possible, use similes and metaphors to make your writing more lively and more interesting. (See 20D.)

- Avoid sexist language. (See 20E.)

Read the following student essay. Then, edit it by creating more effective sentences. Combine simple sentences into compound or complex sentences, use parallelism, create varied sentences, and use words that are concise, specific, and original. The first editing change has been made for you.

Answers will vary.

                    The Donner Party
                    pioneers
        Thousands of ~~people~~ went west in the 1840s. They were

frightened by outbreaks of cholera and malaria in the
                    , and they
east, ~~They~~ wanted to own their own land. Many believed that
                    a Garden of Eden.   *Starting*
California would be ~~wonderful.~~ ~~Wagon trains started~~ in

Illinois or Missouri, ~~The~~ wagon trains traveled two

thousand miles to Oregon and California. The trip west was
                                    , and the
hard. The weather was often very bad, ~~The~~ wagons had to

cross high mountains. Most people survived the trip, but
                    because its
one group became famous, ~~Its~~ experience was disastrous.

This group of pioneers came to be called the Donner Party.
                    Leaving   *, the Donner Party*
        ~~The Donner Party left~~ Missouri in May 1846, ~~The group~~

included nine families and sixteen single men. They
                                                    , who
expected the trip to take four months. George Donner was
                                                    The group
elected the leader, ~~He~~ knew that timing was important. ~~They~~
                                    , and they
could not leave until after the spring rains, ~~They~~ had to

get over the Sierra Mountains before the first snow. At
                                            , which
first, they were delayed by heavy thunderstorms, ~~They~~

caused muddy trails. At Fort Laramie, Wyoming, they heard
                that
about a new route, ~~It~~ would save four hundred miles. ~~They~~
By then, they   *, which*
were a month behind schedule ~~by then.~~ The new route would

go south of the Great Salt Lake, ~~It~~ was supposed to be a

shortcut. They were told that the route would be safe.

Along the way, they could find plenty of grass for the
            and
animals, ~~They could also~~ gather plenty of firewood.

However, experienced travelers warned them not to take this

Covered wagon and pioneer family

shortcut~~,~~ *, saying* ~~They said~~ it would be dangerous. The leaders ~~were~~
had a difficult decision to make.
~~between a rock and a hard place.~~ The Donner Party took the

shortcut.

Unfortunately, it
~~It~~ was very hard~~,~~ ~~unfortunately.~~ The mountains were

barely passable~~,~~ *, and trails* ~~Trails~~ were steep and narrow. The

travelers had to cross eighty miles of the Salt Desert~~,~~ *, which* ~~It~~

was a mix of salt, clay, and mud. *As a result, some* ~~Some~~ of the wagons got

stuck and had to be left behind ~~as a result.~~ Oxen died or

went mad from thirst and ran away. After they crossed the

desert, the travelers checked their food~~,~~ *and* ~~They~~ found they

did not have enough for the rest of the trip.

The shortcut had *actually* delayed them. *Because* ~~Due to the fact that~~ they

were delayed, they had run out of time. *By late October, deep* ~~Deep~~ snow blocked

the pass across the Sierra Nevada mountains ~~by late~~

~~October.~~ *Trapped* ~~They were trapped~~ by the snow~~,~~ *, they* ~~They~~ encountered

snowdrifts that were as much as twenty feet high. The

Donner Party had to spend the winter in the mountains.

Hoping for the best, they built cabins and set up tents.
However, food was scarce~~,~~ *, and people* ~~People~~ became thinner and weaker.
By the time search
~~Search~~ parties brought out all the survivors~~,~~ ~~By that~~

~~time,~~ members of the Donner Party had eaten their animals.

They had eaten mice, twigs, bark, and even their own shoes.

~~were also eaten.~~ Eventually, some of them ate their dead.

Of the original eighty-seven travelers, forty-six

survived. George Donner and his wife died~~,~~ *, and so* ~~So~~ did his

brother, his brother's wife, and most of the Donner
Almost a year after they had left Missouri, the
children. ~~The~~ last survivors reached California ~~almost a~~

~~year after they had left Missouri.~~ ~~The Donner Party tragedy~~
Written
~~was written~~ about in many newspapers of the time~~,~~ *, the* ~~The~~ story

of the Donner Party tragedy quickly spread across the

country. Many readers were shocked when they learned some

people had eaten the dead. However, cannibalism was not a

Camp at Donner Lake

Illustration from a book about the Donner Party

crime, ~~No~~ *, and no* survivors were ever charged. After the Donner

Party tragedy, the number of wagon trains to California

dropped sharply, ~~Then,~~ *until* gold was discovered in 1848.

~~Thousands~~ *Then, thousands* of people ~~then~~ rushed to California to try to ~~hit~~ *find gold.*

~~the jackpot.~~ They took the pass over the Sierra Nevada

mountains, ~~It~~ *, which* was now called the Donner Pass.

UNIT FIVE

Solving Common Sentence Problems

Run-Ons and Comma Splices

■ WRITING FIRST

In the picture above, a boy lies in front of the television. Why do you think so many American children are physically out of shape? What do you think can be done about this problem? Look at the picture, and then try to answer these questions.

A Recognizing Run-Ons and Comma Splices

A **run-on** is an error that occurs when two sentences (independent clauses) are joined without punctuation.

RUN-ON [More and more students are earning high school equivalency diplomas] [the value of these diplomas is currently under debate.]

329

● **Writing Tip**

A comma can join two sentences only when it is followed by a coordinating conjunction. (See 16A.)

Teaching Tip

Let students practice reading aloud passages from which you have deleted all end punctuation. Point out how their voices usually stop at the end of a sentence even when it contains no punctuation.

ON THE WEB
For more practice, visit Exercise Central *at <bedfordstmartins.com/ writingfirst>.*

A **comma splice** is an error that occurs when two sentences are joined with just a comma.

COMMA SPLICE   [More and more students are earning high school equivalency diplomas], [the value of these diplomas is currently under debate.]

◆ **PRACTICE 21-1**

Some of the sentences in the following passage are correct, but others are run-ons or comma splices. In the answer space after each sentence, write *C* if the sentence is correct, *RO* if it is a run-on, and *CS* if it is a comma splice.

Example: "Race movies" had all-black casts, they were intended for African-American audiences. __CS__

(1) In 1919, African-American director Oscar Micheaux filmed *Within Our Gates* this movie examined black life in Chicago. __RO__ (2) The film included scenes of violence, it even depicted two lynchings. __CS__ (3) It also treated interracial relationships white censors banned it. __RO__ (4) Race riots had occurred in Chicago that year, the censors feared violence. __CS__ (5) Micheaux appealed to the board they agreed to the film's release in Chicago. __RO__ (6) The movie was shown, twelve hundred feet of film were omitted. __CS__ (7) Micheaux later made many low-budget movies, but few survive today. __C__ (8) Some are musicals others are melodramas. __RO__ (9) Few are socially conscious films like *Within Our Gates*. __C__ (10) One, *Body and Soul*, was Paul Robeson's first film. __C__ (11) Micheaux died in 1951. __C__ (12) In 1990, an uncut version of *Within Our Gates* was discovered in Madrid, it was shown in Chicago for the first time in 1992. __CS__

● **Writing Tip**

Computer grammar checkers sometimes identify a sentence as a run-on or comma splice simply because it is long. However, a long sentence can be correct. Before you make any changes, be sure you actually have an error (two independent clauses joined without punctuation or with just a comma). (See 21B.)

■ WRITING FIRST: Flashback

Look back at your response to the Writing First exercise on page 329. Do you see any run-ons or comma splices? If so, underline them.

B   Correcting Run-Ons and Comma Splices

You can correct a run-on or comma splice in five ways.

1. Create two separate sentences.

> INCORRECT (RUN-ON)   Muslims fast during daylight for a period of thirty days this period is called Ramadan.
>
> INCORRECT (COMMA SPLICE)   Muslims fast during daylight for a period of thirty days, this period is called Ramadan.
>
> CORRECT   Muslims fast during daylight for a period of thirty days. This period is called Ramadan. (two separate sentences)

2. Use a coordinating conjunction.
If you want to indicate a particular relationship between ideas—for example, cause and effect or contrast—you can connect two independent clauses with a coordinating conjunction (*and, but, or, nor, for, so,* or *yet*) that makes this relationship clear. Always place a comma before the coordinating conjunction.

For more on connecting ideas with a coordinating conjunction, see 16A.

> INCORRECT (RUN-ON)   The Emancipation Proclamation freed U.S. slaves in 1863 slaves in Texas were not officially freed until June 19, 1865 ("Juneteenth").
>
> INCORRECT (COMMA SPLICE)   The Emancipation Proclamation freed U.S. slaves in 1863, slaves in Texas were not officially freed until June 19, 1865 ("Juneteenth").
>
> CORRECT   The Emancipation Proclamation freed U.S. slaves in 1863, <u>but</u> slaves in Texas were not officially freed until June 19, 1865 ("Juneteenth"). (clauses connected with a comma followed by a coordinating conjunction)

3. Use a semicolon.
If you want to indicate a particularly close connection—or a strong contrast—between two ideas, use a semicolon.

For more on connecting ideas with a semicolon, see 16B.

> INCORRECT (RUN-ON)   The swastika was an ancient symbol of good luck it was also the official emblem of the Nazi Party.
>
> INCORRECT (COMMA SPLICE)   The swastika was an ancient symbol of good luck, it was also the official emblem of the Nazi Party.
>
> CORRECT   The swastika was an ancient symbol of good luck<u>;</u> it was also the official emblem of the Nazi Party. (clauses connected with a semicolon)

Teaching Tip
Review the use of semicolons, referring students to 16B. Explain that if a period will not work where the semicolon is, then the semicolon is probably incorrect.

4. Use a semicolon followed by a conjunctive adverb or transitional expression.
To clarify a specific relationship between two closely related ideas, add a conjunctive adverb or transitional expression after the semicolon.

> INCORRECT (RUN-ON)   *Its* is a possessive pronoun *it's* is a contraction.
>
> INCORRECT (COMMA SPLICE)   *Its* is a possessive pronoun, *it's* is a contraction.
>
> CORRECT   *Its* is a possessive pronoun<u>; however,</u> *it's* is a contraction. (clauses connected with a semicolon followed by a conjunctive adverb)

● Writing Tip
Conjunctive adverbs include words such as *however* and *therefore;* transitional expressions include *in fact, as a result,* and *for example.* (See 16C.)

<table>
<tr><td colspan="2">

FOCUS **Connecting Ideas with Semicolons**

Run-ons and comma splices often occur when you use a conjunctive adverb or transitional expression to join two independent clauses *without also using a semicolon.*

INCORRECT (RUN-ON)	Some students have microwaves and refrigerators in their dorm rooms as a result, electrical circuits are overloaded.
INCORRECT (COMMA SPLICE)	Some students have microwaves and refrigerators in their dorm rooms, as a result, electrical circuits are overloaded.

To correct this kind of run-on or comma splice, simply add the missing semicolon.

CORRECT	Some students have microwaves and refrigerators in their dorm rooms; as a result, electrical circuits are overloaded.

</td></tr>
</table>

For more on connecting ideas with a subordinating conjunction or relative pronoun, see Chapter 17.

5. Use a subordinating conjunction or relative pronoun. When one idea is dependent on another, you can turn the dependent idea into a dependent clause by adding a subordinating conjunction (such as *when, although,* or *because*) or a relative pronoun (such as *who, which,* or *that*).

INCORRECT (RUN-ON)	Horace Mann was the first president of Antioch College he encouraged the development of students' social consciences.
INCORRECT (COMMA SPLICE)	Horace Mann was the first president of Antioch College, he encouraged the development of students' social consciences.
CORRECT	When Horace Mann was the first president of Antioch College, he encouraged the development of students' social consciences. (clauses connected with a subordinating conjunction)
CORRECT	Horace Mann, who was the first president of Antioch College, encouraged the development of students' social consciences. (clauses connected with a relative pronoun)

● **Writing Tip**

When you use a relative pronoun to correct a run-on or comma splice, the relative pronoun takes the place of another pronoun in the sentence (for example, in the sentence to the right, *who* takes the place of *he*).

◆ **PRACTICE 21-2**

Correct each of the run-ons and comma splices on the next page in one of the following four ways: by creating two separate sentences, by using a coordinating conjunction, by using a semicolon, or by using a semicolon followed by a conjunctive adverb or transitional expression. Be sure punctuation is correct. Remember to put a semicolon before, and a comma after, each conjunctive adverb or transitional expression.

Example: Some people believe chronic sex offenders should be given therapy*; however,* others believe they should be jailed indefinitely.

Answers may vary.

1. Nursing offers job security and high pay*; therefore,* many people are choosing nursing as a career.

2. Anne Boleyn was the second wife of Henry VIII*, and* her daughter was Elizabeth I.

3. The Democratic Republic of the Congo was previously known as Zaire*;* before that*,* it was the Belgian Congo.

4. Housewife Jean Nidetch started Weight Watchers in 1961*. She* sold the company for $100 million in 1978.

5. Millions of Jews were killed during the Holocaust*;* in addition*,* Catholics, Gypsies, homosexuals, and other "undesirables" were killed.

6. Sojourner Truth was born a slave*, but* she eventually became a leading abolitionist and feminist.

7. Japanese athletes now play various positions on American baseball teams*;* at first*,* all the Japanese players were pitchers.

8. Oliver Wendell Holmes Jr. was a Supreme Court Justice*;* his father was a physician and writer.

9. Père Noel is the French name for Santa Claus*;* he is also known as Father Christmas and St. Nicholas.

10. Latin is one classical language*;* Greek is another.

◆ PRACTICE 21-3

Consulting the list of subordinating conjunctions on page 261 and the list of relative pronouns on page 264, correct the following run-ons and comma splices. Be sure to add correct punctuation where necessary.

Examples: Harlem was a rural area until the nineteenth century *when* improved transportation linked it to lower Manhattan.

The community*, which* was soon home to people escaping the crowds of New York City, ~~it~~ became a fashionable suburb.

Answers may vary.

(1) Harlem*, which* was populated mostly by European immigrants at the turn of the last century, ~~it~~ saw an influx of African Americans beginning

As this
in 1910. (2) ~~This~~ migration from the South continued for several decades,
Harlem became one of the largest African-American communities
in the United States. (3) Many African-American artists and writers
which
settled in Harlem during the 1920s, ~~this~~ led to a flowering of African-
American art. (4) This "Harlem Renaissance" was an important era in
although
American literary history it is not even mentioned in some textbooks.
When scholars
(5) ~~Scholars~~ of the era recognize the great works of the Harlem Renaissance, they point to the writers Langston Hughes and Countee Cullen
and the artists Henry Tanner and Sargent Johnson. (6) Zora Neale
, who
Hurston moved to Harlem from her native Florida in 1925, ~~she~~ began
Because
work there on a book of African-American folklore. (7) Harlem was an
exciting place in the 1920s people from all over the city went there to
listen to jazz and to dance. (8) The white playwright Eugene O'Neill went
, which
to Harlem to audition actors for his play *The Emperor Jones* ~~it~~ made an
While contemporary
international star of the great Paul Robeson. (9) ~~Contemporary~~ African-
American artists know about the Harlem Renaissance, it is still not
When the
familiar to many others. (10) ~~The~~ Great Depression occurred in the
1930s it led to the end of the Harlem Renaissance.

◆ PRACTICE 21-4

Correct each run-on and comma splice in the following passage in the way
that best indicates the relationship between ideas. Be sure you use appropriate punctuation.

Example: Coney Island was once a bustling seaside resort it de-
, but
clined considerably over the years.
Answers may vary.
(1) In the late nineteenth century, Coney Island was famous in fact,
;
it was legendary. (2) Every summer, it was crowded, people mailed hun-
and
dreds of thousands of postcards from the resort on some days. (3) Coney
, which
Island was considered exotic and exciting, ~~it~~ even had a hotel shaped like
Although some
an elephant. (4). ~~Some~~ people saw Coney Island as seedy, others thought
it was a wonderful, magical place. (5) It had beaches, hotels, racetracks,
;
and a stadium however by the turn of the century, it was best known for

three amusement parks. (6) These parks were Luna Park, Steeplechase,
and Dreamland. (7) ~~Gaslight~~ *Even though gaslight* was still the norm in New York, a million
electric lights lit Luna Park. (8) *While* Steeplechase offered many rides, its main
attraction was a two-mile ride on mechanical horses. (9) At Dreamland,
people could see a submarine; in addition, they could travel through
an Eskimo village or visit Lilliputia, with its three hundred midgets.
(10) Today, the old Coney Island no longer exists. (11) Fire destroyed
Dreamland in 1911, *and* Luna Park burned down in 1946. (12) In 1964,
Steeplechase closed. (13) The once-grand Coney Island is gone. *Still,* ~~still~~
its beach and its boardwalk remain. (14) Its famous roller coaster, the
Cyclone, still exists, *and* its giant Ferris wheel, the Wonder Wheel, keeps on
turning. (15) Now, a ballpark has been built for a new minor league
baseball team. *The* ~~the~~ new team is called the Brooklyn Cyclones.

■ WRITING FIRST: Flashback

For each run-on or comma splice you identified in the Flashback
exercise on page 330, write two possible corrected versions here.

Answers will vary.

_____

_____

_____

_____

_____

■ WRITING FIRST: Revising and Editing

Look back at your responses to the Writing First exercise on page
329 and the Flashback exercises on page 330 and above. For each
run-on and comma splice you found, choose the revision that best
conveys your meaning, and revise your Writing First exercise accordingly. If you do not find any run-ons or comma splices in your
own writing, work with a classmate to correct his or her writing, or
edit the work you did for another assignment.

CHAPTER REVIEW

◆ EDITING PRACTICE: PARAGRAPH

Read the following student paragraph, and revise it to eliminate run-ons and comma splices. Correct each run-on and comma splice in the way that best indicates the relationship between ideas. The first error has been corrected for you.

Answers may vary.

Blood Sports

    I used to play competitive sports, but I don't anymore.
My parents *, who* encouraged my athletic career *,* they got me
started in sports early on. Between the ages of ten and
seventeen, I was very active in martial arts, *and* I especially
liked karate. As a young child, I competed in karate
tournaments *, where* I was injured frequently. I broke my nose three
times *;* I also broke my hand twice and my foot once. As a
competitor, I enjoyed the thrill of battle *;* however *,* I was
always afraid of serious injury. Eventually, I gave up
karate *;* instead *,* I concentrated on football. Hard tackling
and blocking were very important in high school football, *and* I
often hurt my opponents. I learned that aggressiveness and
pain are part of playing sports. I accept this as part of
the game *,* I just don't want to play anymore.

◆ EDITING PRACTICE: ESSAY

Read the following student essay, into which sentence errors have been introduced. Then, revise it by eliminating run-ons and comma splices and carefully correcting them to indicate the relationships between ideas. Be sure punctuation is correct. The first error has been corrected for you.

Answers may vary.

Dollars and Cents

    Most of us handle money every day, *but* we rarely look
closely at it or think much about what goes into producing
it. However, the U.S. Treasury Department thinks a lot
about our money. The Treasury Department is always looking
for ways to make money more interesting to consumers and

collectors, ~~it~~ *.It* is also always trying to make money harder
for counterfeiters to copy.

In the past few years, some major changes have been made
to our money. Between 1999 and 2008, the U.S. Mint will be
issuing new quarters for every state ~~the~~ *. The* quarters are being
issued in the order in which the states ratified the
Constitution. The design of each quarter is different, *;* each
image represents a unique characteristic of the state or
its history. The coins are very popular, *;* in fact, many
people are collecting sets for their children and
grandchildren.

The Mint has already begun producing new nickels.
The front of one nickel still shows the head of Thomas
Jefferson, our third president, *but* it is a new image. The back
of the nickel features an American bison, *;* the bison is
shown from the side. The new image of Jefferson also
appears on another nickel, ~~on~~ *. On* the other side, this one
shows the Western waters as first seen by Lewis and Clark.
A third nickel pictures a keelboat like the one that
carried Lewis and Clark on their expedition. The image
on the other side of this nickel is still the head of
President Jefferson that was on the older coins.

The U.S. Treasury is always trying to stay ahead of
the counterfeiters. In the spring of 2003, they printed
the first colorful twenty-dollar-bills ~~these~~ *. These* bills are
printed in shades of blue, yellow, and peach rather than
the standard green and black. The picture of Andrew
Jackson is also larger and slightly off center. The type
is bolder, *and* there is a blue eagle in the background. The
Treasury plans to change our bills every seven to ten
years to make them harder to copy, ~~eventually,~~ *. Eventually,* the fifty-
and one hundred-dollar notes will also be printed in
color.

Changes in our money may be hard to get used to, *but* they

serve an important purpose. They help to prevent
counterfeiting and provide us with attractive currency
to collect—or to spend.

◆ COLLABORATIVE ACTIVITIES

1. Find an interesting paragraph in a newspaper or magazine article. Working in a small group, recopy it onto a separate sheet of paper, creating run-ons and comma splices. Exchange exercises with another group.

2. Work in a small group to correct each run-on and comma splice in an exercise prepared by another group of students. When you have finished, return the exercise to the group that created it.

3. Continuing to work with members of your group, evaluate the other group's work on your exercise, comparing it to the original newspaper or magazine paragraph. Pay particular attention to punctuation. Where the students' version differs from the original, decide whether their version is incorrect or whether it represents an acceptable (or even superior) alternative to the original.

ESL Tip
Nonnative speakers may be no more likely to write run-ons or comma splices than the native speakers in the class are. For this reason, you can feel comfortable calling on nonnative students as you review this unit.

Teaching Tip
Have students memorize the five ways to correct run-ons and comma splices.

☑ REVIEW CHECKLIST:
Run-Ons and Comma Splices

☐ A run-on is an error that occurs when two sentences are joined without punctuation. (See 21A.)

☐ A comma splice is an error that occurs when two sentences are joined with just a comma. (See 21A.)

☐ Correct a run-on or comma splice by creating two separate sentences, by using a coordinating conjunction, by using a semicolon, by using a semicolon followed by a conjunctive adverb or transitional expression, or by connecting clauses with a subordinating conjunction or relative pronoun. (See 21B.)

Sentence Fragments

PREVIEW

In this chapter, you will learn

■ to recognize sentence fragments (22A)

■ to correct sentence fragments created when phrases are punctuated as sentences (22B)

■ to correct sentence fragments created when verbs are incomplete (22C)

■ to correct sentence fragments created when dependent clauses are punctuated as sentences (22D)

■ WRITING FIRST

The picture above shows a billboard advertising Pom pomegranate juice. Look at the picture, and then write several lines of copy for a magazine ad for your favorite beverage, footwear, or health or beauty product.

Word Power

unique   the only one

transform   to change completely

empower   to give strength or power to

A   Recognizing Sentence Fragments

A **sentence fragment** is an incomplete sentence. Every sentence must include at least one subject and one verb, and every sentence must express a complete thought. If a group of words does not do *all* these things, it is a fragment and not a sentence—even if it begins with a capital letter and ends with a period.

                     s   v

SENTENCE   The <u>actors</u> in the play <u>were</u> ethnically diverse. (includes both a subject and a verb and expresses a complete thought)

339

● **Writing Tip**

You may see sentence fragments used in advertise-
ments and other informal
writing (*A full head of hair in
just thirty minutes!*), but
fragments are not accept-
able in college writing.

Because a sentence must have both a subject and a verb and express a complete thought, the following groups of words are not complete sentences; they are fragments.

FRAGMENT (NO VERB)   The actors in the play. (What point is being made about the actors?)

FRAGMENT (NO SUBJECT)   Were ethnically diverse. (What was ethnically diverse?)

FOCUS **Identifying Sentence Fragments**

Sentence fragments almost always appear in paragraphs next to complete sentences.

┌─── COMPLETE SENTENCE ───┐ ┌──── FRAGMENT ────┐
Celia took two electives. Physics 320 and Spanish 101.

The fragment above does not have a verb. The complete sentence that precedes it, however, has both a subject (*Celia*) and a verb (*took*).

Often, as in this case, you can correct a sentence fragment by attaching it to an adjacent sentence that supplies the missing words.

Celia took two electives, Physics 320 and Spanish 101.

Teaching Tip
Consider giving students
a pretest to determine the
types of problems they have.
This will help you decide
how much time you need
to spend on fragments.

◆ **PRACTICE 22-1**

Each of the following items is a fragment. On the line following each fragment, indicate what needs to be added or what needs to be changed to make it a complete sentence. There are four possible ways to correct these sentence fragments: (1) add a subject; (2) add a verb; (3) add a subject and a verb; or (if the fragment has a subject and a verb) (4) revise to express a complete thought.

ON THE WEB
For more practice, visit
Exercise Central *at*
<bedfordstmartins.com/
writingfirst>.

Example: At the beginning of the test. *add a subject and a verb*

1. The students in the classroom. *add a verb*

2. Before the teacher handed out the answer sheets. *revise to express a complete thought*

3. With a number-two pencil. *add a subject and a verb*

4. Opened their test booklets. *add a subject*

5. After twenty-five minutes. *add a subject and a verb*

6. Began the second part of the test. *add a subject*

7. The last set of questions. *add a verb*

8. When the teacher called "Time." *revise to express a complete thought*

9. Breathed a sigh of relief. _add a subject_ _____

10. Quickly out into the hallway. _add a subject and a verb_ _____

◆ **PRACTICE 22-2**

In the following passage, some of the numbered groups of words are missing a subject, a verb, or both. Identify each fragment by labeling it *F.* Then,
attach each fragment to a nearby word group to create a complete new
sentence. Finally, rewrite the entire passage, using complete sentences, on
the lines provided.

ESL Tip
Nonnative speakers may not
have any more trouble with
fragments than other stu-
dents. If they aren't having
problems in this area, work
with them on problem areas
such as count and noncount
nouns (discussed in 30E).

Example: Martha Grimes, Ruth Rendell, and Deborah Crombie
write detective novels. _____ Set in England. _F_

Martha Grimes, Ruth Rendell, and Deborah Crombie write detective novels

set in England.

(1) Sara Paretsky writes detective novels. _____ (2) Such as *Burn
Marks* and *Guardian Angel.* _F_ (3) These novels are about V. I. War-
shawski. _____ (4) A private detective. _F_ (5) V. I. lives and works in
Chicago. _____ (6) The Windy City. _F_ (7) Every day as a detective.
_F_ (8) V. I. takes risks. _____ (9) V. I. is tough. _____ (10) She is also a
woman. _____

Rewrite:

Sara Paretsky writes detective novels, such as Burn Marks and Guardian Angel.

These novels are about V. I. Warshawski, a private detective. V. I. lives and works

in Chicago, the Windy City. Every day as a detective, V. I. takes risks. V. I. is

tough. She is also a woman.

■ **WRITING FIRST: Flashback**

Look back at your response to the Writing First exercise on page
339. Do all your sentences seem complete? If you think any are not
complete, copy them here.

Answers will vary.

_____

_____

_____

B Correcting Phrase Fragments

Every sentence must include a subject and a verb. A **phrase** is a group of words that is missing a subject or a verb or both. When you punctuate a phrase as if it is a sentence, you create a fragment.

Two kinds of phrases that are often written as sentence fragments are *appositives* and *prepositional phrases*.

Appositive Fragments

For more on appositives, see 18C. For information on punctuating appositives, see 31C.

An **appositive** is a phrase that identifies, renames, or describes a noun or a pronoun. An appositive cannot stand alone as a sentence. To correct an appositive fragment, add the words needed to make it a complete sentence: the nouns or pronouns that the appositive identifies. (You will usually find these words in an adjacent sentence.)

INCORRECT	He decorated the room in his favorite colors. Brown and black.
CORRECT	He decorated the room in his favorite colors, brown and black.

Sometimes an expression like *such as, for example,* or *for instance* introduces an appositive. Even if an appositive is introduced by one of these expressions, it is still a fragment.

INCORRECT	A balanced diet should include high-fiber foods. Such as leafy vegetables, fruits, beans, and whole-grain bread.
CORRECT	A balanced diet should include high-fiber foods, such as leafy vegetables, fruits, beans, and whole-grain bread.

Prepositional Phrase Fragments

For more on prepositional phrases, see 15B.

A **prepositional phrase** consists of a preposition and its object. A prepositional phrase cannot stand alone as a sentence. To correct a prepositional phrase fragment, add the words needed to make it a complete sentence. (You will usually find these words in an adjacent sentence.)

INCORRECT	She promised to stand by him. In sickness and in health.
CORRECT	She promised to stand by him in sickness and in health.

ON THE WEB
For more practice, visit Exercise Central at <bedfordstmartins.com/ writingfirst>.

◆ PRACTICE 22-3

Each of the following items includes an appositive fragment. In each case, revise to correct the appositive fragment.

Example: The Pledge of Allegiance was written in 1892 by Francis Bellamy. A Baptist minister.

The Pledge of Allegiance was written in 1892 by Francis Bellamy, a Baptist

minister.

1. Most scholars agree that the U.S. flag was designed by Francis Hopkinson. A New Jersey delegate to the Continental Congress.

   Most scholars agree that the U.S. flag was designed by Francis Hopkinson,

   a New Jersey delegate to the Continental Congress.

2. For the new flag, the Continental Congress required certain design features. Such as the original thirteen stars and thirteen stripes.

   For the new flag, the Continental Congress required certain design fea-

   tures, such as the original thirteen stars and thirteen stripes.

3. The first flag may have been sewn by Betsy Ross. A Philadelphia seamstress.

   The first flag may have been sewn by Betsy Ross, a Philadelphia seam-

   stress.

4. The United States has its patriotic rituals. Such as reciting the Pledge of Allegiance and singing "The Star-Spangled Banner."

   The United States has its patriotic rituals, such as reciting the Pledge

   of Allegiance and singing "The Star-Spangled Banner."

5. The Pledge of Allegiance was first recited during a ceremony in 1892. The four-hundredth anniversary of Columbus's arrival in the New World.

   The Pledge of Allegiance was first recited during a ceremony in 1892, the

   four-hundredth anniversary of Columbus's arrival in the New World.

6. Congress officially recognized the Pledge in 1942. The first year the United States participated in World War II.

   Congress officially recognized the Pledge in 1942, the first year the United

   States participated in World War II.

7. In 1814, Francis Scott Key composed "The Star-Spangled Banner" during a fierce naval battle. An attack by a British warship on Fort McHenry in Baltimore's harbor.

   In 1814, Francis Scott Key composed "The Star-Spangled Banner" during

   a fierce naval battle, an attack by a British warship on Fort McHenry in

   Baltimore's harbor.

8. Key's lyrics were later set to the tune of a popular drinking song. "To Anacreon in Heaven."

Key's lyrics were later set to the tune of a popular drinking song, "To

Anacreon in Heaven."

9. Some people wanted a different National Anthem. Such as "America" or "America the Beautiful."

Some people wanted a different National Anthem, such as

"America" or "America the Beautiful."

10. The fact that "The Star-Spangled Banner" is difficult to sing was their main objection. An objection many still have today.

The fact that "The Star-Spangled Banner" is difficult to sing was their

main objection, an objection many still have today.

◆ **PRACTICE 22-4**

Each of the following items includes a prepositional phrase fragment. In each case, revise to correct the prepositional phrase fragment.

Example: A child's birth order has a strong influence. On his or her personality.

A child's birth order has a strong influence on his or her personality.

1. First-born children are reliable, serious, and goal-oriented. In most cases.

First-born children are reliable, serious, and goal-oriented in most cases.

2. First-borns often display distinct leadership qualities. As children and later as adults.

First-borns often display distinct leadership qualities as children and

later as adults.

3. Only children have personality characteristics like those of first-borns. In larger families.

Only children have personality characteristics like those of first-borns in

larger families.

4. In addition to many business leaders. More than half of the U.S. presidents have been first-born or only children.

In addition to many business leaders, more than half of the U.S. presi-

dents have been first-born or only children.

5. Second-born children may compete with their older sibling but more often pursue different interests. In terms of academics and other activities.

Second-born children may compete with their older sibling but more often

pursue different interests in terms of academics and other activities.

6. If the first-born child is a good student, for example, the second-born child might pursue sports or music. As a way to stand out.

If the first-born child is a good student, for example, the second-born

child might pursue sports or music as a way to stand out.

7. In large families, middle-born children often form close personal relationships. Among themselves or with friends outside of the family.

In large families, middle-born children often form close personal relation-

ships among themselves or with friends outside of the family.

8. The youngest child in a family is always seeking ways to get attention. From the older members of the family.

The youngest child in a family is always seeking ways to get attention

from the older members of the family.

9. Youngest children can be charming and funny but sometimes manipulative. In their relationships with other family members.

Youngest children can be charming and funny but sometimes manipula-

tive in their relationships with other family members.

10. As adults, they are likely to be impulsive and to take a while to settle down. Into careers and marriages.

As adults, they are likely to be impulsive and to take a while to settle

down into careers and marriages.

◆ PRACTICE 22-5

Each of the following items is a phrase fragment, not a sentence, because it lacks a subject or a verb or both. Correct each fragment by adding any words needed to turn the fragment into a complete sentence.

Example: During World War I. *A flu epidemic killed millions of people*

during World War I.

Answers will vary.

1. The best player on the Yankees. _____

_____

2. From a developing nation in Africa. _____

_____

Teaching Tip
Remind students that fragments do not usually appear in isolation (as these do). Here, students must *generate* the missing words, not simply find them in an adjacent sentence.

3. Such as tulips or roses. _____

_____

4. Behind door number 3. _____

_____

5. The worst week of my life. _____

_____

6. With a new car in the driveway. _____

_____

7. A very small animal. _____

_____

8. For a long time. _____

_____

9. Turkey, stuffing, potatoes, and cranberry sauce. _____

_____

10. In less than a year. _____

_____

11. A difficult career decision. _____

_____

12. From one end of the neighborhood to the other. _____

_____

13. An amazing money-back guarantee. _____

_____

14. Along the path to the beach. _____

_____

15. King of the beasts. _____

_____

■ **WRITING FIRST: Flashback**

Look back at your response to the Writing First exercise on page 339. Are any phrases incorrectly punctuated as sentences? On the

(continued on the following page)

(continued from the previous page)
lines below, correct each fragment you find by adding any words necessary to create complete sentences. (Hint: You will probably find these words in a sentence that comes right before or right after the fragment.)

Answers will vary.

_____

_____

_____

_____

C   Correcting Incomplete Verbs

Every sentence must include a **complete verb**. Present participles and past participles are not complete verbs. They need **helping verbs** (also known as **auxiliary verbs**) to complete them.

A **present participle**, such as *looking*, is not a complete verb because it cannot stand alone in a sentence without a **helping verb** (*is looking*, *was looking*, *were looking*, and so on). When you use a present participle without a helping verb, you create a fragment.

> FRAGMENT   The twins always looking for trouble.

To correct the fragment, add a helping verb.

> CORRECT   The twins are always looking for trouble.

An irregular **past participle**, such as *hidden*, is not a complete verb because it cannot stand alone in a sentence without a helping verb (*is hidden*, *was hidden*, *has hidden*, and so on). When you use one of these past participles without a helping verb, you create a fragment.

> FRAGMENT   The letter hidden behind the sofa pillow.

To correct the fragment, add a helping verb.

> CORRECT   The letter was hidden behind the sofa pillow.

● **Writing Tip**
Helping verbs include forms of *be, have,* and *do.* (See 15C.)

For a list of irregular past participles, see 27B.

FOCUS   Correcting Participle Fragments

Sometimes you need to add a subject as well as a helping verb to correct a participle fragment. In most cases, you will find the missing subject and verb in an adjacent sentence.

(continued on the following page)

● **Writing Tip**
Be careful not to create dangling modifiers with participles. (See 25C.)

(continued from the previous page)	
INCORRECT	The twins spent most of the day outside. <u>Looking for trouble.</u>
CORRECT	The twins spent most of the day outside, looking for trouble.
INCORRECT	We finally found the letter. <u>Hidden behind the sofa pillow.</u>
CORRECT	We finally found the letter, hidden behind the sofa pillow.

An **infinitive**, which consists of *to* plus the base form of the verb (*to be, to go, to write*), is not a complete verb. An infinitive phrase (*to be free, to go home, to write a novel*) cannot stand alone as a sentence because it does not include a subject or a complete verb.

> INCORRECT   Eric considered dropping out of school. <u>To start his own business.</u>

To correct an infinitive phrase fragment, you can add the words necessary to complete the sentence.

> CORRECT   Eric considered dropping out of school. He thought he might like to start his own business.

Most of the time, however, the easiest way to correct an infinitive phrase fragment is to attach it to an adjacent sentence.

> CORRECT   Eric considered dropping out of school to start his own business.

◆ PRACTICE 22-6

Each of the following items is a fragment because it does not include a complete verb. Correct each fragment by adding a helping verb.

Example: The sun setting behind the clouds. *The sun was setting behind the clouds.*

Answers will vary.

1. The family been worried about money for a long time. _____

2. The Huangs trying to decide where to live. _____

3. Both Luz and Kate chosen to receive a fellowship. _____

4. Janis always complaining about the lab manual. _____

5. Asbestos fallen from the heating ducts. _____

_____

6. Many recent graduates wondering where to find jobs. _____

_____

7. Amanda deciding whether or not to get a new cell phone. _____

_____

8. Romeo and Juliet forbidden to see each other. _____

_____

9. Most people minding their own business. _____

_____

10. Margaret forgotten the name of the reference book she needed. _____

_____

◆ PRACTICE 22-7

Each of the following items is a fragment because it is missing a subject
and does not have a complete verb. Correct each fragment by attaching it
to a new sentence that contains a subject and a complete verb.

Example: Hoping she would be lucky.

Hoping she would be lucky, she bet her last few dollars

on the lottery.

Answers will vary.

1. Confident that he qualified for the job. _____

_____

2. Leaving for an extended trip to Russia. _____

_____

3. Lacking the money to pay his rent. _____

_____

4. To complete the loan application. _____

_____

5. Staying inside during the three-day snowstorm. _____

_____

6. Exhausted from a sleepless night. _____

_____

Teaching Tip
Remind students to be careful not to create dangling
modifiers when they correct
these fragments.

7. Really feeling optimistic about the future. _____
_____

8. Considered very good in math. _____
_____

9. To take the most scenic route through the mountains. _____
_____

10. Ignored by the waiter. _____
_____

11. To help his best friend. _____
_____

12. Reluctantly handing me the car keys. _____
_____

13. Prepared for another rough biology exam. _____
_____

14. Throwing his cards across the table. _____
_____

15. To eat a plate of nachos. _____
_____

Teaching Tip
You may want to refer students to 31D for information on punctuating restrictive and nonrestrictive clauses.

◆ PRACTICE 22-8

Each of the following items includes a participle fragment. In each case, correct the participle fragment by attaching it to the adjacent sentence.

Example: Keeping some buying tips in mind can help grocery shoppers. Saving them a lot of money.

Keeping some buying tips in mind can help grocery shoppers, saving them

a lot of money.

1. Always try to find a store brand. Costs less than the well-known and widely advertised brands.

   Always try to find a store brand that costs less than the well-known and

   widely advertised brands.

2. Look for a product's cost per pound. Comparing it to the cost per pound of similar products.

   Look for a product's cost per pound, comparing it to the cost per pound

   of similar products.

3. Read consumer magazines for their comparisons of products. Tested in their laboratories for quality and value.

Read consumer magazines for their comparisons of products tested in their laboratories for quality and value.

4. Learn which stores are best for different kinds of products. Realizing that some stores are good only for certain items.

Learn which stores are best for different kinds of products, realizing that some stores are good only for certain items.

5. Examine sale-priced fruits and vegetables carefully. Checking for damage or spoilage.

Examine sale-priced fruits and vegetables carefully, checking for damage or spoilage.

6. Check weekly supermarket flyers for sale items. Offered at a special low price for a limited time.

Check weekly supermarket flyers for sale items offered at a special low price for a limited time.

7. Look for stores that sell loose fruits and vegetables. More easily checked for quality than prepackaged produce.

Look for stores that sell loose fruits and vegetables, more easily checked for quality than prepackaged produce.

8. Buy small amounts of different brands of the same product. Trying each one at home to see which brand you like best.

Buy small amounts of different brands of the same product, trying each one at home to see which brand you like best.

9. Make sure you test the different brands fairly. Covering the labels and judging only by taste.

Make sure you test the different brands fairly, covering the labels and judging only by taste.

10. Finally, ask friends and neighbors for shopping suggestions. Based on their own experiences.

Finally, ask friends and neighbors for shopping suggestions based on their own experiences.

◆ PRACTICE 22-9

Each of the following items includes an infinitive phrase fragment. Correct items 1 through 5 by adding the words necessary to make the infinitive fragment a complete sentence.

Example: Most milk we drink today is pasteurized. To destroy disease-causing organisms.

Most milk we drink today is pasteurized. The pasteurization process is

used to destroy disease-causing organisms.

Answers may vary.

1. Emergency medical technicians receive intensive training. To prepare them for saving lives.

   Emergency medical technicians receive intensive training. The training is

   designed to prepare them for saving lives.

2. Many states have adopted standardized testing of students. To rank local school districts.

   Many states have adopted standardized testing of students. They use

   these tests to rank local school districts.

3. Retailers often locate frequently purchased items at the back of their stores. To increase customer traffic.

   Retailers often locate frequently purchased items at the back of their

   stores. They put these items there to increase customer traffic.

4. The handshake originated as an act between suspicious strangers. To show that they were unarmed.

   The handshake originated as an act between suspicious strangers. They

   shook hands to show that they were unarmed.

5. Professional football teams have extra athletes ready to play each position. To substitute for injured players.

   Professional football teams have extra athletes ready to play each

   position. These athletes can substitute for injured players.

Correct items 6 through 10 by attaching the infinitive fragment to the adjacent sentence.

Example: Many wetlands have been destroyed. To create new housing developments.

Many wetlands have been destroyed to create new housing developments.

Answers may vary.

6. Chimpanzees sometimes pick the leaves off twigs. To create a tool for scooping honey.

   Chimpanzees sometimes pick the leaves off twigs to create a tool for

   scooping honey.

7. My father didn't have enough health insurance. To pay for my sister's long hospitalization.

My father didn't have enough health insurance to pay for my sister's long

hospitalization.

8. You need to replace the bottle cap very tightly. To preserve the soda's carbonation.

You need to replace the bottle cap very tightly to preserve the soda's

carbonation.

9. Early telephone users said "Ahoy" instead of "Hello." To greet incoming callers.

Early telephone users said "Ahoy" instead of "Hello" to greet incoming

callers.

10. With patience and skill, some hawks can be trained. To hunt small animals and birds for their human owners.

With patience and skill, some hawks can be trained to hunt small animals

and birds for their human owners.

■ WRITING FIRST: Flashback

Look back at your response to the Writing First exercise on page 339. Underline any present or past participles or infinitives. Are the sentences in which they appear complete? Correct each fragment you find by adding the words necessary to complete it. Write your corrected sentences on the lines below.

_____

_____

_____

_____

D   Correcting Dependent Clause Fragments

Every sentence must express a complete thought. A **dependent clause** is a group of words that includes a subject and a verb but does not express a complete thought. Therefore, it cannot stand alone as a sentence. To correct a dependent clause fragment, you must complete the thought. The following dependent clause is punctuated as if it were a sentence.

FRAGMENT   After Simon won the lottery.

This sentence fragment includes both a subject (*Simon*) and a complete verb (*won*), but it does not express a complete thought. What happened

For more on identifying dependent and independent clauses, see 17A.

after Simon won the lottery? To turn this fragment into a sentence, you need to complete the thought.

SENTENCE After Simon won the lottery, he quit his night job.

Dependent Clauses Introduced by Subordinating Conjunctions

● **Writing Tip**

Subordinating conjunctions include *although, because, even, if,* and *though.* (See 17B.)

Some dependent clauses are introduced by **subordinating conjunctions**.

FRAGMENT Although Marisol had always dreamed of coming to America.

This sentence fragment includes a subject *(Marisol)* and a complete verb *(had dreamed),* but it is not a sentence; it is a dependent clause introduced by the subordinating conjunction *although.*

One way to correct this fragment is to add an **independent clause** (a complete sentence) to complete the idea and finish the sentence.

SENTENCE Although Marisol had always dreamed of coming to America, she did not have enough money for the trip until 1985.

Another way to correct the fragment is to delete the subordinating conjunction *although,* the word that makes the idea incomplete.

SENTENCE Marisol had always dreamed of coming to America.

Dependent Clauses Introduced by Relative Pronouns

For more on relative pronouns, see 17C.

Other dependent clauses are introduced by **relative pronouns** (*who, which, that,* and so on).

FRAGMENT Novelist Richard Wright, who came to Paris in 1947.

FRAGMENT A quinceañera, which celebrates a Latina's fifteenth birthday.

FRAGMENT A key World War II battle that was fought on the Pacific island of Guadalcanal.

Each of the above sentence fragments includes a subject (*Richard Wright, quinceañera, battle*) and a complete verb (*came, celebrates, was fought*). However, they are not sentences because they do not express complete thoughts. In each case, a relative pronoun creates a dependent clause.

One way to correct each fragment is to add the words needed to complete the idea.

SENTENCE Novelist Richard Wright, who came to Paris in 1947, spent the rest of his life there.

SENTENCE A quinceañera, which celebrates a Latina's fifteenth birthday, signifies her entrance into womanhood.

SENTENCE A key World War II battle that was fought on the Pacific island of Guadalcanal took place in 1943.

Another way to correct the fragments is to delete the relative pronouns that make the ideas incomplete.

SENTENCE Novelist Richard Wright came to Paris in 1947.

SENTENCE A quinceañera celebrates a Latina's fifteenth birthday.

SENTENCE   A key World War II battle was fought on the Pacific island
            of Guadalcanal.

◆ PRACTICE 22-10

ON THE WEB

For more practice, visit
Exercise Central *at*
<bedfordstmartins.com/
writingfirst>.

Correct each of these dependent clause fragments in two ways. First, make
the fragment a complete sentence by adding a group of words that completes the idea. Second, delete the subordinating conjunction or relative
pronoun that makes the idea incomplete.

Example: Before it became a state.

            Revised: *Before it became a state, West Virginia was part*
                        of Virginia.

            Revised: *It became a state.*

Teaching Tip
Have students write the sentences in Practice 22-10 on
the board so everyone has a
chance to correct his or her
own sentences and see possible variations.

1. Because many homeless people are mentally ill.

   Revised: *Answers will vary.*

   _____

   Revised: *Many homeless people are mentally ill.*

   _____

2. The film that frightened me.

   Revised: *Answers will vary.*

   _____

   Revised: *The film frightened me.*

   _____

3. Although raccoons can be found living wild in many parts of the United
   States.

   Revised: *Answers will vary.*

   _____

   Revised: *Raccoons can be found living wild in many parts of the United*
   States.

4. People who drink and drive.

   Revised: *Answers will vary.*

   _____

   Revised: *People drink and drive.*

   _____

5. Some parents who are too strict with their children.

Revised: _Answers will vary._

_____

Revised: _Some parents are too strict with their children._

_____

6. Whenever a new semester begins.

Revised: _Answers will vary._

_____

Revised: _A new semester begins._

_____

7. The Vietnam War, which led to widespread protests in the United States.

Revised: _Answers will vary._

_____

Revised: _The Vietnam War led to widespread protests in the United States._

_____

8. Animals that are used in medical research.

Revised: _Answers will vary._

_____

Revised: _Animals are used in medical research._

_____

9. Unless something is likely to change.

Revised: _Answers will vary._

_____

Revised: _Something is likely to change._

_____

10. Although it is a very controversial issue.

Revised: _Answers will vary._

_____

Revised: _It is a very controversial issue._

_____

◆ PRACTICE 22-11

All of the following are fragments. Turn each fragment into a complete sentence, and write the revised sentence on the line below the fragment. Whenever possible, try creating two different revisions.

Example: Waiting in the dugout.

Revised: _Waiting in the dugout, the players chewed tobacco._

Revised: _The players were waiting in the dugout._

Answers will vary.

1. Because three-year-olds are still very attached to their parents.

   Revised: _____

   _____

   Revised: _____

   _____

2. Going around in circles.

   Revised: _____

   _____

   Revised: _____

   _____

3. To win the prize for the most unusual costume.

   Revised: _____

   _____

   Revised: _____

   _____

4. Students who thought they could not afford to go to college.

   Revised: _____

   _____

   Revised: _____

   _____

5. On an important secret mission.

   Revised: _____

   _____

Revised: _____

_____

6. Although many instructors see cheating as a serious problem.

Revised: _____

_____

Revised: _____

_____

7. Hoping to get another helping of chocolate fudge cake.

Revised: _____

_____

Revised: _____

_____

8. The rule that I always felt was the most unfair.

Revised: _____

_____

Revised: _____

_____

9. A really exceptional worker.

Revised: _____

_____

Revised: _____

_____

10. Finished in record time.

Revised: _____

_____

Revised: _____

_____

■ WRITING FIRST: Flashback

Look back at your response to the Writing First exercise on page 339. Underline every subordinating conjunction you find (first, con-

(continued on the following page)

(continued from the previous page)

sult the list on page 261), and underline *which, that,* and *who* wherever you find them. Do any of these words create a dependent clause that is punctuated as if it is a sentence? On the lines below, correct each fragment you find either by crossing out the subordinating conjunction or relative pronoun or by attaching the fragment to another word group to create a complete sentence.

Answers will vary.

_____

_____

_____

_____

_____

■ WRITING FIRST: Revising and Editing

Look back at your response to the Writing First exercise on page 339. Incorporating corrections from all the Flashback exercises in this chapter, revise your work. Then, check one more time to make sure every sentence is complete. If you do not find any fragments, work with a classmate to correct his or her writing, or edit the work you did in response to another assignment.

CHAPTER REVIEW

◆ EDITING PRACTICE: PARAGRAPH

Read the following student paragraph, which includes incomplete sentences. Underline each fragment. Then, correct the fragment by adding the words that complete it or by attaching it to an adjacent sentence that completes the idea. The first fragment has been underlined and corrected for you.

```
                    My First Job

    When I was in high school, I worked as a salesperson,
in
In a retail clothing store. I always seemed to be
            , constantly
running, Constantly straightening the same racks over and

over again. When the store was busy, it was very hectic.

Not all the customers were patient or polite. Some lost
```

their tempers, ~~Because~~ *because* they couldn't find a particular size or color. Then, they took their anger out on me. On slow nights, when the store was almost empty, I was restless and bored. Eventually, I found a more rewarding position, ~~At~~ *at* a preschool for developmentally delayed children.

◆ EDITING PRACTICE: ESSAY

Read the following student essay, into which incomplete sentences have been introduced. Underline each fragment. Then, correct it by adding the words necessary to complete it or by attaching it to an adjacent sentence that completes the idea. The first fragment has been underlined and corrected for you.

A Narrow Escape

It was the summer before my senior year of high school. I thought I was just going to spend a day at the beach, *with* ~~With~~ two of my friends. We live near the beach in Florida, so we decided to drive over to Daytona Beach in the morning, *to* ~~To~~ go swimming. Unfortunately, what happened that day landed me in the hospital.

Sand tiger shark

My friends and I were swimming in about four feet of water, *when* ~~When~~ I felt something grabbing my ankle, *trying* ~~Trying~~ to pull me straight down. I thought I was tangled up in something, *, such* ~~Such~~ as some seaweed. Then one of my friends yelled, "Shark!" I kicked hard, and the shark let go. Although I was able to get out of the water on my own, I had been badly bitten, *on* ~~On~~ the back of my left foot.

My friends took me to Ocean County Hospital, *, where* ~~Where~~ I got eighty-two stitches. The doctors told me that I was lucky, *because* ~~Because~~ my tendons hadn't been cut in two by the bite. I would probably make a full recovery. I never saw the shark, but some people on the beach said that it was about eight feet long. *It looked* ~~Looked~~ like a bull shark. I know that shark

Great white shark

attacks are rare, but I'm still a little scared, To go
                                              ^ to
back in the water.

◆ COLLABORATIVE ACTIVITIES

1. Exchange workbooks with another student, and read each other's responses to the Writing First exercise on page 339. On a separate sheet of paper, list five fragments that describe the product your partner has written about. When your own workbook is returned to you, revise each fragment written by your partner, creating a complete sentence for each one. Finally, add one of these new sentences to your own Writing First exercise.

2. Working in a group of three or four students, add different subordinating conjunctions to sentences *a* through *d* below to create several different fragments. (See 17B for a list of subordinating conjunctions.) Then, turn each of the resulting fragments into a complete sentence by adding a word group that completes the idea.

Example:

SENTENCE	FRAGMENT	NEW SENTENCE
I left the party.	As I left the party	As I left the party, I fell.
	After I left the party	After I left the party, the fun stopped.
	Until I left the party	Until I left the party, I had no idea it was so late.

SENTENCES
a. My mind wanders.
b. She caught the ball.
c. He made a wish.
d. Disaster struck.

3. Working in a group of three or four students, build as many sentences as you can from the fragments listed below, each of which is introduced by a past or present participle. Use your imagination to create as many creative, comical, or even silly sentences as you can.

Example:

FRAGMENT   Known for his incredible memory

SENTENCES   Zack, known for his incredible memory, has somehow managed to forget everything he learned about chemistry.

Known for his incredible memory, Monty the Magnificent mesmerized audiences.

FRAGMENTS
a. wandering in the desert
b. stranded in the jungle
c. looking for his ideal mate
d. always using as much ketchup as possible
e. folded, stapled, and mutilated

☑ REVIEW CHECKLIST:

Sentence Fragments

☐ A sentence fragment is an incomplete sentence. Every sentence must include a subject and a verb and express a complete thought. (See 22A.)

☐ Phrases cannot stand alone as sentences. (See 22B.)

☐ Every sentence must include a complete verb. (See 22C.)

☐ Dependent clauses cannot stand alone as sentences. (See 22D.)

Subject-Verb Agreement

PREVIEW

In this chapter, you will learn

■ to understand subject-verb agreement (23A)

■ to avoid agreement problems with *be, have,* and *do* (23B)

■ to avoid agreement problems when a prepositional phrase comes between the subject and the verb (23C)

■ to avoid agreement problems with indefinite pronouns as subjects (23D)

■ to avoid agreement problems when the verb comes before the subject (23E)

■ to avoid agreement problems with the relative pronouns *who, which,* and *that* (23F)

■ WRITING FIRST

On October 25, 1990, after the *New York Daily News* demanded millions of dollars in concessions from its workers, the newspaper locked them out. Employees picketed for one hundred forty-eight days before returning to work after the unions agreed to salary reductions and major job cuts. The picture above, by the artist Ralph Fasanella, depicts the *Daily News* strike. Look at the picture, and then describe what you think the artist is trying to convey. For example, do you think his sympathy is with the workers or with the *Daily News*? How do you know? Use the **present tense** in your response.

Word Power

compromise a settlement in which the sides agree to accept less than they originally wanted

confront to challenge, usually with hostility, criticism, or defiance

realistic objects presented as they really are

363

A Understanding Subject-Verb Agreement

A sentence's subject (a noun or pronoun) and its verb must **agree**: singular subjects must have singular verbs, and plural subjects must have plural verbs.

     s v
The <u>museum</u> <u>opens</u> at ten o'clock. (singular noun subject *museum* takes singular verb *opens*)

     s v
The <u>museums</u> <u>open</u> at ten o'clock. (plural noun subject *museums* takes plural verb *open*)

 s   v
<u>She</u> always <u>watches</u> the eleven o'clock news. (singular pronoun subject *she* takes singular verb *watches*)

 s   v
<u>They</u> always <u>watch</u> the eleven o'clock news. (plural pronoun subject *they* takes plural verb *watch*)

Most subject-verb agreement problems occur in the present tense, where third-person singular subjects require special verb forms: regular verbs form the third-person singular by adding *-s* or *-es* to the **base form** (the form of the verb used with *I*).

For more on identifying plural noun and pronoun subjects, see 28B and 28C.

> ● **Writing Tip**
> Subject-verb agreement presents special problems with the irregular verb *be*. (See 23B.)

Teaching Tip
On the board, write a sentence with a subject-verb agreement error—for example, *The boss want to hear from you.* Point out that usually an *-s* follows either the subject or the verb but not both. (Consider giving an example of an exception to this rule—for example, *Gladys wants to hear from you.*)

Subject-Verb Agreement with Regular Verbs

	Singular	**Plural**
First person	I play	Molly and I/we play
Second person	you play	you play
Third person	he/she/it plays	they play
	the man plays	the men play
	Molly plays	Molly and Sam play

In verb tenses other than the present, the same form of the regular verb is used with every subject: *I played, he played, they played; I will play, she will play, they will play.*

Teaching Tip
Tell students that the rules that govern compound subjects and *or* also govern compound subjects and *neither . . . nor.*

FOCUS   **Subject-Verb Agreement with Compound Subjects**

The subject of a sentence is not always a single word. It can also be a **compound subject**, consisting of two or more words. Special rules govern subject-verb agreement with compound subjects.

(continued on the following page)

(continued from the previous page)

■ When the parts of a compound subject are connected by *and*, the compound subject takes a plural verb.

s   v

John and Marsha share an office.

■ If both parts of a compound subject connected by *or* are singular, the compound subject takes a singular verb.

s   v

John or Marsha locks up at the end of the day.

■ If both parts of a compound subject connected by *or* are plural, the compound subject takes a plural verb.

s   v

Buses or trains take you to the center of the city.

■ If one part of a compound subject connected by *or* is singular and the other part is plural, the verb agrees with the word that is closer to it.

s   v

The mayor or the council members meet with community groups.

s   v

The council members or the mayor meets with community groups.

> **Teaching Tip**
> Tell students that an *s* following a verb usually means the verb is singular. For example, in the sentence *He plays golf*, because *he* refers to just one person, the verb needs an *s*. (Point out the exception that occurs with *I* and *you*.)

◆ PRACTICE 23-1

Underline the correct form of the verb in each of the following sentences. Make sure the verb agrees with its subject.

Example: Radio stations (broadcast/broadcasts) many kinds of music.

(1) Most music fans (know/knows) about salsa, a popular style of Latin music. (2) However, they (need/needs) a little education when it comes to ranchera, a blend of traditional forms of regional Mexican music. (3) These forms (include/includes) mariachi music as well as rural-influenced ballads and waltz-like tunes. (4) The ranchera style (appeal/appeals) particularly to a wide audience of Americans of Mexican

ON THE WEB
For more practice, visit **Exercise Central** *at* <bedfordstmartins.com/ writingfirst>.

descent. (5) Its performers (sell/<u>sells</u>) millions of records a year, and often they (<u>top</u>/tops) *Billboard*'s Latin charts. (6) In fact, regional Mexican recordings (outsell/<u>outsells</u>) any other form of Latin music in the United States. (7) This popularity (surprise/<u>surprises</u>) many people because the mainstream music industry (give/<u>gives</u>) most of its attention to Latin pop stars who sing in English. (8) Older ranchera lovers (<u>tend</u>/tends) to be first-generation, working-class immigrants, but more and more young listeners (<u>seem</u>/seems) drawn to ranchera because of their pride in their Mexican heritage. (9) When one Los Angeles nightclub (host/<u>hosts</u>) a ranchera night, it (draw/<u>draws</u>) a large number of English-speaking fans in their twenties. (10) Clearly, ranchera stars (<u>deserve</u>/deserves) more attention from the music industry.

◆ PRACTICE 23-2

Fill in the blank with the correct present tense form of the verb.

> **Example:** At some point, most children ___*get*___ chewing gum in their hair. (get)

(1) To get the gum out, parents ___*can*___ cut off some of their children's hair, but they would rather not do that if they can find another method. (can) (2) A less drastic solution ___*involves*___ ice cubes and a plastic bag. (involve) (3) First, the parent ___*puts*___ some ice cubes in a plastic bag and uses a twist tie to close it. (put) (4) Next, the plastic bag is applied to the hair until pieces of gum ___*freeze*___. (freeze) (5) If the ice cubes ___*grow*___ too cold to be held comfortably, the plastic bag can be wrapped in a washcloth. (grow) (6) When the gum is frozen, it ___*becomes*___ hard. (become) (7) Once the chunks of gum ___*harden*___, they can be gently broken away from the hair. (harden) (8) If the ice cube strategy ___*fails*___, another method is to apply a small amount of nontoxic oil, such as olive oil, to the gum and to the hair around it. (fail) (9) After massaging the oil into the hair and gum, the parent ___*leaves*___ it for twenty minutes. (leave) (10) Often, the gum ___*slides*___ out easily when it is gently combed out. (slide)

◆ **PRACTICE 23-3**

Underline the correct form of the verb in each of the following sentences. Make sure that the verb agrees with its compound subject.

Example: Gloves or a scarf (make/<u>makes</u>) a good wintertime gift.

1. Cars and trucks (<u>fill</u>/fills) the municipal parking lot each day.

2. Grapes or an apple (provide/<u>provides</u>) a nutritious addition to a lunch box.

3. A security officer and a video monitoring system (<u>survey</u>/surveys) the bank's lobby during business hours.

4. A vegetable dish or french fries (<u>come</u>/comes) with the entrée.

5. A pianist or a guitarist (play/<u>plays</u>) at the club every weekend.

6. Nurses or nurse practitioners (<u>offer</u>/offers) round-the-clock patient care.

7. According to the old saying, fish and houseguests (<u>smell</u>/smells) after three days.

8. Flowers or a get-well balloon (cheer/<u>cheers</u>) people up when they are ill.

9. The restaurant owner or her daughter always (greet/<u>greets</u>) customers at the door.

10. A sliding glass door or French windows (<u>allow</u>/allows) the greatest amount of light into a room.

■ WRITING FIRST: Flashback

Look back at your response to the Writing First exercise on page 363. Choose two sentences that contain present tense verbs, and rewrite them on the lines below. Underline the subject of each sentence once and the verb twice. If the subject and verb of each sentence do not agree, correct them here.

_____

_____

_____

_____

_____

Teaching Tip
Before students do this Flashback exercise, review the difference between simple and complete subjects. Tell students that in this Flashback, they are being asked to underline the *simple* subject of each of the two sentences.

Teaching Tip
You may need to remind students that standard written
English does not use *be* as a
helping verb. For example,
*He be trying to get my atten-
tion* is incorrect.

*For more on regular and irreg-
ular verbs, see 26A and 26B.*

Teaching Tip
The dialect-related use of *be*
and *have* may be a sensitive
issue for some students. You
may want to address it in individual conferences outside
of class.

B **Avoiding Agreement Problems with *Be, Have,* and *Do***

The verbs *be, have,* and *do* are irregular in the present tense. For this reason, they can present problems with subject-verb agreement. Memorizing
their forms is the only sure way to avoid such problems.

Subject-Verb Agreement with Be

	Singular	Plural
First person	I am	we are
Second person	you are	you are
Third person	he/she/it is	they are
	Tran is	Tran and Ryan are
	the boy is	the boys are

Subject-Verb Agreement with Have

	Singular	Plural
First person	I have	we have
Second person	you have	you have
Third person	he/she/it has	they have
	Shana has	Shana and Robert have
	the student has	the students have

Subject-Verb Agreement with Do

	Singular	Plural
First person	I do	we do
Second person	you do	you do
Third person	he/she/it does	they do
	Ken does	Ken and Mia do
	the book does	the books do

◆ PRACTICE 23-4

ON THE WEB
For more practice, visit
Exercise Central *at*
*<bedfordstmartins.com/
writingfirst>.*

Fill in the blank with the correct present tense form of the verb *be, have,*
or *do.*

Example: Sometimes, people __*do*__ damage without really meaning
to. (do)

(1) Biologists __*have*__ serious worries about the damage that exotic ani-

mals can cause when they move into places where native species have

developed few defenses against them. (have) (2) The English sparrow _is_ one example. (be) (3) It _has_ a role in the decline in the number

of bluebirds. (have) (4) On the Galapagos Islands, cats _are_ another ex-

ample. (be) (5) Introduced by early explorers, they currently _do_ much

damage to the eggs of the giant tortoises that live on the islands. (do)

(6) Scientists today _are_ worried about a new problem. (be) (7) This

_is_ a situation caused by fish and wildlife agencies that deliberately in-

troduce exotic fish into lakes and streams. (be) (8) They _do_ this to

please those who enjoy fishing. (do) (9) Although popular with people

who fish, this policy _has_ major drawbacks. (have) (10) It _has_ one

drawback in particular: many species of fish have been pushed close to

extinction. (have)

■ WRITING FIRST: Flashback

Look back at your response to the Writing First exercise on page
363. Have you used a form of _be, have,_ or _do_ in any of your sentences? If so, write these sentences on the lines that follow. Have
you used the correct forms of _be, have,_ and _do?_ Correct any agreement errors here.

Answers will vary.

_____

_____

_____

_____

C   Avoiding Agreement Problems When a Prepositional Phrase Comes between the Subject and the Verb

A prepositional phrase cannot contain the subject of a sentence. Do not be
confused when a prepositional phrase (a phrase that begins with _of, in, between,_ and so on) comes between the subject and the verb. In such cases,
the object of the preposition appears to be the subject of the sentence
when really it is not. This error can lead to an incorrect verb choice, as in
the three incorrect sentences below.

*For more on prepositional
phrases, see 15B. For a list of
prepositions, see 30N.*

   INCORRECT   High levels of mercury occurs in some fish.

                 s   v
   CORRECT   High <u>levels</u> of mercury <u>occur</u> in some fish.

INCORRECT Water in the fuel lines cause an engine to stall.

CORRECT Water in the fuel lines <u>causes</u> an engine to stall.
                   <u>Water</u> ⁱ   ᵛ

INCORRECT Food between the teeth result in decay.

CORRECT <u>Food</u> between the teeth <u>results</u> in decay.

You can identify the subject by crossing out the prepositional phrase. By doing this, you can easily see if there are any agreement errors.

High levels ~~of mercury~~ occur in some fish.

Water ~~in the fuel lines~~ causes an engine to stall.

Food ~~between the teeth~~ results in decay.

FOCUS **Words That Come between Subject and Verb**

Look out for prepositional phrases introduced by words such as *in addition to, along with, together with, as well as, except,* and *including.* A noun or pronoun that follows such a phrase is an object of the preposition and cannot be the subject of the sentence.

               ˢ   ᵛ
<u>St. Thomas</u>, ~~along with St. Croix and St. John~~, <u>is</u> part of the United States Virgin Islands.

ON THE WEB
For more practice, visit
Exercise Central *at*
*<bedfordstmartins.com/
writingfirst>.*

Writing Tip

An agreement error can also occur when any long group of words comes between the subject and the verb. To check for agreement, find the subject and the verb, and then cross out the words between them.

◆ **PRACTICE 23-5**

In each of the following sentences, cross out the prepositional phrase that separates the subject and the verb. Then, underline the subject of the sentence once and the verb that agrees with the subject twice.

Example: The <u>food</u> ~~on the carpet~~ (suggest/<u>suggests</u>) that Hiro and Mika had a party.

1. The <u>cupids</u> ~~in the painting~~ (<u>symbolize</u>/symbolizes) lost innocence.

2. <u>Fans</u> ~~at a concert~~ (<u>get</u>/gets) angry if the band is late.

3. The <u>appliances</u> ~~in the kitchen~~ (<u>make</u>/makes) strange noises.

4. The <u>United States</u>, ~~along with Germany and Japan,~~ (produce/<u>produces</u>) most of the world's cars.

5. A good <u>set</u> ~~of skis and poles~~ (cost/<u>costs</u>) a lot.

6. Unfortunately, <u>one</u> ~~out of ten men~~ eventually (<u>gets</u>/get) prostate cancer.

7. Workers ~~in the city~~ (pays/<u>pay</u>) a high wage tax.

8. Each summer, <u>fires</u> ~~from lightning~~ (cause/<u>causes</u>) hundreds of millions of dollars in property damage.

9. <u>Volunteers</u>, ~~including people like my father,~~ (<u>help</u>/helps) paramedics in my community.

10. A <u>doctor</u>, ~~together with two nurses,~~ (<u>staff</u>/staffs) the clinic at the health center.

■ WRITING FIRST: Flashback

Look back at your response to the Writing First exercise on page 363. Can you find any sentences in which a prepositional phrase comes between the subject and the verb? Write each subject and verb on the lines below.

Subject   *Verb*

Answers will vary.

_____   _____

_____   _____

_____   _____

Now, correct any errors in subject-verb agreement.

D   Avoiding Agreement Problems with Indefinite Pronouns as Subjects

An **indefinite pronoun**—*anybody, everyone,* and so on—is a pronoun that does not refer to a particular person, place, or idea. When an indefinite pronoun is the subject of a sentence, the verb must agree with it.

Most indefinite pronouns are singular and take singular verbs.

       S   V
<u>No one</u> <u>likes</u> getting up early.

     S   V
<u>Everyone</u> <u>likes</u> to sleep late.

     S   V
<u>Somebody</u> <u>likes</u> beets.

● **Writing Tip**

Many indefinite pronouns end in *-one, -body,* or *-thing.* These words are almost always singular.

For information on pronoun-antecedent agreement with indefinite pronouns, see 28E.

Singular Indefinite Pronouns

another	either	neither	one
anybody	everybody	nobody	somebody
anyone	everyone	no one	someone
anything	everything	nothing	something
each	much		

A few indefinite pronouns (*both, many, several, few, others*) are plural and take plural verbs.

$$\text{s} \qquad \text{v}$$
<u>Many</u> <u>were</u> left homeless by the storm.

FOCUS **Indefinite Pronouns as Subjects**

If a prepositional phrase comes between the indefinite pronoun and the verb, cross out the prepositional phrase to help you identify the sentence's subject.

$$\text{s} \qquad\qquad \text{v}$$
<u>Each</u> ~~of the boys~~ <u><u>has</u></u> a bike.

$$\text{s} \qquad\qquad \text{v}$$
<u>Many</u> ~~of the boys~~ <u>have</u> bikes.

ON THE WEB
For more practice, visit
Exercise Central *at*
*<bedfordstmartins.com/
writingfirst>.*

◆ **PRACTICE 23-6**

Circle the correct verb in each sentence.

Example: Each of the three streams in our area (is/are) polluted.

1. One of the streams no longer (have/has) any fish.

2. Another (contain/contains) a lot of algae.

3. Everybody (want/wants) to improve the situation.

4. No one (are/is) willing to do anything.

5. Somebody always (take/takes) the lead.

6. Everyone (know/knows) that pollution is difficult to control.

7. Neither of the candidates (seem/seems) willing to act.

8. Whenever anyone (ask/asks) them for suggestions, neither (have, has) any.

9. According to the candidates, everything (is/are) being done that can be done.

10. One of my friends (say/says) that she will not vote for either candidate.

■ WRITING FIRST: Flashback

Look back at your response to the Writing First exercise on page 363. Do any of the sentences contain indefinite pronouns that act as subjects? Do the verbs in these sentences agree with the indefinite pronoun subjects? If you find any that do not, rewrite the correct form of the verb below.

Indefinite Pronoun Subject   *Verb*

Answers will vary.
_____   _____

_____   _____

_____   _____

_____   _____

**E   Avoiding Agreement Problems
When the Verb Comes before the Subject**

A verb always agrees with its subject—even if the verb comes *before* the subject. In questions, for example, word order is reversed, with the verb coming before the subject or with the subject coming between two parts of the verb.

         V   S
Where <u>is</u> the <u>bank</u>?

   V   S   V
<u>Are</u> <u>you</u> <u>going</u> to the party?

If you have trouble identifying the subject of a question, answer the question with a statement.

         V   S
Where <u>is</u> the <u>bank</u>?

    S   V
The <u>bank</u> <u>is</u> on Walnut Street.

> **ESL Tip**
> Point out that questions depart from conventional English word order. Write a series of statements on the board, and have students change them into questions.

┌───┐
│ **FOCUS** *There Is and There Are*   │
│   │
│ In a sentence that begins with *there is* or *there │
│ are,* the word *there* can never be the subject of   │
│ the sentence. The subject comes after the form of   │
│ the verb *be.*   │
│   │
│   V   S   │
│   There are nine justices on the Supreme Court. │
│   │
│   V   S   │
│   There is one chief justice on the Court.   │
└───┘

◆ PRACTICE 23-7

Underline the subject of each sentence, and circle the correct form of the verb.

Example: Who (is/are) the writer who won the 1992 Nobel Prize in literature?

1. Where (is/are) the Bering Straits?

2. Why (do/does) the compound change color after being exposed to light?

3. (Is/Are) the twins identical or fraternal?

4. How (do/does) Congress override a presidential veto?

5. What (have/has) this got to do with me?

6. There (is/are) ten computers in the writing center.

7. There (is/are) more than nine million people living in Mexico City.

8. There (is/are) several reference books in this library that can help you with your research.

9. There (is/are) four reasons why we should save the spotted owl from extinction.

10. There (is/are) more than one way to answer the question.

■ WRITING FIRST: Flashback

Look back at your response to the Writing First exercise on page 363. Do you have any sentences in which the verb comes before the

(continued on the following page)

(continued from the previous page)

subject? If so, write those sentences on the lines below. If the subject and verb of any sentence do not agree, correct the sentence here.

_____

_____

_____

_____

F Avoiding Agreement Problems with the Relative Pronouns *Who, Which,* and *That*

The relative pronouns *who, which,* and *that* are singular when they refer to a singular word and plural when they refer to a plural word. The verb in a dependent clause introduced by the relative pronoun must agree with the word to which the relative pronoun refers.

> The author, who writes about Chinese immigrants, spoke at our college. (The verb *writes* is singular because the relative pronoun *who* refers to *author.*)

> This course, which has a waiting list, is open only to juniors and seniors. (The verb *has* is singular because the relative pronoun *which* refers to *course,* which is singular.)

> Computers that have flat-screen monitors are expensive. (The verb *have* is plural because the relative pronoun *that* refers to *computers,* which is plural.)

For more on who, which, that, and other relative pronouns, see 17C.

> **Writing Tip**
> The verb in the relative clause (introduced by the relative pronoun) must agree with the word to which the relative pronoun refers.

◆ PRACTICE 23-8

Draw an arrow from *who, which,* or *that* to the word to which it refers. Then, circle the correct form of the verb.

Example: Edgar Allan Poe, who (tell/tells) tales of horror, was born in 1809.

(1) Poe's "The Fall of the House of Usher" is a story that (have/has) entertained many readers. (2) The story, which (contain/contains) the poem "The Haunted Palace," was published in 1839. (3) The narrator, who (have/has) not seen Roderick Usher for many years, is summoned to the House of Usher. (4) The decaying mansion, which (is/are) dark and dreary, stands at the edge of a swamp. (5) Roderick's twin sister,

ON THE WEB
For more practice, visit Exercise Central at <bedfordstmartins.com/writingfirst>.

Madeline, who (live/lives) in the house, is very ill. (6) At one point in the story, Roderick's sister, who (is/are) in a trance, is thought to be dead. (7) Roderick buries her in the family vault that (is/are) under the house. (8) Later, Madeline, who (is/are) dressed in her shroud, walks into the room. (9) Roderick, who (is/are) terrified, falls down dead. (10) Running outside, the narrator sees the house, which (have/has) split apart, sink into the swamp.

■ WRITING FIRST: Flashback

Look back at your response to the Writing First exercise on page 363. Can you find any sentences that include a relative pronoun (*who, which,* or *that*)? Write any such sentences on the lines below. Check to make sure you have used a singular verb when *who, which,* or *that* refers to a singular word, and a plural verb when the reference is to a plural word. Make any corrections here.

_____

_____

_____

_____

_____

■ WRITING FIRST: Revising and Editing

Look back at your response to the Writing First exercise on page 363. Incorporating changes and corrections from this chapter's Flashback exercises, revise your work, making sure all your verbs agree with their subjects. When you have finished, rewrite the entire paragraph on a separate sheet of paper, changing all the singular subjects to plural subjects and the plural subjects to singular ones. (For example, *picture* would become *pictures,* and *he* or *she* would become *they.*) Then, change the verbs so they agree with their new subjects.

CHAPTER REVIEW

◆ EDITING PRACTICE: PARAGRAPH

Read the following student paragraph, which includes errors in subject-verb agreement. Decide whether each of the underlined verbs agrees with its subject. If it does not, cross out the verb, and write in the correct form. If it does, write **C** above the verb. The first sentence has been done for you.

Watching Movies

          C
I <u>believe</u> that to be appreciated fully, movies <u>~~has~~</u> *have*
                           are
to be seen in a theater on a big screen. There <u>~~is~~</u> many
                       feel
reasons why I and other movie-goers <u>~~feels~~</u> this way. In
many cases, a blockbuster movie's sound or its other
                require
special effects <u>~~requires~~</u> a theater screening if the movie
C
is to have its full impact on viewers. Even movies that
have   *benefit*
<u>~~has~~</u> no special effects <u>~~benefits~~</u> from being seen on a large
                  C
screen. There <u>is</u> something about sitting with other people
                        respond
in a darkened theater that audiences <u>~~responds~~</u> to in a
                                C
special way. Although it is true that members of a theater
      do
audience <u>~~does~~</u> sometimes cause disruptions, I <u>see</u> these as
                have
minor disturbances that <u>~~has~~</u> little effect on my enjoyment.

◆ EDITING PRACTICE: ESSAY

Read the following student essay, which includes errors of subject-verb agreement. Decide whether each of the underlined verbs agrees with its subject. If it does not, cross out the verb, and write in the correct form. If it does, write **C** above the verb. The first sentence has been done for you.

Party in the Parking Lot

                    is
    Fun at football games <u>~~are~~</u> not limited to cheering for
                            arrive
the home team. Nowadays, many people <u>~~arrives~~</u> four or five
     set   *C*
hours early, <u>~~sets~~</u> up a grill in the parking lot, and <u>start</u>
cooking. Typically, fans, together with their friends and
      drive
families, <u>~~drives~~</u> to the stadium in a pickup truck, a
                       C   *lay*
station wagon, or an SUV. They <u>open</u> up the tailgate, <u>~~lays~~</u>

out the food, and ~~enjoys~~ *enjoy* the atmosphere. Everyone who
tailgates ~~participate~~ *participates* in an American tradition. In fact,
tailgating is so popular that, for some fans, it ~~rival~~ *rivals* the
game itself.

What ~~do~~ *does* it take to tailgate? First, most tailgaters
plan their menus in advance, choosing simple recipes. To
avoid forgetting anything, they ~~makes~~ *make* lists of what to
bring. Disposable paper plates, along with a set of
plastic glasses and cutlery, make it unnecessary to bring
home lots of dirty dishes. Jugs of water ~~is~~ *are* essential, and
damp towels ~~helps~~ *help* clean up hands and faces. Also,
lightweight chairs or another type of seating is important.
At the game, parking near a grassy area or at the end of a
parking row ~~are~~ *is* best. This strategy ~~give~~ *gives* tailgaters more
space to cook and eat. If the food ~~are~~ *is* ready to eat by two
hours before the game ~~start~~ *starts*, there is plenty of time to
put out the fire in the grill and clean up.

Some tailgaters ~~wants~~ *want* more and more impressive
equipment. The simple charcoal grill ~~have~~ *has* turned into a
combination grill, cooler, and fold-out table, with a
portable awning and a pull-out flagpole for the team's
colors. There ~~is~~ *are* grills that ~~has~~ *have* their own storage space,
and others that ~~swings~~ *swing* out from the tailgate to provide
access to the vehicle's storage area. Some deluxe grills
even ~~carries~~ *carry* their own beer tap, stereo system, and sink,
as well as a 12-volt plug for a TV or blender.

Whatever equipment tailgaters ~~brings~~ *bring* to the game, the
most important factors ~~is~~ *are* food and companionship. There is
a tradition of sharing food and swapping recipes with other
tailgaters. In fact, the friendly relations and positive
atmosphere among tailgaters are often the best part of the

Tailgaters deep-frying a turkey

*Tailgating in stadium
parking lot*

love
experience. Most tailgaters ~~loves~~ to meet one another and
compare
~~compares~~ notes on recipes. For many, the tailgating
^   C
experience <u>is</u> as important as the game itself.

◆ COLLABORATIVE ACTIVITIES

1. Working in a group of four students, list ten nouns (five singular and five plural)—people, places, or things—on the left-hand side of a sheet of paper. Beside each noun, write the present tense form of a verb that could logically be used with the noun. Exchange papers with another group, and check to see that singular nouns have singular verbs and plural nouns have plural verbs.

2. Working with your group, expand each noun-and-verb combination you listed in Collaborative Activity 1 into a complete sentence. Next, write a sentence that could logically follow each of these sentences, using a pronoun as the subject of the new sentence. Make sure the pronoun you choose refers to the noun in the previous sentence, as in this example: *Alan watches three movies a week. <u>He</u> is addicted to films.* Check to be certain the subjects in your sentences agree with the verbs.

3. Exchange the final version of your edited Writing First exercise with another student in your group. Answer the following questions about each sentence in your partner's exercise.

   ■ Does the sentence contain a prepositional phrase that comes between the subject and the verb?
   ■ Does the sentence contain an indefinite pronoun used as a subject?
   ■ Does the sentence contain a verb that comes before the subject?
   ■ Does the sentence include a dependent clause introduced by a relative pronoun (*who, which,* or *that*)?

   As you answer these questions, check to make sure all the verbs agree with their subjects. When your own exercise is returned to you, make any necessary corrections.

☑ REVIEW CHECKLIST:
Subject-Verb Agreement

   Singular subjects (nouns and pronouns) take singular verbs, and plural subjects take plural verbs. Special rules govern subject-verb agreement with compound subjects. (See 23A.)

   The irregular verbs *be, have,* and *do* often present problems with subject-verb agreement in the present tense. (See 23B.)

   Prepositional phrases that come between the subject and the verb do not affect subject-verb agreement. (See 23C.)

(continued on the following page)

(continued from the previous page)

- Most indefinite pronouns, such as *no one* and *everyone,* are singular and take a singular verb when they serve as the subject of a sentence. A few are plural and take plural verbs. (See 23D.)

- A sentence's subject and verb must always agree, even if the verb comes before the subject. (See 23E.)

- The relative pronouns *who, which,* and *that* are singular when they refer to a singular word and plural when they refer to a plural word. The verb in a dependent clause introduced by a relative pronoun must agree with the word to which the relative pronoun refers. (See 23F.)

Illogical Shifts

PREVIEW

In this chapter, you will learn

- to avoid illogical shifts in tense (24A)

- to avoid illogical shifts in person (24B)

- to avoid illogical shifts in number (24C)

- to avoid illogical shifts in voice (24D)

■ WRITING FIRST

The picture above shows a mother and daughter in an office on Take Your Daughter to Work Day. Look at the picture, and then write about what parents can do to help their children succeed in life. How can parents motivate their children to set appropriate goals and work to achieve them?

Word Power

aspire to strive toward an end

encourage to inspire with hope or confidence

nurture to nourish; to bring up

A **shift** occurs whenever a writer changes *tense, person, number,* or *voice.* As you write and revise, be sure that any shifts you make are logical. An **illogical shift** occurs when a writer changes tense, person, number, or voice for no apparent reason.

A   Avoiding Illogical Shifts in Tense

An **illogical shift in tense** occurs when a writer shifts from one tense to another for no apparent reason.

381

For more on tense, see Chapters 26 and 27.

ILLOGICAL SHIFT IN TENSE	The dog <u>walked</u> to the fireplace. Then, he <u>circles</u> twice and <u>lies</u> down in front of the fire. (past to present)
REVISED	The dog <u>walked</u> to the fireplace. Then, he <u>circled</u> twice and <u>lay</u> down in front of the fire. (consistent past)
REVISED	The dog <u>walks</u> to the fireplace. Then, he <u>circles</u> twice and <u>lies</u> down in front of the fire. (consistent present)

Of course, some tense shifts (even within a single sentence) are necessary—to indicate a change from past time to present time, for example. In the following sentence, notice how the writer needs to shift from the past tense to the present tense to make a point.

| LOGICAL SHIFT | When they first came out, cell phones <u>were</u> large and bulky, but now they <u>are</u> small and compact. |

◆ **PRACTICE 24-1**

Edit the following sentences for illogical shifts in tense. If a sentence is correct, write **C** in the blank.

Examples:

During World War II, the 100th Battalion of the 442nd Combat Infantry Regiment was made up of young Japanese Americans who <s>are</s> *were* eager to serve in the U.S. Army. _____ (illogical shift)

The 100th Battalion of the 442nd Infantry is the only remaining United States Army Reserve ground combat unit that fought in World War II. __*C*__ (logical shift)

(1) At the start of World War II, 120,000 Japanese Americans <s>are</s> *were* sent to relocation camps because the government feared that they might be disloyal to the United States. _____ (2) However, in 1943, the United States needed more soldiers, so it <s>sends</s> *sent* recruiters to the camps to ask for volunteers. _____ (3) The Japanese-American soldiers <s>are</s> *were* organized into the 442nd Combat Infantry Regiment, which took as its motto "Go for Broke," a Hawaiian slang expression meaning "risk everything you have." _____ (4) The soldiers of the 442nd Infantry fought in some of the bloodiest battles of the war, including the invasion of Italy at Anzio and the battle at the town of Bruyeres in France, where, in bitter house-

moted. (5) A young designer may receive a big raise if *he or she is* ~~you are~~ very tal-

ented, but this is unusual. (6) New employees have to pay their dues, and

they ~~you~~ soon realize that most of *their* ~~your~~ duties are tedious. (7) Employees may be

excited to land a job as an assistant designer but then find that *they color* ~~you color~~

in designs that have already been drawn. (8) Other beginners in fashion

houses discover that *they* ~~you~~ spend most of *their* ~~your~~ time sewing or typing up

orders. (9) If a person is serious about working in the fashion industry, ~~you~~

he or she has ~~have~~ to be realistic. (10) For most newcomers to the industry, the ability

to do what *they* ~~you~~ are told to do is more important than *their* ~~your~~ artistic talent

or fashion sense.

■ WRITING FIRST: Flashback

Look back at your response to the Writing First exercise on page 381. Check each sentence to make sure it includes no illogical shifts in person. If you find an incorrect sentence, rewrite it on the lines below, correcting any illogical shifts in person.

Answers will vary.

_____

_____

_____

C Avoiding Illogical Shifts in Number

Number is the form a noun, pronoun, or verb takes to indicate whether it is singular (one) or plural (more than one).

Number	
Singular	**Plural**
I	we
he, she	they
Fred	Fred and Ethel
man	men
an encyclopedia	encyclopedias
his, her	their
am, is, was	are, were

● **Writing Tip**

A pronoun must agree in
number with the word it
refers to (its antecedent).
(See 28D.) A verb must
agree in number with its
subject. (See 23A.)

ON THE WEB

For more practice, visit
Exercise Central *at*
<bedfordstmartins.com/
writingfirst>.

An **illogical shift in number** occurs when a writer shifts from singular to plural (or the other way around) for no apparent reason.

ILLOGICAL SHIFT IN NUMBER — Each <u>visitor</u> to the museum must check <u>their</u> cameras at the entrance. (singular to plural)

REVISED — Each <u>visitor</u> to the museum must check <u>his or her</u> camera at the entrance. (consistent singular)

REVISED — <u>Visitors</u> to the museum must check <u>their</u> cameras at the entrance. (consistent plural)

◆ **PRACTICE 24-3**

Edit the following sentences for illogical shifts between singular and plural. You can either change the singular element to the plural or change the plural element to the singular. Be sure to change the verb so it agrees with the new subject. If the sentence is correct, write **C** in the blank.

Examples:

his or her
Each attorney first makes ~~their~~ opening speech. _____

Good jurors
~~A good juror~~ takes their time when making a decision. _____

Answers may vary.
(1) According to recent studies, a juror may have ~~their~~ *his or her* mind made up before the trial even begins. _____ (2) As attorneys offer their opening arguments, a juror may immediately decide whether ~~they think~~ *he or she thinks* the defendant is innocent or guilty. _____ (3) This conclusion often depends on which attorney makes ~~their~~ *his or her* initial description of the case the most dramatic. _____ (4) During the trial, this juror will pay attention only to evidence that supports the decision ~~they have~~ *he or she has* already made. _____ (5) Jurors like these are also not likely to listen to challenges to ~~his~~ *their* opinions when the full jury comes together to deliberate. _____ (6) No matter how wrong they are, such ~~a juror argues~~ *jurors argue* their positions strongly. _____ (7) These jurors believe their responsibility is to argue for their version of the truth rather than to weigh all the evidence and alternative possibilities. _C_ (8) Such ~~a juror~~ *jurors* will even make up their own evidence to support their case. _____ (9) For example, one juror argued that a man being tried for murder was acting in ~~their~~ *his* own defense because the victim was probably carrying a knife, but no knife was mentioned during the trial. _____ (10) Studies suggest that people who jump to conclusions

Teaching Tip

Ask students to decide how
many individuals are being
discussed in each sentence.
For example, sentence 2
mentions "a juror" (how
many people is that?) and
then mentions "they" (how
many is that?) Remind students that a pronoun and
its antecedent must agree.

on a jury probably will not take their time when making other important

decisions in life. ___C___

■ WRITING FIRST: Flashback

Look back at your response to the Writing First exercise on page 381. Find all the sentences in which you use the pronoun *they* or *their*. Check every sentence to make sure each of these pronouns refers to a plural noun or pronoun. If you find an incorrect sentence, rewrite it on the lines below, correcting any illogical shifts in number.

Answers will vary.

_____

_____

_____

_____

D   Avoiding Illogical Shifts in Voice

When the subject of a sentence *performs* the action, the sentence is in the **active voice**. When the subject of a sentence *receives* the action (that is, it is acted on), the sentence is in the **passive voice**.

ACTIVE VOICE   Nat Turner organized a slave rebellion in August 1831. (Subject *Nat Turner* performs the action.)

PASSIVE VOICE   A slave rebellion was organized by Nat Turner in 1831. (Subject *rebellion* receives the action.)

An **illogical shift in voice** occurs when a writer shifts from active to passive voice or from passive to active voice for no apparent reason.

ILLOGICAL SHIFT IN VOICE   J. D. Salinger wrote *The Catcher in the Rye,* and *Franny and Zooey* was also written by him. (active to passive)

REVISED   J. D. Salinger wrote *The Catcher in the Rye,* and he also wrote *Franny and Zooey.* (consistent use of active voice)

ILLOGICAL SHIFT IN VOICE   Radium was discovered by Marie Curie in 1910, and she won a Nobel Prize in chemistry in 1911. (passive to active)

REVISED   Marie Curie discovered radium in 1910, and she won a Nobel Prize in chemistry in 1911. (consistent use of active voice)

Teaching Tip
Tell students that to convert the passive voice to the active voice, they should ask themselves, "Who carried out the action?" and make the answer the subject of the sentence.

● **Writing Tip**
To see if your writing over-uses the passive voice, use your computer's Search or Find command to look for *is, are, was,* and *were,* which often appear as part of passive-voice verbs.

ON THE WEB
For more practice, visit
Exercise Central *at*
<*bedfordstmartins.com/ writingfirst*>.

ESL Tip
Have students label passive and active verbs before they make their corrections.

FOCUS **Correcting Illogical Shifts in Voice**

The active voice is stronger and more direct than the passive voice. For this reason, you should usually use the active voice in your college writing. To change a sentence from the passive to the active voice, determine who or what performs the action, and make this noun the subject of a new active voice sentence.

> PASSIVE VOICE The campus escort service <u>is used</u> by my friends. (*My friends* perform the action.)
>
> ACTIVE VOICE My friends <u>use</u> the campus escort service.

Use the passive voice in your college writing only when the action being performed is more important than the person performing it. To change a sentence from the active to the passive voice, determine who or what receives the action, and make this noun the subject of a new passive voice sentence.

> ACTIVE VOICE I <u>completed</u> the report on schedule. (*Report* receives the action.)
>
> PASSIVE VOICE The report <u>was completed</u> on schedule.

◆ **PRACTICE 24-4**

The following sentences contain illogical shifts in voice. Revise each sentence by changing the underlined passive-voice verb to the active voice.

> **Example:**
> Several researchers are interested in leadership qualities, and a study of decision making <u>was conducted</u> by them recently.
>
> Several researchers are interested in leadership qualities, *and they recently conducted a study of decision making.*

1. A local university funded the study, and the research team <u>was led</u> by Dr. Alicia Flynn.

   A local university funded the study, *and Dr. Alicia Flynn led the research team.*

2. The researchers developed a series of questions about decision making, and then a hundred subjects <u>were interviewed</u> by them.

   The researchers developed a series of questions about decision making, *and then they interviewed a hundred subjects.*

3. Intuition <u>was relied on</u> by two-thirds of the subjects, and only one-third used logic.

  <u>*Two-thirds of the subjects relied on intuition*</u> , and only one-third used

  logic.

4. After the researchers completed the study, a report <u>was written</u> about their findings.

  After the researchers completed the study, *they wrote a report about*

  their findings.

5. The report <u>was read</u> by many experts, and most of them found the results surprising.

  <u>*Many experts read the report*</u> , and most

  of them found the results surprising.

■ WRITING FIRST: Flashback

Look back at your response to the Writing First exercise on page 381. Check each sentence to make sure it includes no illogical shifts in voice. If you find an incorrect sentence, rewrite it on the lines below, correcting any illogical shifts in voice.

Answers will vary.

_____

_____

_____

_____

_____

_____

■ WRITING FIRST: Revising and Editing

Look back at your response to the Writing First exercise on page 381. Revise any illogical shifts in tense, person, number, or voice by incorporating the changes and corrections you made in this chapter's Flashback exercises. When you have finished, do the same for another assignment you are currently working on.

CHAPTER REVIEW

◆ EDITING PRACTICE: PARAGRAPH

Read the following student paragraph, which includes illogical shifts in tense, person, number, and voice. Edit the passage to eliminate the unnecessary shifts, making sure subjects and verbs agree. The first error has been corrected for you.

> The Origin of Baseball Cards
>
> The first baseball cards appeared in the late 1800s. These cardboard pictures ~~are~~ *were* inserted in packs of cigarettes to prevent them from being accidentally crushed. Some people collected the cards, and the cigarette companies ~~use~~ *used* the cards to encourage ~~you~~ *people* to buy ~~its~~ *their* products. By the early twentieth century, ~~it was found by~~ candy makers *found* that they could use baseball cards to sell candy to children, and so they developed new marketing strategies. For example, each box of Cracker Jacks ~~contain~~ *contained* a baseball card. In 1933, gum manufacturers packaged pieces of bubblegum with several baseball cards to make "bubblegum cards." The Topps Company was famous for its Bazooka bubblegum cards, which children could trade with one another. Sometimes ~~a child~~ *children* would put cards in the spokes of their bike wheels; the cards made noise when the wheels ~~turns~~ *turned.* Eventually, the bubblegum ~~is~~ *was* dropped by the card manufacturers, and people collected the cards themselves. Still, collecting baseball cards was seen as just a hobby for children until the 1970s, when dealers began to offer ~~his or her~~ *their* rarest cards at high prices. Nowadays, baseball-card collectors ~~were~~ *are* mainly adults who are interested in investment, not baseball.

◆ EDITING PRACTICE: ESSAY

Read the following student essay, which includes illogical shifts in tense,
person, number, and voice. Edit the passage to eliminate the unnecessary
shifts, making sure subjects and verbs agree. The first sentence has been
edited for you.

Answers may vary.

The Mixing of Cultures

Because the United States is the melting pot of the
world, it ~~drew~~ *draws* thousands of immigrants from Europe, Asia,
and Africa. Many of them come to the United States because
they ~~wanted~~ *want* to become Americans. At the same time, they
also want to keep parts of their original cultures. This
conflict confuses many immigrants. Some immigrants think
that to become American, ~~you~~ *they* have to give up ~~your~~ *their* ethnic
identity. Others, however, realize that it is possible to
become an American without losing ~~your~~ *their* ethnic identity.
To me, this is the strength of the United States: as a
Filipino American, I am able to be both Filipino and
American. I know of no other country in the world where
this ~~was~~ *is* true.

Many Filipino Americans are able to maintain their
Filipino culture in the United States. For example, they
decorate their houses to remind themselves of houses in
the Philippines. Filipinos also try to keep their native
language. Although ~~every Filipino speaks~~ *all Filipinos speak* English, Tagalog
~~is also spoken by them~~ *they also speak*—usually at home. On holidays,
Filipinos follow the traditions of the Philippines. They
sing Filipino folk songs, do traditional dances, and cook
Filipino foods. ~~Everyone tries~~ *They all try* to visit their relatives
in the Philippines as often as they can. In this way, a
Filipino child can experience ~~their~~ *his or her* ethnic culture
firsthand.

A Filipino family that wants to hold on to ~~their~~ *its* ethnic
background can enjoy life in America. Here, cultures mix

Filipino-American family

Flag of the Philippines

Teaching Tip
Remind students that a collective noun such as *family*
is usually singular and is
used with a singular pro-
noun. Refer them to 28E.

and enrich one another. Each culture has something to offer

America—~~their~~ *its* food, language, and traditions. At the same

time, America ~~had~~ *has* something to offer each culture—economic

opportunity, education, and freedom.

◆ COLLABORATIVE ACTIVITIES

1. On a separate sheet of paper, write five sentences that include shifts from present to past tense, some logical and some illogical. Exchange papers with another person in your group, and revise any incorrect sentences.

2. As a group, make up a test with five sentences containing illogical shifts in tense, person, number, and voice. Exchange tests with another group in the class. After you have taken their test, compare your answers with theirs.

3. As a group, choose five words from the list below, and use each as the subject of a sentence. Make sure each sentence includes a pronoun that refers to the subject.

   Example: Teachers must know their students.

anybody	children	a parent	something
anyone	everybody	people	teachers
anything	everyone	raccoons	a woman
a book	no one	someone	workers

   Make sure the sentences you have written do not include any illogical shifts in person or number.

☑ REVIEW CHECKLIST:
Illogical Shifts

■ An illogical shift in tense occurs when a writer shifts from one tense to another for no apparent reason. (See 24A.)

■ An illogical shift in person occurs when a writer shifts from one person to another for no apparent reason. (See 24B.)

■ An illogical shift in number occurs when a writer shifts from singular to plural (or the other way around) for no apparent reason. (See 24C.)

■ An illogical shift in voice occurs when a writer shifts from active to passive voice or from passive to active voice for no apparent reason. (See 24D.)

Dangling and Misplaced Modifiers

PREVIEW

In this chapter, you will learn

- to identify present participle modifiers (25A)

- to identify past participle modifiers (25B)

- to recognize and correct dangling modifiers (25C)

- to recognize and correct misplaced modifiers (25D)

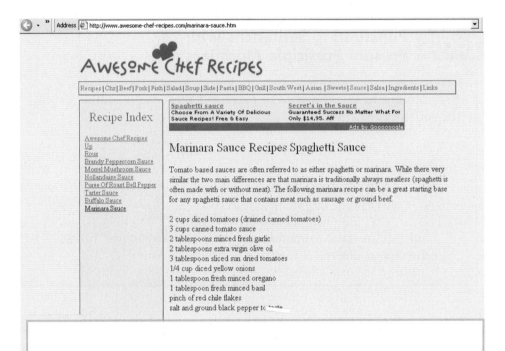

■ WRITING FIRST

Above is a recipe for marinara sauce that appeared on a cooking Web site. Read this recipe, and then write a recipe for your favorite dish. Begin by introducing the recipe; then, list the ingredients, and explain how to prepare the dish.

A **modifier** is a word or word group that functions as an adjective or an adverb. Thus, a modifier describes or limits other words in a sentence. To avoid confusion, a modifier should be placed as close as possible to the word or words it modifies—ideally, directly before or directly after. Many word groups that act as modifiers are introduced by present or past participles.

Word Power

assemble   to put together into a whole

ingredient   something required to form a mixture

Writing Tip

Modifiers can function as adjectives or as adverbs. An adjective modifies a noun or a pronoun. An adverb modifies a verb, an adjective, or another adverb. (See Chapter 29.)

A   Identifying Present Participle Modifiers

A **present participle modifier** consists of the present participle form of the verb (the *-ing* form) along with the words it introduces. A present participle

For more on present participles, see 18C.

modifier provides information about a noun or pronoun that appears right before or right after it in the sentence.

PRESENT PARTICIPLE MODIFIER

Running through the streets, Archimedes could not wait to tell people what he had discovered.

PRESENT PARTICIPLE MODIFIER

Steve Jobs, using his garage as a workshop, invented the personal computer.

Teaching Tip
Review the formation of past participles, referring students to 27A and 27B.

FOCUS | **Punctuating Sentences with Present Participle Modifiers**

Use commas to set off a present participle modifier from the rest of the sentence.

PRESENT PARTICIPLE MODIFIER

Remembering his working-class roots, Paul McCartney returned to Liverpool to give a concert.

PRESENT PARTICIPLE MODIFIER

Paul McCartney, remembering his working-class roots, returned to Liverpool to give a concert.

Teaching Tip
Remind students that beginning every sentence with the same opening strategy can cause readers to lose interest in their writing. Refer them to 18B.

◆ PRACTICE 25-1

Underline the present participle modifier in each of the following sentences. Draw an arrow from the modifier to the word or word group it modifies.

Example: To travel to California before 1869, people either had to take a ship south around the tip of South America or go west by horse and wagon across the country.

(1) Believing that improving transportation would be good for the nation, Congress in 1862 proposed that a transcontinental rail line be built. (2) The new tracks, roughly following the forty-second parallel, would be built by two different railroad companies and would extend all the way to Sacramento, California. (3) Laying track westward from Omaha, the Union Pacific Railroad had to cross the barren plains and the Rocky Mountains. (4) Moving eastward from Sacramento, the Central Pacific

Railroad had to cross the high Sierra Nevada mountains. (5) Carrying supplies long distances in both directions, the railroads needed many workers. (6) The Central Pacific Railroad, hiring thousands of Chinese laborers, hurried to lay as much track as possible each day. (7) Using thousands of European immigrants and Civil War veterans, the Union Pacific Railroad rushed west. (8) Pushing across difficult terrain in the worst kinds of weather, workers raced toward the meeting point. (9) The two railroads, meeting at last at Promontory Point, Utah, marked the completion of the task by driving in a golden spike to mark the spot where the tracks joined. (10) Paving the way for the development of the West, the Transcontinental Railroad was a great engineering feat.

■ WRITING FIRST: Flashback

Look back at your response to the Writing First exercise on page 393. Find any sentences that contain present participle modifiers, and write them on the lines below. (If you cannot find any, write two new sentences that contain present participle modifiers.) Check to make sure you have punctuated your sentences correctly.

Answers will vary.

_____

_____

_____

_____

B Identifying Past Participle Modifiers

A **past participle modifier** consists of the past participle form of the verb (usually ending in *-d* or *-ed*) along with the words it introduces. Like a present participle modifier, a past participle modifier provides information about a noun or a pronoun that is located right before or right after it in the sentence.

● **Writing Tip**

Not all past participles end in *-d* or *-ed*. Irregular verbs have irregular past participle forms—*known, cut,* and *written,* for example. (See 18C and 27B.)

PAST PARTICIPLE MODIFIER

Rejected by Hamlet, Ophelia goes mad and drowns herself.

PAST PARTICIPLE MODIFIER

Hamlet, written by William Shakespeare, is a tragedy.

For more on irregular past participles, see 27B.

FOCUS	**Punctuating Sentences with Past Participle Modifiers**

Use commas to set off a past participle modifier from the rest of the sentence.

PAST PARTICIPLE MODIFIER

Terrorized by bandits, the villagers decided to fight back.

PAST PARTICIPLE MODIFIER

The villagers, terrorized by bandits, decided to fight back.

Teaching Tip
Have students write Practice 25-2 on the board so that other students can check their own work and ask questions. Let students explain why they wrote what they wrote.

◆ **PRACTICE 25-2**

Underline the past participle modifier in each of the following sentences. Draw an arrow from each past participle modifier to the word or word group it modifies.

Example: Often considered a modern phenomenon, graffiti actually has prehistoric roots.

(1) Rarely welcomed by property owners, graffiti covers the walls and sidewalks in some urban neighborhoods. (2) Similar drawings on ancient walls, believed to be done by prehistoric cave dwellers, can also be seen in parts of Africa and Europe. (3) Preserved by the eruptions of Mt. Vesuvius, graffiti provides insight into the street life of the ancient city of Pompeii. (4) This city, destroyed by the volcano, has graffiti that expresses love and personal insults. (5) Found in Rome, Viking graffiti tells about great military victories. (6) Another example of graffiti is an inscription, carved into a boulder in the rim of the Grand Canyon, with the name of a member of the 1904 U.S. Geological Survey team. (7) A popular graffiti slogan, painted by American soldiers during World War II, was "Kilroy Was Here." (8) Some graffiti, sprayed on walls by local gangs, identifies gang turf and warns away outsiders. (9) Sometimes called "tags," such graffiti can be a threat. (10) Regarded as a nuisance by some people, graffiti is seen by others as art.

■ WRITING FIRST: Flashback

Look back at your response to the Writing First exercise on page
393. Identify any sentences that contain past participle modifiers,
and write them on the lines below. (If you cannot find any, write
two new sentences that contain past participle modifiers.) Check to
make sure you have punctuated your sentences correctly.

Answers will vary.

_____

_____

_____

_____

C   Correcting Dangling Modifiers

A modifier describes or limits other words in a sentence. A modifier "dangles" because it cannot logically describe any word or word group in the
sentence. Often a dangling modifier comes at the beginning of a sentence
and appears to modify the noun or pronoun that follows it.

Using my computer, the report was finished in two days.

In the sentence above, the present participle modifier *Using my computer*
appears to refer to *the report*, but this makes no sense. (How can the report
use a computer?) The word to which the modifier should logically refer is
not included in the sentence. To correct this sentence, you need to supply
the missing word.

Using my computer, I finished the report in two days.

As in the example above, the easiest way to correct a dangling modifier
is to supply a word or word group to which the dangling modifier can logically refer.

INCORRECT   Moving the microscope's mirror, the light can be directed
            onto the slide. (Did the light move the mirror?)

CORRECT   Moving the microscope's mirror, you can direct the light
            onto the slide.

INCORRECT   Paid in advance, the furniture was delivered. (Was the
            furniture paid in advance?)

CORRECT   Paid in advance, the movers delivered the furniture.

Teaching Tip
Spend extra time explaining
why these examples are incorrect. This concept is difficult for many students to
grasp.

25 C

ON THE WEB
For more practice, visit
Exercise Central *at*
<bedfordstmartins.com/
writingfirst>.

Teaching Tip
Have students explain the
errors in these sentences.
Show them how to correct
dangling modifiers by asking
questions (for example, "Was
the bus waiting inside?") to
help them identify the missing subject.

◆ **PRACTICE 25-3**

Each of the following sentences contains a dangling modifier. To correct each
sentence, add a word or word group to which the modifier can logically refer.

Example: Waiting inside, my bus passed by.

Waiting inside, I missed my bus.

Answers will vary.

1. Paid by the school, the books were sorted in the library.

   _____

   _____

2. Pushing on the brakes, my car would not stop for the red light.

   _____

   _____

3. Short of money, the trip was canceled.

   _____

4. Working overtime, his salary almost doubled.

   _____

5. Angered by the noise, the concert was called off.

   _____

   _____

6. Using the proper formula, the problem was easily solved.

   _____

   _____

7. Tired and hungry, the assignment was finished by midnight.

   _____

   _____

8. Sitting in the park, the pigeons were fed.

   _____

9. Staying in bed on Sunday, the newspaper was read from beginning to end.

   _____

   _____

10. Driving for a long time, my leg began to hurt.

   _____

   _____

◆ **PRACTICE 25-4**

Complete the following sentences, making sure to include a word or word
group to which the modifiers can logically refer.

    Example: Dancing with the man of her dreams, *she decided that it*

was time to wake up.

Answers will vary.

1. Given one last chance to beg for forgiveness, _____

_____

2. Soaked by the rain, _____

_____

3. Seeing a strange light in the sky, _____

_____

4. Running down the steps as the clock struck twelve, _____

_____

5. Alerted by a sound from outside, _____

_____

6. Sent to fight in a foreign land, _____

_____

7. Jumping over the rail and grabbing the chandelier, _____

_____

8. Disgusted by the horrible meal, _____

_____

9. Wanting desperately to go to the concert, _____

_____

10. Distrusting the advice he got from his friends, _____

_____

  ■ WRITING FIRST: Flashback

Look back at your response to the Writing First exercise on page
393. Do any of your sentences contain dangling modifiers? On the
lines below, rewrite any sentence that contains a dangling modifier,

(continued on the following page)

(continued from the previous page)

making sure to include a word or word group to which the modifier can logically refer.

1. *Answers will vary.* _____

   _____

   _____

2. _____

   _____

   _____

D Correcting Misplaced Modifiers

Teaching Tip
To help students understand the difference between a dangling modifier and a misplaced modifier, point out that a misplaced modifier modifies a word that actually appears in the sentence.

A modifier should be placed as close as possible to the word it modifies. A **misplaced modifier** is a modifier (often introduced by a present or past participle) that has no clear relationship to the word it modifies because it is too far from it. As a result, it appears to modify the wrong word. Frequently, the result is confusing, illogical, or even silly.

To correct this problem, you need to place the modifier as close as possible to the word or words it modifies—usually directly before or directly after it.

INCORRECT Sarah fed the dog <u>wearing her pajamas</u>. (Was the dog wearing Sarah's pajamas?)

CORRECT <u>Wearing her pajamas</u>, Sarah fed the dog.

INCORRECT <u>Dressed in a raincoat and boots</u>, I thought my son was prepared for the storm. (Who was dressed in a raincoat and boots?)

CORRECT I thought my son, <u>dressed in a raincoat and boots</u>, was prepared for the storm.

For more on prepositional phrases, see 15B.

Not all misplaced modifiers are participles. Prepositional phrases, too, can modify other words in the sentence, and so prepositional phrases must also be placed carefully.

INCORRECT At the wedding, she danced with the groom <u>in a beautiful white gown</u>. (Was the groom wearing a white gown?)

CORRECT At the wedding, she danced <u>in a beautiful white gown</u> with the groom.

FOCUS Misplaced Modifiers

Be especially careful when placing **limiting modifiers** such as *almost, even, hardly, just, nearly, only,* and *simply.* Notice how the meaning of the following sentences changes when the modifier *only* is placed in different positions.

<u>Only</u> David could go to the movies yesterday.

David could <u>only</u> go to the movies yesterday.

David could go <u>only</u> to the movies yesterday.

David could go to the movies <u>only</u> yesterday.

Teaching Tip
Ask students to explain the meaning of each sentence.

ESL Tip
Nonnative speakers may have a hard time placing limiting modifiers. Consider giving them additional practice exercises.

◆ PRACTICE 25-5

Rewrite the following sentences, which contain misplaced modifiers, so that each modifier clearly refers to the word it logically modifies.

ON THE WEB
For more practice, visit Exercise Central at <bedfordstmartins.com/ writingfirst>.

Example: Mark ate a pizza standing in front of the refrigerator.

Standing in front of the refrigerator, Mark ate a pizza.

1. The cat broke the vase frightened by a noise.

   Frightened by a noise, the cat broke the vase.

2. Running across my bathroom ceiling, I saw two large, hairy bugs.

   I saw two large, hairy bugs running across my bathroom ceiling.

3. Lori looked at the man sitting in the chair with red hair.

   Lori looked at the man with red hair sitting in the chair.

4. *ET* is a film about an alien directed by Steven Spielberg.

   ET is a film directed by Steven Spielberg about an alien.

5. With their deadly venom, people are sometimes killed by snakes.

   People are sometimes killed by snakes with their deadly venom.

6. *Pudd'nhead Wilson* is a book about an exchange of identities by Mark Twain.

   Pudd'nhead Wilson by Mark Twain is a book about an exchange of identities.

7. I ran outside and saw eight tiny reindeer in my bathrobe.

   I ran outside in my bathrobe and saw eight tiny reindeer.

8. Barking all night, I listened to my neighbor's dog.

   I listened to my neighbor's dog barking all night.

9. The exterminator sprayed the insect wearing a mask.

   Wearing a mask, the exterminator sprayed the insect.

10. With a mysterious smile, Leonardo da Vinci painted the *Mona Lisa*.

    Leonardo da Vinci painted the Mona Lisa with a mysterious smile.

■ **WRITING FIRST: Flashback**

Look back at your response to the Writing First exercise on page 393. Do any sentences contain misplaced modifiers? On the lines below, rewrite any such sentences by placing the modifiers as close as possible to a word or word group they can logically modify.

1. *Answers will vary.*

2. _____

■ **WRITING FIRST: Revising and Editing**

Look back at your response to the Writing First exercise on page 393. Then, add two sentences, one with a present participle modifier and one with a past participle modifier. If you like, you

(continued on the following page)

(continued from the previous page)
can use the new sentences you wrote for the Flashback exercises
on pages 395 and 397. Finally, check your work for any dangling or
misplaced modifiers.

CHAPTER REVIEW

◆ EDITING PRACTICE: PARAGRAPH

Read the following student paragraph, which includes modification errors. Rewrite sentences where necessary to correct dangling and misplaced modifiers. In some cases, you may have to supply a word or word
group to which the modifier can logically refer. The first incorrect sentence has been corrected for you.

Answers may vary.

The Mystery of Stonehenge

~~Traveling to England,~~ Stonehenge is a popular

                    for tourists traveling to England.
destination. Everyone who has seen the massive stone

circles has wondered where they came from. ~~Used for~~

                                Some
~~worshipping ancient gods,~~ some researchers have speculated
                         used for worshipping ancient gods.
that Stonehenge was a temple. Others have thought it was a

sacred burial site. Now, however, researchers have found

that Stonehenge was an astronomical observatory used for

watching eclipses and summer and winter solstices. Although

the stones we see now are only the ruins of the original

circles, historians have figured out how Stonehenge was

built. Taking a great deal of time, effort, and labor, the

people who created Stonehenge accomplished an impressive

engineering feat. About five thousand years ago, ancient

people used tools made of antlers to dig a ditch into the

chalky earth. The first stone circle was set up about a

                        People
thousand years later. ~~To the Stonehenge site, people~~ used
                              to the Stonehenge site.
wheeled sleds to drag eighty stones for 240 miles. ~~Loaded~~

    They
~~on barges, they~~ may have been able to float the stones

, loaded on barges,

on two rivers part of the way. ~~Weighing more than fifty~~

Six

~~tons each, six~~ hundred people would have been needed to

, weighing more than fifty tons each,

drag the biggest stones over the steepest part of the trip.

Levers

~~Raising the stones to an upright position, levers~~ and

to raise the stones to an upright position.

ropes were employed by workers, ~~Probably finished about~~

People

, probably finished about 1500 B.C.,

~~1500 B.C., people~~ clearly felt that Stonehenge was very

important.

◆ EDITING PRACTICE: ESSAY

Read the following student essay, which has modification errors. Rewrite sentences to correct dangling and misplaced modifiers. In some cases, you may have to supply a word or word group to which the modifier can logically refer. The first incorrect sentence has been corrected for you.
Answers may vary.

The ABCs of My Education

I spent

Born in New York City, my early years ~~were spent~~ in

the Bronx. My parents worked hard but made just enough

I saw

money to get by. Raised in this environment, ~~there was~~

violence everywhere. I watched my friends get involved

with gangs and drugs and ruin their lives. Concerned

one of my parents   *me*

about me, ~~I~~ walked to school every day ~~with one of my~~

Believing that school was a safe place for me, they

~~parents. They~~ took a lot of time out of their lives to

see that I got an education, ~~believing that school was~~

~~a safe place for me.~~ Agreeing with them, ~~school was the~~

at school

~~place where~~ I stayed longer and longer. After a while,

I started getting good grades, and my guidance counselor

, seeing my potential,

recommended me to the A Better Chance (A.B.C.) program,

~~seeing my potential.~~

The A.B.C. program is nationally acclaimed.

Participating in the program, ~~the extra classes help~~

take classes to

children with limited opportunities improve their academic

Based on my record,

skills. I was able to go to a suburban high school,

~~based on my record.~~ Arriving at my new school, ~~it was~~

I found

difficult ~~for me~~ to adjust. My teachers encouraged every

in the program

student to aim for college ~~in the program~~, and I was no

exception. With the help of my teachers, my friends, and

Suburban high school

Inner-city high school

especially my parents, I began to excel. Graduating in the
top 20 percent of my class, *I felt* my dreams had come true.

The A.B.C. program helped me realize the importance
of a good education. I hope to return to the South Bronx, *Finished with my schooling,*
~~finished with my schooling,~~ to become a teacher. Teaching
in the Bronx, my students *I will show* ~~will be shown~~ the value of
education. I will also tell them that they themselves can
~~only~~ choose to make something *only* positive of their lives.

◆ COLLABORATIVE ACTIVITIES

1. Working in a group of five or six students, make a list of five present
   participle modifiers and five past participle modifiers. Exchange your
   list with another group, and complete one another's sentences.

   Example:

   Typing as fast as he could, *John could not wait to finish writing his*
   screenplay.

2. Working in a team of three students, compete with other teams to compose sentences that contain outrageous and confusing dangling or misplaced modifiers. As a class, correct the sentences. Then, vote on which
   group wrote the most challenging sentences.

3. In a group of four or five students, find examples of confusing dangling
   and misplaced modifiers in magazines and newspapers. Rewrite the
   sentences, making sure each modifier is placed as close as possible to
   the word or word group it describes.

☑ REVIEW CHECKLIST:

Dangling and Misplaced Modifiers

- A present participle modifier consists of the present participle
  (the *-ing* form of the verb) along with the words it introduces.
  (See 25A.)

- A past participle modifier consists of the past participle form
  of the verb (usually ending in *-d* or *-ed*) along with the words it
  introduces. (See 25B.)

- Correct a dangling modifier by supplying a word or word
  group to which the dangling modifier can logically refer. (See
  25C.)

- Correct a misplaced modifier by placing the modifier as close
  as possible to the word or word group it modifies. (See 25D.)

Read the following student essay, which contains run-ons and comma splices, sentence fragments, errors with subject-verb and pronoun-antecedent agreement, illogical shifts, and dangling and misplaced modifiers. Edit the essay to correct the errors. The first sentence has been corrected for you.

Answers may vary.

Students from the Caribbean

Immigrant children are
~~An immigrant child is~~ entitled to be taught in their
                    in
native language, ~~In~~ many states. This instruction, which
gives
~~give~~ them time to adjust to their new country, is required
                        do
by law. But these laws ~~does~~ not apply to children who come
                                        They
from English-speaking Caribbean countries. ~~You~~ are not
     and
tested, they are not offered any special programs. One high

school principal, whose students are largely West Indian,
says,   *are*
~~say,~~ "These kids ~~is~~ definitely getting a bad deal." Even

though they may have trouble speaking standard English,
they
~~They~~ are ignored.

In New York City, students from the English-speaking
                make
Caribbean ~~makes~~ up more than 20 percent of the new
                                                are
immigrants enrolled in schools. For example, there ~~is~~

many Jamaican and Dominican children in New York schools.
                            do not
The teachers and the principal ~~does not~~ always recognize
                                        because
that these students have a language problem, ~~Because~~ they

comes from countries where English is spoken. However,
                                    ;   *, which*
they do not speak standard English they speak Creole, ~~Which~~
is
~~was~~ a mix of grammar and vocabulary from several languages.
                    was
What happened ~~were~~ that European settlers brought an
                                        , such
official language from their own country, ~~Such~~ as Spanish,
                                        brought
French, Dutch, or English. But these Europeans also ~~bring~~

millions of West African slaves to the Caribbean islands.

Map of the Caribbean

Creole takes
~~Taking~~ the vocabulary from a European language, *but* the

pronunciation and grammar ~~of Creole came~~ from a West

African language. In many Caribbean societies, Creole

languages are looked down on even by the people who speak

them every day.

children
   When a ~~child~~ who speak Creole come to American schools,

, teachers
~~Teachers~~ often have a difficult time understanding them.

feel   *are*
The children ~~feeling~~ that their teachers ~~were~~ laughing at

say
them. Many students ~~said~~ that other children and teachers

they
tell them that ~~you~~ are not speaking proper English. Not

need
realizing that these students ~~needs~~ help mastering standard

, teachers
English, ~~Teachers~~ may automatically assume~~s~~ they are not

. As
intelligent, ~~as~~ a result, a Creole-speaking student often

does
~~do~~ not succeed in school.

are
   However, there ~~is~~ signs that the situation is changing.

Recently, some states have agreed to pay for special

children
programs for immigrant ~~child~~ from ~~an~~ English-speaking

countries, such   *Since the*
Caribbean ~~country. Such~~ as Jamaica and Belize. ~~The~~ teachers

programs are
in such ~~a program is~~ all fluent in Creole-based languages,

they understand these students. Educated as teachers of

they see   *as*
English as a second language, Creole ~~is~~ another language

~~to them.~~ They know that the teachers, as well as the

have
principal, ~~has~~ to create an atmosphere of respect for this

The
language. ~~For these students, the~~ teachers learn that it

for these students   *, one*
may be best to use two different languages, ~~One~~ for home

Teachers can use a
and one for school. ~~A~~ tape player ~~can be used by teachers~~

so
to record and replay examples of students' speech, they

can hear their pronunciation and sentence structure. One

is
of the most useful strategies ~~are~~ to have different

policies for different assignments; for instance, students

might use Creole to discuss marriage customs around the

Stamps of Jamaica

Stamps of Belize

407

world but be expected to switch to standard English, ~~When~~ *when*
they write about these customs.

People
~~Anyone~~ who speak Creole need to learn to value their
own language, they also need to learn standard English,
which
~~Which~~ they will need for success in school and in the
workplace. Making sure that they learn both, ~~it is~~
~~necessary to have~~ well-trained teachers will give these
students the language skills they need.

UNIT SIX

Understanding Basic Grammar

Verbs: Past Tense

PREVIEW

In this chapter, you will learn

■ to understand regular verbs in the past tense (26A)

■ to understand irregular verbs in the past tense (26B)

■ to deal with problem verbs in the past tense (26C and 26D)

Obituaries

June 23, 1988   *The St. James Times*

Edward J. DeRoo dies—writer, scholar, naturalist

Edward John DeRoo

Author and professor emeritus Edward John DeRoo of Head of the Harbor, Saint James, died of heart failure Monday, June 20, at University Hospital at Stony Brook. He was 65. Dr. DeRoo was a professor of communications at Nassau Community College until he retired two years ago following open heart surgery.

During his 23 years at the college, he taught TV and film production, mass media, and interpersonal communications, and was recipient of a state university fellowship grant for filmmaking.

He wrote five novels, which were published in the United States and England. They included *The Fires of Youth, The Young Wolves,* and *The Little Caesars.* In the 1960s he was also the weekly drama columnist for the *Long Island Post* and *The West Side News.*

Before coming to Long Island, he had taught at the University of New Mexico, Texas at El Paso, and the University of Southern California. While in California in the 1950s he had his own TV program, *The Halls of Science,* for five years, and also several small roles as an actor in Hollywood films.

In the late 1940s he had been a playwright, director and actor with The Cleveland Playhouse. Four of his comedies saw local productions by the Salisbury Players in libraries in Nassau.

His degrees include a doctorate in education from Columbia, a master of fine arts from the Yale Drama School, master of arts from the University of Denver and bachelor of arts from the University of Rochester. He was a World War II veteran.

Since retirement he had returned to writing and was active in the Smithtown Writers Guild and Suffolk County's Taproots writing group. One of his short stories was recently purchased by the PEN syndicate affiliated with the National Endowment for the Arts. He was a Friend of the Arts at the State University at Stony Brook, and for many years was a linesman with the National Lawn Tennis Umpires Association. Under the auspices of the National Wildlife Federation, Dr. DeRoo and his wife created a certified wildlife habitat at their Head of the Harbor home.

Dr. DeRoo leaves his wife R. Deborah DeRoo, a son, Adrian of Riverdale, a daughter, Deborah of Montreal, and a stepdaughter, Andrea Kovacs of Manhattan.

Services were held at the St. James Funeral Home on Wednesday, June 22.

■ WRITING FIRST

Look at the newspaper obituary that is printed above, and then write your own obituary. (Refer to yourself by name or by *he* or *she*.) As you write, assume that you have led a long life and have achieved almost everything you hoped you would. Be sure to include the accomplishments for which you would most like to be remembered. Remember to use transitional words and phrases that clearly show how one event in your life relates to another.

Word Power

accomplishment something completed successfully; an achievement

longevity long life

objective a goal

A   Understanding Regular Verbs in the Past Tense

● **Writing Tip**

Not all verbs ending in *-ed*
or *-d* are in the past tense.
Some are past participles.
(See 27A.)

Tense is the form a verb takes to show when an action or situation took place. The **past tense** is the form a verb takes to show that an action occurred in the past. **Regular verbs** form the past tense by adding either *-ed* or *-d* to the **base form** of the verb (the present tense form of the verb that is used with the pronoun *I*).

ESL Tip

Verb tense is a challenge for
nonnative speakers. Check
everything they write, and
have them write often.

● **Writing Tip**

All regular verbs use the
same form for singular and
plural in the past tense: *I
cheered. They cheered.*

> **FOCUS** Regular Verbs in the Past Tense
>
> ■ Most regular verbs form the past tense by adding *-ed* to the base form of the verb.
>
>   I <u>registered</u> for classes yesterday.
>
>   Juan <u>walked</u> to the concert.
>
> ■ Regular verbs that end in *-e* form the past tense by adding *-d*.
>
>   Walt Disney <u>produced</u> short cartoons in 1928.
>
>   Tisha <u>liked</u> to read romance novels.
>
> ■ Regular verbs that end in *-y* form the past tense by changing the *y* to *i* and adding *-ed*.
>
>   tr<u>y</u>   tr<u>ied</u>
>
>   appl<u>y</u>   appl<u>ied</u>

◆ PRACTICE 26-1

ON THE WEB

For more practice, visit
Exercise Central *at*
<bedfordstmartins.com/
writingfirst>.

Change the verbs in the following sentences to the past tense. Cross out the present tense form of each underlined verb, and write the past tense form above it.

Example: Every year, my mother ~~visits~~ her family in Bombay, India. *(visited)*

(1) She always ~~returns~~ with intricate designs on her hands and feet. *(returned)*

(2) In India, women called henna artists ~~create~~ these complex patterns. *(created)*

(3) Henna ~~originates~~ in a plant found in the Middle East, India, Indonesia, and northern Africa. (4) Many women in these areas ~~use~~ henna to color their hands, nails, and parts of their feet. (5) Men ~~dye~~ their beards, as well as the manes and hooves of their horses, with henna. (6) They also ~~color~~ animal skins with henna. (7) In India, my mother always *(originated)* *(used)* *(dyed)* *(colored)*

celebrated
~~celebrates~~ the end of the Ramadan religious fast by going to a "henna
                                attended
party." (8) A professional henna artist ~~attends~~ the party to apply new

henna decorations to the palms and feet of the women. (9) After a few
                           washed
weeks, the henna designs ~~wash~~ off. (10) In the United States, my
                        attracted
mother's henna designs ~~attract~~ the attention of many people.

■ WRITING FIRST: Flashback

Look back at your response to the Writing First exercise on page
411. Underline the past tense verbs that end in *-ed* and *-d*. Then,
write them on the lines below.

Answers will vary.

_____   _____   _____

_____   _____   _____

_____   _____   _____

_____   _____   _____

Teaching Tip
This Flashback works well
as a proofreading exercise. If
students have omitted necessary endings, they usually
recognize their errors.

B Understanding Irregular Verbs in the Past Tense

Unlike regular verbs, whose past tense forms end in *-ed* or *-d*, **irregular
verbs** have irregular forms in the past tense. In fact, their past tense forms
may look very different from their present tense forms.

The following chart lists the base form and past tense form of many of
the most commonly used irregular verbs.

Irregular Verbs in the Past Tense

Base Form	Past	Base Form	Past
awake	awoke	catch	caught
be	was, were	choose	chose
beat	beat	come	came
become	became	cost	cost
begin	began	cut	cut
bet	bet	dive	dove (dived)
bite	bit	do	did
blow	blew	draw	drew
break	broke	drink	drank
bring	brought	drive	drove
build	built	eat	ate
buy	bought	fall	fell

(continued on the following page)

● **Writing Tip**

When you edit your writing,
use the Search or Find command on your computer
to locate the irregular verbs
that give you the most
trouble.

ESL Tip
Ask students to give ex-
amples of irregular verbs
in their native languages.

ESL Tip
Irregular past tense verb
forms are challenging for
native speakers and even
more so for nonnative ones.
Have students write sen-
tences using some of the
verbs in the chart.

(continued from the previous page)

Base Form	Past	Base Form	Past
feed	fed	rise	rose
feel	felt	run	ran
fight	fought	say	said
find	found	see	saw
fly	flew	sell	sold
forgive	forgave	send	sent
freeze	froze	set	set
get	got	shake	shook
give	gave	shine	shone (shined)
go (goes)	went	sing	sang
grow	grew	sit	sat
have	had	sleep	slept
hear	heard	speak	spoke
hide	hid	spend	spent
hold	held	spring	sprang
hurt	hurt	stand	stood
keep	kept	steal	stole
know	knew	stick	stuck
lay (to place)	laid	sting	stung
lead	led	swear	swore
leave	left	swim	swam
let	let	take	took
lie (to recline)	lay	teach	taught
light	lit	tear	tore
lose	lost	tell	told
make	made	think	thought
meet	met	throw	threw
pay	paid	understand	understood
quit	quit	wake	woke
read	read	wear	wore
ride	rode	win	won
ring	rang	write	wrote

◆ PRACTICE 26-2

ON THE WEB
For more practice, visit
Exercise Central *at*
*<bedfordstmartins.com/
writingfirst>.*

In the following sentences, fill in the correct past tense form of the irregular verb in parentheses. Use the chart above to help you find the correct irregular verb form. If you do not find a verb on the chart, look it up in the dictionary.

Example: Dr. David Ho and his research team ___*found*___ (find) ways to treat AIDS at a time when many patients were dying of the disease.

(1) Ho ___*came*___ (come) to the United States from Taiwan when he ___*was*___ (be) twelve years old. (2) He ___*knew*___ (know) no

English at first, but he ___kept___ (keep) studying hard. (3) He

___went___ (go) to M.I.T. for one year. (4) Then he ___got___ (get)

a B.S. in physics from Caltech. (5) Soon he ___became___ (become)

interested in molecular biology and gene splicing. (6) While studying

for his medical degree at the Harvard-M.I.T. School of Medicine, he

___saw___ (see) some of the first documented cases of AIDS. (7) Dr. Ho

___thought___ (think) that he could fight the disease by strengthening pa-

tients' immune systems. (8) He ___had___ (have) the idea of treating

patients in the early stages of the disease with an AIDS "cocktail," which

combined several AIDS medications. (9) Because of his work, deaths

from AIDS ___began___ (begin) to decline. (10) In 1996, *Time* magazine

___gave___ (give) Dr. Ho the honor of being named its Man of the Year.

■ WRITING FIRST: Flashback

Look back at your response to the Writing First exercise on page 411. Circle each irregular past tense verb you find. Then, write each one in the column on the left. In the column on the right, write the verb's base form. (If necessary, consult the list of irregular verbs on pages 413–414 or a dictionary.)

Past Tense	Base Form
Answers will vary.	

C Problem Verbs in the Past Tense: *Be*

● **Writing Tip**

Be is the only verb in English with more than one past tense form. For detailed information about subject-verb agreement with *be*, see 23B.

The irregular verb *be* can be especially troublesome because it has two differ-ent past tense forms—*was* for singular subjects and *were* for plural subjects.

Carlo <u>was</u> interested in becoming a city planner. (singular)

They <u>were</u> happy to help out at the school. (plural)

Past Tense Forms of the Verb Be

	Singular	**Plural**
First person	I was tired.	We were tired.
Second person	You were tired.	You were tired.
Third person	He was tired.	
	She was tired.	They were tired.
	It was tired.	
	The man was tired.	Frank and Billy were tired.

◆ **PRACTICE 26-3**

Edit the following passage for errors in the use of the verb *be*. Cross out any underlined verbs that are incorrect, and write the correct forms above them. If a verb form is correct, label it *C*.

Example: Until the success of Margaret Cho, there ~~was~~ *were* no well-known Korean-American comics.

(1) When Cho was *C* only sixteen, she started performing her stand-up comedy act in a San Francisco comedy club. (2) Although an agent refused to sign her as a client because he said no Asians ~~was~~ *were* ever going to succeed in stand-up comedy, Cho did not back down. (3) She toured college campuses and was *C* a big hit. (4) Cho was *C* booked on television specials with Arsenio Hall and Bob Hope. (5) Then, she ~~were~~ *was* given her own ABC sitcom, *All-American Girl*. (6) Although the show ~~were~~ *was* cancelled after only one season, Cho's fans ~~was~~ *were* still eager to see her. (7) So far, she has had national tours of her four one-woman shows, which were *C* all very successful. (8) Her most recent show, *State of Emergency*, was *C* focused on political humor. (9) To Cho, this show ~~were~~ *was* a way to get out the vote in the November 2004 presidential election. (10) Margaret Cho ~~were~~ *was* honored by several organizations for her activist principles and for her promotion of equal rights for all people.

■ WRITING FIRST: Flashback

Look back at your response to the Writing First exercise on page 411. Find all the sentences in which you use the past tense of *be*.

(continued on the following page)

(continued from the previous page)

Copy two or three of these sentences on the lines below, and underline each subject of the verb *be*. Make sure you have used the correct form of the verb in each case.

1. *Answers will vary.* _____

   _____

2. _____

   _____

3. _____

   _____

Teaching Tip
Use this exercise, coupled with the list of irregular past forms on pages 413–414, as a review.

D Problem Verbs in the Past Tense: *Can/Could* and *Will/Would*

The helping verbs *can/could* and *will/would* present problems because their past tense forms are sometimes confused with their present tense forms.

For more on helping verbs, see 15C.

Can/Could

Can, a present tense verb, means "is able to" or "are able to."

    First-year students <u>can</u> apply for financial aid.

Could, the past tense of *can*, means "was able to" or "were able to."

    Escape artist Harry Houdini claimed that he <u>could</u> escape from any prison.

Will/Would

Will, a present tense verb, talks about the future from a point in the present.

    A solar eclipse <u>will</u> occur in ten months.

Would, the past tense of *will*, talks about the future from a point in the past.

    I told him yesterday that I <u>would</u> think about it.

Would is also used to express a possibility or wish.

    If we stuck to our budget, we <u>would</u> be better off.

    Laurie <u>would</u> like a new stuffed animal.

FOCUS Will and Would

Note that *will* is used with *can* and that *would* is used with *could*.

I <u>will</u> feed the cats if I <u>can</u> find their food.

I <u>would</u> feed the cats if I <u>could</u> find their food.

ON THE WEB
*For more practice, visit
Exercise Central at
<bedfordstmartins.com/
writingfirst>.*

◆ **PRACTICE 26-4**

Circle the appropriate helping verb from the choices in parentheses.

Example: Grandparents and many parents (can) could) still remember summers when children were kept indoors, even in hot weather.

(1) Every year, as summer approached, parents (will, would) worry that their children (will, would) become victims of polio, a terrible disease. (2) An infection of the brain and spinal cord, polio (will, would) spread wherever people gathered in large groups, such as in movie theaters and swimming pools. (3) Polio epidemics (will, would) seem to occur every summer. (4) Doctors (can, could) not predict when polio would strike a community. (5) Often, young and healthy people (will, would) develop the disease. (6) Some people (will, would) show symptoms, such as fever and headache, for only twenty-four hours, but others (can, could) become paralyzed, sometimes permanently. (7) Although no cure for polio existed, patients (can, could) be treated with complete bed rest, hot bandages, and physical therapy. (8) During the 1940s and 1950s, researchers tried to find a way in which they (can, could) prevent polio. (9) Two doctors, Jonas Salk and Albert S. Sabin, (will, would) eventually be successful in discovering a vaccine that would protect against polio. (10) Today, parents whose children have been vaccinated against polio (can, could) be sure that this disease (will, would) not affect them.

■ WRITING FIRST: Flashback

Look back at your response to the Writing First exercise on page 411. On the following lines, write a few sentences that describe what you would have accomplished if you had had the chance. Be sure to use *could* and *would* in your sentences.

Answers will vary.

_____

_____

_____

_____

_____

_____

■ WRITING FIRST: Revising and Editing

Look back at your response to the Writing First exercise on page 411. Make sure you have used the correct past tense form for each of your verbs. If you have not, cross out the incorrect form, and write the proper past tense form of the verb above the line.

CHAPTER REVIEW

◆ EDITING PRACTICE

Read the following student essay, which includes errors in past tense verb forms. Decide whether each of the underlined past tense verbs is correct. If the verb is correct, write **C** above it. If it is not, cross out the verb, and write in the correct past tense form. The first sentence has been corrected for you. (If necessary, consult the list of irregular verbs on pages 413–414.)

Healing

The window seat ~~were~~ ^{was} our favorite place to sit. I piled comfortable pillows on the ledge and ~~spended~~ ^{spent} several minutes rearranging them. Then, my friend and I ~~lied~~ ^{lay} on our backs and propped our feet on the wall. We <u>sat</u> ^C with our

Teaching Tip
Refer students to 34E for more on using *lie* and *lay*.

*Singer Karen Carpenter, who
died as a result of an eating
disorder*

Anorexic girl on scale

arms around our legs and ~~thinked~~ *thought* about the mysteries of

life. We also stared at the people on the street below and

~~wonder~~ *wondered* who they ~~was~~ *were* and where they ~~was~~ *were* going. We imagined

that they ~~can~~ *could* be millionaires, foreign spies, or ruthless

drug smugglers. We believed that everyone except us ~~leaded~~ *led*

wonderful and exciting lives.

   I *C* heard a voice call my name. Reluctantly, I ~~standed~~ *stood*

up, tearing myself away from my imaginary world. My dearest

and oldest friend—my teddy bear—and I came back to the

real world. I grabbed Teddy and ~~brung~~ *brought* him close to my

chest. Together we ~~go~~ *went* into the cold sitting room, where

twelve other girls ~~sit~~ *sat* around a table eating breakfast.

None of them looked happy. In the unit for eating

disorders, meals ~~was~~ *were* always tense. Nobody ~~wants~~ *wanted* to eat, but

the nurses watched us until we ~~eated~~ *ate* every crumb. I set *C*

Teddy on the chair beside me and stared gloomily at the

food on our plate. I closed my eyes and ~~taked~~ *took* the first

bite. I ~~feeled~~ *felt* the calories adding inches of ugly fat. Each

swallow ~~were~~ *was* like a nail being ripped from my finger. At

last, it was *C* over. I had survived breakfast.

   Days passed slowly; each passing minute was *C* a victory.

After a while, I learned how to eat properly. I learned

about other people's problems. I also learned that people

loved me. Eventually, even Teddy stopped feeling sorry for

me. I ~~begun~~ *began* to smile—and laugh. Sometimes, I even

considered myself happy. My doctors challenged me—and,

surprisingly, I ~~rised~~ *rose* to the occasion.

◆ COLLABORATIVE ACTIVITIES

1. Working in a group of three or four students, choose a famous living
   figure—an actor, a sports star, or a musician, for example—and brainstorm together to list details about this person's life. Then, working on
   your own, use the details to write a profile of the famous person.

2. Working in a group, list several contemporary problems that you think
   will be solved within ten or fifteen years. Each member of the group
   should then select a problem from the list and write a paragraph or
   two describing how the problem could be solved. As a group, arrange

the paragraphs so that they form the body of an essay. Develop a thesis statement, write an introduction and a conclusion, and then revise the body paragraphs of the essay.

3. Form a group with three other students. What national or world events do you remember most vividly? Take ten minutes to list news events that you think have defined the last five years. On your own, write a short essay in which you discuss the significance of the three or four events that the members of your group agree were the most important.

✔ REVIEW CHECKLIST:

Verbs: Past Tense

- The past tense is the form a verb takes to show that an action occurred in the past. (See 26A.)

- Regular verbs form the past tense by adding either -ed or -d to the base form of the verb. (See 26A.)

- Irregular verbs have irregular forms in the past tense. (See 26B.)

- *Be* has two different past tense forms—*was* for singular subjects and *were* for plural subjects (See 26C.)

- *Could* is the past tense of *can. Would* is the past tense of *will.* (See 26D.)

Teaching Tip
Have students write a paragraph using a certain number of past tense verbs from the list on pages 413–414.

27

Verbs: Past Participles

Word Power

benefit something that promotes well-being

diversion something that distracts or relaxes the mind

■ WRITING FIRST

The picture above shows a dance class. Look at the picture, and then write about an activity—a hobby or a sport, for example— that you have been involved in for a relatively long time. Begin by identifying the activity and stating why it has been important to you. Then, describe the activity, paying particular attention to what you have gained from it over the years.

A   Identifying Regular Past Participles

Every verb has a past participle form. The **past participle** form of a regular verb is identical to its past tense form. Both are formed by adding *-d* or *-ed* to the **base form** of the verb (the present tense form of the verb that is used with the pronoun *I*).

PAST TENSE
He earned.

PAST PARTICIPLE
He has earned.

Together with a **helping verb** (a form of the verb *have*), past participles form the **present perfect** (see 27C) and **past perfect** tenses (see 27D).

HELPING VERB   PAST PARTICIPLE
PRESENT PERFECT   The government <u>has changed</u> its policy on illegal
TENSE   immigration.

HELPING VERB   PAST PARTICIPLE
PAST PERFECT   I <u>had finished</u> studying for the test by Tuesday.
TENSE

> ● **Writing Tip**
> Note that the helping verb changes its form to agree with the subject but that the past participle always has the same form: *I have earned. She has earned.*

For more on the present perfect and past perfect tenses, see 27C and 27D.

◆ PRACTICE 27-1

Fill in the correct past participle form of each verb in parentheses.

Example: Recently, vacationers have __*discovered*__ (discover) some new opportunities to get away from it all and to do good at the same time.

ON THE WEB
For more practice, visit Exercise Central *at* <bedfordstmartins.com/ writingfirst>.

(1) Volunteer vacationers have __*visited*__ (visit) remote locations to help build footpaths, cabins, and shelters. (2) Groups such as Habitat for Humanity have __*offered*__ (offer) volunteers a chance to help build homes in low-income areas. (3) Habitat's Global Village trips have __*raised*__ (raise) awareness about the lack of affordable housing in many countries of the world. (4) Participants in Sierra Club programs have __*donated*__ (donate) thousands of work hours to groups all over the United States. (5) Sometimes, these volunteers have __*joined*__ (join) forest service workers to help restore wilderness areas. (6) They have __*cleaned*__ (clean) up trash and campsites. (7) They have also __*removed*__ (remove) nonnative plants. (8) Some vacationers have __*traveled*__ (travel) to countries such as Costa Rica, Russia, and Thailand to help with local projects. (9) Other vacationers have __*served*__ (serve) as teachers of English. (10) Volunteering vacations have __*helped*__ (help) to strengthen cross-cultural understanding.

■ WRITING FIRST: Flashback

Look back at your response to the Writing First exercise on page 422. Identify each helping verb (a form of the verb *have*) that is followed by a regular past participle (ending in *-ed* or *-d*). Write both the helping verb and the past participle on the following lines.

Helping Verb

Answers will vary.

_____

_____

_____

_____

Regular Past Participle

_____

_____

_____

_____

B   Identifying Irregular Past Participles

Irregular verbs nearly always have irregular past participles. They do not form the past participle by adding *-ed* or *-d* to the base form of the verb.

Base Form	*Past Tense*	*Past Participle*
buy	bought	bought
choose	chose	chosen
ride	rode	ridden

The following chart lists the base form, the past tense form, and the past participle of the most commonly used irregular verbs.

Irregular Past Participles

Base Form	**Past Tense**	**Past Participle**
awake	awoke	awoken
be (am, are)	was (were)	been
beat	beat	beaten
become	became	become
begin	began	begun
bet	bet	bet
bite	bit	bitten
blow	blew	blown
break	broke	broken

(continued on the following page)

(continued from the previous page)

Base Form	Past Tense	Past Participle
bring	brought	brought
build	built	built
buy	bought	bought
catch	caught	caught
choose	chose	chosen
come	came	come
cost	cost	cost
cut	cut	cut
dive	dove, dived	dived
do	did	done
draw	drew	drawn
drink	drank	drunk
drive	drove	driven
eat	ate	eaten
fall	fell	fallen
feed	fed	fed
feel	felt	felt
fight	fought	fought
find	found	found
fly	flew	flown
forgive	forgave	forgiven
freeze	froze	frozen
get	got	got, gotten
give	gave	given
go	went	gone
grow	grew	grown
have	had	had
hear	heard	heard
hide	hid	hidden
hold	held	held
hurt	hurt	hurt
keep	kept	kept
know	knew	known
lay (to place)	laid	laid
lead	led	led
leave	left	left
let	let	let
lie (to recline)	lay	lain
light	lit	lit
lose	lost	lost
make	made	made
meet	met	met
pay	paid	paid
quit	quit	quit

(continued on the following page)

(continued from the previous page)

Base Form	Past Tense	Past Participle
read	read	read
ride	rode	ridden
ring	rang	rung
rise	rose	risen
run	ran	run
say	said	said
see	saw	seen
sell	sold	sold
send	sent	sent
set	set	set
shake	shook	shaken
shine	shone, shined	shone, shined
sing	sang	sung
sit	sat	sat
sleep	slept	slept
speak	spoke	spoken
spend	spent	spent
spring	sprang	sprung
stand	stood	stood
steal	stole	stolen
stick	stuck	stuck
sting	stung	stung
swear	swore	sworn
swim	swam	swum
take	took	taken
teach	taught	taught
tear	tore	torn
tell	told	told
think	thought	thought
throw	threw	thrown
understand	understood	understood
wake	woke, waked	woken, waked
wear	wore	worn
win	won	won
write	wrote	written

● **Writing Tip**

When you edit your work, use the Find or Search command on your computer to find all uses of *have, has,* and *had.* See if the correct past participle form follows each helping verb.

◆ **PRACTICE 27-2**

Fill in the correct past participle of each verb in parentheses. Refer to the chart above as needed. If you cannot find a particular verb on the chart, look it up in the dictionary.

Example: Since 1836, the Alamo has _____*been*_____ (be) one of the most famous American historical sites.

(1) American schoolteachers have _____ _taught_ _____ (teach) their students about the patriotism and sacrifice of the defenders of the Alamo during Texas's battle for independence from Mexico. (2) Americans have _____ _heard_ _____ (hear) about how 189 Texan colonists held off a Mexican army of thousands for thirteen days. (3) Many children have _____ _built_ _____ (build) models of the Alamo, which was once a home for Spanish missionaries. (4) Visitors have _____ _come_ _____ (come) to see the place where many American heroes, including Davy Crockett and Jim Bowie, died. (5) The slogan "Remember the Alamo" has _____ _become_ _____ (become) famous among Texans and many other Americans. (6) Now, however, one historian has _____ _made_ _____ (make) a startling claim. (7) Dr. Will Fowler, of St. Andrews University in Scotland, has _____ _written_ _____ (write) a book that suggests that perhaps we should forget the Alamo. (8) According to Fowler, the story that many people have _____ _read_ _____ (read) may not be accurate. (9) He has _____ _said_ _____ (say) that the Texans wanted not only to grab the land from Mexico but also to preserve slavery in that territory. (10) Those who have always _____ _seen_ _____ (see) the defenders of the Alamo as heroes strongly disagree with Fowler's position.

◆ **PRACTICE 27-3**

Edit the following passage for errors in irregular past participles. Cross out any underlined past participles that are incorrect, and write in the correct form above them. If the verb form is correct, label it *C*.

> **Example:** In recent years, some people have ~~standed~~ _stood_ up against overseas sweatshops.

(1) Buying products from overseas sweatshops has ~~became~~ _become_ controversial over the last few decades. (2) American manufacturers have ~~sended~~ _sent_ their materials to developing countries where employees work under terrible conditions for very low wages. (3) Violations of basic U.S. labor laws—such as using time cards, getting extra pay for overtime, and being paid on time—have ~~lead~~ _led_ to severe criticism. (4) Low-wage

ON THE WEB
For more practice, visit
Exercise Central *at*
*<bedfordstmartins.com/
writingfirst>.*

ESL Tip
After students have completed Practice 27-3, give them a correct version of the exercise. Have them copy the paragraph and then compare it with their own version.

Teaching Tip
Point out that some words
(such as *not, also, even,* and
hardly) can come between
the helping verb and the
past participle.

workers in developing countries have ~~finded~~ ^*found*^ dangerous working con-

ditions as well as verbal and sexual abuse. (5) Even well-known retail-

ers like Sears, Tommy Hilfiger, and Target have <u>gotten</u> ^*C*^ in trouble with

consumers when sweatshop-made items were found on their shelves.

(6) Recently, colleges have ~~be~~ ^*been*^ criticized for using overseas sweatshops

to make clothing and other items featuring school names. (7) Students

have ~~spoke~~ ^*spoken*^ out against such practices, and schools have <u>had</u> ^*C*^ to respond.

(8) While some manufacturers may have ~~losed~~ ^*lost*^ money by increasing

wages for overseas workers, they have ~~understanded~~ ^*understood*^ that this is the

right thing to do. (9) They have <u>made</u> ^*C*^ a promise to their customers

that they will not employ sweatshop labor. (10) Still, consumers

have not always ~~forgave~~ ^*forgiven*^ manufacturers who have a history of such

practices.

■ WRITING FIRST: Flashback

Look back at your response to the Writing First exercise on page
422, and identify each form of the helping verb *have* that is
followed by an irregular past participle. Then, write both the helping verb and the irregular past participle below.

Helping Verb	*Irregular Past Participle*
Answers will vary.	

C **Using the Present Perfect Tense**

The past participle can be used to form different verb tenses. For example,
the past participle can be combined with the present tense forms of *have*
to form the **present perfect tense**.

The Present Perfect Tense
(have or has + *past participle*)

Singular	**Plural**
I have gained.	We have gained.
You have gained.	You have gained.
He has gained.	They have gained.
She has gained.	
It has gained.	

As you have already learned, the **past tense** is used to indicate an action that began and ended in the past. The **present perfect tense** is used to indicate other past actions.

Use the present perfect tense to indicate an action that began in the past and continues into the present.

PRESENT PERFECT   The nurse <u>has worked</u> at the Welsh Mountain clinic for two years. (The working began in the past and continues into the present.)

Use the present perfect tense to indicate that an action has just occurred.

PRESENT PERFECT   I <u>have</u> just <u>eaten</u>. (The eating has just occurred.)

> ● **Writing Tip**
> The words *just, now, already,* and *recently* show that an action has just occurred.

◆ PRACTICE 27-4

Circle the appropriate verb tense (past tense or present perfect) from the choices in parentheses.

ON THE WEB
For more practice, visit Exercise Central *at* <*bedfordstmartins.com/ writingfirst*>.

Example: When I (visited, have visited) the city of Montreal, I was surprised to find that it is truly bilingual.

(1) I (came, have come) to other foreign cities expecting to hear a language other than English, but when I was in Montreal, I (heard, have heard) both English and French. (2) Montreal (kept, has kept) two languages as a result of its history. (3) Until 1763, Montreal (belonged, has belonged) to France. (4) Then, when France (lost, has lost) the Seven Years War, the city (became, has become) part of England. (5) When I was there last year, most people (spoke, have spoken) both French and English even though French is the official language. (6) Although I (knew, have known) no French, I (found, have found) that I was able to get along quite well. (7) For example, all the museums (made, have made) their guided tours available in English. (8) Most restaurants

(offered, have offered) bilingual menus. (9) There (were, have been) even English radio and television stations, as well as English newspapers. (10) In Montreal, I (felt, have felt) both at home and in a foreign country at the same time.

◆ PRACTICE 27-5

Fill in the appropriate verb tense (past tense or present perfect) of the verb in parentheses.

> **Example:** Most Americans _____*have had*_____ (have) a special interest in the results of presidential election polls.

(1) During the 2004 presidential campaign, at least eight different polls _____*measured*_____ (measure) people's views. (2) Until 1986, interviewers _____*knocked*_____ (knock) on doors to determine the opinions of randomly selected individuals. (3) More recently, public opinion polls _____*have used*_____ (use) the technique of random sampling, in which a computer randomly dials phone numbers taken from a national directory. (4) Using this technique, pollsters _____*have had*_____ (have) to interview only about one thousand people to get an accurate cross-section of the American people. (5) It _____*has taken*_____ (take) great skill for pollsters to learn to ask unbiased questions. (6) Gallup Poll interviewers _____*have asked*_____ (ask) one particular question since the time when Franklin D. Roosevelt was president: "Do you approve or disapprove of the job the president is doing?" (7) Using the same wording _____*has ensured*_____ (ensure) an accurate view of people's feelings about the president over the years. (8) Despite the care that pollsters take to provide an accurate view of public opinion, some people _____*have questioned*_____ (question) the strategy of random sampling. (9) Also, some worry that the wide publicity that polls _____*have received*_____ (receive) encourages some prospective voters to support the candidate who appears to be ahead. (10) Still, when Americans were asked recently to evaluate the accuracy of polls, most _____*said*_____ (say) that they forecast election results accurately.

■ **WRITING FIRST: Flashback**

Look back at your response to the Writing First exercise on page 422. Choose three sentences with past tense verbs, and rewrite them below, changing past tense to present perfect tense. How does your revision change the meaning of each sentence?

1. *Answers will vary.* _____

_____

_____

2. _____

_____

_____

3. _____

_____

_____

D Using the Past Perfect Tense

The past participle can also be used to form the **past perfect tense**, which consists of the past tense of *have* plus the past participle.

The Past Perfect Tense
(had + *past participle*)

Singular
I had returned.
You had returned.
He had returned.
She had returned.
It had returned.

Plural
We had returned.
You had returned.
They had returned.

Use the past perfect tense to show that an action occurred before another past action.

PAST PERFECT TENSE   PAST TENSE
Chief Sitting Bull had fought many battles before he defeated
General Custer.

This sentence identifies two actions that happened in the past—the fighting done by Sitting Bull and his defeat of Custer. The verb in the first part of the sentence (*had fought*) is in the past perfect tense. The verb in the second part of the sentence (*defeated*) is in the past tense. The use of the past perfect tense indicates that Sitting Bull's battles took place *before* he defeated Custer.

ON THE WEB

For more practice, visit
Exercise Central *at*
*<bedfordstmartins.com/
writingfirst>.*

◆ PRACTICE 27-6

Circle the appropriate verb tense (present perfect or past perfect) from the choices in parentheses.

Example: Although the children (have eaten/(had eaten)) dinner, they still had room for ice cream.

1. Ren wondered where he (has left/(had left)) his keys.

2. He now believes he ((has lost)/had lost) them.

3. The receptionist told the interviewer that the applicant (has arrived/ (had arrived)).

4. The interviewer says that she ((has waited)/had waited) for an hour.

5. The jury decided that the defendant (has lied/(had lied)) on the witness stand.

6. The jury members are still discussing the case although they ((have been)/had been) in the jury room for three days.

7. By the time I reached the restaurant, I (have decided/(had decided)) to order a pepperoni pizza.

8. By the time my pizza is ready, I usually ((have finished)/had finished) my pinball game.

9. The movie ((has been)/had been) on for only ten minutes when I turned it off.

10. This movie is excellent; I ((have seen)/had seen) it at least five times.

■ WRITING FIRST: Flashback

Look back at your response to the Flashback on page 431. Rewrite your three present perfect tense sentences on the following lines, this time changing them to the past perfect tense. How do your revisions change the meaning of each sentence?

(continued on the following page)

(continued from the previous page)

1. *Answers will vary.*
   _____
   _____
   _____

2. _____
   _____
   _____

3. _____
   _____

E   Using Past Participles as Adjectives

In addition to functioning as a verb, the past participle can function as an adjective after a **linking verb**—*be, seem, become,* and so on. In the following sentences, notice that the past participle acts as an adjective that describes the subject.

> Jason seemed <u>surprised</u>.

> He looked <u>shocked</u>.

The past participle can also function as an adjective before a noun.

> I cleaned up the <u>broken</u> glass.

> The <u>exhausted</u> runner finally crossed the finish line.

◆ PRACTICE 27-7

Edit the following passage for errors in past participle forms used as adjectives. Cross out any underlined participles that are incorrect, and write the correct form above them. If the participle form is correct, label it *C.*

Example: College students are often <u>strapped</u> for cash.   *C*

   (1) College students are <u>~~surprise~~</u> *surprised* when they find <u>~~preapprove~~</u> *preapproved* applications for credit cards in their mail. (2) Credit-card companies also recruit <u>targeted</u> *C* students through booths that are <u>~~locate~~</u> *located* near student unions and libraries. (3) The booths are <u>~~design~~</u> *designed* to attract new customers with offers of <u>~~inscribe~~</u> *inscribed* coffee mugs and tote bags. (4) Why have companies gone to all this effort to attract <u>qualified</u> *C* students? (5) Most older Americans already have at least five credit cards that are <u>~~stuff~~</u> *stuffed*

● **Writing Tip**

A linking verb—such as *seemed* or *looked*—connects a subject to the word that describes it. (See 15C.)

● **Writing Tip**

The passive voice is formed with the past participle and a form of the verb *to be: The article <u>was written</u> by my instructor.* Use the passive voice only when an action is more important than the person performing it. In all other cases, use the active voice: *My instructor <u>wrote</u> the article.* For more on changing a sentence from passive to active voice, see 24D.

Teaching Tip

Students often omit *-ed* endings in past participles because they do not pronounce them.

Teaching Tip

Refer students to 29A for more on the use of adjectives as modifiers.

in their billfolds. (6) Banks and credit-card companies see younger

college students as a major <u>untapped</u>ᶜ market. (7) According to experts,

students are also a good credit risk because ~~concern~~ *concerned* parents may

bail them out when they are not able to pay a bill. (8) Finally, people

tend to feel ~~tie~~ *tied* to their first credit card. (9) Companies want to be the

first card that is ~~acquire~~ *acquired* by a customer. (10) For this reason, it is a

<u>known</u>ᶜ fact that credit-card companies target ~~uninform~~ *uninformed* college students.

■ WRITING FIRST: Flashback

Look back at your response to the Writing First exercise on page 422. Choose three nouns you used in your writing, and list them in the right-hand column below. Then, think of a past participle that can modify each noun, and write the modifier in the left-hand column.

Past Participle   *Noun*

1. *Answers will vary.* _____   _____

2. _____   _____

3. _____   _____

      Now, use each of these nouns and its past participle modifier in an original sentence.

1. *Answers will vary.* _____

   _____

2. _____

   _____

3. _____

   _____

■ WRITING FIRST: Revising and Editing

Look back at your response to the Writing First exercise on page 422. Do you need to revise any sentences to add the correct present perfect and past perfect tense verb forms? If so, cross out the incorrect verb forms, and write your corrections above them. When you have finished, check the past participles and perfect tenses in another writing assignment on which you are currently working.

CHAPTER REVIEW

◆ EDITING PRACTICE

Read the following student essay, which includes errors in the use of past participles and the perfect tenses. Decide whether each of the underlined verbs or participles is correct. If it is correct, write *C* above it. If it is not, write in the correct verb form. The first error has been corrected for you.

Using the Internet to Get Out the Vote

The number of people who have ~~vote~~ *voted* in recent U.S.

elections has ~~drop~~ *dropped.* One factor is age. The younger a

person is, the less likely it is that he or she will vote.

Even though voting is very important, far too many young

people have not ~~took~~ *taken* part. Now, however, the Internet

has become *C* an essential way to reach voters, raise money

for election campaigns, and motivate young people.

Many businesses have ~~turn~~ *turned* to the Internet to reach

others, especially the young. Similarly, political

campaigns have ~~find~~ *found* that they can attract potential voters

and election workers by using the Internet. For example,

both Democrats and Republicans ~~had~~ *have* used email to persuade

voters to support candidates, and to provide vote-by-mail

ballots. At the same time, their Web sites and blogs

have ~~stimulate~~ *stimulated* interest in politics and have ~~provide~~ *provided* ways

for young people to meet each other and work for their

candidates.

For example, in 2004, Democrats ~~have wanted~~ *wanted* to

motivate young people to work and vote for John Kerry in

the presidential election. As a result, the Moveon.org site

has ~~organize~~ *organized* and ~~promote~~ *promoted* a tour of some popular musicians,

like Bruce Springsteen and the Dixie Chicks. It also sold *C*

anti-Bush T-shirts and bumper stickers with ironic slogans

like "4 More Wars." Similarly, GeorgeWBush.com ~~had offered~~ *offered*

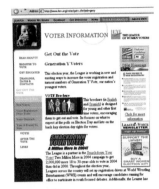

*League of Women Voters
Web site*

John Kerry Web site

young Republicans ways to use the Internet to create a pro-Bush poster, download pro-Bush screensavers, and shop for pro-Bush items at an online store. With such Web sites, the two main political parties have catched *caught* the interest of many young people.

In the recent past, many young Americans have not express *expressed* much interest in politics. However, their interest in the Internet has teached *taught* them about government and politics and has gave *given* them a new way to participate in the democratic process.

George W. Bush Web site

◆ COLLABORATIVE ACTIVITIES

1. Exchange Writing First exercises with another student. Read each other's work, making sure that present perfect and past perfect tenses are used correctly.

2. Assume that you are a restaurant employee who has been nominated for the prestigious Employee of the Year Award. To win this award (along with a thousand-dollar prize), you have to explain in writing what you have done during the past year to deserve this honor. Write a letter to your supervisor and the awards committee. When you have finished, trade papers with another student, and edit his or her letter. Read all the letters to the class, and have the class decide which is the most convincing.

Teaching Tip
Collaborative Activity 2 works well for getting students involved in a classroom discussion.

☑ REVIEW CHECKLIST:
Verbs: Past Participles

☐ The past participle of regular verbs is formed by adding *-ed* or *-d* to the base form. (See 27A.)

☐ Irregular verbs usually have irregular past participles. (See 27B.)

☐ The past participle can be used to form different verb tenses. For example, the past participle can be combined with the present tense forms of *have* to form the present perfect tense. It shows a continuing action, usually one that began in the past and continues into the present. (See 27C.)

☐ The past participle is also used to form the past perfect tense, which consists of the past tense of *have* plus the past participle. It describes an action that occurred before another past tense action. (See 27D.)

☐ The past participle can function as an adjective. (See 27E.)

Nouns and Pronouns

PREVIEW

In this chapter, you will learn

- to identify nouns (28A)

- to form plural nouns (28B)

- to identify pronouns (28C)

- to understand pronoun-antecedent agreement (28D)

- to solve special problems with pronoun-antecedent agreement (28E)

- to understand pronoun case (28F)

- to solve special problems with pronoun case (28G)

- to identify reflexive and intensive pronouns (28H)

■ WRITING FIRST

The picture above shows a scene from the TV show *The Simpsons*. Look at the picture, and then explain why you like a particular TV show, musician or group, or movie. Assume your readers are not familiar with the subject you are writing about.

A Identifying Nouns

A **noun** is a word that names a person *(singer, Jennifer Lopez),* an animal *(dolphin, Flipper),* a place *(downtown, Houston),* an object *(game, Scrabble),* or an idea *(happiness, Darwinism).*

A **singular noun** names one thing. A **plural noun** names more than one thing.

28 B

For information on capitalizing proper nouns, see 33A.

FOCUS **Common and Proper Nouns**

Most nouns, called **common nouns**, begin with lowercase letters.

character   holiday

Some nouns, called **proper nouns**, name particular people, animals, places, objects, or events. A proper noun always begins with a capital letter.

Homer Simpson   Labor Day

B **Forming Plural Nouns**

Most nouns add *-s* to form plurals. Other nouns, whose singular forms end in *-s*, *-ss*, *-sh*, *-ch*, *-x*, or *-z*, add *-es* to form plurals. Some nouns that end in *-s* or *-z* double the *s* or *z* before adding *-es*.

Singular	*Plural*
street	streets
gas	gases
class	classes
bush	bushes
church	churches
fox	foxes
quiz	quizzes

ESL Tip
Briefly review subject-verb agreement. Remind students that if the subject ends in *-s*, the verb usually does not. Refer students to Chapter 23.

Irregular Noun Plurals

Some nouns form plurals in unusual ways.

■ Nouns whose plural forms are the same as their singular forms

Singular	**Plural**
a deer	a few deer
this species	these species
a television series	two television series

■ Nouns ending in *-f* or *-fe*

Singular	**Plural**
each half	both halves
my life	our lives
a lone thief	a gang of thieves

ESL Tip
Tell students that they can sometimes tell whether a word is singular or plural by the word that introduces it. For example, *each* always introduces a singular noun, and *many* always introduces a plural noun. Refer students to 30E.

(continued on the following page)

(continued from the previous page)

Singular	Plural
one loaf	two loaves
the third shelf	several shelves

Familiar exceptions: *roof* (plural *roofs*), *proof* (plural *proofs*), *belief* (plural *beliefs)*

■ Nouns ending in -*y*

Singular	Plural
another baby	more babies
every worry	many worries

Note that when a vowel (*a, e, i, o, u*) comes before the *y*, the noun has a regular plural form: *monkey* (plural *monkeys*), *day* (plural *days*).

■ Hyphenated compound nouns

Singular	Plural
Lucia's sister-in-law	Lucia's two favorite sisters-in-law
a mother-to-be	twin mothers-to-be
the first runner-up	all the runners-up

■ Miscellaneous irregular plurals

Singular	Plural
that child	all children
a good man	a few good men
the woman	lots of women
my left foot	both feet
a wisdom tooth	my two front teeth
this bacterium	some bacteria

◆ PRACTICE 28-1

Next to each of the following singular nouns, write the plural form of the noun. Then, circle the irregular noun plurals.

Examples: bottle _____*bottles*_____   child _____(*children*)_____

1. headache ___*headaches*___

2. life ___(*lives*)___

3. foot ___(*feet*)___

4. chain ___*chains*___

5. deer ___(*deer*)___

6. honey ___*honeys*___

7. bride-to-be ___(*brides-to-be*)___

8. woman ___(*women*)___

9. loaf ___(*loaves*)___

10. kiss ___*kisses*___

11. beach ___*beaches*___

12. duty ___(*duties*)___

● **Writing Tip**

When a noun has an irregular plural, the dictionary lists its plural form.

13. son-in-law _____(sons-in-law)_____   17. elf _____(elves)_____

14. species _____(species)_____   18. tooth _____(teeth)_____

15. wife _____(wives)_____   19. catalog _____catalogs_____

16. city _____(cities)_____   20. patty _____(patties)_____

◆ **PRACTICE 28-2**

Proofread the underlined nouns in the following paragraph, checking to make sure singular and plural forms are correct. If a correction needs to be made, cross out the noun, and write the correct form above it. If the noun is correct, write **C** above it.

Example: Getting through security lines at ~~airportes~~ _airports_ has become difficult.

(1) Since September 11, 2001, ~~traveler-to-bes~~ _travelers-to-be_ need to think carefully about what they pack in their carry-on luggage. (2) All airlines have to protect the ~~lifes~~ _lives_ of the men _C_ and ~~woman~~ _women_ who fly on their planes. (3) On some days _C_, long ~~delayes~~ _delays_ in the security lines occur as screeners carry out their ~~dutys~~ _duties_. (4) Most people _C_ understand that they should never carry weapons and explosives onto a plane. (5) Immediately after the ~~attackes~~ _attacks_ on the World Trade Center, security ~~personnels~~ _personnel_ began to take away certain personal items _C_, like nail clippers and eyelash curlers, from passengers. (6) Now, these things are allowed, but it is still forbidden to bring sharp ~~tooles~~ _tools_ on board. (7) Vacationers who expect to go snorkeling can bring their ~~finz~~ _fins_ and ~~maskes~~ _masks_ into the cabin, but scuba divers must allow their dive ~~tankes~~ _tanks_ to be placed in the baggage ~~compartmentes~~ _compartments._ (8) Compressed ~~gasses~~ _gases_ in pressurized cylinders can be taken on board by scuba divers only if they are unsealed and can be inspected visually.

(9) Hunters must also think about how to transport their equipment: all firearms _C_ must be unloaded and checked in at the gate, and ~~boxs~~ _boxes_ of ammunition should be packed separately. (10) Most airlines allow two pieces _C_ of carry-on luggage, including ~~pursess~~ _purses,_ laptop ~~computeres~~ _computers,_ and briefcases _C_.

C   Identifying Pronouns

A **pronoun** is a word that refers to and takes the place of a noun or another pronoun.

> Michelle was really excited. She had finally found a job that made her happy. (*She* refers to *Michelle; her* refers to *she.*)

In the two sentences above, the pronouns *she* and *her* take the place of the noun *Michelle*.

Without pronouns, your sentences would be tedious and awkward because you would have to repeat the same nouns over and over again.

> Michelle was really excited. Michelle had finally found a job that made Michelle happy.

Pronouns, like nouns, can be singular or plural. The pronouns *I*, *he*, *she*, and *it* are always singular and take the place of singular nouns or pronouns.

> Geoff left his jacket at work, so he went back to get it before it could be stolen. (*He* refers to *Geoff; it* refers to *jacket.*)

The pronouns *we* and *they* are always plural and take the place of plural nouns or pronouns.

> Jessie and Dan got up early, but they still missed their train. (*They* refers to *Jessie and Dan; their* refers to *they.*)

The pronoun *you* can be either singular or plural.

> When the volunteers met the mayor, they said, "We really admire you." The mayor replied, "I admire you, too."

For lists of pronouns, see 28E, 28F, and 28H.

◆ PRACTICE 28-3

In the following sentences, fill in each blank with an appropriate pronoun.

Example: Whenever __*I*__ have hiccups, my parents have suggestions for how to get rid of them.

(1) First, my mother says that __I__ should relax. (2) __I__ answer that having hiccups is not exactly relaxing. (3) Next, my father tells me to stand on my head while __he__ pinches the back of my shoulders. (4) When that doesn't work, __they__ both offer to massage my eyeballs while __I__ keep my eyes closed. (5) Although __I__ have always turned down this offer, __it__ would be tempting to try __it__. (6) What harm could __it__ do? (7) My mother usually has another proposal; __she__ will help by blowing on my thumb while __I__ think of all the bald men that __I__ can. (8) Of course, after __I__ try this, __I__ am generally still hic-cupping. (9) Finally, my father will say, "__I__ give up; __you__ are just going to have the hiccups forever." (10) Fortunately, __he__ is always wrong; as soon as __I__ stop thinking about my hiccups, __they__ stop.

■ WRITING FIRST: Flashback

Look back at your response to the Writing First exercise on page 437. In the column on the left, list all the pronouns (*I, he, she, it, we, you, they*) you used. In the column on the right, list the noun or pronoun each pronoun takes the place of.

Pronoun	*Noun*
Answers will vary.	

D   **Understanding Pronoun-Antecedent Agreement**

The word that a pronoun refers to is called the pronoun's **antecedent**. In the following sentence, the noun *leaf* is the antecedent of the pronoun *it*.

The leaf turned yellow, but it did not fall.

Teaching Tip
Try to assign every Practice in 28D. Pronoun-antecedent agreement errors are very common in student writing.

A pronoun must always agree in **number** with its antecedent. If an antecedent is singular, as it is in the sentence above, the pronoun must be singular. If the antecedent is plural, as it is in the sentence below, the pronoun must also be plural.

The leaves turned yellow, but they did not fall.

Pronouns must also agree with their antecedents in **gender**. If an antecedent is feminine, the pronoun that refers to it must also be feminine.

Melissa passed her driver's exam with flying colors.

If an antecedent is masculine, the pronoun that refers to it must be masculine.

Matt wondered what courses he should take.

If an antecedent is **neuter** (neither masculine nor feminine), the pronoun that refers to it must also be neuter.

Lee's car broke down, but she refused to fix it again.

FOCUS **Vague Pronoun References**

A pronoun should always refer to a specific antecedent.

VAGUE   On the evening news, they said a baseball strike was inevitable.

REVISED   On the evening news, the sportscaster said a baseball strike was inevitable.

◆ **PRACTICE 28-4**

In the following sentences, circle the antecedent of each underlined pronoun. Then, draw an arrow from the pronoun to the antecedent it refers to.

ON THE WEB
For more practice, visit
Exercise Central at
<bedfordstmartins.com/
writingfirst>.

Example: College students today often fear they will be the victims of crime on campus.

(1) Few campuses are as safe as they should be, experts say. (2) However, crime on most campuses is probably no worse than it is in any other community. (3) Still, students have a right to know how safe their campuses are. (4) My friend Joyce never sets foot on campus without her can of Mace. (5) Joyce believes she must be prepared for the worst. (6) Her boyfriend attended a self-defense program that he said was very helpful.

(7) My friends do not let fear of crime keep them from enjoying the college experience. (8) We know that our school is doing all it can to provide a safe environment.

◆ PRACTICE 28-5

Fill in each blank in the following passage with an appropriate pronoun.

Example: Multiplexes are springing up everywhere; in many communities _they_ have replaced drive-ins.

(1) Drive-in movie theaters used to be common in the United States, but now _they_ are fairly rare. (2) In 1958, there were more than four thousand drive-ins across the country, but _they_ are seen far less often today. (3) One of the most amazing is the Thunderbird Drive-In in Ft. Lauderdale, Florida; _it_ has twelve different screens. (4) Owner Preston Henn says _it_ is the largest drive-in theater in the world. (5) _He_ opened the theater with only one screen in 1963. (6) _He_ also opened a flea market on the property. (7) _It_ is now one of the largest flea markets in the state, with over two thousand vendors. (8) The vendors think _they_ are getting a good deal, and so do moviegoers.

■ WRITING FIRST: Flashback

Look back at your response to the Writing First exercise on page 437. Underline each pronoun in your paragraph, circle its antecedent, and draw an arrow from each pronoun to its antecedent. Do all your pronouns agree in number and gender with their antecedents? If not, correct your pronouns.

E   **Solving Special Problems with Pronoun-Antecedent Agreement**

Certain situations present special problems with pronoun-antecedent agreement.

Compound Antecedents

A **compound antecedent** consists of two or more words connected by *and* or *or*. Compound antecedents connected by *and* are plural, and they are used with plural pronouns.

> During World War II, Belgium and France tried to protect their borders.

Compound antecedents connected by *or* may take a singular or a plural pronoun. When both elements of a compound antecedent connected by *or* are singular, use a singular pronoun to refer to the compound antecedent.

For information on subject-verb agreement with compound subjects, see 23A.

> Either a dog or a cat must have put its paw in the frosting.

When both elements are plural, use a plural pronoun.

> Are dogs or cats more loyal to their owners?

When one element of a compound antecedent connected by *or* is singular and one is plural, use the pronoun that agrees with the word closer to it.

> Is it possible that European nations or Russia may send its [not *their*] troops?

> Is it possible that Russia or European nations may send their [not *its*] troops?

◆ PRACTICE 28-6

In each of the following sentences, underline the compound antecedent, and circle the connecting word *(and* or *or)*. Then, circle the appropriate pronoun in parentheses.

Example: Groucho (and) Harpo were younger than (his/(their)) brother Chico.

1. Larry (and) Curly were younger than (his/(their)) partner Moe.

2. Either Chip (or) Dale has a stripe down ((his)/their) back.

3. Most critics believe Laurel (and) Hardy did (his/(their)) best work in silent comedies.

4. Lucy (and) Ethel never seem to learn (her/(their)) lesson.

5. Either *MASH* (or) *The Fugitive* had the highest ratings for any television show in ((its)/their) final episode.

6. Was it Francis Ford Coppola (or) Martin Scorcese who achieved the triumph of ((his)/their) career with *The Godfather?*

7. Either film (or) videotapes lose (its/(their)) clarity over time.

8. Either Tower or Blockbuster is having (its/their) grand opening today.

9. The popcorn and soft drinks here are expensive for (its/their) size.

10. Do comedies or dramas have a greater impact on (its/their) audiences?

Indefinite Pronoun Antecedents

Most pronouns refer to a specific person or thing. However, **indefinite pronouns** do not refer to any particular person or thing.

Most indefinite pronouns are singular.

> ### Singular Indefinite Pronouns
>
> | | | |
> |---|---|---|
> | another | everybody | no one |
> | anybody | everyone | nothing |
> | anyone | everything | one |
> | anything | much | somebody |
> | each | neither | someone |
> | either | nobody | something |

● **Writing Tip**

Some indefinite pronouns (such as *all, any, more, most, none,* and *some*) can be either singular or plural. (*All* is quiet. *All* were qualified.)

For information on subject-verb agreement with indefinite pronouns, see 23D.

When an indefinite pronoun antecedent is singular, use a singular pronoun to refer to it.

Everything was in <u>its</u> place. (*Everything* is singular, so it is used with the singular pronoun *its*.)

> **FOCUS** **Indefinite Pronouns with *Of***
>
> The singular indefinite pronouns *each, either, neither,* and *one* are often used in phrases with *of*—*each of, either of, neither of,* or *one of*— followed by a plural noun. Even in such phrases, these indefinite pronoun antecedents are always singular and take singular pronouns.
>
> Each of the routes has <u>its</u> [not *their*] own special challenges.

ESL Tip
Remind students that singular indefinite pronouns do not have plural forms.

A few indefinite pronouns are plural.

> ### Plural Indefinite Pronouns
>
> both
> few
> many
> others
> several

When an indefinite pronoun antecedent is plural, use a plural pronoun to refer to it.

They all wanted to graduate early, but few received their diplomas in January. (*Few* is plural, so it is used with the plural pronoun *their.*)

FOCUS **Using *His or Her* with Indefinite Pronouns**

Even though the indefinite pronouns *anybody, anyone, everybody, everyone, somebody, someone,* and so on are singular, many people use plural pronouns to refer to them.

Everyone must hand in their completed work before 2 P.M.

This usage is widely accepted in spoken English. Nevertheless, indefinite pronouns like *everyone* are singular, and written English requires a singular pronoun.

Although using the singular pronoun *his* to refer to *everyone* is technically correct, doing so assumes that *everyone* refers to an individual who is male. Using *his or her* allows for the possibility that the indefinite pronoun may refer to either a male or a female.

Everyone must hand in his or her completed work before 2 P.M.

When used repeatedly, however, *he or she, him or her,* and *his or her* can create wordy or awkward sentences. Whenever possible, use plural forms.

All students must hand in their completed work before 2 P.M.

◆ PRACTICE 28-7

In the following sentences, first circle the indefinite pronoun. Then, circle the pronoun in parentheses that refers to the indefinite pronoun antecedent.

Example: (Each) of the artists will have (his or her/their) own exhibit.

1. (Either) of those paintings will be sold with (its/their) frame.

2. (Each) of the artist's brushes has (its/their) own use.

3. (Everything) in the room made (its/their) contribution to the whole design.

4. (Everyone) must remember to take (his or her/their) paint box.

5. (Neither) of my sisters wanted (her/their) picture displayed.

6. (Many) of the men brought (his/their) children to the exhibit.

7. (Several) of the colors must be mixed with (its/their) contrasting colors.

8. When (someone) compliments your work, be sure to tell (him or her/them) that it is for sale.

9. (Anyone) can improve (his or her/their) skills as an artist.

10. (Both) of these workrooms have (its/their) own advantages.

◆ **PRACTICE 28-8**

Edit the following sentences for errors in pronoun-antecedent agreement. When you edit, you have two options: either substitute *his or her* for *their* to refer to the singular antecedent, or replace the singular antecedent with a plural word.

Examples:

Everyone will be responsible for ~~their~~ *his or her* own transportation.

All
~~Each of~~ the children took their books out of their backpacks.

Answers may vary.
1. Everyone has the right to ~~their~~ *his or her* own opinion.

All students
2. ~~Everyone~~ can eat their lunches in the cafeteria.

3. Somebody forgot ~~their~~ *his or her* backpack.

All
4. ~~Each of~~ the patients had their own rooms, with their own televisions and their own private baths.

5. Someone in the store has left ~~their~~ *his or her* car's lights on.

6. Simone keeps everything in her kitchen in ~~their~~ *its* own little container.

7. Each of the applicants must have ~~their~~ *his or her* driver's license.

8. Anybody who has ever juggled a job and children knows how valuable ~~their~~ *his or her* free time can be.

9. Either of the coffeemakers comes with ~~their~~ *its* own filter.

Most people wait
10. ~~Almost everyone waits~~ until the last minute to file their income tax returns.

● **Writing Tip**

Plural forms of collective nouns (*bands, teams*) take plural pronouns. (*The bands played their best tunes.*)

Collective Noun Antecedents

Collective nouns are words (like *band* and *team*) that name a group of people or things but are singular. Because they are singular, collective noun antecedents are used with singular pronouns.

The band played on, but <u>it</u> never played our song.

Frequently Used Collective Nouns			
army	club	gang	mob
association	committee	government	posse
band	company	group	team
class	family	jury	union

◆ PRACTICE 28-9

Circle the collective noun antecedent in the following sentences. Then, circle the correct pronoun in parentheses.

Example: The (jury) returned with ((its)/their) verdict.

1. The (company) offers generous benefits to ((its)/their) employees.

2. All five study (groups) are supposed to hand in (its/(their)) projects by Tuesday.

3. Any (government) should be concerned for the welfare of ((its)/their) citizens.

4. The Asian Students (Union) is sponsoring a party to celebrate ((its)/their) twentieth anniversary.

5. Every (family) has ((its)/their) share of problems.

6. To join the electricians' (union), applicants had to pass ((its)/their) test.

7. Even the best (teams) have (its/(their)) off days.

8. The (orchestra) has just signed a contract to make ((its)/their) first recording.

9. The math (class) did very well with ((its)/their) new teacher.

10. The (club) voted to expand ((its)/their) membership.

◆ PRACTICE 28-10

Edit the following passage for correct pronoun-antecedent agreement. First, circle the antecedent of each underlined pronoun. Then, cross out any pronoun that does not agree with its antecedent, and write the correct form above it. If the pronoun is correct, write **C** above it.

Example: The history of woman suffrage in the United States shows

that (women) were determined to achieve ~~her~~ *their* equal rights.

> ● **Writing Tip**
>
> Note that antecedents may be compounds, indefinite pronouns, or collective nouns.

(1) Before 1920, most American (women) were not allowed to vote
for the candidates they [C] preferred. (2) Men ran the government, and (a
woman) could not express their [her] views at the ballot box. (3) However, in
the mid-1800s, (women) began to demand her [their] right to vote—or "woman
suffrage." (4) Supporters of woman suffrage believed (everyone) regardless of their [his or her] gender, should be able to vote. (5) At the first woman suffrage
convention, (Elizabeth Cady Stanton and Lucretia Mott) gave speeches
explaining his or her [their] views. (6) Susan B. Anthony started the National
Woman Suffrage Association, which opposed the (Fifteenth Amendment)
to the Constitution because it [C] gave the vote to black men but not to
women. (7) The first state to permit (women) to vote was Wyoming, and
then other states became more friendly to her [their] cause. (8) Many (women)
called themselves "suffragettes" and participated in marches where he
or she [they] carried banners and posters for their [C] cause. (9) During World
War I, (the U.S. government) found that the cooperation of women was
essential to their [its] military success. (10) Finally, in 1919, (the House of
Representatives and the states) gave its [their] approval to the Nineteenth
Amendment, which gave American women the right to vote.

■ WRITING FIRST: Flashback

Look back at your response to the Writing First exercise on page 437.
Does your paragraph contain any antecedents that are compounds,
indefinite pronouns, or collective nouns? If so, list them below.

Compounds	Indefinite Pronouns	Collective Nouns
Answers will vary.		

Have you used the correct pronoun to refer to each of these antecedents? If not, correct your pronouns.

F **Understanding Pronoun Case**

A **personal pronoun** refers to a particular person or thing. Personal pronouns change form according to the way they function in a sentence. Personal pronouns can be *subjective, objective,* or *possessive.*

Personal Pronouns

Subjective Case	Objective Case	Possessive Case
I	me	my, mine
he	him	his
she	her	her, hers
it	it	its
we	us	our, ours
you	you	your, yours
they	them	their, theirs
who	whom	whose
whoever	whomever	

Subjective Case

When a pronoun functions as a sentence's subject, it is in the **subjective case**.

Finally, <u>she</u> realized that dreams could come true.

Objective Case

When a pronoun functions as an object, it is in the **objective case**.

If Joanna hurries, she can stop <u>him</u>. (The pronoun *him* is the direct object of the verb *can stop*.)

Professor Miller sent <u>us</u> information about his research. (The pronoun *us* is the indirect object of the verb *sent*.)

Marc threw the ball to <u>them</u>. (The pronoun *them* is the object of the preposition *to*.)

FOCUS **Objects**

A **direct object** is a noun or pronoun to which the verb's action is directed.

DIRECT OBJECT
What did I send yesterday? I sent a <u>fax</u> yesterday.

DIRECT OBJECT
Whom will I call today? I'll call <u>him</u> today.

(continued on the following page)

> *(continued from the previous page)*
>
> An **indirect object** is the noun or pronoun that tells to whom or for whom the verb's action was done.
>
> INDIRECT OBJECT
>
> To whom did I send a fax? I sent <u>Adam</u> a fax.
>
> INDIRECT OBJECT
>
> To whom did I give money? I gave <u>her</u> money.
>
> A word or word group introduced by a preposition is called the **object of the preposition**. (See 15B.)
>
> OBJECT OF PREPOSITION
>
> From what did she run? She ran from the <u>fire</u>.
>
> OBJECT OF PREPOSITION
>
> For whom did Kelly work? Kelly worked for <u>them</u>.

Possessive Case

When a pronoun shows ownership, it is in the **possessive case**.

> Hieu took <u>his</u> lunch to the meeting. (The pronoun *his* indicates that the lunch belongs to Hieu.)
>
> Debbie and Kim decided to take <u>their</u> lunches, too. (The pronoun *their* indicates that the lunches belong to Debbie and Kim.)

◆ PRACTICE 28-11

Teaching Tip
Tell your students that they may consult the chart on page 451.

In the following passage, fill in the blank after each pronoun to indicate whether the pronoun is subjective (**S**), objective (**O**), or possessive (**P**).

Example: Famous criminals Bonnie Parker and Clyde Barrow committed their __*P*__ crimes during the Great Depression.

(1) With their __*P*__ gang, Bonnie and Clyde robbed a dozen banks, as well as many stores and gas stations, between 1932 and 1934. (2) In small towns, they __*S*__ terrorized the police; capturing them __*O*__ seemed impossible. (3) To many Americans, however, their __*P*__ crimes seemed exciting. (4) Many people resented the greed of big business, and they __*S*__ believed Bonnie and Clyde were striking back at it __*O*__. (5) The fact that a woman was in the gang made it __*O*__ especially fascinating. (6) During their __*P*__ crimes, they __*S*__ would often carry a camera, take photographs of themselves, and send them __*O*__ to the

newspapers, which were happy to publish them __O__. (7) Bonnie wrote a poem about their __P__ exploits and the brutal end that she __S__ knew was ahead of them __O__; it __S__ was also published in the newspapers. (8) Both of them __O__ knew that, if caught, they __S__ would be executed. (9) By the time they __S__ were killed in an ambush by Texas and Louisiana law officers, Bonnie and Clyde were famous all over the United States. (10) They __S__ were the first celebrity criminals.

■ WRITING FIRST: Flashback

Look back at your response to the Writing First exercise on page 437. On the following lines, list all the personal pronouns you have used, classifying them as subjective, objective, or possessive.

Subjective	*Objective*	*Possessive*
_____	_____	_____
_____	_____	_____
_____	_____	_____

Have you used correct pronoun case in every sentence? Make any necessary corrections.

G   Solving Special Problems with Pronoun Case

When you are trying to determine which pronoun case to use, three kinds of pronouns can cause problems: pronouns in compounds, pronouns in comparisons, and the pronouns *who* and *whom*.

Pronouns in Compounds

Sometimes a pronoun is linked to a noun or to another pronoun with *and* or *or* to form a **compound**.

> The teacher and I met for an hour.

> She and I had a good meeting.

To determine whether to use the subjective or objective case for a pronoun in a compound, follow the same rules that apply for a pronoun that is not part of a compound.

● **Writing Tip**

The first-person pronoun always comes last in compounds like *Toby and I* and *My father and me*.

Teaching Tip

Explain that the objective case is used with the contraction *let's*: *Let's (let us) you and me* (not *I*) *go swimming*. Remind students that *let's* includes the objective case pronoun *us*.

Teaching Tip

You may want to have students do Practice 28-12 (page 455) before moving on to the next section.

● **Writing Tip**

To decide whether to use the subjective or objective form of a pronoun, add in brackets the words needed to complete the comparison.

■ If the compound in which the pronoun appears is the sentence's subject, use the subjective case.

Toby and I [not *me*] like jazz.

He and I [not *me*] went to the movies.

■ If the compound in which the pronoun appears is the object of the verb or the object of a preposition, use the objective case.

The school sent my father and me [not *I*] the financial aid forms.

This fight is between her and me [not *I*].

FOCUS **Choosing Pronouns in Compounds**

To determine which pronoun case to use in a compound that joins a noun and a pronoun, rewrite the sentence with just the pronoun.

Toby and [*I* or *me?*] like jazz.

I like jazz. (not *Me like jazz*)

Toby and I like jazz.

Pronouns in Comparisons

Sometimes a pronoun appears after the word *than* or *as* in a **comparison**.

John is luckier than I.

The inheritance changed Raymond as much as her.

■ If the pronoun is a subject, use the subjective case.

John is luckier than I [am].

■ If the pronoun is an object, use the objective case.

The inheritance changed Raymond as much as [it changed] her.

FOCUS **Choosing Pronouns in Comparisons**

Sometimes the pronoun you use can change your sentence's meaning. For example, if you say, "I like Cheerios more than he," you mean that you like Cheerios more than the other person likes them.

I like Cheerios more than he [does].

(continued on the following page)

(continued from the previous page)

If, however, you say, "I like Cheerios more than him," you mean that you like Cheerios more than you like the other person.

I like Cheerios more than [I like] him.

Teaching Tip
You may want to have students do Practice 28-13 (page 456) before moving on to the next section.

The Pronouns *Who* and *Whom, Whoever* and *Whomever*

To determine whether to use *who* or *whom* (or *whoever* or *whomever*), you need to know how the pronoun functions within the clause in which it appears.

■ When the pronoun is the subject of the clause, use *who* or *whoever*.

I wonder <u>who</u> wrote that song. *(Who is the subject of the clause who wrote that song.)*

I will vote for <u>whoever</u> supports the youth center. *(Whoever is the subject of the clause whoever supports the youth center.)*

■ When the pronoun is the object, use *whom* or *whomever.*

<u>Whom</u> do the police suspect? *(Whom is the direct object of the verb suspect.)*

I wonder <u>whom</u> the song is about. *(Whom is the object of the preposition about in the clause whom the song is about.)*

Vote for <u>whomever</u> you prefer. *(Whomever is the object of the verb prefer in the clause whomever you prefer.)*

● **Writing Tip**
In conversation, people often use *who* for both subjective case (<u>Who</u> wrote that song?) and objective case (<u>Who</u> are you going with?). In writing, always use *whom* for the objective case: With <u>whom</u> are you going?

FOCUS *Who* and *Whom*

To determine whether to use *who* or *whom*, try substituting another pronoun for *who* or *whom* in the clause. If you can substitute *he* or *she,* use *who;* if you can substitute *him* or *her,* use *whom.*

[Who/Whom] wrote a love song? <u>He</u> wrote a love song.

[Who/<u>Whom</u>] was the song about? The song was about <u>her</u>.

The same test will work for *whoever* and *whomever.*

◆ PRACTICE 28-12

In the following sentences, the underlined pronouns are part of compound constructions. Check them for correct subjective or objective case. If a correction needs to be made, cross out the pronoun, and write the correct form above it. If the pronoun is correct, write **C** above it.

Example: My sister and ~~me~~ heard a strange sound one night last year.

ON THE WEB
For more practice, visit Exercise Central *at* <bedfordstmartins.com/ writingfirst>.

(1) Julia and I̲ [*C*] were about to go to sleep when we heard eerie howls.
(2) At first, we thought that our mom and dad had forgotten to turn off
the television, but then we remembered that ~~him~~ [*he*] and ~~her~~ [*she*] had gone away
for the weekend. (3) Alone in the house, Julia and me [*I*] were in a panic.
(4) Deciding what to do was up to ~~she~~ [*her*] and ~~I.~~ [*me.*] (5) We considered calling
911, but we thought the police wouldn't believe us if we said that strange
howls had been heard by my sister and me [*C*]. (6) ~~Them~~ [*They*] and the 911 oper-
ators might just think that Julia and me [*I*] were playing a trick on them.
(7) Finally, we decided to wait until morning, when ~~her~~ [*she*] and me [*I*] would
be able to figure out what had frightened her [*C*] and ~~I.~~ [*me.*] (8) During the night,
we remembered that our cat Annie and her kitten, Sam, were out-
side, and we began to worry about ~~she~~ [*her*] and ~~he.~~ [*him.*] (9) The next morning, we
found traces of blood and scraps of fur in our backyard, but we never
found ~~she~~ [*her*] and her kitten. (10) Now we suspect that coyotes had been
prowling around our neighborhood and that ~~them~~ [*they*] or other wild animals
may have carried off our pets.

◆ PRACTICE 28-13

Each of the following sentences includes a comparison with a pronoun
following the word *than* or *as*. Write in each blank the correct form (subjective or objective) of the pronoun in parentheses. In brackets, add the
word or words needed to complete the comparison.

> **Example:** Many people are better poker players than ___*I [am]*___
> (I/me).

1. Denzel Washington has received more awards than ___*she [has]*___
   (she/her).

2. The survey showed that most people like the incumbent as much as
   ___*[they like] him*___ (he/him).

3. No one enjoys shopping more than ___*she [does]*___ (she/her).

4. My brother and our Aunt Cecile were very close. Her death affected
   him more than ___*[it affected] me*___ (I/me).

5. No two people could have a closer relationship than ___*they [have]*___
   (they/them).

6. My neighbor drives better than _____I [drive]_____ (I/me).

7. We at Steer Hut serve juicier steaks than _____they [serve]_____ (they/them) at Steak 'n Sizzle.

8. He may be as old as _____I [am]_____ (I/me), but he does not have as much work experience.

9. That jacket fits you better than _____[it fits] me_____ (I/me).

10. The other company had a lower bid than _____we [did]_____ (we/us), but we were awarded the contract.

◆ PRACTICE 28-14

Circle the correct form of *who* or *whom* (or *whoever* or *whomever*) in parentheses in each sentence.

Example: With (who/<u>whom</u>) did Rob collaborate?

1. The defense team learned (<u>who</u>/whom) was going to testify for the prosecution.

2. (Who/<u>Whom</u>) does she think she can find to be a witness?

3. I think the runner (<u>who</u>/whom) crosses the finish line first will be the winner.

4. They will argue their case to (<u>whoever</u>/whomever) will listen.

5. It will take time to decide (<u>who</u>/whom) the record holder is.

6. Take these forms to the clerk (<u>who</u>/whom) is at the front desk.

7. We will have to penalize (<u>whoever</u>/whomever) misses the first training session.

8. (Who/<u>Whom</u>) did Kobe take to the prom?

9. We saw the man (<u>who</u>/whom) fired the shots.

10. To (who/<u>whom</u>) am I speaking?

■ WRITING FIRST: Flashback

Look back at your response to the Writing First exercise on page 437. Can you find any sentences that contain a pronoun used in a

(continued on the following page)

(continued from the previous page)

compound or a comparison? If so, write the sentences here, making sure to use the appropriate pronoun case.

Answers will vary.

_____

_____

Circle any uses of *who* and *whom*. Have you used these pronouns correctly?

H   Identifying Reflexive and Intensive Pronouns

Two special kinds of pronouns, *reflexive pronouns* and *intensive pronouns,* also always agree with their antecedents in person and number. Although the functions of the two kinds of pronouns are different, their forms are identical.

Reflexive and Intensive Pronouns

Singular Forms

Antecedent	*Reflexive or Intensive Pronoun*
I	myself
you	yourself
he	himself
she	herself
it	itself

Plural Forms

Antecedent	*Reflexive or Intensive Pronoun*
we	ourselves
you	yourselves
they	themselves

Reflexive Pronouns

Reflexive pronouns always end in *-self* (singular) or *-selves* (plural). They indicate that people or things did something to themselves or for themselves.

Rosanna lost <u>herself</u> in the novel.

You need to watch <u>yourself</u> when you mix those solutions.

Mehul and Paul made <u>themselves</u> cold drinks.

Intensive Pronouns

Intensive pronouns also end in *-self* or *-selves*. However, they always appear directly after their antecedents, and they are used for emphasis.

I <u>myself</u> have had some experience in sales and marketing.

The victim <u>himself</u> collected the reward.

They <u>themselves</u> were uncertain of the significance of their findings.

◆ PRACTICE 28-15

Fill in the correct reflexive or intensive pronoun in each of the following sentences.

ON THE WEB
For more practice, visit **Exercise Central** *at* *<bedfordstmartins.com/ writingfirst>.*

Example: The opening act was exciting, but the main attraction _____*itself*_____ was boring.

1. My aunt welcomed her visitors and told them to make _____*themselves*_____ at home.

2. Mysteriously, migrating birds can direct _____*themselves*_____ through clouds, storms, and moonless nights.

3. The First Lady _____*herself*_____ gave a speech at the political rally.

4. We all finished the marathon without injuring _____*ourselves*_____.

5. Even though the government offered help to people who lived in the flooded areas, the homeowners _____*themselves*_____ did most of the rebuilding.

6. Sometimes he finds _____*himself*_____ daydreaming in class.

7. The guide warned us to watch _____*ourselves*_____ because the path was slippery.

8. The senators were not happy about committing _____*themselves*_____ to vote for the plan to lower taxes.

9. She gave _____*herself*_____ a manicure.

10. Although everyone else in my family can sing or play a musical instrument, I _____*myself*_____ am tone deaf.

■ WRITING FIRST: Flashback

Look back at your response to the Writing First exercise on page
437. Have you used any reflexive or intensive pronouns? If so, list
them here.

Reflexive pronouns: _____

Intensive pronouns: _____

If not, write two new sentences, one using a reflexive pronoun and
one using an intensive pronoun.

■ WRITING FIRST: Revising and Editing

Look back at your response to the Writing First exercise on page
437. Change every singular noun to a plural noun and every plural
noun to a singular noun. Then, edit your pronouns so singular pronouns refer to singular nouns and plural pronouns refer to plural
nouns. You might also do this exercise with a piece of writing you
did for another class.

CHAPTER REVIEW

◆ EDITING PRACTICE

Read the following student essay, which includes noun and pronoun errors. Check for errors in plural noun forms, pronoun case, and pronoun-
antecedent agreement. Then, make any editing changes you think are
necessary. The first sentence has been edited for you.

Cell Phone Misbehavior

Good ~~manneres~~ *manners* used to mean using the right fork and

holding the door open for others. Today, however, people

may find that good manners are more complicated than ~~it~~ *they*

used to be. New inventions have led to new challenges. Cell

phones, in particular, have created problems. As a cell-

phone user, I admit that I sometimes forget my manners *myself*

~~myself.~~ I am not alone.

One problem is the "cell yell," which is the tendency

of ~~a person~~ *people* to shout while they are using their cell

phones. Why do we do this? Maybe we do not realize how

loud we are talking. Maybe we yell out of frustration. All

cell-phone users can become angry when they lose a call.

Dead ~~batterys~~ *batteries* can be infuriating. Unfortunately, ~~the yeller~~ *yellers*

can annoy everyone around them.

Even if ~~the~~ cell-phone ~~user theirselves~~ *users themselves* speak normally,

other people can hear. Don't people like ~~I~~ *me* know this? We

do, but we forget. ~~Me and my~~ *My* friends *and I* are always calling

each other, and we do not always pay attention to ~~whom~~ *who* can

hear us. The result is that other people are victims of

secondhand conversations. These are not as bad for their

health as secondhand smoke, but they are just as annoying.

~~Whom~~ *Who* really wants to hear about the private ~~lifes~~ *lives* of

strangers? Public restrooms used to be ~~a place~~ *places* of privacy;

now, ~~whomever~~ *whoever* is in the next stall can overhear someone's

private conversation.

Also, some cell-phone ~~user~~ *users* seem to think that getting

~~his~~ *their* calls is more important than anything else that might

be going on. We hear phones ringing, chirping, or playing

silly tunes at ~~concertes,~~ *concerts,* in classrooms, at weddings, in

~~churchs,~~ *churches,* and even at funerals. Can you picture a grieving

family at a cemetery having ~~their~~ *its* service interrupted

by a ringing phone? People should not have to be told to

turn off their cell phones at times like these.

In the United States, there are more than 150 million

cell phones. Many people hate their cell phones, but they

do not think they can live without ~~it.~~ *them.* The problem is that

cell phones became popular before there were any rules for

using ~~it.~~ *them.* However, if the government passed laws about

cell-phone behavior, ~~they~~ *it* would have a tough time enforcing

~~it.~~ *them.* It seems obvious that those of us who use cell phones

should not need laws to make us behave ~~ourself~~ *ourselves* and use

ordinary courtesy.

Cell phone

Woman on cell phone

◆ COLLABORATIVE ACTIVITIES

1. Working in a group, fill in the following chart, writing one noun on each line. If the noun is a proper noun, be sure to capitalize it.

Cars	Trees	Foods	Famous Couples	Cities
Answers will vary.				

Now, using as many of the nouns listed above as you can, write a one-paragraph news article that describes an imaginary event. Exchange your work with another group, and check the other group's article to be sure the correct pronoun refers to each noun. Return the articles to their original groups for editing.

2. Working in a group, write a silly story that uses each of these nouns at least once: *Martians, eggplant, MTV, toupee, kangaroo, Iceland, bat, herd,* and *kayak.* Then, exchange stories with another group. After you have read the other group's story, edit it so that it includes all of the following pronouns: *it, its, itself, they, their, them, themselves.* Return the edited story to its authors. Finally, reread your group's story, and check to make sure pronoun-antecedent agreement is clear and correct.

☑ **REVIEW CHECKLIST:**

Nouns and Pronouns

▢ A noun is a word that names something. A singular noun names one thing; a plural noun names more than one thing. (See 28A.)

▢ Most nouns add *-s* to form plurals. Some nouns have irregular plural forms. (See 28B.)

▢ A pronoun is a word that refers to and takes the place of a noun or another pronoun. (See 28C.)

▢ The word a pronoun refers to is called the pronoun's antecedent. A pronoun and its antecedent must always agree in number and gender. (See 28D.)

(continued on the following page)

(continued from the previous page)

- Compound antecedents connected by *and* are plural and are used with plural pronouns. Compound antecedents connected by *or* may take singular or plural pronouns. (See 28E.)

- Most indefinite pronoun antecedents are singular and are used with singular pronouns; some are plural and are used with plural pronouns. (See 28E.)

- Collective noun antecedents are singular and are used with singular pronouns. (See 28E.)

- Personal pronouns can be in the subjective, objective, or possessive case. (See 28F.)

- Pronouns present special problems when they are used in compounds and comparisons. The pronouns *who* and *whom* and *whoever* and *whomever* can also cause problems. (See 28G.)

- Reflexive and intensive pronouns must agree with their antecedents in person and number. (See 28H.)

CHAPTER 29

Adjectives and Adverbs

PREVIEW

In this chapter, you will learn

- to understand the difference between adjectives and adverbs (29A)

- to identify demonstrative adjectives (29A)

- to form comparatives and superlatives of adjectives and adverbs (29B)

Word Power

tutor a private instructor

extracurricular outside the regular course of study

socialize to make fit for companionship with others

cohort a group united by common experiences

■ WRITING FIRST

The picture above shows children being home schooled by their mother. Look at the picture, and then write about the advantages and disadvantages of being educated at home by parents or other relatives instead of at school by professional teachers.

A Identifying Adjectives and Adverbs

Adjectives and adverbs are words that modify—that is, describe or limit—other words. They help make sentences more specific and more interesting.

An **adjective** answers the question *What kind? Which one?* or *How many?* Adjectives modify nouns or pronouns.

464

The Turkish city of Istanbul spans two continents. (*Turkish* modifies the noun *city,* and *two* modifies the noun *continents.*)

It is fascinating because of its location and history. (*Fascinating* modifies the pronoun *it.*)

● **Writing Tip**

Some adjectives, such as *Turkish,* are capitalized because they are formed from proper nouns. Proper nouns name particular people, places, and things. For more on proper nouns, see 28A.

FOCUS **Demonstrative Adjectives**

Demonstrative adjectives—*this, that, these,* and *those*—do not describe other words. They simply identify particular nouns.

This and *that* identify singular nouns and pronouns.

This Web site is much more up-to-date than that one.

These and *those* identify plural nouns.

These words and phrases are French, but those expressions are Creole.

An **adverb** answers the question *How? Why? When? Where?* or *To what extent?* Adverbs modify verbs, adjectives, or other adverbs.

Traffic moved steadily. (*Steadily* modifies the verb *moved.*)

Still, we were quite impatient. (*Quite* modifies the adjective *impatient.*)

Very slowly, we moved into the center lane. (*Very* modifies the adverb *slowly.*)

FOCUS **Distinguishing Adjectives from Adverbs**

Many adverbs are formed when *-ly* is added to an adjective form.

Adjective	Adverb
slow	slowly
nice	nicely
quick	quickly
real	really

(continued on the following page)

● **Writing Tip**

Some adjectives—*lovely, friendly,* and *lively,* for example—end in *-ly.* Do not mistake these words for adverbs.

> *(continued from the previous page)*
>
> ADJECTIVE   Let me give you one quick reminder. *(Quick modifies the noun reminder.)*
>
> ADVERB   He quickly changed the subject. *(Quickly modifies the verb changed.)*
>
> ADJECTIVE   Tell me your real name. *(Real modifies the noun name.)*
>
> ADVERB   It was really rude of her to ignore me. *(Really modifies the adjective rude.)*

ON THE WEB
For more practice, visit
Exercise Central *at*
<bedfordstmartins.com/ writingfirst>.

◆ PRACTICE 29-1

In the following sentences, circle the correct form (adjective or adverb) from the choices in parentheses.

Example: Women who are (*serious*/seriously) walkers or runners need to wear athletic shoes that fit.

(1) Doctors have found that many athletic shoes are (poor/*poorly*) designed for women. (2) Women's athletic shoes are actual/(*actually*) just smaller versions of men's shoes. (3) Consequently, they cannot provide a (true/*truly*) comfortable fit. (4) Studies have shown that to get a shoe that fits (comfortable/*comfortably*) in the heel, most women must buy one that is too (*tight*/tightly) for the front of the foot. (5) This can have a (real/*really*) negative impact on athletic performance. (6) It can also cause (*serious*/seriously) pain and even physical deformity. (7) Some athletic shoe manufacturers now market athletic shoes that are designed (specific/*specifically*) for women. (8) Experts say that women must become informed consumers and choose (careful/*carefully*) when they shop for athletic shoes. (9) One (*important*/importantly) piece of advice is to shop for shoes (immediate/*immediately*) after exercising or at the end of a work day, when the foot is at its largest. (10) Experts advise that athletic shoes should feel (*comfortable*/comfortably) from the moment they are tried on—or else be returned to the box.

Teaching Tip
Explain that a linking verb such as *feel* is followed by an adjective, not an adverb. Refer students to 15C.

FOCUS *Good and Well*

Be careful not to confuse *good* and *well*. Unlike regular adjectives, whose adverb form adds *-ly*, the adjective *good* is irregular. Its adverb form is *well*.

ADJECTIVE Fred Astaire was a good dancer. (*Good* modifies the noun *dancer.*)

ADVERB He danced especially well with Ginger Rogers. (*Well* modifies the verb *danced.*)

Always use *well* when you are describing a person's health.

He really didn't feel well [not *good*] after eating an entire pizza.

◆ PRACTICE 29-2

Circle the correct form (*good* or *well*) in the sentences below.

Example: It can be hard for some people to find a (good/well) job that they really like.

(1) They may not do (good/well) sitting in an office. (2) Instead, they prefer to use the (good/well) physical condition of their bodies in their work. (3) Such people might consider becoming smoke jumpers—firefighters who are (good/well) at parachuting into remote areas to battle forest fires. (4) Dropped from small planes as low as fifteen hundred feet in altitude, they must be able to work (good/well) even without much sleep. (5) Smoke jumpers must also handle danger (good/well). (6) They look forward to the (good/well) feeling of saving a forest or someone's home. (7) As they battle fires, surrounded by smoke and fumes, smoke jumpers may not feel very (good/well). (8) Sometimes, things go wrong; for example, when their parachutes fail to work (good/well), jumpers may be injured or even killed. (9) Smoke jumpers do not get paid (good/well). (10) However, they are proud of their strength and endurance and feel (good/well) about the excitement of their work.

■ **WRITING FIRST: Flashback**

Look back at your response to the Writing First exercise on page 464. Underline each adjective and adverb, and draw an arrow from each to the word it describes or identifies. Do all adjectives modify nouns or pronouns? Do all adverbs modify verbs, adjectives, or other adverbs? Have you used *good* and *well* correctly? On the lines below, revise any sentences that use adjectives or adverbs incorrectly.

Answers will vary.

B | **Understanding Comparatives and Superlatives**

As you have seen, adjectives and adverbs describe other words. In some cases, an adjective or adverb describes something by comparing it to something else. The **comparative** form of an adjective or adverb compares two people or things. Adjectives and adverbs form the comparative with *-er* or *more*. The **superlative** form of an adjective or adverb compares more than two things. Adjectives and adverbs form the superlative with *-est* or *most*.

> ● **Writing Tip**
> Some adverbs—such as *very, somewhat, quite, extremely, rather,* and *moderately*—do not have comparative or superlative forms.

ADJECTIVES This film is <u>dull</u> and <u>predictable</u>.

COMPARATIVE The film I saw last week was even <u>duller</u> and <u>more predictable</u> than this one.

SUPERLATIVE The film I saw last night was the <u>dullest</u> and <u>most predictable</u> one I've ever seen.

> ● **Writing Tip**
> Demonstrative adjectives (*this, that, these,* and *those*) do not have comparative or superlative forms.

ADVERB For a beginner, Jane did needlepoint <u>skillfully</u>.

COMPARATIVE After she had watched the demonstration, Jane did needlepoint <u>more skillfully</u> than Rosie.

SUPERLATIVE Of the twelve beginners, Jane did needlepoint the <u>most skillfully</u>.

> ● **Writing Tip**
> The adjective *unique* means "the only one." For this reason, it has no comparative or superlative form (*more unique* and *most unique* are incorrect).

Forming Comparatives and Superlatives

Adjectives

■ One-syllable adjectives generally form the comparative with *-er* and the superlative with *-est*.

great   greater   greatest

■ Adjectives with two or more syllables form the comparative with *more* and the superlative with *most*.

> wonderful   more wonderful   most wonderful

Exception: Two-syllable adjectives ending in *-y* add *-er* or *-est* after changing the *y* to an *i*.

> funny   funnier   funniest

Adverbs

■ All adverbs ending in *-ly* form the comparative with *more* and the superlative with *most*.

> efficiently   more efficiently   most efficiently

■ Some other adverbs form the comparative with *-er* and the superlative with *-est*.

> soon   sooner   soonest

Solving Special Problems with Comparatives and Superlatives

The following three rules will help you avoid errors with comparatives and superlatives.

■ Never use both *-er* and *more* to form the comparative or both *-est* and *most* to form the superlative.

> Nothing could have been <u>more awful</u>. (not *more awfuller*)
>
> Space Mountain is the <u>most frightening</u> (not *most frighteningest*) ride at Disney World.

■ Never use the superlative when you are comparing only two things.

> This is the <u>more serious</u> (not *most serious*) of the two problems.

■ Never use the comparative when you are comparing more than two things.

> This is the <u>worst</u> (not *worse*) day of my life.

> **Teaching Tip**
> Tell students that when they form comparatives, they should have only one ending with an *r* sound (not *more greater* or *more better*, for example).

◆ PRACTICE 29-3

Fill in the correct comparative form of the word supplied in parentheses.

> **ON THE WEB**
> *For more practice, visit Exercise Central at <bedfordstmartins.com/ writingfirst>.*

    Example: Children tend to be _____*noisier*_____ (noisy) than adults.

1. Traffic always moves _____*more slowly*_____ (slow) during rush hour than late at night.

2. The weather report says temperatures will be _____*colder*_____ (cold) tomorrow.

3. Some elderly people are _____*healthier*_____ (healthy) than younger people.

4. It has been proven that pigs are _____more intelligent_____ (intelligent) than dogs.

5. When someone asks you to repeat yourself, you usually answer _____more loudly_____ (loud).

6. The _____taller_____ (tall) the building, the more damage the earthquake caused.

7. They want to teach their son to be _____more respectful_____ (respectful) of women than many young men are.

8. Las Vegas is _____more famous_____ (famous) for its casinos than for its natural resources.

9. The WaterDrop is _____wilder_____ (wild) than any other ride in the park.

10. You must move _____more quickly_____ (quick) if you expect to catch the ball.

◆ PRACTICE 29-4

Fill in the correct superlative form of the word supplied in parentheses.

Example: Consumers now pay the _____highest_____ (high) surcharge ever when they buy tickets for arena events.

(1) Ticketmaster is the _____largest_____ (large) seller of sports and entertainment tickets in the country. (2) The company was the _____earliest_____ (early) to sell concert and sporting event tickets both by phone and through retail outlets. (3) It has also been the _____most successful_____ (successful) at making deals to keep rival agencies from selling tickets for large arenas and stadiums. (4) Ticketmaster's markup on tickets adds at least 20 percent to the cost of each ticket sold and is by far the _____highest_____ (high) in the business. (5) Because Ticketmaster is the _____most powerful_____ (powerful) ticket outlet in the country, however, fans have no choice but to pay the price. (6) Critics have argued that Ticketmaster's control of the market is the _____strongest_____ (strong) monopoly in the country. (7) Back in 1994, the

rock group Pearl Jam launched what remains the ___*most serious*___ (seri-

ous) offensive to date against the ticket giant. (8) Wanting its fans to be

able to buy the ___*cheapest*___ (cheap) tickets possible, Pearl Jam pro-

posed to lower its own profits as well as Ticketmaster's for its 1994 sum-

mer tour. Ticketmaster refused. (9) Still one of the ___*most popular*___

(popular) groups in the country, Pearl Jam tried to use arenas that were

not controlled by Ticketmaster for its later tours. (10) Ticketmaster's

president argues that business is business and that his company has suc-

ceeded because it has worked the ___*hardest*___ (hard) and is the

___*most aggressive*___ (aggressive).

FOCUS   *Good/Well and Bad/Badly*

Most adjectives and adverbs form the comparative with *-er* or *more*
and the superlative with *-est* or *most*. The adjectives *good* and *bad*
and their adverb forms *well* and *badly* are exceptions.

Adjective	Comparative Form	Superlative Form
good	better	best
bad	worse	worst

Adverb	Comparative Form	Superlative Form
well	better	best
badly	worse	worst

◆ **PRACTICE 29-5**

Fill in the correct comparative or superlative form of *good, well, bad,* or
badly.

> **Example:** She is at her ___*best*___ (good) when she is under
>
> pressure.

1. Today in track practice, Luisa performed ___*better*___ (well) than she

   has in weeks.

2. In fact, she ran her ___*best*___ (good) time ever in the fifty meter.

3. When things are bad, we wonder whether they will get ___*better*___

   (good) or ___*worse*___ (bad).

4. I've had some bad meals before, but this is the _____worst_____ (bad).

5. The world always looks _____better_____ (good) when you're in love than when you're not.

6. Athletes generally play the _____worst_____ (badly) when their concentration is poorest.

7. The Sport Shop's prices may be good, but Athletic Attic's are the _____best_____ (good) in town.

8. There are _____better_____ (good) ways to solve conflicts than by fighting.

9. People seem to hear _____better_____ (well) when they agree with what you're saying than when they don't agree with you.

10. Of all the children, Manda took the _____best_____ (good) care of her toys.

Teaching Tip
Remind students that absolute adjectives such as *perfect, unique, dead, impossible,* and *infinite* do not have comparative or superlative forms.

■ WRITING FIRST: Flashback

Look back at your response to the Writing First exercise on page 464. Copy the adjectives and adverbs from your paragraph in the column on the left. Then, write the comparative and superlative forms for each adjective or adverb in the other columns.

Adjective or Adverb	Comparative Form	Superlative Form
Answers will vary.		

■ WRITING FIRST: Revising and Editing

Look back at your response to the Writing First exercise on page 464. Have you used adjectives and adverbs that effectively communicate the situation you describe? Have you used enough adjectives and adverbs to explain your ideas to readers? Add or substitute modifying words as needed to make your writing more precise and more interesting. Delete any unnecessary adjectives and adverbs.

CHAPTER REVIEW

◆ EDITING PRACTICE

Read the following student essay, which includes errors in the use of adjectives and adverbs. Make any changes necessary to correct adjectives incorrectly used for adverbs and adverbs incorrectly used for adjectives. Also correct any errors in the use of comparatives and superlatives and in the use of demonstrative adjectives. If you like, you may add adjectives and adverbs that you feel would make the writer's ideas clearer or more specific. The first sentence has been edited for you.
Answers may vary.

                    Starting Over
                              most joyful
     A wedding can be the ~~joyfullest~~ occasion in two

people's lives, the beginning of a couple's ~~most~~ happiest

years. For some unlucky women, however, a wedding can be
       worst
the ~~worse~~ thing that ever happens; it is the beginning not

of their happiness but of their battered lives. As I went
                                             badly
through the joyful day of my wedding, I wanted ~~bad~~ to find

happiness for the rest of my life, but what I hoped and

wished for did not come true.

     I was married in the savannah belt of the Sudan in

the eastern part of Africa, where I grew up. I was barely

twenty-two years old. The first two years of my marriage
           peacefully,
progressed ~~peaceful,~~ but problems started as soon as our

first child was born.

     Many American women say, "If my husband gave me just
                                             this modern
one beating, that would be it. I'd leave." But ~~those~~

attitude does not work in cultures where tradition has

overshadowed women's rights and divorce is not accepted.
                                        sad
All women can do is accept their ~~sadly~~ fate. Battered women
                                   abusive
give many reasons for staying in their marriages, but fear
       most common.
is the ~~commonest.~~ Fear immobilizes these women, ruling

their decisions, their actions, and their very lives. This

is how it was for me.
              really
     Of course, I was ~~real~~ afraid whenever my husband hit

me. I would run to my mother's house and cry, but she

Map of Sudan

Sudanese wedding ceremony

would always talk me into going back and being more *patient* patiently with my husband. Our tradition discourages divorce, and wife-beating is taken for granted. The situation is really quite ironic: Islam, the religion I practice, sets harsh punishments for abusive husbands, but tradition has so overpowered religion that the laws do not really work very *well.* good.

One night, after nine years of torture, I asked myself whether life had treated me *fairly.* fair. True, I had a high school diploma and two of the *most beautiful* beautifullest children in the world, but all this was not enough. I realized that to stand up to the husband who treated me so *badly,* bad, I would have to achieve a more better education than he had. That night, I decided to get a college education in the United States. My husband *strongly* opposed my decision, but with the support of my father and mother, I was able to begin to change my life.

This period has been *really* real difficult for me. I miss my children every day. But I hope that one day I will be able to fight our traditions so that my little daughters will remember even when I am gone that their mother fought back and won.

◆ COLLABORATIVE ACTIVITIES

1. Working in a small group, write a plot summary for an imaginary film. Begin with one of the following three sentences:

   ■ Dirk and Clive were sworn enemies, but that night on Boulder Ridge they vowed to work together just this once, for the good of their country.

   ■ Genevieve entered the room in a cloud of perfume, and when she spoke, her voice was like velvet.

   ■ The desert sun beat down on her head, but Susanna was determined to protect what was hers, no matter what the cost.

2. Trade summaries with another group. Add as many adjectives and adverbs as you can to the other group's summary. Make sure each modifier is appropriate.

3. Reread your group's plot summary and edit it carefully, paying special attention to the way adjectives and adverbs are used.

Teaching Tip
Students tend to use the same adjectives over and over again. Encourage them to move beyond *great, nice, unique,* and so on.

✔ REVIEW CHECKLIST:
Adjectives and Adverbs

- Adjectives modify nouns or pronouns. (See 29A.)

- Demonstrative adjectives—*this, that, these,* and *those*—identify particular nouns. (See 29A.)

- Adverbs modify verbs, adjectives, or other adverbs. (See 29A.)

- To compare two people or things, use the comparative form of an adjective or adverb. To compare more than two people or things, use the superlative form of an adjective or adverb. Adjectives and adverbs form the comparative with *-er* or *more* and the superlative with *-est* or *most.* (See 29B.)

- The adjectives *good* and *bad* and their adverb forms *well* and *badly* have irregular comparative and superlative forms. (See 29B.)

ESL Tip
You may want to refer students to 30L.

Grammar and Usage
for ESL Writers

■ WRITING FIRST

The painting above shows American flags displayed on the Fourth of July, Independence Day. Look at the picture, and then explain how you and your family celebrate a holiday that is important to you.

Learning English as a second language involves more than just learning grammar. In fact, if you have been studying English as a second language, you may know as much about English grammar as many native speakers do—or even more. However, you will still need to learn the conventions and rules that are second nature to most (though by no means all) native speakers. This chapter covers the grammar and usage issues that give non-native speakers the most trouble.

A   Including Subjects in Sentences

English requires that every sentence state its subject. In addition, every dependent clause must also have a subject.

INCORRECT   Elvis Presley was only forty-two years old when died.

CORRECT   Elvis Presley was only forty-two years old when <u>he</u> died.

English even requires a false or "dummy" subject to fill the subject position in sentences like the following one.

<u>It</u> is hot in this room.

It is not correct to write just *Hot in this room* or *Is hot in this room*.

◆ PRACTICE 30-1

Each of the following sentences is missing the subject of a dependent or an independent clause. On the lines after each sentence, rewrite it, adding an appropriate subject. Then, underline the subject you have added.

ON THE WEB
For more practice, visit
Exercise Central *at*
*<bedfordstmartins.com/
writingfirst>.*

Example: Reality TV programs are very popular, but some people believe are going too far.

Reality TV programs are very popular, but some people believe <u>they</u> are

going too far.

1. When the first season of the reality show *Survivor* aired, was an immediate hit.

   When the first season of the reality show Survivor aired, <u>it</u> was an imme-

   diate hit.

2. At first, media experts thought was strange that a show like *Survivor* would be so successful.

   At first, media experts thought <u>it</u> was strange that a show like Survivor

   would be so successful.

3. For a while, *Survivor* became a cultural phenomenon—probably because was seldom in bad taste.

   For a while, Survivor became a cultural phenomenon—probably because <u>it</u>

   was seldom in bad taste.

4. Millions of Americans planned their evening so that could be sure not to miss the next episode.

   Millions of Americans planned their evening so that <u>they</u> could be sure

   not to miss the next episode.

5. Was surprising to see the many other reality shows that suddenly appeared on the air.

   It was surprising to see the many other reality shows that suddenly

   appeared on the air.

6. Many people refused to watch shows that felt were "morally corrupt," such as *The Bachelor.*

   Many people refused to watch shows that they felt were "morally

   corrupt," such as The Bachelor.

7. A recent poll asked viewers: "Do enjoy reality TV, or has it gone too far?"

   A recent poll asked viewers: "Do you enjoy reality TV, or has it gone too

   far?"

8. Most viewers thought that reality TV had gone too far even though enjoyed shows like *Fear Factor* and *The Apprentice.*

   Most viewers thought that reality TV had gone too far even though they

   enjoyed shows like Fear Factor and The Apprentice.

9. Turns out that reality TV is nothing new.

   It turns out that reality TV is nothing new.

10. The 1973 documentary series *An American Family* showed members of the Loud family as went about their daily lives.

    The 1973 documentary series An American Family showed members of

    the Loud family as they went about their daily lives.

B   Avoiding Special Problems with Subjects

● **Writing Tip**

Special dictionaries help nonnative speakers answer usage questions. Your college librarian or English instructor can help you find a dictionary that meets your needs.

Some languages commonly begin a sentence with a word or phrase that has no grammatical link to the sentence but that states clearly what the sentence is about. If you speak such a language, you might write a sentence like this one.

INCORRECT   Career plan I am studying to be an engineer.

A sentence like this cannot occur in English. The phrase *career plan* cannot be a subject because the sentence already includes one: the pronoun *I*, which agrees with the verb *am studying.* In addition, *career plan* is not connected to the rest of the sentence in any other way. One way to revise this sentence is to rewrite it so that *career plan* is the subject.

For more on subjects, see 15A.

CORRECT   My career plan is to be an engineer.

Another way to revise the sentence is to make *career plan* the object of a preposition.

CORRECT   In terms of my career plan, I am studying to be an engineer.

Standard English also does not permit a two-part subject in which the second part is a pronoun referring to the same person or thing as the first part.

INCORRECT   The Caspian Sea it is the largest lake in the world.

CORRECT   The Caspian Sea is the largest lake in the world.

When the real subject follows the verb, and the normal subject position before the verb is empty, it must be filled by a "dummy" subject, such as *there*.

INCORRECT   Are many rivers in my country.

CORRECT   <u>There</u> are many rivers in my country.

◆ **PRACTICE 30-2**

The following sentences contain problems with subjects. Rewrite each sentence correctly on the lines provided. (Some of the sentences can be corrected in more than one way.)

ON THE WEB
For more practice, visit
Exercise Central *at*
<bedfordstmartins.com/
writingfirst>.

Example: Travelers to China they often visit the Great Wall.

Travelers to China often visit the Great Wall.

Answers will vary.

1. Took hundreds of years to finish building the Great Wall.

   It took hundreds of years to finish building the Great Wall.

   _____

2. The first parts of the Great Wall they were built around 200 A.D.

   The first parts of the Great Wall were built around 200 A.D.

   _____

3. The purpose of the Great Wall it was built to keep out invading armies.

   The Great Wall was built to keep out invading armies.

   _____

4. Building the Great Wall it was built entirely by hand.

   The Great Wall was built entirely by hand.

   _____

5. Is as long as the distance from New York City to Omaha, Nebraska.

   The Great Wall is as long as the distance from New York City to Omaha,

   Nebraska.

   _____

6. Path of the Great Wall it follows a winding path through high mountains and deep valleys.

The Great Wall follows a winding path through high mountains and deep

valleys.

7. The sides of the Great Wall they are made of stone, brick, and earth.

The sides of the Great Wall are made of stone, brick, and earth.

8. The top of the Great Wall it is paved with bricks, forming a roadway for horses.

The top of the Great Wall is paved with bricks, forming a roadway for

horses.

9. Was a great feat of engineering.

It was a great feat of engineering.

10. The Great Wall it is the only man-made object that can be seen by astronauts in space.

The Great Wall is the only man-made object that can be seen by astro-

nauts in space.

■ WRITING FIRST: Flashback

Look back at your response to the Writing First exercise on page 476. Does every sentence state its subject? Underline the subject of each sentence. If a sentence does not have a subject, add one. If any sentence has a two-part subject, cross out the unnecessary pronoun.

C Identifying Plural Nouns

In English, most nouns add -s to form plurals. Every time you use a noun, ask yourself whether you are talking about one item or more than one, and choose a singular or plural form accordingly. Consider this sentence.

CORRECT   The <u>books</u> in both <u>branches</u> of the <u>library</u> are deteriorating.

For more on singular and plural nouns, see 28A and 28B.

The three nouns in this sentence are underlined: one is singular (*library*), and the other two are plural (*books, branches*). The word *both* is not enough to indicate that *branch* is plural, even though it might be obvious that there are many books in any branch of a library. But even if a sentence includes information that tells you that a noun is plural, you must always use a form that shows explicitly that the noun is plural.

◆ PRACTICE 30-3

Underline the plural nouns in the following sentences. (Not all the sentences contain plural nouns.)

Example: The shark is one of the earth's most feared <u>animals</u>.

1. There are about 360 <u>species</u> of <u>sharks</u>.

2. These <u>fish</u> live in <u>oceans</u> and <u>seas</u> throughout the world but are most commonly found in warm water.

3. <u>Sharks</u> vary greatly in size and behavior.

4. Whale <u>sharks</u> are the largest, growing up to 40 <u>feet</u> long and weighing over 15 <u>tons</u>.

5. The smallest shark measures as little as half a foot and weighs less than an ounce.

6. Some <u>sharks</u> live in the deepest <u>areas</u> of the ocean, while other <u>sharks</u> stay near the water's surface.

7. Although all <u>sharks</u> are <u>meat-eaters</u>, only a few <u>species</u> are a danger to <u>people</u>.

8. Most <u>sharks</u> eat live <u>fish</u>, including their fellow <u>sharks</u>.

9. Since the <u>1950s</u>, <u>sharks</u> have been used more and more in scientific research.

10. Few <u>sharks</u> have ever been found with cancer, and <u>scientists</u> hope to find out what protects these <u>creatures</u> from this disease.

ON THE WEB
For more practice, visit **Exercise Central** *at <bedfordstmartins.com/ writingfirst>.*

Teaching Tip
Before students do this exercise, direct them to 28B, which deals with irregular noun plurals.

■ WRITING FIRST: Flashback

Look back at your response to the Writing First exercise on page 476. On the lines below, list all the plural nouns you used.

Answers will vary. _____ _____ _____

_____ _____ _____ _____

Does each plural noun have a form that shows the noun is plural? Correct any errors you find.

D Understanding Count and Noncount Nouns

A **count noun** names one particular thing or a group of particular things: *a teacher, a panther, a bed, an ocean, a cloud, an ice cube; two teachers, many panthers, three beds, two oceans, several clouds, some ice cubes.* A **noncount noun**, however, names things that cannot be counted: *gold, cream, sand, blood, smoke, water.*

Count nouns usually have a singular form and a plural form: *cube, cubes.* Noncount nouns usually have only a singular form: *water.* Note how the nouns *cube* and *water* differ in the way they are used in sentences.

CORRECT   The glass is full of ice cubes.

CORRECT   The glass is full of water.

INCORRECT   The glass is full of waters.

CORRECT   The glass contains five ice cubes.

INCORRECT   The glass contains five waters.

Often, the same idea can be represented with either a count noun or a noncount noun.

Count	*Noncount*
people (plural of *person*)	humanity [*not* humanities]
tables, chairs, beds	furniture [*not* furnitures]
letters	mail [*not* mails]
tools	equipment [*not* equipments]
facts	information [*not* informations]

Some words can be either count or noncount, depending on the meaning intended.

COUNT   He had many interesting <u>experiences</u> at his first job.

NONCOUNT   It is often difficult to get a job if you do not have <u>experience</u>.

FOCUS **Count and Noncount Nouns**

Here are some guidelines for using count and noncount nouns.

■ Use a count noun to refer to a living animal, but use a noncount noun to refer to the food that comes from that animal.

COUNT   There are three live <u>lobsters</u> in the tank.

NONCOUNT   This restaurant specializes in <u>lobster</u>.

■ If you use a noncount noun for a substance or class of things that can come in different varieties, you can often make that noun plural if you want to talk about those varieties.

(continued on the following page)

(continued from the previous page)

> NONCOUNT Cheese is a rich source of calcium.
>
> COUNT Many different cheeses come from Italy.

■ If you want to shift attention from a concept in general to specific examples of it, you can often use a noncount noun as a count noun.

> NONCOUNT You have a great deal of talent.
>
> COUNT My talents do not include singing.

◆ PRACTICE 30-4

In each of the following sentences, identify the underlined word as a count or noncount noun. If it is a noncount noun, circle the *N* following the sentence, but do not write in the blank. If it is a count noun, circle the *C*, and then write the plural form of the noun in the blank.

ON THE WEB

For more practice, visit
Exercise Central *at*
<bedfordstmartins.com/
writingfirst>.

Examples: Psychologists, sociologists, and anthropologists work in the field of behavioral science. (N) C _____

They all have the same goal: to understand human behavior.   N (C)

_____goals_____

1. Each type of scientist has a different approach to solving a problem.

   N (C) ____approaches____

2. An example is the problem of homeless people on our cities' streets.

   N (C) ____examples____

3. Sociologists concentrate on the social causes of homelessness. (N) C

   _____

4. They might study how unemployment contributes to a rise in the number of homeless people. (N) C _____

5. A shortage of inexpensive housing can also cause someone to lose his or her home.   N (C) ____shortages____

6. A sociologist's next question could be: How does society deal with homeless people? (N) C _____

7. Psychologists, on the other hand, are interested in the individual.

   N (C) ____individuals____

8. Their focus would be on how a homeless <u>person</u> feels and thinks.

   N Ⓒ _____ *people* _____

9. Anthropologists are interested in studying culture, a society's <u>system</u> of

   beliefs and its ways of doing things.   N Ⓒ _____ *systems* _____

10. An anthropologist might focus on how the <u>homeless</u> find food and

    shelter and on how they raise their children. Ⓝ C _____

E   Using Determiners with Count and Noncount Nouns

Determiners are adjectives that *identify* rather than describe the nouns they modify. Determiners may also *quantify* nouns (that is, indicate an amount or a number).

Determiners include the following words:

- Articles: *a, an, the*
- Demonstrative pronouns: *this, these, that, those*
- Possessive pronouns: *my, our, your, his, her, its, their*
- Possessive nouns: *Sheila's, my friend's,* and so on
- *Whose, which, what*
- *All, both, each, every, some, any, either, no, neither, many, most, much, a few, a little, few, little, several, enough*
- All numerals: *one, two,* and so on

When a determiner is accompanied by one or more other adjectives, the determiner always comes first. For example, in the phrase *my expensive new digital watch, my* is a determiner; you cannot put *expensive, new, digital,* or any other adjective before *my.*

A singular count noun must always be accompanied by a determiner—for example, *my watch* or *the new digital watch,* not just *watch* or *new digital watch.* However, noncount nouns and plural count nouns sometimes have determiners but sometimes do not. *This honey is sweet* and *Honey is sweet* are both acceptable, as are *These berries are juicy* and *Berries are juicy.* (In each case, the meaning is different.) You cannot say, *Berry is juicy,* however; say instead, *This berry is juicy, Every berry is juicy,* or *A berry is juicy.*

FOCUS   Determiners

Some determiners can be used only with certain types of nouns.

- *This* and *that* can be used only with singular nouns (count or noncount): *this berry, that honey.*

(continued on the following page)

(continued from the previous page)

■ *These, those, a few, few, many, both,* and *several* can be used only with plural count nouns: *these berries, those apples, a few ideas, few people, many students, both sides, several directions.*

■ *Much* and *a little* can be used only with noncount nouns: *much affection, a little honey.*

■ *Some* and *enough* can be used only with noncount or plural count nouns: *some honey, some berries, enough trouble, enough problems.*

■ *A, an, every,* and *each* can be used only with singular count nouns: *a berry, an elephant, every possibility, each citizen.*

Teaching Tip
You might point out to students that *a few* and *a little* have positive connotations (*A few seats are left*), while *few* and *little* have negative connotations (*Few seats are left*).

◆ PRACTICE 30-5

In each of the following sentences, circle the more appropriate choice from each pair of words or phrases in parentheses.

ON THE WEB
For more practice, visit Exercise Central *at* <bedfordstmartins.com/ writingfirst>.

Examples:
Volcanoes are among the most destructive of (all/every) natural forces on earth.

People have always been fascinated and terrified by (this/these) force of nature.

1. Not (all/every) volcano is considered a danger.

2. In (major some/some major) volcanic eruptions, huge clouds rise over the mountain.

3. (A few violent/Violent a few) eruptions are so dramatic that they blow the mountain apart.

4. (Most/Much) volcanic eruptions cannot be predicted.

5. Since the 1400s, (many/much) people—almost 200,000—have lost their lives in volcanic eruptions.

6. When a volcano erupts, (little/a little) can be done to prevent property damage.

7. (Many/Much) lives can be saved, however, if people in the area are evacuated in time.

8. Unfortunately, when people realize an eruption is about to take place, there rarely is (every/enough) time to escape.

9. Volcanoes can be dangerous, but they also produce (a little/some) benefits.

10. For example, (a few/a little) countries around the world use geothermal energy—from underground steam in volcanic areas—to produce electric power.

■ WRITING FIRST: Flashback

Look back at your response to the Writing First exercise on page 476. List all the count nouns in the column on the left and all the noncount nouns in the column on the right.

Count Nouns	*Noncount Nouns*
Answers will vary.	_____
_____	_____
_____	_____
_____	_____

Have you used count and noncount nouns correctly? Correct any errors you find.

F   Understanding Articles

The definite article *the* and the indefinite articles *a* and *an* are determiners that tell readers whether the noun that follows is one they can identify (*the book*) or one they cannot yet identify (*a book*).

The Definite Article

When the definite article *the* is used with a noun, the writer is saying to readers, "You can identify which particular thing or things I have in mind. The information you need to make that identification is available to you. Either you have it already, or I am about to give it to you."

Readers can find the necessary information in the following ways.

■ By looking at other information in the sentence

Meet me at the corner of Main Street and Lafayette Road.

In this example, *the* is used with the noun *corner* because other words in the sentence tell readers which particular corner the writer has in mind: the one located at Main and Lafayette.

■ By looking at information in other sentences

Aisha ordered a slice of pie and a cup of coffee. The pie was delicious. She asked for a second slice.

Here, *the* is used before the word *pie* in the second sentence to indicate that it is the same pie identified in the first sentence. Notice, however, that the noun *slice* in the third sentence is preceded by an indefinite article (*a*) because it is not the same slice referred to in the first sentence.

■ By drawing on general knowledge

> The earth revolves around the sun.

Here, *the* is used with the nouns *earth* and *sun* because readers are expected to know which particular things the writer is referring to.

FOCUS   **Definite Articles**

Always use *the* (rather than *a* or *an*) in the following situations.

■ Before the word *same: the same day*
■ Before the superlative form of an adjective: *the youngest son*
■ Before a number indicating order or sequence: *the third time*

For information on the superlative forms of adjectives and adverbs, see 29B.

Indefinite Articles

When an indefinite article is used with a noun, the writer is saying to readers, "I don't expect you to have enough information right now to identify a particular thing that I have in mind. I do, however, expect you to recognize that I'm referring to only one item."

Consider the following sentences.

> We need a table for our computer.

> I have a folding table; maybe you can use that.

In the first sentence, the writer is referring to a hypothetical table, not an actual one. Because the table is indefinite to the writer, it is clearly indefinite to the reader, so *a* is used, not *the*. The second sentence refers to an actual table, but because the writer does not expect the reader to be able to identify the table specifically, it is also used with *a* rather than *the*.

FOCUS   **Indefinite Articles**

Unlike the definite article (*the*), the indefinite articles *a* and *an* occur only with singular count nouns. *A* is used when the next sound is a consonant, and *an* is used when the next sound is a vowel. In choosing *a* or *an*, pay attention to sound rather than to spelling: *a house, a year, a union,* but *an hour, an uncle.*

Teaching Tip
Refer students to the box
on page 557 for a review
of vowels and consonants.

30 F

For more on count and non-count nouns, see 30D.

For more on proper nouns, see 28A and 33A.

No Article

Only noncount and plural count nouns can stand without articles: *butter, chocolate, cookies, strawberries* (but *a cookie* or *the strawberry*).

Nouns without articles can be used to make generalizations.

<u>Infants</u> need <u>affection</u> as well as <u>food</u>.

Here, the absence of articles before the nouns *infants, affection,* and *food* indicates that the statement is not about particular infants, affection, or food but about infants, affection, and food in general. Remember not to use *the* in such sentences; in English, a sentence like *The infants need affection as well as food* can only refer to particular, identifiable infants, not to infants in general.

Articles with Proper Nouns

Proper nouns can be divided into two classes: names that take *the* and names that take no article.

- Names of people usually take no article unless they are used in the plural to refer to members of a family, in which case they take *the: Napoleon, Mahatma Gandhi,* but *the Parkers.*
- Names of places that are plural in form usually take *the: the Andes, the United States.*
- The names of most places on land (cities, states, provinces, and countries) take no article: *Salt Lake City, Mississippi, Alberta, Japan.* The names of most bodies of water (rivers, seas, and oceans, although not lakes or bays) take *the: the Mississippi, the Mediterranean, the Pacific* (but *Lake Erie* and *San Francisco Bay*).
- Names of streets take no article: *Main Street.* Names of highways take *the: the Belt Parkway.*

◆ PRACTICE 30-6

Teaching Tip
Sometimes no article is used for particular (actual) things, usually to suggest quantity: *I can hear dogs barking.*

Teaching Tip
Remind students that plurals of proper nouns (such as *the Parkers*) do not include apostrophes unless they are possessive.

ON THE WEB
For more practice, visit Exercise Central *at* <bedfordstmartins.com/writingfirst>.

In the following passage, decide whether each blank needs a definite article (*the*), an indefinite article (*a* or *an*), or no article. If a definite or indefinite article is needed, write it in the space provided. If no article is needed, leave the space blank.

Example: Vicente Fox was born on _____ July 2, 1942, in *the* Mexican capital of Mexico City.

(1) Vicente was *the* second of nine children born to José Luis Fox, *a* wealthy farmer, and Mercedes Quesada. (2) When Vicente was only four days old, *the* Fox family went to live in San Francisco del Rincón, in *the* state of Guanajuato. (3) Vicente Fox studied _____ business administration at the Universidad Iberoamericana in Mexico City. (4) He then moved to *the* United States, where he received *a* degree in

management at _____ Harvard University. (5) When he returned to Mexico, he went to work for Coca-Cola, and over _the_ next fifteen years, he climbed _the_ corporate ladder and became _the_ company's youngest manager and eventually Coca-Cola's president for Mexico and _____ Latin America. (6) Fox entered _____ politics by joining _the_ National Action Party during _the_ 1980s. (7) In 1988, he was elected to _____ Congress. (8) _A_ few years later, in 1991, he ran for _the_ post of governor of Guanajuato but lost. (9) Four years later, however, he won by _a_ landslide. (10) In 1999, Fox took _a_ leave of absence as governor to run in _the_ presidential elections. (11) In one interview during his campaign, he said he wanted to rebuild Mexico into _a_ country "where _____ security and _____ justice prevail, where no one is above _the_ law." (12) After promoting himself as _a_ "down-to-earth man of _the_ people," on July 2, 2000, Vicente Fox became _the_ first opposition candidate to reach _the_ presidency of _the_ Republic of Mexico.

■ WRITING FIRST: Flashback

Look back at your response to the Writing First exercise on page 476. Circle each definite article (*the*) and indefinite article (*a* or *an*) you have used. Have you used articles correctly? Correct any errors you find.

G Forming Negative Statements and Questions

Negative Statements

To form a negative statement, add the word *not* directly after the first helping verb of the complete verb.

For more on helping verbs, see 15C.

Global warming has been getting worse.

Global warming has <u>not</u> been getting worse.

When there is no helping verb, a form of the verb *do* must be inserted before *not*.

Automobile traffic contributes to pollution.

Automobile traffic <u>does not</u> contribute to pollution.

For information on subject-verb agreement with the verb do, see 23B.

Exception: If the main verb is *am, is, are, was,* or *were,* do not insert a form of *do* before *not: Harry was late. Harry was <u>not</u> late.*

Remember that when *do* is used as a helping verb, the form of *do* used must match the tense and number of the original main verb. Note that in the negative statement on the preceding page, the main verb loses its tense and appears in the base form (*contribute,* not *contributes*).

Questions

To form a question, move the helping verb that follows the subject to the position directly before the subject.

> The governor <u>is</u> trying to compromise.
>
> <u>Is</u> the governor trying to compromise?
>
> The governor <u>is</u> working on the budget.
>
> <u>Is</u> the governor working on the budget?

ESL Tip

If a statement includes more than one helping verb (*The governor <u>will be</u> working on the budget*), move only the *first* helping verb when you form a question (<u>*Will*</u> *the governor <u>be</u> working on the budget?*).

The same rule stated above applies even when the verb is in the past or future tense.

> The governor <u>was</u> trying to lower state taxes.
>
> <u>Was</u> the governor trying to lower state taxes?
>
> The governor <u>will</u> try to get reelected.
>
> <u>Will</u> the governor try to get reelected?

When the verb does not include a helping verb, you must supply a form of *do.* To form a question, put *do* directly before the subject.

> The governor <u>works</u> hard.
>
> <u>Does</u> the governor <u>work</u> hard?
>
> The governor <u>improved</u> life in his state.
>
> <u>Did</u> the governor <u>improve</u> life in his state?

Teaching Tip

Tell students that if a sentence includes the word *some* (*He had <u>some</u> money*), when it is turned into a question, *any* replaces *some* (*Did he have <u>any</u> money?*)

Exception: If the main verb is *am, is, are, was,* or *were,* do not insert a form of *do* before the verb. Instead, move the main verb to before the suject: *Harry was late. <u>Was</u> Harry late?*

Note: The helping verb never comes before the subject in a question that begins with a subject like *who* or *which.*

> <u>Who</u> is talking to the governor?
>
> <u>Which</u> bills have been vetoed by the governor?

◆ PRACTICE 30-7

Rewrite each of the following sentences in two ways: first, turn the sentence into a question; then, rewrite the original sentence as a negative statement.

ON THE WEB

For more practice, visit
Exercise Central *at*
<bedfordstmartins.com/ writingfirst>.

Example: Her newest album is selling as well as her first one.

Question: Is her newest album selling as well as her first one?

Negative statement: Her newest album is not selling as well as her first one.

1. Converting metric measurements to English measurements is difficult.

   Question: Is converting metric measurements to English measurements difficult?

   Negative statement: Converting metric measurements to English measurements is not difficult.

2. The early frost damaged many crops.

   Question: Did the early frost damage many crops?

   Negative statement: The early frost did not damage many crops.

3. That family was very influential in the early 1900s.

   Question: Was that family very influential in the early 1900s?

   Negative statement: That family was not very influential in the early 1900s.

4. Most stores in malls open on Sundays.

   Question: Do most stores in malls open on Sundays?

   Negative statement: Most stores in malls do not open on Sundays.

5. Choosing the right gift is a difficult task.

   Question: Is choosing the right gift a difficult task?

   Negative statement: Choosing the right gift is not a difficult task.

6. Many great artists attain recognition and success during their lifetimes.

   Question: Do many great artists attain recognition and success during their lifetimes?

   Negative statement: Many great artists do not attain recognition and success during their lifetimes.

7. The lawyer can verify the witness's story.

Question: _Can the lawyer verify the witness's story?_

Negative statement: _The lawyer cannot verify the witness's story._

8. New York City is as dangerous as it was thirty years ago.

Question: _Is New York City as dangerous as it was thirty years ago?_

Negative statement: _New York City is not as dangerous as it was thirty years ago._

9. The British royal family is loved by most of the British people.

Question: _Is the British royal family loved by most of the British people?_

Negative statement: _The British royal family is not loved by most of the British people._

10. The policy of segregation of blacks and whites in the American South ended with the Civil War.

Question: _Did the policy of segregation of blacks and whites in the American South end with the Civil War?_

Negative statement: _The policy of segregation of blacks and whites in the American South did not end with the Civil War._

■ WRITING FIRST: Flashback

Look back at your response to the Writing First exercise on page 476. Do you see any negative statements? If so, check to make sure you have formed them correctly. Then, on the lines below, write a question that you could add to your Writing First exercise.

Question: _Answers will vary._

Check carefully to make sure you have formed the question correctly.

H Indicating Verb Tense

In English, a verb's form must always indicate when an action took place (for instance, in the past or in the present). Use the appropriate tense of the verb, even if the time is obvious or if the sentence includes other indications of time (such as *two years ago* or *at present*).

For more on verb tense, see Chapters 26 and 27.

CORRECT Albert Einstein <u>emigrated</u> from Germany in 1933.

INCORRECT Albert Einstein <u>emigrate</u> from Germany in 1933.

■ WRITING FIRST: Flashback

Look back at your response to the Writing First exercise on page 476. Are all your verbs in the present tense? Correct any errors you find.

I Recognizing Stative Verbs

Stative verbs usually tell us that someone or something is in a state that will not change, at least for a while.

Hiro <u>knows</u> American history very well.

The **present progressive** tense consists of the present tense of *be* plus the present participle (*I am going*). The **past progressive** tense consists of the past tense of *be* plus the present participle (*I was going*). Most English verbs show action, and these action verbs can be used in the progressive tenses. Stative verbs, however, are rarely used in the progressive tenses.

INCORRECT Hiro <u>is knowing</u> American history very well.

FOCUS Stative Verbs

Verbs that are stative—such as *know, understand, think, believe, want, like, love,* and *hate*—often refer to mental states. Other stative verbs include *be, have, need, own, belong, weigh, cost,* and *mean.* Certain verbs of sense perception, like *see* and *hear,* are also stative even though they can refer to momentary events as well as to unchanging states.

Many verbs have more than one meaning, and some of these verbs are active with one meaning but stative with another. An example is the verb *weigh.*

ACTIVE The butcher <u>weighs</u> the meat.

STATIVE The meat <u>weighs</u> three pounds.

In the first sentence above, the verb *weigh* means "to put on a scale"; it is active, not stative. In the second sentence, however, the same verb means "to have weight," so it is stative, not active. It would be unacceptable to say, "The meat is weighing three pounds," but "The butcher is weighing the meat" would be correct.

ON THE WEB

For more practice, visit
Exercise Central *at*
<bedfordstmartins.com/
writingfirst>.

◆ **PRACTICE 30-8**

In each of the following sentences, circle the verb or verbs. Then, correct any problems with stative verbs by crossing out the incorrect verb tense and writing the correct verb tense above the line. If the verb is correct, write **C** above it.

Example: Police officers (are knowing) *know* that fingerprint identification (is) *C* one of the best ways to catch criminals.

1. As early as 1750 B.C., ancient Babylonians (were signing) *C* their identities on clay tablets.

2. By 220 A.D., the Chinese (were becoming) *C* aware that ink fingerprints (could identify) *C* people.

3. However, it (was) *C* not until the late 1800s that anyone (was believing) *believed* that criminal identification (was) *C* possible with fingerprints.

4. Nowadays, we (know) *C* that each person (is having) *has* unique patterns on the tips of his or her fingers.

5. When police (study) *C* a crime scene, they (want) *C* to see whether the criminals (have left) *C* any fingerprint evidence.

6. There (is) *C* always a layer of oil on the skin, and police (are liking) *like* to use it to get fingerprints.

7. Crime scene experts (are often seeing) *often see* cases when the criminals (are touching) *touch* their hair and (pick up) *C* enough oil to leave a good fingerprint.

8. The police (are needing) *need* to judge whether the fingerprint evidence (has been damaged) *C* by sunlight, rain, or heat.

9. In the courtroom, juries often (weigh) *C* fingerprint evidence before they (are deciding) *decide* on their verdict.

10. The FBI (is collecting) *C* millions of fingerprints, which police departments (can compare) *C* with the fingerprints they (find) *C* at crime scenes.

■ **WRITING FIRST: Flashback**

Look back at your response to the Writing First exercise on page 476. Can you identify any stative verbs? If so, list them here.

Stative verbs: *Answers will vary.* _____ _____

_____ _____ _____

Check carefully to be sure you have not used any of these verbs in a progressive tense. Correct any errors you find.

J   Using Modal Auxiliaries

A **modal auxiliary** (such as *can, may, might,* or *must*) is a helping verb that is used with another verb to express ability, possibility, necessity, intent, obligation, and so on.

> I *can imagine* myself in Hawaii.

Modal auxiliaries usually intensify the dominant verb's meaning:

> I *must run* as fast as I can.

> You *ought to lose* some weight.

For more on helping verbs, see 15C.

Modal Auxiliaries

can	ought to
could	shall
may	should
might	will
must	would

> **ESL Tip**
> Students should understand the definition of modal auxiliary verbs as expressions of will, probability, permission, and obligation. Students should memorize the list of modals.

FOCUS Modals

Modal auxiliaries can be used to

■ Express physical ability

  I <u>can</u> walk faster than my brother.

■ Express the possibility of something occurring

  He <u>might</u> get the job if his interview goes well.

(continued on the following page)

(continued from the previous page)

- Express or request permission

  <u>May</u> I use the restroom in the hallway?

- Express necessity

  I <u>must</u> get to the train station on time.

- Express a suggestion or advice

  To be healthy, you <u>should</u> [or <u>ought to</u>] exercise and eat balanced meals.

- Express intent

  I <u>will</u> try to study harder next time.

- Express a desire

  <u>Would</u> you please answer the telephone?

◆ PRACTICE 30-9

In the exercise below, circle the correct modal auxiliary.

   Example: (May/Would) you help me complete the assignment?

1. It doesn't rain very often in Arizona, but today it looks like it (can/might).

2. I know I (will/ought to) call my aunt on her birthday, but I always find an excuse.

3. Sarah (should/must) study for her English exam, but she is happier spending time with her friends.

4. John (can/would) be the best person to represent our class.

5. Since the close presidential election of 2000, many people now believe they (could/should) vote in every election.

6. All students (will/must) bring two pencils, a notebook, and a dictionary to class every day.

7. (Would/May) you show me the way to the post office?

8. I (could/should) not ask for more than my health, my family, and my job.

9. Do you think they (could/can) come back tomorrow to finish the painting job?

10. A dog (should/might) be a helpful companion for your disabled father.

K   Using Gerunds

A **gerund** is a verb form ending in *-ing* that always acts as a noun.

> <u>Reading</u> the newspaper is one of my favorite things to do on Sundays.

Just like a noun, a gerund can be used as a subject, a direct object, a subject complement, or the object of a preposition.

FOCUS   **Gerunds**

- A gerund can be the subject of a sentence.

  <u>Playing</u> tennis is one of my hobbies.

- A gerund can be a direct object.

  My brother influenced my <u>racing</u>.

- A gerund can be a subject complement.

  The most important thing is <u>winning</u>.

- A gerund can be the object of a preposition.

  The teacher rewarded him for <u>passing</u>.

◆ PRACTICE 30-10

To complete the sentences below, fill in the blanks with the gerund form of the verb provided in parentheses.

Example: _____*Typing*_____ (type) is a skill that every girl used to learn in high school.

1. _____*Eating*_____ (eat) five or six smaller meals throughout the day is healthier than eating two or three big meals.

2. In the winter, there is nothing better than _____*skating*_____ (skate) outdoors on a frozen pond.

3. The household task I dread the most is _____*cleaning*_____ (clean).

4. The fish avoided the net by _____*swimming*_____ (swim) faster.

5. _____*Quitting*_____ (quit) is easier than accomplishing a goal.

6. Her parents praised her for ___*remembering*___ (remember) their anniversary.

7. The job she enjoyed the most was ___*organizing*___ (organize) the files.

8. I did not like his ___*singing*___ (sing).

9. For me, ___*cooking*___ (cook) is a relaxing way to spend the evening.

10. The best possible way to prepare for the concert is by ___*practicing*___ (practice).

L Placing Modifiers in Order

Adjectives and other modifiers that come before a noun usually follow a set order.

Required Order

For more on determiners, see 30E.

■ Determiners always come first in a series of modifiers: *these fragile glasses*. The determiners *all* or *both* always precede any other determiners: *all these glasses*.
■ If one of the modifiers is a noun, it must come directly before the noun it modifies: *these wine glasses*.
■ Descriptive adjectives are placed between the determiners and the noun modifiers: *these fragile wine glasses*. If there are two or more descriptive adjectives, the following order is preferred.

Preferred Order

■ Adjectives that show the writer's attitude generally precede adjectives that merely describe: *these lovely fragile wine glasses*.
■ Adjectives that indicate size generally come early: *these lovely large fragile wine glasses*.

◆ PRACTICE 30-11

ON THE WEB
For more practice, visit
Exercise Central *at*
*<bedfordstmartins.com/
writingfirst>.*

Arrange each group of modifiers in the correct order, and rewrite the complete phrase in the blank.

Example: (annual, impressive, the, publisher's) report

the publisher's impressive annual report

1. (brand-new, a, apartment, high-rise) building

a brand-new high-rise apartment building

2. (gifted, twenty-five-year-old, Venezuelan, this) author

   this gifted twenty-five-year-old Venezuelan author

3. (successful, short-story, numerous) collections

   numerous successful short-story collections

4. (her, all, intriguing, suspense) novels

   all her intriguing suspense novels

5. (publisher's, best-selling, the, three) works

   the publisher's three best-selling works

6. (main, story's, two, this) characters

   this story's two main characters

7. (young, a, strong-willed) woman

   a strong-willed young woman

8. (middle-aged, attractive, the, British) poet

   the attractive middle-aged British poet

9. (exquisite, wedding, an, white) gown

   an exquisite white wedding gown

10. (elaborate, wedding, an, million-dollar) reception

    an elaborate million-dollar wedding reception

■ WRITING FIRST: Flashback

Look back at your response to the Writing First exercise on page 476. Have you used several modifiers before a single noun? If so, list here all the modifiers and the noun that follows them.

Modifiers: _*Answers will vary.*_ _____ _____ Noun: _____

Modifiers: _____ _____ _____ Noun: _____

Have you arranged the modifiers in the correct order? Make any necessary corrections.

M **Choosing Correct Prepositions**

A **preposition** links a noun (or a word or word group that functions as a noun) to a verb, an adjective, or another noun in the sentence. Thus, prepositions show the precise relationships between words—for example, whether a book is *on, near,* or *under* a table.

> I thought I had left the book <u>on</u> the table or somewhere <u>near</u> the table, but I found it <u>under</u> the table.

The prepositions *at, in,* and *on* sometimes cause problems for non-native speakers of English. For example, to identify the location of a place or an event, you can use *at, in,* or *on.*

■ The preposition *at* specifies an exact point in space or time.

> The museum is <u>at</u> 1000 Fifth Avenue. Let's meet there <u>at</u> 10:00 tomorrow morning.

■ Expanses of space or time are treated as containers and therefore require *in.*

> Women used to wear long skirts <u>in</u> the 1900s.

■ *On* must be used in two cases: with names of streets (but not with exact addresses), and with days of the week or month.

> We will move into our new office <u>on</u> 18th Street either <u>on</u> Monday or <u>on</u> March 12.

N   Using Prepositions in Familiar Expressions

Many familiar expressions end with prepositions. Learning to write clearly and **idiomatically**—in keeping with the conventions of written English—means learning which preposition is used in such expressions. Even native speakers of English sometimes have trouble choosing the correct preposition.

The sentences that follow illustrate idiomatic use of prepositions in various expressions. Note that sometimes different prepositions are used with the same word. For example, both *on* and *for* can be used with *wait* to form two different expressions with two different meanings (*He waited <u>on</u> their table; She waited <u>for</u> the bus*). Which preposition you choose depends on your meaning. (In the list that follows, pairs of similar expressions that end with different prepositions are bracketed.)

ESL Tip
Have each student write an additional sentence for two or three of the expressions listed. Ask students to share their sentences with the class.

Expression with Preposition	*Sample Sentence*
acquainted with	During orientation, the university offers workshops to make sure that students are <u>acquainted with</u> its rules and regulations.
addicted to	I think Abby is becoming <u>addicted to</u> pretzels.
agree on (a plan or objective)	It is vital that all members of the school board <u>agree on</u> goals for the coming year.
agree to (a proposal)	Striking workers finally <u>agreed to</u> the terms of management's offer.

angry about or at (a situation)	Taxpayers are understandably <u>angry about</u> (or <u>at</u>) the deterioration of city recreation facilities.
angry with (a person)	When the mayor refused to hire more police officers, his constituents became <u>angry with</u> him.
approve of	Amy's adviser <u>approved of</u> her decision to study in Guatemala.
bored with	Salah got <u>bored with</u> economics, so he changed his major to psychology.
capable of	Hannah is a good talker, but she is not <u>capable of</u> acting as her own lawyer.
consist of	The deluxe fruit basket <u>consisted of</u> five pathetic pears, two tiny apples, a few limp bunches of grapes, and one lonely kiwi.
contrast with	Coach Headley's relaxed style <u>contrasts</u> sharply <u>with</u> the previous coach's more formal approach.
convenient for	The proposed location of the new day-care center is <u>convenient for</u> many families.
deal with	Many parents and educators believe it is possible to <u>deal with</u> the special needs of autistic children in a regular classroom.
depend on	Children <u>depend on</u> their parents for emotional as well as financial support.
differ from (something else)	A capitalist system <u>differs from</u> a socialist system in its view of private ownership.
differ with (someone else)	When Miles realized that he <u>differed with</u> his boss on most important issues, he handed in his resignation.
emigrate from	My grandfather and his brother <u>emigrated from</u> the part of Russia that is now Ukraine.
grateful for (a favor)	If you can arrange an interview next week, I will be very <u>grateful for</u> your time and trouble.
grateful to (someone)	Jerry Garcia was always <u>grateful to</u> his loyal fans.
immigrate to	Many Cubans want to leave their country and <u>immigrate to</u> the United States.
impatient with	Keshia often gets <u>impatient with</u> her four younger brothers.
interested in	Tomiko had always been <u>interested in</u> computers, so no one was surprised when she became a Web designer.
interfere with	College athletes often find that their dedication to sports <u>interferes with</u> their schoolwork.
meet with	I hope I can <u>meet with</u> you soon to discuss my research projects.
object to	The defense attorney <u>objected to</u> the prosecutor's treatment of the witness.

pleased with	Most of the residents are <u>pleased with</u> the mayor's crackdown on crime.
protect against	Nobel Prize winner Linus Pauling believed that large doses of vitamin C could <u>protect</u> people <u>against</u> the common cold.
reason with	When two-year-olds are having tantrums, it is nearly impossible to <u>reason with</u> them.
reply to	If no one <u>replies to</u> our ad within two weeks, we will advertise again.
responsible for	Should teachers be held <u>responsible for</u> their students' low test scores?
similar to	The blood sample found at the crime scene was remarkably <u>similar to</u> one found in the suspect's residence.
specialize in	Dr. Casullo is a dentist who <u>specializes in</u> periodontal surgery.
succeed in	Lisa hoped her M.B.A. would help her <u>succeed in</u> a business career.
take advantage of	Some consumer laws are designed to prevent door-to-door salespeople from <u>taking advantage of</u> buyers.
wait for (something to happen)	Many parents of teenagers experience tremendous anxiety while <u>waiting for</u> their children to come home at night.
wait on (in a restaurant)	We sat at the table for twenty minutes before someone <u>waited on</u> us.
worry about	Why <u>worry about</u> things you cannot change?

Teaching Tip

You may want to remind students that although *wait on* is often used for *wait for* in casual speech (*I'm waiting on my adviser, but he's late*), this usage is not acceptable in college writing.

FOCUS **Using Prepositions in Familiar Expressions: Synonyms**

Below is a list of familiar expressions that have similar meanings. They can be used in almost exactly the same contexts.

acquainted with, familiar with
addicted to, hooked on
angry with (a person), upset with
approve of, authorize
bored with, tired of
capable of, able to
consists of, has, contains, includes

deal with (a problem), address
depend on, rely on
differ from (something else), be different from
differ with (someone else), disagree
emigrate from, move from (another country)

(continued on the following page)

(continued from the previous page)

grateful for (a favor), thankful for	similar to, almost the same as
immigrate to, move to (another country)	specialize in, devote oneself to (a special area of work)
interested in, fascinated by	succeed in, attain success, reach a goal
interfere with, disrupt	take advantage of, use an opportunity
meet with, get together with	
object to, oppose	wait for (something to happen), expect
pleased with, happy with	wait on (in a restaurant), serve
protect against, guard against	
reply to, answer	
responsible for, accountable for	

◆ **PRACTICE 30-12**

In the following passage, fill in each blank with the correct preposition.

Example: Tony Bartoli is ___*in*___ his second year ___*at*___ a large state college.

(1) There have been many changes ___*in*___ Tony's life ___*in*___ the past few years. (2) ___*In*___ 1997, Tony's family emigrated ___*from*___ Argentina. (3) Although Tony had studied English ___*in*___ Argentina, he was amazed ___*at*___ how little he seemed to know when he got ___*to*___ the States. (4) ___*On*___ his first day ___*of*___ high school, he met ___*with*___ a guidance counselor who convinced him to take advantage ___*of*___ the special English classes that were being offered ___*at*___ the vocational-technical school. (5) Since Tony was very interested ___*in*___ improving his English (and knew he would have to do that if he wanted to succeed ___*in*___ his new world), he enrolled ___*in*___ a class. (6) Now, Tony is grateful not only ___*to*___ his guidance counselor but also ___*to*___ all the teachers who supported him and showed him that he was capable ___*of*___ succeeding. (7) Adjusting ___*to*___ a new life ___*in*___ a new country and getting acquainted ___*with*___ a culture that differs greatly ___*from*___ the one that he was used ___*to*___ were challenges that he met ___*with*___

ON THE WEB
For more practice, visit Exercise Central *at* *<bedfordstmartins.com/ writingfirst>*.

enthusiasm and ____*with*____ success. (8) Last year, when he first arrived
____*at*____ Florida State, he was worried ____*about*____ taking regular col-
lege courses____*in*____ his second language, English. (9) Some of the
first-year classes were difficult, but he was pleased ____*with*____ his grades
____*at*____ the end ____*of*____ the year. (10) This year, Tony went back
____*to*____ school early so that he could look ____*for*____ a part-time job
and somewhere to live. (11) When he found the apartment ____*on*____
College Avenue, he called his parents ____*on*____ the phone. (12) ____*At*____
first, they objected ____*to*____ his decision to live on his own, but they
finally agreed ____*to*____ the idea. (13) It is going to be a great year, and
Tony is looking forward ____*to*____ it.

■ WRITING FIRST: Flashback

Look back at your response to the Writing First exercise on page
476. Have you used any of the idiomatic expressions listed on pages
500–502? If so, bracket each expression. Have you used the correct
prepositions? Make any necessary corrections.

O Using Prepositions in Phrasal Verbs

A **phrasal verb** consists of two words, a verb and a preposition. Some
phrasal verbs are **inseparable**: that is, the preposition must always come
immediately after the verb. Other phrasal verbs are **separable**. This means
that other words may come between the verb and the preposition.

Inseparable Phrasal Verbs

Some phrasal verbs cannot be separated. If the preposition in a phrasal
verb introduces a prepositional phrase, the preposition always comes right
after the verb. In the following sentence, the word *over* introduces the
prepositional phrase *over the manual*; therefore, *over* must come right
after the verb (*go*).

CORRECT Please <u>go over</u> the manual carefully.

INCORRECT Please <u>go</u> the manual <u>over</u> carefully.

In other phrasal verbs, words that look like prepositions do not function as prepositions. For example, in the sentence on the following page,
the second word of the verb (*up*) does not introduce a prepositional
phrase; instead, it combines with the first word of the verb to form a two-

word verb with its own meaning. Phrasal verbs like these are also not usually separated; the preposition must come right after the verb.

    CORRECT The student <u>spoke up</u> without hesitation.

    INCORRECT The student <u>spoke</u> without hesitation <u>up</u>.

Some Common Inseparable Phrasal Verbs

come across	grow up
get along	run into
give in	speak up
go over	stay away

Separable Phrasal Verbs

In some cases, however, a phrasal verb may be split. For example, some phrasal verbs are **transitive verbs**; that is, they express an action toward an object. When the object is a noun, the second word of the phrasal verb can come either before or after the object. In the sentence below, the phrasal verb *fill out* is a transitive verb. Because the object of the verb *fill out* is a noun *(form)*, the second word of the verb can come either before or after the verb's object.

    CORRECT Please <u>fill out</u> the form.

    CORRECT Please <u>fill</u> the form <u>out</u>.

When the object is a pronoun, however, these phrasal verbs *must* be split, and the pronoun must come between the two parts of the verb.

    CORRECT Please <u>fill</u> it <u>out</u>.

    INCORRECT Please <u>fill out</u> it.

Some Common Separable Phrasal Verbs

ask out	give away	put back	throw away
bring up	hang up	put on	try out
call up	let out	shut off	turn down
drop off	make up	take down	turn off
fill out	put away	think over	wake up

Remember, when the object of the verb is a pronoun, these phrasal verbs must be split, and the pronoun must come between the two parts (for example, *take (it) down, put (it) on, let (it) out,* and *make (it) up*).

◆ PRACTICE 30-13

In each of the following sentences, look closely at the phrasal verb, and decide whether the preposition is placed correctly in the sentence. If it is, write **C** in the blank after the sentence. If the preposition needs to be moved, edit the sentence.

ON THE WEB
For more practice, visit
Exercise Central *at*
*<bedfordstmartins.com/
writingfirst>.*

Example: People who live in American suburbs are often surprised to come across evidence of wild animals in their neighborhoods. __C__

1. In one case, a New Jersey woman found that a hungry bear woke ~~up~~ her ^up^ from a nap one afternoon. _____

2. She called the police, hung up the phone, and ran for her life. __C__

3. Actually, although it is a good idea to stay ^away^ from bears ~~away,~~ , most wild bears are timid. _____

4. When there is a drought, people are more likely to run into bears and other wild animals. __C__

5. The amount of blueberries and other wild fruit that bears eat usually drops ^off^ in dry weather ~~off.~~ . _____

6. Bears need to put on weight before the winter, so they may have to find food in suburban garbage cans. __C__

7. It is a good idea for families to go ^over^ their plans ~~over~~ to safeguard their property against bears. _____

8. People should not leave pet food out overnight, or else their dog may be disappointed to find that a hungry bear has eaten its dinner. __C__

9. If people have a bird feeder in the yard, they should put ~~away~~ it ^away^ during the autumn. _____

10. As the human population grows, more and more houses are built in formerly wild areas, with the result that bears and people have to learn to get along with each other. __C__

■ WRITING FIRST: Flashback

Look back at your response to the Writing First exercise on page 476. Have you used any phrasal verbs? If so, list them here.

_____

_____

_____

Have you placed the preposition correctly in each case? Make any necessary corrections.

■ WRITING FIRST: Revising and Editing

Look back at your response to the Writing First exercise on page 476. Then, review all your Flashback exercises, and be sure you have made all necessary corrections in grammar and usage. When you have finished, add any additional transitional words and phrases you need to make the celebration you have described clear to your readers.

CHAPTER REVIEW

◆ EDITING PRACTICE

Read the following student essay, which includes errors in the use of subjects, articles and determiners, and stative verbs, as well as errors with prepositions in idiomatic expressions. Check each underlined word or phrase. If it is not used correctly, cross it out, and write the correct word or phrase above the line. If the underlined word or phrase is correct, write *C* above it. The title of the essay has been edited for you.

in
How to Succeed ~~on~~ Multinational Business
                        ^
                                                     on
Success in multinational business often depends ~~in~~ the
                                                     ^
the ability to understand other countries' cultures.
                          from
Understanding how cultures differ ~~to~~ our own, however, is
            these   ^   *it*
only one key to ~~this~~ enterprises. Also, is crucial that
                                            ^
businesses learn to adapt to different cultures. ~~The~~
Ethnocentrism   *the*
~~ethnocentrism~~ is the belief that one's own culture has ~~a~~
^   *it*   ^
best way of doing things. In international business, is
                                                     ^
            C   *use*
necessary to set aside this belief. A company cannot ~~uses~~
                                                     ^
the same methods overseas as it uses at home. If a company

tries to sell exactly the same product in a different
        there
country, ~~it~~ could be problems.
         ^
          ethnocentrism,
    To avoid ~~ethnocentrisms,~~ a company that wants to sell
           ^
                                          some
its product internationally ~~it~~ should do ~~a few~~ market
                            ^   ^
research. For example, when McDonald's opened restaurants
in   *it*
~~on~~ India, realized that beef burgers would not work in a
        ^
country where many people believe that cows are sacred.

McDonald's in Egypt

Instead, burgers were created out of ground ~~chickens~~ *chicken*. For India's many vegetarians, McDonald's created several different vegetable ~~patty~~ *patties*. McDonald's understood that both the religious and cultural ~~characteristic~~ *characteristics* of the country had to be considered if its new restaurants were going to succeed.

Similarly, *an* American company should always find out what the name of the product means in the new language. ~~With~~ *In* one famous example, ~~the~~ General Motors tried to sell a car called the Chevy Nova in Spanish-speaking countries. The car was not a success. Then, the company discovered that although *nova* means "bright star" in English, *no va* means "doesn't go" in Spanish, so it was not *a* good name to use in Spanish-speaking countries. If General Motors' businesspeople had been capable ~~to~~ *of* speaking and understanding the language, they ~~must~~ *might* have avoided this embarassing situation. Communicating directly with customers ~~make~~ *makes* everyone more comfortable and efficient.

~~It is~~ *There are* many aspects of a country that must be understood before successful international business can be carried out. To protect ~~from~~ *against* legal errors, a company needs to understand the country's legal system, which may be very different from its home country's legal system. ~~May be~~ *It may* be necessary to get licenses to export products ~~onto~~ *into* other countries. The role of women is likely to be different; without knowing this, businesspeople might offend people unintentionally. Also, ~~much~~ *many* personal interactions in other countries may give the wrong impression to someone who is inexperienced. For example, in Latin American countries, people ~~are~~ often ~~standing~~ *stand* close together and touch each other when they are talking. Americans may feel uncomfortable in such a situation unless *they* understand it.

Over time, the marketplace is becoming more global. In ~~those~~ *this* setting, individuals from numerous cultures come together. To perform effectively, an international company

Business meeting in Kuwait

must hire people with the right ~~experiences.~~ *experience.* To deal with *C*

other cultures, multinational companies ~~inside~~ *in* today's

global market must have good ~~informations~~ *information* and show other

cultures the highest ~~respects.~~ *respect.*

◆ COLLABORATIVE ACTIVITIES

1. Working in a small group, make a list of ten prepositional phrases that include the prepositions *above, around, at, between, from, in, on, over, under,* and *with.* Use specific nouns as objects of these prepositions, and use as many modifying words as you wish. (Try, for example, to write something like *above their hideous wedding portrait,* not just *above the picture.*)

2. Exchange lists with another group. Still working collaboratively, compose a list of ten sentences, each including one of the other group's ten prepositional phrases. Give your list of ten sentences to another group.

3. Working with this new list of ten sentences, substitute a different prepositional phrase for each one that appears in a sentence. Make sure each sentence still makes sense.

> **Teaching Tip**
> Collaborative Activity 1 is an effective review. It can also be fun, especially if students use a lot of modifying words.

☑ REVIEW CHECKLIST:
Grammar and Usage for ESL Writers

▪ In almost all cases, English sentences must state their subjects. (See 30A and 30B.)

▪ In English, most nouns add *-s* to form plurals. Always use a form that indicates that a noun is plural. (See 30C.)

▪ English nouns may be count nouns or noncount nouns. A count noun names one particular thing or a group of particular things (*a teacher, oceans*). A noncount noun names something that cannot be counted (*gold, sand*). (See 30D.)

▪ Determiners are adjectives that identify rather than describe the nouns they modify. Determiners may also indicate amount or number. (See 30E.)

▪ The definite article *the* and the indefinite articles *a* and *an* are determiners that indicate whether the noun that follows is one readers can identify (*the book*) or one they cannot yet identify (*a book*). (See 30F.)

▪ To form a negative statement, add the word *not* directly after the first helping verb of the complete verb. To form a question, move the helping verb that follows the subject to the position directly before the subject. (See 30G.)

(continued on the following page)

(continued from the previous page)

☐ A verb's form must indicate when an action took place. (See 30H.)

☐ Stative verbs indicate that someone or something is in a state that will not change, at least for a while. Stative verbs are rarely used in the progressive tenses. (See 30I.)

☐ A modal auxiliary is a helping verb that expresses ability, possibility, necessity, intent, obligation, and so on. (See 30J.)

☐ A gerund is a verb form ending in *-ing* that is always used as a noun. (See 30K.)

☐ Adjectives and other modifiers that come before a noun usually follow a set order. (See 30L.)

☐ The prepositions *at, in,* and *on* sometimes cause problems for nonnative speakers of English. (See 30M.)

☐ Many familiar expressions end with prepositions. (See 30N.)

☐ When the preposition in a phrasal verb introduces a prepositional phrase, the preposition comes right after the verb. In some cases, however, a phrasal verb may be split. (See 30O.)

UNIT REVIEW

Read the following student essay, which includes errors in the use of verbs, nouns, pronouns, adjectives, and adverbs, as well as ESL errors. Make any changes necessary to correct the basic grammar of the sentences. The first sentence has been edited for you.

The Mystery of the Bermuda Triangle

The Bermuda Triangle is an area in the Atlantic Ocean
known
~~know~~ as the Devil's Triangle, or the Hoodoo Sea. Its size,
between 500,000 and 1.5 million square miles, depends on
whom *believe.*
~~who~~ you ~~are believing.~~ Strange events happen there.

During the past century, more than fifty ships and twenty
in this
airplanes have disappeared ~~to these~~ area, which extends
from Puerto Rico to Florida to Bermuda. According to
popular belief, a mysterious force causes ships and planes
to vanish in the Bermuda Triangle. Everyone who hears
himself or herself
about the mystery has to decide for ~~themselves~~ what they
believe. However, according to the U.S. Coast Guard, the
explanations are not mysterious.

odd
The stories about ~~odd~~ these occurrences in the area ~~they~~
may have started as early as 1492. When Columbus sailed
he *saw*
through the area, ~~him~~ and his crew ~~seen~~ unusual lights in
it
the sky, and his compass reacted strangely. Now, is
believed that the lights came from a meteor that crashed
into the ocean. The peculiar compass readings were probably
caused by
~~cause from~~ the fact that, in this area, magnetic compasses
point toward true north, rather than magnetic north. Unless
experienced navigators understand this situation, the
them
variation can cause ~~him~~ to sail far off course.

The more famous Bermuda Triangle legend started in 1945,
composed
when Flight 19, ~~compose~~ of five U.S. Navy Avenger torpedo
bombers, disappeared while on a routine training mission.
A rescue *had*
~~Rescue~~ plane that ~~has~~ been sent to search for them also
men
disappeared. Six aircraft and twenty-seven ~~man~~ vanished.
lives
Not only were their ~~lifes~~ lost, but no bodies were ever

Map of Bermuda Triangle

511

found. *Was* ~~Were~~ the mysterious force responsible? Although the events themselves seem strange, there are convincing ~~explanation.~~ *explanations.* First, all the crewmen except ~~his~~ *their* leader were inexperienced trainees. It is quite *possible* ~~possibly~~ that they ~~flied~~ *flew* through a magnetic storm or that the leader's compass was not working. If so, they would have become confused ~~of~~ *about* their location. Radio transmissions were unreliable because of ~~a~~ bad weather and a faulty receiver in one of the planes. The crew leader may have had a hangover; if so, he was not functioning ~~good.~~ *well.* The leader ~~telled~~ *told* his pilots to head east; he evidently ~~thinked~~ *thought* that they were over the Gulf of Mexico. However, they were flying up the Atlantic coastline, so the instructions sent ~~him~~ *them* further out to sea. If the planes crashed into the ocean at night, it is not likely that ~~no one~~ *anyone* survived. No wreckage was ever ~~recover,~~ *recovered,* possibly because the planes went down in the deepest point of the Atlantic Ocean, the 30,100-foot-deep Puerto Rico Trench.

After Flight 19 disappeared, ~~storys start~~ *stories started* to appear about the events that ~~have~~ *had* occurred. The peculiar compass readings, the problems with radio transmissions, and the missing wreckage ~~lead~~ *led* to tales of time warps and alien abductions. Some people believe that the missing ships and planes were taken by UFOs (unidentified flying objects) to a different dimension. Others think that those ~~whom~~ *who* disappeared were kidnapped ~~from~~ *by* aliens from other planets. However, other factors offer ~~most~~ *more* convincing explanations. The possibility that magnetic compasses point true north in this area is now well known. It is a phenomenon that ~~could~~ *can* also be found in ~~a~~ *an* area of the Pacific Ocean, off the coast of Japan. It is also well known that the weather patterns in the southern Atlantic and Caribbean areas ~~is~~ *are* extremely unpredictable. In addition, human error may have been involved. For these ~~reason,~~ *reasons,* the tales of the Bermuda Triangle are probably science fiction, not fact.

Missing Ship Recalls
1918 Disappearance

Coast Guard Hunting
Tanker With 43 Men

512

UNIT SEVEN

Understanding Punctuation, Mechanics, and Spelling

Using Commas

PREVIEW

In this chapter, you will learn

- to use commas in a series (31A)

- to use commas to set off introductory phrases, conjunctive adverbs, and transitional expressions (31B)

- to use commas with appositives (31C)

- to use commas to set off nonrestrictive clauses (31D)

- to use commas in dates and addresses (31E)

- to avoid unnecessary commas (31F)

■ WRITING FIRST

The picture above shows new single-family public housing units. Look at the picture, and then describe an ideal public housing complex for low-income families. Where should it be located? What kinds of buildings should be constructed? What facilities and services should be offered to residents?

Word Power
subsidized assisted or supported financially

low-density sparsely settled; not crowded

A **comma** is a punctuation mark that separates words or word groups within sentences. In this way, commas keep ideas distinct from one another. In earlier chapters, you learned to use a comma between two independent clauses linked by a coordinating conjunction (16A) and to use a comma after a dependent clause that comes before an independent clause (17B). Commas have several other uses, as you will learn in this chapter.

Teaching Tip
Students often use commas
where they do not belong
and omit them from where
they are needed. Begin this
chapter by telling students
to use commas only in the
situations outlined in 31A
through 31E and referring
them to the discussion of
unnecessary commas in 31F.

A   Using Commas in a Series

Use commas to separate all elements in a **series** of three or more words or word groups (phrases or clauses).

> Leyla, Zack, and Kathleen campaigned for Representative Fattah.
>
> Leyla, Zack, or Kathleen will be elected president of Students for Fattah.
>
> Leyla made phone calls, licked envelopes, and ran errands for the campaign.
>
> Leyla is president, Zack is vice president, and Kathleen is treasurer.

● **Writing Tip**
Do not use a comma before
the first item in a series
or after the last item in a
series. (See 31F.)

> **FOCUS**   Using Commas in a Series
>
> Newspapers and magazines usually omit the comma before the co-ordinating conjunction in a series. However, in college writing you should always use a comma before the coordinating conjunction.
>
>   Leyla, Zack, and Kathleen worked on the campaign.
>
> Exception: Do not use *any* commas if all the items in a series are separated by coordinating conjunctions.
>
>   Leyla or Zack or Kathleen will be elected president of Students for Fattah.

◆ PRACTICE 31-1

Edit the following sentences for the use of commas in a series. If the sentence is correct, write **C** in the blank.

ON THE WEB
For more practice, visit
Exercise Central *at*
<bedfordstmartins.com/
writingfirst>.

Examples:

Costa Rica produces bananas, cocoa, and sugar cane. __*C*__

The pool rules state that there is no running, or jumping, or diving.

_____

1. The musician plays guitar, bass, and drums. _____

2. The organization's goals are feeding the hungry, housing the homeless and helping the unemployed find work. _____

3. *The Price Is Right, Let's Make a Deal,* and *Jeopardy!* are three of the longest-running game shows in television history. __*C*__

4. In native Hawaiian culture, yellow was worn by the royalty͵ red was worn by priests͵ and a mixture of the two colors was worn by others of high rank. ____

5. The remarkable diary kept by young Anne Frank while her family hid from the Nazis is insightful, touching͵ and sometimes humorous. ____

6. A standard bookcase is sixty inches tall͵ forty-eight inches wide͵ and twelve inches deep. ____

7. Most coffins manufactured in the United States are lined with bronze, ~~or~~ copper, or lead. ____

8. Young͵ handsome͵ and sensitive, Leonardo DiCaprio was the 1990s answer to the 1950s actor James Dean. ____

9. California's capital is Sacramento, its largest city is Los Angeles͵ and its oldest settlement is San Diego. ____

10. Watching television, playing video games, and riding a bicycle are the average ten-year-old boy's favorite pastimes. __*C*__

■ WRITING FIRST: Flashback

Look back at your response to the Writing First exercise on page 515. If you have included a series of three or more words or word groups in any of your sentences, copy it here. Did you use commas correctly to separate elements in the series? If not, correct your punctuation. If no sentence includes a series, write a new sentence that does on the lines below.

Answers will vary. _____

_____

| **B** | **Using Commas to Set Off Introductory Phrases, Conjunctive Adverbs, and Transitional Expressions** |

Use a comma to set off an **introductory phrase** from the rest of the sentence.

<u>In the event of a fire</u>, proceed to the nearest exit.

● **Writing Tip**

When an introductory prepositional phrase has fewer than three words, a comma is not required (*In 1969 Neil Armstrong walked on the moon*), but your sentences will be clearer if you include a comma after *every* introductory phrase.

For lists of frequently used conjunctive adverbs and transitional expressions, see 16C.

Walking home, Nelida decided to change her major.

To keep fit, people should try to exercise regularly.

Also use commas to set off **conjunctive adverbs** or **transitional expressions** whether they appear at the beginning, in the middle, or at the end of a sentence.

In fact, Thoreau spent only one night in jail.

He was, of course, bailed out by a friend.

He did spend more than two years at Walden Pond, however.

● **Writing Tip**

A conjunctive adverb or transitional expression that joins two complete sentences requires a semicolon and a comma: *Thoreau spent only one night in jail; however, he spent more than two years at Walden Pond.*

FOCUS **Using Commas in Direct Address**

Always use commas to set off the name of someone whom you are **addressing** (speaking to) directly, whether the name appears at the beginning, in the middle, or at the end of a sentence.

Molly, come here and look at this.

Come here, Molly, and look at this.

Come here and look at this, Molly.

◆ **PRACTICE 31-2**

Edit the following sentences for the use of commas with introductory phrases. If the sentence is correct, write **C** in the blank.

ON THE WEB
For more practice, visit Exercise Central *at* <bedfordstmartins.com/ writingfirst>.

Examples:

From professional athletes to teenagers‚ people have begun to find
                                      ^
alternatives to steroids.

Regulated by the Drug Enforcement Administration, steroids are a

controlled substance and can be legally obtained only with a prescrip-

tion. __C__

Teaching Tip
Review the use of commas in introductory phrases, asking students to read sentences aloud so they can hear where the natural pauses occur.

(1) In recent years‚ many Olympic athletes have been disqualified be-
                  ^
cause they tested positive for banned drugs. ____ (2) Only five days be-

fore the 2004 Athens Olympics‚ sixteen athletes were ejected from the
                              ^
games or stripped of their medals. ____ (3) In the past, banned steroids

were the most common cause of positive drug tests. __C__ (4) Recently‚
                                                                      ^
other banned substances have often been used, including erythropoietin

(EPO), which stimulates an athlete's delivery of oxygen to the blood-stream. _____ (5) In other doping scandals, athletes have tested positive for male hormones and human growth hormones. __C__ (6) Among track and field athletes͵ doping has been especially common. _____ (7) Disappointing thousands of Greeks͵ two Greek sprinting stars refused to participate in a drug test at the Athens Olympics. _____ (8) Because of their failure to take the test, they were not allowed to run. __C__ (9) For using a banned stimulant in April 2004͵ American sprinter Torri Edwards was banned from competition for two years. _____ (10) Even in the sport of baseball͵ the records of home-run hitters like Sammy Sosa and Barry Bonds have been questioned because of the possibility that the athletes were helped by banned substances. _____

◆ PRACTICE 31-3

Edit the following sentences for the use of commas with conjunctive adverbs and transitional expressions. If the sentence is correct, write **C** in the blank.

Example: Some holidays͵ of course͵ are fairly new.

(1) For example͵ the African-American celebration of Kwanzaa was introduced in the 1960s. _____ (2) This holiday celebrating important African traditions has, however͵ attracted many people over its short life. _____ (3) By the way͵ the word *Kwanzaa* means "first fruits" in Swahili. _____ (4) In other words, Kwanzaa stands for renewal. __C__ (5) This can͵ of course͵ be demonstrated in some of the seven principles of Kwanzaa. _____ (6) Kwanzaa is, in fact͵ celebrated over seven days to focus on each of these seven principles. _____ (7) The focus͵ first of all͵ is on unity *(umoja)*. _____ (8) Also͵ Kwanzaa focuses on personal self-determination *(kujichagulia)*. _____ (9) In addition͵ Kwanzaa celebrations emphasize three kinds of community responsibility *(ujima, ujamaa,* and *nia)*. _____ (10) The other principles of Kwanzaa are creativity *(kuumba)* and͵ finally, faith *(imani)*. _____

■ WRITING FIRST: Flashback

Look back at your response to the Writing First exercise on page 515. Underline any introductory phrases, conjunctive adverbs, or transitional expressions. Have you set off each of these with commas where appropriate? Revise any incorrect sentences on the lines below, adding commas where needed.

Answers will vary.

C Using Commas with Appositives

Use commas to set off an **appositive**—a word or word group that identifies, renames, or describes a noun or pronoun.

> I have visited only one country, <u>Canada</u>, outside the United States. (*Canada* is an appositive that identifies the noun *country*.)

> Carlos Santana, <u>leader of the group Santana</u>, played at Woodstock in 1969. (*Leader of the group Santana* is an appositive that identifies *Carlos Santana*.)

> <u>A really gifted artist</u>, he is also a wonderful father. (*A really gifted artist* is an appositive that describes the pronoun *he*.)

FOCUS Using Commas with Appositives

Most appositives are set off by commas, whether they fall at the beginning, in the middle, or at the end of a sentence.

> <u>A dreamer</u>, he spent his life thinking about what he could not have.

> He always wanted to build a house, <u>a big white one</u>, overlooking the ocean.

> He finally built his dream house, <u>a log cabin</u>.

ON THE WEB

For more practice, visit **Exercise Central** *at* <*bedfordstmartins.com/ writingfirst*>.

◆ **PRACTICE 31-4**

Edit the following sentences for the correct use of commas to set off appositives. If the sentence is correct, write **C** in the blank.

Examples:

The Buccaneers have not joined the Cheese League, the group of NFL teams that holds summer training in Wisconsin. _____

William Filene, the Boston merchant who founded Filene's department store, invented the concept of the "bargain basement." _____

1. Traditional Chinese medicine is based on meridians, channels of energy believed to run in regular patterns through the body. _____

2. Acupuncture, the insertion of thin needles at precise points in the body, stimulates these meridians. _____

3. Herbal medicine, the basis of many Chinese healing techniques, requires twelve years of study. _____

4. Gary Larson, creator of the popular *Far Side* cartoons, ended the series in 1995. _____

5. A musician at heart, Larson said he wanted to spend more time practicing the guitar. __C__

6. *Far Side* calendars and other product tie-ins earned Larson over $500 million, a lot of money for guitar lessons. _____

7. Nigeria, the most populous country in Africa, is also one of the fastest-growing nations in the world. _____

8. On the southwest coast of Nigeria lies Lagos, a major port. _____

9. The Yoruban people, the Nigerian settlers of Lagos, are unusual in Africa because they tend to form large urban communities. _____

10. A predominantly Christian people, the Yoruba have incorporated many native religious rituals into their practice of Christianity. _____

■ WRITING FIRST: Flashback

Look back at your response to the Writing First exercise on page 515. Have you used any appositives? Underline each one. Have you set off appositives with commas? Revise any incorrect sentences on the lines that follow.

(continued on the following page)

(continued from the previous page)

Answers will vary.

D   Using Commas to Set Off Nonrestrictive Clauses

Use commas to set off **nonrestrictive clauses**, clauses that are not essential to a sentence's meaning. Do not use commas to set off **restrictive
clauses**.

A **nonrestrictive** clause does *not* contain essential information. It does
not restrict the meaning of the sentence; therefore, it is set off from the
rest of the sentence by commas.

> Telephone calling-card fraud, <u>which cost consumers and phone
> companies four billion dollars last year</u>, is increasing.

Here, the clause between the commas (underlined) provides extra information to help readers understand the sentence, but the sentence communicates the same idea without this information.

> Telephone calling-card fraud is increasing.

A **restrictive** clause contains essential information. It restricts the
meaning of the sentence; therefore, it is *not* set off from the rest of the sentence by commas.

> Many rock stars <u>who recorded hits in the 1950s</u> made little money
> from their songs.

In the sentence above, the clause *who recorded hits in the 1950s* supplies
specific information that is essential to the idea the sentence is communicating: it tells readers which group of rock stars made little money. Without the clause, the sentence does not communicate the same idea because
it does not tell which rock stars made little money.

> Many rock stars made little money from their songs.

FOCUS   *Who, Which,* and *That*

■ *Who* can introduce either a restrictive or a nonrestrictive clause.

> RESTRICTIVE   Many parents <u>who work</u> feel a lot of stress.
> (no commas)

(continued on the following page)

(continued from the previous page)

NONRESTRICTIVE Both of my parents, <u>who have always wanted</u> <u>the best for their children</u>, have worked two jobs for years. (clause set off by commas)

■ *Which* always introduces a nonrestrictive clause.

The job, <u>which had excellent benefits</u>, did not pay well. (clause set off by commas)

■ *That* always introduces a restrictive clause.

He accepted the job <u>that had the best benefits.</u> (no commas)

◆ PRACTICE 31-5

Edit the following sentences so that commas set off all nonrestrictive clauses. (Remember, commas are *not* used to set off restrictive clauses.) If a sentence is correct, write **C** in the blank.

ON THE WEB
For more practice, visit Exercise Central *at* *<bedfordstmartins.com/ writingfirst>.*

Example: An Alaska museum exhibition that celebrates the Alaska highway tells the story of its construction. __*C*__

Teaching Tip
Have students do Practice 31-5 in groups. (Fewer papers allow you more time for careful grading.) Students can also form groups to look over the graded assignment.

(1) During the 1940s, a group of African-American soldiers who defied the forces of nature and human prejudice were shipped to Alaska. __*C*__ (2) They built the Alaska highway which stretches twelve hundred miles across Alaska. _____ (3) The troops who worked on the highway have received little attention in most historical accounts. __*C*__ (4) The highway which cut through some of the roughest terrain in the world was begun in 1942. _____ (5) The Japanese had just landed in the Aleutian Islands which lie west of the tip of the Alaska Peninsula. _____ (6) Military officials who oversaw the project doubted the ability of the African-American troops. _____ (7) As a result, they made them work under conditions that made construction difficult. _____ (8) The troops who worked on the road proved their commanders wrong by finishing the highway months ahead of schedule. __*C*__ (9) In one case, white engineers who surveyed a river said it would take two weeks to bridge. _____ (10) To the engineers' surprise, the soldiers who worked on the project beat the estimate by half a day. __*C*__ (11) A military report that was

issued in 1945 praised them. _____^C (12) It said the goals that the

African-American regiments achieved would be remembered through

the ages. _____^C

■ WRITING FIRST: Flashback

Look back at your response to the Writing First exercise on page
515. Make sure you have included commas to set off nonrestrictive
clauses and have *not* set off restrictive elements with commas.

E   Using Commas in Dates and Addresses

Dates

Use commas in dates to separate the day of the week from the month and
the day of the month from the year.

> The first Cinco de Mayo we celebrated in the United States was
> Tuesday, May 5, 1998.

When a date that includes commas does not fall at the end of a sentence,
place a comma after the date.

> Tuesday, May 5, 1998, was the first Cinco de Mayo we celebrated in
> the United States.

Addresses

Use commas in addresses to separate the street address from the city and
the city from the state or country.

> The office of the famous fictional detective Sherlock Holmes was
> located at 221b Baker Street, London, England.

When an address that includes commas does not fall at the end of a sentence, place a comma after the state or country.

> The office at 221b Baker Street, London, England, belonged to the
> famous fictional detective Sherlock Holmes.

◆ PRACTICE 31-6

Edit the following sentences for the correct use of commas in dates and
addresses. Add any missing commas, and cross out any unnecessary commas. If the sentence is correct, write *C* in the blank.

Examples:

June 3, 1968, is the day my parents were married. ____

Their wedding took place in Santiago, Chile. ____

1. The American Declaration of Independence was approved on July 4,

   1776. ____

2. The Pelican Man's Bird Sanctuary is located at 1705 Ken Thompson

   Parkway, Sarasota, Florida. ____

3. At 175 Carlton Avenue, Brooklyn, New York, is the house where Richard

   Wright began writing *Native Son*. ____

4. I found this information in the February 12, 1994, issue of the *New York*

   Times. ____

5. The Mexican hero Father Miguel Hidalgo y Costilla was shot by a fir-

   ing squad on June 30, 1811. __C__

6. The Palacio de Gobierno at Plaza de Armas, Guadalajara, Mexico,

   houses a mural of the famous revolutionary. ____

7. The Pueblo Grande Museum is located at 1469 East Washington Street,

   Phoenix, Arizona. ____

8. Brigham Young led the first settlers into the valley that is now Salt

   Lake City, Utah, in July, 1847. ____

9. St. Louis, Missouri, was the birthplace of writer Maya Angelou, but she

   spent most of her childhood in Stamps, Arkansas. ____

10. Some records list the writer's birthday as May 19, 1928, while others

    indicate she was born on April 4, 1928. ____

F   Avoiding Unnecessary Commas

In addition to knowing where commas are required, it is also important to
know when *not* to use commas.

■ Do not use a comma before the first item in a series.

    INCORRECT   *Duck Soup* starred, Groucho, Chico, and Harpo Marx.

    CORRECT   *Duck Soup* starred Groucho, Chico, and Harpo Marx.

> ● **Writing Tip**
> Use a comma between items
> in a series. (See 31A.)

■ Do not use a comma after the last item in a series.

INCORRECT   Groucho, Chico, and Harpo Marx, starred in *Duck Soup.*

CORRECT   Groucho, Chico, and Harpo Marx starred in *Duck Soup.*

■ Do not use a comma between a subject and a verb.

INCORRECT   Students and their teachers, should try to respect one another.

CORRECT   Students and their teachers should try to respect one another.

■ Do not use a comma before the coordinating conjunction that separates the two parts of a compound predicate.

INCORRECT   The transit workers voted to strike, and walked off the job.

CORRECT   The transit workers voted to strike and walked off the job.

■ Do not use a comma before the coordinating conjunction that separates the two parts of a compound subject.

INCORRECT   The transit workers, and the sanitation workers voted to strike.

CORRECT   The transit workers and the sanitation workers voted to strike.

■ Do not use a comma to set off a restrictive clause.

INCORRECT   People, who live in glass houses, should not throw stones.

CORRECT   People who live in glass houses should not throw stones.

■ Finally, do not use a comma before a dependent clause that follows an independent clause.

INCORRECT   He was exhausted, because he had driven all night.

CORRECT   He was exhausted because he had driven all night.

> ● **Writing Tip**
>
> Do use a comma before a coordinating conjunction that links independent clauses in a compound sentence: *The transit workers voted to strike, and they walked off the job.*

> **Teaching Tip**
>
> Remind students that not every *and* and *but* is preceded by a comma.

> ● **Writing Tip**
>
> Do use commas to set off a nonrestrictive clause. (See 31D.)

> ● **Writing Tip**
>
> Do use a comma after a dependent clause that comes before an independent clause: *Because he had driven all night, he was exhausted.*

◆ PRACTICE 31-7

Some of the following sentences contain unnecessary commas. Edit to eliminate unnecessary commas. If the sentence is correct, write **C** in the blank following it.

Example: Both the Dominican Republic/ and the republic of Haiti occupy the West Indian island of Hispaniola. ____

1. The capital of the Dominican Republic/ is Santo Domingo. ____

2. The country's tropical climate, generous rainfall, and fertile soil/ make the Dominican Republic suitable for many kinds of crops. ____

3. Chief among these are/ sugarcane, coffee, cocoa, and rice. ____

4. Mining is also important to the country's economy, because the land is rich in many ores. _____

5. Spanish is the official language of the Dominican Republic, and Roman Catholicism is the state religion. __C__

6. In recent years, resort areas have opened, and brought many tourists to the country. _____

7. Tourists who visit the Dominican Republic, remark on its tropical beauty. _____

8. Military attacks from abroad, and internal political unrest have marked much of the Dominican Republic's history. _____

9. Because the republic's economy has not always been strong, many Dominicans have immigrated to the United States. __C__

10. However, most Dominican immigrants maintain close ties to their home country, and return often to visit. _____

■ WRITING FIRST: Flashback

Look back at your response to the Writing First exercise on page 515. Check your work carefully to make sure you have not used commas in any of the situations listed in 31F. Make any necessary corrections.

■ WRITING FIRST: Revising and Editing

Look back at your response to the Writing First exercise on page 515. Then, make the following additions:

1. Add a sentence that includes a series of three or more words or word groups.
2. Add introductory phrases to two of your sentences.
3. Add an appositive to one of your sentences.
4. Add a conjunctive adverb or transitional expression to one of your sentences (at the beginning, in the middle, or at the end).
5. Add a nonrestrictive clause to one of your sentences.

When you have made all the additions, reread your work to check your use of commas in the new material.

CHAPTER REVIEW

◆ EDITING PRACTICE

Read the following student essay, which includes errors in comma use. Add commas where necessary between items in a series and with introductory phrases, conjunctive adverbs or transitional expressions, appositives, and nonrestrictive clauses. Cross out any unnecessary commas. The first sentence has been edited for you.

Answers may vary.

Maxine Hong Kingston

Map of China

Brave Orchid

One of the most important characters in The Woman Warrior, Maxine Hong Kingston's autobiographical work, is Brave Orchid, Kingston's mother. Brave Orchid, a complex character, is an imaginative storyteller, who tells vivid tales of China. A quiet woman, she nevertheless impresses her classmates with her intelligence. She is also a traditional woman. However, she will stop at nothing to make her family exactly what she wants it to be. Brave Orchid strongly believes in herself; even so, she sees herself as a failure.

In her native China, Brave Orchid trains to be a midwife. The other women in her class envy her independence, brilliance, and courage. One day, Brave Orchid proves her courageousness by confronting the Fox Spirit, and telling him he will not win. First of all, she tells him she can endure any pain that he inflicts on her. Next, she gathers together the women in the dormitory to burn the ghost away. After this event, the other women admire her even more.

Working hard, Brave Orchid becomes a midwife in China. After coming to America, however, she cannot work as a midwife. Instead, she works in a Chinese laundry, and picks tomatoes. None of her classmates in China would have imagined this outcome. During her later years in America, Brave Orchid becomes a woman, who is overbearing and domineering. She bosses her children around, she tries to ruin her sister's life and she criticizes everyone and everything around her. Her daughter, a straight-A student is the object of her worst criticism.

Brave Orchid's intentions are good. Nevertheless she devotes her energy to the wrong things. She wants the people around her to be as strong as she is. Because she bullies them however she eventually loses them. In addition she is too busy criticizing her daughter's faults to see all her accomplishments. Brave Orchid an independent woman and a brilliant student never achieves her goals. She is hard on the people around her/ because she is disappointed in herself.

◆ COLLABORATIVE ACTIVITIES

1. Bring a homemaking, sports, or fashion magazine to class. Working in a small group, look at the people pictured in the ads. In what roles are men most often depicted? In what roles are women most often presented? Identify the three or four most common roles for each sex, and give each kind of character a descriptive name—*jock* or *mother,* for example.

2. Working on your own, choose one type of character from the list your group made in the preceding activity. Then, write a paragraph in which you describe this character's typical appearance and habits. Refer to the appropriate magazine pictures to support your characterization.

3. Collaborating with other members of your group, write two paragraphs, one discussing how men are portrayed in ads and one discussing how women are portrayed.

4. Circle every comma in the paragraph you wrote for Collaborative Activity 2. Then, work with your group to explain why each comma is used. If no one in your group can justify a particular comma's use, cross it out.

✔ REVIEW CHECKLIST:
Using Commas

- Use commas to separate all elements in a series of three or more words or word groups. (See 31A.)

(continued on the following page)

(continued from the previous page)

- Use commas to set off introductory phrases, conjunctive adverbs, and transitional expressions from the rest of the sentence. (See 31B.)

- Use commas to set off appositives from the rest of the sentence. (See 31C.)

- Use commas to set off nonrestrictive clauses. (See 31D.)

- Use commas to separate parts of dates and addresses. (See 31E.)

- Avoid unnecessary commas. (See 31F.)

Using Apostrophes

■ WRITING FIRST

The picture above shows a female mechanic working on a car—a fairly unusual sight. Like certain jobs, certain household tasks have traditionally been considered "men's work," and others have been viewed as "women's work." Although the family, like the workplace, has changed considerably in recent years, some habits and behavior patterns have remained the same. Look at the picture above, and then discuss the tasks that are considered "men's work" and "women's work" in your current household (or in the household in which you grew up). Be sure to give examples of the responsibilities of different people in your household. (Note: Contractions, such as *isn't* or *don't*, are acceptable in this informal response.)

Word Power

gender sexual identity (male or female)

stereotype (n) a conventional, usually oversimplified, opinion or belief; (v) to develop a fixed opinion

An **apostrophe** is a punctuation mark that is used in two situations: to form a contraction and to form the possessive of a noun or an indefinite pronoun.

A **Using Apostrophes to Form Contractions**

A **contraction** is a word that uses an apostrophe to combine two words.
The apostrophe takes the place of the omitted letters.

> I didn't (*did not*) realize how late it was.
>
> It's (*it is*) not right for cheaters to go unpunished.

Frequently Used Contractions

I + am = I'm	are + not = aren't
we + are = we're	can + not = can't
you + are = you're	do + not = don't
it + is = it's	will + not = won't
I + have = I've	should + not = shouldn't
I + will = I'll	let + us = let's
there + is = there's	that + is = that's
is + not = isn't	who + is = who's

◆ PRACTICE 32-1

In the following sentences, add apostrophes to contractions if needed. If
the sentence is correct, write **C** in the blank.

Example: ~~Whats~~ the deadliest creature on earth? _____
(*What's*)

(1) Bacteria and viruses, which we ~~cant~~ (*can't*) see without a microscope,
certainly kill many people every year. _____ (2) But when we speak about
the deadliest creature, usually ~~were~~ (*we're*) talking about creatures that cause ill-
ness or death from their poison, which is called venom. _____ (3) After
~~your~~ (*you're*) bitten, stung, or stuck, how long does it take to die? _____ (4) The
fastest killer is a creature called the sea wasp, but it isn't a wasp at all.
_C_ (5) The sea wasp is actually a fifteen-foot-long jellyfish, and although ~~its~~ (*it's*) not aggressive, it can be deadly. _____ (6) People who've gone
swimming off the coast of Australia may encounter this creature. _C_
(7) While jellyfish found off the Atlantic coast of the United States
can sting, they ~~arent~~ (*aren't*) as dangerous as the sea wasp, whose venom is
deadly enough to kill sixty adults. _____ (8) A person ~~whos~~ (*who's*) been stung
by a sea wasp has anywhere from thirty seconds to four minutes to get
help or die. _____ (9) Oddly, it's been found that something as thin and
flimsy as pantyhose worn over the skin will prevent these stings. _C_

(10) Also, ~~theres~~ *there's* an antidote to the poison in the stings that can save the

lives of victims. ____

■ WRITING FIRST: Flashback

Look back at your response to the Writing First exercise on page 531, and underline any contractions. Have you used apostrophes correctly to replace the missing letters? Recopy all the contractions correctly on the lines below. Then, rewrite the contractions as two separate words.

Answers will vary.

Contractions   *Separate Words*

_____   _____   _____

_____   _____   _____

_____   _____   _____

B   Using Apostrophes to Form Possessives

Possessive forms indicate ownership. Nouns and indefinite pronouns do not have special possessive forms. Instead, they use apostrophes to indicate ownership.

● **Writing Tip**

Possessive pronouns have special forms, such as *its* and *his*, and these forms never include apostrophes. For information on possessive pronouns, see 28F.

Singular Nouns and Indefinite Pronouns

To form the possessive of singular nouns (including names) and indefinite pronouns, add an apostrophe plus an *s*.

> <u>Cesar Chavez's</u> goal *(the goal of Cesar Chavez)* was justice for American farm workers.
>
> The <u>strike's</u> outcome *(the outcome of the strike)* was uncertain.
>
> Whether it would succeed was <u>anyone's</u> guess *(the guess of anyone)*.

For more on indefinite pronouns, see 23D and 28E.

FOCUS   Singular Nouns Ending in *-s*

Even if a singular noun already ends in *-s*, add an apostrophe plus an *-s* to form the possessive.

> The <u>class's</u> next assignment was a research paper.
>
> <u>Dr. Ramos's</u> patients are participating in a clinical trial.

Plural Nouns

Most plural nouns end in -s. To form the possessive of plural nouns ending in -s (including names), add just an apostrophe (not an apostrophe plus an s).

> The two <u>drugs'</u> side effects (*the side effects of the two drugs*) were quite different.

> The <u>Johnsons'</u> front door (*the front door of the Johnsons*) is red.

Some irregular noun plurals do not end in -s. If a plural noun does not end in -s, add an apostrophe plus an s to form the possessive.

> The <u>men's</u> room is right next to the <u>women's</u> room.

● **Writing Tip**

Most nouns form the plural by adding -s. For a list of frequently used irregular noun plurals, see 28B.

ON THE WEB

For more practice, visit Exercise Central at <bedfordstmartins.com/ writingfirst>.

◆ PRACTICE 32-2

Rewrite the following phrases, changing the noun or indefinite pronoun that follows *of* to the possessive form. Be sure to distinguish between singular and plural nouns.

Examples:

the mayor of the city _the city's mayor_

the uniforms of the players _the players' uniforms_

1. the video of the singer _the singer's video_

2. the scores of the students _the students' scores_

3. the favorite band of everybody _everybody's favorite band_

4. the office of the boss _the boss's office_

5. the union of the players _the players' union_

6. the specialty of the restaurant _the restaurant's specialty_

7. the bedroom of the children _the children's bedroom_

8. the high cost of the tickets _the tickets' high cost_

9. the dreams of everyone _everyone's dreams_

10. the owner of the dogs _the dogs' owner_

■ WRITING FIRST: Flashback

Look back at your response to the Writing First exercise on page 531. Circle any possessive forms of nouns or indefinite pronouns. Have you used apostrophes correctly to form these possessives? If not, rewrite them correctly in the appropriate columns on the next page.

(continued on the following page)

(continued from the previous page)

Singular Nouns	Indefinite Pronouns	Plural Nouns
Answers will vary.		

C   Revising Incorrect Use of Apostrophes

Be careful not to confuse a plural noun *(boys)* with the singular possessive form of the noun *(boy's)*. Never use an apostrophe with a plural noun unless the noun is possessive.

Termites can be dangerous pests [not *pest's*].

The Velezes [not *Velez's*] live on Maple Drive, right next door to the Browns [not *Brown's*].

Also be careful not to use apostrophes with possessive pronouns that end in *-s: theirs* (not *their's*), *hers* (not *her's*), *its* (not *it's*), *ours* (not *our's*), and *yours* (not *your's*).

FOCUS **Possessive Pronouns**

Be especially careful not to confuse possessive pronouns with sound-alike contractions. Possessive pronouns never include apostrophes.

Possessive Pronoun	Contraction
The dog bit its master.	It's (*it is*) time for breakfast.
The choice is theirs.	There's (*there is*) no place like home.
Whose house is this?	Who's (*who is*) on first?
Is this your house?	You're (*you are*) late again.

● **Writing Tip**
Your computer's spell checker will not tell you when you have used a contraction for a possessive form—*it's* for *its*, for example. If you are not sure you have used the correct form, consult a dictionary.

◆ PRACTICE 32-3

Check the underlined words in the following sentences for correct use of apostrophes. If a correction needs to be made, cross out the word, and write the correct version above it. If the noun or pronoun is correct, write **C** above it.

Example: The president's views were presented after several other
    speakers   *theirs.*
    ~~speaker's~~ first presented ~~their's.~~

ON THE WEB
For more practice, visit
Exercise Central *at*
<bedfordstmartins.com/ writingfirst>.

32 C

Teaching Tip
Even strong writers often
have trouble distinguishing
plural nouns from singular
possessive forms and using
apostrophes correctly with
possessive pronouns. You
may want to review 32C and
Practice 32-3 in class.

1. *Parents*
   ~~Parent's~~ should realize that when it comes to disciplining children, the
   theirs.
   responsibility is ~~their's.~~
   C   *C*
2. It's also important that parents offer praise for a child's good behavior.
   its   *weeks*
3. In ~~it's~~ first few ~~week's~~ of life, a child is already developing a personality.
   hers   *couples,*   *C*
4. His and ~~her's~~ towels used to be popular with ~~couple's,~~ but it's not so
   common to see them today.
   Ryans   *years*
5. All the ~~Ryan's~~ spent four ~~year's~~ in college and then went on to graduate
   school.
   C   *whose*
6. From the radio came the lyrics "You're the one ~~who's~~ love I've been
   waiting for."
   classes,
7. If you expect to miss any ~~class's,~~ you will have to make arrangements
   C   *your*
   with someone who's willing to tell you ~~you're~~ assignment.
   C
8. No other school's cheerleading squad ever tried as many tricky stunts
   ours
   as ~~our's~~ did.
   tests   *C*
9. Surprise ~~test's~~ are a regular feature of my economics teacher's class.
   C   *musicians*   *C*
10. Jazz's influence on many mainstream ~~musician's~~ is one of the book's
    subjects.
    main ~~subject's.~~

■ WRITING FIRST: Flashback

Look back at your response to the Writing First exercise on page
531. Circle each plural noun. Then, circle each possessive pronoun
that ends in -s. Have you incorrectly used an apostrophe with any
of the circled words? If so, revise your work.

■ WRITING FIRST: Revising and Editing

Look back at your response to the Writing First exercise on page
531. Because this is an informal exercise, contractions are acceptable; in fact, they may be preferable because they give your writing
a conversational tone. Edit your writing so that you have used contractions in all possible situations.

(continued on the following page)

(continued from the previous page)

Now, add two sentences—one that includes a singular possessive noun and one that includes a plural possessive noun. Make
sure these two new sentences fit smoothly into your writing and
that they, too, use contractions wherever possible.

CHAPTER REVIEW

◆ EDITING PRACTICE

Read the following student essay, which includes errors in the use of apostrophes. Edit it to eliminate errors by crossing out incorrect words and
writing corrections above them. (Note that this is an informal response
paper, so contractions are acceptable.) The first sentence has been edited
for you.

The Women of Messina

In William ~~Shakespeares'~~ *Shakespeare's* play <u>Much Ado about Nothing</u>,
the women of Messina, whether they are seen as love objects
or as ~~shrew's,~~ *shrews,* have very few options. A ~~womans~~ *woman's* role is to
please a man. She can try to resist, but she will probably
wind up giving in. The ~~plays~~ *play's* two women, Hero and Beatrice,
are very different. Hero is the obedient one. ~~Heroes~~ *Hero's*
cousin, Beatrice, tries to challenge the rules of the ~~mans~~ *man's*
world in which she lives. However, in a place like Messina,
even women like Beatrice find it hard to get the respect
that should be ~~their's.~~ *theirs.*

Right from the start, we are drawn to Beatrice. ~~Shes~~ *She's*
funny, she has a clever comment for most ~~situation's,~~ *situations,* and
she always speaks her mind about other ~~peoples~~ *people's* behavior.
Unlike Hero, she tries to stand up to the men in her life,
as we see in her and ~~Benedicks~~ *Benedick's* conversations. But even
though Beatrice's intelligence is obvious, she often
mocks herself. ~~Its~~ *It's* clear that she doesn't have much self-
esteem. In fact, Beatrice ~~is'nt~~ *isn't* the strong woman she seems
to be.

William Shakespeare

Shakespeare's Globe Theater

Ultimately, Beatrice does get her man, and she will be happy—but at what cost? ~~Benedicks'~~ *Benedick's* last ~~word's~~ *words* to her are "Peace! I will stop your mouth." Then, he kisses her. The kiss is a symbolic end to their bickering. It is also the mark of ~~Beatrices~~ *Beatrice's* defeat. She has lost. Benedick has shut her up. Now, she will be Benedick's wife and do what he wants her to do. Granted, she will have more say in her marriage than Hero will have in ~~her's,~~ *hers,* but she is still defeated. Even Beatrice, the most rebellious of ~~Messinas~~ *Messina's* women, finds it impossible to achieve anything of importance in this male-dominated society.

◆ COLLABORATIVE ACTIVITIES

1. Working in a group of four and building on your individual responses to the Writing First exercise at the beginning of the chapter, consider which specific occupational and professional roles are still associated largely with men and which are associated primarily with women. Make two lists, heading one "women's jobs" and one "men's jobs."

2. Now, work in pairs, with one pair of students in each group concentrating on men and the other pair on women. Write a paragraph that attempts to justify why the particular jobs you listed should or should not be restricted to one gender. In your discussion, list the various qualities men or women possess that qualify (or disqualify) them for particular jobs. Use possessive forms whenever possible—for example, *women's energy* (not *women have energy*).

3. Bring to class a book, magazine, or newspaper whose style is informal—for example, a romance novel, *TV Guide,* your school newspaper, or even a comic book. Working in a group, circle every contraction you can find on one page of each publication, and substitute for each contraction the words it combines. Are your substitutions an improvement? (You may want to read a few paragraphs aloud before you reach a conclusion.)

☑ REVIEW CHECKLIST:
Using Apostrophes

- Use apostrophes to form contractions. (See 32A.)

- Use an apostrophe plus an *s* to form the possessive of singular nouns and indefinite pronouns, even when a noun ends in *-s*. (See 32B.)

(continued on the following page)

(continued from the previous page)

☐ Use an apostrophe alone to form the possessive of plural nouns ending in *-s,* including names. If a plural noun does not end in *-s,* add an apostrophe plus an *s.* (See 32B.)

☐ Do not use apostrophes with plural nouns unless they are possessive. Do not use apostrophes with possessive pronouns. (See 32C.)

Understanding Mechanics

■ **WRITING FIRST**

The picture above shows a familiar scene from the 1939 film *The Wizard of Oz*. Look at the picture, and then describe a memorable scene from your favorite movie. Begin by giving the film's title and listing the names of the major stars and the characters they play. Then, tell what happens in the scene, quoting a few lines of dialogue if possible.

A   Capitalizing Proper Nouns

A **proper noun** names a particular person, animal, place, object, or idea. Proper nouns are always capitalized. The list that follows explains and illustrates specific rules for capitalizing proper nouns and also includes some important exceptions to those rules.

1. Always capitalize names of races, ethnic groups, tribes, nationalities, languages, and religions.

   The census data revealed a diverse community of <u>C</u>aucasians, <u>A</u>frican <u>A</u>mericans, and <u>A</u>sian <u>A</u>mericans, with a few <u>L</u>atino and <u>N</u>avajo residents. Native languages included <u>E</u>nglish, <u>K</u>orean, and <u>S</u>panish. Most people identified themselves as <u>C</u>atholic, <u>P</u>rotestant, or <u>M</u>uslim.

● **Writing Tip**
The words *black* and *white* are generally not capitalized when they name racial groups. However, *African American* and *Caucasian* are always capitalized.

2. Capitalize names of specific people and the titles that accompany them. In general, do not capitalize titles used without a name.

   In 1994, <u>P</u>resident <u>N</u>elson <u>M</u>andela was elected to lead South Africa.

   The newly elected fraternity <u>p</u>resident addressed the crowd.

3. Capitalize names of specific family members and their titles. Do not capitalize words that identify family relationships, including those introduced by possessive pronouns.

   The twins, <u>A</u>unt <u>E</u>dna and <u>A</u>unt <u>E</u>velyn, are <u>D</u>ad's sisters.

   My <u>a</u>unts, my <u>f</u>ather's sisters, are twins.

4. Capitalize names of specific countries, cities, towns, bodies of water, streets, and so forth. Do not capitalize words that do not name particular places.

   The <u>S</u>eine runs through <u>P</u>aris, <u>F</u>rance.

   The <u>r</u>iver runs through the <u>c</u>ity.

5. Capitalize names of specific geographical regions. Do not capitalize such words when they specify direction.

   William Faulkner's novels are set in the American <u>S</u>outh.

   Turn right at the golf course, and go <u>s</u>outh for about a mile.

6. Capitalize names of specific buildings and monuments. Do not capitalize general references to buildings and monuments.

   He drove past the <u>L</u>iberty <u>B</u>ell and looked for a parking space near City <u>H</u>all.

   He drove past the <u>m</u>onument and looked for a parking space near the <u>b</u>uilding.

7. Capitalize names of specific groups, clubs, teams, and associations. Do not capitalize general references to such groups.

   The Teamsters <u>U</u>nion represents workers who were at the stadium for the <u>R</u>epublican <u>P</u>arty convention, the <u>R</u>olling <u>S</u>tones concert, and the <u>P</u>hillies-<u>A</u>stros game.

   The <u>u</u>nion represents workers who were at the stadium for the <u>p</u>olitical <u>p</u>arty's convention, the <u>r</u>ock <u>g</u>roup's concert, and the <u>b</u>aseball <u>t</u>eams' game.

8. Capitalize names of specific historical periods, events, and documents. Do not capitalize nonspecific references to periods, events, or documents.

The Emancipation Proclamation was signed during the Civil War, not during Reconstruction.

The document was signed during the war, not during the postwar period.

9. Capitalize names of businesses, government agencies, schools, and other institutions. Do not capitalize nonspecific references to such institutions.

The Department of Education and Apple Computer have launched a partnership project with Central High School.

A government agency and a computer company have launched a partnership project with a high school.

10. Capitalize brand names. Do not capitalize general references to kinds of products.

While Jeff waited for his turn at the Xerox machine, he drank a can of Coke.

While Jeff waited for his turn at the copier, he drank a can of soda.

11. Capitalize titles of specific academic courses. Do not capitalize names of general academic subject areas, except for proper nouns—for example, a language or a country.

Are Introduction to American Government and Biology 200 closed yet?

Are the introductory American government course and the biology course closed yet?

12. Capitalize days of the week, months of the year, and holidays. Do not capitalize the names of seasons.

The Jewish holiday of Passover usually falls in April.

The Jewish holiday of Passover falls in the spring.

◆ PRACTICE 33-1

Edit the following sentences, capitalizing letters or changing capitals to lowercase where necessary.

Example: The third largest ~~C~~ity in the ~~u~~nited ~~s~~tates is ~~c~~hicago, ~~i~~llinois.

(1) Located in the ~~m~~idwest on ~~l~~ake Michigan, ~~c~~hicago is an important port city, a rail and highway hub, and the site of ~~o~~'~~h~~are ~~i~~nternational ~~a~~irport, one of the ~~N~~ation's busiest. (2) The financial center of the city is

ON THE WEB

For more practice, visit
Exercise Central *at*
<bedfordstmartins.com/
writingfirst>.

Lasalle street, and the lakefront is home to Grant park, where there are many Museums and monuments. (3) To the North of the city, soldier field is home to the chicago bears, the city's football team, and wrigley field is home to the chicago cubs, a national league Baseball Team. (4) In the mid-1600s, the site of what is now Chicago was visited by father jacques marquette, a catholic missionary to the ottawa and huron tribes, who were native to the area. (5) By the 1700s, the city was a trading post run by john kinzie. (6) The city grew rapidly in the 1800s, and immigrants included germans, irish, italians, poles, greeks, and chinese, along with african americans who migrated from the south. (7) In 1871, much of the city was destroyed in one of the worst fires in united states history; the fire started when, according to legend, mrs. O'Leary's Cow kicked over a burning lantern. (8) Today, Chicago's skyline is marked by many Skyscrapers, built by businesses like the john hancock company, sears, and amoco. (9) I know Chicago well because my Mother grew up there and my aunt jean and uncle amos still live there. (10) I also got information from the Chicago Chamber of Commerce when I wrote a paper for introductory research writing, a course I took at Graystone high school.

■ WRITING FIRST: Flashback

Look back at your response to the Writing First exercise on page 540. Underline every proper noun. Does each proper noun begin with a capital letter? On the lines below, correct any that do not.

Answers will vary. _____ _____

_____ _____ _____

B Punctuating Direct Quotations

A **direct quotation** reproduces the *exact* words of a speaker or writer. Direct quotations are always placed within quotation marks.

> Lauren said, "My brother and Tina have gotten engaged."

> A famous advertiser wrote, "Don't sell the steak; sell the sizzle."

When a quotation is a complete sentence, it begins with a capital letter. When a quotation falls at the end of a sentence, as in the two examples on the preceding page, the period is placed inside the quotation marks. If the quotation is a question or an exclamation, the question mark or an exclamation point is also placed inside the quotation marks.

The instructor asked, "Has anyone read *Sula*?"

Officer Warren shouted, "Hold it right there!"

If the quotation itself is not a question or an exclamation, the question mark or exclamation point goes *outside* the quotation marks.

Did Joe really say, "I quit"?

I can't believe he really said, "I quit"!

FOCUS Indirect Quotations

Be careful not to confuse direct and indirect quotations. A direct quotation reproduces someone's *exact* words, but an **indirect quotation** simply summarizes what was said or written.

Indirect quotations are not placed within quotation marks.

> DIRECT QUOTATION   Martin Luther King Jr. said, "I have a dream."

> INDIRECT QUOTATION   Martin Luther King Jr. said that he had a dream.

● **Writing Tip**

Note that an indirect quotation is usually introduced by the word *that* (*She told me that she was cold*).

Teaching Tip

You may need to explain what an identifying tag is by literally pointing it out.

FOCUS Identifying Tags

A direct quotation is usually accompanied by an **identifying tag**, a phrase that names the person or work being quoted.

■ **Identifying tag at the beginning** When the identifying tag comes *before* the quotation, it is followed by a comma.

Alexandre Dumas wrote, "Nothing succeeds like success."

■ **Identifying tag at the end** When the identifying tag comes at the *end* of the sentence, it is followed by a period. A comma (or, sometimes, a question mark or exclamation point) inside the closing quotation marks separates the quotation from the identifying tag.

"Life is like a box of chocolates," stated Forrest Gump.

"Is that so?" his friends wondered.

(continued on the following page)

(continued from the previous page)

■ **Identifying tag in the middle** When the identifying tag comes in the *middle* of the quoted sentence, it is followed by a comma. The first part of the quotation is also followed by a comma, placed inside the quotation marks. Because the part of the quotation that follows the tag is not a new sentence, it does not begin with a capital letter.

"This is my life," Bette insisted, "and I'll live it as I please."

■ **Identifying tag between two sentences** When the identifying tag comes between two quoted sentences, it is followed by a period, and the second quoted sentence begins with a capital letter.

"Producer Barry Gordy is an important figure in the history of music," Tony explained. "He was the creative force behind Motown records."

◆ PRACTICE 33-2

The following sentences contain direct quotations. First, underline the identifying tag. Then, punctuate the quotation correctly, adding capital letters as necessary.

ON THE WEB
For more practice, visit
Exercise Central *at*
*<bedfordstmartins.com/
writingfirst>.*

Example: " Why Darryl asked " are teachers so strict about deadlines? "

1. We who are about to die salute you said <u>the gladiators</u> to the emperor.

2. When we turned on the television, <u>the newscaster was saying</u> ladies and gentlemen, we have a new president-elect.

3. The bigger they are said <u>boxer John L. Sullivan</u> the harder they fall.

4. Do you take Michael to be your lawfully wedded husband asked <u>the minister.</u>

5. <u>Lisa Marie replied</u> I do.

6. If you believe the *National Enquirer* <u>my friend always says</u> then you'll believe anything.

7. When asked for the jury's verdict, <u>the foreperson replied</u> we find the defendant not guilty.

8. I had felt for a long time that if I was ever told to get up so a white person could sit <u>Rosa Parks recalled</u> I would refuse to do so.

9. Yabba dabba doo <u>Fred exclaimed</u> this brontoburger looks great.

10. Where's my money <u>Addie Pray asked</u> you give me my money!

Teaching Tip
Have students write sentences from Practice 33-2 on the board. Review fragments, which can be caused by incorrect punctuation of tags. Refer students to Chapter 22.

◆ **PRACTICE 33-3**

The following quotations are followed in parentheses by the names of the people who wrote or spoke them. On the blank lines, write a sentence that includes the quotation and places the identifying tag in the position that the directions specify. Be sure to punctuate and capitalize correctly.

Example: Nothing endures but change. (written by the Greek philosopher Heraclitus)

Identifying tag in the middle _"Nothing endures," wrote the Greek philoso-_

pher Heraclitus, "but change."

Answers will vary.

1. One is not born a woman; one becomes one. (written by essayist Simone de Beauvoir)

   Identifying tag at the beginning _Essayist Simone de Beauvoir wrote, "One_

   is not born a woman; one becomes one."

2. I want a kinder, gentler nation. (spoken by former president George Herbert Walker Bush)

   Identifying tag at the end _"I want a kinder, gentler nation," said former_

   president George Herbert Walker Bush.

3. Tribe follows tribe, and nation follows nation. (spoken by Suquamish Chief Seattle in 1854)

   Identifying tag in the middle _"Tribe follows tribe," said Suquamish Chief_

   Seattle in 1854, "and nation follows nation."

4. When I'm good, I'm very good. When I'm bad, I'm better. (spoken by actress Mae West in the classic film *I'm No Angel*)

   Identifying tag in the middle _"When I'm good, I'm very good," said_

   actress Mae West in the classic film I'm No Angel. "When I'm bad,

   I'm better."

5. The rich rob the poor, and the poor rob one another. (spoken by abolitionist Sojourner Truth)

   Identifying tag at the beginning _Abolitionist Sojourner Truth said, "The_

   rich rob the poor, and the poor rob one another."

6. Heaven is like an egg, and the earth is like the yolk of the egg. (written by Chinese philosopher Chang Heng)

   Identifying tag in the middle _"Heaven is like an egg." wrote the Chinese_

   philosopher Chang Heng, "and the earth is like the yolk of the egg."

7. When I found I had crossed that line, I looked at my hands to see if I was the same person. (spoken by former slave Harriet Tubman)

Identifying tag at the beginning *Former slave Harriet Tubman said, "When I found I had crossed that line, I looked at my hands to see if I was the same person."*

8. If a man hasn't discovered something he will die for, then he isn't fit to live. (spoken by Martin Luther King Jr.)

Identifying tag at the end *"If a man hasn't discovered something he will die for, then he isn't fit to live," said Martin Luther King Jr.*

9. No man chooses evil because it is evil. He only mistakes it for happiness. (written in 1790 by Mary Wollstonecraft)

Identifying tag in the middle *"No man chooses evil because it is evil," wrote Mary Wollstonecraft in 1790. "He only mistakes it for happiness."*

10. Marriage is an evil, but a necessary evil. (written by the ancient Greek poet Menander)

Identifying tag at the beginning *The ancient Greek poet Menander wrote, "Marriage is an evil, but a necessary evil."*

■ WRITING FIRST: Flashback

Look back at your response to the Writing First exercise on page 540. Make sure that you have enclosed any direct quotations in quotation marks, placed other punctuation correctly, and capitalized where necessary. Revise any incorrectly punctuated quotations on the following lines.

Answers will vary.

C Setting Off Titles of Books, Stories, and Other Works

Some titles are typed in *italics* (or <u>underlined</u> to indicate italics). Others are enclosed in quotation marks. The following box shows how to set off different kinds of titles.

Teaching Tip
Remind students that they should underline to indicate italics in handwritten work. MLA style recommends underlining in typed work as well, but you may prefer that students use italics.

Teaching Tip
Remind students not to use underlining and quotation marks together (as in "America the Beautiful").

● **Writing Tip**
When you type your own papers, do not underline your title or enclose it in quotation marks. (Only titles of *published* works are set off in this way.)

ESL Tip
Students may forget to include articles in titles. Remind them to include them—but not to capitalize an article unless it is the first word of the title.

Italicized Titles

Books: *How the García Girls Lost Their Accents*
Newspapers: the *Miami Herald*
Magazines: *People*
Long poems: *John Brown's Body*
Plays: *Death of a Salesman*
Films: *The Rocky Horror Picture Show*
Television or radio series: *Star Trek: The Next Generation*

Titles in Quotation Marks

Book chapters: "Understanding Mechanics"
Short stories: "The Tell-Tale Heart"
Essays and articles: "The Suspected Shopper"
Short poems: "Richard Cory"
Songs: "America the Beautiful"
Individual episodes of television or radio series: "The Montgomery Bus Boycott" (an episode of the PBS series *Eyes on the Prize*)

FOCUS Capital Letters in Titles

The first letters of all important words in a title are capitalized. Do not capitalize an article (*a, an, the*), a preposition (*to, of, around,* and so on), or a coordinating conjunction (*and, but,* and so on) unless it is the first or last word of the title or subtitle (*On the Road;* "To an Athlete Dying Young"; *No Way Out; And Quiet Flows the Don*).

◆ **PRACTICE 33-4**

Edit the following sentences, capitalizing letters as necessary in titles.

         A W P
Example: Eudora Welty's "a worn path" is a very moving short story.

                                       P   N   O
1. Directed by the wacky Ed Wood, the 1959 movie *plan nine from outer*
   S
space has been called the worst picture of all time.

                                           A P
2. Gary Larson's cartoon collections include the books *a prehistory of the*
  F S   W   D A
far side and *weiner dog art.*

                                       I H   D
3. Everyone should read Martin Luther King Jr.'s "i have a dream" speech
      L   B   J
and "letter from birmingham jail."

                           T R   L
4. Bruce Springsteen's album *the rising* includes the songs "lonesome
  D   I   F   M C   R
day," "into the fire," and "my city of ruins."

                  CSI CSI M   CSI N Y
5. CBS has had hits with *csi, csi: miami,* and *csi: new york.*

ON THE WEB
For more practice, visit Exercise Central *at* <bedfordstmartins.com/ writingfirst>.

◆ **PRACTICE 33-5**

In the following sentences, underline or insert quotation marks around titles. (Remember that titles of books and other long works are underlined, and titles of stories, essays, and other shorter works are enclosed in quotation marks.)

> **Example:**   An article in the <u>New York Times</u> called "It's Not Easy Being Green" is a profile of former Chicago Bulls player Dennis Rodman, who once had green hair.

1. Sui Sin Far's short story "The Wisdom of the New," from her book <u>Mrs. Spring Fragrance</u>, is about the clash between Chinese and American cultures in the early twentieth century.

2. Major league baseball games traditionally open with fans singing "The Star-Spangled Banner."

3. Interesting information about fighting skin cancer can be found in the article "Putting Sunscreens to the Test," which appeared in the magazine <u>Consumer Reports</u>.

4. One of the best-known poems of the twentieth century is Robert Frost's "The Road Not Taken."

5. Ang Lee has directed several well-received films, including <u>Crouching Tiger, Hidden Dragon</u>.

6. It is surprising how many people enjoy reruns of two 1960s television series: <u>Bewitched</u> and <u>I Dream of Jeannie</u>.

7. The title of Lorraine Hansberry's play <u>A Raisin in the Sun</u> comes from Langston Hughes's poem "Harlem."

8. In his autobiography, <u>Breaking the Surface</u>, Olympic diving champion Greg Louganis wrote about his struggle with AIDS.

■ WRITING FIRST: Flashback

Look back at your response to the Writing First exercise on page 540. Circle the film's title. Have you underlined it? Are capital letters used where necessary? Make any corrections on the lines below.

Answers will vary.

*For information on sentence
types, see 18A.*

D   **Using Minor Punctuation Marks**

A sentence may end with a period, a question mark, or an exclamation point. If a sentence is a statement, it ends with a **period**; if it is a question, it ends with a **question mark**; if it is an exclamation, it ends with an **exclamation point**. Other important punctuation marks are the **comma** (Chapter 31), the **apostrophe** (Chapter 32), and the **semicolon** (16B).

Three additional punctuation marks—*colons, dashes,* and *parentheses*—are used to set off material from the rest of the sentence.

The Colon

Use a **colon** to introduce a quotation.

> Our family motto is a simple one: "Accept no substitutes."

Use a colon to introduce an explanation, a clarification, or an example.

> Only one thing kept him from climbing Mt. Everest: fear of heights.

Also use a colon to introduce a list.

> I left my job for four reasons: boring work, poor working conditions, low pay, and a terrible supervisor.

● **Writing Tip**

When a colon introduces a quotation, an example, or a list, a complete sentence must precede the colon.

● **Writing Tip**

All items in a list should be parallel. (See Chapter 19.)

The Dash

Use **dashes** to emphasize information by setting it off from the rest of the sentence.

> She parked her car—a red Firebird—in a towaway zone.

● **Writing Tip**

Dashes give writing an informal tone. Use them sparingly in college and professional writing.

Parentheses

Use **parentheses** to set off material that is not an essential part of the sentence.

> The weather in Portland (a city in Oregon) was overcast.

ON THE WEB
For more practice, visit
Exercise Central *at*
*<bedfordstmartins.com/
writingfirst>.*

◆ PRACTICE 33-6

Add colons, dashes, and parentheses to the following sentences where necessary.

> **Example:**   New Orleans (population 465,000) is the largest city in Louisiana.
>
> *Answers will vary.*

1. New Orleans has two nicknames: the "Crescent City" and the "City that Care Forgot."

2. The oldest part of the city known as the French Quarter dates to the early 1700s.

3. The French Quarter is famous for several attractions¦its unique build-

   ings, its fine food, its street musicians, and its wild nightlife.

4. Jackson Square (called Place d'Armes by the original French settlers)

   lies at the heart of the French Quarter.

5. At the center of the square—a gathering place for artists—is a monument

   to Andrew Jackson.

6. Located next to Jackson Square is a famous coffee house¦the Café du

   Monde.

7. Its popular beignets (pronounced ben-*yeas*) are deep-fried pastries

   covered with sugar.

8. Visitors to New Orleans can try many traditional foods¦crayfish,

   gumbos, blackened fish, and "dirty" rice.

9. New Orleans visitors—people from all over the world—particularly enjoy

   the laid-back atmosphere of the city.

10. This atmosphere is summed up in the city's unofficial motto¦"Let the

    good times roll."

■ WRITING FIRST: Flashback

Look back at your response to the Writing First exercise on page
540. Do you see places where you might add a quotation, an example, or a list that could be introduced by a colon? Write your
possible additions here.

Quotation: _____

Example: _____

List: _____

■ WRITING FIRST: Revising and Editing

Look back at your response to the Writing First exercise on page
540. If you have quoted specific lines of dialogue from the film, try
varying the placement of the identifying tags you have used. If you
did not include quotations, try adding one or two. Then, add the

(continued on the following page)

(continued from the previous page)
quotation, example, or list from the Flashback exercise on page 551 to your Writing First exercise, introducing it with a colon. Finally, edit for proper use of capital letters, quotation marks, and under-lining.

CHAPTER REVIEW

◆ EDITING PRACTICE

Read the following student essay, which includes errors in capitalization and punctuation and in the use of direct quotations and titles. Edit the passage to correct any such errors. The first sentence has been edited for you.

Answers may vary.

Gary Soto

The World of Gary Soto

My favorite Author is Gary Soto, a mexican-american poet and fiction writer whose first book of poetry, "The Elements of San Joaquin," was published in 1977. Soto was born in 1952 in fresno, california, and grew up in a large spanish-speaking family. His Father he died when Soto was five worked in a factory, and his Mother picked grapes and other crops in the farms of the san joaquin valley. Much of Soto's writing is influenced by childhood memories. "These are the pictures I take with me when I write" he once said. "they stir the past, the memories that are so vivid."

Soto attended fresno city college and later studied at the university of California at fresno, where he originally majored in Geology. There, according to Soto, "One day I came across a book of poetry on a shelf in the college library. I read it, liked it, and began to write poems of my own"/

One of Soto's best poems is Oranges, from his 1985 book "Black Hair." In this poem, he describes the events of a cold december afternoon when a boy takes his girlfriend

into a drugstore to buy her a treat. She wants a chocolate
that costs a Dime, but he only has a Nickel. He gives the
Saleslady the coin plus an orange he has in his pocket,
and, knowing what is going on, she lets him pay for the
candy this way. In another poem, "How things Work," Soto
also writes about money. This poem is about how people are
connected by one important thing the money they spend.

   This theme of money is picked up again in the Title
of one of Soto's books of stories, "Nickel And Dime." The
first story is called "We Ain't Asking Much" and is about
Roberto, who loses his job, cannot pay his rent, and ends
up on the Street, trying to sell Christmas ornaments made
of twigs to rich people. Silver, a Character in another
story, has something in common with Soto he is a poet but
he also has trouble making enough money to live on. It
is interesting that Silver lives in Oakland near San
Francisco, where Soto himself lives.

   Does Soto write from Personal Experience? He admits
that this is partly true. He says, however, "Although the
experiences in my stories, poems, and novels may seem
autobiographical, much of what I write is the stuff of
imagination."

Book jacket of Nickel and Dime

◆ COLLABORATIVE ACTIVITIES

1. Imagine that you and the other members of your group are the nomi-
nations committee for this year's Emmy, Oscar, or Grammy Awards.
Work together to compile a list of categories and several nominees for
each category, deciding as a group when to use capital letters.

   Trade lists with another group. From each category, select the individual artist or work you believe deserves to win the award. Write
a sentence about each winner, explaining why each is the best in its
category.

   When you have finished, exchange papers with another group.
Check one another's papers for correct use of capitals, quotation
marks, and underlining.

2. Using a separate sheet of paper, work in groups to list as many items
in each of the following five categories as you can: planets, islands,
musicians or bands, automobile models, sports teams. Be sure all your
items are proper nouns, and use capital letters where necessary.

On the lines below, write five original sentences using one proper noun from each category in each sentence.

Answers will vary.

_____

_____

_____

_____

_____

_____

_____

_____

_____

_____

_____

Teaching Tip
Encourage students to write at least five or six sentences of dialogue.

3. Working in pairs, write a conversation between two characters, real or fictional, who have very different positions on a particular issue. Place all direct quotations within quotation marks, and include identifying tags that clearly indicate which character is speaking. (Begin a new paragraph each time a new person speaks.)

Exchange your conversations with another pair of students, and check their work to see that all directly quoted speech is set within quotation marks and that capital letters and all other punctuation are used correctly.

☑ **REVIEW CHECKLIST:**

Understanding Mechanics

☐ Capitalize proper nouns. (See 33A.)

☐ Always place direct quotations within quotation marks. (See 33B.)

☐ In titles, capitalize all important words. Use italics or quotation marks to set off titles. (See 33C.)

☐ Use colons, dashes, and parentheses to set off material from the rest of the sentence. (See 33D.)

Understanding Spelling

PREVIEW

In this chapter, you will learn

■ to become a better speller (34A)

■ to know when to use *ie* and *ei* (34B)

■ to understand prefixes (34C)

■ to understand suffixes (34D)

■ to identify commonly confused words (34E)

■ WRITING FIRST

In an effort to improve discipline and boost self-esteem, a number of schools across the country have begun requiring students to wear uniforms. The picture above shows a group of students at one such elementary school. Look at the picture, and then write about whether or not you think elementary school students should be required to wear uniforms such as the ones in the picture.

Word Power
conducive to   leading to; contributing to

economical   thrifty

individuality   the quality of being distinct from others

A   Becoming a Better Speller

Improving your spelling may take time, but the following steps can make this task a lot easier.

1. *Use a spell checker.* When you write on a computer, use your spell checker. It will correct most misspelled words and also identify many typos, such as transposed or omitted letters. Keep in mind, however,

that spell checkers have limitations. They do not identify typos that create other words (*then/than, form/from,* or *big/beg,* for example) or words that you have used incorrectly (*their/there* or *its/it's,* for example). For this reason, even if you use a spell checker, you still have to know how to spell.

2. *Proofread carefully.* Even if you have used a spell checker, always proofread your papers for spelling before you hand them in.

3. *Use a dictionary.* As you proofread your papers, circle words whose spellings you are unsure of. After you have finished your draft, look up these words in a college dictionary. It will give you the spelling of a word, tell you how to pronounce the word, and show you which syllables to stress.

4. *Keep a personal spelling list.* Write down all the words you misspell. If you keep a writing journal, set aside a few pages in the back for your personal spelling list. Whenever your instructor returns one of your papers, look for misspelled words—usually circled and marked *sp.* Add these to your personal spelling list.

5. *Look for patterns in your misspelling.* Do you consistently misspell words with *ei* combinations? Do you have trouble forming plurals? Once you figure out which errors you make most frequently, you can take steps to eliminate them.

6. *Learn the basic spelling rules.* Memorize the spelling rules in this chapter, especially those that apply to areas in which you are weak. Remember that each rule can help you spell many words correctly.

7. *Review the list of commonly confused words in 34E.* If you have problems with any of these word pairs, add them to your personal spelling list.

8. *Make flash cards.* If you consistently have trouble with spelling, put individual words on 3- by 5-inch cards. You can use them to test yourself periodically.

9. *Use memory cues.* Memory cues help you remember how to spell certain words. For example, remembering that *definite* contains the word *finite* will help you remember that *definite* is spelled with an *i,* not an *a.*

10. *Learn to spell some of the most frequently misspelled words.* Identify those on the list below that give you trouble, and add them to your personal spelling list.

Frequently Misspelled Words

across	calendar	describe	finally
all right	cannot	develop	forty
a lot	careful	disappoint	fulfill
already	careless	early	generally
argument	cemetery	embarrass	government
beautiful	certain	entrance	grammar
becoming	conscience	environment	harass
beginning	definite	everything	height
believe	definitely	exercise	holiday
benefit	dependent	experience	integration

(continued on the following page)

(continued from the previous page)

intelligence	occurrences	receive	tomatoes
interest	occurring	recognize	truly
interfere	occurs	reference	until
judgment	personnel	restaurant	usually
loneliness	possible	roommate	Wednesday
medicine	potato	secretary	weird
minute	potatoes	sentence	window
necessary	prejudice	separate	withhold
noticeable	prescription	speech	woman
occasion	privilege	studying	women
occur	privilege	surprise	writing
occurred	probably	tomato	written
	professor		

Because English pronunciation is not always a reliable guide for spelling, most people find it useful to memorize some spelling rules.

Teaching Tip
Discuss the fact that English spelling is complex and unpredictable. Mention that many languages have more regular spelling than English does.

FOCUS   Vowels and Consonants

Knowing which letters are vowels and which are consonants will help you understand the spelling rules presented in this chapter.

> *Vowels: a, e, i, o, u*

> *Consonants: b, c, d, f, g, h, j, k, l, m, n, p, q, r, s, t, v, w, x, z*

The letter *y* may be considered either a vowel or a consonant, depending on how it is pronounced. In *young, y* acts as a consonant because it has the sound of *y;* in *truly,* it acts as a vowel because it has the sound of *ee.*

B   Deciding between *ie* and *ei*

Memorize this rule: *i* comes before *e* except after *c,* or when the *ei* sound is pronounced *ay* (as in *neighbor*).

Teaching Tip
Have students memorize spelling rules. Test them on these rules.

i before *e*	except after *c*	or when *ei* is pronounced *ay*
achieve	ceiling	eight
believe	conceive	freight
friend	deceive	neighbor
		weigh

Teaching Tip
Tell students that when the
i and *e* in a word are not
pronounced as a unit (as in
science), the "*i* before *e*" rule
does not apply.

ON THE WEB
For more practice, visit
Exercise Central *at*
<bedfordstmartins.com/
writingfirst>.

FOCUS **Exceptions to the "*i* before *e*" Rule**

There are some exceptions to the "*i* before *e*" rule. The exceptions
follow no pattern, so you must memorize them.

ancient	either	leisure	seize
caffeine	foreign	neither	species
conscience	height	science	weird

◆ PRACTICE 34-1

Proofread the underlined words in the following sentences for correct
spelling. If a correction needs to be made, cross out the incorrect word,
and write the correct spelling above it. If the word is spelled correctly,
write **C** above it.

    Example: It was a <u>relief</u> to ~~recieve~~ the good news. [C, *receive*]

1. Be sure to ~~wiegh~~ [weigh] the pros and cons before making important decisions, particularly those involving <u>friends</u>. [C]

2. When your <u>beliefs</u> [C] are tested, you may be able to ~~acheive~~ [achieve] a better
understanding of yourself.

3. In our <u>society</u> [C], many people ~~decieve~~ [deceive] themselves into ~~beleiving~~ [believing] that they
are better than everyone else.

4. ~~Cheifly~~ [Chiefly] because they have been lucky, they have reached a certain
<u>height</u> [C] in the world.

5. They think that the blood running through <u>their</u> [C] ~~viens~~ [veins] makes them
belong to a higher <u>species</u> [C] than the average person.

6. In fact, they are probably ~~niether~~ [neither] smarter nor more talented than others, but they are certainly <u>deficient</u> [C] in humility.

7. ~~Thier~~ [Their] <u>impatient</u> [C] attitude can cause others a lot of ~~greif.~~ [grief.]

8. I have always ~~percieved~~ [perceived] myself as thoughtful of others, and my
<u>conscience</u> [C] leads me to treat everyone with respect.

9. There are a ~~vareity~~ [variety] of ways to learn a ~~foriegn~~ [foreign] language.

10. *Dark City* is a really <u>weird</u> [C] movie, even for <u>science</u> [C] fiction.

■ **WRITING FIRST**

Look back at your response to the Writing First exercise on page 555. Underline any words that have *ie* or *ei* combinations, and check a dictionary to make sure they are spelled correctly. Correct any spelling errors on the lines below.

Answers will vary.

C   Understanding Prefixes

A **prefix** is a group of letters added at the beginning of a word that changes the word's meaning. Adding a prefix to a word never affects the spelling of the original word.

dis + service = disservice   pre + heat = preheat
un + able = unable   un + natural = unnatural
co + operate = cooperate   over + rate = overrate

◆ **PRACTICE 34-2**

Write in the blank the new word that results when the specified prefix is added to each of the following words.

ON THE WEB
For more practice, visit Exercise Central *at* <bedfordstmartins.com/ writingfirst>.

Example: dis + respect = ___disrespect___

1. un + happy = _unhappy_   6. non + negotiable = _nonnegotiable_

2. tele + vision = _television_   7. im + patient = _impatient_

3. pre + existing = _preexisting_   8. out + think = _outthink_

4. dis + satisfied = _dissatisfied_ 9. over + react = _overreact_

5. un + necessary = _unnecessary_   10. dis + solve = _dissolve_

■ **WRITING FIRST: Flashback**

Look back at your response to the Writing First exercise on page 555. Underline any words that have prefixes, and check a dictionary to make sure each word is spelled correctly. Correct any spelling errors on the lines below.

Answers will vary.

D Understanding Suffixes

A **suffix** is a group of letters added to the end of a word that changes the word's meaning or its part of speech. Adding a suffix to a word can change the spelling of the original word.

Words Ending in Silent *e*

If a word ends with a silent (unpronounced) *e*, drop the *e* if the suffix begins with a vowel.

DROP THE *E*

hope + <u>ing</u> = hoping   dance + <u>er</u> = dancer

continue + <u>ous</u> = continuous   insure + <u>able</u> = insurable

EXCEPTIONS

change + able = changeable   courage + ous = courageous

notice + able = noticeable   replace + able = replaceable

Keep the *e* if the suffix begins with a consonant.

KEEP THE *E*

hope + <u>ful</u> = hopeful   bore + <u>dom</u> = boredom

excite + <u>ment</u> = excitement   same + <u>ness</u> = sameness

EXCEPTIONS

argue + ment = argument   true + ly = truly

judge + ment = judgment   nine + th = ninth

◆ **PRACTICE 34-3**

ON THE WEB

For more practice, visit
Exercise Central *at*
*<bedfordstmartins.com/
writingfirst>.*

Write in the blank the new word that results from adding the specified suffix to each of the following words.

Examples:

insure + ance = _____ *insurance* _____

love + ly = _____ *lovely* _____

1. lone + ly = ____ *lonely* _____   7. microscope + ic = ____ *microscopic* ____

2. use + ful = ____ *useful* _____   8. prepare + ation = ____ *preparation* ____

3. revise + ing = ____ *revising* _____   9. nine + th = ____ *ninth* _____

4. base + ment = ____ *basement* _____   10. indicate + ion = ____ *indication* ____

5. desire + able = ____ *desirable* ____   11. effective + ness = ____ *effectiveness* ____

6. true + ly = ____ *truly* _____   12. arrange + ment = ____ *arrangement* ____

13. fortune + ate = _fortunate_   17. advertise + ment = _advertisement_

14. taste + ful = _tasteful_   18. notice + able = _noticeable_

15. argue + ment = _argument_   19. care + less = _careless_

16. disable + ed = _disabled_   20. judge + ment = _judgment_

Words Ending in -y

When you add a suffix to a word that ends in -y, change the y to an i if the letter before the y is a consonant.

CHANGE Y TO I

beauty + ful = beautiful   busy + ly = busily

try + ed = tried   friendly + er = friendlier

EXCEPTIONS

■ Keep the y if the suffix starts with an i.

cry + ing = crying   baby + ish = babyish

■ Keep the y when you add a suffix to certain one-syllable words.

shy + er = shyer   dry + ness = dryness

Keep the y if the letter before the y is a vowel.

KEEP THE Y

annoy + ance = annoyance   enjoy + ment = enjoyment

play + ful = playful   display + ed = displayed

EXCEPTIONS

day + ly = daily   say + ed = said

gay + ly = gaily   pay + ed = paid

◆ PRACTICE 34-4

Write in the blank the new word that results from adding the specified suffix to each of the following words.

Examples:

study + ed = _studied_

employ + ment = _employment_

1. happy + ness = _happiness_   4. carry + ed = _carried_

2. convey + or = _conveyor_   5. ready + ness = _readiness_

3. deny + ing = _denying_   6. annoy + ing = _annoying_

7. destroy + er = _destroyer_

8. twenty + eth = _twentieth_

9. forty + ish = _fortyish_

10. day + ly = _daily_

11. cry + ed = _cried_

12. delay + ed = _delayed_

13. busy + ness = _business_

14. lonely + ness = _loneliness_

15. spy + ing = _spying_

16. prepay + ed = _prepaid_

17. lively + hood = _livelihood_

18. ally + ance = _alliance_

19. joy + ful = _joyful_

20. marry + ing = _marrying_

Doubling the Final Consonant

For more information on vowels and consonants, see the Focus box in 34A.

When you add a suffix that begins with a vowel—for example, *-ed, -er,* or *-ing*—sometimes you need to double the final consonant in the original word. Do this (1) if the last three letters of the word have a consonant-vowel-consonant (cvc) pattern and (2) if the word has one syllable or the last syllable is stressed.

FINAL CONSONANT DOUBLED

drum	+	ing	=	drumming (cvc—one syllable)
bat	+	er	=	batter (cvc—one syllable)
pet	+	ed	=	petted (cvc—one syllable)
commit	+	ed	=	committed (cvc—stress is on last syllable)
occur	+	ing	=	occurring (cvc—stress is on last syllable)

FINAL CONSONANT NOT DOUBLED

answer	+	ed	=	answered (cvc—stress is not on last syllable)
happen	+	ing	=	happening (cvc—stress is not on last syllable)
act	+	ing	=	acting (no cvc)

Teaching Tip

As a homework assignment, have students think of other examples to add to the suffix lists in 34D.

◆ PRACTICE 34-5

Write in the blank the new word that results from adding the specified suffix to each of the following words.

Examples:

rot + ing = _rotting_

narrow + er = _narrower_

1. hope + ed = _hoped_

2. shop + er = _shopper_

3. rest + ing = _resting_

4. combat + ed = _combatted_

5. reveal + ing = _revealing_

6. open + er = _opener_

7. unzip + ed = _unzipped_

8. trap + ed = _trapped_

9. cram + ing = _cramming_ 15. omit + ed = _omitted_

10. star + ing = _starring_ 16. want + ing = _wanting_

11. appeal + ing = _appealing_ 17. fat + er = _fatter_

12. resist + ed = _resisted_ 18. fast + er = _faster_

13. refer + ing = _referring_ 19. repel + ed = _repelled_

14. skip + er = _skipper_ 20. repeal + ed = _repealed_

■ WRITING FIRST: Flashback

Look back at your response to the Writing First exercise on page 555. Underline any words that have suffixes, and check a dictionary to make sure each word is spelled correctly. Correct any spelling errors on the lines below.

Answers will vary.

E   Learning Commonly Confused Words

Accept/Except   *Accept* means "to receive something." *Except* means "with the exception of" or "to leave out or exclude."

"I <u>accept</u> your challenge," said Alexander Hamilton to Aaron Burr.

Everyone <u>except</u> Darryl visited the museum.

Affect/Effect   *Affect* is a verb meaning "to influence." *Effect* is a noun meaning "result" and sometimes a verb meaning "to bring about."

Carmen's job could <u>affect</u> her grades.

Overexposure to sun can have a long-term <u>effect</u> on skin.

Commissioner Williams tried to <u>effect</u> changes in police procedure.

All ready/Already   *All ready* means "completely prepared." *Already* means "previously, before."

Serge was <u>all ready</u> to take the history test.

Gina had <u>already</u> been to Italy.

Brake/Break   *Brake* is a noun that means "a device to slow or stop a vehicle." *Break* is a verb meaning "to smash" or "to detach" and sometimes a noun meaning either "a gap" or "an interruption" or "a stroke of luck."

Peter got into an accident because his foot slipped off the <u>brake</u>.

Babe Ruth thought no one would ever <u>break</u> his home run record.

● **Writing Tip**

Delete commonly confused words from your computer's spell checker so they will always be flagged as possible errors.

Teaching Tip

Teach students how to use mnemonic devices to remember spellings. (For example, *their* refers to ownership, and so does *heir*; *there* refers to location, and so does *here*.)

The baseball game was postponed until there was a <u>break</u> in the bad weather.

Buy/By   *Buy* means "to purchase." *By* is a preposition meaning "close to" or "next to" or "by means of."

The Stamp Act forced colonists to <u>buy</u> stamps for many public documents.

He drove <u>by</u> but did not stop.

He stayed <u>by</u> her side all the way to the hospital.

Malcolm X wanted "freedom <u>by</u> any means necessary."

◆ **PRACTICE 34-6**

ON THE WEB
For more practice, visit
Exercise Central *at*
<bedfordstmartins.com/
writingfirst>.

Proofread the underlined words in the following sentences for correct spelling. If a correction needs to be made, cross out the incorrect word, and write the correct spelling above it. If the word is spelled correctly, write **C** above it.

Example: We must ~~except~~ [*accept*] the fact that the human heart can <u>break</u> [*C*].

1. The ~~affects~~ [*effects*] of several new AIDS drugs have ~~all ready~~ [*already*] been reported.

2. *Consumer Reports* gave high ratings to the ~~breaks~~ [*brakes*] on all the new cars tested ~~accept~~ [*except*] one.

3. Advertisements urge us to ~~by~~ [*buy*] a new product even if we <u>already</u> [*C*] own a similar item.

4. If you ~~except~~ [*accept*] the charges for a collect telephone call, you will probably have to ~~brake~~ [*break*] your piggy bank to pay their bill.

5. Cigarette smoking <u>affects</u> [*C*] the lungs <u>by</u> [*C*] creating deposits of tar that make breathing difficult.

6. The show was ~~already~~ [*all ready*] to begin <u>except</u> [*C*] that the star had not arrived.

7. People who live ~~buy~~ [*by*] the landfill have complained for years about its ~~affects~~ [*effects*] on the neighborhood.

8. The physical therapy program has ~~all ready~~ [*already*] ~~excepted~~ [*accepted*] 20 percent more students than it admitted last year.

9. Even a tiny <u>break</u> [*C*] in a bone can strongly ~~effect~~ [*affect*] an athlete's performance.

10. When they ~~by~~ [*buy*] their textbooks, most students <u>accept</u> [*C*] the fact that they will lose money if they resell them.

Conscience/Conscious *Conscience* is a noun that refers to the part of the mind that urges a person to choose right over wrong. *Conscious* is an adjective that means "aware" or "deliberate."

After he cheated at cards, his <u>conscience</u> started to bother him.

As she walked through the woods, she became <u>conscious</u> of the hum of insects.

Elliott made a <u>conscious</u> decision to stop smoking.

Everyday/Every day *Everyday* is a single word that means "ordinary" or "common." *Every day* is two words that mean "occurring daily."

I Love Lucy was a successful comedy show because it appealed to <u>everyday</u> people.

<u>Every day</u>, Lucy and Ethel would find a new way to get into trouble.

Fine/Find *Fine* means "superior quality" or "a sum of money paid as a penalty." *Find* means "to locate."

He sang a <u>fine</u> solo at church last Sunday.

Demi had to pay a <u>fine</u> for speeding.

Some people still use a willow rod to <u>find</u> water.

Hear/Here *Hear* means "to perceive sound by ear." *Here* means "at or in this place."

I moved to the front so I could <u>hear</u> the speaker.

My great-grandfather came <u>here</u> in 1883.

Its/It's *Its* is the possessive form of *it*. *It's* is the contraction of *it is* or *it has*.

The airline canceled <u>its</u> flights because of the snow.

<u>It's</u> twelve o'clock, and we are late.

Ever since <u>it's</u> been in the accident, the car has rattled.

◆ **PRACTICE 34-7**

Proofread the underlined words in the following sentences for correct spelling. If a correction needs to be made, cross out the incorrect word, and write the correct spelling above it. If the word is spelled correctly, write **C** above it.

Example: <u>It's</u> [C] often difficult for celebrities to adjust to ~~every day~~ [everyday] life.

1. <u>Hear</u> [Here] at Simonson's Fashions, we try to make our customers feel that ~~everyday~~ [every day] is a sale day.

2. My uncle was a ~~find~~ [fine] person, and ~~its~~ [it's] a shame that he died so young.

3. That inner voice you <u>hear</u> [C] is your ~~conscious~~ [conscience] telling you how you should behave.

Teaching Tip
Students often use *it's* instead of *its*. Read aloud a sentence containing this error, replacing the contraction with the two words it stands for (for example, *The baby fell out of it is high chair*). The error should be immediately apparent.

4. In the ~~every day~~ *everyday* world of work and school, it can be hard to ~~fine~~ *find* the time to relax and enjoy life.

5. By the time I became ~~conscience~~ *conscious* of the leaking pipe, ~~it's~~ *its* damage had run to more than a hundred dollars.

6. The judge ordered the company to pay a thousand-dollar fine *C* for ~~everyday~~ *every day* that it violated federal safety codes.

7. When immigrants first arrive ~~hear~~ *here* in the United States, they may find *C* that ~~its~~ *it's* difficult to adjust to their new home.

8. In ~~every day~~ *everyday* decision making, let your conscience *C* be your guide.

9. Even though they ~~here~~ *hear* about the dangers of drinking and driving, young people always think, "It's *C* not going to happen to me."

10. The college is holding ~~it's~~ *its* fourth annual survey to ~~fine~~ *find* the most popular teacher on campus.

Know/No/Knew/New   *Know* means "to have an understanding of" or "to have fixed in the mind." *No* means "not any," "not at all," or "not one." *Knew* is the past tense form of the verb *know. New* means "recent or never used."

I <u>know</u> there will be a lunar eclipse tonight.

You have <u>no</u> right to say that.

He <u>knew</u> how to install a <u>new</u> light switch.

Lie/Lay   *Lie* means "to rest or recline." The past tense of *lie* is *lay. Lay* means "to put or place something down." The past tense of *lay* is *laid.*

Every Sunday, I <u>lie</u> in bed until noon.

They <u>lay</u> on the grass until it began to rain, and then they went home.

Tammy told Carl to <u>lay</u> his cards on the table.

Brooke and Cassia finally <u>laid</u> down their hockey sticks.

Loose/Lose   *Loose* means "not fixed or rigid" or "not attached securely." *Lose* means "to mislay" or "to misplace."

In the 1940s, many women wore <u>loose</u>-fitting pants.

I don't gamble because I hate to <u>lose</u>.

Mine/Mind   *Mine* is a possessive pronoun that indicates ownership. *Mind* can be a noun meaning "human consciousness" or "intelligence" or a verb meaning "to obey" or "to attend to."

That red mountain bike is <u>mine</u>.

A <u>mind</u> is a terrible thing to waste.

"<u>Mind</u> your manners when you visit your grandmother," Dad said.

Passed/Past   *Passed* is the past tense of the verb *pass*. It means "moved by" or "succeeded in." *Past* is a noun meaning "earlier than the present time."

> The car that <u>passed</u> me was doing more than eighty miles an hour.
>
> David finally <u>passed</u> his driving test.
>
> The novel was set in the <u>past</u>.

Peace/Piece   *Peace* means "the absence of war" or "calm." *Piece* means "a part of something."

> The British prime minister thought he had achieved <u>peace</u> with honor.
>
> My <u>peace</u> of mind was destroyed when the flying saucer landed.
>
> "Have a <u>piece</u> of cake," said Marie.

◆ PRACTICE 34-8

Proofread the underlined words in the following sentences for correct spelling. If a correction needs to be made, cross out the incorrect word, and write the correct spelling above it. If the word is spelled correctly, write **C** above it.

> **Example:**   Although the soldiers stopped fighting, a ~~piece~~ *peace* treaty was never signed.

1. The *C* <u>loose</u> soil around the house was washed away during the storm.

2. Because he was late for the job interview, he was afraid he would ~~loose~~ *lose* his chance to work for the company.

3. While she ~~laid~~ *lay* down to rest, her children cooked dinner and cleaned the house.

4. There will be ~~know~~ *no* wool sweaters on sale before the holidays.

5. I tried to ~~mine~~ *mind* my own business, but I couldn't resist asking my new neighbors why they painted their house pink.

6. I don't ~~no~~ *know* whether I can buy a *C* <u>new</u> car this year.

7. The *C* <u>past</u> chair of the committee left a lot of unfinished business.

8. According to the ~~knew~~ *new* professor, any student who set his or her *C* <u>mind</u> to it should be able to *C* <u>pass</u> the course.

9. ~~Lie~~ *Lay* the pen on the counter when you are finished filling out the form.

10. The broken knife found in the trash turned out to be a ~~peace~~ *piece* of the murder weapon.

Plain/Plane   *Plain* means "simple, not elaborate." *Plane* is the shortened form of *airplane*.

Sometimes the Amish are referred to as the <u>plain</u> people.

Chuck Yeager was the first person to fly a <u>plane</u> faster than the speed of sound.

Principal/Principle   *Principal* means "first" or "highest" or "the head of a school." *Principle* means "a law or basic assumption."

She had the <u>principal</u> role in the movie.

I'll never forget the day the <u>principal</u> called me into his office.

It was against his <u>principles</u> to lie.

Quiet/Quit/Quite   *Quiet* means "free of noise" or "still." *Quit* means "to leave a job" or "to give up." *Quite* means "actually" or "very."

Jane looked forward to the <u>quiet</u> evenings at the lake.

Sammy <u>quit</u> his job and followed the girls into the parking lot.

"You haven't <u>quite</u> got the hang of it yet," she said.

After practicing all summer, Tamika got <u>quite</u> good at tennis.

Raise/Rise   *Raise* means "to elevate" or "to increase in size, quantity, or worth." The past tense of *raise* is *raised*. *Rise* means "to stand up" or "to move from a lower position to a higher position." The past tense of *rise* is *rose*.

Carlos <u>raises</u> his hand whenever the teacher asks for volunteers.

They finally <u>raised</u> the money for the down payment.

The crowd <u>rises</u> every time their team scores a touchdown.

Sarah <u>rose</u> before dawn so she could see the eclipse.

Right/Write   *Right* means "correct" or "the opposite of left." *Write* means "to form letters with a writing instrument."

If you turn <u>right</u> at the corner, you will be going in the <u>right</u> direction.

All students must <u>write</u> three short papers.

Sit/Set   *Sit* means "to assume a sitting position." The past tense of *sit* is *sat*. *Set* means "to put down or place" or "to adjust something to a desired position." The past tense of *set* is *set*.

I usually <u>sit</u> in the front row at the movies.

They <u>sat</u> at the clinic waiting for their names to be called.

Elizabeth <u>set</u> the mail on the kitchen table and left for work.

Every semester I <u>set</u> goals for myself.

Suppose/Supposed   *Suppose* means "to consider" or "to assume." *Supposed* is both the past tense and the past participle of *suppose*. *Supposed* also means "expected" or "required." (Note that when *supposed* has this meaning, it is followed by *to*.)

● **Writing Tip**
Be careful not to drop the *d* of *supposed* before *to: He is* <u>supposed</u> *to study* (not *He is* <u>suppose</u> *to study*.)

Suppose researchers were to find a cure for AIDS.

We supposed the movie would be over by ten o'clock.

You were supposed to finish a draft of the report by today.

◆ PRACTICE 34-9

Proofread the underlined words in the following sentences for correct spelling. If a correction needs to be made, cross out the incorrect word, and write the correct spelling above it. If the word is spelled correctly, write **C** above it.

plane   *C*
Example: Boarding the ~~plain~~ to San Francisco took quite a long time because of the security process.

supposed
1. Jackie was ~~suppose~~ to mow the lawn and trim the bushes last week-end.

set
2. It is important to ~~sit~~ the computer in a place where the on-off switch can be reached.

C
3. If you raise the window, a pleasant breeze will blow into the bedroom.

principal   *rise*   *C*
4. The ~~principle~~ reason for her ~~raise~~ to the position of principal of the school was hard work.

C   *quiet.*
5. We were all told to sit and wait for the crowd to become ~~quite.~~

right
6. It would be easier to vote for the ~~write~~ candidate for class president if
write   *principles.*
all of them were required to ~~right~~ essays stating their ~~principals.~~

C
7. Suppose that the defense is correct and the district attorney is wrong.

plain,   *quite*
8. The furniture in his old house was very ~~plane,~~ but it was ~~quiet~~ functional.

C
9. Quit complaining!

C   *C*
10. My father never raised his voice in anger, and this set a good example for us children.

Their/There/They're *Their* is the possessive form of the pronoun *they*. *There* means "at or in that place." *There* is also used in the phrases *there is* and *there are*. *They're* is the contraction of "they are."

Jane Addams wanted poor people to improve their living conditions.

I put the book over there.

There are three reasons I will not eat meat.

They're the best volunteer firefighters I've ever seen.

Then/Than   *Then* means "at that time" or "next in time." *Than* is used to introduce the second element in a comparison.

> He was young and naive <u>then</u>.
>
> I went to the job interview and <u>then</u> stopped off for a chocolate shake.
>
> My dog is smarter <u>than</u> your dog.

Threw/Through   *Threw* is the past tense of *throw*. *Through* means "in one side and out the opposite side" or "finished."

> Satchel Paige <u>threw</u> a baseball more than ninety-five miles an hour.
>
> It takes almost thirty minutes to go <u>through</u> the tunnel.
>
> "I'm <u>through</u>," said Clark Kent, storming out of Perry White's office.

To/Too/Two   *To* means "in the direction of." *Too* means "also" or "more than enough." *Two* denotes the numeral 2.

> During spring break, I am going <u>to</u> Disney World.
>
> My roommates are coming <u>too</u>.
>
> The microwave popcorn is <u>too</u> hot to eat.
>
> "If we get rid of the Tin Man and the Cowardly Lion, the <u>two</u> of us can go to Oz," said the Scarecrow to Dorothy.

Use/Used   *Use* means "to put into service" or "to consume." *Used* is both the past tense and past participle of *use*. *Used* also means "accustomed." (Note that when *used* has this meaning, it is followed by *to*.)

> I <u>use</u> a soft cloth to clean my glasses.
>
> "Hey! Who <u>used</u> all the hot water?" he yelled from the shower.
>
> Mary had <u>used</u> all the firewood during the storm.
>
> After two years in Alaska, they got <u>used</u> to the short winter days.

● **Writing Tip**

Do not use the informal spelling *thru* for *through*.

◆ PRACTICE 34-10

Proofread the underlined words in the following sentences for correct spelling. If a correction needs to be made, cross out the incorrect word, and write the correct spelling above it. If the word is spelled correctly, write *C* above it.

Example: Because of good nutrition, people are taller *than* ~~then~~ they were in the past.

1. After the power went out in the dorms, many students *C* <u>then</u> went *to* ~~too~~ the library to study.

2. Whenever he ~~through~~ *threw* out the trash, he walked ~~threw~~ *through* the back yard on his way *to* ~~two~~ the alley.

3. Get your tickets before ~~their~~ *they're* all gone.

4. I ~~use~~ *used* to think that my ancestors all came from northern Europe, but I

recently learned that one of my great-grandparents <u>used</u> to live in

South Africa.

5. The countries that signed the peace treaty have not lived up to ~~they're~~ *their*

responsibilities.

6. The local supermarkets all reduced ~~there~~ *their* prices for produce when local

fruits and vegetables were available, and, as a result, many of their cus-

tomers <u>used</u> more of these foods.

7. Political polls may be more important <u>than</u> they ~~use~~ *used* to be.

8. It ~~use~~ *used* to take more ~~then~~ *than* thirty hours to drive from New York to

Miami.

9. When the president <u>threw</u> out the first ball of the baseball season this

afternoon, he ~~use~~ *used* his left hand.

10. When ~~too~~ *two* people are in love, ~~their~~ *they're* often unable to see any faults in each

other.

Weather/Whether   *Weather* refers to the state of the atmosphere with respect to temperature, humidity, precipitation, and so on. *Whether* is used
to introduce alternative possibilities.

> The *Farmer's Almanac* says that the <u>weather</u> this winter will be
> severe.

> <u>Whether</u> or not this prediction will be correct is anyone's guess.

Where/Were/We're   *Where* means "at or in what place." *Were* is the past
tense of *are*. *We're* is the contraction of "we are."

> <u>Where</u> are you going, and <u>where</u> have you been?
> Charlie Chaplin and Mary Pickford <u>were</u> popular stars of silent
> movies.
> <u>We're</u> doing our back-to-school shopping early this year.

Whose/Who's   *Whose* is the possessive form of *who*. *Who's* is the contraction of either "who is" or "who has."

> My roommate asked, "<u>Whose</u> book is this?"
> "<u>Who's</u> there?" squealed the second little pig as he leaned against
> the door.
> <u>Who's</u> left a yellow 1957 Chevrolet blocking the driveway?

Your/You're   *Your* is the possessive form of *you*. *You're* is the contraction
of "you are."

> "You should have worn <u>your</u> running shoes," said the hare as he
> passed the tortoise.
> "<u>You're</u> too kind," said the tortoise sarcastically.

◆ **PRACTICE 34-11**

Proofread the underlined words in the following sentences for correct spelling. If a correction needs to be made, cross out the incorrect word, and write the correct spelling above it. If the word is spelled correctly, write **C** above it.

    Example: As citizens, ~~were~~ *we're* all concerned with where our country is *C* going.

1. Authorities are attempting to discover ~~who's~~ *whose* fingerprints were *C* left at the scene of the crime.

2. Cancer does not care ~~weather your~~ *whether you're* rich or poor, young or old; it can strike anyone.

3. Santa Fe, ~~were~~ *where* I lived for many years, has better weather *C* than New Jersey has.

4. Whenever we listen to politicians debate, ~~were~~ *we're* likely to be wondering ~~whose~~ *who's* telling the truth.

5. You should take your *C* time before deciding ~~weather~~ *whether* to focus your *C* energy on school or on work.

6. The people ~~who's~~ *whose* lives influenced me the most were *C* my grandmother and grandfather.

7. You cannot just sit around wondering ~~whose~~ *who's* going to make ~~you're~~ *your* dreams come true.

8. Even when the weather *C* report advises us that it's going to be sunny, ~~were~~ *we're* always careful to carry an umbrella.

9. By the time ~~your~~ *you're* in high school, people expect you to have decided ~~were~~ *where* you want to be ten years from now.

10. Only someone who's *C* experienced in combat knows ~~weather~~ *whether* to stand and fight or retreat.

■ **WRITING FIRST: Flashback**

Look back at your response to the Writing First exercise on page 555. Identify any words that appear on the lists of commonly confused words (on the preceding pages), and check to make sure you

(continued on the following page)

(continued from the previous page)

have spelled them correctly. Correct any misspelled words, and
then write them here.

Answers will vary.

_____   _____

_____   _____

■ WRITING FIRST: Revising and Editing

Type your response to the Writing First exercise on page 555 if you
have not already done so. Now, run a spell check. Did the computer
pick up all the errors? Which did it identify? Which did it miss?
Correct the spelling errors the computer identified as well as the
ones that you found while proofreading. (You can also check
spelling in this way in a longer writing assignment you are currently working on.)

CHAPTER REVIEW

◆ **EDITING PRACTICE**

Read the following student essay, which includes spelling errors. Identify
the words you think are misspelled; then, look them up in a dictionary. Finally, cross out each incorrectly spelled word, and write the correct
spelling above the line. The first sentence has been edited for you.

Answers may vary.

Coming Home

When my Uncle Joe, a private in the United States Marine
                    returned
Corps, ~~returnned~~ from Iraq, I remember being glad that he
                                     fulfilled
was home. He had ~~fullfilled~~ his responsibility, had served

honorably, and was safe. With my family, I welcomed him at
                                          hugged
the airport with flags and flowers. He ~~huged~~ us all and
         thrilled
looked ~~thriled~~ to be home. However, returning to civilian

life turned out to be more difficult for him than any of

us had expected.

   Being in the military is very different from any other
experience.   *Soldiers*
~~expereince.~~ ~~Soldeirs~~ have to kill people and see them

Marines fighting in Iraq

killed. To do this, they have to forget what they have

been taught since they were children about not harming

                                                    conscience
others. They sometimes have to ignore their ~~conscious~~

and become less sensitive to others' feelings. Also, to

                            suspicious
survive, they have to be ~~suspitious~~ of everything around

them. They must be alert at all times. Most important,
their   *controlled.*
~~thier~~ emotions must be ~~controled.~~ In a way, they have to

function like a machine in combat: when given an order,

they must follow it. Their own lives and those of their
                              obedience.
fellow soldiers depend on instant ~~obedeince.~~

In the case of Uncle Joe, war changed him, and I

learned that this was true of many veterans. Although
                            necessary
insensitivity and suspicion are ~~necesary~~ for a soldier,
neither
~~niether~~ is of much use in civilian life. For example, when
              overreacted
my uncle ~~overeacted~~ and spoke harshly to his wife about a

dirty dish left on the kitchen counter, she became confused

and angry. Similarly, when his family asked him about the
              annoyed   *refused*
war, he became ~~annoied~~ and ~~refussed~~ to talk about it. His

family did not understand. He felt isolated from his
friends
~~freinds~~ and family, and when he slept, he had nightmares

of being back in Iraq, under fire. He also missed the

closeness of his fellow Marines.

Soldiers training in Iraq

Before he returned home, Uncle Joe had looked forward to
                          insurance
returning to his job in an ~~insurence~~ company. However, his
                                    too.
feelings about his career changed, ~~to.~~ He had become used
              strict *discipline*
to the ~~strick~~ ~~dicsipline~~ of the military, which included

respecting authority and following orders. As a Marine, my
                            appropriate
uncle always knew what ~~apropriate~~ behavior was. But at

work, there was no officer to give him orders; although he
                            a lot
had a boss, there seemed to be ~~alot~~ of leeway in what was
              acceptable.
considered ~~acceptible.~~ He had much more freedom, but he

did not know quite what to do with it. Also, Uncle Joe

missed the job security of the military. At home,
everything   *uncertain;*
~~everthing~~ seemed to be so ~~uncertin;~~ people lost their jobs

without much warning, and entire companies went bankrupt.

                                                                         similar
     What my uncle went through as a returning soldier was
                                               buddies
~~similiar~~ to what many of his ~~buddys~~ have experienced. Even
  ^

with counseling, it took him a long time to be able to

trust the people around him. Eventually, he was able to

become more sensitive to the feelings of others, and he
tried
~~tryed~~ to rely on his civilian friends and family the way
^
                                         Occasionally,
he had relied on his fellow Marines. ~~Ocasionaly,~~ he still
        ^
                                      occur
has nightmares about the war, but they ~~ocurr~~ less often.
         ^

For Uncle Joe, the war did not end when he came home;
                                    beginning
returning home was just the ~~begining~~ of his own personal
      ^

struggle.

◆ COLLABORATIVE ACTIVITIES

1. Working in pairs, compare responses to the Writing First exercise on page 555. How many misspelled words did each of you find? How many errors did you and your partner have in common?

2. Are there any patterns of misspelling in your Writing First exercises? What types of spelling errors seem most common?

3. Collaborate with your partner to make a spelling list for the two of you, and then work with other groups to create a spelling list for the whole class. When you have finished, determine which types of errors are most common.

☑ REVIEW CHECKLIST:
Understanding Spelling

> Follow the steps to becoming a better speller. (See 34A.)

> *I* comes before *e*, except after *c* or in any *ay* sound, as in *neighbor*. (See 34B.)

> Adding a prefix to a word never affects the word's spelling. (See 34C.)

> Adding a suffix to a word may change the word's spelling. (See 34D.)

> When a word ends with silent *e*, drop the *e* if the suffix begins with a vowel. Keep the *e* if the suffix begins with a consonant. (See 34D.)

(continued on the following page)

(continued from the previous page)

☐ When you add a suffix to a word that ends with a *y*, change the *y* to an *i* if the letter before the *y* is a consonant. Keep the *y* if the letter before the *y* is a vowel. (See 34D.)

☐ When you add a suffix that begins in a vowel, double the final consonant in the original word (1) if the last three letters of the word have a consonant-vowel-consonant pattern (cvc) and the word has one syllable or (2) if the last three letters have a cvc pattern and the last syllable is stressed. (See 34D.)

☐ Memorize the most commonly confused words. (See 34E.)

UNIT REVIEW

Read the following student essay, which includes various errors. Then, edit the essay by correcting errors in punctuation, mechanics, and spelling. The first sentence has been corrected for you. (Because this is an informal essay, contractions are acceptable.)

Answers may vary.

Education Internship: First Year

On ~~september 15 2004~~ *September 15, 2004,* I ~~recieved~~ *received* a copy of my college schedule in the ~~male.~~ *mail.* I learned that from nine to ten on ~~monday's~~ *Mondays* and ~~wednesday's,~~ *Wednesdays,* I would be an intern at the ~~accellerated learning laboratory school~~ *Accelerated Learning Laboratory School* (the ALL ~~school~~ *School*).

This would be my first chance to be in a classroom when I ~~wasnt~~ *wasn't* a student. On the first day of class I got to the school extra early. After I signed in I put on my yellow visitors badge~~,~~ and met the teacher ~~irene~~ *, Irene* Dennis. I was ~~nervus~~ *nervous* but ready.

Ms. ~~dennis~~ *Dennis* told me that most of the children were in third~~,~~ or fourth grade, ~~accept~~ *except* for ~~too~~ *two* girls. One of them was ~~sue~~ *Sue,* a sixth grader. She ~~coudnt~~ *couldn't* read at all. At the ~~beggining~~ *beginning* of the day, the children were ~~suppose~~ *supposed* to be reading, ~~writting~~ *writing,* or ~~studing~~ *studying* math. When I looked at them, though I saw that most of them were ~~daydreamming.~~ *daydreaming.* It was hard to get them to pay ~~attenntion~~ *attention* to ~~there~~ *their* work.

At nine ~~oclock~~ *o'clock,* it was time for ~~they're~~ *their* group work. Ms ~~dennis~~ *Dennis's* students all went to ~~diferrent~~ *different* classrooms~~,~~ and ~~interrracted~~ *interacted* with other children. The students were studying ~~africa,~~ *Africa,* with three ~~teacher's~~ *teachers* teaching about thirty children. Each group had been given one country to ~~focuss~~ *focus* on. They had to learn about the food that people ate~~,~~ and the ~~close~~ *clothes* they wore. Because it was the end of the month~~,~~ the students were ~~wraping~~ *wrapping* up ~~they're~~ *their* study of the ~~Continent~~ *continent* and ~~completeing~~ *completing* worksheets.

My first job was to help Luke~~,~~ a fifth grader. ~~Lukes~~ *Luke's* problem was that he tended to ~~waist~~ *waste* time and get distracted. However I gave him ~~alot~~ *a lot* of firm ~~advise~~ *advice* and

Intern and students in a classroom

577

Classroom bulletin boards

eventually got him to work independently. Next, I moved on to help Randy, a boy who thought he knew all the answers. Randy had a hard time expressing himself. "It's an easy question," he'd say, but then he'd give the wrong answer. By the time I had both Luke and Randy working on their own, it was time for us to return to our original classroom.

Now, Ms. Dennis asked me to work with a girl named Tien. Originally from Vietnam, she was twelve years old and didn't speak English very well. On a piece of paper she had written, "Happy birthen to you." I pointed to <u>birthen</u> and wrote "birthday." She wrote "birthday" and then she wrote the whole sentence again, this time with the correct spelling. I asked her when her birthday was, and she counted on her fingers and wrote "4/30." I pointed to the 4, and wrote "April." Then, she wrote "Happy birthday to you, April 30." I wanted to spend more time with her, but it was almost time for me to leave.

The principal was making an announcement over the loudspeaker as I put my coat on. I waved goodbye when I left, and I heard all these little voices saying, "Goodbye, Rebecca." They seemed disappointed that I was leaving. "Don't worry," I told them, "I'll be back." I didn't come every day, but every Monday and Wednesday for the rest of the year, I was there. I loved working with the children and helping them to improve. I really felt I was making a difference in their lives.

In May 2005, right before the end of the spring semester, I was walking across campus when I passed a little kid. All of a sudden, I heard him yell out, "Hey, she goes to our school." He was pointing at me. I remembered this boy who was from the ALL School. His words had an incredible effect on me. I always used to wonder whether I'd be a teacher one day. Now I knew I would. I used to think that teachers' effect on their students was overrated. Now I knew better.

Classroom bulletin boards

578

UNIT EIGHT

Reading Essays

Reading for College

PREVIEW

In this chapter, you will learn

- to preview a reading assignment (35A)

- to highlight a reading assignment (35B)

- to annotate a reading assignment (35C)

- to outline a reading assignment (35D)

- to summarize a reading assignment (35E)

- to write a response paragraph (35F)

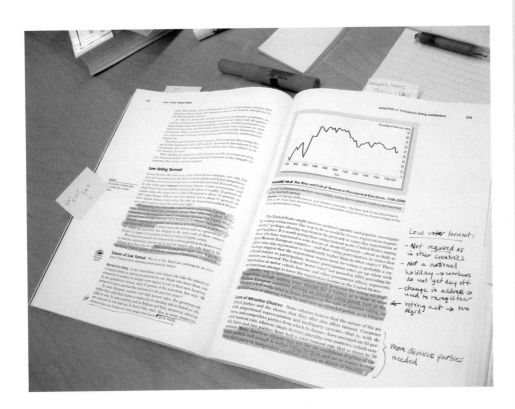

Reading is essential to all your college courses. To get the most out of your reading, you should approach the books and articles you read in a practical way, always asking yourself what they can offer you. You should also approach assigned readings critically, just as you approach your own writing when you revise.

Reading critically does not mean finding fault with every point and challenging or arguing with every idea, but it does mean wondering, commenting, questioning, and judging. Most of all, it means being an active rather than a passive reader. Being an **active reader** means participating in the reading process: approaching a reading assignment with a clear understanding of your purpose, previewing a selection, highlighting and annotating it, and perhaps outlining it—all *before* you begin to respond in writing to what you have read.

To gain an understanding of your **purpose**—your reason for reading—you should start by answering some questions.

581

35 A

Questions about Your Purpose

■ Why are you reading?

■ Will you be expected to discuss what you are reading? If so, will you discuss it in class or in a conference with your instructor?

■ Will you have to write about what you are reading? If so, will you be expected to write an informal response (for example, a journal entry) or a more formal one (for example, an essay)?

■ Will you be tested on the material?

Once you understand your purpose, you are ready to begin reading.

A Previewing a Reading Assignment

When you **preview**, you skim a passage to get a sense of the writer's main idea and key supporting points as well as the general emphasis of the passage. You can begin by focusing on the title, the first paragraph (which often contains a purpose statement or overview), and the last paragraph (which often contains a summary of the writer's points). You should also look for clues to the writer's message in the passage's other **visual signals** (headings, boxes, and so on) as well as in its **verbal signals** (the words and phrases the writer uses to convey order and emphasis).

Using Visual Signals

■ Look at the essay's title.

■ Look at the essay's **headnote**, the paragraph that introduces the author and gives background about the reading.

■ Look at the essay's opening and closing paragraphs.

■ Look at each paragraph's first sentence.

■ Look at headings.

■ Look at *italicized* and **boldfaced** words.

■ Look at numbered lists.

■ Look at bulleted lists (like this one).

■ Look at visuals (graphs, charts, tables, photographs, and so on).

■ Look at any information that is boxed.

■ Look at any information that is in color.

Using Verbal Signals

■ Look for phrases that signal emphasis ("The *primary* reason"; "The *most important* idea").

■ Look for repeated words and phrases.

■ Look for words that signal addition (*also, in addition, furthermore*).

■ Look for words that signal time sequence (*first, after, then, next, finally*).

■ Look for words that identify causes and effects (*because, as a result, for this reason*).

(continued on the following page)

(continued from the previous page)

- Look for words that introduce examples (*for example, for instance*).
- Look for words that signal comparison (*likewise, similarly*).
- Look for words that signal contrast (*unlike, although, in contrast*).
- Look for words that signal contradiction (*however, on the contrary*).
- Look for words that signal a narrowing of the writer's focus (*in fact, specifically, in other words*).
- Look for words that signal summaries or conclusions (*to sum up, in conclusion*).

When you have finished previewing the passage, you should have a general sense of what the writer wants to communicate.

◆ PRACTICE 35-1

"No Comprendo" ("I Don't Understand") is a newspaper article by Barbara Mujica, a professor of Spanish at Georgetown University in Washington, D.C. In this article, which was published in the *New York Times* on February 21, 1992, Mujica argues against bilingual education (teaching students in their native language as well as in English).

In preparation for class discussion and for other activities that will be assigned later in this chapter, preview the article. As you read, try to identify the writer's main idea and key supporting points, and then write them on the lines that follow the article on pages 584–585.

> **Teaching Tip**
> Direct students' attention to this essay's title, thesis statement, topic sentences, and opening and closing paragraphs.

No Comprendo

Last spring, my niece phoned me in tears. She was graduating from high school and had to make a decision. An outstanding soccer player, she was offered athletic scholarships by several colleges. So why was she crying?

My niece came to the United States from South America as a child. Although she had received good grades in her schools in Miami, she spoke English with a heavy accent, and her comprehension and writing skills were deficient. She was afraid that once she left the Miami environment, she would feel uncomfortable and, worse still, have difficulty keeping up with class work.

Programs that keep foreign-born children in Spanish-language classrooms for years are only part of the problem. During a visit to my niece's former school, I observed that all business, not just teaching, was conducted in Spanish. In the office, secretaries spoke to the administrators and the children in Spanish. Announcements over the public-address system were made in an English so fractured that it was almost incomprehensible.

I asked my niece's mother why, after years in public schools, her 4 daughter had poor English skills. "It's the whole environment," she replied. "All kinds of services are available in Spanish or Spanglish.[1] Sports and after-school activities are conducted in Spanglish. That's what the kids hear on the radio and in the street."

Until recently, immigrants made learning English a priority. But 5 even when they didn't learn English themselves, their children grew up speaking it. Thousands of first-generation Americans still strive to learn English, but others face reduced educational and career opportunities because they have not mastered this basic skill they need to get ahead.

According to the 1990 census, 40 percent of the Hispanics born in 6 the United States do not graduate from high school, and the Department of Education says that a lack of proficiency in English is an important factor in the drop-out rate.

People and agencies that favor providing services only in foreign 7 languages want to help people who do not speak English, but they may be doing these people a disservice by condemning them to a linguistic ghetto from which they cannot easily escape.

And my niece? She turned down all of her scholarship opportuni- 8 ties, deciding instead to attend a small college in Miami, where she will never have to put her English to the test.

Writer's main idea

Because Hispanics are not being encouraged to learn English, their opportunities are limited.

Key supporting points

1. *Writer's niece is afraid to accept a scholarship away from Miami.*

---

1. A mixture of Spanish and English.

2. *Foreign-born students are kept in Spanish-language classes.*

3. *Many services are provided in Spanish.*

4. *Many (40%) Hispanics do not graduate from high school.*

B   Highlighting a Reading Assignment

After you have previewed a passage, read through it carefully, highlighting as you read. **Highlighting** means using underlining and symbols to identify key ideas. This active reading strategy will help you to understand the writer's ideas and to make connections among these ideas when you reread. Be selective; don't highlight too much. Remember, you will eventually be rereading every highlighted word, phrase, and sentence—so highlight only the most important, most useful information.

When you highlight, use different symbols to indicate different things. These symbols will convey specific information to you when you reread before you take an exam or write a paper. The number and kinds of highlighting symbols you use are up to you. All that matters is that your symbols are clear and easy to remember.

Using Highlighting Symbols

- <u>Underline</u> key ideas—for example, topic sentences.
- Box or circle words or phrases you want to remember.
- Place a check mark (✔) or star (✱) next to an important idea.
- Place a double check mark (✔✔) or double star (✱✱) next to an especially significant idea.
- Draw lines or arrows to connect related ideas.
- Put a question mark (?) beside a word or idea that you need to look up.
- Number the writer's key supporting points or examples.

FOCUS   Knowing What to Highlight

You want to highlight what's important—but how do you *know* what's important? As a general rule, you should look for the same **visual signals** you looked for when you did your previewing. Many of the ideas you will need to highlight will probably be found in material that is visually set off from the rest of the text—opening and closing paragraphs, lists, and the like. Also, continue to look for **verbal signals**—words and phrases like *however, therefore, another reason, the most important point,* and so on—that often introduce key points. Together, these visual and verbal signals will give you clues to the writer's meaning and emphasis.

Here is how a student highlighted an excerpt from a newspaper column, "Barbie at Thirty-Five" by Anna Quindlen.

But consider the recent study at the University of Arizona investigating the <u>attitudes of white and black teenage girls toward body</u> ✳ <u>image</u>. The attitudes of the ⬚white girls⬚ were a nightmare. Ninety percent expressed <u>dissatisfaction with their own bodies</u>, and many said ✔ they saw dieting as a kind of all-purpose ⬭panacea.⬭ ? "I think the reason I would diet would be to gain self-confidence," said one. "I'd feel like it was a way of getting control," said another. And they were curiously united in their description of the ⬭perfect girl⬭ She's 5 feet 7 inches, weighs just over 100 pounds, has long legs and flowing hair. The researchers concluded, "The ideal girl was a living manifestation of the ⬭Barbie doll."⬭

While white girls described an ⬭impossible ideal,⬭ ⬚black teenagers⬚ talked about appearance in terms of style, attitude, pride, and personality. White respondents talked "thin," black ones "shapely." Seventy percent of the black teenagers said they were <u>satisfied with their</u> ✔ <u>weight</u>, and there was little emphasis on dieting. "We're all brought up and taught to be realistic about life," said one, "and we don't look at things the way you want them to be. You look at them the way they are."

The student who highlighted this passage was preparing to write an essay about eating disorders. She began her highlighting by underlining and starring the writer's main idea. She then boxed the names of the two key groups the passage compares—*white girls* and *black teenagers*—and underlined two phrases that illustrate how the attitudes of the two groups differ (*dissatisfaction with their own bodies* and *satisfied with their weight*). Check marks in the margin remind the student of the importance of these two phrases, and arrows connect each phrase to the appropriate group of girls.

The student also circled three related terms that characterize white girls' attitudes—*perfect girl*, *Barbie doll*, and *impossible ideal*—drawing lines to connect them to one another. Finally, she circled the unfamiliar word *panacea* and put a question mark above it to remind herself to look the word up in a dictionary.

◆ PRACTICE 35-2

Review the highlighted passage above. How would your own highlighting of this passage be similar to or different from the sample student highlighting?

◆ PRACTICE 35-3

Reread "No Comprendo" (pages 583–584). As you reread, highlight the article by underlining and starring main ideas, boxing and circling key words, checkmarking important points, and, if you wish, drawing lines and arrows to connect related ideas. Be sure to circle each unfamiliar word and to put a question mark above it.

C Annotating a Reading Assignment

As you highlight, you should also *annotate* what you are reading. **Annotating** a passage means making notes—of questions, reactions, reminders, ideas for writing or discussion—in the margins or between the lines. Keeping an informal record of ideas as they occur to you will prepare you for class discussion and provide a useful source of material for writing.

As you read a passage, asking yourself the following questions will help you make useful annotations.

Questions for Annotating

■ What is the writer saying? What do you think the writer is suggesting or implying? What makes you think so?
■ What is the writer's purpose (his or her reason for writing)?
■ What kind of audience is the writer addressing?
■ Is the writer responding to another writer's ideas?
■ What is the writer's main idea?
■ How does the writer support his or her points? Does the writer use facts? Opinions? Both?
■ What kind of supporting details and examples does the writer use?
■ Does the writer include enough supporting details and examples?
■ What pattern of development does the writer use to arrange his or her ideas? Is this pattern the best choice?
■ Does the writer seem well informed? Reasonable? Fair?
■ Do you understand the writer's vocabulary?
■ Do you understand the writer's ideas?
■ Do you agree with the points the writer is making?
■ How are the ideas presented in this reading selection like (or unlike) those presented in other selections you have read?

Teaching Tip
Encourage students to write notes in the margin as they read, even if a thought seems irrelevant. Such notes are often useful for class discussion.

For more on purpose and audience, see 1B.

For more on patterns of essay development, see Chapter 14.

The following passage reproduces the student's highlighting from page 586 and also illustrates her annotations.

But consider the recent study at the University of Arizona investigating the attitudes of white and black teenage girls toward body ✳

= cure-all

Need for control, perfection. Why? Media? Parents?

Barbie doll = plastic, unreal

"Thin" vs. "shapely"

Only 30% dissatisfied — but 90% of white girls

image. The attitudes of the white girls were a nightmare. Ninety percent expressed dissatisfaction with their own bodies, and many said they saw dieting as a kind of all-purpose panacea. "I think the reason I would diet would be to gain self-confidence," said one. "I'd feel like it was a way of getting control," said another. And they were curiously united in their description of the perfect girl. She's 5 feet 7 inches, weighs just over 100 pounds, has long legs and flowing hair. The researchers concluded, "The ideal girl was a living manifestation of the Barbie doll."

While white girls described an impossible ideal, black teenagers talked about appearance in terms of style, attitude, pride, and personality. White respondents talked "thin," black ones "shapely." Seventy percent of the black teenagers said they were satisfied with their weight, and there was little emphasis on dieting. "We're all brought up and taught to be realistic about life," said one, "and we don't look at things the way you want them to be. You look at them the way they are." *vs. Barbie doll (= unrealistic)* *overgeneralization?*

With her annotations, this student wrote down the meaning of the word *panacea*, put the study's conclusions and the contrasting statistics into her own words, and recorded questions she intended to explore further.

◆ PRACTICE 35-4

Reread "No Comprendo" (pages 583–584). As you reread, refer to the Questions for Annotating (page 587), and use them to help you annotate the article by writing down your own thoughts and questions in the margins. Note where you agree or disagree with the writer, and briefly explain why. Quickly summarize any points you think are particularly important. Take time to look up any unfamiliar words you have circled and to write brief definitions. Think of these annotations as your preparation for discussing the article in class and eventually writing about it.

◆ PRACTICE 35-5

Trade workbooks with another student, and read over his or her highlighting and annotating of "No Comprendo." How are your written responses similar to the other student's? How are they different? Do your classmate's responses help you see anything new about the article?

D Outlining a Reading Assignment

Outlining is another technique you can use to help you understand a reading assignment. Unlike a **formal outline**, which follows strict conventions, an **informal outline** enables you to record a passage's ideas in the order in which they are presented. After you have finished an informal outline of a passage, you should be able to see the writer's emphasis (which ideas are more important than others) as well as how the ideas are related.

● **Writing Tip**

Formal outlines can help you keep track of ideas in long essays or research papers. See 12E and Appendix B, section 7, for examples of formal outlines.

FOCUS Making an Informal Outline

1. Write or type the passage's main idea across the top of a sheet of paper. (This will remind you of the writer's focus and help keep your outline on track.)
2. At the left margin, write down the most important idea of the first body paragraph or first part of the passage.
3. Indent the next line a few spaces, and list the examples or details that support this idea. (You can use your computer's Tab key to help you set up your outline.)
4. As ideas become more specific, indent further. (Ideas that have the same degree of importance are indented the same distance from the left margin.)
5. Repeat the process with each body paragraph or part of the passage.

The student who highlighted and annotated the excerpt from Anna Quindlen's "Barbie at Thirty-Five" (page 586) made the following informal outline to help her understand the writer's ideas.

```
Main idea: Black and white teenage girls have very
different attitudes about their body images.

White girls dissatisfied
     90% dissatisfied with appearance
     Dieting=cure-all
          —self-confidence
          —control
     Ideal=unrealistic
          —tall and thin
          —Barbie doll
Black girls satisfied
     70% satisfied with weight
     Dieting not important
     Ideal=realistic
          —shapely
          —not thin
```

◆ PRACTICE 35-6

Working on your own or in a small group, make an informal outline of "No Comprendo" (pages 583–584). Refer to your highlighting and annotations as you construct your outline. When you have finished, check to make certain your outline indicates the writer's emphasis and the relationships among her ideas.

E Summarizing a Reading Assignment

Once you have highlighted, annotated, and outlined a passage, you may want to try summarizing it to help you understand it better. A **summary** retells, *in your own words*, what a passage is about. A summary condenses a passage, so it leaves out all but the main idea and key supporting points. A summary omits examples and details, and it does *not* include your own ideas or opinions.

FOCUS Summarizing a Reading Assignment

1. Review your outline.
2. Consulting your outline, restate the passage's main idea *in your own words*.
3. Consulting your outline, restate the passage's key supporting points. Add transitional words and phrases between sentences where necessary.
4. Reread the original passage to make sure you haven't left out anything significant.

Note: To avoid accidentally using the exact language of the original, do not look at the passage while you are writing your summary. If you want to use a distinctive word or phrase from the original passage, put it in quotation marks.

The student who highlighted, annotated, and outlined the excerpt from "Barbie at Thirty-Five" (page 586) wrote the following summary.

As Anna Quindlen reports in "Barbie at Thirty-Five," a University of Arizona study found that black and white teenage girls have very different attitudes about their body images. Almost all white girls (90 percent) said they were dissatisfied with their appearance. They seemed to think dieting would solve all their problems and give them confidence and control. To them, the "perfect girl" would look like a Barbie doll (tall and very thin). Quindlen sees this attitude as unrealistic, calling it an "impossible ideal." Black girls in the

study, however, were generally satisfied with their
appearance. In fact, 70 percent said that they were
happy with their weight and that dieting was not
important to them. They did not say they wanted to be
thin; they said they wanted to be "shapely."

◆ PRACTICE 35-7

Write a brief summary of "No Comprendo" (pages 583–584). Use your outline to guide you, and keep your summary short and to the point. Your
summary should be about one-quarter to one-third the length of the original article.

F   Writing a Response Paragraph

Once you have highlighted and annotated a reading selection, you are
ready to write about it—perhaps in a **response paragraph** in which you
record your informal reactions to the writer's ideas.

Because a response paragraph is informal, no special guidelines or
rules govern its format or structure. As in any paragraph, however, you
should include a topic sentence, write in complete sentences, and link sentences with appropriate transitions. Informal style and personal opinions
are acceptable.

*For more on writing a para-
graph, see Chapters 1 and 2.*

The student who highlighted, annotated, outlined, and summarized
the Quindlen passage wrote this response paragraph.

> Why are white and black girls' body images so
> different? Why do black girls think it's okay to be
> "shapely" while white girls want to be thin? Maybe it's
> because music videos and movies and fashion magazines
> show so many more white models, all half-starved,
> with perfect hair and legs. Or maybe white girls get
> different messages from their parents or the people they
> date. Do white and black girls' attitudes about their
> bodies stay the same when they get older? And what about
> male teenagers' self-images? Do white and black guys
> have different body images too?

Teaching Tip
Remind students that con-
tractions are acceptable here
only because this is an informal paragraph.

The process of writing this paragraph was very helpful to the student. The
questions she asked suggested some interesting ideas that she could explore in class discussion or in a longer, more formal, and more fully
developed piece of writing.

◆ PRACTICE 35-8

On a separate sheet of paper, write an informal response paragraph expressing your reactions to "No Comprendo" (pages 583–584) and to the
issue of bilingual education.

☑ REVIEW CHECKLIST:
Reading for College

- Preview the reading assignment. (See 35A.)
- Highlight the reading assignment. (See 35B.)
- Annotate the reading assignment. (See 35C.)
- Outline the reading assignment. (See 35D.)
- Summarize the reading assignment. (See 35E.)
- Write a response paragraph. (See 35F.)

Readings for Writers

PREVIEW

In this chapter, you will learn to react critically to essays by professional writers.

The following nineteen essays by professional writers offer interesting material to read, react to, think critically about, discuss, and write about. In addition, these essays illustrate some of the ways you can organize ideas in your own writing.

The essays in this chapter use the nine patterns of development you learned about in Units 1 through 3 of this book: exemplification, narration, description, process, cause and effect, comparison and contrast, classification, definition, and argument. Of course, these patterns are not your only options for arranging ideas in essays; in fact, many essays combine several patterns of development. Still, understanding how each of these nine patterns works will help you choose the most effective organization strategy when you are writing for a particular purpose and audience.

In this chapter, two essays by professional writers illustrate each pattern of development. (For argument, three model essays are included.) Each essay is preceded by a short **headnote**, an introduction that tells you something about the writer and suggests what to look for as you read. Following each selection are five sets of questions. Questions that you can work on in collaboration with other students are marked with an **asterisk** (*).

See Chapters 3 through 11 for information on using various patterns for developing paragraphs. See Chapter 14 for information on writing essays that use these patterns of development.

- **Reacting to the Reading** questions suggest guidelines for previewing, highlighting, and annotating the essay.
- **Reacting to Words** questions focus on the writer's word choice.
- **Reacting to Ideas** questions encourage you to respond critically to the writer's ideas and perhaps to consider his or her audience or purpose.
- **Reacting to the Pattern** questions ask you to consider how ideas are arranged within the essay and how they are connected to one another.
- **Writing Practice** suggestions give you opportunities to explore in writing ideas related to the section's readings.

For more on previewing, highlighting, and annotating, see Chapter 35.

A   Exemplification

For more on how to write an exemplification essay, see 14A.

An **exemplification** essay uses one or more specific examples to support a thesis statement. The two selections that follow, "Don't Call Me a Hot Tamale" by Judith Ortiz Cofer and "The Suspected Shopper" by Ellen

Goodman, are exemplification essays. The first uses a series of short examples to support a thesis; the second uses a single extended example.

DON'T CALL ME A HOT TAMALE

Judith Ortiz Cofer

Award-winning poet, novelist, and essayist Judith Ortiz Cofer often writes about her experiences as a Latina—a Hispanic woman—living in a non-Hispanic culture. In "Don't Call Me a Hot Tamale," she discusses how being Puerto Rican has affected her in the world beyond Puerto Rico. Note that all her examples illustrate the stereotypes she encounters in reaction to both her heritage and her gender.

On a bus to London from Oxford University, where I was earning some graduate credits one summer, a young man, obviously fresh from a pub, approached my seat. With both hands over his heart, he went down on his knees in the aisle and broke into an Irish tenor's rendition of "Maria" from *West Side Story.* I was not amused. "Maria" had followed me to London, reminding me of a prime fact of my life: You can leave the island of Puerto Rico, master the English language, and travel as far as you can, but if you're a Latina, especially one who so clearly belongs to Rita Moreno's[1] gene pool, the island travels with you.

Growing up in New Jersey and wanting most of all to belong, I lived in two completely different worlds. My parents designed our life as a microcosm of their *casas* on the island—we spoke in Spanish, ate Puerto Rican food bought at the *bodega,* and practiced strict Catholicism complete with Sunday mass in Spanish.

I was kept under tight surveillance by my parents, since my virtue and modesty were, by their cultural equation, the same as their honor. As teenagers, my friends and I were lectured constantly on how to behave as proper *señoritas.* But it was a conflicting message we received, since our Puerto Rican mothers also encouraged us to look and act like women by dressing us in clothes our Anglo schoolmates and their mothers found too "mature" and flashy. I often felt humiliated when I appeared at an American friend's birthday party wearing a dress more suitable for a semiformal. At Puerto Rican festivities, neither the music nor the colors we wore could be too loud.

I remember Career Day in high school, when our teachers told us to come dressed as if for a job interview. That morning, I agonized in front of my closet, trying to figure out what a "career girl" would wear, because the only model I had was Marlo Thomas[2] on TV. To me and my Puerto Rican girlfriends, dressing up meant wearing our mother's ornate jewelry and clothing.

At school that day, the teachers assailed us for wearing "everything at once"—meaning too much jewelry and too many accessories. And it was

1

2

3

4

5

---

1. A Puerto Rican actress, dancer, and singer. She is well known for her role in the movie musical *West Side Story,* a version of Shakespeare's *Romeo and Juliet* featuring Anglos and Puerto Ricans in New York City.

2. Star of a 1966–71 television comedy about a young woman living on her own in New York City.

painfully obvious that the other students in their tailored skirts and silk blouses thought we were hopeless and vulgar. The way they looked at us was a taste of the cultural clash that awaited us in the real world, where prospective employers and men on the street would often misinterpret our tight skirts and bright colors as a come-on.

It is custom, not chromosomes, that leads us to choose scarlet over pale pink. Our mothers had grown up on a tropical island where the natural environment was a riot of primary colors, where showing your skin was one way to keep cool as well as to look sexy. On the island, women felt freer to dress and move provocatively since they were protected by the traditions and laws of a Spanish/Catholic system of morality and machismo, the main rule of which was: *You may look at my sister, but if you touch her I will kill you.* The extended family and church structure provided them with a circle of safety on the island; if a man "wronged" a girl, everyone would close in to save her family honor.

Off-island, signals often get mixed. When a Puerto Rican girl who is dressed in her idea of what is attractive meets a man from the mainstream culture who has been trained to react to certain types of clothing as a sexual signal, a clash is likely to take place. She is seen as a Hot Tamale, a sexual firebrand. I learned this lesson at my first formal dance when my date leaned over and painfully planted a sloppy, overeager kiss on my mouth. When I didn't respond with sufficient passion, he said in a resentful tone: "I thought you Latin girls were supposed to mature early." It was only the first time I would feel like a fruit or vegetable—I was supposed to *ripen*, not just grow into womanhood like other girls.

These stereotypes, though rarer, still surface in my life. I recently stayed at a classy metropolitan hotel. After having dinner with a friend, I was returning to my room when a middle-aged man in a tuxedo stepped directly into my path. With his champagne glass extended toward me, he exclaimed, "Evita!"[3]

Blocking my way, he bellowed the song "Don't Cry for Me, Argentina." Playing to the gathering crowd, he began to sing loudly a ditty to the tune of "La Bamba"[4]—except the lyrics were about a girl named Maria whose exploits all rhymed with her name and gonorrhea.

I knew that this same man—probably a corporate executive, even worldly by most standards—would never have regaled a white woman with a dirty song in public. But to him, I was just a character in his universe of "others," all cartoons.

Still, I am one of the lucky ones. There are thousands of Latinas without the privilege of the education that my parents gave me. For them every day is a struggle against the misconceptions perpetuated by the myth of the Latina as whore, domestic worker or criminal.

Rather than fight these pervasive stereotypes, I try to replace them with a more interesting set of realities. I travel around the U.S. reading from my books of poetry and my novel. With the stories I tell, the dreams and fears I examine in my work, I try to get my audience past the particulars of my skin color, my accent or my clothes.

3. Eva Perón, wife of Juan Perón, president of Argentina in the 1940s and 1950s. She is the subject of the musical *Evita*.
4. A song with Spanish lyrics popular in the late 1950s.

I once wrote a poem in which I called Latinas "God's brown daugh- 13 ters." It is really a prayer, of sorts, for communication and respect. In it, Latin women pray "in Spanish to an Anglo God/with a Jewish heritage," and they are "fervently hoping/that if not omnipotent,/at least He be bilingual."

Reacting to the Reading

1. Underline the essay's thesis statement.
2. In the margins of the essay, number the examples Cofer uses to support this thesis.

Reacting to Words

Teaching Tip
Students may need help defining words. With nonnative students, consider going over the definitions in class before assigning the reading.

*1. Define these words: *tamale* (title), *rendition* (paragraph 1), *microcosm* (2), *ornate* (4), *assailed* (5), *riot* (6), *machismo* (6), *firebrand* (7), *regaled* (10), *perpetuated* (11), *pervasive* (12), *omnipotent* (13). Can you suggest a synonym for each word that will work in the essay?
2. What does the phrase *hot tamale* suggest to you? What do you think Cofer intends it to suggest? Can you think of a word or phrase that might be more effective?

Reacting to Ideas

Teaching Tip
Remind students to answer all questions in complete sentences.

*1. Cofer states her thesis in paragraph 1: "You can leave the island of Puerto Rico, master the English language, and travel as far as you can, but if you're a Latina, . . . the island travels with you." Restate this thesis in your own words. Do you think this statement applies only to Latinas or to other ethnic groups as well? Explain.
2. How, according to Cofer, are the signals sent by dress and appearance interpreted differently in Puerto Rico and "off-island" (paragraph 7)? How does this difference create problems for Cofer? Do you think there is anything she can do to avoid these problems?

Reacting to the Pattern

1. What examples does Cofer use to support her thesis? Do you think she uses enough examples to convince readers that her thesis is reasonable?
2. Cofer begins her essay with an example. Do you think this is an effective opening strategy? Why or why not? How else might she have begun her essay?
3. All of Cofer's examples are personal experiences. Are they as convincing as statistics or examples from current news articles would be? Are they *more* convincing? Explain.

Writing Practice

Teaching Tip
Before assigning Writing Practice 2, discuss with class members whether they believe Cofer *should* take steps to change how others see her. (You can also have this discussion after students finish the assignment.)

1. What kinds of positive examples can you think of to counteract the stereotype of the Latina as "whore, domestic worker or criminal" (paragraph 11)? Write a letter to a television network in which you propose the addition of several different Latina characters to actual programs in which they might appear.
2. What do you think Cofer can do to avoid being stereotyped? Write an essay that gives examples of specific things she might do to change the

way others see her. In your thesis, state why she should (or should not) make these changes.

3. Do you think others stereotype you because of your heritage—or because of your age, your gender, your dress, or where you live? Discuss some specific instances of such stereotyping.

THE SUSPECTED SHOPPER

Ellen Goodman

Journalist Ellen Goodman wrote "The Suspected Shopper" for her syndicated newspaper column. Note that although Goodman develops a single extended example of a "suspected shopper"—herself—throughout her essay, she supports her thesis with specific examples of incidents in which she was suspected. As you read, consider whether the essay (written in 1981) is still relevant to readers today—or whether it is perhaps even more relevant.

It is Saturday, Shopping Saturday, as it's called by the merchants who spread their wares like plush welcome mats across the pages of my newspaper.

But the real market I discover is a different, less eager place than the one I read about. On this Shopping Saturday I don't find welcomes, I find warnings and wariness.

At the first store, a bold sign of the times confronts me: SHOPLIFTERS WILL BE PROSECUTED TO THE FULL EXTENT OF THE LAW.

At the second store, instead of a greeter, I find a doorkeeper. It is his job, his duty, to bar my entrance. To pass, I must give up the shopping bag on my arm. I check it in and check it out.

At the third store, I venture as far as the dressing room. Here I meet another worker paid to protect the merchandise rather than to sell it. The guard of this dressing room counts the number of items I carry in and will count the number of items I carry out.

In the mirror, a long, white, plastic security tag juts out from the blouse tucked into the skirt. I try futilely to pat it down along my left hip, try futilely to zip the skirt.

Finally, during these strange gyrations, a thought seeps through years of dulled consciousness, layers of denial. Something has happened to the relationship between shops and shoppers. I no longer feel like a woman in search of a shirt. I feel like an enemy at Checkpoint Charlie.[1]

I finally, belatedly, realize that I am treated less like a customer these days and more like a criminal. And I hate it. This change happened gradually, and understandably. Security rose in tandem with theft. The defenses of the shopkeepers went up, step by step, with the offenses of the thieves.

But now as the weapons escalate, it's the average consumer, the innocent bystander, who is hit by friendly fire.

I don't remember the first time an errant security tag buzzed at the doorway, the first time I saw a camera eye in a dress department. I accepted it as part of the price of living in a tight honesty market.

---

1. A military security checkpoint.

In the supermarket, they began to insist on a mug shot before they would cash my check. I tried not to take it personally. At the drugstore, the cashier began to staple my bags closed. And I tried not to take it personally. 11

Now, these experiences have accumulated until I feel routinely treated like a suspect. At the jewelry store, the door is unlocked only for those who pass judgment. In the junior department, the suede pants are permanently attached to the hangers. In the gift shop, the cases are only opened with a key. 12

I am not surprised anymore, but I am finally aware of just how unpleasant it is to be dealt with as guilty until we prove our innocence. Anyplace we are not known, we are not trusted. The old slogan, "Let the Consumer Beware," has been replaced with a new slogan: "Beware of the Consumer." 13

It is no fun to be Belgium[2] in the war between sales and security. Thievery has changed the atmosphere of the marketplace. Merchant distrust has spread through the ventilation system of a whole business, a whole city, and it infects all of us. 14

At the cashier counter today, with my shirt in hand, I the Accused stand quietly while the saleswoman takes my credit card. I watch her round up the usual suspicions. In front of my face, without a hint of embarrassment, she checks my charge number against the list of stolen credit vehicles. While I stand there, she calls the clearinghouse of bad debtors. 15

Having passed both tests, I am instructed to add my name, address, serial number to the bottom of the charge. She checks one signature against another, the picture against the person. Only then does she release the shirt into my custody. 16

And so this Shopping Saturday I take home six ounces of silk and a load of resentment. 17

Reacting to the Reading

1. Goodman gives a number of examples of incidents in which she was suspected of shoplifting. Highlight these examples.

2. In the margins of the essay, supplement Goodman's examples with one or two examples from your personal experience (or from the experiences of your friends) that support her thesis.

Reacting to Words

*1. Define these words: *futilely* (paragraph 6), *gyrations* (7), *belatedly* (8), *tandem* (8), *errant* (10). Can you suggest a synonym for each word that will work in the essay?

2. What is Goodman's purpose in choosing words like *enemy* (paragraph 7) and *mug shot* (11)? How do they help to support her thesis? Can you find additional words or expressions that serve the same purpose?

Reacting to Ideas

*1. Goodman, a middle-class white woman, uses *we* in the sentence "Anyplace we are not known, we are not trusted" (paragraph 13). Who

2. Country located between France and Germany, which were enemies in several wars.

is this *we?* Do you think Goodman is really part of the group with which she identifies?

2. In paragraph 8, Goodman says the change in attitude she observes is understandable. Do you think she is right?

3. Do you think shoplifting is more or less of a problem today than it was in 1981 when Goodman wrote her essay? What makes you think so?

Reacting to the Pattern

1. In paragraph 8, Goodman states her thesis: "I finally, belatedly, realize that I am treated less like a customer these days and more like a criminal." However, she introduces a number of her examples even before she states this thesis. Why do you think she does this?

2. List the specific examples of times when Goodman was "treated less like a customer . . . and more like a criminal" (paragraph 8).

3. How does Goodman arrange the specific examples that support her thesis? Is each discussed in an individual paragraph, or are examples grouped together?

Writing Practice

1. Why do you think people shoplift? Write an exemplification essay in which you discuss a different reason in each body paragraph.

2. Have you ever been torn between giving in to peer pressure and maintaining your own sense of right and wrong? Develop an extended example that illustrates what it was like to be caught in the middle and explains how you resolved the problem.

3. What do you think merchants can do to reduce shoplifting without making shoppers feel like criminals? Using exemplification to organize your ideas, write a letter to a store where you are a regular customer.

B Narration

A **narrative** essay tells a story by presenting a series of events in chronological order. In the first of the two essays that follow, "The Sanctuary of School," Lynda Barry tells a story about home and family. In the second, "Thirty-Eight Who Saw Murder Didn't Call the Police," Martin Gansberg reports the story of a tragic murder.

For more on how to write a narrative essay, see 14B.

THE SANCTUARY OF SCHOOL

Lynda Barry

In her cartoon strip "Ernie Pook's Comeek," which appears in a number of newspapers and magazines, Lynda Barry looks at the world through the eyes of children. Her characters remind adult readers of the complicated world of young people and of the clarity with which they see social situations. In "The Sanctuary of School," Barry tells a

> **Teaching Tip**
> Remind students to familiarize themselves with the end-of-essay questions before they read the essay.

story from her own childhood. As you read this essay, note how Barry relates her personal experience to a broader issue.

1   I was 7 years old the first time I snuck out of the house in the dark. It was winter and my parents had been fighting all night. They were short on money and long on relatives who kept "temporarily" moving into our house because they had nowhere else to go.

2   My brother and I were used to giving up our bedroom. We slept on the couch, something we actually liked because it put us that much closer to the light of our lives, our television.

3   At night when everyone was asleep, we lay on our pillows watching it with the sound off. We watched Steve Allen's mouth moving. We watched Johnny Carson's mouth moving.[1] We watched movies filled with gangsters shooting machine guns into packed rooms, dying soldiers hurling a last grenade and beautiful women crying at windows. Then the sign-off finally came and we tried to sleep.

4   The morning I snuck out, I woke up filled with a panic about needing to get to school. The sun wasn't quite up yet but my anxiety was so fierce that I just got dressed, walked quietly across the kitchen and let myself out the back door.

5   It was quiet outside. Stars were still out. Nothing moved and no one was in the street. It was as if someone had turned the sound off on the world.

6   I walked the alley, breaking thin ice over the puddles with my shoes. I didn't know why I was walking to school in the dark. I didn't think about it. All I knew was a feeling of panic, like the panic that strikes kids when they realize they are lost.

7   That feeling eased the moment I turned the corner and saw the dark outline of my school at the top of the hill. My school was made up of about 15 nondescript portable classrooms set down on a fenced concrete lot in a rundown Seattle neighborhood, but it had the most beautiful view of the Cascade Mountains. You could see them from anywhere on the playfield and you could see them from the windows of my classroom—Room 2.

8   I walked over to the monkey bars and hooked my arms around the cold metal. I stood for a long time just looking across Rainier Valley. The sky was beginning to whiten and I could hear a few birds.

9   In a perfect world my absence at home would not have gone unnoticed. I would have had two parents in a panic to locate me, instead of two parents in a panic to locate an answer to the hard question of survival during a deep financial and emotional crisis.

10   But in an overcrowded and unhappy home, it's incredibly easy for any child to slip away. The high levels of frustration, depression and anger in my house made my brother and me invisible. We were children with the sound turned off. And for us, as for the steadily increasing number of neglected children in this country, the only place where we could count on being noticed was at school.

11   "Hey there, young lady. Did you forget to go home last night?" It was Mr. Gunderson, our janitor, whom we all loved. He was nice and he was funny and he was old with white hair, thick glasses and an unbelievable number of keys. I could hear them jingling as he walked across the playfield. I felt incredibly happy to see him.

---

1. Steve Allen and Johnny Carson were late-night television hosts.

He let me push his wheeled garbage can between the different portables as he unlocked each room. He let me turn on the lights and raise the window shades and I saw my school slowly come to life. I saw Mrs. Holman, our school secretary, walk into the office without her orange lipstick on yet. She waved.

I saw the fifth-grade teacher Mr. Cunningham, walking under the breezeway eating a hard roll. He waved.

And I saw my teacher, Mrs. Claire LeSane, walking toward us in a red coat and calling my name in a very happy and surprised way, and suddenly my throat got tight and my eyes stung and I ran toward her crying. It was something that surprised us both.

It's only thinking about it now, 28 years later, that I realize I was crying from relief. I was with my teacher, and in a while I was going to sit at my desk, with my crayons and pencils and books and classmates all around me, and for the next six hours I was going to enjoy a thoroughly secure, warm and stable world. It was a world I absolutely relied on. Without it, I don't know where I would have gone that morning.

Mrs. LeSane asked me what was wrong and when I said "Nothing," she seemingly left it at that. But she asked me if I would carry her purse for her, an honor above all honors, and she asked if I wanted to come into Room 2 early and paint.

She believed in the natural healing power of painting and drawing for troubled children. In the back of her room there was always a drawing table and an easel with plenty of supplies, and sometimes during the day she would come up to you for what seemed like no good reason and quietly ask if you wanted to go to the back table and "make some pictures for Mrs. LeSane." We all had a chance at it—to sit apart from the class for a while to paint, draw and silently work out impossible problems on 11×17 sheets of newsprint.

Drawing came to mean everything to me. At the back table in Room 2, I learned to build myself a life preserver that I could carry into my home.

We all know that a good education system saves lives, but the people of this country are still told that cutting the budget for public schools is necessary, that poor salaries for teachers are all we can manage and that art, music and all creative activities must be the first to go when times are lean.

Before- and after-school programs are cut and we are told that public schools are not made for baby-sitting children. If parents are neglectful temporarily or permanently, for whatever reason, it's certainly sad, but their unlucky children must fend for themselves. Or slip through the cracks. Or wander in a dark night alone.

We are told in a thousand ways that not only are public schools not important, but that the children who attend them, the children who need them most, are not important either. We leave them to learn from the blind eye of a television, or to the mercy of "a thousand points of light"[2] that can be as far away as stars.

I was lucky. I had Mrs. LeSane. I had Mr. Gunderson. I had an abundance of art supplies. And I had a particular brand of neglect in my home that allowed me to slip away and get to them. But what about the rest of the kids who weren't as lucky? What happened to them?

---

2. Phrase used by former president George Herbert Walker Bush to promote volunteerism.

By the time the bell rang that morning I had finished my drawing and   23
Mrs. LeSane pinned it up on the special bulletin board she reserved for
drawings from the back table. It was the same picture I always drew—a
sun in the corner of a blue sky over a nice house with flowers all around it.

Mrs. LeSane asked us to please stand, face the flag, place our right   24
hands over our hearts and say the Pledge of Allegiance. Children across the
country do it faithfully. I wonder now when the country will face its children and say a pledge right back.

Reacting to the Reading

1. Underline passages that describe Barry's home life in negative terms
   and her school life in positive terms.
2. In the margins of the essay, note the specific features of the two places
   (home and school) that are contrasted.

Reacting to Words

*1. Define these words: *nondescript* (paragraph 7), *fend* (20). Can you suggest a synonym for each word that will work in the essay?
2. Look up the word *sanctuary* in a dictionary. Which of the listed definitions do you think comes closest to Barry's meaning?

Teaching Tip
Students may need help
defining words. With nonnative students, consider going
over the definitions in class
before assigning the reading.

Teaching Tip
Remind students to answer
all questions in complete
sentences.

Reacting to Ideas

1. In paragraph 10, Barry characterizes herself and her brother as "children with the sound turned off." What do you think she means?
2. List the ways in which Barry's home and school worlds are different.
*3. What is the main point of Barry's essay—the idea that she wants to
   convince readers to accept? Is this idea actually stated in her essay? If
   so, where? If not, do you think it should be?

Reacting to the Pattern

1. Paragraphs 9–10 and 19–22 interrupt Barry's story. What purpose do
   these paragraphs serve? Do you think the essay would be more effective if paragraphs 9 and 10 came earlier? If paragraphs 19–22 came
   after paragraph 24? Explain.
2. What transitional words and phrases does Barry use to move readers
   from one event to the next? Do you think her essay needs more transitions? If so, where should they be added?

Writing Practice

1. Did you see elementary school as a sanctuary or as something quite
   different? Write a narrative essay that conveys to readers what school
   meant to you when you were a child.
2. In addition to school, television was a sanctuary for Barry and her
   brother. Did television watching (or some other activity) serve this function for you when you were younger? Is there some activity that fills
   this role now? In a narrative essay, write about your own "sanctuary."
3. What role does college play in your life? Write an article for your
   school newspaper in which you use narration to tell what school
   means to you now that you are an adult.

THIRTY-EIGHT WHO SAW MURDER
DIDN'T CALL THE POLICE

Martin Gansberg

This newspaper story uses objective language to tell about an incident that occurred in New York City in 1964. As Gansberg reconstructs the crime two weeks after it happened, he gives readers a detailed picture of the sequence of events that led up to a young woman's murder—in full view of thirty-eight of her "respectable, law-abiding" neighbors. As you read, consider how you might have acted if you had been a witness to this tragedy.

1   For more than half an hour 38 respectable, law-abiding citizens in Queens watched a killer stalk and stab a woman in three separate attacks in Kew Gardens.

2   Twice their chatter and the sudden glow of their bedroom lights inter- rupted him and frightened him off. Each time he returned, sought her out, and stabbed her again. Not one person telephoned the police during the assault; one witness called after the woman was dead.

3   That was two weeks ago today.

4   Still shocked is Assistant Chief Inspector Frederick M. Lussen, in charge of the borough's detectives and a veteran of 25 years of homicide investigations. He can give a matter-of-fact recitation on many murders. But the Kew Gardens slaying baffles him—not because it is a murder, but because the "good people" failed to call the police.

5   "As we have reconstructed the crime," he said, "the assailant had three chances to kill this woman during a 35-minute period. He returned twice to complete the job. If we had been called when he first attacked, the woman might not be dead now."

6   This is what the police say happened beginning at 3:20 a.m. in the staid, middle-class, tree-lined Austin Street area:

7   Twenty-eight-year-old Catherine Genovese, who was called Kitty by almost everyone in the neighborhood, was returning home from her job as manager of a bar in Hollis. She parked her red Fiat in a lot adjacent to the Kew Gardens Long Island Rail Road Station, facing Mowbray Place. Like many residents of the neighborhood, she had parked there day after day since her arrival from Connecticut a year ago, although the railroad frowns on the practice.

8   She turned off the lights of her car, locked the door, and started to walk the 100 feet to the entrance of her apartment at 82-70 Austin Street, which is in a Tudor building, with stores on the first floor and apartments on the second.

9   The entrance to the apartment is in the rear of the building because the front is rented to retail stores. At night the quiet neighborhood is shrouded in the slumbering darkness that marks most residential areas.

10   Miss Genovese noticed a man at the far end of the lot, near a seven- story apartment house at 82-40 Austin Street. She halted. Then, nervously, she headed up Austin Street toward Lefferts Boulevard, where there is a call box to the 102nd Police Precinct in nearby Richmond Hill.

11   She got as far as a street light in front of a bookstore before the man grabbed her. She screamed. Lights went on in the 10-story apartment house at 82-67 Austin Street, which faces the bookstore. Windows slid open and voices punctuated the early-morning stillness.

Miss Genovese screamed: "Oh, my God, he stabbed me! Please help 12
me! Please help me!"

From one of the upper windows in the apartment house, a man called 13
down: "Let that girl alone!"

The assailant looked up at him, shrugged, and walked down Austin 14
Street toward a white sedan parked a short distance away. Miss Genovese
struggled to her feet.

Lights went out. The killer returned to Miss Genovese, now trying to 15
make her way around the side of the building by the parking lot to get to
her apartment. The assailant stabbed her again.

"I'm dying!" she shrieked. "I'm dying!" 16

Windows were opened again, and lights went on in many apartments. 17
The assailant got into his car and drove away. Miss Genovese staggered to
her feet. A city bus, O-10, the Lefferts Boulevard line to Kennedy International Airport, passed. It was 3:35 a.m.

The assailant returned. By then, Miss Genovese had crawled to the 18
back of the building, where the freshly painted brown doors to the apartment house held out hope for safety. The killer tried the first door;
she wasn't there. At the second door, 82-62 Austin Street, he saw her
slumped on the floor at the foot of the stairs. He stabbed her a third
time—fatally.

It was 3:50 by the time the police received their first call, from a man 19
who was a neighbor of Miss Genovese. In two minutes they were at the
scene. The neighbor, a 70-year-old woman, and another woman were the
only persons on the street. Nobody else came forward.

The man explained that he had called the police after much delibera- 20
tion. He had phoned a friend in Nassau County for advice and then he had
crossed the roof of the building to the apartment of the elderly woman to
get her to make the call.

"I didn't want to get involved," he sheepishly told police. 21

Six days later, the police arrested Winston Moseley, a 29-year-old busi- 22
ness machine operator, and charged him with homicide. Moseley had
no previous record. He is married, has two children and owns a home at
133-19 Sutter Avenue, South Ozone Park, Queens. On Wednesday, a court
committed him to Kings County Hospital for psychiatric observation.

When questioned by the police, Moseley also said that he had slain 23
Mrs. Annie May Johnson, 24, of 146-12 133d Avenue, Jamaica, on Feb. 29
and Barbara Kralik, 15, of 174-17 140th Avenue, Springfield Gardens, last
July. In the Kralik case, the police are holding Alvin L. Mitchell, who is said
to have confessed to that slaying.

The police stressed how simple it would have been to have gotten in 24
touch with them. "A phone call," said one of the detectives, "would have
done it." The police may be reached by dialing "O" for operator or SPring
7-3100.

Today witnesses from the neighborhood, which is made up of one- 25
family homes in the $35,000 to $60,000 range with the exception of the
two apartment houses near the railroad station, find it difficult to explain
why they didn't call the police.

A housewife, knowingly if quite casually, said, "We thought it was a 26
lovers' quarrel." A husband and wife both said, "Frankly, we were afraid."
They seemed aware of the fact that events might have been different. A
distraught woman, wiping her hands in her apron, said, "I didn't want my
husband to get involved."

One couple, now willing to talk about that night, said they heard the 27 first screams. The husband looked thoughtfully at the bookstore where the killer first grabbed Miss Genovese.

"We went to the window to see what was happening," he said, "but the 28 light from our bedroom made it difficult to see the street." The wife, still apprehensive, added: "I put out the light and we were able to see better."

Asked why they hadn't called the police, she shrugged and replied: "I 29 don't know."

A man peeked out from a slight opening in the doorway to his apart- 30 ment and rattled off an account of the killer's second attack. Why hadn't he called the police at the time? "I was tired," he said without emotion. "I went back to bed."

It was 4:25 a.m. when the ambulance arrived to take the body of Miss 31 Genovese. It drove off. "Then," a solemn police detective said, "the people came out."

Reacting to the Reading

1. Place a check mark beside each passage of dialogue Gansberg uses.
2. Add brief marginal annotations next to three of these passages of dialogue.

Reacting to Words

*1. Define these words: *staid* (paragraph 6), *shrouded* (9). Can you suggest a synonym for each word that will work in the essay?

2. What is Gansberg's purpose in using terms like *respectable* (paragraph 1), *law-abiding* (1), and *good people* (4)? What is your reaction to these words?

> **Teaching Tip**
> Students may need help defining words. With nonnative students, consider going over the definitions in class before assigning the reading.

Reacting to Ideas

1. What reasons do the witnesses give for not coming to Kitty Genovese's aid? Why do *you* think no one helped her? Do you think the witnesses should be held accountable for their lack of action?

*2. Suppose Genovese's attack were to occur today. How do you think her neighbors would react? What might be different about the situation?

> **Teaching Tip**
> Remind students to answer all questions in complete sentences.

Reacting to the Pattern

1. What other patterns could Gansberg have used to develop his essay? For instance, could he have used comparison and contrast? Exemplification? Given the alternatives, do you think narration is the best choice? Why or why not?

*2. Gansberg uses many transitional words and phrases, including references to specific times, to move readers from one event to the next. List as many of these transitions as you can. Do you think more transitions should be added?

Writing Practice

1. Write a narrative essay about a time when you were a witness who chose not to become involved in events you were observing.

2. Find a brief newspaper article that tells a story about a similar incident in which bystanders witnessed a crime. Expand the article into a longer essay, inventing characters, dialogue, and additional details.
3. Retell Kitty Genovese's story—but this time, have a witness come to her rescue.

C Description

For more on how to write a descriptive essay, see 14C.

A **descriptive** essay tells what something looks, sounds, smells, tastes, or feels like. It uses details to give readers a clear, vivid picture of a person, place, or object. In "Summer Picnic Fish Fry," Maya Angelou describes a community picnic. In "Guavas," Esmeralda Santiago describes a fruit.

SUMMER PICNIC FISH FRY

Maya Angelou

Maya Angelou is a poet, historian, playwright, civil rights activist, producer, and director. At the request of President Bill Clinton, she wrote and delivered a poem at his 1993 inauguration. "Summer Picnic Fish Fry," from her autobiographical *I Know Why the Caged Bird Sings* (1969), presents a vivid picture of a specific time (the 1930s) and place (the rural Arkansas town of Stamps). As you read, notice how Angelou, from her place on the grass, takes in the entire picnic, one scene at a time.

> "Acka Backa, Sody Cracka
> Acka Backa, Boo
> Acka Backa, Sody Cracka
> I'm in love with you."

The sounds of tag beat through the trees while the top branches waved   1
in contrapuntal rhythms. I lay on a moment of green grass and telescoped the children's game to my vision. The girls ran about wild, now here, now there, never here, never was, they seemed to have no more direction than a splattered egg. But it was a shared if seldom voiced knowledge that all movements fitted, and worked according to a larger plan. I raised a platform for my mind's eye and marveled down on the outcome of "Acka Backa." The gay picnic dresses dashed, stopped and darted like beautiful dragonflies over a dark pool. The boys, black whips in the sunlight, popped behind the trees where their girls had fled, half hidden and throbbing in the shadows.

The summer picnic fish fry in the clearing by the pond was the biggest   2
outdoor event of the year. Everyone was there. All churches were represented, as well as the social groups (Elks, Eastern Star, Masons, Knights of Columbus, Daughters of Pythias), professional people (Negro teachers from Lafayette county) and all the excited children.

Musicians brought cigar-box guitars, harmonicas, juice harps, combs 3
wrapped in tissue paper and even bathtub basses.

The amount and variety of foods would have found approval on the 4
menu of a Roman epicure. Pans of fried chicken, covered with dishtowels,
sat under benches next to a mountain of potato salad crammed with hard-
boiled eggs. Whole rust-red sticks of bologna were clothed in cheese-cloth.
Homemade pickles and chow-chow, and baked country hams, aromatic
with cloves and pineapples, vied for prominence. Our steady customers
had ordered cold watermelons, so Bailey[1] and I chugged the striped-green
fruit into the Coca-Cola box and filled all the tubs with ice as well as the
big black wash pot that Momma used to boil her laundry. Now they too lay
sweating in the happy afternoon air.

The summer picnic gave ladies a chance to show off their baking 5
hands. On the barbecue pit, chickens and spareribs sputtered in their own
fat and a sauce whose recipe was guarded in the family like a scandalous
affair. However, in the ecumenical light of the summer picnic every true
baking artist could reveal her prize to the delight and criticism of the town.
Orange sponge cakes and dark brown mounds dripping Hershey's chocolate stood layer to layer with ice-white coconuts and light brown caramels.
Pound cakes sagged with their buttery weight and small children could no
more resist licking the icings than their mothers could avoid slapping the
sticky fingers.

Proven fishermen and weekend amateurs sat on the trunks of trees at 6
the pond. They pulled the struggling bass and the silver perch from the
swift water. A rotating crew of young girls scaled and cleaned the catch
and busy women in starched aprons salted and rolled the fish in corn
meal, then dropped them in Dutch ovens trembling with boiling fat.

On one corner of the clearing a gospel group was rehearsing. Their 7
harmony, packed as tight as sardines, floated over the music of the county
singers and melted into the songs of the small children's ring games.

"Boys, don'chew let that ball fall on none of my cakes, you do and it'll 8
be me on you."

"Yes, ma'am," and nothing changed. The boys continued hitting the 9
tennis ball with pailings snatched from a fence and running holes in the
ground, colliding with everyone.

Reacting to the Reading

1. Circle all the words and phrases in the essay that designate colors.
2. In the margins, write brief notes explaining what these words and
   phrases add to the essay.

Reacting to Words

*1. Define these words: *contrapuntal* (paragraph 1), *epicure* (4), *aromatic*
   (4), *vied* (4), *ecumenical* (5), *colliding* (9). Can you suggest a synonym
   for each word that will work in the essay?
2. Find several examples of vivid action verbs (for example, *sagged* in
   paragraph 5). What does each verb mean? What does it suggest?

> **Teaching Tip**
> Students may need help
> defining words. With nonna-
> tive students, consider going
> over the definitions in class
> before assigning the reading.

---

1. The author's brother.

For more on metaphors and similes, see 20D.

*3. Angelou uses some unusual **metaphors** (for example, "boys, black whips in the sunlight" in paragraph 1) and **similes** (for example, "harmony, packed as tight as sardines" in paragraph 7). Find as many similes and metaphors as you can. Which ones are most effective? Why?

Reacting to Ideas

1. What do you think Angelou means in paragraph 1 when she says that she "raised a platform for [her] mind's eye"?
2. What is it about the picnic that makes it so memorable to Angelou and the other townspeople?

Reacting to the Pattern

*1. In paragraph 2, Angelou says, "The summer picnic fish fry in the clearing by the pond was the biggest outdoor event of the year. Everyone was there." How do these statements establish her essay's mood? What mood does Angelou want her details to convey?
2. Angelou, seated on the grass, begins her description with the sights and sounds of children playing tag and ends with her observation of another children's game. What does she see in between these two scenes? Trace her observations as she moves her gaze around the picnic.
3. Is this essay primarily subjective or objective description? Explain.

Writing Practice

1. Describe a large outdoor family or community event that you have attended. Be sure to include concrete, sensory details about the setting, food, guests, and activities, and make your description as visual and vivid as possible.
2. Describe a scene at which you, like Angelou, were an observer rather than a participant. Begin by describing the location from which you viewed the scene.

GUAVAS

Esmeralda Santiago

Esmeralda Santiago grew up in Puerto Rico as the oldest of eleven children raised by a single mother. The family moved to New York when she was thirteen years old. She has written a childhood memoir, *When I Was Puerto Rican* (1993), and its sequel, *Almost a Woman* (1998), describing the family's move to Brooklyn. After graduating from the High School of the Performing Arts in Manhattan, Santiago spent eight years studying part-time at community colleges before being accepted on full scholarship to Harvard University. In recent years, Santiago has also founded a film and production company, helped found a shelter for battered women, and most recently worked as an editor. As you read this selection, take note of which of the five senses Santiago uses to describe the experience of eating a guava.

Barco que no anda, no llega a puerto.

A ship that doesn't sail, never reaches port.

There are guavas at the Shop & Save. I pick one the size of a tennis ball 1
and finger the prickly stem end. It feels familiarly bumpy and firm. The
guava is not quite ripe; the skin is still a dark green. I smell it and imagine
a pale pink center, the seeds tightly embedded in the flesh.

A ripe guava is yellow, although some varieties have a pink tinge. The 2
skin is thick, firm, and sweet. Its heart is bright pink and almost solid with
seeds. The most delicious part of the guava surrounds the tiny seeds. If you
don't know how to eat a guava, the seeds end up in the crevices between
your teeth.

When you bite into a ripe guava, your teeth must grip the bumpy sur- 3
face and sink into the thick edible skin without hitting the center. It takes
experience to do this, as it's quite tricky to determine how far beyond the
skin the seeds begin.

Some years, when the rains have been plentiful and the nights cool, 4
you can bite into a guava and not find many seeds. The guava bushes grow
close to the ground, their branches laden with green then yellow fruit that
seem to ripen overnight. These guavas are large and juicy, almost seedless,
their roundness enticing you to have one more, just one more, because
next year the rains may not come.

As children, we didn't always wait for the fruit to ripen. We raided the 5
bushes as soon as the guavas were large enough to bend the branch.

A green guava is sour and hard. You bite into it at its widest point, 6
because it's easier to grasp with your teeth. You hear the skin, meat, and
seeds crunching inside your head, while the inside of your mouth explodes
in little spurts of sour.

You grimace, your eyes water, and your cheeks disappear as your lips 7
purse into a tight O. But you have another and then another, enjoying the
crunchy sounds, the acid taste, the gritty texture of the unripe center. At
night, your mother makes you drink castor oil, which she says tastes better
than a green guava. That's when you know for sure that you're a child and
she has stopped being one.

I had my last guava the day we left Puerto Rico. It was large and juicy, 8
almost red in the center, and so fragrant that I didn't want to eat it because
I would lose the smell. All the way to the airport I scratched at it with my
teeth, making little dents in the skin, chewing small pieces with my front
teeth, so that I could feel the texture against my tongue, the tiny pink
pellets of sweet.

Today, I stand before a stack of dark green guavas, each perfectly 9
round and hard, each $1.59. The one in my hand is tempting. It smells
faintly of late summer afternoons and hopscotch under the mango tree.
But this is autumn in New York, and I'm no longer a child.

The guava joins its sisters under the harsh fluorescent lights of the 10
exotic fruit display. I push my cart away, toward the apples and pears of
my adulthood, their nearly seedless ripeness predictable and bittersweet.

Reacting to the Reading

1. The essay begins with a quotation in Spanish, followed by its English
   translation. In a marginal note, explain why you think Santiago opens
   with this quotation.

2. Circle all the words in the essay that convey information about guavas' physical appearance (how they look).

Reacting to Words

Teaching Tip

Students may need help defining words. With nonnative students, consider going over the definitions in class before assigning the reading.

*1. Define these words: *guava* (title), *edible* (paragraph 3), *laden* (4), *enticing* (4), *spurts* (6), *grimace* (7), *pellets* (8). Can you suggest a synonym for each word that will work in the essay?

*2. Write an alternate one-word title for this selection.

Reacting to Ideas

Teaching Tip

Remind students to answer all questions in complete sentences.

1. How is the fruit in the Shop & Save different from the fruit of Santiago's childhood?

*2. Is this essay just about guavas, or is it really about something else? Explain.

Reacting to the Pattern

1. Santiago begins and ends her essay at the Shop & Save, but her imagination takes her somewhere else. Where? What sends her thoughts away from the supermarket?

2. Santiago describes several kinds of guavas. How are they different?

*3. In addition to describing how guavas look, Santiago also describes their smell, taste, and feel. Where does she use language that conveys how guavas taste? How they smell? How they feel?

4. If Santiago had written a purely objective description, what would she have left out? What might she have added?

Writing Practice

1. Write a subjective description of a food you loved when you were a child. Try to describe the smell, taste, and feel of the food as well as its appearance.

2. Write an essay about a friend or family member with whom you associate a particular food or meal. Include descriptions of that person engaged in eating or in preparing the food.

3. How have your tastes in food changed since you were a child? Trace the development of your food preferences, beginning as far back as you can remember. Be sure to describe the foods that defined each stage of your life.

D   Process

For more on how to write a process essay, see 14D.

A **process** essay explains the steps in a procedure, telling how something is (or was) done. In "Slice of Life," Russell Baker gives a set of instructions for carving a turkey. In "About a Bird," Patrick Martins explains how turkeys are raised.

SLICE OF LIFE

Russell Baker

Pulitzer Prize–winning columnist and author Russell Baker was known for his keen political insight and sharp social commentary. He was also known for being funny. The source of much of Baker's humor is his deadpan approach, in which he pretends to be completely serious. In the following essay, note how he uses this approach to turn what seems to be a straightforward set of instructions into a humorous discussion of a holiday ritual.

Teaching Tip
Remind students to familiarize themselves with the end-of-essay questions before they read the essay.

1   How to carve a turkey:

2   Assemble the following tools—carving knife, stone for sharpening carving knife, hot water, soap, wash cloth, two bath towels, barbells, meat cleaver. If the house lacks a meat cleaver, an ax may be substituted. If it is, add bandages, sutures, and iodine to above list.

3   Begin by moving the turkey from the roasting pan to a suitable carving area. This is done by inserting the carving knife into the posterior stuffed area of the turkey and the knife-sharpening stone into the stuffed area under the neck.

4   Thus skewered, the turkey may be lifted out of the hot grease with relative safety. Should the turkey drop to the floor, however, remove the knife and stone, roll the turkey gingerly into the two bath towels, wrap them several times around it and lift the encased fowl to the carving place.

5   You are now ready to begin carving. Sharpen the knife on the stone and insert it where the thigh joins the torso. If you do this correctly, which is improbable, the knife will almost immediately encounter a barrier of bone and gristle. This may very well be the joint. It could, however, be your thumb. If not, execute a vigorous sawing motion until satisfied that the knife has been defeated. Withdraw the knife and ask someone nearby, in as testy a manner as possible, why the knives at your house are not kept in better carving condition.

6   Exercise the biceps and forearms by lifting barbells until they are strong enough for you to tackle the leg joint with bare hands. Wrapping one hand firmly around the thigh, seize the turkey's torso in the other hand and scream. Run cold water over hands to relieve pain of burns.

7   Now, take a bath towel in each hand and repeat the above maneuver. The entire leg should snap away from the chassis with a distinct crack, and the rest of the turkey, obedient to Newton's law[1] about equal and opposite reactions, should roll in the opposite direction, which means that if you are carving at the table the turkey will probably come to rest in someone's lap.

8   Get the turkey out of the lap with as little fuss as possible, and concentrate on the leg. Use the meat cleaver to sever the sinewy leather which binds the thigh to the drumstick.

9   If using the alternate, ax method, this operation should be performed on a cement walk outside the house in order to preserve the table.

10   Repeat the above operation on the turkey's uncarved side. You now have two thighs and two drumsticks. Using the wash cloth, soap and hot

1. Sir Isaac Newton, seventeenth-century physicist and mathematician known for formulating the laws of gravity and light and for inventing calculus.

water, bathe thoroughly and, if possible, go to a movie. Otherwise, look each person in the eye and say, "I don't suppose anyone wants white meat."

If compelled to carve the breast anyhow, sharpen the knife on the stone   11 again with sufficient awkwardness to tip over the gravy bowl on the person who started the stampede for white meat.

While everyone is rushing about to mop the gravy off her slacks, hack   12 at the turkey breast until it starts crumbling off the carcass in ugly chunks.

The alternative method for carving white meat is to visit around the   13 neighborhood until you find someone who has a good carving knife and borrow it, if you find one, which is unlikely.

This method enables you to watch the football game on neighbors'   14 television sets and also creates the possibility that somebody back at your table will grow tired of waiting and do the carving herself.

In this case, upon returning home, cast a pained stare upon the mound   15 of chopped white meat that has been hacked out by the family carving knife and refuse to do any more carving that day. No one who cares about the artistry of carving can be expected to work upon the mutilations of amateurs, and it would be a betrayal of the carver's art to do so.

Reacting to the Reading

1. Number the steps in the process.
2. Underline or star the cautions and warnings Baker provides for readers.

Reacting to Words

*1. Define these words: *sutures* (paragraph 2), *gingerly* (4), *encased* (4), *torso* (5), *execute* (5), *testy* (5), *chassis* (7). Can you suggest a synonym for each word that will work in the essay?

2. In paragraph 14, Baker uses *herself* to refer to *somebody*. What is your reaction to this pronoun use? What other options did Baker have? Why do you think he chose to use *herself*?

Reacting to Ideas

1. This process is not intended to be taken seriously or followed exactly. How can you tell?
*2. Referring to your response to Reacting to the Reading question 1, list the steps in Baker's process of carving a turkey. Then, cross out all nonessential or humorous material. Are the instructions that remain logically ordered? Clear? Accurate?

Reacting to the Pattern

1. What stylistic signals tell you that this essay is a set of instructions and not an explanation of a process?
*2. Do you think the phrase "How to carve a turkey" is an adequate introduction for this essay? What other kind of introduction might Baker have written?
3. Review the various cautions and warnings that you identified in Reacting to the Reading question 2. Are they all necessary? Explain.

Writing Practice

1. Write a new introductory paragraph for this essay. Then, turn Baker's instructions into a straightforward process explanation, deleting any material you consider irrelevant to your purpose. Be sure to include all necessary articles (*a, an, the*) and transitions.

2. List the steps in a recipe for preparing one of your favorite dishes. Then, expand your recipe into an essay, adding transitions and cautions and reminders. Finally, add opening and closing paragraphs that describe the finished product and tell readers why the dish is worth preparing.

3. Write an essay that explains to your fellow students how you juggle the demands of family, work, and school in a typical day. Organize your essay either as a process explanation or as a set of instructions.

Teaching Tip
When students write process essays, they often use very simple subject-verb-object sentences. Remind students to vary their sentence structure. Refer them to Chapter 17 if necessary.

ABOUT A BIRD

Patrick Martins

In 1998, Patrick Martins brought the slow-food movement to the United States by founding Slow Food U.S.A. Begun in Italy in 1986, the movement encourages hurried people to slow down and enjoy cooking, eating, and learning about how their food is produced. In the following 2003 article, Martins outlines the life of a factory-farmed turkey, the Broad-Breasted White variety, and asks readers to think twice about which Thanksgiving turkey they will buy. As you read, note how Martins structures his essay by following the life of a farm-raised turkey from egg to kitchen table.

Teaching Tip
Remind students to familiarize themselves with the end-of-essay questions before they read the essay.

1   When you sit down to your Thanksgiving meal on Thursday, waiting for the main attraction to be brought in on a platter, take a moment to think about where it came from and how it found its way to your table. After all, your turkey is not the same wily, energetic, tasty bird that struck our ancestors as the perfect centerpiece for an American holiday.

2   Most Americans know that the turkey is a native game bird and that Benjamin Franklin thought it would have been a better national symbol than the bald eagle. For good reason: in the wild, *Meleagris gallopavo* is a fast runner and a notoriously difficult prize for hunters. Even after they were domesticated, turkeys remained spirited, traditionally spending the bulk of their lives outdoors, exploring, climbing trees, socializing, and, of course, breeding.

3   Now consider the bird that will soon be on your plate. It probably hatched in an incubator on a huge farm, most likely in the Midwest or the South. Its life went downhill from there. A few days after hatching—in the first of many unnatural if not necessarily painful indignities—it had its upper beak and toenails snipped off. A turkey is normally a very discriminating eater (left to its own devices, it will search out the exact food it wants to eat). In order to fatten it up quickly, farmers clip the beak, transforming it into a kind of shovel. With its altered beak, it can no longer pick and choose what it will eat. Instead, it will do nothing but gorge on the highly fortified corn-based mash that it is offered, even though that is far removed from the varied diet of insects, grass, and seeds turkeys prefer.

And the toenails? They're removed so that they won't do harm later on: in the crowded conditions of industrial production, mature turkeys are prone to picking at the feathers of their neighbors—and even cannibalizing them.

After their beaks are clipped, mass-produced turkeys spend the first three weeks of their lives confined with hundreds of other birds in what is known as a brooder, a heated room where they are kept warm, dry and safe from disease and predators. The next rite of passage comes in the fourth week, when turkeys reach puberty and grow feathers. For centuries, it was at this point that a domesticated turkey would move outdoors for the rest of its life.

But with the arrival of factory turkey farming in the 1960s, all that changed. Factory-farm turkeys don't even see the outdoors. Instead, as many as 10,000 turkeys that hatched at the same time are herded from brooders into a giant barn. These barns generally are windowless, but are illuminated by bright lights 24 hours a day, keeping the turkeys awake and eating.

These turkeys are destined to spend their lives not on grass but on wood shavings, laid down to absorb the overwhelming amount of waste that the flock produces. Still, the ammonia fumes rising from the floor are enough to burn the eyes, even at those operations where the top level of the shavings is occasionally scraped away during the flock's time in the barn.

Not only do these turkeys have no room to move around in the barn, they don't have any way to indulge their instinct to roost (clutching onto something with their claws when they sleep). Instead, the turkeys are forced to rest in an unnatural position—analogous to what sleeping sitting up is for humans.

Not only are the turkeys in the barn all the same age, they—and the roughly 270 million turkeys raised on factory farms each year—are all the same variety, the appropriately named Broad-Breasted White. Every bit of natural instinct and intelligence has been bred out of these turkeys, so much so that they are famously stupid (to the point where farmers joke they'll drown themselves by looking up at the rain). Broad-Breasted Whites have been developed for a single trait at the expense of all others: producing disproportionately large amounts of white meat in as little time as possible.

Industrial turkeys pay a high price for the desire of producers and consumers for lots of white breast meat. By their eighth week, these turkeys are severely overweight. Their breasts are so large that they are unable to walk or even have sex. (All industrial turkeys today are the product of artificial insemination.)

Needless to say, no Broad-Breasted White could hope to survive in nature. These turkeys' immune systems are weak from the start, and to prevent even the mildest pathogen from killing them, farmers add large amounts of antibiotics to their feed. The antibiotics also help the turkeys grow faster and prevent ailments like diabetes, respiratory problems, heart disease and joint pains that result from an unvaried diet and lack of exercise. Because the health of these turkeys is so delicate, the few humans who come in contact with them generally wear masks for fear of infecting them.

On nonindustrial farms, it takes turkeys 24 weeks to arrive at slaughter weight, about 15 pounds for a hen and 24 pounds for a tom. Industrial turkeys, however, need half that time. By 12 to 14 weeks, the whole flock is ready for the slaughterhouse. Once slaughtered, turkeys have to suffer one more indignity before arriving in your grocer's meat case. Because of their monotonous diet, their flesh is so bland that processors inject them with saline solution and vegetable oils, improving "mouthfeel" while at the same time increasing shelf life and adding weight.

Anyone who cooks knows that salt alone won't do the trick. Once, simply sticking a turkey in the oven for a few hours was enough. Today, chefs have to go to heroic lengths to try to counteract the turkey's cracker-like dryness and lack of flavor. Cooks must brine, marinate, deep fry, and hide the taste with maple syrup, herbs, spices, butter and olive oil. It's no surprise that side dishes have moved to the center of the Thanksgiving menu.

Even so, 45 million turkeys will be sold this Thanksgiving, so turkey producers aren't doing badly for themselves. But could they be sowing the seeds of their own misfortune? By relying solely on a single strain of the Broad-Breasted White, and producing it in huge vertically integrated companies that control every aspect of production, entire flocks and even the species itself is one novel pathogen away from being wiped off the American dinner table. The future of the turkey as we know it rests on only one genetic strain. And the fewer genetic strains of an animal that exist, the less chance that the genes necessary to resist a lethal pathogen are present.

It's for this reason that maintaining genetic diversity within any species is crucial to a secure and sustainable food supply. Sadly for the turkey and for us, the rise of the Broad-Breasted White means that dozens of other turkey varieties, including the Bourbon Red, Narragansett, and Jersey Buff, have been pushed to the brink of extinction because there is no longer a market for them.

What to do? One solution is to bypass Broad-Breasted Whites altogether. A few nonprofit groups—including my own, Slow Food U.S.A., and the American Livestock Breeds Conservancy—are working with independent family farms to ensure that a handful of older, preindustrial turkey varieties, known as heritage breeds, are still being grown. These varieties are slowly gaining recognition for their dark, rich, and succulent meat. (My group, which encourages the preservation of artisanal foods, sells turkeys on behalf of these farmers, but we don't profit from the transactions.)

While it might be too late to get your hands on a heritage bird this year, there are some other options available to consumers who would like a turkey raised in a more humane fashion, even if it is a Broad-Breasted White. Farmers' markets often have meat purveyors who raise their turkeys the way they should be, free ranging and outdoors.

At the market, you can often meet the person who grew your turkey and ask about how it was raised. Many independent butcher shops have developed relationships with local farmers who deliver fresh turkeys, especially for special occasions like Thanksgiving. A few environmentally conscious supermarkets get their turkeys from small family farms.

But as you shop, you need to look for more than just labels like "organic," "free range," and "naturally raised." They have been coopted by big business and are no guarantee of a healthier and more humanely raised bird.

The key word to keep in mind is "traceability." If the person behind the counter where you buy your turkey can name the farm or farmer who raised it, you are taking a step in the right direction. You'll help give turkeys a better life. You'll be kinder to the environment. And you might even wind up with a turkey that tastes, well, like a turkey.

Reacting to the Reading

1. In the margins of the essay, number the steps in the process Martins describes in paragraphs 3 through 12.

2. What purpose do paragraphs 1 and 2 serve? In the margin, write a one- or two-sentence summary of these two paragraphs.

Reacting to Words

*1. Define these words: *wily* (paragraph 1), *domesticated* (2), *altered* (3), *gorge* (3), *fortified* (3), *indulge* (7), *analogous* (7), *pathogen* (9), *indignity* (10), *artisanal* (14), *coopted* (17). Can you suggest a synonym for each word that will work in the essay?

2. In paragraph 4, Martins defines *brooder;* in paragraph 7, he defines *roost*. Why does he define these words and not others?

Reacting to Ideas

*1. What process is Martins explaining? What is his motive in explaining this process?

2. Starting with the question "What to do?" in paragraph 15, Martins makes some recommendations to readers. What are they? Has he convinced you that his recommendations make sense?

*3. Martins compares factory-farmed turkeys with turkeys raised on non-industrial farms. How are the two systems of raising turkeys different? What purpose does this contrast serve in the essay?

Reacting to the Pattern

1. How can you tell that this is a process explanation and not a set of instructions?

2. What transitional words and phrases does Martins use to guide readers through his essay?

*3. How does Martins signal the beginning and end of the process explanation? Do you think these signals should be clearer? If so, why?

Writing Practice

1. Write an essay explaining a distasteful process that you have performed. In your essay, try to convince readers that this process should be changed (or eliminated).

2. Write a process essay explaining the daily routine you follow in a job you hold (or held). Include a thesis statement that tells readers how you feel about the job.

3. Write a process essay in which you explain how to perform a particular task at a job—for example, how to keep a potential customer on the phone during a sales call, how to clean a deep-fat fryer, or how to stock shelves in a convenience store.

E   Cause and Effect

For more on how to write a cause-and-effect essay, see 14E.

A **cause-and-effect** essay identifies causes or predicts effects; sometimes it does both. In "Too Close for Comfort," Katherine S. Newman explains why mass shootings are more likely to take place in small towns than in cities. In "The 'Black Table' Is Still There," Lawrence Otis Graham focuses on a troubling social situation at his junior high school.

TOO CLOSE FOR COMFORT

Katherine S. Newman

Urban anthropologist and Harvard professor Katherine S. Newman is the author of *Falling from Grace* (1988), *Declining Fortunes* (1993), *No Shame in My Game: The Working Poor in the Inner City* (1999), and *A Different Shade of Gray: Mid-Life and Beyond in the Inner City* (2003). Her work has examined the lives of the working poor, elderly city-dwellers, and the middle class. As you read her 2004 essay "Too Close for Comfort," notice how Newman works backward from a discussion of school violence to the possible causes for such extreme behavior.

Teaching Tip
Remind students to familiarize themselves with the end-of-essay questions before they read the essay.

1   On Tuesday the nation will mark the fifth anniversary of the Columbine High School massacre. The memory of that tragedy is fresh in the minds of parents and students in the tiny community of Malcolm, Neb., where 17-year-old Josh Magee was stopped in the high school parking lot last month with 20 homemade bombs and a bolt-action rifle at the ready.

2   Deadly violence is usually considered an urban problem. Yet this brand of murder—attacks on schools by their own students—almost never happens in cities. Malcolm has a population of 437. Two other communities where colleagues and I researched school violence—Westside, Ark., and Heath, Ky.—are also small towns hours away from urban areas. In these places, schools are small, church is important, and everyone really does know your name. So why do rampage shootings tend to happen in communities like this?

3   For all their virtues, small towns are hard on misfits. In big cities, oddballs might find like-minded friends, a comic-book clique, or a band to hang out with. But in Heath and Westside, for example, Friday night football is the center of community social life; hence alternatives for marginal teenagers are harder to find.

4   Social networks overlap in small towns: your next-door neighbor is your former high school classmate, your child's teacher, a church group leader, and the fourth-grade baseball coach. If a child gets a bad reputation in one of these arenas, it spreads like wildfire to the others. As a result, misfits can feel like there is no exit from their misery.

5   Heath and Westside are remarkably stable. Teenagers stay close to home, even after high school graduation. That solidarity is a source of pride for most residents. For the marginal boy, however, stability is a life sentence: once a loser, always a loser.

6   Murderous violence is inconsistent with the view that small towns have of their virtues, which causes them to lower their guard. Moreover, because school shooters are as likely to come from good families as from dysfunctional homes, no one picks up on the signals they are broadcasting. And small-town teenagers, who believe that adults are watching over them, tend to work harder to conceal deviant behavior. For all these reasons, it is hard to see rampage attacks coming.

Since the Columbine incident, children have begun to recognize the significance of warnings they hear from attention-seeking boys. Concerned students are coming forward more often, which is why we hear more about "near miss" plots than actual shootings. Yet the social forces that push misfit boys over the edge are still alive in isolated communities. This means that adults—teachers, parents, coaches, counselors—need to remember that disaffected teenagers who get into minor scrapes or complain about being bullied may be more troubled than they appear. 7

We need to create alternatives to an adolescent culture that prizes a boy's prowess at sports over his artistic, academic, "nerdy" accomplishments so that the oddballs can find a social niche more easily. As the memory of Columbine fades, we can't let our resolve to prevent school shootings disappear along with it. 8

Reacting to the Reading

1. Underline the question Newman asks at the end of paragraph 2.
2. Highlight the answers Newman gives to this question in her essay.

Reacting to Words

*1. Define these words: *rampage* (paragraph 2), *clique* (3), *marginal* (3), *solidarity* (5), *dysfunctional* (6), *deviant* (6), *disaffected* (7), *prowess* (8). Can you suggest a synonym for each word that will work in the essay?
2. List the different words Newman uses to characterize the "marginal teenagers" (3) she discusses. What do all these words suggest to you?

Reacting to Ideas

1. What do the small towns Newman mentions have in common?
*2. Why do "marginal teenagers" (3) have a harder time in small towns than in cities?
3. Why is the stability of small-town life a problem for the marginal boys?

Reacting to the Pattern

1. List the causes of "rampage shootings" (2) identified in this essay.
*2. According to Newman, how have the Columbine shootings and similar incidents affected students' behavior? Have you seen evidence of this change in your own life?
3. Is this essay's emphasis on causes, on effects, or on both causes and effects? Explain.

Writing Practice

1. Inventing people and events to explain his motives, write a biography of Josh Magee, the seventeen-year-old Newman introduces in paragraph 1.
2. After reading the last paragraph of Newman's essay, write an article for your school newspaper in which you discuss the steps you think school officials should take to prevent violent attacks by students.
3. Newman's essay focuses on teenage boys who have been the perpetrators of school shootings. Write an essay in which you consider why teenage girls do not generally commit such violent acts.

THE "BLACK TABLE" IS STILL THERE

Lawrence Otis Graham

A corporate lawyer and best-selling author, Lawrence Otis Graham is best known for "Invisible Man," an article he wrote about the racism he encountered while working as a busboy at an exclusive country club during a leave from his job as a lawyer. In the following essay, Graham reflects on the "black table," a situation that has continued in the school cafeteria since his junior high days. As you read, note how his conclusions about what motivates people to sit where they sit have changed over the years.

Teaching Tip
A reading such as "The 'Black Table' Is Still There" may create some racial tension in the classroom. Before assigning the reading, decide whether you are ready to handle students' possible reactions.

1   During a recent visit to my old junior high school in Westchester County, I came upon something that I never expected to see again, something that was a source of fear and dread for three hours each school morning of my early adolescence: the all-black lunch table in the cafeteria of my predominantly white suburban junior high school.

2   As I look back on 27 years of often being the first and only black person integrating such activities and institutions as the college newspaper, the high school tennis team, summer music camps, our all-white suburban neighborhood, my eating club at Princeton or my private social club at Harvard Law School, the one scenario that puzzled me the most then and now is the all-black lunch table.

Teaching Tip
Remind students to familiarize themselves with the end-of-essay questions before they read the essay.

3   Why was it there? Why did the black kids separate themselves? What did the table say about the integration that was supposedly going on in home rooms and gym classes? What did it say about the black kids? The white kids? What did it say about me when I refused to sit there, day after day, for three years?

4   Each afternoon, at 12:03 p.m., after the fourth period ended, I found myself among 600 12-, 13- and 14-year-olds who marched into the brightly-lit cafeteria and dashed for a seat at one of the 27 blue formica lunch tables.

5   No matter who I walked in with—usually a white friend—no matter what mood I was in, there was one thing that was certain: I would not sit at the black table.

6   I would never consider sitting at the black table.

7   What was wrong with me? What was I afraid of?

8   I would like to think that my decision was a heroic one, made in order to express my solidarity with the theories of integration that my community was espousing. But I was just 12 at the time, and there was nothing heroic in my actions.

9   I avoided the black table for a very simple reason: I was afraid that by sitting at the black table I'd lose all my white friends. I thought that by sitting there I'd be making a racist, anti-white statement.

10   Is that what the all-black table means? Is it a rejection of white people? I no longer think so.

11   At the time, I was angry that there was a black lunch table. I believed that the black kids were the reason why other kids didn't mix more. I was ready to believe that their self-segregation was the cause of white bigotry.

12   Ironically, I even believed this after my best friend (who was white) told me I probably shouldn't come to his bar mitzvah because I'd be the

only black and people would feel uncomfortable. I even believed this after my Saturday afternoon visit, at age 10, to a private country club pool prompted incensed white parents to pull their kids from the pool in terror.

In the face of this blatantly racist (anti-black) behavior, I still somehow   13
managed to blame only the black kids for being the barrier to integration in my school and my little world. What was I thinking?

I realize now how wrong I was. During that same time, there were at   14
least two tables of athletes, an Italian table, a Jewish girls' table, a Jewish boys' table (where I usually sat), a table of kids who were into heavy metal music and smoking pot, a table of middle class Irish kids. Weren't these tables just as segregationist as the black table? At the time, no one thought so. At the time, no one even acknowledged the segregated nature of these other tables.

Maybe it's the color difference that makes all-black tables or all-black   15
groups attract the scrutiny and wrath of so many people. It scares and angers people; it exasperates. It did those things to me, and I'm black.

As an integrating black person, I know that my decision *not* to join the   16
black lunch table attracted its own kind of scrutiny and wrath from my classmates. At the same time that I heard angry words like "Oreo" and "white boy" being hurled at me from the black table, I was also dodging impatient questions from white classmates: "Why do all those black kids sit together?" or "Why don't you ever sit with the other blacks?"

The black lunch table, like those other segregated tables, is a comment   17
on the superficial inroads that integration has made in society. Perhaps I should be happy that even this is a long way from where we started. Yet, I can't get over the fact that the 27th table in my junior high school cafeteria is still known as the "black table"—14 years after my adolescence.

Reacting to the Reading

1. Underline what you consider the three or four most important points Graham makes.

2. Graham asks a number of questions in this essay—for example, in paragraph 3 and in paragraph 7. In marginal annotations, answer two or three of these questions.

Reacting to Words

*1. Define these words: *scenario* (paragraph 2), *espousing* (8), *bar mitzvah* (12), *incensed* (12), *blatantly* (13), *scrutiny* (15), *wrath* (15), *inroads* (17). Can you suggest a synonym for each word that will work in the essay?

2. What images does the phrase *black table* bring to mind? Does it have positive or negative connotations to you? Can you think of another term Graham might use to identify the black table?

Reacting to Ideas

*1. Why didn't Graham sit at the black table? Do you understand the forces that motivated him? Do you think he should have sat with the other African-American students?

2. When he was in junior high school, who did Graham think was at fault for the existence of the black table? Who does he now think was at fault? Do you agree with him?

3. In paragraph 14, Graham considers other lunch tables and asks, "Weren't these tables just as segregationist as the black table?" Answer his question.

Reacting to the Pattern

1. Is Graham's essay primarily about causes or about effects? Explain your answer.

*2. Graham focuses largely on his own experiences and actions. Where, if anywhere, does he consider other forces that could have created segregated lunch tables? Do you think he should have considered other causes? For example, should he have discussed the school administration's role? Housing patterns in his community? Explain your position.

Writing Practice

1. Try to recall the lunch tables in the cafeteria of your own junior high school or middle school. Were they segregated as they were in Graham's school? What factors do you believe led students to sit where they did? Write a cause-and-effect essay that discusses the possible causes of the seating patterns you remember.

2. What do you see as the *effects* of segregated lunch tables? Do you think they are necessarily a bad thing, or do they have advantages? Write a cause-and-effect essay that explores the possible results of such seating patterns.

3. What kinds of self-segregation (by race, gender, class, and so on) do you observe in your school, workplace, or community? In an essay, discuss both causes and effects.

F   Comparison and Contrast

A **comparison-and-contrast** essay explains how two things are alike or how they are different; sometimes it discusses both similarities and differences. In "Resisting My Family History," Indira Ganesan compares her life in India to her life in the United States. In "Men Are from Mars, Women Are from Venus," John Gray compares men and women.

For more on how to write a comparison-and-contrast essay, see 14F.

RESISTING MY FAMILY HISTORY

Indira Ganesan

At the age of five, Indira Ganesan emigrated with her family from India to the United States. Now a professor at Long Island University, Ganesan has written two novels about the challenges of being both Indian and American—*The Journey* (1990) and *Inheritance* (1998). The following essay, "Resisting My Family History," describes her visit to India after graduating from high school and compares her life in America with the experiences she has with her relatives in India.

Teaching Tip
Before beginning this section, review the difference between point-by-point and subject-by-subject comparison. Refer students to 14F.

In June 1978, in suburban Nanuet, New York, home to a famous mall,   1
I wore a sari to my high school graduation. The next day it was raining,
and my family and I set off for India. Watch out for the cows, wrote my favorite English teacher, tongue-in-cheek, in my yearbook. I'd keep a wary
eye out, I thought, packing a dozen cassettes on which I'd recorded my favorite music. My friends stood in the rain with a banner proclaiming
"Goodbye, Indira!" I was a heroine, a star for the moment. I was leaving
the country.

Though I'd been born there, I didn't want to go to India. What I wanted   2
was to knock on a Broadway producer's door and say, "I'm brown, I'm talented, let me write you a play." My parents, however, believed I needed to
embrace my Indian past. I wanted only to escape it, as I wanted to escape
anything that spoke to me of tradition or old-fashioned ideas. I was too
cool for India, too smart.

I remember the heat in Bombay's airport, so thick it was sliceable; the   3
crush of people who wanted to help or state an opinion after our car developed engine trouble on our way home; the glare of the outdoors; the
cool dark of the interiors. My uncle's family welcomed my mother and me
into their home in Madras, a city on the southeastern part of the subcon-
tinent, famed for its music festivals and its beach. In Madras I enrolled in
a Catholic women's college. Nuns were the teachers, the English language
was the norm.

In high school I had edited an underground newspaper, bought my   4
first copy of the *Village Voice*, read the *New York Times* regularly. I believed
I was a feminist. In India I was unsure of my role. Above all, I was deeply
worried that I'd be married off, that I'd be forced to become a housewife,
horror of horrors, and would lose my freedom.

What I discovered in India: people who looked like me. Girls who be-   5
friended me instantly. Girls who told me the truth at once. I was an American, and how everyone knew that—for they all did—escaped me. Wasn't
I as brown as they? Or was I giving off an American aura, wearing Wrangler jeans and a T-shirt, speaking hesitant Tamil?

I attended a wedding. I watched some of the funeral preparations fol-   6
lowing the death of my great-uncle. I climbed 500 steps to reach a Jain
temple where a priest gave me a blessing that translated roughly as "You
will have seven years of good luck followed by seven years more of the
same." During a ten-day tour of famous temples, I saw a snake charmer in
a parking lot and visited an entire city of priests and ascetics. They let us
into a temple's sanctum sanctorum, where we saw the God image in all its
splendor. On the day that I returned to my uncle's, I announced to my
grandmother that I was going to become a *sannyasi*, a holy woman. I was
17; my grandmother just laughed.

In India I had the unswerving consideration of my relatives, 25 of   7
whom I met in my first six months. I remember our meals together, and
the preparations: the pile of freshly shredded coconut—white, flaky, fragrant with milk; the way sweet dough for *jellabies* would be dropped in hot
oil and bob up to perfection. In America I picked at pizza and baked ziti
on the school lunch menu; in India I feasted. There were scores of delicious meals, piles of snacks in tins, water always available in an earthen
vessel in the kitchen.

And still I felt I was missing out on a superlative year in America, and   8
I was determined to dislike India. I dragged my aunt to see a Woody Allen

movie and felt it superior to Indian films, even though they managed to reduce me to tears.

In all of this, I, the *yanqui,* was a source of amusement to the family. 9
They bent over backward to please me that year, and I finally admitted to enjoying myself. I can still recall the din of the streets as I rushed to college in the mornings—bicycles, rickshaws, buses, pedestrians, bikes and yes, even a bull here and there.

Upon arrival at school, we lined up for assembly and the college pres- 10
ident led the prayers as hundreds of girls listened, long, sleek braids shining with oil. As a fine arts major, I learned from Sister Mary Ann about Buddhist art and how to apply lapis lazuli. We practiced calligraphy with Sister Bernard, a nun in her nineties who wrote "God Is Great" with a beautiful, firm hand. I remember the broad, wooden desks, the way the crows would gather on the windowsills. Goats ambled through the nearby flower gardens.

Now a teacher myself in San Diego, I have just come back from giving 11
a class on "the travel essay." One of my students suggested that the writer we were studying had formed her opinion of the country she was visiting before traveling there. In a sense, I thought, that is what I did with my year in India. I knew before going that I would like the temples and the food and the embrace of my relatives; I just didn't think it was a place for me, a newly graduated high school senior who dreamed of travel. How wrong I was. It was my year abroad, a high-seas adventure from which I would draw for years to come. In India I took my dreams of becoming a someone and began to be a someone. A someone connected to a history, to a family, to a distinct geography. A someone who had traveled after all.

Reacting to the Reading

1. Identify three points of contrast between India and the United States that Ganesan points out. Draw arrows to link these contrasts, connecting each point about life in India to a corresponding point about life in the United States.

2. In the margins of the essay, label the content of each paragraph "Life in India," "Life in the U.S.," or "India vs. U.S."

Reacting to Words

*1. Define these words: *sari* (paragraph 1), *aura* (5), *ascetics* (6), *sanctum sanctorum* (6), *unswerving* (7), *din* (9), *rickshaws* (9), *lapis lazuli* (10), *calligraphy (10).* Can you suggest a synonym for each word that will work in the essay?

2. Ganesan uses a few words in Tamil (the language spoken in Madras, India) in her essay. Why does she use these words? Does she define them? Do you think she should have used more?

Reacting to Ideas

1. According to Ganesan, what are the major differences between her life in the United States and her life in India?

*2. Which country do you think Ganesan considers her home? Why?

> **Teaching Tip**
> Students may need help defining words. With nonnative students, consider going over the definitions in class before assigning the reading.

> **Teaching Tip**
> Remind students to answer all questions in complete sentences.

3. In paragraph 2, Ganesan says, "I was too cool for India, too smart." What does she mean? Does she change her mind after her year in India? How does India change her?

Reacting to the Pattern

For more on point-by-point and subject-by-subject comparison, see 14F.

1. Is this a point-by-point or a subject-by-subject comparison? Explain.

*2. This essay contrasts Indian and American life, but the writer includes much more information about India than about the United States. Why do you think she does this?

*3. What specific points does Ganesan make about India that she does not make about the United States? Can you supply the missing information?

4. Ganesan begins her essay with a discussion of her high school graduation. Why do you think she mentions that she wore a sari to her graduation?

Writing Practice

1. Write an essay in which you contrast two worlds of your own—for example, your home life and your school life, your life in your native country and your life in the United States, or your childhood and your adulthood.

2. Write an essay in which you contrast the food, the dress, or another aspect of two different cultures or geographical regions.

3. Write an article for the travel section of a newspaper about a trip you took. Structure your article as a comparison-and-contrast essay, comparing the place you visited with the place in which you and your readers live.

MEN ARE FROM MARS, WOMEN ARE FROM VENUS

John Gray

Marriage counselor, seminar leader, and author John Gray has written a number of books that examine relationships between men and women. His best-known book, *Men Are from Mars, Women Are from Venus* (1992), uses a two-planet model to show how, in his view, men and women are at times so different that they might as well come from different planets. In the following excerpt from this book, Gray contrasts the different communication styles that he believes are characteristic of men and women. As you read, consider whether Gray's comparison oversimplifies the gender differences he discusses.

The most frequently expressed complaint women have about men is   1
that men don't listen. Either a man completely ignores [a woman] when she speaks to him, or he listens for a few beats, assesses what is bothering her, and then proudly puts on his Mr. Fix-It cap and offers her a solution to make her feel better. He is confused when she doesn't appreciate this gesture of love. No matter how many times she tells him that he's not listening, he doesn't get it and keeps doing the same thing. She wants empathy, but he thinks she wants solutions.

The most frequently expressed complaint men have about women is   2
that women are always trying to change them. When a woman loves a
man she feels responsible to assist him in growing and tries to help him
improve the way he does things. She forms a home-improvement committee, and he becomes her primary focus. No matter how much he resists
her help, she persists—waiting for any opportunity to help him or tell him
what to do. She thinks she's nurturing him, while he feels he's being controlled. Instead, he wants her acceptance.

These two problems can finally be solved by first understanding why   3
men offer solutions and why women seek to improve. Let's pretend to go
back in time, where by observing life on Mars and Venus—before the
planets discovered one another or came to Earth—we can gain some
insights into men and women.

Martians value power, competency, efficiency, and achievement. They   4
are always doing things to prove themselves and develop their power and
skills. Their sense of self is defined through their ability to achieve results.
They experience fulfillment primarily through success and accomplishment.

Everything on Mars is a reflection of these values. Even their dress is   5
designed to reflect their skills and competence. Police officers, soldiers,
businessmen, scientists, cab drivers, technicians, and chefs all wear uniforms or at least hats to reflect their competence and power.

They don't read magazines like *Psychology Today, Self,* or *People.* They   6
are more concerned with outdoor activities, like hunting, fishing, and racing cars. They are interested in the news, weather, and sports and couldn't
care less about romance novels and self-help books.

They are more interested in "objects" and "things" rather than people   7
and feelings. Even today on Earth, while women fantasize about romance,
men fantasize about powerful cars, faster computers, gadgets, gizmos, and
new more powerful technology. Men are preoccupied with the "things" that
can help them express power by creating results and achieving their goals.

Achieving goals is very important to a Martian because it is a way for   8
him to prove his competence and thus feel good about himself. And for
him to feel good about himself he must achieve these goals by himself.
Someone else can't achieve them for him. Martians pride themselves in
doing things all by themselves. Autonomy is a symbol of efficiency, power,
and competence.

Understanding this Martian characteristic can help women under-   9
stand why men resist so much being corrected or being told what to do. To
offer a man unsolicited advice is to presume that he doesn't know what to
do or that he can't do it on his own. Men are very touchy about this, because the issue of competence is so very important to them.

Because he is handling his problems on his own, a Martian rarely talks   10
about his problems unless he needs expert advice. He reasons: "Why
involve someone else when I can do it by myself?" He keeps his problems
to himself unless he requires help from another to find a solution. Asking
for help when you can do it yourself is perceived as a sign of weakness.

However, if he truly does need help, then it is a sign of wisdom to get it.   11
In this case, he will find someone he respects and then talk about his prob-
lem. Talking about a problem on Mars is an invitation for advice. Another
Martian feels honored by the opportunity. Automatically he puts on his Mr.
Fix-It hat, listens for a while, and then offers some jewels of advice.

This Martian custom is one of the reasons men instinctively offer solu-   12
tions when women talk about problems. When a woman innocently shares

upset feelings or explores out loud the problems of her day, a man mistakenly assumes she is looking for some expert advice. He puts on his Mr. Fix-It hat and begins giving advice; this is his way of showing love and of trying to help.

He wants to help her feel better by solving her problems. He wants to 13 be useful to her. He feels he can be valued and thus worthy of her love when his abilities are used to solve her problems.

Once he has offered a solution, however, and she continues to be upset 14 it becomes increasingly difficult for him to listen because his solution is being rejected and he feels increasingly useless.

He has no idea that by just listening with empathy and interest he can 15 be supportive. He does not know that on Venus talking about problems is not an invitation to offer a solution.

Venusians have different values. They value love, communication, 16 beauty, and relationships. They spend a lot of time supporting, helping, and nurturing one another. Their sense of self is defined through their feelings and the quality of their relationships. They experience fulfillment through sharing and relating.

Everything on Venus reflects these values. Rather than building high- 17 ways and tall buildings, the Venusians are more concerned with living together in harmony, community, and loving cooperation. Relationships are more important than work and technology. In most ways their world is the opposite of Mars.

They do not wear uniforms like the Martians (to reveal their compe- 18 tence). On the contrary, they enjoy wearing a different outfit every day, according to how they are feeling. Personal expression, especially of their feelings, is very important. They may even change outfits several times a day as their mood changes.

Communication is of primary importance. To share their personal feel- 19 ings is much more important than achieving goals and success. Talking and relating to one another is a source of tremendous fulfillment.

This is hard for a man to comprehend. He can come close to under- 20 standing a woman's experience of sharing and relating by comparing it to the satisfaction he feels when he wins a race, achieves a goal, or solves a problem.

Instead of being goal oriented, women are relationship oriented; they 21 are more concerned with expressing their goodness, love, and caring. Two Martians go to lunch to discuss a project or business goal; they have a problem to solve. In addition, Martians view going to a restaurant as an efficient way to approach food: no shopping, no cooking, and no washing dishes. For Venusians, going to lunch is an opportunity to nurture a relationship, for both giving support to and receiving support from a friend. Women's restaurant talk can be very open and intimate, almost like the dialogue that occurs between therapist and patient.

On Venus, everyone studies psychology and has at least a master's 22 degree in counseling. They are very involved in personal growth, spirituality, and everything that can nurture life, healing, and growth. Venus is covered with parks, organic gardens, shopping centers, and restaurants.

Venusians are very intuitive. They have developed this ability through 23 centuries of anticipating the needs of others. They pride themselves in being considerate of the needs and feelings of others. A sign of great love is to offer help and assistance to another Venusian without being asked.

Because proving one's competence is not as important to a Venusian, 24
offering help is not offensive, and needing help is not a sign of weakness.
A man, however, may feel offended because when a woman offers advice
he doesn't feel she trusts his ability to do it himself.

A woman has no conception of this male sensitivity because for her it 25
is another feather in her hat if someone offers to help her. It makes her feel
loved and cherished. But offering help to a man can make him feel incom-
petent, weak, and even unloved.

On Venus it is a sign of caring to give advice and suggestions. Venu- 26
sians firmly believe that when something is working it can always work
better. Their nature is to want to improve things. When they care about
someone, they freely point out what can be improved and suggest how to
do it. Offering advice and constructive criticism is an act of love.

Mars is very different. Martians are more solution oriented. If some- 27
thing is working, their motto is don't change it. Their instinct is to leave
it alone if it is working. "Don't fix it unless it is broken" is a common
expression.

When a woman tries to improve a man, he feels she is trying to fix him. 28
He receives the message that he is broken. She doesn't realize her caring
attempts to help him may humiliate him. She mistakenly thinks she is just
helping him to grow.

Reacting to the Reading

1. In marginal annotations, number the specific characteristics of men
   and women that Gray identifies.
2. Using these characteristics as a guide, make an outline for a point-by-
   point comparison.

Reacting to Words

*1. Define these words: *empathy* (paragraph 1), *nurturing* (2), *autonomy*
   (8), *unsolicited* (9). Can you suggest a synonym for each word that will
   work in the essay?
2. Do you think referring to men as Martians and women as Venusians is
   an effective strategy? What other contrasting labels might work?

> **Teaching Tip**
> Students may need help
> defining words. With nonna-
> tive students, consider going
> over the definitions in class
> before assigning the reading.

Reacting to Ideas

*1. Do you think Gray is serious? Why or why not?
*2. Do you think Gray's specific observations about men and women are
   accurate? Is he stereotyping men and women? Explain.
*3. Do you agree with Gray's general point that men and women seem to
   be from two different planets? Why or why not?

> **Teaching Tip**
> Remind students to answer
> all questions in complete
> sentences.

Reacting to the Pattern

1. This essay is a subject-by-subject comparison. How does Gray signal
   the movement from the first subject to the second subject? Why do you
   suppose he chose to write a subject-by-subject rather than a point-by-
   point comparison?

*2. If you were going to add a more fully developed conclusion to sum up this selection's points, what closing strategy would you use? Do you think the selection needs such a conclusion?

Writing Practice

1. Are young (or adolescent) boys and girls also from two different planets? Take a position on this issue, and support it in a subject-by-subject comparison. In your thesis statement, try to account for the differences you identify between boys and girls.

2. Identify one general area in which you believe men's and women's attitudes, behavior, or expectations are very different—for example, dating, careers, eating habits, sports, housekeeping, or driving. Write a comparison-and-contrast essay (serious or humorous) that explores the differences you identify.

3. Are men and women portrayed differently in television dramas (including soap operas) and comedies? Choose a program that has several well-developed male and female characters, and contrast the men and the women in terms of their actions and their conversations.

G   Classification

For more on how to write a classification essay, see 14G.

A **classification** essay divides a whole into parts and sorts various items into categories. Jo-Ellan Dimitrius and Mark Mazzarella's "Liars" considers four different kinds of liars. Scott Russell Sanders's "The Men We Carry in Our Minds" classifies the working men he has known.

LIARS

Jo-Ellan Dimitrius and Mark Mazzarella

Los Angeles lawyer Jo-Ellan Dimitrius is a jury consultant who worked on some of the best-known criminal trials of the 1980s and 1990s, including the Rodney King, O. J. Simpson, and Reginald Denny cases. Dimitrius has worked in civil and criminal trials to assist lawyers in selecting juries and evaluating witnesses by predicting human behavior. Mark Mazzarella is a practicing trial lawyer in San Diego, California, who writes about the formation and management of impressions in juries. He and Jo-Ellan Dimitrius have cowritten *Put Your Best Foot Forward* (2000) and *Reading People* (1998). In this essay, Dimitrius and Mazzarella classify liars; as you read, think about how their classification of liars could be useful beyond the courtroom.

If people were all honest with one another, reading them would be a 1 lot easier. The problem is that people lie. I'm not talking about those who are wrong but sincerely believe they are correct, or about the delusional few who genuinely can't tell fact from fantasy. Rather, I'm referring to the one characteristic that is probably the most important in any relationship: truthfulness. And if we assume it's there when it's not—watch out!

Much of the information we gather about someone comes directly
from the horse's mouth. If he is lying, the information is wrong, and we're
likely to misjudge him. That's why it's so crucial to identify liars as soon as
possible, and, if you have reason to doubt a person's honesty, to continue
to test it until you're entirely at ease with your conclusion.

I have found that most liars fall into one of four basic categories: the
occasional liar, the frequent liar, the habitual liar, and the professional liar.

The Occasional Liar

The occasional liar, like most of us, will lie now and then to avoid an unpleasant situation or because he doesn't want to admit doing something
wrong or embarrassing. Also like most of us, he does not like to lie and
feels very uncomfortable when he does. Because he's uncomfortable, he'll
usually reveal his lie through his appearance, body language, and voice.
The stress lying causes him will leak out through such things as poor eye
contact, fidgeting, or a change in the tone, volume, or patterns of his
speech.

The occasional liar often gives his lie some thought, so it may be logical and consistent with the rest of his story. Because it's well thought out,
you probably won't be able to spot the lie by its content or context, or by
information from third-party sources. In fact, the occasional liar will seldom lie about something that could be easily verified. Consequently, when
dealing with an occasional liar, you need to focus on the various visual and
oral clues he exhibits.

The Frequent Liar

The frequent liar recognizes what she's doing but doesn't mind it as much
as the occasional liar does, so she lies more regularly. Practice makes
perfect: the frequent liar is much less likely to reveal her lie through her
appearance, body language, and voice. Also, since it doesn't bother her as
much to lie, the typical stress-related symptoms won't be as obvious. Any
clues in her appearance, voice, and body language might be rather subtle.
Often a better way to detect a frequent liar is to focus on the internal con-
sistency and logic of her statements. Since the frequent liar lies more
often, and tends to think her lies through less carefully than the occasional
liar, she can get sloppy.

The Habitual Liar

The habitual liar lies so frequently that he has lost sight of what he is doing
much of the time. In most cases, if he actually thought about it, he would
realize he was lying. But he doesn't much care whether what he's saying is
true or false. He simply says whatever comes to mind. Because he doesn't
care that he's lying, the habitual liar will give very few, if any, physical or
vocal clues that he's being dishonest. But because he gives so little thought
to his lies and they come so thick and fast, the habitual liar doesn't bother
to keep track of them. As a result they are often inconsistent and obvious.
So while it's hard to detect the physical and vocal clues in a habitual liar,
it's easier to spot his inconsistencies. Listen carefully and ask yourself
whether the liar is contradicting himself and whether what he's saying
makes sense. Asking a third party about the liar's stories will also help you
confirm your suspicions.

The habitual liar is fairly uncommon, so most of us are temporarily taken in when we encounter one. An acquaintance of mine told me she worked with a woman for several months before her suspicions that the co-worker was a habitual liar were confirmed by an obvious and quite ridiculous lie. The liar, a brown-eyed brunette, came to work one day sporting blue contact lenses of an almost alien hue. When my friend commented on her lenses, the liar said, "These aren't contacts. They're my real eye color. It's just that I've always worn brown contact lenses before."

More than once, a client has told me that his adversary lies all the time and will undoubtedly lie on the witness stand. I counsel my client not to worry: the habitual liar is the easiest target in a lawsuit. In real life, she can run from one person to another, from one situation to the next, lying as she goes, and no one compares notes. There are no court reporters or transcripts of testimony; no one reveals what every witness has said to every other witness, and nobody pores over everything the liar has written on the subject to see whether it's all consistent. But in litigation, that is exactly what happens—and suddenly the habitual liar is exposed. It's very rewarding to see.

The Professional Liar

The professional liar is the hardest to identify. He doesn't lie indiscriminately, like the habitual liar. He lies for a purpose. For example, a mechanic who routinely cons motorists about their "faulty" transmissions will have his diagnosis carefully prepared. A real estate salesman who doesn't want to acknowledge a leaky roof will respond quickly to an inquiry about the stains on the ceiling with a rehearsed, very spontaneous sounding statement: "That was old damage from a water leak in the attic. All it needs is a little touch-up paint."

The professional liar has thought the lie through and knows exactly what he's going to say, how it will fly, and whether the customer can easily verify it. Such a well-practiced lie will not be revealed by the liar's voice, body language, or appearance. The lie will be consistent, both internally and logically. The only sure way to detect it is to check the liar's statements against entirely independent sources. Have the roof inspected. Get a second opinion from another mechanic. Take nothing for granted.

Before you make a definitive call about someone who is truly important to you, always ask yourself whether the information you have about him is reliable. Is he being truthful? If your goal is to accurately evaluate someone, you can't afford to skip this step.

Reacting to the Reading

1. Circle the names of the four categories of liar the essay identifies.
2. In the margins of the essay, write a one-sentence definition of each of the four categories. Be sure to use your own words for the definitions.

Reacting to Words

*1. Define these words: *delusional* (paragraph 1), *crucial* (2), *context* (5), *verified* (5), *adversary* (9), *pores* (9), *litigation* (9). Can you suggest a synonym for each word that will work in the essay?
2. When referring to the different types of liars, the writers alternate the pronouns *he* and *she*. Why do you think they do this? Do you find it confusing? What other alternatives do they have?

Teaching Tip
Students may need help defining words. With nonnative students, consider going over the definitions in class before assigning the reading.

Reacting to Ideas

1. According to the authors, why is it important to identify liars?
*2. Which kind of liar do you see as most dangerous? Why?
*3. Do you think a lie is ever acceptable? Explain.

Teaching Tip
Remind students to answer
all questions in complete
sentences.

Reacting to the Pattern

1. What determines the order in which the four kinds of liars are presented? Does this arrangement make sense to you?
2. The writers devote considerably more space to the "habitual liar" and the "professional liar" than to the other two kinds. What material do they include for these two categories and not for the other two? Why do you think they do this?

Writing Practice

1. Write an essay about the different kinds of lies told by "occasional liars." Be sure to include at least three different categories.
2. Using "Liars" as a model, write a classification essay that discusses three or four categories of cheaters. Give each category a name.
3. Write a classification essay about different kinds of heroes. In setting up your categories, consider what motivates people to perform heroic acts.

THE MEN WE CARRY IN OUR MINDS

Scott Russell Sanders

Scott Russell Sanders is a professor of English and an essayist. His essays are personal reflections that include social commentary and philosophical reflection and are often set in the Midwest, where he was born and raised. In "The Men We Carry in Our Minds," Sanders reflects on the working lives of the men he knew when he was a boy and classifies them according to their work. His essay discusses not only his boyhood impressions of the work these men did but also the direction his own professional life has taken. As you read, notice how Sanders moves from classifying men's work to comparing men's lives to women's lives.

Teaching Tip
Remind students to familiarize themselves with the end-of-essay questions before they read the essay.

The first men, besides my father, I remember seeing were black convicts and white guards, in the cottonfield across the road from our farm on the outskirts of Memphis. I must have been three or four. The prisoners wore dingy gray-and-black zebra suits, heavy as canvas, sodden with sweat. Hatless, stooped, they chopped weeds in the fierce heat, row after row, breathing the acrid dust of boll-weevil poison. The overseers wore dazzling white shirts and broad shadowy hats. The oiled barrels of their shotguns flashed in the sunlight. Their faces in memory are utterly blank. Of course those men, white and black, have become for me an emblem of racial hatred. But they have also come to stand for the twin poles of my early vision of manhood—the brute toiling animal and the boss. 1

When I was a boy, the men I knew labored with their bodies. They were marginal farmers, just scraping by, or welders, steelworkers, carpenters; they swept floors, dug ditches, mined coal, or drove trucks, their forearms ropy with muscle; they trained horses, stoked furnaces, built tires, stood 2 on assembly lines wrestling parts onto cars and refrigerators. They got up before light, worked all day long whatever the weather, and when they came home at night they looked as though somebody had been whipping them. In the evenings and on weekends they worked on their own places, tilling gardens that were lumpy with clay, fixing broken-down cars, hammering on houses that were always too drafty, too leaky, too small.

The bodies of the men I knew were twisted and maimed in ways visible 3 and invisible. The nails of their hands were black and split, the hands tattooed with scars. Some had lost fingers. Heavy lifting had given many of them finicky backs and guts weak from hernias. Racing against conveyor belts had given them ulcers. Their ankles and knees ached from years of standing on concrete. Anyone who had worked for long around machines was hard of hearing. They squinted, and the skin of their faces was creased like the leather of old work gloves. There were times, studying them, when I dreaded growing up. Most of them coughed, from dust or cigarettes, and most of them drank cheap wine or whiskey, so their eyes looked bloodshot and bruised. The fathers of my friends always seemed older than the mothers. Men wore out sooner. Only women lived into old age.

As a boy I also knew another sort of men, who did not sweat and break 4 down like mules. They were soldiers, and so far as I could tell they scarcely worked at all. During my early school years we lived on a military base, an arsenal in Ohio, and every day I saw GIs in the guardshacks, on the stoops of barracks, at the wheels of olive drab Chevrolets. The chief fact of their lives was boredom. Long after I left the Arsenal I came to recognize the sour smell the soldiers gave off as that of souls in limbo. They were all waiting—for wars, for transfers, for leaves, for promotions, for the end of their hitch—like so many braves waiting for the hunt to begin. Unlike the warriors of older tribes, however, they would have no say about when the battle would start or how it would be waged. Their waiting was broken only when they practiced for war. They fired guns at targets, drove tanks across the churned-up fields of the military reservation, set off bombs in the wrecks of old fighter planes. I knew this was all play. But I also felt certain that when the hour for killing arrived, they would kill. When the real shooting started, many of them would die. This was what soldiers were *for*, just as a hammer was for driving nails.

Warriors and toilers: those seemed, in my boyhood vision, to be the 5 chief destinies for men. They weren't the only destinies, as I learned from having a few male teachers, from reading books, and from watching television. But the men on television—the politicians, the astronauts, the generals, the savvy lawyers, the philosophical doctors, the bosses who gave orders to both soldiers and laborers—seemed as removed and unreal to me as the figures in tapestries. I could no more imagine growing up to become one of these cool, potent creatures than I could imagine becoming a prince.

A nearer and more hopeful example was that of my father, who had es- 6 caped from a red-dirt farm to a tire factory, and from the assembly line to the front office. Eventually he dressed in a white shirt and tie. He carried himself as if he had been born to work with his mind. But his body, remembering the earlier years of slogging work, began to give out on him in his fifties, and it quit on him entirely before he turned sixty-five. Even such a partial escape from man's fate as he had accomplished did not seem possible for most of the boys I knew. They joined the Army, stood in line for jobs in the smoky plants, helped build highways. They were bound to work as their fathers had worked, killing themselves or preparing to kill others.

A scholarship enabled me not only to attend college, a rare enough feat in my circle, but even to study in a university meant for the children of the rich. Here I met for the first time young men who had assumed from birth that they would lead lives of comfort and power. And for the first time I met women who told me that men were guilty of having kept all the joys and privileges of the earth for themselves. I was baffled. What privileges? What joys? I thought about the maimed, dismal lives of most of the men back home. What had they stolen from their wives and daughters? The right to go five days a week, twelve months a year, for thirty or forty years to a steel mill or a coal mine? The right to drop bombs and die in war? The right to feel every leak in the roof, every gap in the fence, every cough in the engine, as a wound they must mend? The right to feel, when the lay-off comes or the plant shuts down, not only afraid but ashamed?

I was slow to understand the deep grievances of women. This was because, as a boy, I had envied them. Before college, the only people I had ever known who were interested in art or music or literature, the only ones who read books, the only ones who ever seemed to enjoy a sense of ease and grace were the mothers and daughters. Like the menfolk, they fretted about money, they scrimped and made-do. But, when the pay stopped coming in, they were not the ones who had failed. Nor did they have to go to war, and that seemed to me a blessed fact. By comparison with the narrow, ironclad days of fathers, there was an expansiveness, I thought, in the days of mothers. They went to see neighbors, to shop in town, to run errands at school, at the library, at church. No doubt, had I looked harder at their lives, I would have envied them less. It was not my fate to become a woman, so it was easier for me to see the graces. Few of them held jobs outside the home, and those who did filled thankless roles as clerks and waitresses. I didn't see, then, what a prison a house could be, since houses seemed to me brighter, handsomer places than any factory. I did not realize—because such things were never spoken of—how often women suffered from men's bullying. I did learn about the wretchedness of abandoned wives, single mothers, widows; but I also learned about the wretchedness of lone men. Even then I could see how exhausting it was for a mother to cater all day to the needs of young children. But if I had been asked, as a boy, to choose between tending a baby and tending a machine, I think I would have chosen the baby. (Having now tended both, I know I would choose the baby.)

So I was baffled when the women at college accused me and my sex of having cornered the world's pleasures. I think something like my bafflement has been felt by other boys (and by girls as well) who grew up in dirt-poor farm country, in mining country, in black ghettos, in Hispanic barrios, in the shadows of factories, in Third World nations—any place where the fate of men is as grim and bleak as the fate of women. Toilers and warriors. I realize now how ancient these identities are, how deep the tug they exert on men, the undertow of a thousand generations. The miseries I saw, as a boy, in the lives of nearly all men I continue to see in the lives of many—the body-breaking toil, the tedium, the call to be tough, the humiliating powerlessness, the battle for a living and for territory.

When the women I met at college thought about the joys and privileges of men, they did not carry in their minds the sort of men I had known in my childhood. They thought of their fathers, who were bankers, physicians, architects, stockbrokers, the big wheels of the big cities. These fathers rode the train to work or drove cars that cost more than any of my childhood houses. They were attended from morning to night by female helpers, wives and nurses and secretaries. They were never laid off, never short of cash at month's end, never lined up for welfare. These fathers made decisions that mattered. They ran the world.

The daughters of such men wanted to share in this power, this glory. 11 So did I. They yearned for a say over their future, for jobs worthy of their abilities, for the right to live at peace, unmolested, whole. Yes, I thought, yes yes. The difference between me and these daughters was that they saw me, because of my sex, as destined from birth to become like their fathers, and therefore as an enemy to their desires. But I knew better. I wasn't an enemy, in fact or in feeling. I was an ally. If I had known, then, how to tell them so, would they have believed me? Would they now?

Reacting to the Reading

1. In the margins of the essay, name and number the categories Sanders identifies. If he does not name a particular category, supply a suitable name.
2. Highlight paragraph 8. Then, write a brief summary of this paragraph's ideas in the margin.

Reacting to Words

*1. Define these words: *sodden* (paragraph 1), *acrid* (1), *overseers* (1), *tilling* (2), *finicky* (3), *toilers* (5), *savvy* (5), *expansiveness* (8), *undertow* (9), *yearned* (11). Can you suggest a synonym for each word that will work in the essay?
2. Suggest two or three alternative names for the categories *warriors* and *toilers* (paragraph 5). Do you think any of your suggestions are better than Sanders's choices?

> **Teaching Tip**
> Students may need help defining words. With nonnative students, consider going over the definitions in class before assigning the reading.

Reacting to Ideas

1. When Sanders was young, what did he see as his destiny? How did he escape his fate? How else might he have escaped?
2. What were the grievances of the women Sanders met at college? Why did Sanders have trouble understanding these grievances?
*3. Who do you believe has an easier life—men or women? Explain.

> **Teaching Tip**
> Remind students to answer all questions in complete sentences.

Reacting to the Pattern

1. What two types of men did Sanders know when he was young? How are they different? What do they have in common?
2. What kinds of men discussed in the essay do not fit into the two categories Sanders identifies in paragraphs 2 through 4? Why don't they fit?
*3. Sanders does not categorize the women he discusses. Can you think of a few categories into which these women could fit?

Writing Practice

1. Write a classification essay in which you identify and discuss three or four categories of workers (females as well as males) you observed in your community when you were growing up. In your thesis statement, draw a conclusion about the relative status and rewards of these workers' jobs.

2. Consider your own work history as well as your future career. Write a classification essay in which you discuss your experience in several different categories of employment in the past, present, and future. Give each category a descriptive title, and include a thesis statement that sums up your progress.

3. Categorize the workers in your current place of employment or on your college campus.

H   Definition

A **definition** essay presents an extended definition, using other patterns of development to move beyond a simple dictionary definition. In "The Wife-Beater," Gayle Rosenwald Smith defines an item of clothing. In "Why I Want a Wife," Judy Brady defines a family role.

For more on how to write a definition essay, see 14H.

THE WIFE-BEATER

Gayle Rosenwald Smith

Philadelphia lawyer Gayle Rosenwald Smith, who specializes in family law, has coauthored *What Every Woman Should Know about Divorce and Custody* (1998). Her articles have been published in newspapers such as the *Chicago Tribune* and the *Philadelphia Inquirer* (where this essay appeared). As you read, think about the connotations of violence and masculinity in Smith's definition of a "wife-beater."

Teaching Tip
Remind students to familiarize themselves with the end-of-essay questions before they read the essay.

Everybody wears them. The Gap sells them. Fashion designers Dolce and Gabbana have lavished them with jewels. Their previous greatest resurgence occurred in the 1950s, when Marlon Brando's Stanley Kowalski wore one in Tennessee Williams' *A Streetcar Named Desire.* They are all the rage. 1

What are they called? 2

The name is the issue. For they are known as "wife-beaters." 3

A Web search shows that kids nationwide are wearing the skinny-ribbed white T-shirts that can be worn alone or under another shirt. Women have adopted them with the same gusto as men. A search of boutiques shows that these wearers include professionals who wear them, adorned with designer accessories, under their pricey suits. They are available in all colors, sizes and price ranges. 4

Wearers under 25 do not seem to be disturbed by the name. But I sure am. 5

It's an odd name for an undershirt. And even though the ugly stereotypes behind the name are both obvious and toxic, it appears to be cool to say the name without fear of (or without caring about) hurting anyone. 6

That the name is fueled by stereotype is now an academically established fact, although various sources disagree on exactly when shirt and name came together. The *Oxford Dictionary* defines the term *wife-beater* as:
"1. A man who physically abuses his wife and
2. Tank-style underwear shirts. Origin: based on the stereotype that physically abusive husbands wear that particular type of shirt." 7

The *World Book Dictionary* locates the origin of the term *wife-beater* in 8 the 1970s, from the stereotype of the Midwestern male wearing an undershirt while beating his wife. The shirts are said to have been popular in the 1980s at all types of sporting events, especially ones at which one sits in the sun and develops "wife-beater marks." The undershirts also attained popularity at wet T-shirt contests, in which the wet, ribbed tees accentuated contestants' breasts.

In an article in the style section of the New York Times, Jesse Sheidlower, principal editor of the *Oxford English Dictionary*'s American office, says the association of the undershirt and the term *wife-beater* arose in 1997 from varied sources, including gay and gang subcultures and rap music. 9

In the article, some sources argued that the reference in the term was not to spousal abuse per se but to popular-culture figures such as Ralph Cramden and Tony Soprano. And what about Archie Bunker?[1] 10

It's not just the name that worries me. Fashion headlines reveal that we want to overthrow '90s grunge and return to shoulder pads and hardware-studded suits. Am I reading too much into a fashion statement that the return is also to male dominance where physical abuse is acceptable as a means of control? 11

There has to be a better term. After all, it's a pretty rare piece of clothing that can make both men and women look sexier. You'd expect a term connoting flattery—not violence. 12

Wearers under 25 may not want to hear this, but here it is. More than 4 million women are victims of severe assaults by boyfriends and husbands each year. By conservative estimate, family violence occurs in 2 million families each year in the United States. Average age of the batterer: 31. 13

Possibly the last statistic is telling. Maybe youth today would rather ignore the overtones of the term *wife-beater*. It is also true, however, that the children of abusers often learn the behavior from their elders. 14

Therein lies perhaps the worst difficulty: that this name for this shirt teaches the wrong thing about men. Some articles quote women who felt the shirts looked great, especially on guys with great bodies. One woman stated that it even made guys look "manly." 15

So *manly* equals *violent*? Not by me, and I hope not by anyone on any side of age 25. 16

Reacting to the Reading

1. Smith's essay opens with the sentence, "Everybody wears them." Underline this sentence (if you have not already done so).
2. Place a check mark beside each sentence in the essay that supports this opening statement.

Reacting to Words

*1. Define these words: *lavished* (paragraph 1), *resurgence* (1), *gusto* (4), *toxic* (6), *connoting* (12). Can you suggest a synonym for each word that will work in the essay?
2. Smith uses informal words and expressions—*kids* (4), *pricey* (4), and *Not by me* (16)—as well as contractions. Do you think this informal style undercuts her serious message? Explain.

---

1. Characters in the 1950s sitcom *The Honeymooners,* the HBO series *The Sopranos,* and the 1970s sitcom *All in the Family.*

Reacting to Ideas

*1. Beyond defining the term *wife-beater*, what is Smith's purpose for writing this essay? How can you tell?

2. What does Smith actually propose or recommend to her readers? For example, does she think people should stop wearing "wife-beater" T-shirts?

*3. In paragraph 11, Smith asks, "Am I reading too much into a fashion statement . . . ?" Answer her question.

Reacting to the Pattern

*1. Where in her essay does Smith develop her definition with examples? Where does she use description? Can you identify any other patterns of development?

2. Where does Smith present a formal (dictionary) definition of *wife-beater*? Where does she give information about the term's origin? Why does she include these two sections?

Writing Practice

1. Define another article of clothing that, like the "wife-beater" T-shirt, has taken on some special significance. (For example, you could write about baggy jeans or baseball caps.) Focus on the garment and its wearers (not on its name), discussing the impression the article of clothing makes and the associations it has for its wearers and for others. You can use description, exemplification, or classification to develop your essay.

2. Think of an item or activity that has a name with a negative, even offensive, connotation—for example, the name *bobos* for generic-brand sneakers. Define the item, developing your definition with description and examples, and try in your definition to persuade people why they should stop using the negative term.

WHY I WANT A WIFE

Judy Brady

Judy Brady helped found the Toxic Links Coalition, an organization dedicated to exposing the dangers of environmental toxins and their impact on public health. She was also an activist in the women's movement, and her classic essay "Why I Want a Wife" was published in the first issue of *Ms.* magazine (1971). As you read, note how Brady uses examples to support her definition of a wife.

1   I belong to that classification of people known as wives. I am A Wife. And, not altogether incidentally, I am a mother.

2   Not too long ago a male friend of mine appeared on the scene fresh from a recent divorce. He had one child, who is, of course, with his ex-wife. He is looking for another wife. As I thought about him while I was ironing one evening, it suddenly occurred to me that I, too, would like to have a wife. Why do I want a wife?

3   I would like to go back to school so that I can become economically independent, support myself, and, if need be, support those dependent upon

me. I want a wife who will work and send me to school. And while I am going to school I want a wife to take care of my children. I want a wife to keep track of the children's doctor and dentist appointments. And to keep track of mine, too. I want a wife to make sure my children eat properly and are kept clean. I want a wife who will wash the children's clothes and keep them mended. I want a wife who is a good nurturant attendant to my children, who arranges for their schooling, makes sure that they have an adequate social life with their peers, takes them to the park, the zoo, etc. I want a wife who takes care of the children when they are sick, a wife who arranges to be around when the children need special care, because, of course, I cannot miss classes at school. My wife must arrange to lose time at work and not lose the job. It may mean a small cut in my wife's income from time to time, but I guess I can tolerate that. Needless to say, my wife will arrange and pay for the care of the children while my wife is working.

I want a wife who will take care of *my* physical needs. I want a wife who will keep my house clean. A wife who will pick up after my children, a wife who will pick up after me. I want a wife who will keep my clothes clean, ironed, mended, replaced when need be, and who will see to it that my personal things are kept in their proper place so that I can find what I need the minute I need it. I want a wife who cooks the meals, a wife who is a *good* cook. I want a wife who will plan the menus, do the necessary grocery shopping, prepare the meals, serve them pleasantly, and then do the cleaning up while I do my studying. I want a wife who will care for me when I am sick and sympathize with my pain and loss of time from school. I want a wife to go along when our family takes a vacation so that someone can continue to care for me and my children when I need a rest and change of scene.

I want a wife who will not bother me with rambling complaints about a wife's duties. But I want a wife who will listen to me when I feel the need to explain a rather difficult point I have come across in my course of studies. And I want a wife who will type my papers for me when I have written them.

I want a wife who will take care of the details of my social life. When my wife and I are invited out by my friends, I want a wife who will take care of the babysitting arrangements. When I meet people at school that I like and want to entertain, I want a wife who will have the house clean, will prepare a special meal, serve it to me and my friends, and not interrupt when I talk about things that interest me and my friends. I want a wife who will have arranged that the children are fed and ready for bed before my guests arrive so that the children do not bother us. I want a wife who takes care of the needs of my guests so that they feel comfortable, who makes sure that they have an ashtray, that they are passed the hors d'oeuvres, that they are offered a second helping of the food, that their wine glasses are replenished when necessary, that their coffee is served to them as they like it. And I want a wife who knows that sometimes I need a night out by myself.

I want a wife who is sensitive to my sexual needs, a wife who makes love passionately and eagerly when I feel like it, a wife who makes sure that I am satisfied. And, of course, I want a wife who will not demand sexual attention when I am not in the mood for it. I want a wife who assumes the complete responsibility for birth control, because I do not want more children. I want a wife who will remain sexually faithful to me so that I do not have to clutter up my intellectual life with jealousies. And I want a wife who understands that *my* sexual needs may entail more than strict adherence to monogamy. I must, after all, be able to relate to people as fully as possible.

If, by chance, I find another person more suitable as a wife than the wife I already have, I want the liberty to replace my present wife with another one. Naturally, I will expect a fresh new life; my wife will take the children and be solely responsible for them so that I am left free.   8

When I am through with school and have a job, I want my wife to quit working and remain at home so that my wife can more fully and completely take care of a wife's duties.   9

My God, who *wouldn't* want a wife?   10

Reacting to the Reading

1. Review all the characteristics of a wife Brady mentions, and in the margin, write a one-sentence definition of *wife* that summarizes these characteristics.

2. In the margin beside paragraph 10, answer Brady's concluding question.

Reacting to Words

*1. Define these words: *nurturant* (paragraph 3), *peers* (3), *hors d'oeuvres* (6), *replenished* (6), *adherence* (7), *monogamy* (7). Can you suggest a synonym for each word that will work in the essay?

*2. Brady repeats the word *wife* over and over in her essay. Can you think of other words she could have used instead? How would these words change her essay?

> **Teaching Tip**
> Students may need help defining words. With nonnative students, consider going over the definitions in class before assigning the reading.

Reacting to Ideas

1. How do you define *wife*? Is your idea of a wife different from Brady's? If so, how do you define the differences?

2. What central point or idea do you think Brady wants to communicate to her readers? Does she ever actually state this idea? If not, do you think she should?

*3. Brady's essay was written in 1971. Does her idea of a wife seem dated, or does it still seem accurate to you?

> **Teaching Tip**
> Remind students to answer all questions in complete sentences.

Reacting to the Pattern

1. Does Brady include a formal definition of *wife* anywhere in her essay? If so, where? If not, do you think she should? Explain.

*2. Brady develops her definition with examples. List some of her most important examples.

3. What other patterns of development does Brady use to develop her definition?

Writing Practice

1. Assume you are married to Brady and feel unjustly attacked by her essay. Write her a letter in which you define *husband*, using as many examples as you can to show how you are overworked and underappreciated.

2. Write an essay in which you define your ideal teacher, parent, spouse, or boss.

For more on how to write an argument essay, see 14I.

An **argument** essay takes a stand on one side of a debatable issue, using facts, examples, and expert opinion to persuade readers to accept a position. The writers of the three essays that follow—Ji-Yeon Yuh in "Let's Tell the Story of All America's Cultures," Dave Eggers in "Serve or Fail," and Martin Luther King Jr. in "I Have a Dream"—attempt to convince readers to accept their positions or at least to acknowledge that they are reasonable.

Teaching Tip
Before you begin this unit, you may want to review the difference between an inductive argument and a deductive argument. Refer students to 14I.

LET'S TELL THE STORY OF ALL AMERICA'S CULTURES

Ji-Yeon Yuh

In 1970, at the age of five, Ji-Yeon Yuh immigrated to Chicago from Seoul, Korea. After working at *Newsday* and the *Ohama World-Reporter*, she completed a doctorate at the University of Pennsylvania and now teaches history at Northwestern University. She is the author of *Beyond the Shadow of Camptown: Korean Military Brides in America* (2002). The following essay, "Let's Tell the Story of All America's Cultures," was originally published in the *Philadelphia Inquirer*. As you read the essay, consider how Yuh includes opposing viewpoints while still successfully arguing her case.

Teaching Tip
Remind students to familiarize themselves with the end-of-essay questions before they read the essay.

I grew up hearing, seeing, and almost believing that America was white—albeit with a little black tinged here and there—and that white was best.   1

The white people were everywhere in my 1970s Chicago childhood: Founding Fathers, Lewis and Clark, Lincoln, Daniel Boone, Carnegie, presidents, explorers, and industrialists galore. The only black people were slaves. The only Indians were scalpers.   2

I never heard one word about how Benjamin Franklin was so impressed by the Iroquois federation of nations that he adapted that model into our system of state and federal government. Or that the Indian tribes were systematically betrayed and massacred by a greedy young nation that stole their land and called it the United States.   3

I never heard one word about how Asian immigrants were among the first to turn California's desert into fields of plenty. Or about Chinese immigrant Ah Bing, who bred the cherry now on sale in groceries across the nation. Or that plantation owners in Hawaii imported labor from China, Japan, Korea, and the Philippines to work the sugar cane fields. I never learned that Asian immigrants were the only immigrants denied U.S. citizenship, even though they served honorably in World War I. All the immigrants in my textbook were white.   4

I never learned about Frederick Douglass, the runaway slave who became a leading abolitionist and statesman, or about black scholar W.E.B. Du Bois. I never learned that black people rose up in arms against slavery. Nat Turner wasn't one of the heroes in my childhood history class.   5

I never learned that the American Southwest and California were al-   6 ready settled by Mexicans when they were annexed after the Mexican-American War. I never learned that Mexico once had a problem keeping land-hungry white men on the U.S. side of the border.

So when other children called me a slant-eyed chink and told me to go   7
back where I came from, I was ready to believe that I wasn't really an American because I wasn't white.

America's bittersweet legacy of struggling and failing and getting an-   8
other step closer to democratic ideals of liberty and equality and justice for all wasn't for the likes of me, an immigrant child from Korea. The history books said so.

Well, the history books were wrong.   9

Educators around the country are finally realizing what I realized as a   10
teenager in the library, looking up the history I wasn't getting in school. America is a multicultural nation, composed of many people with varying histories and varying traditions who have little in common except their humanity, a belief in democracy, and a desire for freedom.

America changed them, but they changed America too.   11

A committee of scholars and teachers gathered by the New York State   12
Department of Education recognizes this in their recent report, "One Nation, Many Peoples: A Declaration of Cultural Interdependence."

They recommend that public schools provide a "multicultural educa-   13
tion, anchored to the shared principles of a liberal democracy."

What that means, according to the report, is recognizing that America   14
was shaped and continues to be shaped by people of diverse backgrounds. It calls for students to be taught that history is an ongoing process of discovery and interpretation of the past, and that there is more than one way of viewing the world.

Thus, the westward migration of white Americans is not just a heroic   15
settling of an untamed wild, but also the conquest of indigenous peoples. Immigrants were not just white, but Asian as well. Blacks were not merely passive slaves freed by northern whites, but active fighters for their own liberation.

In particular, according to the report, the curriculum should help chil-   16
dren "to assess critically the reasons for the inconsistencies between the ideals of the U.S. and social realities. It should provide information and intellectual tools that can permit them to contribute to bringing reality closer to the ideals."

In other words, show children the good with the bad, and give them   17
the skills to help improve their country. What could be more patriotic?

Several dissenting members of the New York committee publicly   18
worry that America will splinter into ethnic fragments if this multicultural curriculum is adopted. They argue that the committee's report puts the focus on ethnicity at the expense of national unity.

But downplaying ethnicity will not bolster national unity. The history   19
of America is the story of how and why people from all over the world came to the United States, and how in struggling to make a better life for themselves, they changed each other, they changed the country, and they all came to call themselves Americans.

E pluribus unum. Out of many, one.   20

This is why I, with my Korean background, and my childhood tor-   21
mentors, with their lost-in-the-mist-of-time European backgrounds, are all Americans.

It is the unique beauty of this country. It is high time we let all our chil- 22
dren gaze upon it.

Reacting to the Reading

1. Underline Yuh's thesis statement.
2. In the margin beside the thesis statement, rewrite it in your own words.

Reacting to Words

*1. Define these words: *albeit* (paragraph 1), *galore* (2), *abolitionist* (5), *annexed* (6), *multicultural* (10), *indigenous* (15), *ethnicity* (19). Can you suggest a synonym for each word that will work in the essay?
*2. List the words Yuh uses to refer to various ethnic and racial groups. Do you think any other words would be more appropriate?

Reacting to Ideas

*1. In Yuh's "1970s Chicago childhood" (2), she learned little about the achievements of nonwhites. Is this true for you as well?
2. In paragraphs 2 through 6, Yuh lists the things she didn't learn in school. Can you give additional examples?
*3. Do you agree with Yuh that the public school curriculum should "tell the story of all America's cultures"? Do you see any problems in such an approach?

Reacting to the Pattern

1. Does Yuh arrange her essay as an inductive argument or as a deductive argument (see 14I)? Explain.
2. Where in her essay does Yuh present an argument against her position? Paraphrase this argument.
3. How does Yuh refute (argue against) the opposing argument she presents? Is her refutation convincing? Why or why not?

Writing Practice

1. Write a letter to your high school American history teacher arguing in favor of (or against) a more multicultural curriculum for your school. Like Yuh, use examples from your own educational experiences to support your thesis.
2. Review a high school or college history textbook—either a recent text or one a parent or older sibling used. Do you think there is too little coverage of minority groups' contributions? Too much? Write an email to the publisher arguing for changes.
3. Do you think public schools should "tell the story of all America's cultures"? Write an essay in which you consider what would be gained (or lost) if such an approach were adopted in all American public schools.

SERVE OR FAIL

Dave Eggers

Author, editor, and publisher Dave Eggers is best known for his memoir *A Heartbreaking Work of Staggering Genius* (2000). The book describes how he raised his brother, Christopher, after his parents' death.
Eggers also founded McSweeney's, an independent publishing house,
as well as writing centers for children in San Francisco and Brooklyn.
In "Serve or Fail" (2004), he suggests that public service should be required for college students. As you read this essay, consider facts and
examples that Eggers uses to persuade his audience.

Teaching Tip
Remind students to familiarize themselves with the end-
of-essay questions before
they read the essay.

About now, most recent college graduates, a mere week or two beyond 1
their last final, are giving themselves a nice respite. Maybe they're on a
beach, maybe they're on a road trip, maybe they're in their rooms, painting their toenails black with a Q-tip and shoe polish. Does it matter?
What's important is that they have some time off.

Do they deserve the time off? Well, yes and no. Yes, because finals week 2
is stressful and sleep-deprived and possibly involves trucker-style stimu-
lants. No, because a good deal of the four years of college is spent playing
foosball.

I went to a large state school—the University of Illinois—and during 3
my time there, I became one of the best two or three foosball players in the
Land of Lincoln. I learned to pass deftly between my rigid players, to play
the corners, to strike the ball like a cobra would strike something a cobra
would want to strike. I also mastered the dart game called Cricket, and the
billiards contest called Nine-ball. I became expert at whiffle ball, at backyard archery, and at a sport we invented that involved one person tossing
roasted chickens from a balcony to a group of us waiting below. We got to
eat the parts that didn't land on the patio.

The point is that college is too long—it should be three years—and 4
that even with a full course load and part-time jobs (I had my share) there
are many hours in the days and weeks that need killing. And because most
of us, as students, saw our hours as in need of killing—as opposed to
thinking about giving a few of these hours to our communities in one way
or another—colleges should consider instituting a service requirement for
graduation.

I volunteered a few times in Urbana-Champaign—at a Y.M.C.A. and at 5
a home for senior citizens—and in both cases it was much too easy to quit.
I thought the senior home smelled odd, so I left, and though the Y.M.C.A.
was a perfect fit, I could have used nudging to continue—nudging the university might have provided. Just as parents and schools need to foster in
young people a "reading habit"—a love of reading that becomes a need,
almost an addiction—colleges are best-poised to create in their students a
lifelong commitment to volunteering even a few hours a month.

Some colleges, and many high schools, have such a thing in place, and 6
last year Michael R. Veon, a Democratic member of Pennsylvania's House
of Representatives, introduced a bill that would require the more than
90,000 students at 14 state-run universities to perform 25 hours of community service annually. That comes out to more than two million volunteer hours a year.

College students are, for the most part, uniquely suited to have time for and to benefit from getting involved and addressing the needs of those around them. Unlike high school students, they're less programmed, less boxed-in by family and after-school obligations. They're also more mature, and better able to handle a wide range of tasks. Finally, they're at a stage where exposure to service—and to the people whose lives nonprofit service organizations touch—would have a profound effect on them. Meeting a World War II veteran who needs meals brought to him would be educational for the deliverer of that meal, I would think. A college history major might learn something by tutoring a local middle school class that's studying the Underground Railroad. A connection would be forged; a potential career might be discovered.

A service requirement won't work everywhere. It probably wouldn't be feasible, for example, for community college students, who tend to be transient and who generally have considerable family and work demands. But exempt community colleges and you would still have almost 10 million college students enrolled in four-year colleges in the United States. If you exempted a third of them for various reasons, that would leave more than 6 million able-bodied young people at the ready. Even with a modest 10-hour-a-year requirement (the equivalent of two mornings a year) America would gain 60 million volunteer hours to invigorate the nation's nonprofit organizations, churches, job corps, conservation groups and college outreach programs.

And with some flexibility, it wouldn't have to be too onerous. Colleges could give credit for service. That is, at the beginning of each year, a student could opt for service, and in return he or she might get credits equal to one class period. Perhaps every 25 hours of service could be traded for one class credit, with a maximum of three credits a year. What a student would learn from working in a shelter for the victims of domestic abuse would surely equal or surpass his or her time spent in racquetball class—at my college worth one full unit.

Alternatively, colleges could limit the service requirement to a student's junior year—a time when the students are settled and have more hours and stability in their schedules. Turning the junior year into a year when volunteering figures prominently could also help colleges bridge the chasm that usually stands between the academic world and the one that lies beyond it.

When Gov. Gray Davis of California proposed a service requirement in 1999, an editorial in *The Daily Californian*, the student newspaper at the University of California at Berkeley, opposed the plan: "Forced philanthropy will be as much an oxymoron in action as it is in terms. Who would want to receive community service from someone who is forced to serve? Is forced community service in California not generally reserved for criminals and delinquents?"

First of all, that's putting forth a pretty dim view of the soul of the average student. What, is the unwilling college volunteer going to *throw food* at visitors to the soup kitchen? Volunteering is by nature transformative—reluctant participants become quick converts every day, once they meet those who need their help.

Second, college is largely about fulfilling requirements, isn't it? Students have to complete this much work in the sciences, that much work in the arts. Incoming freshmen accept a tacit contract, submitting to the wisdom of the college's founders and shapers, who decide which experiences are necessary to create a well-rounded scholar, one ready to make a contribution to the world. But while colleges give their students the intellectual tools for life beyond campus, they largely ignore the part about how they might contribute to the world. That is, until the commencement speech, at which time all the "go forth's" and "be helpful's" happen.

But what if such a sentiment happened on the student's first day? What   14 if graduating seniors already knew full well how to balance jobs, studies, family, and volunteer work in the surrounding community? What if campuses were full of underserved high school students meeting with their college tutors? What if the tired and clogged veins of thousands of towns and cities had the energy of millions of college students coursing through them? What if the student who might have become a foosball power—and I say this knowing how much those skills have enhanced my life and those who had the good fortune to have watched me—became instead a lifelong volunteer? That might be pretty good for everybody.

Reacting to the Reading

1. Where does Eggers state his thesis? Place a star in the margin beside it.
2. Underline any statements in the essay with which you disagree. In the margins, briefly explain why.

Reacting to Words

*1. Define these words: *respite* (paragraph 1), *deftly* (3), *forged* (7), *onerous* (9), *surpass* (9), *chasm* (10), *philanthropy* (11), *oxymoron* (11), *transformative* (12). Can you suggest a synonym for each word that will work in the essay?

2. What does the phrase *service requirement* suggest to you? Is the connotation positive or negative? What other terms could Eggers have used?

Teaching Tip
Students may need help defining words. With nonnative students, consider going over the definitions in class before assigning the reading.

Reacting to Ideas

1. In paragraphs 1 through 4, Eggers discusses the ways college students waste time. Does his assessment seem accurate to you? If not, do these paragraphs undermine his argument in favor of required community service for college students?
2. Do you agree with Eggers that it is colleges that are "best-poised to create in their students a lifelong commitment to volunteering" (5), or do you think this responsibility lies elsewhere? Explain.
*3. Do you think Eggers is too optimistic about the value of community service to the college student? To the community?

Teaching Tip
Remind students to answer all questions in complete sentences.

Reacting to the Pattern

1. Is this argument inductive, deductive, or a combination of the two (see 14I)?
2. Do you think Eggers spends enough time considering (and refuting) possible objections to his proposal? Can you think of any objections that he doesn't discuss?
3. Identify some of the many questions Eggers asks in his essay. How do they help to move his argument along?

Writing Practice

1. What is your position on required community service for college students? Write a proposal to your school's president arguing for a community-service requirement—or write an editorial for your school newspaper arguing against such a requirement.

2. Write an essay in which you argue that it is not college students but high school students (or recent college graduates) who are "uniquely suited to have time for and to benefit from getting involved and addressing the needs of those around them" (7).

I HAVE A DREAM

Martin Luther King Jr.

On August 28, 1963, Martin Luther King Jr. delivered the following speech on the steps in front of the Lincoln Memorial in Washington, D.C. King used the occasion of this speech—the March on Washington, in which more than 200,000 people participated—to reinforce his ideas about racial equality and nonviolent protest. The speech itself is a deductive argument that makes a compelling case for racial justice in the United States. As you read, notice King's effective use of repetition.

Teaching Tip
Consider using Writing Practice 2 (on page 649) as a discussion topic or a written assignment before having students read the King selection.

Teaching Tip
Remind students to familiarize themselves with the end-of-essay questions before they read the essay.

Five score years ago, a great American, in whose symbolic shadow we stand, signed the Emancipation Proclamation. This momentous decree came as a great beacon light of hope to millions of Negro slaves who had been seared in the flames of withering injustice. It came as a joyous daybreak to end the long night of captivity.

But one hundred years later, we must face the tragic fact that the Negro is still not free. One hundred years later, the life of the Negro is still sadly crippled by the manacles of segregation and the chains of discrimination. One hundred years later, the Negro lives on a lonely island of poverty in the midst of a vast ocean of material prosperity. One hundred years later, the Negro is still languishing in the corners of American society and finds himself an exile in his own land. So we have come here today to dramatize an appalling condition.

In a sense we have come to our nation's capital to cash a check. When the architects of our republic wrote the magnificent words of the Constitution and the Declaration of Independence, they were signing a promissory note to which every American was to fall heir. This note was a promise that all men—yes, black men as well as white men—would be guaranteed the unalienable rights of life, liberty, and the pursuit of happiness.

It is obvious today that America has defaulted on this promissory note insofar as her citizens of color are concerned. Instead of honoring this sacred obligation, America has given the Negro people a bad check, a check which has come back marked "insufficient funds." But we refuse to believe that there are insufficient funds in the great vaults of opportunity of this nation. So we have come to cash this check—a check that will give us upon demand the riches of freedom and the security of justice. We have also come to this hallowed spot to remind America of the fierce urgency of *now*. This is no time to engage in the luxury of cooling off or to take the tranquilizing drugs of gradualism. *Now* is the time to make real the

promises of Democracy. *Now* is the time to rise from the dark and deso-
late valley of segregation to the sunlit path of racial justice. *Now* is the time
to open the doors of opportunity to all of God's children. *Now* is the time
to lift our nation from the quicksands of racial injustice to the solid rock
of brotherhood.

It would be fatal for the nation to overlook the urgency of the moment 5
and to underestimate the determination of the Negro. This sweltering
summer of the Negro's legitimate discontent will not pass until there is an
invigorating autumn of freedom and equality; 1963 is not an end, but a
beginning. Those who hope that the Negro needed to blow off steam and
will now be content will have a rude awakening if the nation returns to
business as usual. There will be neither rest nor tranquility in America
until the Negro is granted his citizenship rights. The whirlwinds of revolt
will continue to shake the foundations of our nation until the bright day
of justice emerges.

But there is something that I must say to my people who stand on the 6
warm threshold which leads into the palace of justice. In the process of
gaining our rightful place we must not be guilty of wrongful deeds. Let us
not seek to satisfy our thirst for freedom by drinking from the cup of bit-
terness and hatred. We must forever conduct our struggle on the high
plane of dignity and discipline. We must not allow our creative protest to
degenerate into physical violence. Again and again we must rise to the
majestic heights of meeting physical force with soul force. The marvelous
new militancy which has engulfed the Negro community must not lead us
to a distrust of all white people, for many of our white brothers, as
evidenced by their presence here today, have come to realize that their
destiny is tied up with our destiny and their freedom is inextricably bound
to our freedom. We cannot walk alone.

And as we walk, we must make the pledge that we shall march ahead. 7
We cannot turn back. There are those who are asking the devotees of civil
rights, "When will you be satisfied?" We can never be satisfied as long as
the Negro is the victim of the unspeakable horrors of police brutality. We
can never be satisfied as long as our bodies, heavy with the fatigue of
travel, cannot gain lodging in the motels of the highways and the hotels of
the cities. We cannot be satisfied as long as the Negro's basic mobility is
from a smaller ghetto to a larger one. We can never be satisfied as long as
a Negro in Mississippi cannot vote and a Negro in New York believes he
has nothing for which to vote. No, no, we are not satisfied, and we will not
be satisfied until justice rolls down like waters and righteousness like a
mighty stream.

I am not unmindful that some of you have come here out of great trials 8
and tribulations. Some of you have come fresh from narrow jail cells.
Some of you have come from areas where your quest for freedom left you
battered by the storms of persecution and staggered by the winds of police
brutality. You have been the veterans of creative suffering. Continue to
work with the faith that unearned suffering is redemptive.

Go back to Mississippi, go back to Alabama, go back to South Car- 9
olina, go back to Georgia, go back to Louisiana, go back to the slums and
ghettos of our northern cities, knowing that somehow this situation can
and will be changed. Let us not wallow in the valley of despair.

I say to you today, my friends, that in spite of the difficulties and frus- 10
trations of the moment I still have a dream. It is a dream deeply rooted in
the American dream.

I have a dream that one day this nation will rise up and live out the true 11
meaning of its creed: "We hold these truths to be self-evident, that all men
are created equal."

I have a dream that one day on the red hills of Georgia the sons of 12
former slaves and the sons of former slaveowners will be able to sit down
together at the table of brotherhood.

I have a dream that one day even the state of Mississippi, a desert state 13
sweltering with the heat of injustice and oppression, will be transformed
into an oasis of freedom and justice.

I have a dream that my four little children will one day live in a nation 14
where they will not be judged by the color of their skin but by the content
of their character.

I have a dream today. 15

I have a dream that one day the state of Alabama, whose governor's lips 16
are presently dripping with the words of interposition and nullification,
will be transformed into a situation where little black boys and black girls
will be able to join hands with little white boys and white girls and walk
together as sisters and brothers.

I have a dream today. 17

I have a dream that one day every valley shall be exalted, every hill and 18
mountain shall be made low, the rough places will be made plain, and the
crooked places will be made straight, and the glory of the Lord shall be
revealed, and all flesh shall see it together.

This is our hope. This is the faith with which I return to the South. With 19
this faith we will be able to hew out of the mountain of despair a stone of
hope. With this faith we will be able to transform the jangling discords of
our nation into a beautiful symphony of brotherhood. With this faith we will
be able to work together, to pray together, to struggle together, to go to jail together, to stand up for freedom together, knowing that we will be free one day.

This will be the day when all of God's children will be able to sing with 20
new meaning

> My country, 'tis of thee,
> Sweet land of liberty,
>   Of thee I sing:
> Land where my fathers died,
> Land of the pilgrim's pride,
> From every mountainside,
>   Let freedom ring.

So let freedom ring from the prodigious hilltops of New Hampshire. 21
Let freedom ring from the mighty mountains of New York. Let freedom
ring from the heightening Alleghenies of Pennsylvania. Let freedom ring
from the snowcapped Rockies of Colorado. Let freedom ring from the curvaceous peaks of California.

But not only that. Let freedom ring from Stone Mountain of Georgia. 22
Let freedom ring from Lookout Mountain of Tennessee. Let freedom ring
from every hill and molehill of Mississippi. From every mountainside, let
freedom ring.

When we let freedom ring, when we let it ring from every village and 23
every hamlet, from every state and every city, we will be able to speed up
that day when all of God's children, black men and white men, Jews and
Gentiles, Protestants and Catholics, will be able to join hands and sing in

the words of the old Negro spiritual, "Free at last! Free at last! Thank God almighty, we are free at last!"

Reacting to the Reading

1. Highlight the passage in which King outlines his dream for the United States.
2. In a marginal annotation, explain what King means when he says his dream is "deeply rooted in the American dream" (paragraph 10).

Reacting to Words

*1. Define these words: *score* (paragraph 1), *beacon* (1), *withering* (1), *languishing* (2), *appalling* (2), *promissory* (3), *unalienable* (3), *hallowed* (4), *gradualism* (4), *invigorating* (5), *inextricably* (6), *redemptive* (8), *wallow* (9), *prodigious* (21), *curvaceous* (21). Can you suggest a synonym for each word that will work in the essay?

2. King uses a number of words again and again in his speech. Identify some of these words. Why do you think he repeats them? Would the speech have been more (or less) effective without this repetition?

Teaching Tip
Students may need help defining words. With nonnative students, consider going over the definitions in class before assigning the reading.

Reacting to Ideas

1. In paragraph 3, King says that he and the other marchers have come to Washington "to cash a check." How does this image convey what he and the other protesters want to achieve? Can you think of another image that might also work here?

2. In this speech, King addresses the marchers who have come to Washington. Whom else do you think he is addressing?

3. Do you think the current racial climate in the United States still warrants King's criticism? Are we any closer today than we were in 1963 to realizing his dream?

Teaching Tip
Remind students to answer all questions in complete sentences.

Reacting to the Pattern

*1. King uses a deductive argument to present his ideas about racial justice. Do you think an inductive argument would have been more effective?

2. King's argument reaches its conclusion in paragraph 4. What does he do in the rest of his speech?

3. Why do you think King chose to include only a few specific examples to illustrate his points? Should he have provided more evidence?

For more on deductive arguments, see 14I.

Writing Practice

1. In paragraph 4, King says, "America has defaulted on this promissory note. . . ." Can you think of some person or organization that has defaulted on its promissory note to you? Write an argument essay in which you make your case. If you wish, you may use King's image of a bad check.

2. Write an essay in which you argue that if King were alive today, he would (or would not) think his dream of racial justice had been realized.

3. Choose an issue you feel strongly about. Write a letter to the editor of your local paper in which you take a strong stand on this issue.

Strategies for College Success

Learning the time-tested strategies discussed in this appendix can help to make your life as a college student more productive and less stressful.

1 Learning Orientation Strategies

Some strategies come in handy even before school begins, as you orient yourself to life as a college student. In fact, you may already have discovered some of them.

- Make sure you have a college catalog, a photo ID, a student handbook, a parking permit, and any other items that entering students at your school are expected to have.
- Read your school's orientation materials (distributed as handouts or posted on the school Web site) carefully. These materials will help you to familiarize yourself with campus buildings and offices, course offerings, faculty members, extracurricular activities, and so on.
- Be sure you know your academic adviser's name (and how to spell it), email address, office location, and office hours. Copy this information into your personal address book.
- Get a copy of the library's orientation materials. These will tell you about the library's hours and services and explain procedures such as how to use the online catalog.
- Be sure you know where things are—not just how to find the library and the parking lot, but also where you can do photocopying or buy a newspaper. You might as well learn to find your way around before things get too hectic.

2 Learning First-Week Strategies

College can seem like a confusing place at first, but from your first day as a college student, there are steps you can take to help you get your bearings.

1. *Make yourself at home*. Find places on campus where you can get something to eat or drink, and find a good place to study or relax before or between classes. As you explore the campus, try to locate all the things you need to feel comfortable—for example, ATMs, rest rooms, and vending machines.

2. *Know where you are going and when you need to be there*. Check the building and room number for each of your classes and the days and hours the class meets. Copy this information onto the front cover of the appropriate notebook. Pay particular attention to classes with irregular schedules (for example, a class that meets from 9 a.m. to 10 a.m. on Tuesdays but from 11 a.m. to 12 noon on Thursdays).

3. *Get to know your fellow students*. **Networking** with other students is an important part of the college experience. Get the name, phone number, and email address of two students in each of your classes. If you miss class, you will need to get in touch with someone to find out what material you missed.

4. *Familiarize yourself with each course's syllabus*. At the first meeting of every course, your instructor will hand out a **syllabus**, an outline or summary of course requirements, policies, and procedures. (The syllabus may also be posted on the course's Web page.) A syllabus gives you three kinds of useful information.

   ■ Practical information, such as the instructor's office number and email address and what books and supplies to buy
   ■ Information that can help you plan a study schedule—for example, when assignments are due and when exams are scheduled
   ■ Information about the instructor's policies on absences, grading, class participation, and so on

   Read each syllabus carefully, ask questions about anything you do not understand, refer to all your course syllabi regularly—and do not lose them.

5. *Buy books and supplies*. When you buy your books and supplies, be sure to keep the receipts, and do not write your name in your books until you are certain that you are not going to drop a course. (If you write in a book, you will not be able to return it.) If your schedule of courses is not definite, wait a few days to buy your texts. You should, however, buy some items right away: a separate notebook and folder for each course you are taking, a college dictionary, and a pocket organizer (see A4). In addition to the books and other items required

Teaching Tip
Tell students not to email their instructors asking them to fill them in on work they missed. It is the student's responsibility to get this information from a classmate.

Word Power

networking engaging in informal communication for mutual help and support

---

FOCUS **Using a Dictionary**

Even though your computer has a spell checker, you still need to buy a dictionary. A college dictionary tells you not only how to spell words but also what words mean and how to use them.

ESL Tip
Students whose first language is not English may need to buy a special ESL dictionary as well.

for a particular course (for example, a lab notebook, a programmable calculator, art supplies), you should buy pens and pencils in different colors, blank computer disks, paper clips or a stapler, Post-It notes, highlighter pens, and so on. Finally, you will need to buy a backpack or bookbag in which to keep all these items.

6. *Set up your notebooks*. Establish a separate notebook (or a separate section of a divided notebook) for each of your classes. Copy your instructor's name, email address, phone number, and office hours and location into the inside front cover of the notebook; write your own name, address, and phone number on the outside, along with the class location and meeting time. (Notebooks with pocket folders can help you keep graded papers, handouts, and the class syllabus all in one place, near your notes.)

3 Learning Day-to-Day Strategies

As you get busier and busier, you may find that it is hard to keep everything under control. Here are some strategies to help you as you move through the semester.

1. *Find a place to study*. As a college student, you will need your own private place to work and study. Even if it is just a desk in one corner of your dorm room (or, if you are living at home, in one corner of your bedroom or at the back of your basement or garage), you will need a place that is yours alone, a place that will be undisturbed when you leave it. (The kitchen table, which you share with roommates or family members, is far from ideal.) This space should include everything you will need to make your work easier—quiet, good lighting, a comfortable chair, a clean work surface, storage for supplies, and so on.

2. *Set up a bookshelf*. Keep your textbooks, dictionary, calculator, supplies, and everything else you use regularly for your coursework in one place—ideally, in your own workspace. That way, when you need something, you will know exactly where it is.

3. *Set up a study schedule*. Identify thirty- to forty-five-minute blocks of free time before, between, and after classes. Set this time aside for review. Remember, studying should be part of your regular routine, not something you do only the night before an exam.

FOCUS Skills Check

Do not wait until you have a paper to write to discover that your computer skills need improvement. Be sure your basic word-processing skills are at the level you need for your work. If you need help, get it right away. Your school's computer lab should be the first place you turn for help with word processing, but writing lab and library staff members may also be able to help you.

4. ***Establish priorities***. It is very important to understand what your priorities are. Before you can establish priorities, however, you have to know which assignments are due first, which ones can be done in steps, and which tasks or steps will be most time consuming. Then, you must decide which tasks are most pressing. For example, studying for a test to be given the next day is more pressing than reviewing notes for a test scheduled for the following week. Finally, you have to decide which tasks are more important than others. For example, studying for a midterm is more important than studying for a quiz, and the midterm for a course you are in danger of failing is more important than the midterm for a course in which you are doing well. Remember, you cannot do everything at once; you need to know what must be done immediately and what can wait.

5. ***Check your mail***. Check your campus mailbox and email account regularly—if possible, several times a day. If you miss a message, you may miss important information about changes in assignments, canceled classes, or rescheduled quizzes.

6. ***Schedule conferences***. Try to meet with each of your instructors during the semester even if you are not required to do so. You might schedule one conference during the second or third week of school and another a week or two before a major exam or paper is due. Your instructors will appreciate and respect your initiative.

7. ***Become familiar with the student services available on your campus***. College is hard work, and you cannot do everything on your own. There is nothing shameful about getting help from your school's writing lab or tutoring center or from the center for disabled students (which serves students with learning disabilities as well as physical challenges), the office of international students, or the counseling center, as well as from your adviser or course instructors. Think of yourself as a consumer. You are paying for your education, and you are entitled to—and should take advantage of—all the available services you need.

Teaching Tip
Tell students that once they establish priorities, they can use this information to help them set up a calendar and an organizer. Refer students to section 4 of this appendix.

Teaching Tip
Let students know if you plan to use email for class announcements and assignments. Be sure to have another method of contacting commuting students who do not have regular access to email from home. Also, be sure that students give you the email address they check regularly (which may not be their school email account).

Teaching Tip
Give students a sheet with information about the writing lab and the tutoring center. Consider having a representative from one or both places talk to the class.

FOCUS **Asking for Help**

Despite all your careful planning, you may still run into trouble. For example, you may miss an exam and have to make it up; you may miss several days of classes in a row and fall behind in your work; you may have trouble understanding the material in one of your courses; or a family member may get sick. Do not wait until you are overwhelmed to ask for help. If you have an ongoing personal problem or a family emergency, let your instructors know immediately.

---

4   **Learning Time-Management Strategies**

Learning to manage your time is very important for success in college. Here are some strategies you can adopt to make this task easier.

1. *Use an organizer*. Whether you prefer a print organizer or an electronic one, you should certainly use one—and use it *consistently*. If you are most comfortable with paper and pencil, purchase a "week-on-two-pages" academic year organizer (one that begins in September, not January); the "week-on-two-pages" format (see below) gives you more writing room for Monday through Friday than for the weekend, and it also lets you view an entire week at once.

Carry your organizer with you at all times. At the beginning of the semester, copy down key pieces of information from your course syllabi—for example, the date of every quiz and exam and the due date of every paper. As the semester progresses, continue to write in assignments and deadlines. In addition, enter information such as days when a class will be canceled or will meet in the computer lab or in the library, reminders to bring a particular book or piece of equipment to class, and appointments with instructors or other college personnel. You can also jot down reminders and schedule appointments that are not related to school—for example, changes in your work hours, a dental appointment, or lunch with a friend. (In addition to writing notes on the pages for each date, some students like to keep a separate month-by-month "to do" list. Crossing out completed items can give you a feeling of accomplishment—and make the road ahead look shorter.)

The first sample organizer below shows how you can use an organizer to keep track of deadlines, appointments, and reminders. The second sample organizer (p. 655) includes not only this information

Sample Organizer Page: Deadlines, Appointments, and Reminders Only

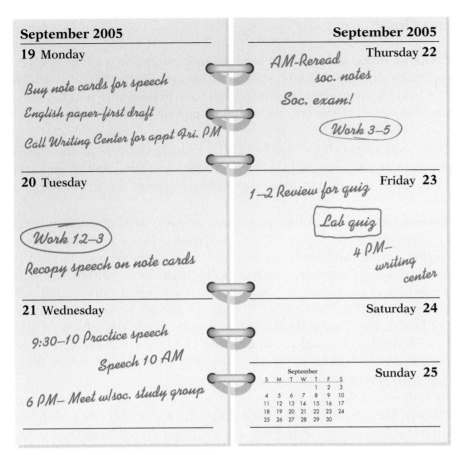

September 2005

19 Monday

Buy note cards for speech

English paper—first draft

Call Writing Center for appt Fri. PM

20 Tuesday

Work 12–3

Recopy speech on note cards

21 Wednesday

9:30–10 Practice speech

Speech 10 AM

6 PM— Meet w/soc. study group

September 2005

Thursday **22**

AM—Reread
soc. notes

Soc. exam!

Work 3–5

Friday **23**

1–2 Review for quiz

Lab quiz

4 PM—
writing
center

Saturday **24**

Sunday **25**

September
S	M	T	W	T	F	S
				1	2	3
4	5	6	7	8	9	10
11	12	13	14	15	16	17
18	19	20	21	22	23	24
25	26	27	28	29	30	

Sample Organizer Page: Deadlines, Appointments, Reminders, and Study Schedule

but also a study schedule, with notes about particular tasks to be done each day.

2. *Use a calendar*. Buy a large calendar, and post it where you will see it every morning—on your desk, on the refrigerator, or wherever you keep your keys and your ID. At the beginning of the semester, fill in important dates such as school holidays, work commitments, exam dates, and due dates for papers and projects. When you return from school each day, update the calendar with any new information you have entered into your organizer.

3. *Plan ahead*. If you think you will need help from a writing lab tutor to revise a paper that is due in two weeks, don't wait until day thirteen to make an appointment; all the time slots may be filled by then. To be safe, make an appointment for help about a week in advance.

4. *Learn to enjoy downtime*. One final—and important—point to remember is that you are entitled to "waste" a little time. When you have a free minute, take time for yourself—and don't feel guilty about it.

5   Learning Note-Taking Strategies

Learning to take notes in a college class takes practice, but taking good notes is essential for success in college. Here are some basic guidelines that will help you develop and improve your note-taking skills.

A 5

During Class

1. ***Come to class***. If you miss class, you miss notes—so come to class, and come on time. In class, sit where you can see the board or screen and hear the instructor. Do not feel you have to keep sitting in the same place in each class every day; change your seat until you find a spot that is comfortable for you.

2. ***Date your notes***. Begin each class by writing the date at the top of the page. Instructors frequently identify material that will be on a test by dates. If you do not date your notes, you may not know what to study.

3. ***Know what to write down***. You cannot possibly write down everything an instructor says. If you try, you will miss a lot of important information. Listen carefully *before* you write, and listen for cues to what is important. For example, sometimes the instructor will tell you that something is important, or that a particular piece of information will be on a test. If the instructor emphasizes an idea or underlines it on the board, you should do the same in your notes. (Of course, if you have done the assigned reading before class, you will recognize important topics and know to take especially careful notes when these topics are introduced in class.)

4. ***Include examples***. Try to write down an example for each important concept introduced in class—something that will help you remember what the instructor was talking about. (If you do not have time to include examples as you take notes during class, add them when you review your notes.) For instance, if your world history instructor is explaining *nationalism,* you should write down not only a definition but also an example, such as "Germany in 1848."

5. ***Write legibly, and use helpful signals***. Use dark (blue or black) ink for your note-taking, but keep a red or green pen handy to highlight important information, jot down announcements (such as a change in a test date), note gaps in your notes, or question confusing points. Do not take notes in pencil, which is hard to read and not as permanent as ink.

6. ***Ask questions***. If you do not hear (or do not understand) something your instructor said, or if you need an example to help you understand something, *ask!* But do not immediately turn to another student for clarification. Instead, wait to see if the instructor explains further, or if he or she pauses to ask if anyone has a question. If you are not comfortable asking a question during class, make a note of the question and ask the instructor—or send an email—after class.

After Class

1. ***Review your notes***. After every class, try to spend ten or fifteen minutes rereading your notes, filling in gaps and examples while the material is still fresh in your mind.

2. ***Recopy information***. When you have a break between classes, or when you get home, recopy important pieces of information from your notes. (Some students even find it helpful to recopy their notes after every class to reinforce what they have learned.)

> **Teaching Tip**
> Suggest that students try dividing their notebook page into two sections by drawing a vertical line down the middle. One side can be for notes on lectures or readings; the other side can be for their responses to and questions about the material.

- Copy announcements (such as quiz dates) onto your calendar.

- Copy reminders (for example, a note to schedule a conference before your next paper is due) into your organizer.

- Copy questions you have to ask the instructor onto the top of the next blank page in your class notebook.

For information on calendars and organizers, see section 4 of this appendix.

Before the Next Class

1. *Reread your notes*. Leave time to skim the previous class's notes once more just before each class. This strategy will get you oriented for the class to come and will remind you of anything that needs clarification or further explanation. (You might want to give each day's notes a title so you can remember the topic of each class. This can help you find information when you study.)

2. *Ask for help*. Call a classmate if you need to fill in missing information; if you still need help, see the instructor during his or her office hours, or come to class early so you can ask your question before class begins.

6   Learning Homework Strategies

Doing homework is an important part of your education. Homework gives you a chance to practice your skills and measure your progress. If you are having trouble with the homework, chances are you are having trouble with the course. Ask the instructor or teaching assistant for help *now;* do not wait until the day before the exam. Here are some tips for getting the most out of your homework.

1. *Write down the assignment*. Do not expect to remember an assignment; copy it down. If you are not sure exactly what you are supposed to do, check with your instructor or with another student.

2. *Do your homework, and do it on time*. Teachers assign homework to reinforce classwork, and they expect homework to be done on a regular basis. It is easy to fall behind in college, but trying to do three—or five—nights' worth of homework in one night is not a good idea. If you do several assignments at once, you not only overload yourself, you also miss important day-to-day connections with classwork.

3. *Be an active reader*. Get into the habit of highlighting your textbooks and other material as you read.

4. *Join study groups*. A study group of three or four students can be a valuable support system for homework as well as for exams. If your schedule permits, do some homework assignments—or at least review your homework—with other students on a regular basis. In addition to learning information, you will learn different strategies for doing assignments.

Teaching Tip
You might help students establish study groups for your class by passing around a sign-up sheet. However, students may prefer to form groups without your direct involvement.

For information on active reading strategies, see Chapter 35.

7 Learning Exam-Taking Strategies

For specific information on how to take an exit exam, see Appendix C.

Preparation for an exam should begin well before the exam is announced. In a sense, you begin this preparation on the first day of class.

Before the Exam

1. *Attend every class*. Regular attendance in class—where you can listen, ask questions, and take notes—is the best possible preparation for exams. If you do have to miss a class, arrange to copy (and read) another student's notes *before the next class* so you will be able to follow the discussion.

2. *Keep up with the reading*. Read every assignment, and read it before the class in which it will be discussed. If you do not, you may have trouble understanding what is going on in class.

3. *Take careful notes*. Take careful, thorough notes, but be selective. If you can, compare your notes on a regular basis with those of other students in the class; working together, you can fill in gaps or correct errors. Establishing a buddy system will also force you to review your notes regularly instead of just on the night before the exam.

4. *Study on your own*. When an exam is announced, adjust your study schedule—and your priorities—so you have time to review everything. (This is especially important if you have more than one exam in a short period of time.) Over a period of several days, review all your material (class notes, readings, and so on), and then review it again. Make a note of anything you do not understand, and keep track of topics you need to review. Try to predict the most likely questions, and—if you have time—practice answering them.

5. *Study with a group*. If you can set up a study group, you should certainly do so. Studying with others can help you understand the material better. However, do not come to group sessions unprepared and expect to get everything from the other students. You must first study on your own.

6. *Make an appointment with your instructor*. Set up a conference with the instructor or with the course's teaching assistant a few days before the exam. Bring to this meeting any specific questions you have about course content and about the format of the upcoming exam. (Be sure to review all your study material before the conference.)

7. *Review the material one last time*. The night before the exam is not the time to begin your studying; it is the time to review. When you have finished your review, get a good night's sleep.

Teaching Tip
If you give exams in your course, be sure to give students specific information about the kinds of questions you will be asking. You might even consider giving a practice exam.

During the Exam

By the time you walk into the exam room, you will already have done all you could to get ready for the test. Your goal now is to keep the momentum going and not do anything to undermine all your hard work.

> ### FOCUS Writing Essay Exams
>
> If you are asked to write an essay on an exam, remember that what you are really being asked to do is write a **thesis-and-support essay**. Chapter 12 of this text tells you how to do this.

1. *Read through the entire exam*. Be sure you understand how much time you have, how many points each question is worth, and exactly what each question is asking you to do. Many exam questions call for just a short answer—*yes* or *no, true* or *false*. Others ask you to fill in a blank with a few words, and still others require you to select the best answer from among several choices. If you are not absolutely certain what kind of answer a particular question calls for, ask the instructor or the proctor *before* you begin to write. (Remember, on some tests there is no penalty for guessing, but on other tests it is best to answer only those questions you have time to read and consider carefully.)

2. *Budget your time*. Once you understand how much each section of the exam and each question are worth, plan your time and set your priorities, devoting the most time to the most important questions. If you know you tend to rush through exams, or if you find you often run out of time before you get to the end of a test, you might try putting a mark on your paper when about one-third of the allotted time has passed (for a one-hour exam, put a mark on your paper after twenty minutes) to make sure you are pacing yourself appropriately.

3. *Reread each question*. Carefully reread each question *before* you start to answer it. Underline the **key words**—the words that give specific information about how to approach the question and how to phrase your answer.

   Remember, even if everything you write is correct, your response is not acceptable if you do not answer the question. If a question asks you to *compare* two novels, writing a *summary* of one of them will not be acceptable.

> **Teaching Tip**
> Encourage students to practice timing themselves at home, or have them do practice timed tests in class.

> ### FOCUS Key Words
>
> Here are some helpful key words to look for on exams.
>
> | | | |
> |---|---|---|
> | analyze | explain | suggest results, effects, outcomes |
> | argue | give examples | |
> | compare | identify | summarize |
> | contrast | illustrate | support |
> | define | recount | take a stand |
> | demonstrate | suggest causes, origins, contributing factors | trace |
> | describe | | |
> | evaluate | | |

For more on brainstorming, see 1C and 12C.

For more on topic sentences, see 2A and 2C. For more on thesis statements, see 12D.

ESL Tip

Brainstorming may be an unfamiliar term for non-native speakers. Make sure all students understand this concept.

4. ***Brainstorm to help yourself recall the material***. If you are writing a paragraph or an essay, look frequently at the question as you brainstorm. (You can write your brainstorming notes on the inside cover of the exam book.) Quickly write down all the relevant points you can think of—what the textbook had to say, your instructor's comments, and so on. The more you can think of now, the more you will have to choose from when you write your answer.

5. ***Write down the main idea***. Looking closely at the way the question is worded and at your brainstorming notes, write a sentence that states the main idea of your answer. If you are writing a paragraph, this sentence will be your **topic sentence**; if you are writing an essay, it will be your **thesis statement**.

6. ***List your main points***. You do not want to waste your limited (and valuable) time making a detailed outline, but an informal outline that lists just your key points is worth the little time it takes. An informal outline will help you plan a clear direction for your paragraph or essay.

7. ***Draft your answer***. You will spend most of your time actually writing the answers to the questions on the exam. Follow your outline, keep track of time, and consult your brainstorming notes when you need to—but stay focused on your writing.

8. ***Reread, revise, and edit***. When you have finished drafting your answer, reread it carefully to make sure it says everything you want it to say—and that it answers the question.

Using Research in Your Writing

In many essays, you use your own ideas to support your points. In other essays—such as argument essays—you may need to supplement your own ideas with **research**: information from outside sources, such as books, magazines, and Internet sites. An expert's opinion, a memorable quotation, or a helpful fact or statistic from an outside source can make your writing more interesting, more authoritative, and more convincing. Consider the following paragraph.

Teaching Tip
Although in a developmental writing class you probably will not need to spend a lot of time on research, keep in mind that students need basic research skills for other courses, often before they complete freshman composition.

> Many of the sports injuries that occur in the United States each year are preventable. These injuries have a number of causes. Over-working of muscles causes most of these injuries. For example, I have been running since I was in high school, and over the years I have had my share of injuries. Most of these occurred because I did not take the time to rest after I had run long distances.

The writer supports the main idea of this paragraph with an example from her own experience. Although it is relevant, this single example is not enough to support the claim she makes in her topic sentence (that most sports injuries are preventable).

Now, consider the following revised version of the paragraph above, which includes information from the writer's research.

> Many of the sports injuries that occur in the United States each year are preventable. *According to the National Institutes of Health (NIH) Web site, over ten million people annually are treated for sports injuries.* Overworking of muscles is the major cause of most of these injuries. *Every time a muscle is used, says the National Center for Sports Injury (NCSI), some fibers are destroyed. However, simple resting for forty-eight hours after an intense workout could eliminate many problems* ("Avoiding Injury" 17). For example, I have been running since I was in high school, and over the years I have had my share of injuries. Most of these occurred because I did not take the time to rest after I had run long distances. *As the NCSI points out, I probably could have avoided many of my problems by exercising regularly and by warming up and stretching before running* ("Avoiding Injury" 22).

Notice that the paragraph now contains facts, examples, statistics, and the opinions of experts. This material from outside sources—for example, an article from the National Institutes of Health's Web site and a pamphlet published by the National Center for Sports Injury—strengthens the original paragraph by providing clear, convincing support.

When you write an essay that calls for research, you use material from books, periodicals (journals, magazines, and newspapers), and the Internet to support your ideas. You will have an easier time writing your essay if you follow these steps:

1. Choose a topic.
2. Test your topic.
3. Do research.
4. Take notes.
5. Watch out for plagiarism.
6. Draft a thesis statement.
7. Make an outline.
8. Write your paper.
9. Document your sources.

Teaching Tip
Encourage students to choose a research topic they find interesting and know something about.

1 Choosing a Topic

The first step in writing an essay that calls for research is finding a topic to write about. Before you choose a topic, ask yourself the following questions:

- What is your page limit?
- When is your paper due?
- How many sources are you expected to use?
- What kind of sources are you expected to use?

The answers to these questions will help you tell if your topic is too broad or too narrow.

When Allison Rogers, a student in a composition course, was asked to write a three- to four-page essay that was due in five weeks, she decided that she wanted to write about the violence she saw in society. She knew, however, that the general topic "violence" would be too broad for her essay. After considering a number of possible topics, Allison decided to write about the effect of violent movies on behavior.

In her film class, she had just seen the movie *Natural Born Killers* and was shocked by its graphic violence. She remembered her instructor saying that the movie had caused a great deal of controversy and that two teenagers who committed murder had actually used it as a defense in their trial. This led Allison to narrow her focus to the link between film violence and behavior. Because she was majoring in early childhood education, she decided to examine the effects of violent movies on the behavior of children. Allison thought this topic would work well because she could discuss it in the required number of pages and because she would be able to finish her paper within the five-week time limit.

Teaching Tip
If your college library offers tours, encourage students to take one to familiarize themselves with the library's resources.

2 Testing Your Topic

Before you buy a car, you take it for a test drive. Similarly, before you choose a topic for an essay that calls for research, you should test it to see if it will work—that is, you will be able to find enough material. You can begin testing your topic by quickly surveying the resources of your library. (It is a good idea to arrange a meeting with your college librarian, who can answer questions, give suggestions, and point you toward helpful sources.)

Start your survey by searching your library's catalog by subject to see what books it lists on your topic. For example, under the general subject of *violence*, Allison saw the related headings *movie violence* and *media violence*. Under each of these headings, she saw a variety of books and government studies on her topic.

In addition to books, look for articles. To do this, consult an index such as *Readers' Guide to Periodical Literature*, which lists articles in newspapers and magazines, or *InfoTrac*, a computer database that contains the texts of many articles. (Your librarian can show you how to use these resources.) A quick look at *Readers' Guide* showed Allison that many articles had been written about violence in the media. A few focused specifically on children, examining the effect of violent movies and television on their behavior.

The Internet can also help you get an overview of your topic. Begin by carrying out an Internet search with a **search engine**, a program (such as Google) that helps you find information available on the Internet. When Allison entered the key words *movie violence* and *Natural Born Killers*, she saw many articles that related to her topic. (Ask your librarian to demonstrate effective searching techniques.)

For information about using the Internet for research, see section 3 of this appendix.

3 Doing Research

Finding Information in the Library

The best place to start your research is in your college library, which contains resources that you cannot find anywhere else—including on the Internet. For the best results, you should do your library research systematically: begin by looking at reference works; then, search the library's card catalog and periodical indexes; and finally, look for any additional facts or statistics that you need to support your ideas.

FOCUS **The Resources of the Library**

Reference Works

It is a good idea to begin your research in the reference section of the library. There you can consult works that will give you an overview of your topic as well as key facts, dates, and names that you can use in your paper. **General encyclopedias**—like the *New Encyclopaedia Britannica*—contain articles on a wide variety of topics. **Specialized encyclopedias** contain articles that give you detailed information about a specific field—psychology or sociology, for

(continued on the following page)

(continued from the previous page)

example. Other reference works—such as *Who's Who in America*—provide information about people's lives.

The Library's Catalog

Once you get a general sense of your topic, you can consult the library's catalog. Most libraries have replaced print catalogs with **online catalogs** that enable you to use a computer to search all the resources held by the library. By typing in words or phrases related to your topic on computer terminals located around the library, you can find books, periodicals, and other materials that you can use in your paper. If you know exactly what you are looking for, you can find it by typing in the title of a book or its author.

Periodical Indexes

After consulting the online catalog, you may want to look at the periodical indexes that your library subscribes to. **Periodical indexes** enable you to access information from newspapers, magazines, and journals. Some indexes list just citations, while others enable you to retrieve the full text of articles. You can usually search the periodical indexes by using the same computer terminals that you use to search the library's online catalog. Many college libraries have classes that teach you how to use this resource.

Sources for Facts and Statistics

As you write your paper, you may find that you need certain facts or statistics to support particular points. Works like *Facts on File,* the *Information Please Almanac,* and the *Statistical Abstract of the United States* can help you get such information. These resources are available in the reference section of your college library, where your librarian can help you find sources of factual and statistical information specific to your topic.

Word Power

tabloid a newspaper that emphasizes stories with sensational content

Remember, once you find information in the library, you still have to **evaluate** it—that is, to determine its usefulness and reliability. For example, an article in a respected periodical such as the *New York Times* or the *Wall Street Journal* is more trustworthy and believable than one in a tabloid such as the *National Enquirer* or the *Sun.* You should also look at the date of publication to decide if the book or article is up to date. Finally, look at the author's biographical information. Is he or she an expert? Does the author's background suggest that he or she has a particular point of view to advance? Your instructor or college librarian can help you select sources that are both appropriate and reliable.

Teaching Tip

At the start of the semester, assess your students' levels of computer and Internet expertise.

Finding Information on the Internet

The Internet can give you access to a great deal of information that can help you support your points and develop your essay. To use the Internet, you need an Internet **browser**, a tool that enables you to display Web pages. The most popular browsers are Netscape Navigator and Microsoft Internet Explorer. Most new computers come with one of these browsers already installed.

Before you can access the Internet, you have to be **online**—that is, connected to an **Internet service provider (ISP)**. Many colleges and universities provide Internet access free of charge to students. Once you are online, you need to connect to a **search engine**, a program that helps you find information by sorting through the millions of documents that are available on the Internet. Among the most popular search engines are Google (www.google.com), AltaVista <www.altavista.com>, Infoseek <www .infoseek.com>, and Yahoo <www.yahoo.com>.

There are three ways to use a search engine to find information.

1. *You can enter a Web site's URL.* All search engines have a box in which you can enter a Web site's electronic address, or **uniform resource locator** (**URL**). When you click on the URL or hit your computer's Enter or Return key, the search engine connects you to the Web site. For example, to find information about family members who entered the United States through Ellis Island, you would enter this URL: *www.ellisislandrecords.com.*

2. *You can do a keyword search.* All search engines let you do a **keyword search**. You type a term into a box, and the search engine looks for documents that contain the term, listing all the **hits** (documents containing one or both of these words) that it found. If you type in a broad term like *civil war,* you might get hundreds of thousands of hits—more than you could possibly consider. If this occurs, narrow your search by using a more specific term—*the Battle of Gettysburg,* for example. You can focus your search even further by putting quotation marks around the term (*"Battle of Gettysburg"*). When you do this, the search engine will search only for documents that contain this specific phrase.

3. *You can do a subject search.* Some search engines, such as Yahoo, let you do a **subject search**. First, you choose a broad subject from a list of subjects: *The Humanities, The Arts, Entertainment, Business,* and so on. Each of these general subjects leads you to more specific subjects, until eventually you get to the subtopic that you want. For example, you could start your search on Yahoo with the general topic *Entertainment.* Clicking on this topic would lead you to *Movies* and then to *Movie Reviews.* Finally, you would get to a list of movie reviews that might link to a review of the specific movie you are interested in.

● **Writing Tip**

It is a good idea to **bookmark** useful sites by selecting the Bookmark or Favorites option at the top of your Internet browser's screen. Once you bookmark a site, you can easily return to it.

FOCUS **Accessing Web Sites: Troubleshooting**

Sometimes your computer will tell you that a site you want to visit is unavailable or does not exist. When this occurs, consider the following possibilities before moving on to another site:

■ *Check to make sure you are connected to the Internet.* To reach a site, you have to be connected to the Internet. If you are not properly connected, your computer will indicate this.

(continued on the following page)

(continued from the previous page)

■ *Check to make sure the URL is correct.* To reach a site, you have to type its URL accurately. Do not add spaces between items in the address or put a period at the end. Any error will send you to the wrong site—or to no site at all.

■ *Try using just part of the URL.* If the URL is very long, use just the part that ends in *.com* or *.gov*. If this part of the URL doesn't take you where you want to go, you have an incorrect address.

■ *Try revisiting the site later.* Sometimes Web sites experience technical problems that prevent them from being accessed. Your computer will tell you if a site is temporarily unreachable.

● **Writing Tip**

A Web site's URL can give you information about the site's purpose. For example, the abbreviation *.edu* indicates that the site is sponsored by an educational institution, *.gov* indicates a government agency, *.org* indicates a nonprofit organization, and *.com* indicates a business.

Not every site you access is a valuable source of information. In fact, anyone can put information on the Internet. For this reason, it is a good idea to approach Internet sites with skepticism. Just as you would with a print source, you should determine whether information you find on the Internet is believable and useful.

FOCUS **Avoiding Plagiarism**

When you transfer information from Web sites into your notes, you may be tempted to "cut and paste" text without noting where the text came from. If you then copy this text into a draft of your paper, you are committing **plagiarism**—and plagiarism is the theft of ideas. Every college has rules that students must follow when using words, ideas, and visuals from books, articles, and Internet sources. Consult your school's Web site or student handbook for information on the appropriate use of such information.

● **Writing Tip**

Do not forget to record the page numbers of all material you copy.

When Allison searched a periodical database in her college library for the term *media violence,* she found the National Institute of Mental Health (NIMH) Web site, which contained an article titled "Child and Adolescent Violence Research at the NIMH." Using the terms *Natural Born Killers* and *movie violence,* Allison also found an article by John Grisham attacking the violence in *Natural Born Killers* and an article by Oliver Stone, the movie's director, in which he responds to Grisham's criticism.

● **Writing Tip**

Record full publication information (including page numbers) for all material you photocopy or download. You will need this information when you document your sources.

4 **Taking Notes**

Once you have gathered the material you will need, read it carefully, recording any information you think you can use in your essay. As you take notes, keep your topic in mind; this will help you decide what material is useful. Record your notes on 3 × 5 inch cards, on separate sheets of paper, or in a computer file you have created for this purpose.

Paraphrasing

When you **paraphrase**, you use your own words to present the main ideas of a source, but you keep the order and emphasis of the original. You paraphrase when you want detailed information from the source but not the author's exact words. Paraphrase is useful when you want to make a difficult discussion easier to understand while still giving a clear sense of the original.

Begin by reading the source until you are sure you understand it. As you write, go through the source sentence by sentence, writing down ideas in the order in which they occur. Include only the author's ideas; keep your own opinions to yourself. Also be sure to present only the main idea and key supporting points of the passage, eliminating the examples or comments that are not essential to meaning. Remember, *because a paraphrase contains the original ideas of the source's author, you must include documentation.*

For information on documentation, see section 9 of this appendix.

FOCUS **Writing a Paraphrase**

1. Read the passage until you understand it.
2. Jot down the main idea of the passage, and list all key supporting points.
3. As you write, follow the order and emphasis of the original.
4. When you revise, make sure you have used your own words and phrasing, and not the words or sentence structure of the original.
5. Document your source.

Here is a passage from the article "Child and Adolescent Violence Research at the NIMH," which Allison downloaded from a Web site, followed by her paraphrase.

ORIGINAL

Many studies indicate that a single factor or a single defining situation does not cause child and adolescent antisocial behavior. Rather, multiple factors contribute to and shape antisocial behavior over the course of development. Some factors relate to characteristics within the child, but many others relate to factors within the social environment (e.g., family, peers, school, neighborhood, and community contexts) that enable, shape, and maintain aggression, antisocial behavior, and related behavioral problems.

PARAPHRASE

```
Studies by the National Institute of Mental Health
(NIMH) indicate that no one thing causes a child to
```

Teaching Tip
Remind students that they should read a passage several times and then put it aside before trying to paraphrase it. Looking at the material as they write is likely to lead to plagiarism.

behave in antisocial ways. In fact, a number of possible factors can cause children to act in antisocial ways. For example, a child's own problems can cause antisocial behavior. More likely, however, other things in the child's family and community are the cause of his or her problems ("Child and Adolescent Violence Research").

Summarizing

● **Writing Tip**

In a paraphrase or summary, you present only the source's ideas, not your own ideas or opinions about the source.

For information on documenting sources, see section 9 of this appendix.

Unlike a paraphrase, which restates the ideas of a source in detail, a **summary** is a general restatement, in your own words, of the main ideas of a passage. For this reason, a summary is always much shorter than the original. Unlike a paraphrase, a summary does not necessarily follow the order or emphasis of the original.

Before you begin to write, make sure you understand the passage you are going to summarize. Read it several times, identifying the writer's main idea. As you write, make sure that you use your own words, not those of your source. Keep in mind that a summary can be one sentence or several sentences in length, depending on the complexity of the ideas in the original passage. As you revise, make sure that your summary contains just the ideas of your source, not your own opinions or conclusions. Remember, *because a summary contains the original ideas of the source's author, you must include documentation.*

FOCUS | **Writing a Summary**

1. Read the passage until you understand it.
2. Jot down the main idea of the passage.
3. As you write, make sure you use your own words, not those of your source.
4. When you revise, make sure your summary contains only the ideas of the source.
5. Document your source.

Here is Allison's summary of the original passage on page 667.

SUMMARY

A study conducted by the National Institute of Mental Health (NIMH) indicates that many factors—some within the child and some in his or her environment—can work together to create antisocial behavior ("Child and Adolescent Violence Research").

Quoting

When you quote, you use the author's exact words as they appear in the source, including all punctuation and capitalization. Enclose all words from your source in quotation marks—*followed by appropriate documentation.* Because quotations distract readers, use them only when you think that the author's exact words will add something to your discussion.

For information on documenting sources, see section 9 of this appendix.

FOCUS **When to Quote**

1. Quote when the words of a source are so memorable that to put them into your own words would lessen their impact.
2. Quote when the words of a source are so concise that a paraphrase or summary would change the meaning of the original.
3. Quote when the words of a source add authority to your discussion. The words of a recognized expert can help you make your point convincingly.

Teaching Tip
Make sure that you reinforce to students the importance of documenting all words and ideas that they borrow from their sources.

Teaching Tip
Use this opportunity to introduce a discussion of plagiarism.

QUOTATION

According to NIMH researchers, "multiple factors contribute to and shape antisocial behavior over the course of development" ("Child and Adolescent Violence Research").

● **Writing Tip**
Explain that Internet sources often do not contain page numbers. For this reason, parenthetical documentation of Internet sources may consist of just the author's last name (or, as in this case, a shortened title of an article).

Integrating Sources

To show readers why you are using a source and to help you integrate source material smoothly into your essay, introduce paraphrases, summaries, and quotations with a phrase that identifies the source or its author. You can position this identifying phrase at various places in a sentence.

As one NIMH study points out, "multiple factors contribute to and shape antisocial behavior over the course of development" ("Child and Adolescent Violence Research").

"Multiple factors," claim NIMH researchers, "contribute to and shape antisocial behavior over the course of development" ("Child and Adolescent Violence Research").

"Multiple factors contribute to and shape antisocial behavior over the course of development," observe NIMH researchers ("Child and Adolescent Violence Research").

For information on documentation, see section 9 of this appendix.

FOCUS **Integrating Sources**

Instead of repeating the word *says,* use some of the words below when you introduce quotations.

admits	concludes	points out
believes	explains	remarks
claims	notes	states
comments	observes	suggests

---

5 Watching Out for Plagiarism

As a rule, you must **document** (give source information for) all words, ideas, or statistics from an outside source. (It is not necessary, however, to document **common knowledge**, factual information widely available in reference works.) When you present information from another source as if it is your own (whether you do it intentionally or unintentionally), you commit **plagiarism**—and plagiarism is theft. You can avoid plagiarism by understanding what you must document and what you do not have to document.

FOCUS **Avoiding Plagiarism**

You should document

- All word-for-word quotations from a source
- All summaries and paraphrases of material from a source
- All ideas—opinions, judgments, and insights—of others
- All tables, graphs, charts, and statistics that you get from a source

You do not need to document

- Your own ideas
- Common knowledge
- Familiar quotations

Read the following paragraph from "Frankenstein Must Be Destroyed: Chasing the Monster of TV Violence," an essay by Brian Siano, and the four rules that follow. This material will help you understand and correct the most common causes of plagiarism.

ORIGINAL

Of course, there are a few crazies out there who will be unfavorably influenced by what they see on TV. But even assuming that somehow the TV show (or movie or record) shares some of the blame, how does one predict what future crazies will take for inspiration? What guidelines would ensure that people write, act, or produce something that *will not upset a psychotic?* Not only is this a ridiculous demand, it's insulting to the public as well. We would all be treated as potential murderers in order to gain a hypothetical 5 percent reduction in violence.

1. Document Ideas from Your Sources

PLAGIARISM

```
Even if we were to control the programs that are shown
on television, we would decrease violence in society by
only perhaps 5 percent.
```

Even though the writer does not quote Siano directly, she must still identify him as the source of the paraphrased material.

CORRECT

```
According to Brian Siano, even if we were to control
the programs that are shown on television, we would
decrease violence in society by only perhaps 5 percent
(24).
```

2. Place Borrowed Words in Quotation Marks

PLAGIARISM

```
According to Brian Siano, there will always be a few
crazies out there who will be unfavorably influenced by
what they see on television (24).
```

Although the writer cites Siano as the source, the passage incorrectly uses Siano's exact words without quoting them. The writer must either quote the borrowed words or paraphrase the material.

CORRECT (BORROWED WORDS IN QUOTATION MARKS)

```
According to Brian Siano, there will always be "a few
crazies out there who will be unfavorably influenced by
what they see on TV" (24).
```

CORRECT (BORROWED WORDS REPHRASED)

```
According to Brian Siano, some unstable people will
commit crimes because of the violence they see in the
media (24).
```

3. Use Your Own Phrasing

PLAGIARISM

```
Naturally, there will always be people who are affected
```

by what they view on television. But even if we agree
that television programs can influence people, how can
we really know what will make people commit crimes? How
can we be absolutely sure that a show will not disturb
someone who is insane? The answer is that we cannot.
To pretend that we can is insulting to law-abiding
citizens. We cannot treat everyone as if they were
criminals just to reduce violence by a small number
of people (Siano 24).

Even though the writer acknowledges Siano as her source, and even though she does not use Siano's exact words, her passage closely follows the order, emphasis, sentence structure, and phrasing of the original. In the following passage, the writer uses her own wording, quoting one distinctive phrase from Siano's essay.

CORRECT

According to Brian Siano, we should not censor a
television program just because "a few crazies" may
be incited to violence (24). Not only would such
censorship deprive the majority of people of the right
to watch what they want, but it will not significantly
lessen the violence in society (24).

● **Writing Tip**

Even though the paragraph ends with documentation, the quotation requires its own citation.

4. Distinguish Your Ideas from the Source's Ideas

PLAGIARISM

Any attempt to control television violence will quickly
reach the point of diminishing returns. There is no way
to make absolutely certain that a particular television
program will not cause a disturbed person to commit a
crime. It seems silly, then, to treat the majority of
people as "potential murderers" just to control the
behavior of a few (Siano 24).

In the preceding passage, only the quotation in the last sentence appears to be borrowed from Siano's article. In fact, the ideas in the second sentence are also Siano's. The writer should use an identifying phrase (such as "According to Siano") to acknowledge the borrowed material in this sentence and to show where it begins.

CORRECT

Any attempt to control television violence will quickly
reach the point of diminishing returns. According to
Brian Siano, we cannot be absolutely certain that a
particular television program will not cause a disturbed
person to commit a crime (24). It seems silly, then, to
treat the majority of people as "potential murderers"
just to control the behavior of a few (24).

● **Writing Tip**

Each quotation requires its own separate parenthetical documentation.

6 Drafting a Thesis Statement

After you have taken notes, review the information you have gathered, and draft a thesis statement. Your **thesis statement** is a single sentence that states the main idea of your paper and tells readers what to expect. After reviewing her notes, Allison Rogers came up with the following thesis statement for her paper on media violence.

For information on thesis statements, see 12D.

Thesis Statement

> For most people, no amount of on-screen violence is an excuse for violent behavior; when it comes to young children, however, violent movies may present a real danger.

● **Writing Tip**

At this stage, your thesis statement is tentative. You will probably change it as you write your paper.

7 Making an Outline

Once you have drafted a thesis statement, you are ready to make an outline. Your outline, which covers just the body paragraphs of your paper, can be either a **topic outline** (in which each idea is expressed in a word or a short phrase) or a **sentence outline** (in which each idea is expressed in a complete sentence). After reviewing her notes, Allison Rogers wrote the following sentence outline for her paper.

  I. Teenagers claim the movie <u>Natural Born Killers</u> made them commit murder.
    A. According to John Grisham, the movie inspired the teenagers to commit their crimes.
    B. Grisham says that several murders have been committed by teenagers who say they were influenced by the movie.
  II. The idea that movie violence causes violent behavior is not supported.
    A. Other factors could have influenced the teenagers.
    B. No clear link between media violence and aggressive behavior has been discovered.
  III. Evidence supporting the link between "copycat crimes" and media violence is based on secondhand accounts.
    A. Movies are seldom directly linked to crimes.
    B. Secondhand accounts are not representative.
  IV. Young children are easily influenced by what they see.
    A. Parents, not the media, should protect young children.
      1. Parents should monitor what children see on TV and in the movies.

For more on outlining, see 12E.

● **Writing Tip**

Allison's outline uses roman numerals for first-level headings, capital letters for second-level headings, and numbers for third-level headings. All the outline's points are stated in parallel terms. (For more on parallelism, see Chapter 19.)

2. Parents should limit their children's TV viewing and discuss the content of movies and TV shows with their children.

V. The right of the majority to watch movies and television shows of their choice should not be limited because some unbalanced people may commit crimes.

   A. Movie theaters should enforce rating systems.

   B. Violent programs should not be shown on stations whose audience is primarily children.

8   Writing Your Paper

> ● **Writing Tip**
>
> Use a thesis-and-support structure to organize your essay (See 12A.)

Once you have decided on a thesis and written an outline, you are ready to write a draft of your essay. Begin with an **introduction** that includes your thesis statement. Usually, your introduction will be a single paragraph, but sometimes it will be longer.

In the **body** of your essay, support your thesis statement, with each body paragraph developing a single point. These paragraphs should have clear topic sentences so that your readers will know exactly what points you are making. Use transitional words and phrases to help readers follow your ideas.

For more on introductions and conclusions, see 13A and 13B.

Finally, write a **conclusion** that gives readers a sense of completion. Like your introduction, your conclusion will usually be a single paragraph, but it could be longer. It should reinforce your thesis statement and should end with a memorable sentence.

> ● **Writing Tip**
>
> Check carefully to make sure you have not committed plagiarism. (See section 5 of this appendix.)

Remember, you will probably write several drafts of your essay before you hand it in. You can use the Self-Assessment Checklists on pages 142 and 143 to help you revise and edit your paper.

Allison Rogers's completed essay on media violence begins on page 681.

9   Documenting Your Sources

When you **document** your sources, you tell readers where you found the ideas you used in your essay. The Modern Language Association (MLA) recommends the following documentation style for essays that use research. This format consists of *parenthetical references* in the body of the paper that refer to a *works-cited list* at the end the paper.

Parenthetical References in the Text

A parenthetical reference should include just enough information to lead readers to a specific entry in your works-cited list. A typical parenthetical reference consists of the author's last name and the page number (Grisham 2). If you use more than one work by the same author, include a shortened form of the title in the parenthetical reference (Grisham, "Killers" 4). Notice that there is no comma and no *p* or *p.* before the page number.

Whenever possible, introduce information from a source with a phrase that includes the author's name. (If you do this, include only the page number in parentheses.) Place documentation so that it does not interrupt the flow of your ideas, preferably at the end of a sentence.

```
As John Grisham observes in "Unnatural Killers," Oliver
Stone celebrates gratuitous violence (4).
```

In the four special situations listed below, the format for parenthetical references departs from these guidelines:

1. When You Are Citing a Work by Two Authors

```
Film violence has been increasing during the past ten
years (Williams and Yorst 34).
```

2. When You Are Citing a Work without a Listed Author

```
Ever since cable television came on the scene, shows
with graphically violent content have been common
("Cable Wars" 76).
```

3. When You Are Citing a Statement by One Author That Is Quoted in a Work by Another Author

```
When speaking of television drama, Leonard Eron, of the
University of Illinois, says "perpetrators of violence
should not be rewarded for violent acts" (qtd. in Siano
23).
```

4. When You Are Citing an Electronic Source

```
While observing participants, researchers saw "real
differences between the children who watched the violent
shows and those who watch nonviolent ones" ("Childhood
Exposure to Media Violence").
```

Note: Material downloaded from the Internet or from the library's periodical indexes frequently lacks publication information—for example, page numbers. For this reason, the parenthetical references that cite it may contain just the author's name or—as in the case of the example above—just a shortened title, if the article appears without an author.

FOCUS **Formatting Quotations**

■ **Short quotations** Quotations of no more than four typed lines are run in with the text of your paper. End punctuation comes after the parenthetical reference (which follows the quotation marks). *(continued on the following page)*

(continued from the previous page)

```
According to Grisham, there are "only two ways to
curb the excessive violence of films like Natural
Born Killers" (576).
```

■ **Long quotations**   Quotations of more than four lines are set off from the text of your paper. Begin a long quotation ten spaces (or one inch) from the left-hand margin, and do not enclose it in quotation marks. Do not indent the first line of a single paragraph or part of a paragraph. If a quoted passage has more than one paragraph, indent the first line of each paragraph (including the first) three additional spaces (or one-quarter inch). Introduce a long quotation with a complete sentence followed by a colon, and place the parenthetical reference one space *after* the end punctuation.

```
Grisham believes that eventually the courts will
act to force studio executives to accept
responsibility for the effects of their products:
        But the laughing will soon stop. It will
        take only one large verdict against the
        likes of Oliver Stone, and his production
        company, and perhaps the screenwriter,
        and the studio itself, and then the party
        will be over. The verdict will come from
        the heartland, far away from Southern
        California, in some small courtroom with
        no cameras. (577)
```

The Works-Cited List

The works-cited list includes all the works you cite (refer to) in your essay. Use the guidelines in the box on page 680 to prepare your list.

The following sample works-cited entries cover the situations you will encounter most often. Follow the formats exactly as they appear here.

Books

Books by One Author

List the author with last name first. Underline the title. Include the city of publication and a shortened form of the publisher's name—for example, *Prentice* for *Prentice Hall* or *Bedford* for *Bedford/St. Martin's*. Use the abbreviation *UP* for *University Press,* as in *Princeton UP* and *U of Chicago P.* End with the date of publication.

```
Goldsmith, Martin. The Beatles Come to America. Hoboken:
     Wiley, 2004.
```

● **Writing Tip**

For more examples of MLA documentation style, see the *MLA Handbook for Writers of Research Papers,* 6th ed. (New York: MLA, 2003), or the MLA Web site <http://www.mla.org>.

● **Writing Tip**

MLA recommends that you underline book titles, not put them in italics.

Books by Two or Three Authors

List second and subsequent authors with first name first, in the order in which they are listed on the book's title page.

> Bigelow, Fran, and Helene Siegel. Pure Chocolate. New
>   York: Broadway, 2004.

Book by More than Three Authors

List only the first author, followed by the abbreviation *et al.* ("and others").

> Ordeman, John T., et al. Artists of the North American
>   Wilderness: George and Belmore Browne. New York:
>   Warwick, 2004.

Two or More Books by the Same Author

List two or more books by the same author in alphabetical order according to title. In each entry after the first, use three unspaced hyphens (followed by a period) instead of the author's name.

> Angelou, Maya. Hallelujah! The Welcome Table: A Lifetime
>   of Memories with Recipes. New York: Random, 2004.
>
> ---. I Know Why the Caged Bird Sings. New York: Bantam,
>   1985.

Edited Book

> Whitman, Walt. The Portable Walt Whitman. Ed. Michael
>   Warner. New York: Penguin, 2004.

Translation

> Garcia Marquez, Gabriel. Living to Tell the Tale. Trans.
>   Edith Grossman. New York: Knopf, 2004.

Revised Edition

> Bjelajac, David. American Art: A Cultural History. 2nd
>   ed. New York: Prentice, 2004.

Anthology

> Kirszner, Laurie G., and Stephen R. Mandell, eds.
>   Patterns for College Writing. 8th ed. New York:
>   Bedford, 2001.

Essay in an Anthology

> Grisham, John. "Unnatural Killers." Patterns for College
>   Writing. Ed. Laurie G. Kirszner and Stephen R.
>   Mandell. 8th ed. New York: Bedford, 2001. 566-75.

More than One Essay in the Same Anthology

List each essay separately with a cross-reference to the entire anthology.

> Grisham, John. "Unnatural Killers." Kirszner and Mandell
>   566-75.
>
> Kirszner, Laurie G., and Stephen R. Mandell, eds.
>   Patterns for College Writing. 8th ed. New York:
>   Bedford, 2001.

● **Writing Tip**

When the abbreviation *ed.* follows a name, it means "editor" (*eds.* means "editors"). When the abbreviation *Ed.* comes before one or more names, it means "edited by."

Stone, Oliver. "Memo to John Grisham: What's Next—'A Movie Made Me Do It'?" Kirszner and Mandell 576-80.

Section or Chapter of a Book

Gordimer, Nadine. "Loot." "Loot" and Other Stories. New York: Penguin, 2004. 1-6.

> **● Writing Tip**
>
> When one title enclosed in quotation marks falls within another, use single quotation marks for the inside title.

Periodicals

JOURNALS

A **journal** is a publication aimed at readers who know a lot about a particular subject—literature or history, for example. The articles they contain can sometimes be challenging.

Article in a Journal with Continuous Pagination throughout Annual Volume

Some scholarly journals have continuous pagination; that is, one issue might end on page 234, and the next would then begin with page 235. In this case, the volume number is followed by the date of publication in parentheses.

Markley, Robert. "Gulliver and the Japanese: The Limits of the Postcolonial Past." Modern Language Quarterly 65 (2004): 457-80.

Article in a Journal with Separate Pagination in Each Issue

For a journal in which each issue begins with page 1, the volume number is followed by a period and the issue number and then by the date. Leave no space after the period.

Rushdie, Salman. "The Ministry of False Alarms." Virginia Quarterly Review, 80.4 (2004): 7-23.

MAGAZINES

A **magazine** is a publication aimed at general readers. For this reason, it contains articles that are easier to understand than those in journals. Frequently, an article in a magazine does not appear on consecutive pages. For example, it may begin on page 40, skip to page 47, and continue on page 49. If this is the case, include only the first page, followed by a plus sign.

Article in a Monthly or Bimonthly Magazine

Edwards, Owen. "Kilroy Was Here." Smithsonian Oct. 2004: 40+.

Article in a Weekly or Biweekly Magazine (Signed or Unsigned)

Schley, Jim. "Laid Off, and Working Harder Than Ever." Newsweek 20 Sept. 2004: 16.

"Real Reform Post-Enron." The Nation 4 Mar. 2002: 3.

Article in a Newspaper

Bykowicz, Julie. "Man Faces Identity Theft Counts: College Worker Accused of Taking Students' Data." Sun 18 Sept. 2004: 2B.

Editorial or Letter to the Editor

> "An Un-American Way to Campaign." Editorial. <u>New York
>   Times</u> 25 Sept. 2004, late ed.: A14.

Internet Sources

Full source information is not always available for Internet sources. When citing Internet sources, include whatever information you can reasonably find—for example, the title of the Internet site (underlined), the date of electronic publication (if available), and the date you accessed the source. (Some of the following examples include only the date of access; this indicates that the date of publication was not available.) Always include the electronic address (URL) enclosed in angle brackets.

Entire Web Site

> <u>Words of the Year</u>. 2004. American Dialect Society. 18 Jan.
>   2002 <http://www.americandialect.org/woty.html>.

Document within a Web Site

> "Child and Adolescent Violence Research at the NIMH."
>   <u>National Institute of Mental Health Web Site</u>. 2000.
>   2 Oct. 2004 <http://www.nimh.nih.gov/publicat/
>   violenceresfact.cfm>.

Personal Site

> Lynch, Jack. Home page. 21 Dec. 2001 <http://
>   andromeda.rutgers.edu/~jlynch>.

Article in an Online Reference Book or Encyclopedia

> "Croatia." <u>The World Factbook 2001</u>. 30 Mar. 2002.
>   Central Intelligence Agency. 30 Dec. 2002 <http://
>   www.odci.gov/cia/publications/factbook>.

> "World Trade Center." <u>Grolier Online 2001</u>. 4 Oct. 2004
>   <http://go.grolier.com>.

Article in a Newspaper

> Meller, Paul. "European Court Reviews Two Cases Central
>   to Issue of Competition." <u>New York Times on the Web</u>
>   27 Sept. 2004. 4 Oct. 2004 <http://
>   query.nytimes.com>.

Editorial

> "Clarifying What Mr. Rumsfeld Meant." Editorial.
>   <u>Washington Post</u> 27 Sept. 2004. 4 Oct. 2004 <http://
>   proquest.umi.com>.

Article in a Magazine

> Nobel, Philip. "Head for the Hills." <u>Metropolis Magazine</u>
>   Feb. 2002. 20 Feb. 2002 <http://
>   www.metropolismag.com/html/content_0202/
>   far/index.html>.

B 9

FOCUS **Preparing the Works-Cited List**

- Begin the works-cited list on a new page after the last page of your essay.
- Number the works-cited page as the next page of your essay.
- Center the heading *Works Cited* one inch from the top of the page; do not underline the heading or place it in quotation marks.
- Double-space the list.
- List entries alphabetically according to the author's last name.
- Alphabetize unsigned articles according to the first major word of the title.
- Begin typing each entry at the left-hand margin.
- Indent second and subsequent lines five spaces (or one-half inch).
- Separate major divisions of each entry—author, title, and publication information—by a period and one space.

Sample Essay Using MLA Style

Following is Allison Rogers's completed essay on the topic of media violence. The essay follows the MLA documentation style. Note that it has been reproduced in a narrower format than a standard (8½- by 11-inch) sheet of paper.

Rogers 1

Allison Rogers

Professor Sullivan

English 122-83

8 March 2005

Violence in the Media

Mickey and Mallory, two characters in
Oliver Stone's film Natural Born Killers,
travel across the Southwest, killing fifty-two
people. After watching this movie, two
teenagers went on a crime spree and killed one
person and wounded another, paralyzing her for
life. At their trial, their defense was that
watching Natural Born Killers had made them
commit their crimes and that Hollywood, along
with the director of the movie, Oliver Stone,
was to blame. As creative as this defense is,
it is hard to accept. For most people, no
amount of on-screen violence is an excuse for
violent behavior; when it comes to young
children, however, violent movies may present
a real danger.

According to John Grisham, Oliver Stone's
Natural Born Killers "inspired two teenagers
to commit murder" (5). Grisham goes on to say
that since the movie was released, several
murders have been committed by troubled
adolescents who claimed they were "under the
influence" of Mickey and Mallory (5). This type
of defense keeps reappearing as the violence in
our everyday lives increases: "I am not to
blame," says the perpetrator. "That movie (or
television show) made me do it."

The idea that violence in the media causes
violent behavior is not supported by the facts.
When we look at Ben and Sarah, the two
teenagers who supposedly imitated Mickey and

Introduction

Thesis statement

Paragraph combines quotation and paraphrase from Grisham article with Allison's observations

Paragraph combines Allison's own conclusions with paraphrases of Stone's article and article from NIMH Web site

Mallory, it is clear that factors other than Natural Born Killers could have influenced their decision to commit murder. Both young adults had long histories of drug and alcohol abuse as well as psychiatric treatment (Stone 39). In addition, no clear link between violent movies and television shows and aggressive behavior has been established. In fact, recent studies suggest that no single factor causes antisocial behavior. Rather, such behavior develops over time and is influenced by the makeup of the individual as well as his or her social environment ("Child and Adolescent Violence Research").

> Paragraph contains Allison's own ideas so no documentation needed

What are we supposed to make of crimes that seem to be inspired by the media? The evidence for most of these so-called copycat crimes is usually based on secondhand accounts rather than firsthand experience. Two problems exist with this type of "evidence." The first problem is that in most cases the movie or television show is never directly linked to the crime. For example, a Kentucky high school student fired an automatic weapon into a crowd of students in the school lobby. He killed three and wounded five, claiming he had seen this done by Leonardo DiCaprio's character in the movie Basketball Diaries. Naturally, it appeared as if the movie had inspired the crime. However, similar crimes had occurred throughout the country before the movie's release. So the question remains: Did the movie really cause the violence in this particular case or did it simply reflect a kind of violent mood that was already present in society? The truth is that we cannot answer this question. The second problem with secondhand accounts as evidence is that these

Rogers 3

accounts are not representative. Crimes that are actually inspired by the media are extremely rare. Only a few people have had such unusual reactions, and because they were mentally unbalanced, no one could have predicted what would set them off. It could have been a movie like Natural Born Killers, but it could also have been a Bugs Bunny cartoon or a Three Stooges movie.

Even though no direct link between media violence and violent behavior has been found, most people agree that young children are easily influenced by what they see. According to the American Academy of Pediatrics, the level of violence in children's cartoons is five times that on prime time television ("Some Things"). One study showed that children who watch violent shows "identify with aggressive same-sex TV characters" and believe that TV violence is real. These children tend to show aggressive behavior as young adults ("Childhood Exposure to Media Violence"). For this reason, young children should be protected. However, the responsibility for this protection should lie with the parents, not the media. First, parents need to understand their responsibility for monitoring what their children see on television and in the movies. Second, as the American Academy of Pediatrics suggests, parents should limit their children's TV viewing and discuss the content of the movies and shows they are allowed to watch ("Some Things").

There is no doubt that violence is learned and that violent media images encourage violent behavior in young children. It is not clear, however, that violent movies and television shows will actually cause an adult to commit a

Paragraph combines Allison's own ideas with quotation from APA article and paraphrase of an article from the American Academy of Pediatrics Web site

Conclusion

B 9

crime. Society should not limit the right of the majority to watch movies and television shows just because a few unbalanced individuals might go out and commit crimes. Placing blame on the media is just an easy way to sidestep the hard questions, such as what is causing so much violence in our society and what we can do about it. If we prohibit violent programs, we will deprive many adults of their right to view the programs of their choice, and we will prevent artists from expressing themselves freely. In the process, these restrictions will deprive society of a good deal of worthwhile entertainment.

Conclusion needs no documentation because it contains Allison's own ideas

Rogers 5

Works Cited

"Child and Adolescent Violence Research at the
      NIMH." National Institute of Mental Health
      Web Site. 2000. 2 Oct. 2004 <http://
      www.nimh.nih.gov/publicat/
      violenceresfact.cfm>.

"Childhood Exposure to Media Violence Predicts
      Young Adult Aggressive Behavior." American
      Psychological Association Web Site. 9 Mar.
      2003. 27 Oct. 2004 <http://www.uncg.edu/
      edu/ericcass/violence/index/htm>.

Grisham, John. "Unnatural Killers." The Oxford
      American Spring, 1996: 2-5.

"Some Things You Should Know about Media
      Violence and Media Literacy." American
      Academy of Pediatrics Web Site. June 1995.
      2 Oct. 2004 <http://www.aap.org/advocacy/
      childhealthmonth/media.htm>.

Stone, Oliver. "Memo to John Grisham: What's
      Next—A Movie Made Me Do It?" LA Weekly 29
      Mar.-4 Apr. 1996: 39.

Articles from Web sites are listed by title
because authors' names are not easily
obtainable

Taking Standardized Assessment Tests

Standardized testing is one way colleges find out who you are and what skills you have mastered. The first section of this appendix introduces you to three national assessment tests (the Accuplacer test, the COMPASS and ASSET test, and the CUNY/ACT), one state assessment test (from Texas), and two state exit exams (Florida and Georgia). Sections 2 to 8 give you tips on how you can use *Writing First* to help prepare for these tests.

1 Common Exit Exams and Placement Tests

To graduate from high school, you might have taken a standardized test called an **exit exam**, a test designed to determine whether you have the skills you need to leave high school. Some colleges use exit exams to determine whether you should graduate from college (like the Georgia Regents' Testing Program). During your college experience, you also might be given a standardized test called a **placement test**. These exams are designed to place you in classes that are right for your skill level (like the Accuplacer and the COMPASS and ASSET tests).

The following pages offer brief overviews of placement tests and exit exams commonly used by colleges. If you know you will have to take one, use the information here to prepare for it. Study the test outline and the sample question, and visit the test's Web site for extra practice. Being prepared for standardized tests will give you a better chance of achieving a good score.

National Assessment Tests

Accuplacer

Accuplacer, administered by the College Board, is a placement test for students entering college. It helps to determine what level of college classes students are ready for.

Accuplacer has a multiple-choice test consisting of five parts (reading comprehension, sentence skills, arithmetic, elementary algebra, and college-level mathematics) and an essay assessment. Both tests are administered on a computer. Your college may wish to test you in all or only in some of these areas. A sample of an Accuplacer question for reading comprehension is shown on page 687.

Accuplacer, Sample Question

Reading Comprehension

Question 1

Every sip of milk contains 59 different bioactive hormones according to endocrinologist Clark Grosvenor. Imagine taking 59 different hormone pills every morning, afternoon and evening. These hormones cause mood swings, irritability and depression. Imagine the devastation that is created in your body by the cumulative effect of taking those powerful drugs. What is the gross effect on the total behavior of a society, so dosed?

As we drink more and more milk and increase the amount of genetically engineered milk and cheese and ice cream products containing increased levels of naturally occurring milk hormones, we most certainly have influenced the way we act as a society.

The author's argument is that:

A. Many people are drug addicts
B. Milk has an effect on the way our society acts
C. Women need to take hormones
D. Everyone should drink more milk

FOCUS   **Accuplacer**

To read more about how to prepare for the test, visit Accuplacer's on-line Student Guide at **<http://cpts.accuplacer.com/docs/Student Guide.html>**. General information is also available at **<http://www.collegeboard.com/highered/apr/accu/accu.html>**.

COMPASS and ASSET

Like the College Board, ACT (American College Testing) also administers a test that helps colleges place students in courses appropriate to their skill level. COMPASS is an electronic version of the test, and the ASSET is a paper-based version of the test. The COMPASS test is computer adaptive. This means that the test gets more difficult when a question is answered correctly, and it gets easier if a question is answered incorrectly. This test uses software to assess your writing.

The COMPASS and ASSET tests consist of two sets of multiple-choice questions—the Basic Skills Tests (which test writing, reading, and numerical skills) and the Advanced Mathematics Tests. The writing skills tested include grammar, sentence construction, and argumentation. The reading skills tested include reading comprehension and critical thinking. A sample ASSET test question is shown on page 688.

ASSET test, Sample Questions

The following paragraphs may or may not be in the most logical order. Each paragraph is numbered in brackets, and item 11 will ask you to choose the sequence of paragraph numbers that is in the most logical order.

[1]

In the end, everyone gives up jogging. Some find that their strenuous efforts to earn a living <u>drains</u> away the energy
                                    1

necessary for running. Others <u>suffering</u>
                                        2

from defeat by the hazards of the course, which can range from hard pavement to muddy tracks and smog to sleet and snow. <u>Person's can also</u> simple collapse in their
            3

Sneakers. My experience was different, however; I had a revelation.

1. A. NO CHANGE
    B. drain
    C. has drained
    D. is draining

2. A. NO CHANGE
    B. suffered
    C. suffer
    D. suffering with

3. A. NO CHANGE
    B. Still others
    C. One may also
    D. It's also possible to

FOCUS **COMPASS/ASSET**

To get more information about the COMPASS and ASSET tests, and to view student guides and samples, visit these Web sites: **<http://www.act.org/compass/>** and **<http://www.act.org/asset/>**.

CUNY/ACT

The City University of New York (CUNY) uses the CUNY/ACT test to test students entering college and to place them in appropriate college courses. Students also take the test if they are exiting remedial, developmental, and English as a Second Language (ESL) courses. The CUNY/ACT test is very similar to the COMPASS/ASSET test, with sections on reading, writing, and mathematic skills. A sample test question from the CUNY/ACT Reading Skills Test is shown below.

CUNY/ACT test, Sample Questions

Sample Practical Reading Passage (Placement)

Regular tune-ups of your heating system will cut heating costs and will most likely increase the lifetime and safety of the system. When a service technician performs a tune-up, he or she should test the efficiency of your heating system.

The technician should measure the efficiency of your system both before and after servicing it and provide you with a copy of the results. Combustion efficiency is determined indirectly, based on some of the following tests: 1) temperature of the flue (or chimney); 2) percent carbon dioxide or percent oxygen in the atmosphere; 3) presence of carbon monoxide in the atmosphere; and 4) draft. Incomplete combustion of fuel is the main contributor to low efficiency. If the technician cannot raise the combustion efficiency up to at least 75% after tuning your heating system, you should consider installing a new system or at least modifying your present system to increase its efficiency.

Adapted from Alex Wilson and John Morrill, Consumer Guide to Home Energy Savings. 1993 by the American Council for an Energy-Efficient Economy.

Referring

1. The passage suggests that the presence of carbon monoxide in the atmosphere:
   A. can provide information regarding combustion efficiency.
   B. is found in 75% of heating systems tested.
   C. can be reduced by decreasing heating system draft.
   D. is the main cause of low efficiency in heating systems.
   E. is more reliable than flue temperature as an indicator of combustion efficiency.

Reasoning

2. According to the passage, when performing a tune-up of a heating system, the service technician should:
   A. ensure that the combustion efficiency is at least 25%.
   B. modify the heating system before initially measuring efficiency.
   C. measure combustion efficiency both before and after servicing the system.
   D. provide his or her supervisor with a written report of the system's efficiency.
   E. ignore the age of the heating system.

FOCUS **CUNY/ACT**

For more information on the CUNY/ACT test, visit the Skills Assessment Program's Web site at **<http://rwc.hunter.cuny.edu/cuny -act/>**.

State Assessment Test

The Texas Higher Education Assessment (THEA) Test

The Texas Higher Education Assessment (THEA) test (formerly called "the TASP") provides colleges with information about students' reading, math, and writing skills so that they can be placed in the appropriate college courses. Before students enter public colleges and universities and public or private teacher-preparation programs in Texas, they need to take this test. The THEA test is entirely multiple-choice. A sample test question from the writing section is shown below.

THEA, Sample Question

THEA Practice Test—Writing Section

Read the passage below, written in the style of a student letter to a college newspaper. Then answer the questions that follow.

    1The parking situation on this campus is truly outrageous. **2**Sure, for full-time students who live in campus, convenient parking isn't a big deal. **3**But by now everyone—except, evidently, those responsible for campus parking—must know that there are a lot of us commuter students who struggle to balance a job, a family, and academics. **4**We are not the ones you see strolling leisurely from dormitory to class to dining hall to student hangout. **5**Nothing in our lives is leisurely: we race from job to classroom to the library to the daycare center to the grocery store and finally, exhaustedly, back home.

1. Which of the following sentences, if added between Parts 3 and 4 of the first paragraph, would be most consistent with the writer's purpose and intended audience?

    A. We commuter students don't drive to campus just because it's nice to have a car around in case we want to go shopping or to the movies.

    B. Even a cursory survey of the situation should be sufficient to reveal the significant burdens that such a demanding life style must place on the average commuter student.

    C. One must accept the statistically verifiable fact that, as a group, commuter students take more difficult courses than students who live on campus.

    D. I am aware that commuter students cannot and should not request special treatment from campus officials.

FOCUS **THEA**

For more information on the THEA and for access to a practice test, visit the THEA Web site at **<http://www.thea.nesinc.com/>**.

State Exit Exams

The Florida College Level Academic Skills Test (CLAST)

The Florida College Level Academic Skills Test (CLAST) is administered to students who are completing the requirements for an associate degree from a community college or who are transferring from a community college to upper-division classes at a four-year state university in Florida.

The test has four sections: an essay, English language skills, reading, and math. The English language skills, reading, and math sections are multiple-choice. The essay portion of the test requires students to write a composition. Students with grade point averages above 2.5 do not have to take the CLAST. A sample of the English Language Skills section of the test is shown below.

CLAST, Sample Questions

CLAST English Language Skills

Directions: Choose the most effective word or phrase within the context suggested by the sentence.

1. Because the case was not over, Suzanne was _____ to discuss it with anyone other than her fellow jury members.
   a. wanting   b. able   c. forbidden   d. required

Directions: Choose the sentence that logically and correctly expresses the comparison.

2. a. To some people the Empire State Building, is more beautiful than the Chrysler building.
   b. To some people the Empire State Building is more beautiful, than the Chrysler building.
   c. To some people, the Empire State Building is more beautiful than the Chrysler building.

3. a. Hanging in the window of the shop that sold my favorite shoes, I found a "closed" sign.
   b. I found a "closed" sign hanging in the window of the shop that sold my favorite shoes.
   c. In the window of the shop that sold my favorite shoes, I found a "closed" sign hanging.

Directions: Choose the correct option.

4. Mr. Greene taught six sections of the philosophy <u>class. With</u> forty students attending each group.
   a. sections. Of   b. class, with   c. students, attending
   d. No change is necessary.

(continued on the following page)

(continued from the previous page)

5. Tammy <u>has go</u> everywhere with her poodle, today, even to the mall.
   a. have gone   b. has went   c. has gone
   d. No change is necessary.

FOCUS **CLAST**

For sample materials and practice tests, visit this helpful Web site, which is maintained by the University of Central Florida: **<http://sarc.sdes.ucf.edu/clastsamplequestions.html>**. For more information about the test, visit the CLAST Web site at **<http://www.firn.edu/doe/sas/clsthome.htm>**.

The Georgia Regents' Testing Program

Passing the Georgia Regents' Reading Test and Essay Test is required for graduation from a bachelor's program at a Georgia state university. Some students may be exempt from portions of these tests if they performed acceptably on the SAT, ACT, or other approved tests. (Check with your university to see if you qualify for an exemption.) The Georgia Regents' Reading Test is multiple-choice, whereas the Regents' Essay Test requires students to write an essay on a given topic.

A sample of the Regents' Essay Test question is shown below.

Regents' Test, Sample Question

Regents Testing Program Essay Test

Choose one of the following topics. Put an "X" in the box to indicate your choice.

☐ Discuss the influence that advertising has had on your life or the lives of your friends. (4)

☐ Why would you like or dislike owning your own business? (164)

☐ In the development of a national budget, which should be more important—fighting poverty at home or arming to fight an aggressor? Explain. (333)

☐ Discuss why people are fascinated by amusement parks such as Disney World and Six Flags. (340)

Begin your essay on the first lined page. You may use the space below for an outline or notes. (Remember to use a pen to write your essay. Essays written in pencil will not be graded.)

FOCUS **Georgia Regents' Tests**

For more information on this test, including a sample reading skills test and a list of approved essay topics, go to: **<http://www2.gsu.edu/ ~wwwrtp/>**.

---

2 Using *Writing First* to Help You Prepare

Most state placement tests and exit exams require students to show proficiency in writing. *Writing First* can help you improve your performance on these tests. The left-hand column of the Correlation Guide below lists the skills that are necessary for good writing, and the right-hand column shows you where to find appropriate practice exercises in *Writing First*. Use this chart when you study for any standardized writing test you may need to take. Concentrate on practicing the skills you have trouble with and on reviewing the ones you learned recently.

Correlation Guide

Composition Skills and the Writing Process	Pages in *Writing First*
Purpose and audience	4–5
Organizing, drafting, revising, and editing	13–20, 130–151
Main idea	13
Thesis statement and topic sentence	23–30, 112–116, 122–128
Support: general and specific details	14–15, 33–38
Relevant and irrelevant details	30–33
Unity	30–33
Logical order	38–40
Coherence and transitions	41–43, 169–172, 174–178
Essay structure	121–148
Sentence variety	275–297
Examples	52–56, 168–173
Process	72–78, 186–191
Description	65–71, 180–185
Language and Word Usage	
Mechanics	540–552

(continued on the following page)

(continued from the previous page)

Composition Skills and the Writing Process	Pages in *Writing First*
Spelling	555–563
Capitalization	540–543
Punctuation	
Commas	515–527
Semicolons	246–248
Colons, dashes, and parentheses	550–552
Apostrophes	531–537
Quotations	543–547
Titles	547–549
Coordination and subordination	241–246, 258–264
Modifiers	393–403, 498–499
Adjectives and adverbs	464–472
Parallelism	300–306
Verbs and tenses	411–419, 422–434
Pronouns	441–460
Commonly confused and misused words	563–573
Conciseness	310–315
Word usage	310–321

Sentence Structure	
Subjects and verbs	229–232, 234–238, 477–484
Prepositions	232–234, 499–507
Coordination and subordination	241–246, 258–264
Run-ons	329–335
Fragments	339–359
Subject and verb agreement	363–376

3   Dealing with Anxiety

Not knowing what to expect from a standardized test can make you anxious. Test anxiety is natural and can actually be beneficial if you use that extra energy to work harder and faster. If you are too anxious, however, your judgment may be impaired.

The best way to beat test anxiety is to be prepared on test day. First, read about your test in advance so you know what kind of format and content to expect. Then, use the Correlation Guide on pages 693–694 to help you review writing, grammar, and mechanics skills. Finally, study the tips that follow to help you get prepared and beat the test-day jitters.

4   Preparing for Standardized Tests

The best preparation for any standardized test is to pay attention and work hard in class. Here are some extra hints to help you succeed:

1. **Be rested and ready.** Too often, students stay up late cramming the night before a standardized test. Instead, prepare a few days in advance so you can get plenty of sleep the night before your test is scheduled. This will enable you to perform at your best.

2. **Know your test.** Learn about the form and content of your test and how it is scored.

3. **Practice.** If you are taking one of the tests mentioned in this appendix, go to the test's Web site to take a practice test. If your test is not covered here, do some research (ask your teacher, a librarian, or a bookstore clerk, or go online) to see if a practice test is available.

4. **Plan your time.** When you take the practice test, figure out how much time you will need to complete each section: take your time-plan with you on test day. Give yourself extra time for challenging sections, but do not spend all your time there. Remember to reserve time to review your work at the end. During the real test, use your time-plan to help you move efficiently through each section.

5. **Use Writing First.** Use the Correlation Guide on pages 623–624 to help you brush up on your writing and mechanics skills. Also visit **<bedfordstmartins.com/exercisecentral>** and **<bedfordstmartins.com/writingfirst>** for extra practice questions.

6. **Use traditional resources.** Ask at your library, learning center, or bookstore for study materials designed to help you with your test.

5   Preparing for Multiple-Choice Tests

Multiple-choice tests measure both your ability to remember facts and your critical-thinking skills. These tests often have several answers that seem right, but you are expected to find the *best* answer.

1. **Use your time-plan** (see point 4 above). Be careful not to get stuck on one question. Instead, use the time-plan you developed to pace yourself. Ask the exam proctor if you can write on the test. If you are allowed to do so, write your time-plan in the test's margins, and refer back to it as you work.

2. **Read the directions carefully.** The test directions will tell you what specific answering procedures you must follow, how much time you have to answer each question, and how questions will be graded. Keep these directions in mind as you work.

3. **Answer what is asked.** Be sure you know exactly what the question is asking. Read the question carefully and do not make assumptions. Be

sure to highlight the question's key words. Think about how to answer the question before you answer it.

4. *Stay organized.* Answer all questions in order, and identify answers you have doubts about. After you have answered all the questions, recheck the ones you were uncertain of.

5. *Give it your best guess.* Do not linger too long on any one question. Mark your best guess, and move on; return later to troublesome questions if you have time.

6 Approaching a Multiple-Choice Question

1. *Try to anticipate the answer.* Try to determine the correct answer before you read through the answer choices (A, B, C, and D). Then, compare each of the possible choices to the answer you thought of. Be sure to read every word of each possible answer; often, the choices are similar.

2. *Divide and conquer.* If you cannot anticipate the answer, check each answer choice against the question. Eliminate all false answers. Of the true statements, pick the one that most precisely answers the question. If you are having trouble determining which one is most correct, try focusing on the specific differences between the two answers.

3. *Identify negatives and absolutes.* Underline negative words like *not, but,* and *except.* Negative words can change a question from "Choose the answer that is correct" to "Choose the answer that is *not* correct." Also underline absolutes, such as *always, never,* and *only.* Answers containing absolutes are often incorrect because exceptions can be found to almost every statement.

4. *Be especially aware of negatives.* Pay special attention to all questions containing negative words, such as *not* or *never.* These can be confusing. Be especially alert for the use of double or even triple negatives within a sentence. Work out each question's true meaning before you attempt to answer it. (For example, the sentence "He was not unfriendly" means that he *was* friendly.)

5. *Consider "All of the above."* If there is an "All of the above" answer choice and you have determined that at least two answer choices are correct, select "All of the above."

6. *Make an educated guess.* Before guessing, eliminate as many answers as possible. Then, select an answer that uses a qualifying term, like *usually, often,* or *most.* If all else fails, choose the answer that you first thought seemed right. Your first instinct is often correct.

7 Preparing for a Standardized Essay Test

The essays that you write for standardized tests are similar to the essays that you write in class; however, they might be scored differently. In addition, some tests might assign more than one essay—for example, one essay will assess grammar and mechanics and another essay will assess critical thinking. Pay close attention to the instructions on your test. Begin by reviewing the directions for exam-taking strategies in the section "During the Exam" in Appendix A (page 658). Then review the points below.

- *Know how to score points.* Standardized test scorers must work fast, so they look for specific things when scoring your test. (This is especially true for computer-scored tests.) Visit the test's Web site to try to find out what the test emphasizes. If this information is not available, assume that large issues (like ideas, logic, and organization) will be more important than small ones, like spelling and grammar (although all of these elements count).

- *Tackle the easiest questions first.* In class, you often have an entire period in which to write a single essay. Standardized tests, however, often require you to write multiple essays in a limited amount of time. Where should you begin? Read all of the questions, and begin with the one that seems easiest. Starting strong will help ease your anxiety and give you momentum. In addition, you will score higher if you make sure you finish your best work before time runs out.

- *Make a plan.* Make a rough outline of each essay before you begin to write it. The few minutes you spend planning will improve the organization of your essay and keep you on track as you write.

- *Get down to business.* On standardized essay tests, keep your writing lean and efficient. Avoid long-winded introductions; begin your first paragraph with a sentence that directly answers the essay question and states your thesis.

- *Manage your time.* If time allows, quickly proofread your work to correct any grammatical or mechanical mistakes. However, if you see that you are running out of time, quickly jot down an outline of the remaining part of your answer without checking for other errors.

- *Use in-class essays as practice.* As you write essays for your classes, ask yourself how effective your essay would be if you were preparing it for a standardized test and how you would change the essay to score higher.

8 Defining Common Essay Test Directives

Testmakers use words called **directives** to tell you what type of essay to write. To answer a question correctly, you need to know what these directives mean. Here is a list of common directives, organized according to the patterns of essay development you learned in Chapter 14.

Exemplification Essays

An **exemplification essay** uses specific examples to support a thesis. The directives *explain* and *discuss* call for an exemplification essay.

For more information on how to write an exemplification essay, see 14A.

■ **Explain**: Present an idea as well as the facts and examples that support this idea. (If you are asked to explain only one side of an issue, do not explain the other side.)

DIRECTIVE *Explain the benefits of assigning homework to kindergarteners.*

EXAMPLE Assigning homework to kindergarteners will teach them valuable study skills and discipline.

■ **Discuss**: Examine an issue thoroughly. (If you are asked to discuss only one side of an issue, do not discuss the other side.)

DIRECTIVE *Discuss the reasons why homework should not be assigned to kindergarteners.*

EXAMPLE Homework should not be assigned to kindergarteners because it will take time away from play and teach them to dislike school.

Descriptive Essays

For more information on how to write a descriptive essay, see 14C.

A **descriptive essay** uses details to give readers a clear, vivid picture of a person, place, or object. The directive *describe* calls for a descriptive essay.

■ **Describe**: Give details about what something looks like, sounds like, and so on.

DIRECTIVE *Describe your kindergarten classroom.*

EXAMPLE My kindergarten classroom was a colorful place with a giant red, yellow, and blue train in the middle of the room.

Comparison-and-Contrast Essays

For more information on how to write a comparison-and-contrast essay, see 14F.

A **comparison-and-contrast essay** explains how two things are similar or how they are different. Sometimes, this kind of essay discusses both similarities and differences. The directives *compare and contrast* call for a comparison-and-contrast essay.

■ **Compare**: Tell how one thing is similar to another thing.
■ **Contrast**: Identify the differences between two things.

DIRECTIVE *Compare and contrast the arguments for and against assigning homework to kindergarteners.*

EXAMPLE Some people say that assigning homework to kindergarteners burdens them with too much responsibility. Others say that it is a necessary step in learning to develop good study habits.

Argument Essays

An **argument essay** uses evidence—facts, examples, and expert opinion—to persuade readers to accept a position. The directives *criticize, interpret, justify,* and *evaluate* call for an argument essay.

For more information on how to write an argument essay, see 14I.

■ *Criticize*: Say whether a position is right or wrong, and explain why.

DIRECTIVE *Criticize the decision of some schools to assign homework to kindergarten students.*

EXAMPLE Assigning homework to kindergarteners is wrong because children at this age are too young to understand their responsibilities as students.

■ *Interpret*: Decide what you think a text means, and use the details of that text as evidence.

DIRECTIVE *Attached is a graph showing the test scores of kindergarteners who were given homework in relation to kindergarteners who were not given homework. Interpret this graph.*

EXAMPLE According to the data, assigning homework to kindergarteners does not increase test scores. As the graph indicates, the students who were not assigned homework had higher scores than students who were assigned homework.

■ *Justify*: Defend a position. When you defend a position, you emphasize the strengths of your side more than the weaknesses of the other side.

DIRECTIVE *Justify the statement that assigning homework to kindergarteners is beneficial.*

EXAMPLE Assigning homework to kindergarteners teaches children to be responsible for their time and assignments.

■ *Evaluate*: Present a careful assessment of both sides of an issue. Your evaluation should present your position on the issue you are discussing.

DIRECTIVE *Evaluate the statement that homework is bad for kindergarteners.*

EXAMPLE On the one hand, if children are deprived of playtime, they will not learn to think creatively. On the other hand, without some homework, they may not develop good work habits and therefore may suffer academically. In short, too little homework may be bad for children, but too much homework may also be harmful.

C 8

● **Writing Tip**
You can also use the *Writing First* Web site and Exercise Central to help you practice for your standardized test. Visit <**bedfordstmartins .com/exercisecentral**>.

☑ SELF-ASSESSMENT CHECKLIST:
Preparing for Standardized Tests

- ☐ Did you research your test to find out what it covers and how it is scored?

- ☐ Did you take practice tests?

- ☐ Did you use the Correlation Guide on pages 693–694 to help you study?

- ☐ Did you review your in-class essays to see what your common errors are?

- ☐ Did you study the most common test directives and learn what they mean?

- ☐ Did you ask at your library, bookstore, or learning center for more study aids?

Answers to Odd-Numbered Exercise Items

Chapter 15

◆ PRACTICE 15-1, page 230

Answers: **(1)** Complete subject: Derek Walcott **(3)** Complete subject: Walcott's early years; simple subject: years **(5)** Complete subject: His early poems; simple subject: poems **(7)** Complete subject: Walcott **(9)** Complete subject: the renowned poet; simple subject: poet **(11)** Complete subject: the sixty-two-year-old Caribbean poet; simple subject: poet

◆ PRACTICE 15-2, page 231

Possible answers: **(1)** animals **(3)** Pets **(5)** Social workers **(7)** patients **(9)** dogs

◆ PRACTICE 15-3, page 231

Answers: **(1)** a land bridge; singular **(3)** The Channel Tunnel; singular **(5)** The tubes; plural **(7)** The third tube; singular **(9)** cold-water pipes; plural

◆ PRACTICE 15-4, page 233

Answers: **(1)** Prepositional phrases: With more than 27 percent, of the vote, in history; subject: Theodore Roosevelt **(3)** Prepositional phrases: Until Roosevelt, of votes; subject: candidate **(5)** Prepositional phrases: For example, of the Progressive Party, about 16 percent, of the vote, in the 1924 race; subject: Robert M. LaFollette **(7)** Prepositional phrases: In 1980, of the vote; subject: John B. Anderson **(9)** Prepositional phrases: In 2000, with the support, of many environmentalists, for the presidency; subject: Ralph Nader **(11)** Prepositional phrases: To this day, of the United States, despite many challenges, by third-party candidates; subject: system

◆ PRACTICE 15-5, page 235

Answers: **(1)** see **(3)** offers **(5)** enters; wins **(7)** realizes **(9)** enjoy

◆ PRACTICE 15-6, page 236

Answers: **(1)** are **(3)** is **(5)** is **(7)** becomes **(9)** are

◆ PRACTICE 15-7, page 236

Answers: **(1)** wrote **(3)** is; seems **(5)** lives **(7)** dies **(9)** works

◆ PRACTICE 15-8, page 238

Answers: **(1)** Complete verb: had become; helping verb: had **(3)** Complete verb: had become; helping verb: had **(5)** Complete verb: would get; helping verb: would **(7)** Complete verb: did cause; helping verb: did **(9)** Complete verb: would remain; helping verb: would

Chapter 16

◆ PRACTICE 16-1, page 243

Answers: **(1)** and **(3)** and **(5)** and **(7)** so/and **(9)** for

◆ PRACTICE 16-2, page 243

Answers: **(1)** for **(3)** or **(5)** but **(7)** for **(9)** but

◆ PRACTICE 16-3, page 244

Possible edits: Diet, exercise, and family history may account for centenarians' long lives, but this is not the whole story. Recently, a study conducted in Georgia showed surprising common traits among centenarians. They did not necessarily avoid tobacco and alcohol, nor did they have low-fat diets. In fact, they ate relatively large amounts of fat, cholesterol, and sugar, so diet could not explain their long lives. They did, however, share four key survival characteristics. First, all of the centenarians were optimistic about life, and all of them were positive thinkers. They were also involved in religious life and had deep religious faith. In addition, all the centenarians had continued to lead physically active lives, and they remained mobile even as elderly people. Finally, all were able to adapt to loss. They had all experienced the deaths of friends, spouses, or children, but they were able to get on with their lives.

◆ PRACTICE 16-4, page 245

Answers will vary.

PRACTICE 16-5, page 247

Answers: **(1)** Sometimes runners-up are better remembered than winners; the triumphant are forgotten. **(3)** Roald Amundsen was a Norwegian explorer; Robert Falcon Scott was a British naval officer. **(5)** Amundsen's men buried food all along the trail; Scott's men left food in only a few locations. **(7)** Amundsen's men made it to the Pole in December 1911; Scott's party arrived in January 1912. **(9)** Scott's exhausted party could not get to their provisions; none of the men survived the trek.

PRACTICE 16-6, page 247

Answers will vary.

PRACTICE 16-7, page 250

Answers: **(1)** Andrew F. Smith, a food historian, wrote a book about the tomato; subsequently, he wrote a book about ketchup. **(3)** The word *ketchup* may have come from a Chinese word; however, Smith is not certain of the word's origins. **(5)** Ketchup has changed a lot over the years; for example, special dyes were developed in the nineteenth century to make it red. **(7)** Ketchup is now used by people in many cultures; still, salsa is more popular than ketchup in the United States. **(9)** Some of today's ketchups are chunky; in addition, some ketchups are spicy.

PRACTICE 16-8, page 251

Possible edits: **(1)** The Man of the Year has had great influence over the previous year's events; consequently, the choice is often a prominent politician. **(3)** During the war years, Hitler, Stalin, Churchill, and Roosevelt were all chosen; in fact, Stalin was featured twice. **(5)** In 1956, The Hungarian Freedom Fighter was Man of the Year; then, in 1966, *Time* editors chose The Young Generation. **(7)** In 1975, American Women were honored as a group; nevertheless, the Man of the Year has nearly always been male. **(9)** The Man of the Year has almost always been one or more human beings; however, the Computer was selected in 1982 and Endangered Earth in 1988. **(11)** In 2003, *Time* did not choose a politician; instead; it honored The American Soldier.

PRACTICE 16-9, page 251

Possible answers: **(1)** Campus residents may have a better college experience; still, being a commuter has its advantages. **(3)** Commuters have a wide choice of jobs in the community; on the other hand, students living on campus may have to take on-campus jobs. **(5)** There are also some disadvantages to being a commuter; for example, commuters may have trouble joining study groups. **(7)** Commuters might have to help take care of their parents or grandparents; in addition, they might have to babysit for younger siblings. **(9)** Younger commuters may be under the watchful eyes of their parents; of course, parents are likely to be stricter than dorm counselors.

PRACTICE 16-10, page 253

Answers will vary.

Chapter 17

PRACTICE 17-1, page 259

Answers: **(1)** Independent clause **(3)** Dependent clause **(5)** Independent clause **(7)** Independent clause **(9)** Dependent clause

PRACTICE 17-2, page 260

Answers: **(1)** Independent clause **(3)** Independent clause **(5)** Dependent clause **(7)** Dependent clause **(9)** Independent clause

PRACTICE 17-3, page 261

Possible answers: **(1)** when **(3)** Although **(5)** Since **(7)** Although **(9)** that

PRACTICE 17-4, page 263

Possible edits: **(1)** Although professional midwives are used widely in Europe, in the United States, they usually practice only in areas with few doctors. **(3)** Stephen Crane describes battles in *The Red Badge of Courage* even though he never experienced a war. **(5)** After Jonas Salk developed the first polio vaccine in the 1950s, the number of polio cases declined in the United States. **(7)** Before the Du Ponts arrived from France in 1800, American gunpowder was inferior to the kind manufactured by the French. **(9)** Because Thaddeus Stevens thought plantation land should be given to freed slaves, he disagreed with Lincoln's peace terms for the South.

PRACTICE 17-5, page 265

Possible answers: **(1)** Dependent clause: which was performed by a group called the Buggles; relative pronoun: which; noun: video **(3)** Dependent clause: who had been suspicious of MTV at first; relative pronoun: who; noun: executives **(5)** Dependent clause: which aired in September 1984; relative pronoun: which; noun: awards **(7)** Dependent clause: who was its first host; relative pronoun: who; noun: Cindy Crawford **(9)** Dependent clause: who would soon be elected president; relative pronoun: who; noun: Bill Clinton

PRACTICE 17-6, page 266

Possible answers: **(1)** Their work, which benefits both the participants and the communities, is called service-learning. **(3)** The young people, who are not paid, work at projects such as designing neighborhood playgrounds. **(5)** Designing a playground, which requires teamwork, teaches them to communicate. **(7)** They also learn to solve problems that the community cannot solve by itself. **(9)** The young participants, who often lack self-confidence, gain satisfaction from performing a valuable service.

◆ **PRACTICE 17-7, page 268**

(1) Restrictive **(3)** Nonrestrictive **(5)** Nonrestrictive
(7) Nonrestrictive **(9)** Restrictive

◆ **PRACTICE 17-8, page 269**

Answers will vary: **(1)** Zapata was a sharecropper who could not read or write. **(3)** Mexican peasants wanted to regain their land, which they felt foreigners had taken from them. **(5)** He created his own program, which was known as the "Plan of Ayala," for returning the land. **(7)** Zapata, who had gained control of almost all of southern Mexico, entered Mexico City in 1914. **(9)** The government, which wanted to get rid of Zapata, tricked him into meeting with one of its generals.

◆ **PRACTICE 17-9, page 270**

Answers will vary.

Chapter 18

◆ **PRACTICE 18-1, page 276**

Answers will vary.

◆ **PRACTICE 18-2, page 278**

Answers: **(1)** Adverb: however; edited sentence: However, one way to deal with this problem is to shop online. **(3)** Adverb: nevertheless; edited sentence: Nevertheless, access to a wide variety of products can be exhilarating. **(5)** Adverb: then; edited sentence: Then, the search can be narrowed. **(7)** Adverb: often; edited sentence: Often, customer reviews are available to help shoppers make a choice. **(9)** Adverb: generally; edited sentence: Generally, payment is by credit card.

◆ **PRACTICE 18-3, page 280**

Answers will vary.

◆ **PRACTICE 18-4, page 280**

Answers: **(1)** Prepositional phrase: during World War II; edited sentence: During World War II, many male factory workers became soldiers. **(3)** Prepositional phrase: in the war's early years; edited sentence: In the war's early years, the U.S. government encouraged women to take factory jobs. **(5)** Prepositional phrase: in unprecedented numbers; edited sentence: In unprecedented numbers, they entered the industrial workplace. **(7)** Prepositional phrase: with their efforts; edited sentence: With their efforts, productivity rose and quality improved. **(9)** Prepositional phrase: for the first time; edited sentence: For the first time, many women felt comfortable wearing pants.

◆ **PRACTICE 18-5, page 281**

Answers will vary.

◆ **PRACTICE 18-6, page 282**

Answers: **(1)** Martí was born in Havana in 1853, at a time when Cuba was a colony of Spain. **(3)** In 1870, the Span-ish authorities forced him to leave Cuba and go to Spain. **(5)** Working as a journalist and professor, he returned to Cuba but was sent away again. **(7)** During his time in New York, he started the journal of the Cuban Revolutionary Party. **(9)** Passionately following up his words with actions, he died in battle against Spanish soldiers in Cuba.

◆ **PRACTICE 18-7, page 282**

Possible edits: **(1)** Professional football is one of the most popular sports in the country; it is also one of the most dangerous. **(3)** The league has established new rules to make the game safer, and some of these have cut down on serious injuries. **(5)** These precautions, however, do not always protect players. **(7)** Sometimes they do this because they are angry and frustrated, but sometimes it is a calculated strategy. **(9)** Of course, the fans also share the blame for the violence of football. **(11)** They believe their team should do anything to win.

◆ **PRACTICE 18-8, page 284**

Answers: **(1)** Feeling useless to themselves and everyone else, most prisoners do little while in prison. **(3)** Performing a variety of other jobs, about two thousand U.S. prisoners are working for private business. **(5)** Continuing a practice that once was common, these prisoners are able to repay part of their cost to the public. **(7)** Improving prisoners' chances of staying out of prison, this arrangement works well for everyone. **(9)** Fearing competition from low-cost prison labor, many businesses are opposed to prison work programs.

◆ **PRACTICE 18-9, page 286**

Answers will vary.

◆ **PRACTICE 18-10, page 287**

Answers: **(1)** Captured as a young girl by a rival tribe, Sacajawea was later sold into slavery. **(3)** Hired by the explorers Lewis and Clark in 1806, Charbonneau brought his pregnant wife along on their westward expedition. **(5)** Guided by Sacajawea's knowledge of the rugged terrain, the expedition also benefited from her familiarity with native food plants. **(7)** Protected by the presence of the Shoshone woman and her infant, Lewis and Clark encountered little hostility from the tribes they met. **(9)** Celebrated for many years as an American hero, Sacajawea recently received an additional honor.

◆ **PRACTICE 18-11, page 288**

Answers will vary.

◆ **PRACTICE 18-12, page 289**

Answers: **(1)** About 1200, a new language and new customs came to the Hawaiian Islands, brought by travelers from the island of Tahiti. **(3)** At this time, the Hawaiians' culture and religion supported common land ownership for the benefit of all the people. **(5)** A Hawaiian alphabet and a Hawaiian-language Bible were created by Christian missionaries. **(7)** By 1900, many Japanese and Chinese people had immigrated to Hawaii to find work on the plantations. **(9)** Tolerance for others and ethnic harmony are results of the diversity of the Hawaiian population.

◆ PRACTICE 18-13, page 291

Answers: **(1)** Despite his lack of formal education, Edison had a quick mind and showed a talent for problem solving. **(3)** Edison patented the earliest phonograph in 1878 and created the first practical light bulb the following year. **(5)** Edison later developed an electric railroad and produced one of the first batteries to store long-term power. **(7)** His early experiments with sound pictures were surprisingly successful and eventually led to "talking pictures" (movies). **(9)** Edison did much of his work in New Jersey and had laboratories there in West Orange and Menlo Park.

◆ PRACTICE 18-14, page 292

Answers: **(1)** These college presidents and their supporters wanted to improve the academic performance of college athletes. **(3)** A second proposal required athletes to earn a certain number of credits every year and mandated a minimum grade point average for them. **(5)** Many Big East coaches believe standardized test scores are biased and want their use in screening student athletes banned. **(7)** According to supporters, however, many athletes under the old system have failed to advance academically and often finish their eligibility fifty or more hours short of graduation. **(9)** In the supporters' view, poor supervision by athletic directors and lack of support for academic excellence were to blame for the poor performance of student athletes.

◆ PRACTICE 18-15, page 293

Possible edits: **(1)** A playwright who wrote the prize-winning *A Raisin in the Sun*, Lorraine Hansberry was born in Chicago in 1930. **(3)** Hostile neighbors there were responsible for throwing a brick through a window of their house, an act Hansberry never forgot. **(5)** Lena Younger, the mother of the family, is about to receive a ten-thousand-dollar insurance payment following her husband's death. **(7)** Her dream, a house with a yard her grandson can play in, leads her to purchase a home in a white neighborhood. **(9)** One of their new white neighbors has offered the Younger family a bribe not to move into the neighborhood, a deal Walter now decides to accept.

◆ PRACTICE 18-16, page 295

Possible edits: Kente cloth is made in western Africa and produced primarily by the Ashanti people. It has been worn for hundreds of years by African royalty, who consider it a sign of power and status. Many African Americans wear kente cloth because they see it as a link to their heritage. Each pattern on the cloth has a name, and each color has a special significance. For example, red and yellow suggest a long and healthy life, while green and white suggest a good harvest. Although African women may wear kente cloth as a dress or head wrap, African-American women, like men, usually wear strips of cloth around their shoulders. Men and women of African descent wear kente cloth as a sign of racial pride; in fact, it often decorates college students' gowns at graduation.

Chapter 19

◆ PRACTICE 19-1, page 301

Answers: **(1)** I just bought a head of lettuce, a pint of mushrooms, and three pounds of tomatoes. **(3)** The plumber needs to fix a leaky pipe, replace a missing faucet, and fix a running toilet. **(5)** Parallel **(7)** Parallel **(9)** Parallel

◆ PRACTICE 19-2, page 303

Answers will vary.

◆ PRACTICE 19-3, page 304

Answers: **(1)** Pasadena, Claremont, and Pomona are major cities in the valley. **(3)** Watching the big Tournament of Roses Parade is more exciting than watching the Macy's Thanksgiving parade. **(5)** Judges rate the rose-covered floats on their originality, artistic merit, and overall impact. **(7)** The Rose Bowl game is not only America's oldest collegiate championship but also the country's most popular bowl game. **(9)** Visitors come to play challenging skill games and enjoy various ethnic foods.

Chapter 20

◆ PRACTICE 20-1, page 311

Answers: **(1)** three fifty-watt bulbs; coal oil; baking bread **(3)** wooden table; unfinished game of checkers; apple-tree stump **(5)** none

◆ PRACTICE 20-2, page 312

Answers will vary.

◆ PRACTICE 20-3, page 312

Answers will vary.

◆ PRACTICE 20-4, page 314

Possible edits: **(1)** To become an informed used-car buyer, the first thing a person should do is to look on the Internet and in the local newspapers to get an idea of the prices. **(3)** When first seeing the car, search for new paint that looks different from the paint in the surrounding area. **(5)** Check the engine for problems like broken wires, cracked hoses, and leaks. **(7)** Push down suddenly on the accelerator while the car is running, and see if the car hesitates. **(9)** Even if there does not seem to be anything wrong with the car, take it to a mechanic you trust to inspect it.

◆ **PRACTICE 20-5, page 316**

Possible edits: **(1)** Clichés: like a dog; high on the hog. Many people think that a million-dollar lottery jackpot allows the winner to stop working long hours and start living a comfortable life. **(3)** Cliché: hit the jackpot. For one thing, lottery winners who win big prizes do not receive their winnings all at once; instead, payments—for example, $50,000—are usually spread out over twenty years. **(5)** Clichés: with their hands out; between a rock and a hard place. Next come relatives and friends who ask for money, leaving winners with difficult choices to make. **(7)** Cliché: Adding insult to injury. Even worse, many lottery winners have lost their jobs because employers thought that once they were "millionaires," they no longer needed to draw a salary. **(9)** Cliché: In their hour of need. Faced with financial difficulties, many would like to sell their future payments to companies that offer lump-sum payments of forty to forty-five cents on the dollar.

◆ **PRACTICE 20-6, page 318**

Answers will vary.

◆ **PRACTICE 20-7, page 318**

Answers will vary.

◆ **PRACTICE 20-8, page 320**

Answers: **(1)** Many people today would like to see more police officers patrolling the streets. **(3)** The attorneys representing the plaintiff are Geraldo Diaz and Barbara Wilkerson. **(5)** Travel to other planets will be a significant step for humanity.

Chapter 21

◆ **PRACTICE 21-1, page 330**

Answers: **(1)** Run-on **(3)** Run-on **(5)** Run-on **(7)** Correct **(9)** Correct **(11)** Correct

◆ **PRACTICE 21-2, page 332**

Possible edits: **(1)** Nursing offers job security and high pay; therefore, many people are choosing nursing as a career. **(3)** The Democratic Republic of the Congo was previously known as Zaire; before that, it was the Belgian Congo. **(5)** Millions of Jews were killed during the Holocaust; in addition, Catholics, Gypsies, homosexuals, and other "undesirables" were killed. **(7)** Japanese athletes now play various positions on American baseball teams; at first, all the Japanese players were pitchers. **(9)** Père Noel is the French name for Santa Claus; he is also known as Father Christmas and St. Nicholas.

◆ **PRACTICE 21-3, page 333**

Possible edits: **(1)** Harlem, which was populated mostly by European immigrants at the turn of the last century, saw an influx of African Americans beginning in 1910. **(3)** Many African-American artists and writers settled in Harlem during the 1920s, which led to a flowering of African-American art. **(5)** When scholars of the era recognize the great works of the Harlem Renaissance, they point to the writers Langston Hughes and Countee Cullen and the artists Henry Tanner and Sargent Johnson. **(7)** Because Harlem was an exciting place in the 1920s, people from all over the city went there to listen to jazz and to dance. **(9)** While contemporary African-American artists know about the Harlem Renaissance, it is still not familiar to many others.

◆ **PRACTICE 21-4, page 334**

Possible edits: In the late nineteenth century, Coney Island was famous; in fact, it was legendary. Every summer, it was crowded, and people mailed hundreds of thousands of postcards from the resort on some days. Coney Island, which was considered exotic and exciting, even had a hotel shaped like an elephant. Although some people saw Coney Island as seedy, others thought it was a wonderful, magical place. It had beaches, hotels, racetracks, and a stadium; however, by the turn of the century, it was best known for three amusement parks. These parks were Luna Park, Steeplechase, and Dreamland. Even though gaslight was still the norm in New York, a million electric lights lit Luna Park. While Steeplechase offered many rides, its main attraction was a two-mile ride on mechanical horses. At Dreamland, people could see a submarine; in addition, they could travel through an Eskimo village or visit Lilliputia, with its three hundred midgets. Today, the old Coney Island no longer exists. Fire destroyed Dreamland in 1911, and Luna Park burned down in 1946. In 1964, Steeplechase closed. The once-grand Coney Island is gone. Still, its beach and its boardwalk remain. Its famous roller coaster, the Cyclone, still exists, and its giant Ferris wheel, the Wonder Wheel, keeps on turning. Now, a ballpark has been built for a new minor league baseball team. The new team is called the Brooklyn Cyclones.

Chapter 22

◆ **PRACTICE 22-1, page 340**

Answers: **(1)** Add a verb. **(3)** Add a subject and a verb. **(5)** Add a subject and a verb. **(7)** Add a verb. **(9)** Add a subject.

◆ **PRACTICE 22-2, page 341**

Answers: Items 2, 4, 6, and 7 are fragments. *Rewrite:* Sara Paretsky writes detective novels, such as *Burn Marks* and *Guardian Angel*. These novels are about V. I. Warshawski, a private detective. V. I. lives and works in Chicago, the Windy City. Every day as a detective, V. I. takes risks. V. I. is tough. She is also a woman.

◆ PRACTICE 22-3, page 342

Answers: **(1)** Most scholars agree that the U.S. flag was designed by Francis Hopkinson, a New Jersey delegate to the Continental Congress. **(3)** The first flag may have been sewn by Betsy Ross, a Philadelphia seamstress. **(5)** The Pledge of Allegiance was recited first during a ceremony in 1892, the four-hundredth anniversary of Columbus's arrival in the New World. **(7)** In 1814, Francis Scott Key composed "The Star Spangled Banner" during a fierce naval battle, an attack by a British warship on Fort McHenry in Baltimore's harbor. **(9)** Some people wanted a different National Anthem, such as "America" or "America the Beautiful."

◆ PRACTICE 22-4, page 344

Answers: **(1)** First-born children are reliable, serious, and goal-oriented in most cases. **(3)** Only children have personality characteristics like those of first-borns in larger families. **(5)** Second-born children may compete with their older sibling but more often pursue different interests in terms of academics and other activities. **(7)** In large families, middle-born children often form close personal relationships among themselves or with friends outside of the family. **(9)** Youngest children can be charming and funny but sometimes manipulative in their relationships with other family members.

◆ PRACTICE 22-5, page 345

Answers will vary.

◆ PRACTICE 22-6, page 348

Answers will vary.

◆ PRACTICE 22-7, page 349

Answers will vary.

◆ PRACTICE 22-8, page 350

Answers: **(1)** Always try to find a store brand that costs less than the well-known and widely advertised brands. **(3)** Read consumer magazines for their comparisons of products tested in their laboratories for quality and value. **(5)** Examine sale-priced fruits and vegetables carefully, checking for damage or spoilage. **(7)** Look for stores that sell loose fruits and vegetables, more easily checked for quality than prepackaged produce. **(9)** Make sure you test the different brands fairly, covering the labels and judging only by taste.

◆ PRACTICE 22-9, page 351

Answers: **(1)** Emergency medical technicians receive intensive training. The training is designed to prepare them for saving lives. **(3)** Retailers often locate frequently purchased items at the back of their stores. They put these items there to increase customer traffic. **(5)** Professional football teams have extra athletes ready to play each position. These athletes can substitute for injured players. **(7)** My father didn't have enough health insurance to pay for my sister's long hospitalization. **(9)** Early telephone users said "Ahoy" instead of "Hello" to greet incoming calls.

◆ PRACTICE 22-10, page 355

Possible edits: **(1)** Many homeless people are mentally ill. **(3)** Raccoons can be found living wild in many parts of the United States. **(5)** Some parents are too strict with their children. **(7)** The Vietnam War led to widespread protests in the United States. **(9)** Something is likely to change.

◆ PRACTICE 22-11, page 357

Answers will vary.

Chapter 23

◆ PRACTICE 23-1, page 365

Answers: **(1)** know **(3)** include **(5)** sell; top **(7)** surprises; gives **(9)** hosts; draws

◆ PRACTICE 23-2, page 366

Answers: **(1)** can **(3)** puts **(5)** grow **(7)** harden **(9)** leaves

◆ PRACTICE 23-3, page 367

Answers: **(1)** fill **(3)** survey **(5)** plays **(7)** smell **(9)** greets

◆ PRACTICE 23-4, page 368

Answers: **(1)** have **(3)** has **(5)** do **(7)** is **(9)** has

◆ PRACTICE 23-5, page 370

Answers: **(1)** Prepositional phrase: in the painting; subject: cupids; verb: symbolize **(3)** Prepositional phrase: in the kitchen; subject: appliances; verb: make **(5)** Prepositional phrase: of skis and poles; subject: set; verb: costs **(7)** Prepositional phrase: in the city; subject: Workers; verb: pay **(9)** Prepositional phrase: including people like my father; subject: Volunteers; verb: help

◆ PRACTICE 23-6, page 372

Answers: **(1)** has **(3)** wants **(5)** takes **(7)** seems **(9)** is

◆ PRACTICE 23-7, page 374

Answers: **(1)** Subject: Bering Straits; verb: are **(3)** Subject: twins; verb: Are **(5)** Subject: this; verb: has **(7)** Subject: people; verb: are **(9)** Subject: reasons; verb: are

◆ PRACTICE 23-8, page 375

Answers: **(1)** Antecedent: story; verb: has **(3)** Antecedent: narrator; verb: has **(5)** Antecedent: Madeline; verb: lives **(7)** Antecedent: vault; verb: is **(9)** Antecedent: Roderick; verb: is

Chapter 24

◆ **PRACTICE 24-1, page 382**

Answers: **(1)** were **(3)** were **(5)** were **(7)** required **(9)** is

◆ **PRACTICE 24-2, page 384**

Answers: **(1)** Young people who want careers in the fashion industry do not always realize how hard they will have to work. **(3)** In reality, no matter how talented he or she is, a recent college graduate entering the industry is paid only about $22,000 a year. **(5)** A young designer may receive a big raise if he or she is very talented, but this is unusual. **(7)** Employees may be excited to land a job as an assistant designer but then find that they color in designs that have already been drawn. **(9)** If a person is serious about working in the fashion industry, he or she has to be realistic.

◆ **PRACTICE 24-3, page 386**

Possible edits: **(1)** According to recent studies, a juror may have his or her mind made up before the trial even begins. **(3)** This conclusion often depends on which attorney makes his or her initial description of the case the most dramatic. **(5)** Jurors like these are also not likely to listen to challenges to opinions when the full jury comes together to deliberate. **(7)** Correct **(9)** For example, one juror argued that a man being tried for murder was acting in his own defense because the victim was probably carrying a knife, but no knife was mentioned during the trial.

◆ **PRACTICE 24-4, page 388**

Answers: **(1)** A local university funded the study, and Dr. Alicia Flynn led the research team. **(3)** Two-thirds of the subjects relied on intuition, and only one-third used logic. **(5)** Many experts read the report, and most of them found the results surprising.

Chapter 25

◆ **PRACTICE 25-1, page 394**

Answers: **(1)** Present participle modifier: Believing that improving transportation would be good for the nation; modifies: Congress **(3)** Present participle modifier: Laying track westward from Omaha; modifies: Union Pacific Railroad **(5)** Present participle modifier: Carrying supplies long distances in both directions; modifies: railroads **(7)** Present participle modifier: Using thousands of European immigrants and Civil War veterans; modifies: Union Pacific Railroad **(9)** Present participle modifier: meeting at last at Promontory Point, Utah; modifies: railroads

◆ **PRACTICE 25-2, page 396**

Answers: **(1)** Past participle modifier: Rarely welcomed by property owners; modifies: graffiti **(3)** Past participle modifier: Preserved by the eruptions of Mt. Vesuvius; mod-ifies: graffiti **(5)** Past participle modifier: Found in Rome; modifies: graffiti **(7)** Past participle modifier: painted by American soldiers during World War II; modifies: slogan **(9)** Past participle modifier: Sometimes called "tags"; modifies: graffiti

◆ **PRACTICE 25-3, page 398**

Answers will vary.

◆ **PRACTICE 25-4, page 399**

Answers will vary.

◆ **PRACTICE 25-5, page 401**

Answers: **(1)** Frightened by a noise, the cat broke the vase. **(3)** Lori looked at the man with red hair sitting in the chair. **(5)** People are sometimes killed by snakes with their deadly venom. **(7)** I ran outside in my bathrobe and saw eight tiny reindeer. **(9)** Wearing a mask, the exterminator sprayed the insect.

Chapter 26

◆ **PRACTICE 26-1, page 412**

Answers: **(1)** returned **(3)** originated **(5)** dyed **(7)** celebrated **(9)** washed

◆ **PRACTICE 26-2, page 414**

Answers: **(1)** came; was **(3)** went **(5)** became **(7)** thought **(9)** began

◆ **PRACTICE 26-3, page 416**

Answers: **(1)** Correct **(3)** Correct **(5)** was **(7)** Correct **(9)** was

◆ **PRACTICE 26-4, page 418**

Answers: **(1)** would; would **(3)** would **(5)** would **(7)** could **(9)** would

Chapter 27

◆ **PRACTICE 27-1, page 423**

Answers: **(1)** visited **(3)** raised **(5)** joined **(7)** removed **(9)** served

◆ **PRACTICE 27-2, page 426**

Answers: **(1)** taught **(3)** built **(5)** become **(7)** written **(9)** said

◆ **PRACTICE 27-3, page 427**

Answers: **(1)** become **(3)** led **(5)** Correct **(7)** spoken; Correct **(9)** Correct

◆ **PRACTICE 27-4, page 429**

Answers: **(1)** have come; heard **(3)** belonged **(5)** spoke **(7)** made **(9)** were

◆ **PRACTICE 27-5, page 430**

Answers: **(1)** measured **(3)** have used **(5)** has taken **(7)** has ensured **(9)** have received

◆ **PRACTICE 27-6, page 432**

Answers: **(1)** had left **(3)** had arrived **(5)** had lied **(7)** had decided **(9)** had been

◆ **PRACTICE 27-7, page 433**

Answers: **(1)** surprised; preapproved **(3)** designed; inscribed **(5)** stuffed **(7)** concerned **(9)** acquired

Chapter 28

◆ **PRACTICE 28-1, page 439**

Answers: **(1)** headaches (regular) **(3)** feet (irregular) **(5)** deer (irregular) **(7)** brides-to-be (irregular) **(9)** loaves (irregular) **(11)** beaches (regular) **(13)** sons-in-law (irregular) **(15)** wives (irregular) **(17)** elves (irregular) **(19)** catalogs (regular)

◆ **PRACTICE 28-2, page 440**

Answers: **(1)** travelers-to-be **(3)** Correct; delays; duties **(5)** attacks; personnel; Correct **(7)** fins; tanks; compartments **(9)** Correct; boxes

◆ **PRACTICE 28-3, page 441**

Answers: **(1)** I **(3)** he **(5)** I; it; it **(7)** she; I; I **(9)** I; you

◆ **PRACTICE 28-4, page 443**

Answers: **(1)** Antecedent: campuses; pronoun: they **(3)** Antecedent: students; pronoun: their **(5)** Antecedent: Joyce; pronoun: she **(7)** Antecedent: friends; pronoun: them

◆ **PRACTICE 28-5, page 444**

Answers: **(1)** they **(3)** it **(5)** He **(7)** It

◆ **PRACTICE 28-6, page 445**

Answers: **(1)** Compound antecedent: Larry and Curly; connecting word: and; pronoun: their **(3)** Compound antecedent: Laurel and Hardy; connecting word: and; pronoun: their **(5)** Compound antecedent: *MASH* or *The Fugitive*; connecting word: or; pronoun: its **(7)** Compound antecedent: film or videotapes; connecting word: or; pronoun: their **(9)** Compound antecedent: popcorn and soft drinks; connecting word: and; pronoun: their

◆ **PRACTICE 28-7, page 447**

Answers: **(1)** Indefinite pronoun antecedent: Either; pronoun: its **(3)** Indefinite pronoun antecedent: Everything;

pronoun: its **(5)** Indefinite pronoun antecedent: Neither; pronoun: her **(7)** Indefinite pronoun antecedent: Several; pronoun: their **(9)** Indefinite pronoun antecedent: Anyone; pronoun: his or her

◆ **PRACTICE 28-8, page 448**

Possible edits: **(1)** Everyone has the right to his or her own opinion. **(3)** Somebody forgot his or her backpack. **(5)** Someone in the store has left his or her car's lights on. **(7)** Each of the applicants must have his or her driver's license. **(9)** Either of the coffeemakers comes with its own filter.

◆ **PRACTICE 28-9, page 449**

Answers: **(1)** Collective noun antecedent: company; pronoun: its **(3)** Collective noun antecedent: government; pronoun: its **(5)** Collective noun antecedent: family; pronoun: its **(7)** Collective noun antecedent: teams; pronoun: their **(9)** Collective noun antecedent: class; pronoun: its

◆ **PRACTICE 28-10, page 449**

Answers: **(1)** Antecedent: woman; pronoun: Correct **(3)** Antecedent: women; pronoun: their **(5)** Antecedent: Elizabeth Cady Stanton and Lucretia Mott; pronoun: their **(7)** Antecedent: women; pronoun: their **(9)** Antecedent: the U.S. government; pronoun: its

◆ **PRACTICE 28-11, page 452**

Answers: **(1)** Possessive **(3)** Possessive **(5)** Objective **(7)** Possessive; Subjective; Objective; Subjective **(9)** Subjective

◆ **PRACTICE 28-12, page 455**

Answers: **(1)** Correct **(3)** I **(5)** Correct **(7)** she; I; Correct; me **(9)** her

◆ **PRACTICE 28-13, page 456**

Answers: **(1)** she [has] **(3)** she [does] **(5)** they [have] **(7)** they [serve] **(9)** [it fits] me

◆ **PRACTICE 28-14, page 457**

Answers: **(1)** who **(3)** who **(5)** who **(7)** whoever **(9)** who

◆ **PRACTICE 28-15, page 459**

Answers: **(1)** themselves **(3)** herself **(5)** themselves **(7)** ourselves **(9)** herself

Chapter 29

◆ **PRACTICE 29-1, page 466**

Answers: **(1)** poorly **(3)** truly **(5)** really **(7)** specifically **(9)** important; immediately

◆ **PRACTICE 29-2, page 467**

Answers: **(1)** well **(3)** good **(5)** well **(7)** well **(9)** well

◆ **PRACTICE 29-3, page 469**

Answers: **(1)** more slowly **(3)** healthier **(5)** more loudly **(7)** more respectful **(9)** wilder

◆ **PRACTICE 29-4, page 470**

Answers: **(1)** largest **(3)** most successful **(5)** most powerful **(7)** most serious **(9)** most popular

◆ **PRACTICE 29-5, page 471**

Answers: **(1)** better **(3)** better; worse **(5)** better **(7)** best **(9)** better

Chapter 30

◆ **PRACTICE 30-1, page 477**

Possible edits: **(1)** When the first season of the reality show *Survivor* aired, it was an immediate hit. **(3)** For a while, *Survivor* became a cultural phenomenon—probably because it was seldom in bad taste. **(5)** It was surprising to see the many other reality shows that suddenly appeared on the air. **(7)** A recent poll asked viewers: "Do you enjoy reality TV, or has it gone too far?" **(9)** It turns out that reality TV is nothing new.

◆ **PRACTICE 30-2, page 479**

Possible answers: **(1)** It took hundreds of years to finish building the Great Wall. **(3)** The Great Wall was built to keep out invading armies. **(5)** The Great Wall is as long as the distance from New York City to Omaha, Nebraska. **(7)** The sides of the Great Wall are made of stone, brick, and earth. **(9)** It was a great feat of engineering.

◆ **PRACTICE 30-3, page 481**

Answers: **(1)** species; sharks **(3)** Sharks **(5)** No plural nouns **(7)** sharks; meat-eaters; species; people **(9)** 1950s; sharks

◆ **PRACTICE 30-4, page 483**

Answers: **(1)** Count: approaches **(3)** Noncount **(5)** Count: shortages **(7)** Count: individuals **(9)** Count: systems

◆ **PRACTICE 30-5, page 485**

Answers: **(1)** every **(3)** A few violent **(5)** many **(7)** Many **(9)** some

◆ **PRACTICE 30-6, page 488**

Answers: **(1)** the; a **(3)** No article needed **(5)** the; the; the; No article needed **(7)** No article needed **(9)** a **(11)** a; No article needed; No article needed; the

◆ **PRACTICE 30-7, page 490**

Answers: **(1)** Question: Is converting metric measurements to English measurements difficult?; Negative statement: Converting metric measurements to English measurements is not difficult. **(3)** Question: Was that family very influential in the early 1900s?; Negative statement: That family was not very influential in the early 1900s. **(5)** Question: Is choosing the right gift a difficult task?; Negative statement: Choosing the right gift is not a difficult task. **(7)** Question: Can the lawyer verify the witness's story?; Negative statement: The lawyer cannot verify the witness's story. **(9)** Question: Is the British royal family loved by most of the British people?; Negative statement: The British royal family is not loved by most of the British people.

◆ **PRACTICE 30-8, page 494**

Answers: **(1)** Correct **(3)** Correct; believed; Correct **(5)** Correct; Correct; Correct **(7)** often see; touch; Correct **(9)** Correct; decide

◆ **PRACTICE 30-9, page 496**

Answers: **(1)** might **(3)** should **(5)** should **(7)** Would **(9)** can

◆ **PRACTICE 30-10, page 497**

Answers: **(1)** Eating **(3)** cleaning **(5)** Quitting **(7)** organizing **(9)** cooking

◆ **PRACTICE 30-11, page 498**

Answers: **(1)** a brand-new high-rise apartment building **(3)** numerous successful short-story collections **(5)** the publisher's three best-selling works **(7)** a strong-willed young woman **(9)** an exquisite white wedding gown

◆ **PRACTICE 30-12, page 503**

Answers: **(1)** in; in **(3)** in; at; to **(5)** in; in; in **(7)** to; in; with; from; to; with; with **(9)** with; at; of **(11)** on; on **(13)** to

◆ **PRACTICE 30-13, page 505**

Answers: **(1)** In one case, a New Jersey woman found that a hungry bear woke her up from a nap one afternoon. **(3)** Actually, although it is a good idea to stay away from bears, most wild bears are timid. **(5)** The amount of blueberries and other wild fruit that bears eat usually drops off in dry weather. **(7)** It is a good idea for families to go over their plans to safeguard their property against bears. **(9)** If people have a bird feeder in the yard, they should put it away during autumn.

Chapter 31

◆ **PRACTICE 31-1, page 516**

Answers: **(1)** The musician plays guitar, bass, and drums. **(3)** Correct **(5)** The remarkable diary kept by young Anne Frank while her family hid from the Nazis is insightful, touching, and sometimes humorous. **(7)** Most coffins manufactured in the United States are lined with bronze, copper, or lead. **(9)** California's capital is Sacramento, its largest city is Los Angeles, and its oldest settlement is San Diego.

◆ **PRACTICE 31-2, page 518**

Answers: **(1)** In recent years, many Olympic athletes have been disqualified because they tested positive for banned drugs. **(3)** Correct **(5)** Correct **(7)** Disappointing thousands of Greeks, two Greek sprinting stars refused to participate in a drug test at the Athens Olympics. **(9)** For using a banned stimulant in April 2004, American sprinter Torri Edwards was banned from competition for two years.

◆ PRACTICE 31-3, page 519

Answers: **(1)** For example, the African-American celebration of Kwanzaa was introduced in the 1960s. **(3)** By the way, the word *Kwanzaa* means "first fruits" in Swahili. **(5)** This can, of course, be demonstrated in some of the seven principles of Kwanzaa. **(7)** The focus, first of all, is on unity (*umoja*). **(9)** In addition, Kwanzaa celebrations emphasize three kinds of community responsibility (*ujima, ujamaa,* and *nia*).

◆ PRACTICE 31-4, page 520

Answers: **(1)** Traditional Chinese medicine is based on meridians, channels of energy believed to run in regular patterns through the body. **(3)** Herbal medicine, the basis of many Chinese healing techniques, requires twelve years of study. **(5)** Correct **(7)** Nigeria, the most populous country in Africa, is also one of the fastest-growing nations in the world. **(9)** The Yoruban people, the Nigerian settlers of Lagos, are unusual in Africa because they tend to form large urban communities.

◆ PRACTICE 31-5, page 523

Answers: **(1)** Correct **(3)** Correct **(5)** The Japanese had just landed in the Aleutian Islands, which lie west of the tip of the Alaska Peninsula. **(7)** As a result, they made them work under conditions that made construction difficult. **(9)** In one case, white engineers who surveyed a river said it would take two weeks to bridge. **(11)** Correct

◆ PRACTICE 31-6, page 524

Answers: **(1)** The American Declaration of Independence was approved on July 4, 1776. **(3)** At 175 Carlton Avenue, Brooklyn, New York, is the house where Richard Wright began writing *Native Son.* **(5)** Correct **(7)** The Pueblo Grande Museum is located at 1469 East Washington Street, Phoenix, Arizona. **(9)** St. Louis, Missouri, was the birthplace of writer Maya Angelou, but she spent most of her childhood in Stamps, Arkansas.

◆ PRACTICE 31-7, page 526

Answers: **(1)** The capital of the Dominican Republic is Santo Domingo. **(3)** Chief among these are sugarcane, coffee, cocoa, and rice. **(5)** Correct **(7)** Tourists who visit the Dominican Republic remark on its tropical beauty. **(9)** Correct

Chapter 32

◆ PRACTICE 32-1, page 532

Answers: **(1)** Bacteria and viruses, which we can't see without a microscope, certainly kill many people every year. **(3)** After you're bitten, stung, or stuck, how long does it take to die? **(5)** The sea wasp is actually a fifteen-foot-long jellyfish, and although it's not aggressive, it can be deadly. **(7)** While jellyfish found off the Atlantic coast of the United States can sting, they aren't as dangerous as the sea wasp, whose venom is deadly enough to kill sixty adults. **(9)** Correct

◆ PRACTICE 32-2, page 534

Answers: **(1)** the singer's video **(3)** everybody's favorite band **(5)** the players' union **(7)** the children's bedroom **(9)** everyone's dreams

◆ PRACTICE 32-3, page 535

Answers: **(1)** Parents; theirs **(3)** its; weeks **(5)** Ryans; years **(7)** classes; Correct; your **(9)** tests; Correct

Chapter 33

◆ PRACTICE 33-1, page 542

Answers: **(1)** Midwest; Lake; Chicago; O'Hare International Airport; nation's **(3)** north; Soldier Field; Chicago Bears; Wrigley Field; Chicago Cubs; National League baseball team **(5)** John Kinzie **(7)** United States; Mrs.; cow **(9)** mother; Aunt Jean; Uncle Amos

◆ PRACTICE 33-2, page 545

Answers: **(1)** "We who are about to die salute you," said the gladiators to the emperor. **(3)** "The bigger they are," said boxer John L. Sullivan, "the harder they fall." **(5)** Lisa Marie replied, "I do." **(7)** When asked for the jury's verdict, the foreperson replied, "We find the defendant not guilty." **(9)** "Yabba dabba doo!" Fred exclaimed. "This brontoburger looks great."

◆ PRACTICE 33-3, page 546

Answers: **(1)** Essayist Simone de Beauvoir wrote, "One is not born a woman; one becomes one." **(3)** "Tribe follows tribe," said Suquamish Chief Seattle in 1854, "and nation follows nation." **(5)** Abolitionist Sojourner Truth said, "The rich rob the poor, and the poor rob one another." **(7)** Former slave Harriet Tubman said, "When I found I had crossed that line, I looked at my hands to see if I was the same person." **(9)** "No man chooses evil because it is evil," wrote Mary Wollstonecraft in 1790. "He only mistakes it for happiness."

◆ **PRACTICE 33-4, page 548**

Answers: **(1)** *Plan Nine from Outer Space* **(3)** "I Have a Dream"; "Letter from a Birmingham Jail" **(5)** *CSI; CSI: Miami; CSI: New York*

◆ **PRACTICE 33-5, page 549**

Answers: **(1)** Sui Sin Far's short story "The Wisdom of the New," from her book Mrs. Spring Fragrance, is about the clash between Chinese and American cultures in the early twentieth century. **(3)** Interesting information about fighting skin cancer can be found in the article "Putting Sunscreens to the Test," which appeared in the magazine Consumer Reports. **(5)** Ang Lee has directed several well-received films, including Crouching Tiger, Hidden Dragon. **(7)** The title of Lorraine Hansberry's play A Raisin in the Sun comes from Langston Hughes's poem "Harlem."

◆ **PRACTICE 33-6, page 550**

Possible answers: **(1)** New Orleans has two nicknames: the "Crescent City" and the "City that Care Forgot." **(3)** The French Quarter is famous for several attractions: its unique buildings, its fine food, its street musicians, and its wild nightlife. **(5)** At the center of the square—a gathering place for artists—is a monument to Andrew Jackson. **(7)** Its popular beignets (pronounced ben-*yeas*) are deep-fried pastries covered with sugar. **(9)** New Orleans visitors—people from all over the world—particularly enjoy the laid-back atmosphere of the city.

Chapter 34

◆ **PRACTICE 34-1, page 558**

Answers: **(1)** weigh; Correct **(3)** Correct; deceive; believing **(5)** Correct; veins; Correct **(7)** Their; Correct; grief **(9)** variety; foreign

◆ **PRACTICE 34-2, page 559**

Answers: **(1)** unhappy **(3)** preexisting **(5)** unnecessary **(7)** impatient **(9)** overreact

◆ **PRACTICE 34-3, page 560**

Answers: **(1)** lonely **(3)** revising **(5)** desirable **(7)** microscopic **(9)** ninth **(11)** effectiveness **(13)** fortunate **(15)** argument **(17)** advertisement **(19)** careless

◆ **PRACTICE 34-4, page 561**

Answers: **(1)** happiness **(3)** denying **(5)** readiness **(7)** destroyer **(9)** fortyish **(11)** cried **(13)** business **(15)** spying **(17)** livelihood **(19)** joyful

◆ **PRACTICE 34-5, page 562**

Answers: **(1)** hoped **(3)** resting **(5)** revealing **(7)** unzipped **(9)** cramming **(11)** appealing **(13)** referring **(15)** omitted **(17)** fatter **(19)** repelled

◆ **PRACTICE 34-6, page 564**

Answers: **(1)** effects; already **(3)** buy; Correct **(5)** Correct; Correct **(7)** by; effects **(9)** Correct; affect

◆ **PRACTICE 34-7, page 565**

Answers: **(1)** Here; every day **(3)** Correct; conscience **(5)** conscious; its **(7)** here; Correct; it's **(9)** hear; Correct

◆ **PRACTICE 34-8, page 567**

Answers: **(1)** Correct **(3)** lay **(5)** mind **(7)** Correct **(9)** Lay

◆ **PRACTICE 34-9, page 569**

Answers: **(1)** supposed **(3)** Correct **(5)** Correct; quiet **(7)** Correct **(9)** Correct

◆ **PRACTICE 34-10, page 570**

Answers: **(1)** Correct; to **(3)** they're **(5)** their **(7)** Correct; used **(9)** Correct; used

◆ **PRACTICE 34-11, page 572**

Answers: **(1)** whose; Correct **(3)** where; Correct **(5)** Correct; whether; Correct **(7)** who's; your **(8)** Correct; we're **(9)** you're; where

Acknowledgments

Picture acknowledgments

3L Bill Aron/PhotoEdit Inc.; **3R** James Marshall/The Image Works; **23** Bill Bachman/Photo Researchers, Inc.; **45B** Stacy Walsh Rosenstock/NewsCom; **45T** Chris Gardner/AP/Wide World Photos; **46** Hulton/Archive/Getty Images; **51** © Broward Community College; **58** Charles Walker/Topfoto/The Image Works; **65** Vic Bider/PhotoEdit Inc.; **72** TWISTER ® AND © 2005 Hasbro Inc. Used with permission; **79** Michael A. Keller/CORBIS; **87** Photofest; **96** Chuck Savage/CORBIS; **102** Tony Freeman/PhotoEdit Inc.; **109** David Young-Wolff/PhotoEdit Inc.; **121** Photofest; **149** Ken Reid/The Image Bank/Getty Images; **150** David Young-Wolff/PhotoEdit Inc.; **153** Photofest; **164** Jessica Rinaldi/Reuters/Landov; **165** AP/Wide World Photos; **167** David Young-Wolff/PhotoEdit Inc.; **173** Bill Aron/PhotoEdit Inc.; **179** Brand X Pictures/Getty Images; **185** Frank Siteman; **192** Photofest; **199** Darren McCollester/Getty Images; **205B** Richard Pasley/Stock Boston, LLC; **205T** Dennis MacDonald/Index Stock Imagery, Inc.; **211** Michael Newman/PhotoEdit Inc.; **217B** James Wilson/Woodfin Camp & Associates; **217CL** Bob Daemmrich/Stock Boston, LLC; **217CR** Sybil Shackman; **217T** Ken Cavanaugh/Photo Researchers, Inc.; **225** Bob Daemmrich/Stock Boston, LLC; **229** Jeff Zelevansky/Icon SMI/Zuma Press; **239** Leonard Freed/Magnum Photos, Inc.; **241** Stephen Ferry/Getty Images; **255B** Super-Stock; **255T** Courtesy of the University of Texas Libraries, the University of Texas at Austin; **258** David Duprey/AP/Wide World Photos; **272** Greg Martin/SuperStock; **273** Chris Gardner/AP/Wide World Photos; **275** AP/Wide World Photos; **297** SuperStock; **298** The Advertising Archive; **300** Chicagoview/Alamy Images; **307** Mark Lennihan/AP/Wide World Photos; **308** AP/Wide World Photos; **310** Ellen Senisi/The Image Works; **321** Chris Ware/Keystone Features/Getty Images; **322B** Courtesy 3M Corporation; **322T** Library of Congress; **324** National Archives and Records Administration; **325B** Picture Collection, The Branch Libraries, The New York Public Library, Astor, Lenox and Tilden Foundations; **325T** Courtesy of The Bancroft Library, University of California, Berkeley; **329** Jeff Greenberg/Photo Researchers, Inc.; **337** United States Mint Image; **339** Bill Aron/PhotoEdit Inc.; **360B** Jeff Rotman/Index Stock Imagery, Inc.; **360T** Wayne and Karen Brown/Index Stock Imagery, Inc.; **363** Ralph Fasanella/ACA Galleries; **378B** Robert E. Klein/AP/Wide World Photos; **378T** Donna McWilliam/AP/Wide World Photos; **381** Michael Newman/PhotoEdit Inc.; **393** "Marinara Sauce Recipes Spaghetti Sauce" from the Awesome Chef Recipes Web site at *http://www.awesome-chef-recipes.com/marinara-sauce.htm.* Reprinted by permission of Chef Brian Johnson; **391C** PictureQuest; **391T** Michael Newman/PhotoEdit Inc.; **404B** Rudi Von Briel/PhotoEdit Inc.; **404T** Rudi Von Briel/PhotoEdit Inc.; **406** Courtesy of the University of Texas Libraries, the University of Texas at Austin; **407B** Courtesy of Sheldon's, *asksheldon@aol.com;* **407T** Courtesy of Sheldon's, *asksheldon@aol.com;* **411** DeRoo Family; **420B** David Young-Wolff/Alamy Images; **420T** AP/Wide World Photos; **422** Bob Stern/The Image Works; **435T** From the League of Women Voters Web site, June 2005, *http://www.lwv.org/voter/gotv.cfm?pid=geny.* Reprinted by permission; **435B** From *JohnKerry.com,* reprinted by permission of the Press Office for Senator John Kerry; **436** Photograph of President Bush on a September 14, 2001 trip to view the World

Trade Center. Photograph taken by Eric Draper of the White House. Reprinted by permission of the White House; **437** TM and © 20th Century Fox Film Corp./Photofest; **461T** David Young-Wolff/PhotoEdit Inc.; **461B** Jiang Jin/SuperStock; **464** James Marshall/The Image Works; **473** Courtesy of the University of Texas Libraries, the University of Texas at Austin; **474** Abbas/Magnum Photos, Inc.; **476** *Fourth of July, 1916*, by Frederick C. Hassam (detail)/Christie's Images, NY; **507** Stuart Franklin/Magnum Photos, Inc.; **508** James Smalley/Index Stock Imagery, Inc.; **511** *GraphicMaps.com;* **515** Monika Graff/The Image Works; **528T** Eric Risberg/AP/Wide World Photos; **528B** Courtesy of the University of Texas Libraries, the University of Texas at Austin; **531** Tony Freeman/PhotoEdit Inc.; **537** Library of Congress; **538** Art Resource, NY; **540** Photo by Metro-Goldwyn-Mayer/ZUMA Press. © Copyright 1939 by Courtesy of MGM; **552** Courtesy of Gary Soto; **553** University of New Mexico Press; **555** Eric Fowke/PhotoEdit Inc.; **573** Brennan Linsley/AP/Wide World Photos; **574** Anja Niedringhaus/AP/Wide World Photos; **577** Michael Newman/PhotoEdit Inc.; **578** Spencer Grant/PhotoEdit Inc.; **578** Lon C. Diehl/PhotoEdit Inc.; **581** Sherri Zuckerman.

Text acknowledgments

Maya Angelou, "Summer Picnic Fish Fry." From *I Know Why the Caged Bird Sings.* Copyright © 1969 and renewed 1997 by Maya Angelou. Used by permission of Random House, Inc.

Russell Baker, "Slice of Life." From *The New York Times*, November 24, 1974. Copyright © 1974 by the New York Times Co. Reprinted with permission.

Lynda Barry, "The Sanctuary of School." From *The New York Times*, January 25, 1992. Copyright © 1992 by the New York Times Co. Reprinted with permission.

Judy Brady, "I Want a Wife." Used by permission of the author.

Judith Ortiz Cofer, "Don't Call Me a Hot Tamale." From *The Latin Deli: Prose & Poetry.* Copyright © 1993 by Judith Ortiz Cofer. Reprinted by permission of the University of Georgia Press.

Jo-Ellan Dimitrius, Ph.D., and Mark Mazzarella, "Liars." From *Reading People.* Copyright © 1998, 1999 by Jo-Ellan Dimitrius, Ph.D., and Mark Mazzarella. Used by permission of Random House, Inc.

Dave Eggers, "Serve or Fail." From *The New York Times*, June 13, 2004. Copyright © 2004 by the New York Times Co. Reprinted with permission.

Indira Ganesan, "Resisting My Family History." From *Glamour*, September 1994. Reprinted by permission of the author.

Martin Gansberg, "Thirty-Eight Who Saw Murder Didn't Call the Police." From *The New York Times*, March 27, 1964. Copyright © 1964 by the New York Times Co. Reprinted with permission.

Ellen Goodman, "The Suspected Shopper." From *Keeping in Touch.* Copyright © 1985 by The Washington Post Company. All rights reserved. Reprinted with the permission of Simon & Schuster Adult Publishing Group.

Lawrence Otis Graham, "The 'Black Table' Is Still There." From *The New York Times*, February 3, 1991. Copyright © 1991 by The New York Times. Used by permission.

John Gray, excerpt from *Men Are from Mars, Women Are from Venus.* Copyright © 1992 by John Gray. Reprinted by permission of HarperCollins Publishers, Inc.

Martin Luther King Jr., "I Have a Dream." Copyright 1963 by Martin Luther King Jr., copyright renewed 1991 by Coretta Scott King. Reprinted by arrangement with the Estate of Martin Luther King Jr., c/o Writers House as agent for the proprietor, New York, NY.

Patrick Martins, "About a Bird." From *The New York Times*, November 24, 2003. Copyright © 2003 by The New York Times. Used by permission.

Katherine S. Newman, "Too Close for Comfort." From *The New York Times*, April 17, 2004. Copyright © 2004 by the New York Times. Used by permission.

Scott Russell Sanders, "The Men We Carry in Our Minds." From *The Paradise of Bombs.* Reprinted by permission of the Virginia Kidd Agency.

Esmeralda Santiago, "Guavas." From *When I Was Puerto Rican.* Copyright © 1993 by Esmeralda Santiago. Reprinted by permission of Perseus Books PLC, a member of Perseus Books, LLC.

Gayle Rosenwald Smith, "The Wife Beater." From *The Philadelphia Inquirer*, July 2, 2001. Reprinted with permission from the Philadelphia Inquirer.

Ji-Yeon Yuh, "Let's Tell the Story of All America's Cultures." From *The Philadelphia Inquirer*, 1991. Used by permission of the Philadelphia Inquirer.

"WritePlacerPlus" from the College Board Web site. Reprinted by permission of the College Board.

"Sample Writing Skills Test" from the ACT Web site at *http://www.act.org/asset/*. Reprinted by permission of ACT Communications.

Texas Higher Education Assessment (THEA®) Practice Test—Writing Section excerpted from The Official THEA® Test Study Guide, Copyright © 2004 by National Evaluation Systems, Inc. (NES®). Reprinted by permission. "Texas Higher Education Assessment™," "THEA®," and the "THEA®" logo are trademarks of National Evaluation Systems, Inc. (NES®). This product was developed by Laurie G. Kirszner and Stephen R. Mandell. It was not developed in connection with the Texas Higher Education Coordinating Board, the State Board for Education Certification, or National Evaluation Systems, Inc., nor was it reviewed or endorsed by any of these agencies.

"Regent's Testing Program Essay Test" from *http://www2.gsu.edu/~wwwrtp/*. Copyright © Board of Regents University System of Georgia.

Index